CODES & CHEATS 2005

FALL EDITION

Prima Games
A Division of Random House, Inc.
3000 Lava Ridge Court
Roseville, CA 95661
(800) 733-3000
www.primagames.com

Product Manager: Damien Waples
Editor: Amanda Peckham, Fernando Bueno, Alaina Yee
Layout & Design: Graphic Applications Group, Inc.

ISBN: 0-7615-5139-5
Library of Congress Catalog Card Number: 2005925098
Printed in the United States of America

05 06 07 08 AA 10 9 8 7 6 5 4 3 2

ATV Offroad Fury Blazin Trails

To enter these passwords go to the Options menu, select the Player Profile menu, and then enter the Cheat menu.

Unlockable	Code
1,500 Credits	$MONEYBAGS$
All Music Videos	BILLBOARDS
All Rider Gear	DUDS
Unlock Everything (except the Fury Bike)	ALL ACCESS
Unlock Rims	DUBS

Gretzky NHL

In the Gretzky Challenge, go into Unlockable and press Start.

Unlockable	Code
Unlocks Everything	SHOENLOC

Hot Shots Golf Open Tee

Easy Loyalty To gain loyalty much quicker than playing an entire round of golf, start a match play game under challenge mode. Give up on the first three holes by pressing Select then Start to forfeit. After the match you will still gain loyalty for your character.

Metal Gear Acid

Enter the following in the passwords Menu.

Card	Password
Gives Card No.173 - Viper	Viper
Gives Card No.178 - Mika Slayton	Mika
Gives Card No.182 - Karen Houjou	Karen
Gives Card No.184 - Jehuty	Jehuty
Gives Card No.199 - XM8	Xmeight

NFL Street 2 Unleashed

Enter the following in the cheats menu.

Unlockable	Codes
AFC East All Stars	EAASFSCT
AFC North All Stars	NAOFRCTH
AFC South All Stars	SAOFUCTH
AFC West All Stars	WAEFSCT
EA Field	EAField
Fumble Mode (Other team fumbles)	GreasedPig
Gargantuan Players	BIGSmash
Max Catch	MagnetHands
NFC East All Stars	NNOFRCTH
NFC North All-Stars	NNAS66784
NFC South All Stars	SNOFUCTH
NFC West All Stars	ENASFSCT
No Fumble Mode	GlueHands
Reebok Team	Reebok
Unlimited Turbo	NozBoost

Tony Hawk's Underground 2 Remix

Go to Game Options, then Cheat Codes and enter the following codes.

Unlockable	Code
Perfect Rail Balance	Tightrope
Unlock Tony Hawk from Tony Hawk Pro Skater 1	Birdman

Twisted Metal Head On

Input these codes during gameplay.

Unlockable	Code
Invulnerability	→, ←, ↓, ↑ and finally press L1 + R1
Infinite Weapons	▲, ▲, ↓, ↓, L1 + R1

PSP Xbox PS2 GC GBA

Table of Contents - Xbox

Table of Contents - Xbox

PSP

007: Agent Under Fire

Description	Objective
Alpine Guard Skin in Multiplayer Mode	Complete the Streets of Bucharest level with a "Platinum" rank and all 007 icons.
Calypso Gun in Multiplayer Mode	Complete the Fire and Water level with a "Platinum" rank and all 007 icons.
Carrier Guard Multiplayer Skin	Complete the Evil Summit level with a "Platinum" rank and all 007 icons.
Cyclops Oil Guard skin in Multiplayer Mode	Complete the Poseidon level with a "Platinum" rank and all 007 icons.
Full Arsenal in Multiplayer Mode	Complete the Forbidden Depths level with a "Platinum" rank and all 007 icons.
Golden Accuracy Power-Up (This cheat enables you to have greater auto-aim.)	Complete the Bad Diplomacy level with a "Gold" rank.
Golden Armor Power-Up	Complete the Forbidden Depths level with a "Gold" rank.
Golden Bullet Power-Up	Complete the Poseidon level with a "Gold" rank.
Golden CH-6 (This cheat gives you unlimited rockets.)	Complete the Precious Cargo level with a "Gold" rank.
Golden Clip Power-Up	Complete the Cold Reception level with a "Gold" rank.
Golden Grenade Power-Up	Complete the Night of the Jackal level with a "Gold" rank.
Golden Gun (Unlocks the Golden PK2)	Complete the Trouble in Paradise level with a "Gold" rank.
Golden Gun in Multiplayer Mode	Complete the Precious Cargo level with a "Platinum" rank and all 007 icons.
Gravity Boots in Multiplayer Mode	Complete the Bad Diplomacy level with a "Platinum" rank and all 007 icons.
Guard Skin in Multiplayer Mode	Complete the Cold Reception level with a "Platinum" rank and all 007 icons.
Lotus Esprit Car rank.	Complete the Streets of Bucharest level with a "Gold"
Poseidon Guard Skin in Multiplayer Mode	Complete the Mediterranean Crisis level with a "Platinum" rank and all 007 icons.
Rapid Fire Power-Up	Complete the Fire and Water level with a "Gold" rank.
Regenerative Armor Power-Up	Complete the Mediterranean Crisis level with a "Gold" rank.
Rocket Manor Multiplayer Level (This cheat unlocks a new multiplayer level, a large, open area. The map settings allow only rockets.)	Complete the Trouble in Paradise level with a "Platinum" rank and all 007 icons.
Stealth Bond Skin in Multiplayer Mode	Complete the Dangerous Pursuit level with a "Platinum" rank and all 007 icons.
Unlimited Car Missiles	Complete the Dangerous Pursuit level with a "Gold" rank.
Unlimited Golden Gun Ammunition	Complete the Evil Summit level with a "Gold" rank.
Viper Gun in Multiplayer Mode	Complete the Night of the Jackal level with a "Platinum" rank and all 007 icons.

Xbox

PS2

GC

GBA

TIP

Golden Gun Tip:

With this gun, you receive a silencer that the normal P2K doesn't have. To do this easily, get as much accuracy as you can, take as few hits as you can, and do all the Bond moves (shooting barrels to explode, shooting vital enemy characters, and finding secret areas).

007: Everything or Nothing

Unlockable	Objective
003	290 Points
All Weapons	17 Platinum
Baron Samedi	50 Points
Burn Chamber	370 Points
Cayenne Upgrade	12 Gold
Cistern	30 Points
Cloak	13 Platinum
Diavolo Moscow	400 Points
Double Ammo	7 Platinum
Double Damage	9 Platinum
Egypt Commander	90 Points
Egypt Guard	180 Points
Full Ammo	11 Platinum
Full Battery	15 Platinum
Gallery	27 Gold
Golden Gun	1 Platinum
Hazmat Guard	110 Points
Helicopter Upgrade	6 Gold
Improved Battery	5 Platinum
Improved Traction	3 Platinum
Katya	20 Gold
Katya Jumpsuit	320 Points
Le Rouge	260 Points
Moscow Guard	230 Points
MI6 Combat Simulator	Complete all Missions
MI6 Survival Test	Complete all Missions
Miss Nagai	450 Points
Miss Nagai	17 Gold
Mya	130 Points
Mya	14 Gold
Nanotank Upgrade	24 Gold
Odd Job	70 Points
Platinum Gun	27 Platinum
Production Stills 1	1 Gold
Production Stills 2	2 Gold
Production Stills 3	3 Gold
Production Stills 4	4 Gold
Production Stills 5	5 Gold
Production Stills 6	7 Gold
Production Stills 7	9 Gold
Production Stills 8	13 Gold
Production Stills 9	16 Gold
Production Stills 10	18 Gold
Production Stills 11	19 Gold
Production Stills 12	22 Gold
Production Stills 13	23 Gold
Production Stills 14	25 Gold
Serena	350 Points
Serena	430 Points
Serena	8 Gold
Slow Motion Driving	25 Platinum
South Commander	210 Points
Tank Upgrade	10 Gold
Test Lab	160 Points
Triumph Upgrade	21 Gold
Underworld	11 Gold
Unlimited Ammo	23 Platinum
Unlimited Battery	19 Platinum
Vanquish Upgrade	15 Gold

007: Nightfire

Cheat Mode: For the following codes, select the "Codenames" option at the main menu. Select your character and enter one of the following codes at the Secret Unlocks screen. Save your Codename after entering the code. Then exit your Codename and begin gameplay.

Unlockable	Code
All Gadget Upgrades	Q LAB
All Multiplayer Options	GAMEROOM
Alpine Escape Level	POWDER
Bigger Clip for Sniper Rifle	MAGAZINE
Camera Upgrade	SHUTTER
Chain Reaction Level	MELTDOWN
Countdown Level	BLASTOFF
Decrypter Upgrade	SESAME

007: Nightfire (cont'd)

Deep Descent Level	AQUA
Double Cross Level	BONSAI
Enemies Vanquished Level	TRACTION
Equinox Level	VACUUM
Golden P2K	AU P2K
Golden PP7	AU PP7
Grapple Upgrade	LIFTOFF
Island Infiltration Level	PARADISE
Laser Upgrade	PHOTON
Level Select	PASSPORT
Multiplayer Bond Spacesuit	ZERO G
Multiplayer Mode All Characters	PARTY
Multiplayer Mode Assassination Option	TARGET
Multiplayer Mode Baron Samedi	VOODOO
Multiplayer Mode Bond Tuxedo	BLACKTIE
Multiplayer Mode Christmas Jones	NUCLEAR
Multiplayer Mode Demolition Option	TNT
Multiplayer Mode Drake	NUMBER 1 (Don't forget the space in the code.)
Multiplayer Mode Elektra King	Enter SLICK
Multiplayer Mode Explosive Scenery Option	BOOM
Multiplayer Mode GoldenEye Strike Option	ORBIT
Multiplayer Mode Goldfinger	MIDAS
Multiplayer Mode Jaws	DENTAL
Multiplayer Mode Max Zorin	BLIMP
Multiplayer Mode Mayday	BADGIRL
Multiplayer Mode Nick Nack	BITESIZE
Multiplayer Mode Oddjob	BOWLER
Multiplayer Mode Protection Option	GUARDIAN
Multiplayer Mode Pussy Galore	CIRCUS
Multiplayer Mode Renard	HEADCASE
Multiplayer Mode Scaramanga	ASSASSIN
Multiplayer Mode Team King of the Hill Option	TEAMWORK
Multiplayer Mode Uplink Option	TRANSMIT
Vanquish Car Missile Upgrade	LAUNCH
Tranquilizer Dart Upgrade (Your tranquilizer darts are upgraded so enemies stay down longer.)	SLEEPY
Stunner Upgrade	ZAP
Rifle Scope Upgrade	SCOPE
Phoenix Fire Level	FLAME
P2K Upgrade	P2000
Night Shift Level	HIGHRISE
Multiplayer Mode Wai Lin	MARTIAL
Multiplayer Mode Xenia Onatopp	JANUS

007: Nightfire (cont'd)

The following codes can be activated during gameplay.

Unlockable	Code
Berserk Racing	While racing on the Paris Prelude, Enemies Vanquished, Island Infiltration, or Deep Descent levels, press START to pause gameplay, hold L, press X, Y, Y, X, Y, B, then release L.
Faster Gameplay	Press START to pause gameplay, hold L, press X, Y, B, WHT, X, Y, B, WHT, then release L.
Frantic Racing	While racing on the Paris Prelude, Enemies Vanquished, Island Infiltration, or Deep Descent levels, press START to pause gameplay, hold L, press X, Y, B, Y, X, then release L.
Drive a Shelby Cobra	While racing on the Enemies Vanquished level, press START to pause gameplay, hold L, press →, →, ←, ←, ↑, then release L. You can now use the Shelby Cobra from the Paris Prelude level in the race through the Alps.
Drive an SUV	While racing on the Enemies Vanquished level, press START to pause gameplay, hold L, press X, B, Y, X, Y, and then release L.
Double Armor during Racing	While racing on the Paris Prelude, Enemies Vanquished, Island Infiltration, or Deep Descent levels, press START to pause gameplay, hold L, press B, Y, X, B, B, then release L.
Bonus Race in Alps	While racing on the Enemies Vanquished level, press START to pause gameplay, hold L, press B, B, X, X, Y, then release L.
Quadruple Armor during Racing	While racing on the Paris Prelude, Enemies Vanquished, Island Infiltration, or Deep Descent levels, press START to pause gameplay, hold L, press B, Y, X, B, B, B, B, then release L.
Super Bullets during Racing	While racing on the Paris Prelude, Enemies Vanquished, Island Infiltration, or Deep Descent levels, press START to pause gameplay, hold L, press B, B, B, B, then release L. Note: You can also do this when you fly the plane with Alura.
Trails during Racing	While racing on the Paris Prelude, Enemies Vanquished, Island Infiltration, or Deep Descent levels, press START to pause gameplay, hold L, press X, B, B, X, then release L.
Triple Armor during Racing	While racing on the Paris Prelude, Enemies Vanquished, Island Infiltration, or Deep Descent levels, press START to pause gameplay, hold L, press B, Y, X, B, B, B, then release L.

4X4 Evolution 2

Enter these codes at the Main Menu or Title Screen.

Unlockable	Code
Extra Money in Career Mode	Y,X,WHT,Y,X,WHT,X,X,Y,BLK,X,Y
High Reputation (for team selection)	Y,Y,WHT,X,X,WHT,Y,Y,Y,X,X,X
Mission Select	X,X,WHT,WHT,Y,Y,WHT,X,Y,Y,X,WHT

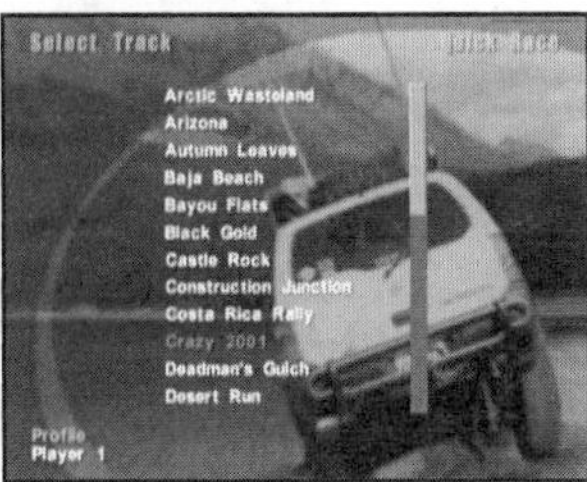

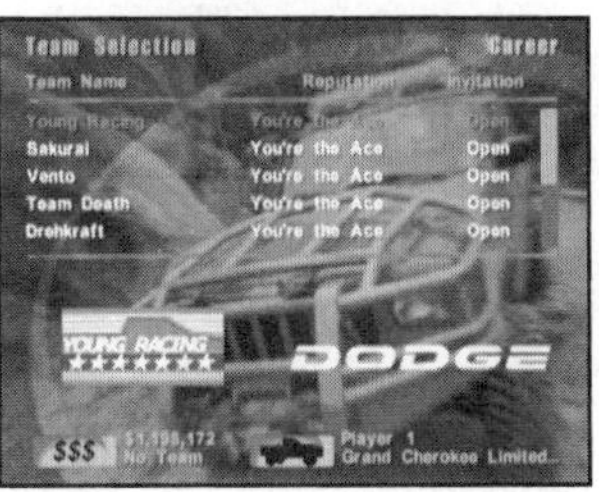

PSP Xbox PS2 GC GBA

Aggressive Inline

Unlockable	Objective
Bonus Characters	Complete the normal and hidden challenges in a level to unlock a bonus character.
Cheats	Collect all juice boxes in a level to reveal a cheat code.
FMV Sequences	Complete the normal challenges in a level to unlock its FMV sequence.
Power Skates	Complete all challenges (normal and hidden) on every level. The Power Skates give you one blue stat point for every attribute.
Ultra Skates	Complete all the levels with 100 percent. The Ultra Skates give you the other blue stat point for every attribute.

Aliens Vs Predator: Extinction

Unlockable	Code
Cheats	Pause the game and press R, R, L, R, L, L, R, L, R, R, L, R, L, L, R, L. The cheats are now available via the options menu.

Alter Echo

Enter these codes during gameplay.

Unlockable	Code
Remove Display	↑,↑,↓,↓,←,→,←,BACK+Y
Restore Health	↑,↑,↓,↓,←,→,←,BACK+→
Restore Time Dilation	↑,↑,↓,↓,←,→,←,BACK+↑

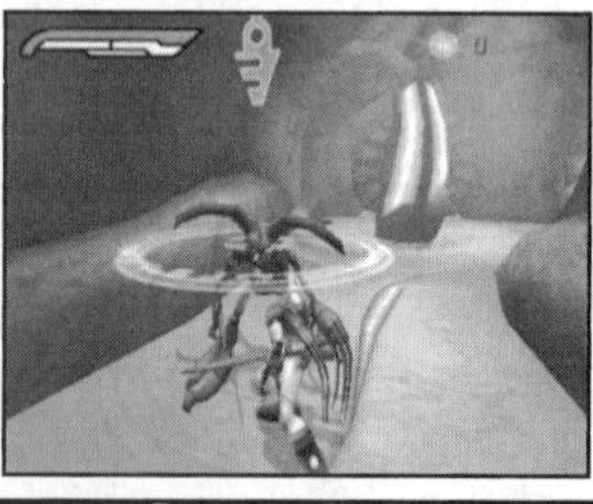

Amped: Freestyle Snowboarding

For the following codes, select "Options" at the main menu, then "Cheats." Enter the following case-sensitive codes to unlock these hidden goodies. A sound will confirm correct code entry. Press B to exit the Cheat menu.

Unlockable	Code
Bouncy Terrain	MegabOUnce
Disable Tree Collisions	buzzsaW
Free Movement (You can move anywhere quickly, even going uphill.)	ZiPster
Harder to Do Flips and Spins	KeepnReal
Level Select, All Costumes, Gear, and Snowboards	GimmeGimme
Low Gravity	MegaLeg
Perfect Jumps	StickiT
Play as Raven, the girl from the original Xbox tech demos, and get an Xbox snowboard	RidinwRaven
Play as Steezy	ChillinwSteezy
Super Spins	WhirlyGig

Amped: Freestyle Snowboarding (cont'd)

Super Statistics	BigsteeZ
View Programmer Replays	Enter the "Replay Theater" and highlight "Hard Disk." Press ⊙ until "Game Disc" appears to find replays generated by the programmers. To play one of those levels, select a replay, then highlight "Watch Replay." Press ⊙ until you see "Challenge," then select it.

Amped 2

Go to Options and enter the following codes in the Cheats menu.

Unlockable	Code
All Courses Are Icy	AllIce
All Secret Boarders	AllMyPeeps
Cheats Are Deactivated	NoCheats
Low Gravity	LowGravity
Max Out Rider Stats	MaxSkills
No Collisions with Other Riders	NoCollisions
Open All Levels	AllLevels
Rider Moves Faster	FastMove
Rider Never Crashes	DontCrash
Spin Faster	SuperSpin
Unlock a Pink Bunny	Bunny

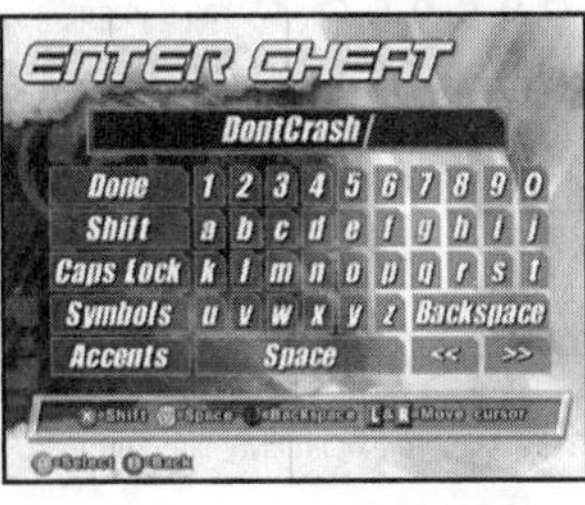

Apex

Enter all codes as brand names in Dream Mode.

Unlockable	Code
All Concept Cars in Arcade Mode	Dreamy
All Production Cars in Arcade Mode	Reality
All Tracks in Arcade Mode	World

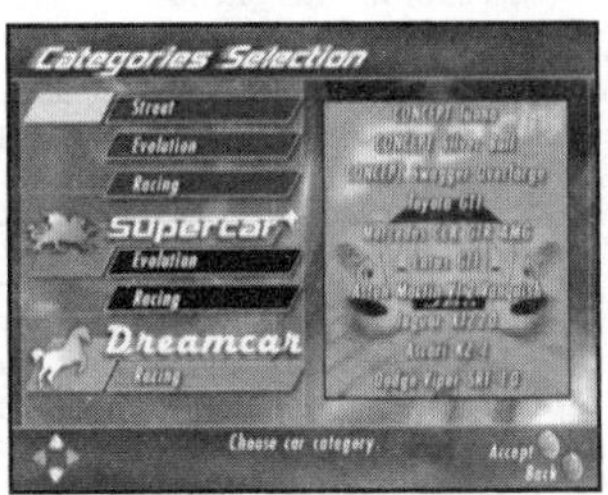

Armed and Dangerous

Enter the following codes at the Cheats screen in the Options Menu.

Unlockable	Code
Big Boots	R, White, Y, A, L, B, White, X
Big Hands	R, White, X, L, White, R, R, Y
Big Heads	L, Black, B, White, White, B, Black, L
Fill Ammo	Black, B, A, R, R, A, L, Black
Fill Health Bar	X, R, A, Y, Black, B, A, R
Invincible	X, X, X, R, A, L, L, Y
Topsy Turvy	X, A, B, B, A, B, White, White

Azurik: Rise of Perathia

Unlockable	Code
Adjust Camera	Quickly press R, ↓, ↑, ↓, ↑, click Right Thumbstick, click Left Thumbstick. The game stops, allowing you to alter the view. See Adjust Camera Tip for camera controls.
Adjust Lighting	Quickly press A, click Right Thumbstick, B, click Right Thumbstick, click Left Thumbstick. Darker areas become easier to see, but at the expense of having less dramatic lighting. Repeat this code to return to normal.
Afro Hairstyle	Quickly press ↓, →, Black + White, click Right Thumbstick, click Left Thumbstick, press Left Thumbstick → + Right Thumbstick ←, B, Y. A sound confirms correct code entry.
Big Heads	Quickly click Right Thumbstick, press R, ↓, ↑, A. A sound confirms correct code entry.
Full Power and Health	Hold ← and rotate the Right Thumbstick from right counter-clockwise to Left. Release ←, then press A, X. You can now restore your health and elemental power.
Gem Mode (You can increase your elemental power storage and get all the Obsidians through this mode.)	Quickly press →, ←, A, B, A, B, →, ←. You can get Earth, Air, Fire, Water, and Obsidian gems by pressing A, B, X, Y, or Black. Any other button exits Gem mode.
God Mode	Quickly press X, Black, White, R + L, click Left Thumbstick + Right Thumbstick. A sound confirms correct code entry. Repeat this code to disable its effect.
Level Select (This cheat also allows you to change your stats and view all FMV sequences.)	Press Left Thumbstick → + Right Thumbstick ←, Left Thumbstick ← + Right Thumbstick →, A, B, click Right Thumbstick, click Left Thumbstick. You must power off the Xbox to exit an FMV sequence.
Save at any point	Quickly press White, ↑, ↓, A, B, click Right Thumbstick during the "swing" animation. A click confirms that the game has been saved.

TIP

Adjust Camera Tip: Camera Controls

Press L or R to move the view up or down. Press Left Thumbstick or Right Thumbstick to move the view forward and back. Press Directional Pad to zoom in and out. Press A to view and remove the elemental power display. Press Back to resume the game.

CAUTION

Gem Mode Caution!

Do not create more gems than are supported! This will crash the game.

CAUTION

Save Point Caution!

While this may be done at any time during the game, remember to choose your save point carefully. Avoid saving on moving platforms, in areas where enemies respawn, while falling, or while dying.

Backyard Wrestling

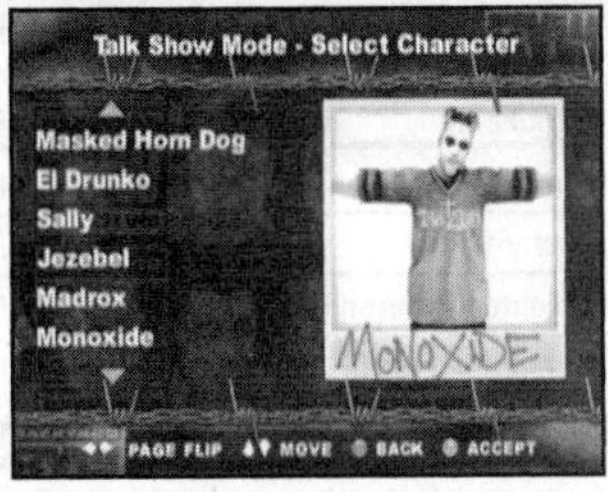

Enter this code at the main menu.

Unlockable	Code
All Wrestlers and Stages	Hold L, then press A,X,Y,B,A,X,Y,B

Bad Boys: Miami Takedown

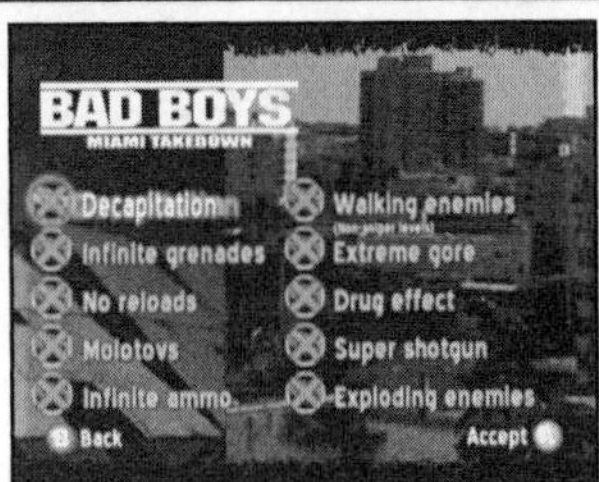

Enter the code at the Title Screen.

Unlockable	Code
Cheat Menu	B,Up,X,Y,Right,Down

Baldur's Gate: Dark Alliance

Enter these codes during gameplay.

Unlockable	Code
All Spells Available	Hold Y+A+L, then hold R down halfway. Now press Left.
Level Warp and Invulnerability Menu	Hold Y+A+L, press Left, hold R down halfway, then press START. All buttons must be held when start is pressed.

The Bard's Tale

While playing, hold L+R, then enter the following codes.

Unlockable	Code
Damage x100	Up,Down,Up,Down,Left,Right,Left,Right
Full Mana and Health	Left,Left,Right,Right,Up,Down,Up,Down
Intangible	Left,Right,Left,Right,Up,Down,Up,Down
Invincible	Right,Left,Right,Left,Up,Down,Up,Down
Silver and Adderstones	Up,Up,Down,Down,Left,Right,Left,Right

Batman: Rise of Sin Tzu

To access the following unlockables, hold both triggers and enter code.

Unlockable	Code
All Upgrades	Down,Up,Down,Left,Down,Right,Up,Down
All Rewards	Left,Down,Left,Right,Left,Left,Down,Right
God Mode	Up,Right,Up,Left,Down,Left,Down,Right

Batman Vengeance

Input the following codes at the main menu. Many of them will make a sound to confirm correct code entry.

Unlockable	Code
Bonus Characters	Press ←, →, ↓, White, L + R, then press START
Master Code	Press L, R, L, R, X, X, Y, Y
Unlimited Batarangs	Press L, R, White, Y
Unlimited Electric Batarangs	Press L, R, B, White, L

Battlestar Galactica

Enter the following codes in the Extras menu. A sound will confirm successful code entry.

Unlockable	Code
Wingmen, Starbuck and Apollo	↓,↓,←,↓,↓,↑,→,→
Production stills and artwork	←,↑,←,←,↓,←,↑,↓
	↑,↑,↓,↓,→,↑,→,↓
	↓,↓,↓,↓,←,←,←,←
	↑,↑,↑,↓,↓,↓,←,→
	→,→,↓,↓,←,←,↑,↑
	→,→,→,→,↓,↓,←,←
	→,→,↑,↑,←,←,↑,↑
	↑,←,↑,→,↑,←,↑,→

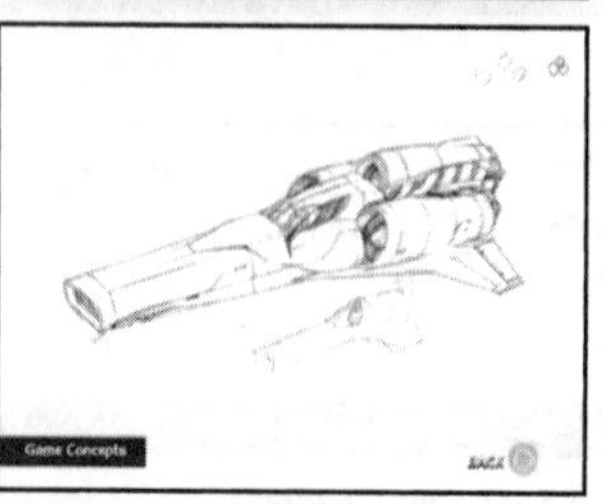

Big Mutha Trucker

Unlockable	Code
All Cheats	CHEATINGMUTHATRUCKER
Automatic Navigation	USETHEFORCE
Diplomatic Immunity	VICTORS
Evil Truck	VARLEY
Extra Money	LOTSAMONEY
Fast Truck	GINGERBEER
Infinite Time	PUBLICTRANSPORT
Level Select	LAZYPLAYER
Small Pedestrians	DAISHI
Toggle Damage	6WL

NOTE

You can also unlock Evil Truck by clearing the 60-Day Trial in Truckin' mode and win the race to Big Mutha Trucking HQ.

Black Stone: Magic and Steel

Unlockable	Code
New Character Class	From the Class selection screen, press R as you highlight each of the following classes: Pirate, Thief, Warrior, Archer, Pirate, Warlock, Thief, Warlock, Thief.

Blade II

At the Main Menu, hold down L, then enter the following codes. Text will appear upon successful code entry.

Unlockable	Code
All Weapons	X,B,Down,Left,B,B,Y
Daywalker Difficulty	Left,B,Up,Down,X,B,A
Level Select	Down,Up,Left,Left,B,Right,Down,X

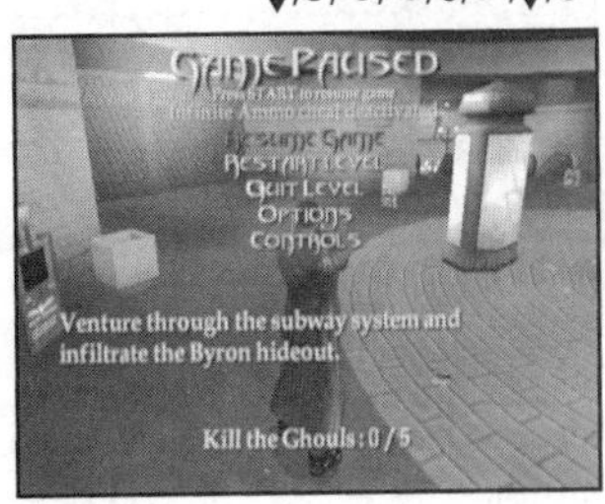

While paused, hold L, then enter the following codes. Text will appear upon successful code entry.

Unlockable	Code
Infinite Ammunition	Left,B,Right,X,Up,Y,Down,A
Infinite Health	Y,X,Y,X,Y,B,Y,B
Infinite Rage	Left,Down,Left,Down,Right,Up,Right,Left
Invincibility for NPCs during escort missions	X,B,Y,A,X,B,Y,A

Blinx

Unlockable	Objective
Bonus FMV Sequence	Complete Levels 1-1 through 8-4 with an "A+" or greater rank. (A game developers' FMV sequence unlocks in the "Collection" option for your prizes.)
Quick Level Completion	As soon as the level starts, quickly perform a low jump, and land back on the level start ring. The game is programmed to think that this is the finish ring. Note: This is very difficult to perform, but it is possible.
Ultimate Sweeper	Collect all 80 Cat Medals. (Now you can buy the Ultimate Sweeper for 90,000 at the last shop before the final boss. This Level 3 Sweeper can sweep any trash size and shoots fire and ice.)

BloodRayne

From the Options screen, go to Enter Cheats and input the following.

Unlockable	Code
Fill Bloodlust	ANGRYXXXINSANEHOOKER
Freeze Enemies	DONTFARTONOSCAR
God Mode	TRIASSASSINDONTDIE
Gratuitous Dismemberment	INSANEGIBSMODEGOOD
Juggy Mode	JUGGYDANCESQUAD

BloodRayne (cont'd)

Level Select	ONTHELEVEL
Restore Health	LAMEYANKEEDONTFEED
Secret Louisiana Level	BRIMSTONEINTHEBAYOU
Show Weapons	SHOWMEMYWEAPONS
Time Factor	NAKEDNASTYDISWASHERDANCE

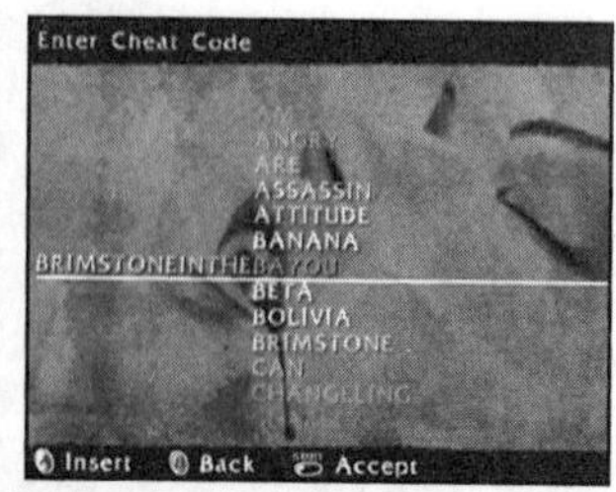

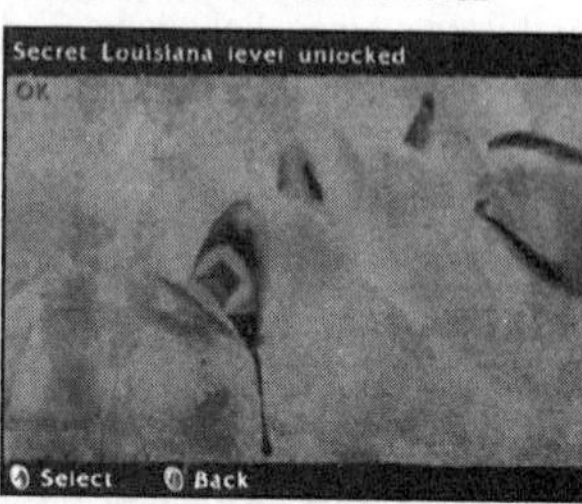

Blood Wake

Input the following codes at the "start game" screen. Listen for the sound to confirm correct code entry.

Unlockable	Code
All Battle Modes	Press Y, A, X, B, click L, click R, Black, White, R, R then press START.
All Boats	Press ↑, ↓, ←, →, L, B, X, X, click R, then press START.
All Levels	Press X, Y, ↑, →, ←, ↓, ↑, ↓, click L, L, then press START.
Blood Ball Mode	Press X, Y, White, Black, B, A, ←, ↑, →, ↓, then press START.
Import Boat Mode	Press Y, B, X, A, L, R, ←, →, click L, click R, then press START.
Invincibility	Click L, click R, press ↓, ←, ↓, ←, B, Y, then press START.
Puffer Fish	Press A, B, Black, White, Y, X, click R, R, click L, L, then press START.
Rubber Duck Mode	Click R, click L, R, L, Black, White, ↑, ↓, ←, →, then press START.
Unlimited Ammunition	Press Black, White, L, R, click R, R, Y, X, then press START.
Unlimited Turbo	Press ↑, ↑, ↓, ↓, ←, →, ←, →, B, A, then press START.

Unlockable	Objective
Basilisk	Complete the "Protection Racket" level under the captain difficulty setting.
Clanbake Battle Mode	Complete the "A Poke in the Eye" level under the ensign difficulty setting.
Fireshark	Complete the "Up the Nagau" level under the ensign difficulty setting.
Guncat Catamaran	Complete the "Protection Racket" level under the ensign difficulty setting.
Gunshark	Complete the "Ships in the Night" level under the ensign difficulty setting.
Hellcat Catamaran	Complete the "The Gauntlet" level under the ensign difficulty setting.
Hydroplane Switchblade	Complete the "Gladiator" level under the ensign difficulty setting.
Jackal	Complete the "Assault on Black Moon" level under the ensign difficulty setting.
Kingdom Come Battle Mode	Complete the "Baptism of Fire" level under the ensign difficulty setting.
Lightning	Complete the "A Friend in Need" level under the ensign difficulty setting.

Blood Wake (cont'd)

Metal Massacre Battle Mode	Complete the "Hurricane of Fire" level under the ensign difficulty setting.
Pike	Complete the "Payment Is Due" level under the ensign difficulty setting.
Salamander	Complete the "Fish in a Barrel" level under the ensign difficulty setting.
Switchblade Hydroplane	Complete the "Gladiator" level under the ensign difficulty setting.
Tigershark	Complete the "Sampan Surprise" level under the ensign difficulty setting.

Bloody Roar Extreme

Unlockable	Objective
Beast Mode	Beat the game fifteen times.
Big Kid Mode	Beat the game four times.
Break Walls Mode	Beat the game eight times.
Com Vs Com Battle Mode	Watch the computer spar against itself by clearing the game twice in Computer Vs Computer mode.
Corn Battle Mode	Beat the game twice.
Cronos	Beat the game twice.
Eliminate All Walls Mode	Beat the game six times.
Expert Mode	Beat the game twelve times.
Fang	Defeat Arcade Mode with all available characters, plus Uranus and Kohryu.
Ganesha	Beat the game once.
High Speed Mode	Beat the game ten times.
Human Mode	Beat the game fourteen times.
Kid Mode	Beat the game three times.
Knock Down Battle Mode	Beat the game thirteen times.
Kohryu	Beat him in the Arcade Mode, then finish the Arcade Mode.
Low Speed Mode	Beat the game nine times.
Movie Player Option	Beat the game once.
No Blocking Mode	Beat the game eleven times.
Super Buff Mode	Beat the game five times.
Weaken All Walls Mode	Beat the game seven times.

Blow Out

Unlockable	Code
All Weapons	charliehustleoverdressedromeo
All Levels	coollevelcheatcode
God Mode	nopainnocane
Unlimited Ammo	fishinabarrel

Breakdown

Unlockable	Objective
Extreme Mode	Complete the game.
Gallery	Complete the game.
Music Player	Complete the game.
Trailer	Complete the game.

Brothers in Arms: Road to Hill 30

Unlockable	Code
Unlock All Levels and Difficulties	BAKERSDOZEN

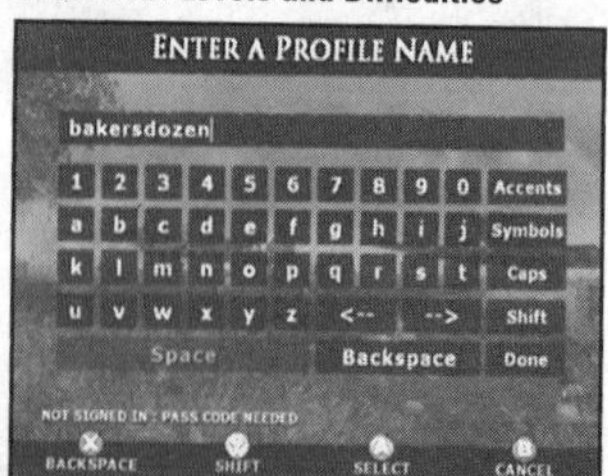

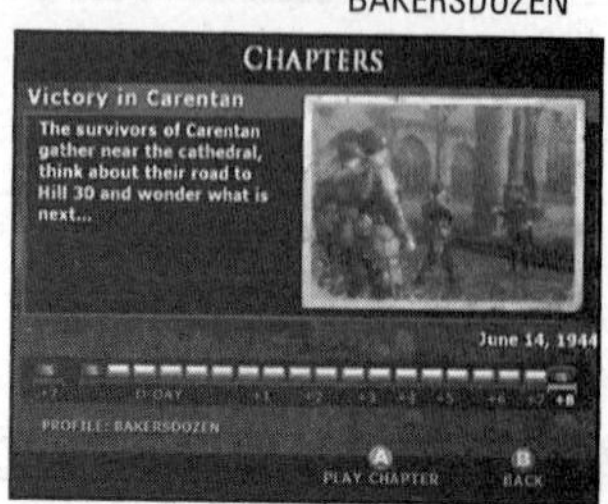

Bruce Lee: Quest of the Dragon

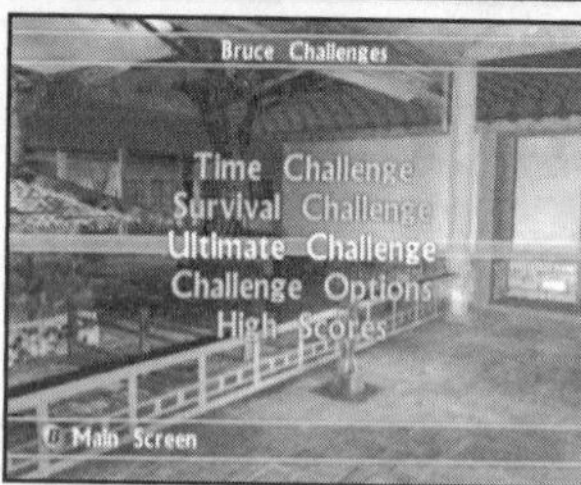

Enter this code at the Title Screen.

Unlockable	Code
Bruce's Challenges	X,Y,X,Y,X,X,Y,Y,L,R

Brute Force

Unlockable	Code
Better Aim	DEADAIM
Better Defense	ERINROBERTS
Cartoon Mode	HVYMTL
Harder Difficulty	BRUTAL
Quick Death	DBLDAY
Rapid Fire Weapons	RAPIDFIRE
Stupid AI	SPRAGNT
Tough Characters	MATTSOELL

Unlockable	Objective
Confed Marine	Find the DNA sequence in Mission 1 or Mission 6
Feral Colonist	Find the DNA sequence in Mission 2
Feral Outcast	Find the DNA sequence in Mission 3
Feral Shaman	Find the DNA sequence in Mission 9
Fire Hound	Find the DNA sequence in Mission 13
Gunthar Ghent	Find the DNA sequence in Mission 10
Hunter Lord	Find the DNA sequence in Mission 18
McTavish	Find the DNA sequence in Mission 14
Militia	Find the DNA sequence in Mission 5 or Mission 11
Outcast Shaman	Find the DNA sequence in Mission 7
Seer Follower	Find the DNA sequence in Mission 4
Seer Priest	Find the DNA sequence in Mission 8
Shadoon	Find the DNA sequence in Mission 12
Shrike Heavy	Find the DNA sequence in Mission 16
Shrike Hound	Find the DNA sequence in Mission 17
Shrike Soldier	Find the DNA sequence in Mission 15

Buffy the Vampire Slayer

Go to the Extras screen and input the following.

Unlockable	Code
All Four Multiplayer Arenas	Y,Y,WHT,BLK,BLK,Y,Y,Y,Y,Y,WHT,BLK
Slayer Power	Y,Y,Y,BLK,BLK,BLK,Y,WHT,BLK,BLK,WHT,Y
Unlimited Health	Y,WHT,BLK,BLK,WHT,Y,BLK,BLK,BLK,Y,Y,Y

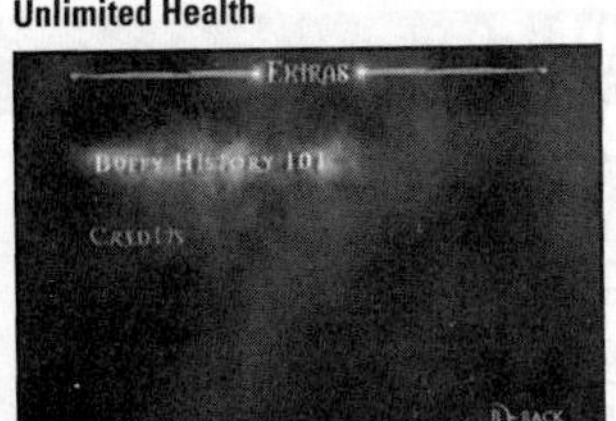

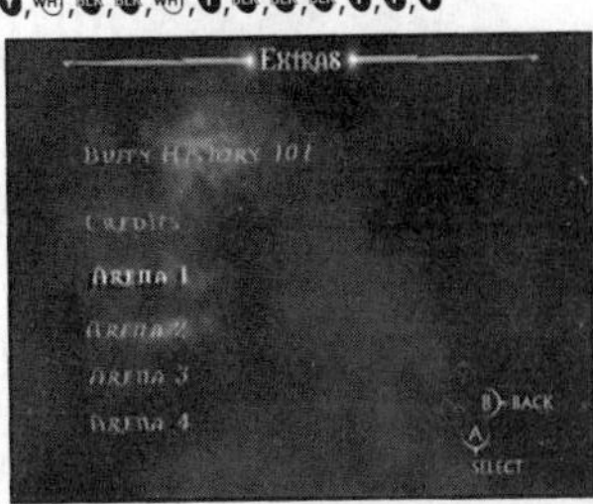

Buffy the Vampire Slayer: Chaos Bleeds

Unlockable	Objective
Abominator	Finish Mission 10 with Professional rating
Amber Benson Interview	Complete Mission 2
Amber Benson Voice Over Session	Complete Mission 8
Anthony Stewart Interview	Complete Mission 1
Anthony Stewart Voice Over Session	Complete Mission 7
Bat Beast	Finish Mission 4 with Professional rating
Cemetery	Finish Mission 2 with Slayer rating
Chainz	Finish Mission 10 with Slayer rating
Chaos Bleeds Comic Book	Complete Mission 5
Chris	Finish Mission 12 with Slayer rating
Faith	Finish Mission 8 with Professional rating
Female Vampire	Finish Mission 1 with Slayer rating
Initiative	Finish Mission 8 with Slayer rating
James Marsters Voice Over Session	Complete Mission 6
Joss Whedon	Finish Mission 12 with Professional rating
Joss Whedon Voice Over Session	Complete Mission 11
Kakistos	Finish Mission 9 with Slayer rating
Male Vampire	Finish Mission 1 with Professional rating
Materani	Finish Mission 5 with Professional rating
Nicholas Brendan Interview	Complete Mission 3
Nicholas Brendon Voice Over Session	Complete Mission 9
Out-Takes	Complete Mission 12
Psycho Patient	Finish Mission 6 with Professional rating
Quarry	Finish Mission 11 with Slayer rating
Robin Sachs Interview	Complete Mission 4
Robin Sachs Voice Over Session	Complete Mission 10
S&M Mistress	Finish Mission 7 with Slayer rating
S&M Slave	Finish Mission 7 with Professional rating
Sid the Dummy	Finish Mission 6 with Slayer rating
Tara	Finish Mission 3 with Slayer rating
Zombie Demon	Finish Mission 3 with Professional rating

Buffy the Vampire Slayer: Chaos Bleeds (cont'd)

Zombie Devil	Finish Mission 4 with Slayer rating
Zombie Gorilla	Finish Mission 11 with Professional rating
Zombie Skeleton	Finish Mission 2 with Professional rating
Zombie Soldier	Finish Mission 9 with Professional rating

Burnout 2: Point of Impact—Developer's Cut

Unlockable	Objective
Cheat Mode Menu	Unlock any cheat and the Cheat Mode menu option will appear at the Options screen.
Classic 1970 Car	Destroy the car with a police car in Pursuit 2.
Custom Compact	Beat Custom Series Qualifier.
Custom Coupe	Get all gold medals at Split Second Grand Prix.
Custom Muscle Car	Beat Pursuit 6.
Custom Pickup Truck	Beat Pursuit 5.
Custom Roadster	Get all gold medals at the Point Of Impact Grand Prix.
Custom Series Championship	Earn gold medals in every race and complete Championship Mode.
Custom Sports Car	Get all gold medals at the Speed Streak Grand Prix.
Custom SUV	Beat Pursuit 4.
Drivers' Ed Car	Get all gold medals in Driving 101.
Freerun	Finish Custom Series Championship.
Gangster Car	Beat Pursuit 3.
Hot Rod Car	Beat Face Off 1.
Invulnerability Option	Finish the Grand Prix Championships with gold medals.
Japanese Muscle Car	Beat Face Off 2.
Oval Racer	Beat the car in Face Off 2.
Police Car	Beat Pursuit 1 and destroy the villain's car.
Super Car	Beat Face Off 4.

Catwoman

Enter this code in the Vault Menu.

Unlockable	Code
Extra Galleries	1941

Conflict Desert Storm

Enter this code at the Main Menu.

Unlockable	Code
Cheat Mode	X,X,Y,Y,L,L,R,R,L,L,R,R

Conflict Vietnam

Enter this code at the Main Menu.

Unlockable	Code
Cheat Menu	R,R,L,L,B,B,Y,Y,X,X,WHT

Conflict Desert Storm II: Back to Baghdad

Unlockable	Code
Cheat Menu	At the Main menu, enter L,L,R,R,X,X,Y,Y,B,B. Go to Options and the Cheat Menu will be at the bottom.

Constantine

To enter these codes, press BACK to open your journal.

Unlockable	Code
Big Headed Demons	BLK,←,→,←,←,→,←,BLK
Big Weapon Mode	←,X,X,X,Y,Y,Y
Explosive Holy Bomb	→,←,X,Y,X,Y,←,→
Rapid Fire Shotgun	WHT,←,BLK,←,Y,X,Y,X
Shoot Fireballs	Y,Y,Y,←,→,→,←,←,→

Corvette

In the Options Menu, select "Change Name," then enter this code.

Unlockable	Code
All Cars and All Tracks	XOPENSEZ

Crash Bandicoot: The Wrath of Cortex

Unlockable	Code
Alternate Ending Sequence	Collect all 46 gems

Crazy Taxi 3: High Roller

Unlockable	Objective
All Drivers	Complete Crazy X Level S-S.
Another Day Mode	Complete Crazy X Level 3.
Bonus Courses— West Coast, Glitter Oasis, and Small Apple	Complete Crazy X Level 1
Bonus Taxis—bike, stroller, and carriage	Complete Crazy X Level 2

Crazy Taxi 3: High Roller (cont'd)

Cheat Mode (All drivers, courses, and taxis unlock.)	Hold L+R+X+Y+click-hold L+click-hold R on controllers one and four simultaneously at the Character Selection screen. A voice confirms correct code entry.
Disable Arrow Indicators	Highlight a driver, hold WHT, and press A at the Character Selection screen. The message "No Arrows" appears to confirm correct code entry.
Disable Destination Indicator	Highlight a driver, hold BLK, and press A at the Character Selection screen. The message "No Destination Markers" appears to confirm correct code entry.
Expert Mode (No destination or arrow indicators appear in this mode.)	Highlight a driver, hold WHT+BLK, and press A at the Character Selection screen. The message "Expert Mode" appears to confirm correct code entry.
Toggle Headlights	Click R to turn your headlights on and off.

Crimson Skies: High Road to Revenge

Enter the following codes during gameplay.

Unlockable	Code	Unlockable	Code
$5,000	A,Y,A,Y,BLK	God Mode	Y,A,X,B,BLK
10 Tokens	X,B,X,B,BLK	Super Primary Weapon	B,X,A,B,BLK
All Planes	Y,X,B,Y,BLK	Ultra Hard Mode	X,B,A,X,BLK

Dakar 2

Unlockable	Code
All Cars	SWEETAS
All Tracks	BONZER

Dark Summit

Input each of the following codes at the main menu. After inputting a code, listen for a sound to confirm correct code entry.

Unlockable	Code
Alien Unlocked (Challenges 43 (Race the Chief), 48 (Bomb #5), 49 (Alien Half Pipe), and 50 (Storm HQ) will be completed. You'll also have Bomb Piece #5.)	Hold BACK + START and press Y, L, X, B, R, A, R, X.
All Boarders	Hold BACK + START and press Y, L, X, B, R, A, R, B
Challenges Completed (All challenges except for 43 (Race the Chief), 48 (Bomb #5), 49 (Alien Half Pipe), and 50 (Storm HQ) will be completed. You'll also have all Bomb Pieces, with the exception of Bomb #5.)	Hold BACK + START and press Y, L, X, B, R, A, R, Y at the main menu.
Extra Points (You'll get 9,100,000 lift points, which unlock all lifts except for the Moon Gate. You'll also get 9,100,000 equipment points, which unlock all boards, accessories, and special tricks.)	Hold BACK + START and press Y, L, X, B, R, A, R, A at the main menu.
Shoot Projectile	Hold BACK + START and press Y, X, B, R. Press L + R to shoot a barrel with a projectile.
Slow Motion	Hold BACK + START and press Y, X, B, L. Press L + R when in the air or during a railslide to activate Slow Motion mode. This mode automatically ends when you reach the ground.

PSP
Xbox
PS2
GC
GBA

Dave Mirra Freestyle BMX 2

Enter all codes at the Main Menu. If done correctly, a sound confirms correct code entry.

Character Bikes	Code
Colin Mackay	Down, Down, Right, Right, Right, Right, Right, Up, X
Dave Mirra	Down, Down, Up, Right, Up, Right, Up, Up, X
Joey Garcia	Down, Down, Up, Right, Left, Left, Down, Right, X
John Englebert	Down, Down, Left, Up, Left, Up, Left, Left, X
Kenan Harkin	Down, Down, Left, Up, Down, Right, Down, Down, X
Leigh Ramsdell	Down, Down, Down, Up, Left, Left, Down, Left, X
Mike Laird	Down, Down, Right, Left, Down, Up, Up, Right, X
Rick Moliterno	Down, Down, Up, Left, Right, Right, Left, Up, X
Ryan Nyquist	Down, Down, Down, Down, Down, Right, Up, Down, X
Scott Wirch	Down, Down, Right, Up, Down, Down, Left, Right, X
Tim Mirra	Down, Down, Right, Left, Down, Right, Down, Up, X
Todd Lyons	Down, Down, Down, Down, Left, Right, Left, Down, X
Troy McMurray	Down, Down, Left, Down, Right, Left, Up, Left, X
Zach Shaw	Down, Down, Left, Down, Up, Right, Right, Down, X

Levels	Code
Colin Mackay	Up, Up, Right, Left, Up, Right, Right, Up, X
Dave Mirra	Up, Up, Up, Right, Up, Left, Up, Up, X
Joey Garcia	Up, Up, Up, Up, Down, Down, Down, Right, X
John Englebert	Up, Up, Left, Down, Right, Down, Left, Left, X
Kenan Harkin	Up, Up, Left, Left, Down, Up, Down, Down, X
Leigh Ramsdell	Up, Up, Down, Up, Left, Down, Down, Left, X
Mike Laird	Up, Up, Right, Down, Down, Right, Up, Right, X
Rick Molitero	Up, Up, Up, Down, Right, Right, Left, Up, X
Ryan Nyquist	Up, Up, Down, Down, Left, Right, Up, Down, X
Scott Wirch	Up, Up, Right, Up, Left, Left, Left, Right, X
Tim Mirra	Up, Up, Right, Down, Right, Left, Down, Up, X
Todd Lyons	Up, Up, Down, Up, Right, Right, Left, Down, X
Troy McMurray	Up, Up, Left, Up, Up, Right, Up, Left, X
Zach Shaw	Up, Up, Left, Right, Down, Down, Right, Down, X

Rider Outfits	Code
Colin Mackay	Right, Right, Right, Left, Right, Up, Right, Up, X
Joey Garcia	Right, Right, Up, Down, Up, Right, Down, Right, X
John Englebert	Right, Right, Left, Right, Up, Up, Left, Left, X
Kenan Harkin	Right, Right, Left, Down, Up, Left, Down, Down, X
Leigh Ramsdell	Right, Right, Down, Left, Up, Down, Down, Left, X
Mike Laird	Right, Right, Right, Up, Down, Down, Up, Right, X
Rick Moliterno	Right, Right, Up, Up, Up, Right, Left, Up, X
Ryan Nyquist	Right, Right, Down, Down, Left, Up, Up, Down, X
Scott Wirch	Right, Right, Right, Up, Left, Left, Left, Right, X
Tim Mirra	Right, Right, Right, Down, Down, Right, Down, Up, X
Todd Lyons	Right, Right, Down, Left, Left, Up, Left, Down, X

Dave Mirra Freestyle BMX 2 (cont'd)

Rider Outfits	Code
Troy McMurray	→,→,←,↑,←,←,↑,←,Ⓧ
Zach Shaw	→,→,←,←,↓,↓,→,↓,Ⓧ

Signature Tricks	Code
Amish Air	←,→,↑,↑,→,↓,→,→,Ⓧ
Colin Mackay	←,→,→,↑,←,→,→,↑,Ⓧ
Dave Mirra	←,→,↑,↑,←,→,↑,↑,Ⓧ
Joey Garcia	←,→,↑,→,↓,↑,↓,→,Ⓧ
John Englebert	←,→,←,←,↓,↑,←,←,Ⓧ
Kenan Harkin	←,→,←,↓,↑,↓,↓,↓,Ⓧ
Leigh Ramsdell	←,→,↓,←,←,→,↓,←,Ⓧ
Mike Laird	←,→,→,→,←,→,↑,→,Ⓧ
Rick Moliterno	←,→,↑,↑,↑,↓,←,↑,Ⓧ
Ryan Nyquist	←,→,↓,↓,↓,↑,↑,↓,Ⓧ
Scott Wirch	←,→,→,→,↑,↓,←,↑,Ⓧ
Slim Jim Guy	←,→,↓,←,↑,←,→,←,Ⓧ
Tim Mirra	←,→,→,↑,↓,↑,↓,↑,Ⓧ
Todd Lyons	←,→,↓,↓,←,→,←,↓,Ⓧ
Troy McMurray	←,→,←,←,↑,↓,↑,←,Ⓧ
Zach Shaw	←,→,←,↓,←,↑,→,↓,Ⓧ

Dead or Alive 3

Unlockable	Code
Alternate Snow Stage Appearance	Select Versus or Training mode and highlight the snow stage. Press Ⓧ for a light snow, press Ⓨ for a blizzard, or press Ⓐ for a random effect.
Control Replays	Hold Ⓐ + Ⓑ + Ⓧ after winning a match. When the replay starts, press Ⓨ to slow it down or go back.
Control Victory View	Press R3 or R4 and use Ⓛ or Ⓡ during the victory scene after a battle to change the camera angle. Ⓛ pans the camera, and Ⓡ zooms in and out.

NOTE

Each character has at least one taunt. All characters do this with Back, Forward, Back, then BLK or Ⓧ + Ⓐ + Ⓑ. Some characters have more, such as Hayabusa, Brad, Ayane, and Lei Fang. To do these extra taunts, press ↓, ↓, BLK or Ⓧ + Ⓐ + Ⓑ. Another one is done by pressing Forward, Back, Forward (BLK or Ⓧ + Ⓐ + Ⓑ). Yet another is done by pressing Back twice (BLK or Ⓧ + Ⓐ + Ⓑ).

NOTE

Only one or two characters have the last two sets of taunt moves.

Dead or Alive Xtreme Beach Volleyball

Unlockable	Objective
Bonus Music Tracks—"How Crazy Are You" (by Meja) and "Is This Love" (by Bob Marley).	Play through the game once. When you resume that saved game file, these two hidden songs are available in the Radio Station.

Dead or Alive Xtreme Beach Volleyball
(cont'd)

Unlockable	Objective
Ending Bonus	Complete the game. When you start a new game, you can immediately advance to the end. Select the "Leave Tomorrow" option at the Hotel or Pool menu to skip to the ending.
Ending Sequence	Wait for the credits to end to see an extra FMV sequence featuring Zack and the remains of his island.
Extra Items	Give many gifts to one character and complete that game. Start a new game with that saved game file, and choose to play as the character that received those gifts. Those items are available in your inventory in the new game.

Dead to Rights

Enter the code at the Main Menu.

Unlockable	Code
Chapter Select	↑,↓,↑,↓,←,→,→,Y,X,X

Def Jam Fight for NY

Enter these codes in the Cheat Menu.

Unlockable	Code
100 Reward Points	NEWJACK
Anything Goes by CNN	MILITAIN
Bust by Outkast	BIGBOI
Comp by Comp	CHOCOCITY
Dragon House by Chiang	AKIRA
Koto by Chiang	GHOSTSHELL
Man Up by Sticky Fingaz	KIRKJONES
Move by Public Enemy	RESPECT
Original Gangster by Ice T	POWER
Take a Look at my Life by Fat Joe	CARTAGENA
Walk with Me by Joe Budden	PUMP

NOTE

The following codes also yield the "100 Reward Points" unlockable: THESOURCE, CROOKLYN, DUCKET, GETSTUFF

Destroy All Humans

To activate these codes, pause the game and hold L, then enter the code and release L.

Unlockable	Code
Ammo-A-Plenty	←,Y,WHT,→,BLK,X
Aware Like a Fox	→,X,WHT,BLK,→,WHT
Bulletproof Crypto	X,Y,←,←,Y,X
Deep Thinker	BLK,WHT,Y,→,WHT,Y
Mmmm...Brains!	BLK,BLK,WHT,WHT,←,→,←,→,WHT,BLK This code increase DNA. (You must be done on the Mothership.)
Nobody Loves You	WHT, →, WHT, BLK, X, →

Disney's Extreme Skate Adventure

Enter these codes in the Cheats Menu.

Unlockable	Code
All Create-a-Skater Items	gethotgear
All Levels	frequentflyers
All Skaters	xtremebuddies
Lion King Video	savannah
Special Meter always full	happyfeet
Tarzan Video	nugget
Toy Story Video	marin

Dr. Muto

In the Options Menu, select "Cheats" to enter these codes.

Unlockable	Code
All Gadgets	TINKERTOY
All Morphs	EUREKA
Death No Touch	NECROSCI
Go Anywhere	BEAMMEUP
Never Take Damage	CHEATERBOY
Secret Morphs	LOGGLOGG
See all Movies	HOTTICKET
Super Ending Unlocked	BUZZOFF

Driv3r

Enter the following codes at the Main Menu.

Unlockable	Code
All Missions	X,X,Y,Y,R,R,L
All Weapons	L,L,X,Y,Y,R,R
Immunity	X,Y,R,R,L,L,Y
Invincibility	X,Y,L,R,L,R,R—NOTE: Does not work in Story Mode
Unlimited Ammo	R,R,L,L,X,Y,Y
Unlock All Vehicles	X,X,Y,Y,L,R,L

Dungeon and Dragons Heroes

To enter these codes, hold L and press A+Y during gameplay.

Unlockable	Code
10 Anti Venom	SPINRAD
10 Berserker Brew	THOMAS
10 Fire Bomb	WEBER
10 Fire Flask	BROPHY
10 Firey Oil	EHOFF
10 Flash Freeze	ESKO
10 Globe Potions	WRIGHT
10 Holy Water	CRAWLEY
10 Insect Plagues	DERISO
10 Keys	SNODGRASS
10 Large Healing Potions	THOMPSON
10 Large Will Potions	GEE
10 Medium Potions of Will	LU
10 Potions of Haste	UHL
10 Pyrokins	SMITH
10 Rod of Destruction	AUSTIN
10 Rod of Fire	DELUCIA
10 Rod of Miracles	JARMAN
10 Rod of Missiles	MILLER
10 Rod of Reflection	WHITTAKE
10 Rod of Shadows	DINOLT
10 Thrown Axe of Ruin	RAMERO
10 Thrown Daggers	MOREL
10 Thrown Daggers of Stunning	BELL
10 Thrown Halcyon Hammer	PRASAD
10 Thrown Hammer	BRATHWAI
10 Thrown Viper Axe	HOWARD
10 Thunderstone	ELSON
10 Tome of Apprentice	BILGER

Dungeon and Dragons Heroes (cont'd)

Unlockable	Code
10 Tome of Lessons	PAQUIN
10 Tome of Teacher	MEFORD
10 Tome of the Master	SPANBURG
10 Warp Stones	HOPPENST
10,000 XP Points	DSP633
500,000 Gold Pieces	KNE637
Add 10 to Constitution	N STINE
Add 10 to Dexterity	YAN
Disable Cheats	UNBUFF
Invincibility	PELOR
Nightmare Setting	MPS LABS
Unlimited Mystical Will	OBADHI
View Concept Art	CONCEPTS
View Credits	Credits

EA Sports Bio Awards

Unlockable	Code
2002 All-American Team	Level 18
Butter Fingers Pennant	Level 4
Orange Bowl Pennant	Level 8
Rose Bowl Pennant	Level 2
Tostitos Bowl Pennant	Level 12

The Elder Scrolls III: Morrowind

During Gameplay, go to the Statistics page to enter the following codes. You can only enter one code at a time.

Unlockable	Code
Restore Fatigue	Highlight Fatigue and press BLK, BLK, WHT, WHT, BLK, then hold A to reach the desired level.
Restore Health	Highlight Health and press BLK, WHT, BLK, BLK, BLK, then hold A to reach the desired level.
Restore Magicka	Highlight Magicka and press BLK, WHT, WHT, BLK, WHT, then hold A to reach the desired level.

Enclave

Unlockable	Code
God Mode and Complete Mission	Pause the game and enter X, Y, X, X, Y, Y, X, Y, X, X, Y, Y

Enter the Matrix

Enable Cheats: Enter the hacking system and enter cheat.exe from the A prompt. Then you can enter the codes below.

CAUTION

Warning! The game can crash with cheats enabled.

Unlockable	Code
All weapons	0034AFFF
Blind Enemies	FFFFFFF1
Bonus level	13D2C77F
Deaf Enemies	4516DF45
Faster Logos	7867F443
Faster Logos	7867F443
Infinite ammo	1DDF2556
Infinite focus	69E5D9E4
Infinite Health	7F4DF451
Invisibility	FFFFFFF1
Low gravity	BB013FFF
Multiplayer	D5C55D1E
Recover Focus Fast	FFF0020A
Taxi Driving	312MF451
Turbo mode	FF00001A

ESPN NBA Basketball

Unlockable	Code
All 24/7 Items	Create a Player wit the first name HUNT and the lastname 4TREASURE.

ESPN NFL 2K5

Get these unlockables by changing your VIP profile name to the following:

Unlockable	Profile Name
1,000,000 Crib Credits	PhatBank
All Crib items	CribMax
All Milestones complete (full trophy room)	MadSkilz

ESPN NHL 2K5

Unlockable	Code
All Skybox	Create a Profile with the name LuvLeafs.

Evil Dead: Fistful of Boomstick

Unlockable	Objective
Unlock Arcade Levels	Finish levels in story mode.
Unlock Gallery Art	Each time you finish a level, concept art for the level will be unlocked at the Extras menu.

Fantastic Four

Enter these codes quickly at the Main menu. You will hear a sound to confirm a correct entry.

Unlockable	Code
Barge Arena and Stan Lee interview #1	X,B,X,↓,↓,B,↑
Bonus Level Hell	→, →, X, B, ←, ↑, ↓
Infinite Cosmic Powers	↑, X, X, X, ←, →, B

Fight Night 2004

Unlockable	Code
All Venues	At the Main Menu, highlight My Corner and press ←,←,←,→,→,→,←,→,→.
Big Tigger	In the Record Book menu, go to most wins and press ↑,↑.
Miniature Fighters	At the Main Menu, hightlight Play Now and press ←,←,←,→,→,→,←,A

Fight Night Round 2

Unlockable	Code
All Venus	At the game mode select screen hold ← until you hear a bell.
Mini Fighters	At the choose Venue screen hold ↑ until you hear a bell ring.
Unlock Fabulous	Create a character with the first name GETFAB then cancel out and Fabulous will be available for Play Now and Career mode.

Finding Nemo

Enter all the codes at the Main Menu and the word Cheat will show up if done correctly.

Unlockable	Code
Credits	Y,X,B,Y,Y,X,B,Y,X,B,Y,X,X,B,Y,X,B,Y,X,B,B,X,Y
Invincibility	Y,X,X,B,B,B,Y,Y,X,X,X,B,B,B,B,X,Y,B, B,B,X,B,Y,B,B,X,B,B,Y,B,X,B,B,B,Y
Level Select	Y,Y,Y,X,X,B,X,Y,B,X,Y,X,Y,X,Y,B,Y,Y
Secret Level	Y,X,B,B,X,Y,Y,X,B,B,X,Y,Y,B,X,Y,X,B,B,X,Y

Flatout

Create a profile using these passwords.

Unlockable	Passwords
Lots of Cash	GIVECASH
Unlocks Everything	GIVEALL
Use the Shift Up Button to Launch the Driver	Ragdoll

Freaky Flyers

Unlockable	Objective
Pilot X	On the last level in Adventure mode, beat Pilot X by destroying his robot.

Freedom Fighters

Enter these codes during gameplay.

Unlockable	Code
Change Spawn Point	Y,A,X,B,A,Up
Fast Motion	Y,A,X,B,B,Down
Heavy Machine Gun	Y,A,X,B,Y,Down
Infinite Ammo	Y,A,X,B,A,Right
Invisibility	Y,A,X,B,B,Left
Max Charisma	Y,A,X,B,A,Down
Nail Gun	Y,A,X,B,A,Left
Ragdolls	Y,A,X,B,X,Up
Rocket Launcher	Y,A,X,B,Y,Left
Shotgun	Y,A,X,B,B,Up
Slow Motion	Y,A,X,B,B,Right
Sniper Rifle	Y,A,X,B,Y,Right
Sub Machine Gun	Y,A,X,B,Y,Up

Freestyle Metal X

Go to Options, then enter the following case-sensitive codes in the Cheat menu.

Unlockable	Code
$1,000,000	sugardaddy
All Bike Parts	garageking
All Costumes	johnnye
All FMV Sequences	watchall
All Levels and Events	universe
All Photos and Posters in the Gallery	seeall
All Riders and Bikes	dudemaster
All Songs	hearall
All Special Stunts	fleximan

Full Spectrum Warrior

Enter the following codes at the Cheat Menu.

Unlockable	Code
Big Head Mode	NICKWEST
Full Version of America's Army	ha2p1py9tur5tle
Play at a harder level with no HUD	SWEDISHARMY
Unlimited ammo	MERCENARIES

Futurama

While playing, hold L and enter the following codes.

Unlockable	Code
All Extras	A, R+X, R+Y, A, R+X, R+Y, R+B, R+A, Black, R+B, R+Back
Full Charge	A, R+X, R+Y, A, R+X, R+Y, R+B, R+A, Black, X, R+Back
Full Health	A, R+X, R+Y, A, R+X, R+Y, R+B, R+A, Black, Y, R+Back
Infinite Ammo	A, R+X, R+Y, A, R+X, R+Y, R+B, R+A, Black, B, R+Back
Invincibility	A, R+X, R+Y, A, R+X, R+Y, R+B, R+A, Black, R+Y, R+Back
Unlimited Lives	A, R+X, R+Y, A, R+X, R+Y, R+B, R+A, Black, A, R+Back

Level	Code
Bender's Breakout	A, R+X, R+Y, A, R+X, R+Y, R+X, R+Y, R+Y, Y, Back
Bogad Swamp Trail	A, R+X, R+Y, A, R+X, R+Y, R+X, R+Y, X, Y, Back
Fry Fights Back	A, R+X, R+Y, A, R+X, R+Y, R+X, R+Y, R+Y, A, Back
Inner Temple	A, R+X, R+Y, A, R+X, R+Y, R+X, R+Y, A, R+Y, Back
Leela's Last Laugh	A, R+X, R+Y, A, R+X, R+Y, R+X, R+Y, R+Y, B, Back
Left Wing	A, R+X, R+Y, A, R+X, R+Y, R+X, R+Y, A, B, Back
Market Square	A, R+X, R+Y, A, R+X, R+Y, R+X, R+Y, A, Y, Back
Old New York	A, R+X, R+Y, A, R+X, R+Y, R+X, R+Y, Y, X, Back
Planet Express	A, R+X, R+Y, A, R+X, R+Y, R+X, R+Y, Y, Y, Back
Red Light District	A, R+X, R+Y, A, R+X, R+Y, R+X, R+Y, Y, Y, Back
Red Rock Creek	A, R+X, R+Y, A, R+X, R+Y, R+X, R+Y, B, X, Back
Right Wing	A, R+X, R+Y, A, R+X, R+Y, R+X, R+Y, A, A, Back
Rumble in the Junkyard	A, R+X, R+Y, A, R+X, R+Y, R+X, R+Y, B, R+B, Back
Run, Bender, Run	A, R+X, R+Y, A, R+X, R+Y, R+X, R+Y, B, B, Back
Sewers	A, R+X, R+Y, A, R+X, R+Y, R+X, R+Y, Y, A, Back
Subway	A, R+X, R+Y, A, R+X, R+Y, R+X, R+Y, Y, B, Back
Temple Courtyard	A, R+X, R+Y, A, R+X, R+Y, R+X, R+Y, A, X, Back
The Junkyard	A, R+X, R+Y, A, R+X, R+Y, R+X, R+Y, B, R+Y, Back
The Mine Facility	A, R+X, R+Y, A, R+X, R+Y, R+X, R+Y, B, A, Back
Uptown	A, R+X, R+Y, A, R+X, R+Y, R+X, R+Y, Y, R+B, Back
Weasel Canyon	A, R+X, R+Y, A, R+X, R+Y, R+X, R+Y, B, Y, Back

Fuzion Frenzy

Enter the following codes after pressing Start to pause gameplay. Repeat each code to disable its effect.

Unlockable	Code
Enable "Real Controls"	Hold L and press Y, Y, Y, B.
First-Person Mode	Hold L and press Y, B, Y, B
Mutant Mode	Hold L and press Y, B, X, X. To get Mutant mode two, repeat the code. To return to Mutant mode, repeat the code again. To disable the code, repeat it one more time.
Squeaky Voices	Hold L and press Y, X, Y, Y
Turbo Mode (during a mini-game)	Hold L and press Y, B, X, X
Welsh Mode	Hold L and press Y, Y, Y, Y

Gauntlet: Dark Legacy

Enter the following codes as names to access these unlockables.

Unlockable	Name
10,000 Gold per Level	10000K

Gauntlet: Dark Legacy (cont'd)

Unlockable	Name
Always Have Nine Potions and Keys	ALLFUL
Dwarf in S&M Costume	NUD069
Dwarf Is a Large Jester	ICE600
Invincibility	INVULN
Jester Is a Stick Figure with Baseball Cap Head	KJH105
Jester Is a Stick Figure with Mohawk Head	PNK666
Jester Is a Stick Figure with Smiley Face	STX222
Knight Is a Bald Man in Street Clothes (Sean Gugler)	STG333
Knight Is a Ninja (Sword and Claws)	TAK118
Knight Is a Quarterback	RIZ721
Knight Is a Roman Centurion	BAT900
Knight Is an Orange-Skirted Waitress	KAO292
Knight Wears Black Karate Outfit with Twin Scythes	SJB964
Knight Wears Black Outfit and Cape	DARTHC
Knight Wears Street Clothes	ARV984
Knight Wears Street Clothes (Chris Sutton)	CSS222
Knight Wears Street Clothes and Baseball Cap	DIB626
Permanent Anti-Death	1ANGEL
Permanent Full Turbo	PURPLE
Permanent Invisibility	000000
Permanent Pojo the Chicken	EGG911
Permanent Reflect Shot	REFLEX
Permanent Shrink Enemy and Growth	DELTA1

Goblin Commander: Unleash the Horde

To access the following unlockables, hold the left and right triggers and Y for three seconds during gameplay, then enter code.

Unlockable	Code
1000 Gold and Souls	R,R,L,R,R,Y,Y,Y,L,L
God Mode	R,R,R,L,L,L,R,L,Y,R
Permanent Super Shot with Large Crossbow	SSHOTS
Permanent Triple Shot	MENAGE
Permanent X-Ray Vision	PEEKIN
Run Quickly	XSPEED
Throw Quickly	QCKSHT
Valkyrie as a Cheerleader with Baton	CEL721
Valkyrie as a Japanese School Girl	AYA555
Valkyrie as the Grim Reaper with Bloody Scythe	TWN300
Warrior as an Orc Boss	MTN200
Warrior with a Rat Head	RAT333
Warrior with an Ogre Costume	CAS400
Wizard as a Pharaoh	DES700
Wizard as an Alien	SKY100
Wizard as an Undead Lich	GARM00
Wizard as Sumner	SUM224
Wizard with an Evil Appearance	GARM99

Goblin Commander: Unleash the Horde (cont'd)

Unlockable	Code
Introduction Sequence	Press (L) at the Midway Games screen to see how the story begins.

Godzilla: Destroy All Monsters Melee

Cheat List: At the main menu, highlight Versus Mode. Then in order, press and hold (L), (B), and (R). Then release them in this order: (B), (R), (L). Then enter the following codes.

Unlockable	Code
Black and white mode	860475
Boxing Level	440499
Extra Military Damage	970432
Godzilla 2000	637522
Unlock All monsters	209697

Unlockable	Objective
Destroyah	Beat Adventure mode with Godzilla 2000.
Gigan	Beat Adventure mode with Aguirus.
Godzilla 2000	Complete the Adventure mode with Godzilla 90's.
King Ghidorah	Beat Adventure mode with Megalon.
Mecha Godzilla	Beat the Adventure mode with Destoroyah, Rodan and Mecha-King Ghidorah
Mecha Godzilla 2	Beat adventure mode with all monsters, then beat it again with Mecha King Ghidrah.
Mecha Godzilla 3	Beat adventure mode with Orga on Hard.
Mecha-King Ghidora	Beat Adventure mode with King Ghidorah.
Mothership Level	Beat the game on adventure mode with Mecha Godzilla.
Orga	Beat Adventure mode with all the characters, then beat the mode once more on medium difficulty with Godzilla 2000.
Rodan	Complete Adventure mode with Gigan.
Vortaak Level	Beat adventure mode with Mecha Godzilla 3 on Medium.

Godzilla: Save the Earth

To activate the Cheat Menu, press and hold (L), then (B), then (R) in that order, then release the keys starting with (B), then (R), then (L)

Unlockable	Code
All Cities	659996
All Monsters	525955
Buildings are Indestructible	812304
Energy doesn't regenerate	122574
Health Regenerates	536117
Player 1 deals 4x damage	259565
Player 1 has Infinite Energy	819324
Player 1 is Invisible	531470
Player 1 is Invulnerable	338592
Player 2 deals 4x damage	927281
Player 2 has Infinite Energy	324511
Player 2 is Invisible	118699
Player 2 is Invulnerable	259333
Player 3 deals 4x damage	500494
Player 3 has Infinite Energy	651417
Player 3 is Invisible	507215
Player 3 is Invulnerable	953598
Player 4 deals 4x damage	988551
Player 4 has Infinite Energy	456719
Player 4 is Invisible	198690
Player 4 is Invulnerable	485542

Golden Eye: Rogue Agent

In the Extras Menu, enter the following:

Unlockable	Code
Paintball Mode	→, ←, →, ←, ↓, ↓, ↑, ↑
Unlock all skins in Multiplayer	↓, ←, ↑, ←, →, ↓, ←, ↑

Grand Theft Auto 3

Unlockable	Code
All Weapons	BLK, BLK, L, BLK, ←, ↓, →, ↑, ←, ↓, →, ↑
Full Health	BLK, BLK, L, R, ←, ↓, →, ↑, ←, ↓, →, ↑
Full Armor	BLK, BLK, L, WHT, ←, ↓, →, ↑, ←, ↓, →, ↑

Grand Theft Auto San Andreas

Enter these codes during gameplay; do not pause the game.

Unlockable	Code
$250,000 Plus Full Health and Armor	R, BLK, L, A, ←, ↓, →, ↑, ←, ↓, →, ↑
Adrenaline Mode	A, A, X, R, L, A, ↓, ←, A
Aggressive Drivers	←, BLK, ↑, ↑, BLK, B, X, BLK, L, ←, ↓, L
Aggressive Traffic	BLK, B, R, WHT, ←, R, L, BLK, WHT
Aiming while Driving	↑, ↑, X, WHT, →, A, R, ↓, BLK, B
All Cars Are Pink	B, L, ↓, WHT, ←, A, R, L, →, B
All Cars Fly Away When Hit	X, BLK, ↓, ↓, ←, ↓, ←, ←, WHT, A
All Cars Have Nitrous	←, Y, R, L, ↑, X, Y, ↓, B, WHT, L, L
All Cars Have Tank Properties	L, WHT, WHT, ↑, ↓, ↓, ↑, R, BLK, BLK
All Cars You Drive Can Drive on Water	→, BLK, B, R, WHT, X, R, BLK
All Cars You Drive Can Fly	X, ↓, WHT, ↑, L, B, ↑, A, ←
All Vehicles Are Black	B, WHT, ↑, R, ←, A, R, L, ←, B
All Vehicles Are Farm Vehicles and Everyone Is Dressed Like Farmers	L, L, R, R, WHT, L, BLK, ↓, ←, ↑
All Vehicles Are Invisible (except motorcycles)	Y, L, Y, BLK, X, L, L
All Vehicles Are Junk Cars	WHT, →, L, ↑, A, L, WHT, BLK, R, L, L, L
Always Midnight	X, L, R, →, A, ↑, L, ←, ←
Beach Mode	↑, ↑, ↓, ↓, X, B, L, R, Y, ↓
Better Car Suspension	X, X, BLK, ←, ↑, X, BLK, A, A, A
Chaos Mode	WHT, →, L, Y, →, →, R, L, →, L, L, L
Cloudy	WHT, ↓, ↓, ←, X, ←, BLK, X, A, R, L, L
Clown Mode	Y, Y, L, X, X, B, X, ↓, B
Destroy All Cars	BLK, WHT, R, L, WHT, BLK, X, Y, B, Y, WHT, L
Faster Cars	→, R, ↑, WHT, WHT, ←, R, L, R, R
Faster Clock	B, B, L, X, L, X, X, X, L, Y, B, Y
Faster Gameplay	Y, ↑, →, ↓, WHT, L, X
Flying Boats	BLK, B, ↑, L, →, R, →, ↑, X, Y
Foggy Weather	BLK, A, L, L, WHT, WHT, WHT, A
Full Wanted Level	B, →, B, →, ←, X, A ↓
Hitman Rank (all weapons)	↓, X, A, ←, R, BLK, ←, ↓, ↓, L, L, L
Increase Car Speed	↑, L, R, ↑, →, ↑, A, WHT, A, L
Infinite Air	↓, ←, L, ↓, ↓, BLK, ↓, WHT, ↓
Infinite Ammo	L, R, X, R, ←, BLK, R, ←, X, ↓, L, L
Infinite Health	↓, A, →, ←, →, R, →, ↓, ↑, Y
Jetpack	←, →, L, WHT, R, BLK, ↑, ↓, ←, →
Lower Wanted Level	R, R, B, BLK, ↑, ↓, ↑, ↓, ↑, ↓

Grand Theft Auto San Andreas (cont'd)

Unlockable	Code
Max Fat	Y, Up, Up, Left, Right, X, B, Down
Max Muscle	Y, Up, Up, Left, Right, X, B, Right
Max Respect	L, R, Y, Down, BLK, A, L, Up, WHT, WHT, L, L
Max Sex Appeal	B, Y, Y, Up, B, R, WHT, Up, Y, L, L, L
Max Stamina	Up, A, Y, A, Y, A, X, BLK, Right
Max Vehicle Stats	X, WHT, A, R, WHT, WHT, Right, R, Right, L, L, L
Morning	BLK, A, L, L, WHT, WHT, WHT, X
Never Hungry	X, WHT, R, Y, Up, X, WHT, Up, A
No Muscle and No Fat	Y, Up, Up, Left, Right, X, B, Right
No Pedestrians and Low Traffic	A, Down, Up, BLK, Down, Y, L, Y, Left
Noon	BLK, A, L, L, WHT, WHT, WHT, Down
Orange Sky	Left, Left, WHT, R, Right, X, X, L, WHT, A
Overcast	BLK, A, L, L, WHT, WHT, WHT, X
Parachute	Left, Right, L, WHT, R, BLK, BLK, Up, Down, Right, L
Pedestrian Attack	Down, Up, Up, Up, A, BLK, R, WHT, WHT This code cannot be turned off.
Pedestrian Riot Mode	Down, Left, Up, Left, A, BLK, R, WHT, L This code cannot be turned off.
Pedestrians Dress Like Elvis	L, B, Y, L, L, X, WHT, Up, Down, Left
Pedestrians Have Guns	A, L, Up, X, Down, A, WHT, Y, Down, R, L, L
Pedestrians Have Weapons	BLK, R, A, Y, A, Y, Up, Down
Perfect Handling in Vehicles	Y, R, R, Left, R, L, BLK, L
Pimp Mode	X, Right, X, X, WHT, A, Y, A, Y
Prostitutes Pay You	Right, WHT, WHT, Down, WHT, Up, Up, WHT, BLK
Recruit Anyone (9mm)	Down, X, Up, BLK, BLK, Up, Right, Right, Up
Recruit Anyone (rockets)	BLK, BLK, BLK, A, WHT, L, BLK, L, Down, A
Sand Storm	Up, Down, L, L, WHT, WHT, L, WHT, R, BLK
Skinny	Y, Up, Up, Left, Right, X, B, Right
Slow Down Gameplay	Y, Up, Right, Down, X, BLK, R
Spawn Bloodring Banger	Down, R, B, WHT, WHT, A, R, L, Left, Left
Spawn Caddy	B, L, Up, R, WHT, A, R, L, B, A
Spawn Dozer	BLK, L, L, Right, Right, Up, Up, A, L, Left
Spawn Hotring Racer #1	R, B, BLK, Right, L, WHT, A, A, X, R
Spawn Hotring Racer #2	BLK, L, B, Right, L, R, Right, Up, B, BLK
Spawn Hunter	B, A, L, B, B, L, B, R, BLK, WHT, L, L
Spawn Hydra	Y, Y, X, B, A, L, L, Down, Up
Spawn Monster	Right, Up, R, R, R, Down, Y, Y, A, B, L, L
Spawn Quadbike	Left, Left, Down, Down, Up, Up, X, B, Y, R, BLK
Spawn Rancher	Up, Right, Right, L, Right, Up, X, WHT
Spawn Rhino	B, B, L, B, B, B, L, WHT, R, Y, B, Y
Spawn Stretch	BLK, Up, WHT, Left, Left, R, L, B, Right
Spawn Stunt Plane	B, Up, L, WHT, Down, R, L, L, Left, Left, A, Y
Spawn Tanker	R, Up, Left, Right, BLK, Up, Right, X, Right, WHT, L, L

Grand Theft Auto San Andreas (cont'd)

Unlockable	Code
Spawn Vortex	Y, Y, X, B, A, L, White, Down, Down
Stormy	Black, A, L, L, White, White, White, B
Super Bike Jumps	Y, X, B, B, X, B, B, L, White, White, R, Black
Super Jumps	Up, Up, Y, Y, Up, Up, Left, Right, X, Black, Black
Super Punches	Up, Left, A, Y, R, B, B, B, White
Traffic Lights Stay Green	Right, R, Up, White, White, Left, R, L, R, R
Unlock Romero	Down, Black, Down, R, White, Left, R, L, Left, Right
Unlock Trashmaster	B, R, B, R, Left, Left, R, L, B, Right
Weapon Set 1	R, Black, L, Black, Left, Down, Right, Up, Left, Down, Right, Up
Weapon Set 2	R, Black, L, Black, Left, Down, Right, Up, Left, Down, Down, Left
Weapon Set 3	R, Black, L, Black, Left, Down, Right, Up, Left, Down, Down, Down
Yakuza Mode	A, A, Down, Black, White, B, R, B, X

Grand Theft Auto: Vice City

Unlockable	Code
Full Armor	R, Black, L, A, Left, Down, Right, Up, Left, Down, Right, Up
Full Health	R, Black, L, B, Left, Down, Right, Up, Left, Down, Right, Up
Lower Wanted Level	R, R, B, Black, Up, Down, Up, Down, Up, Down

Gravity Games: Bike

Unlockable	Code
All Bikes	PIKARIDE
Angus Sigmund	SIGMAN
Bird Brains	FLYAWAY
Bobby Bones	BONEGUY
Fuzzy Yard Level	FUZYDIRT
Dirt Level	MUDPUDLE
Hotty Babe	BADGIRL
Master Code	LOTACRAP
Max Dennis McCoy's Stats	DMCDMAN
Max Stats for All Riders	MAXSTATS
Mount Magma Level	VOLCANO
Museum District Competition	ARTCOMP
Museum District Level	ARTRIDER
Oil Refinery Level	OILSPILL
Ramp Granny	OLDLADY
Street Level	PAVEMENT
Train Depot Level	CHOOCHOO
Vert Level	GGFLYER

Great Escape

Unlockable	Code
Restore Health	While playing, pause when you are equipping a gun and a health kit. Then press Y, X, L, R, L, R, X, Y, L, Y, Y, R, A
Select Levels	From the main menu, press Y, R, Y, X, Y, R, X, L, X, X, X, Y
Unlock all Movies	From the main menu, press L, L, Y, X, X, R, R, Y, Y, X, L, R

Halo

Unlockable	Objective
Talking Grunt	During the last level, you'll come to a group of tunnels after the dropship pick up goes wrong. Take the tunnel on your right and there should be a fork leading to a dead end. If you head in that direction, you can hear a grunt talking about something phenomenonally droll.

Haunted Mansion

To access the following unlockables, hold R on the D-Pad, then enter code.

Unlockable	Code
Level Select	B, B, X, Y, Y, X, B, A
God Mode	X, B, B, B, X, B, Y, A

Hitman 2: Silent Assassin

Unlockable	Code
All Weapons	Press R, L, Up, Down, A, Up, X, A during gameplay.
Bomb Mode	Press R, L, Up, Down, A, Up, White during gameplay.
Full Heal	Press R, L, Up, Down, A, Up, Down during gameplay.
God Mode	Press R, L, Up, Down, A, R, L, Black, White during gameplay.
Hitman AI	During gameplay press R, L, Up, Down, A, Up, Up.
Lethal Charge	Press L, R, Up, Down, A, Black, Black during gameplay.
Level Select	Press R, L, Up, Down, Y, B at the main menu.
Level Skip	Press R, L, Up, Down, A, X, click, and press B, A, B, A during gameplay. Enable this code immediately after starting a level to complete it with a Silent Assassin rank.
Megaforce Mode	Press R, L, Up, Down, A, R, R during gameplay. Restart the level to remove its effect.
Nailgun Mode (Weapons pin people to walls when you activate this code.)	Press R, L, Up, Down, A, White, White during gameplay.
Punch Mode	Press R, L, Up, Down, A, Up, Up during gameplay.
Slow Motion	Press R, L, Up, Down, A, Up, L during gameplay.
SMG and 9mm Pistol SD	Press L,R,Up,Down,A,Up,R,R during gameplay.
Toggle Gravity	Press R, L, Up, Down, A, L, L during gameplay.

Hitman Contracts

Enter the following codes at the Main Menu.

Unlockable	Code
Level Select	X,Y,B,Left,Up,Right,L,R
Level Skip and Silent Assasin Rating	R,L,Up,Down,X,A,L,B,A,B,A

House of the Dead 3

Unlockable	Objective
Extra Items in Original Mode	Complete House of the Dead 3, and then go to House of the Dead 2, by taking an elevator down. On the way down, the door opens a couple of times. Shoot all the enemies as quickly and as accurately as possible to get items for Original mode in House of the Dead 2. Complete House of the Dead 3 again to repeat the process. Every time you do this, you get new items for Original mode. This works best if you unlocked the "Free-Play" option for House of the Dead 3.
Free Play	Complete the game with an "A" rank. Enter the Options screen, and select "House of the Dead 3." You can now increase the credits past nine until "Free Play" appears.
House of the Dead 2	Complete Survival mode in House of the Dead 3 to unlock House of the Dead 2.

The Hulk

Enter these cheats at the Code Input screen in the Options menu.

Unlockable	Code
Double Health for Enemies	BRNGITN
Double Health for Hulk	HLTHDSE
Full Rage Meter Cheat	ANGMNGT
Half Enemies' HP	MMMYHLP
High Score reset	NMBTHIH
Invincibility	GMMSKIN
Level Select	TRUBLVR
Play as Gray Hulk	JANITOR
Puzzle Solved Cheat	BRCESTN
Regenerator	FLSHWND
Unlimited Continues	GRNCHTR
Unlock Desert Battle art	FIFTEEN

The Hulk (cont'd)

Unlockable	Code	Unlockable	Code
Unlock Hulk Movie FMV art	NANOMED	Unlock Hulk vs. Hulk Dogs art	PITBULL
Unlock Hulk Transformed art	SANFRAN	Wicked Punch Cheat	FSTOFRY

Hunter: The Reckoning

Unlockable	Code/Objective
All Weapons	Press Ⓑ, ↑, ←, ↓, →, Ⓑ, Ⓑ during gameplay.
Alternate Ending Sequence	Save at over 50 Innocents before returning to the train to unlock the good ending.
Alternate Hunter Mode	Complete the game to unlock the "Alternate Hunter Mode" option at the Special Features screen.
Nightmare Mode	Complete the game to unlock the "Nightmare Mode" option at the Special Features screen.
Sound Test	Press ←, ←, Ⓑ or →, →, Ⓑ during gameplay.

The Incredibles

Pause the game and go to the Secrets menu and enter the following codes.

Unlockable	Code
Big Heads	EINSTEINIUM
Credits	YOURNAMEINLIGHTS
Destroy All Enemies on Screen	SMARTBOMB
Eye Laser	GAZERBEAM
Feet of Fire	ATHLETESFOOT
One Hit knockout	KRONOS
Restore Health	UUDDLRLRBAS
Slow down Gameplay	BWTHEMOVIE
Small Heads	DEEVOLVE
So many Colors	EMODE
Speed up Gameplay	SASSMODE
Turn off the HUD	BHUD
Unlimited Incredi-Power for Mr. Incredible	SHOWTIME
Unlimited Incredi-Power for Elastigirl	FLEXIBLE
Watch the Intro again	HI

The Italian Job

Unlockable	Objective
All Bonus Content	Complete the story mode.
All Cars in Circuit Racing	Get an A ranking in every level.

Juiced

Enter this passwords in the Password menu.

Unlockable	Password
All Cars in Arcade Mode	PINT

Jurassic Park: Operation Genesis

Unlockable	Code
All Dinosaurs have 55% DNA	During gameplay press Ⓡ, ↑, Ⓛ, ↓.
All research	During gameplay, quickly press ↓, ↓, ↓, ←, →, Ⓛ, ↓, and ↑.
Constant Rain	During gameplay, press Ⓡ, Ⓛ, Ⓡ, ↓, ↑, ↓.

Jurassic Park: Operation Genesis (cont'd)

Unlockable	Code
Crash a Car	During gameplay, press L + R, and repeatedly tap ↑, ↓, ↑, ↓.
Dial-A-Twister	Press ←, ↑, →, ↓, and L + R.
Downgrade all Fences to Low Security	During gameplay press ↓, ↓, ←, →, L, L, ↑, ↑.
Extinction Event	Press L, R, ↓, R, and L.
Gimme Some Money	Press L + ↑ and then L + ↓ to get $10,000.
Guaranteed Immunity	Press ↑, ↑, R, L, ↑, ↑
Hot One	Press R + ↓ and then R + ↓ to cause a heat wave.
Impossible Mission	Press R, →, →, →, →, and R to unlock all missions, exercises, and sites.
Increase Park Budget by $250,000	During gameplay, press L, →, →, L, R, ↓.
Isla Muerta	Press R, R, R, L, and → to make the dinosaurs look like the living dead.
Market Day	Press L + R and then ↓ to make your finances zero.
Mr. DNA	Press R, ↑, R, →, L, and ↓ to set all excavated dinosaur DNA to 100%.
No Red Tape	Press L, R, ←, and ↓, ↓, ↓, ↓.
No Twisters	Press ←, →, release L + R, and then Press L + R again.
Oh No!	Press →, ←, →, ←, →, and R to kill all tourists.
Open to the Public	Press ←, ↓, →, ↑, L + R, and L + R to freely select three dig sites without any stars.
Rampage Time	Press L, L, L, and ←, ←, ← to stress out all carnivores.
Stormy Weather	Press R, R, L, R, ↓, ↑, and ↓.
Tourist Casualties Don't Affect Your Budget	Press R, ←, ↓, ↓, ↓, ↓.
Upgrade all Fences to Maximum Security	Press L, ←, ←, R, R, →.
Where's The Money	Press L, R, L, R, and ↓, ↓ to restock your market with fossils.

Kill.switch

Unlockable	Code
Infinite Ammo	After completing the game, pause the game and press L,R,X,X

Legacy of Kain: Defiance

To access the following, pause the game any time and enter code.

Unlockable	Code
All Bonuses	BLK,↓,WHT,R,←,WHT,↓,L,Y
Infinite Reaver Charge	↓,↓,↑,←,R,BLK,↓,Y,B
Card Board Tube Reaver	↑,↓,←,→,BLK,WHT,Y,↓,B
God Mode	↑,↓,→,↓,R,BLK,↓,Y,L

Legends of Wrestling

Unlockable	Code
All Wrestlers	At the Main Menu, press ↑,↑,↓,↓,←,→,←,→,Y,Y,X. The save prompt appears to let you know the code worked.

LEGO Star Wars

To unlock characters for purchase in Free Play mode, go to Dexter's Diner, then the Codes menu, and enter the following.

Unlockable	Code
Battle Droid	987UYR
Battle Droid (Commander)	EN11K5
Battle Droid (Geonosis)	LK42U6
Battle Droid (Security)	KF999A
Big Blasters	IG72X4
Boba Fett	LA811Y
Brushes	SHRUB1
Classic Blasters	L449HD
Clone	F8B4L6
Clone (Episode III)	ER33JN
Clone (Episode III, Pilot)	BHU72T
Clone (Episode III, Swamp)	N3T6P8
Clone (Episode III, Walker)	RS6E25
Count Dooku	14PGMN
Darth Maul	H35TUX
Darth Sidious	A32CAM
Disguised Clone	VR832U
Droideka	DH382U
General Grievous	SF321Y
Geonosian	19D7NB
Gonk Droid	U63B2A
Grievous' Bodyguard	ZTY392
Invincibility	4PR28U
Jango Fett	PL47NH
Ki-Adi Mundi	DP55MV
Kit Fisto	CBR954
Luminara	A725X4
Mace Windu (Episode III)	MS952L
Minikit Detector	LD116B
Moustaches	RP924W
Padme	92UJ7D
PK Droid	R840JU
Princess Leia	BEQ82H
Purple	YD77GC
Rebel Trooper	L54YUK
Royal Guard	PP43JX
Shaak Ti	EUW862
Silhouettes	MS999Q
Silly Blasters	NR37W1
Super Battle Droid	XZNR21
Tea Cups	PUCEAT

Links 2004

Unlockable	Code
80 Attribute Points	Create a new profile using the name SafariTK.
All courses	At the Main Menu, hold L+R and press X+Y

The Lord of the Rings: The Fellowship of the Ring

Input the following codes during gameplay.

Unlockable	Code
Infinite Ammo	3, 2, 4, 1, 3, 2.
Infinite Health	4, 1, 3, 2, 1, 4.
Infinite Ring Use	4, 2, 1, 2, 4, 3.

Lord of the Rings: Return of the King

To access the following unlockables, hold L+R and enter code.

Unlockable	Code
Legolas 1000 Exp Points	A, Y, Up, A
Gandalf 1000 Exp Points	B, Y, Up, Down
Frodo 1000 Exp Points	Down, Y, Up, Down
Aragorn 1000 Exp Points	Up, X, Y, A
Sam 1000 Exp Points	Y, A, Down, A
1000 Exp Points	B, B, Y, A
Infinite Respawn in Co-Op Mode	B, X, Up, B

Mace Griffin: Bounty Hunter

The following codes require that you select the Electro Cosh and then input the required commands.

Unlockable	Code
Auto-Focus Mode	Press L, R, L, R, A, B, B, A, B, A.
Big Head Mode	Press L, R, L, R, A, B, B, A, B, B.
Detach Camera	Press L, R, L, R, A, B, B, A, Y, X.
Double Damage	Press L, R, L, R, A, B, B, A, Y, Y.
Infinite Ammo	Press L, R, L, R, A, B, B, A, X, X.
Invulnerability	Press L, R, L, R, A, B, B, A, X, Y.
One Hit Kills	Press L, R, L, R, A, B, B, A, A, A.

Input these codes during gameplay.

Unlockable	Code
Skip to Next Level	Press L, R, L, R, A, A, B, B, X, B.
Unlock All Sections	Press L, R, L, R, A, A, B, B, X, X.

Madden NFL 2004

Unlockable	Objective
1990 Eagles Classic Team	Earn Level 4 EA Sports Bio
Bingo! Cheat	Earn Level 2 EA Sports Bio
Steve Spurrier Coach	Earn Level 6 EA Sports Bio

Madden NFL 2005

From My Madden menu, go to Madden Cards, Madden Codes, and enter the following:

Card	Password
Aaron Brooks Gold Card	_J95K1J
Aaron Glenn Gold Card	Q48E9G
Adewale Ogunleye Gold Card	C12E9E
Ahman Green Gold Card	T86L4C
Al Wilson Gold Card	G72G2R
Alan Faneca Gold Card	U32S9C
Amani Toomer Gold Card	Z75G6M
Andre Carter Gold Card	V76E2Q
Andre Johnson Gold Card	E34S1M
Andy Reid Gold Card	N44K1L
Anquan Boldin Gold Card	S32F7K
Antoine Winfield Gold Card	A12V7Z
Bill Cowher Gold Card	S54T6U
Brad Hopkins Gold Card	P44A8B
Bret Favre Gold Card	L61D7B
Brian Billick Gold Card	L27C4K
Brian Dawkins Gold Card	Y47B8Y
Brian Simmons Gold Card	S22M6A
Brian Urlacher Gold Card	Z34J4U
Brian Westbrook Gold Card	V46I2I
Bubba Franks Gold Card	U77F2W
Butch Davis Gold Card	G77L6F
Byron Leftwich Gold Card	C55V5C
Carson Palmer Gold Card	O36V2H
Casey Hampton Gold Card	Z11P9T
Chad Johnson Gold Card	R85S2A
Chad Pennington Gold Card	B64L2F
Champ Bailey Gold Card	K89O9E
Charles Rogers Gold Card	E57K9Y
Charles Woodson Gold Card	F95N9J
Chris Hovan Gold Card	F14C6J
Corey Simon Gold Card	R11D7K
Courtney Brown Gold Card	R42R75
Curtis Martin Gold Card	K47X3G
Dallas Coach Gold Card	O24U1Q
Damien Woody Gold Card	F78I1I
Dante Hall Gold Card	B23P8D
Dat Nguyen Gold Card	Q86I2S
Daunte Culpepper Gold Card	O62O9K
Dave Wannstedt Gold Card	W73D7D
David Boston Gold Card	A25I9F
David Carr Gold Card	C16E2Q
Dennis Erickson Gold Card	J83E3T
Dennis Green Gold Card	C18J7T
Derrick Brooks Gold Card	P93I9Q
Derrick Mason Gold Card	S98P3T
Deuce McAllister Gold Card	D11H4J
Dexter Coakley Gold Card	L35K1A

Madden NFL 2005 (cont'd)

Card	Password
Dexter Jackson Gold Card	G16B2I
Dick Vermeil Gold Card	F68V1W
Dom Capers Gold Card	B97I6R
Domanick Davis Gold Card	L58S3J
Donnie Edwards Gold Card	E18Y5Z
Donovin Darius Gold Card	Q11T7T
Donovon McNabb Gold Card	T98J1I
Donte Stallworth Gold Card	R75W3M
Dre Bly Gold Card	H19Q2O
Drew Bledsoe Gold Card	W73M3E
Dwight Freeney Gold Card	G76U2L
Edgerrin James Gold Card	A75D7X
Ed Reed Gold Card	G18Q2B
Eric Moulds Gold Card	H34Z8K
Flozell Adams Gold Card	R54T1O
Fred Taylor Gold Card	I87X9Y
Grant Wistrom Gold Card	E46M4Y
Herman Edwards Gold Card	O19T2T
Hines Ward Gold Card	M12B8F
Jack Del Rio Gold Card	J22P9I
Jake Delhomme Gold Card	M86N9F
Jake Plummer Gold Card	N74P8X
Jamie Sharper Gold Card	W27I7G
Jason Taylor Gold Card	O33S6I
Jason Webster Gold Card	M74B3E
Jeff Fisher Gold Card	N62B6J
Jeff Garcia Gold Card	H32H7B
Jeremy Newberry Gold Card	J77Y8C
Jeremy Shockey Gold Card	R34X5T
Jerry Porter Gold Card	F71Q9Z
Jerry Rice Gold Card	K34F8S
Jevon Kearse Gold Card	A78B1C
Jim Haslett Gold Card	G78R3W
Jim Mora Jr. Gold Card	N46C3M
Jimmy Smith Gold Card	I22J5W
Joe Horn Gold Card	P91A1Q
Joey Harrington Gold Card	Z68W8J
John Fox Gold Card	Q98R7Y
Jon Gruden Gold Card	H61I8A
Josh McCown Gold Card	O33Y4X
Julian Peterson Gold Card	M89J8A
Julius Peppers Gold Card	X54O4Z
Junior Seau Gold Card	W26K6Q
Kabeer Gbaja-Biamala Gold Card	U16I9Y
Keith Brooking Gold Card	E12P4S
Keith Bulluck Gold Card	M63N6V
Kendrell Bell Gold Card	T96C7J
Kevan Barlow Gold Card	A23T5E
Kevin Mawae Gold Card	L76E6S
Kris Jenkins Gold Card	W63O3K
Kyle Boller Gold Card	A72F9X
Kyle Turley Gold Card	Y46A8V
LaDainian Tomlinson Gold Card	M64D4E
LaVar Arrington Gold Card	F19Q8W
Laveranues Coles Gold Card	R98I5S
Lawyer Milloy Gold Card	M37Y5B
La'Roi Glover Gold Card	K24L9K
Lee Suggs Gold Card	Z94X6Q
Leonard Davis Gold Card	H14M2V
Lovie Smith Gold Card	L38V3A
Marc Bulger Gold Card	U66B4S
Marcel Shipp Gold Card	R42X2L
Marcus Stroud Gold Card	E56I5O
Marcus Trufant Gold Card	R46T5U
Mark Brunell Gold Card	B66D9J
Marshall Faulk Gold Card	U76G1U
Marty Booker Gold Card	P51U4B
Marty Schottenheimer Gold Card	D96A7S
Marvin Harrison Gold Card	T11E8O
Marvin Lewis Gold Card	P24S4H
Matt Hasselback Gold Card	R68D5F
Michael Bennett Gold Card	W81W2J
Michael Strahan Gold Card	O66T6K
Michael Vick Gold Card	H67B1F
Mike Alstott Gold Card	D89F6W
Mike Brown Gold Card	F12J8N
Mike Martz Gold Card	R64A8E
Mike Mularkey Gold Card	C56D6E
Mike Rucker Gold Card	K89O6S
Mike Shanahan Gold Card	H15L5Y
Mike Sherman Gold Card	F84X6K
Mike Tice Gold Card	Y31T6Y
New England Coach Gold Card	N24L4Z
Nick Barnett Gold Card	X95I7S
Norv Turner Gold Card	F24K1M
Olin Kreutz Gold Card	R17R2O
Orlando Pace Gold Card	U42U9U
Patrick Surtain Gold Card	H58T9X
Peerless Price Gold Card	X75V6K
Peter Warrick Gold Card	D86P8O
Peyton Manning Gold Card	L48H4U

Madden NFL 2005 (cont'd)

Card	Password	Card	Password
Plaxico Burress Gold Card	K18P6J	Stephen Davis Gold Card	E39X9L
Priest Holmes Gold Card	X91N1L	Steve Mariucci Gold Card	V74Q3N
Quentin Jammer Gold Card	V55S3Q	Steve McNair Gold Card	S36T1I
Randy Moss Gold Card	W79U7X	Steve Smith Gold Card	W91020
Ray Lewis Gold Card	B94X6V	Takeo Spikes Gold Card	B83A6C
Reggie Wayne Gold Card	R29S8C	Tedy Bruschi Gold Card	K28Q3P
Rex Grossman Gold Card	C46P2A	Terence Newman Gold Card	W57Y5P
Rich Gannon Gold Card	Q69I1Y	Terrell Suggs Gold Card	V71A9Q
Richard Seymour Gold Card	L69T4T	Tiki Barber Gold Card	T43A2V
Ricky Williams Gold Card	P19V1N	T.J. Duckett Gold Card	P67E1I
Rod Smith Gold Card	V22C4L	Todd Heap Gold Card	H19M1G
Rodney Harrison Gold Card	084I3J	Tom Brady Gold Card	X22V7E
Ronde Barber Gold Card	J72X8W	Tom Coughlin Gold Card	S71D6H
Roy Williams Gold Card	J76C6F	Tony Dungy Gold Card	Y96R8V
Rudi Johnson Gold Card	W26J6H	Tony Gonzalez Gold Card	N46E9N
Sam Madison Gold Card	Z87T5C	Torry Holt Gold Card	W96U7E
Samari Rolle Gold Card	C69H4Z	Travis Henry Gold Card	F36M2Q
Santana Moss Gold Card	H79E5B	Trent Green Gold Card	Y46M4S
Seattle Coach Gold Card	V58U4Y	Ty Law Gold Card	F13W1Z
Shaun Alexander Gold Card	C95Z4P	Walter Jones Gold Card	G57P1P
Shaun Ellis Gold Card	Z54F2B	Washington Coach Gold Card	W63V9L
Shawn Rogers Gold Card	J97X8M	Will Shields Gold Card	B52S8A
Shawn Springs Gold Card	Z28D2V	Zach Thomas Gold Card	U63I3H
Simeon Rice Gold Card	S62F9T		

Secret Teams

Card	Password	Card	Password
1958 Colts	_P74X8J	1982 Redskins	F56D6V
1966 Packers	G49P7W	1983 Raiders	D23T8S
1968 Jets	C24W2A	1984 Dolphins	X23Z8H
1970 Browns	G12N1I	1985 Bears	F92M8M
1972 Dolphins	R79W6W	1986 Giants	K44F2Y
1974 Steelers	R12D9B	1988 49ers	F77R8H
1976 Raiders	P96Q8M	1990 Eagles	G95F2Q
1977 Broncos	O18T2A	1991 Lions	I89F4I
1978 Dolphins	G97U5X	1992 Cowboys	I44A10
1980 Raiders	K71K4E	1993 Bills	Y66K30
1981 Chargers	Y27N9A		

Secret Stadiums

Stadium	Password	Stadium	Password
Pro Bowl Hawaii '05	G67F5X	Super Bowl XLII	T67R10
Super Bowl XL	085P6I	Super Bowl XXXIX	D58F1B
Super Bowl XLI	P48Z4D		

Pump Up and Cheerleader Cards

Password	Card	Password	Card
49ers Cheerleader	_X61T6L	Bengals Cheerleader	Y22S6G
Bears Pump Up Crowd	K17F2I	Bills Cheerleader	F26S6X

Madden NFL 2005 (cont'd)

Pump Up and Cheerleader Cards (cont'd)

Password	Card	Password	Card
Broncos Cheerleader	B85U5C	Lions Pump Up Crowd	C18F4G
Browns Pump Up Crowd	B65Q1L	Packers Pump Up Crowd	K26Y4V
Buccaneers Cheerleader	Z55Z7S	Panthers Cheerleader	M66N4D
Cardinals Cheerleader	Q91W5L	Patriots Cheerleader	O59P9C
Chargers Cheerleader	Q68S3F	Raiders Cheerleader	G92L2E
Chiefs Cheerleader	T46M6T	Rams Cheerleader	W73B8X
Colts Cheerleader	M22Z6H	Ravens Cheerleader	P98T6C
Cowboys Cheerleader	J84E3F	Redskins Cheerleader	N19D6Q
Dolphins Cheerleader	E88T2J	Saints Cheerleader	R99G2F
Eagles Cheerleader	Q88P3Q	Seahawks Cheerleader	A35T8R
Falcons Cheerleader	W86F3F	Steelers Pump Up Crowd	C98I2V
Giants Pump Up Crowd	L13Z9J	Texans Cheerleader	R74G3W
Jaguars Cheerleader	K32C2A	Titans Cheerleader	Q81V4N
Jets Pump Up Crowd	S45W1M	Vikings Cheerleader	E26H4L

Gold Cheat Cards

Card	Description	Code
3rd Down	For one half, your opponent has 3 downs to get a first down.	_Z28X8K
5th Down	For one half, you will have 5 downs to get a first down.	P66C4L
Bingo!	Your defensive interceptions increase by 75% for the game.	J33I8F
Da Bomb	You will receive unlimited pass range for one half.	B61A8M
Da Boot	You will receive unlimited field goal range for one half.	I76X3T
Extra Credit	Awards 4 points for every interception and 3 points for every sack.	M89S8G
1st and 15	Requires your opponent to get 15 yards to reach a first down for one half.	V65J8P
1st and 5	Your first down yards to go will be set to 5 for one half.	O72E9B
Fumblitis	Your opponent's fumbles will increase by 75% for the game.	R14B8Z
Human Plow	Your Broken Tackles will increase by 75% for the game.	L96J7P
Lame Duck	Your opponent will throw a lob pass for one half.	D57R5S
Mistake Free	You can't fumble or throw an interception for one half.	X78P9Z
Mr. Mobility	Your QB can't get sacked for one half.	Y59R8R
Super Dive	Your diving distance increases by 75% for the game.	D59K3Y
Tight Fit	Your opponent's uprights will be made very narrow for one half.	V34L6D
Unforced Errors	Your opponent will fumble every time he tries to juke for one half.	L48G1E

Mafia

Unlockable	Objective
Car Selection	Learn to break into cars during missions, which will allow you to use it in Free Ride.
City Selection	Progress through story mode to unlock more areas for Free Ride.
Monster Truck	Take first place in all of the races in Racing Championship mode.
Time of Day	Progress through story mode to unlock a Day/Night option for Free Ride.

Magic the Gathering: Battlegrounds

Unlockable	Code
All Quest	During the quest select, press L+R, ↓, ↑, Left Thumbstick, White, ↑, →, ←, ↓, L+R.
Secret Level for Vs. Mode	At the Arena select, press L+R, ←, ↑, X, ↑, R, Y, L+R.
All Duelists in Arcade Mode	At the Character select screen, press L+R, ↓, ↑, X, White, ↑, X, Black, ↑, X, L+R.

Manhunt

In order to unlock these codes, you must complete each level with 3 stars or better. Then, once you unlock the codes, enter them at the main menu.

Unlockable	Objective	Code
Fully Equipped (all weapons in level and infinite ammo)	Beat Drunk Driving and Graveyard Shift	R, White, L, Black, ↓, ↑, ←, ↑
God Mode	Complete whole game	↓, ↓, B, ↑, X, Y, X, White, ↑, ↑, L
Helium Hunters (explode when hit and speak with squeaky voices)	Beat Strapped for Cash and View of Innocence	R, R, Y, B, X, Black, L, ↓
Invisibility (hunters are blind)	Beat Trained to Kill and Border Patrol	X, X, X, ↓, X, ↓, B, ↑
Monkey Skin	Beat Press Coverage and Wrong Side of the Tracks	X, X, White, ↓, Y, X, B, ↓
Piggsy Skin	Beat Key Personnel and Deliverance	↑, ↓, ←, ←, R, White, L, L
Rabbit Skin	Beat Kill the Rabbit and Divided They Fall	←, R, R, Y, R, R, X, L
Regeneration (Cash's health regenerates)	Beat Fueled by Hate and Grounds for Assault	White, →, B, White, Black, ↓, B, ←
Runner (player has infinite stamina)	Beat Born Again and Doorway Into Hell	White, White, L, White, ←, →, ←, →
Silence (hunters are deaf)	Beat Road to Ruin and White Trash	R, L, White, L, →, ←, ←, ←
Super Punch	Beat Mouth of Madness and Doing Time	L, Y, Y, Y, B, B, B, R

Max Payne

Unlockable	Objective
Additional Difficulty Settings—"Dead on Arrival" and "New York Minute"	Complete the game under the "Fugitive" difficulty setting.
Bonus Level	Complete the game in New York Minute mode to unlock a new bonus level in which you have to kill a lot of enemies, all in bullet time.
Cheat Mode	Start a game. Press Back during gameplay to display the main menu. Then, hold L + R + click Left Thumbstick + click Right Thumbstick, and quickly press White, Black, Black, White, White, Black at the main menu. A cheat option will appear.
Last Challenge Bonus Level	Complete the game under the "Dead on Arrival" difficulty setting.
Level Skip	Press Start during gameplay. Then, hold L and press Black, Black, Black, Black, X, X, X, X, X, X, Y, Y, Y, Back. When you're at the main menu, go back. A sound confirms that the current chapter has been completed.
Secret Programmer Room	Complete the Last Challenge level. The doors in the back of the room will open up to the Remedy Room.

Max Payne 2

Unlockable	Code
All Modes	At any time during the game, pause and enter X,X,X,A,L,R,L,R

Mech Assault

Unlockable	Code
Completion Bonuses	Complete the game to unlock Ragnarok in local multiplayer mode.

Medal of Honor European Assault

To unlock the ability to enter cheats, go to the Pause Menu and enter the Activate Cheat Entry code.

Unlockable	Code
Active Cheat Entry	Hold L+R then press Down,A,X,BLK,B,A
Player Suicide (SP only)	B,R,WHT,Y,L,WHT
Hide HUD	BLK,L,BLK,R,Up,Y
Kill Nemesis	Right,Left,R,L,X,Y
Pickup OSS Document	A,B,R,WHT,BLK,L
Disable Shellshock	X,Y,A,B,L,X

Medal of Honor: Rising Sun

Unlockable	Code
God Mode	banner
Infinite Ammo	jawfish
All Missions	tuskfish

Mercedes-Benz World Racing

Unlockable	Code
All Cars	Enter Full House as a profile name in multi-player mode
All Tracks	Enter Free Ride as a profile name in multi-player mode
All Championships	Enter JamSession as a profile name.
All Missions	Enter Miss World as a profile name in single player mode.
Almost every car	Enter ALLUCANGET as a profile name.
Status 1	Top 10
Status 2	HUIBUH
Status 3	N.I.C.E. 2
Status 4	TaxiDriver
Status 5	Halbzeit
Status 6	No Hat!
Status 7	McRace
Status 8	Jiu-Jitsu
Status 9	Goodzpeed

Midnight Club II

Enter the following codes from the cheat menu.

Unlockable	Code
All car abilities	greasemonkey
All cars	hotwired
All Locations	theworldismine
Change difficulty levels	howhardcanitbe0 (easiest)
Change difficulty levels	howhardcanitbe1
Change difficulty levels	howhardcanitbe2
Change difficulty levels	howhardcanitbe3
Change difficulty levels	howhardcanitbe4
Change difficulty levels	howhardcanitbe5

Midnight Club II (cont'd)

Unlockable	Code
Change difficulty levels	howhardcanitbe6
Change difficulty levels	howhardcanitbe7
Change difficulty levels	howhardcanitbe8
Change difficulty levels	howhardcanitbe9 (hardest)
Change Game Speed	howfastcanitbe0 (slowest)
Change Game Speed	howfastcanitbe1
Change Game Speed	howfastcanitbe2
Change Game Speed	howfastcanitbe3
Change Game Speed	howfastcanitbe4
Change Game Speed	howfastcanitbe5
Change Game Speed	howfastcanitbe6
Change Game Speed	howfastcanitbe7
Change Game Speed	howfastcanitbe8
Change Game Speed	howfastcanitbe9 (fastest)
Infinite Nitrous	zoomzoom4
Machine Gun and Rocket	lovenotwar

Unlockable	Objective
LAPD car in Arcade Mode	Beat all five circuit races for LA in Arcade mode.
Paris Cop Car	Beat all 6 of the Paris arcade circuit tracks.
SLF450X	Complete 100% of the game
Tokyo Cop Car	Beat all 7 Tokyo arcade circuit tracks.
Veloci	Beat all of the World Champion's races.

Midnight Club 3 Dub Edition

Enter these case sensitive passwords in the Cheats section under Options.

Unlockable	Password
All Cities Unlocked in Arcade Mode	crosscountry
Bunny Ears	getheadl
Chrome Body	haveyouseenthisboy
Faster Pedestrians/All Cities in Arcade Mode	urbansprawl
Flaming Head	trythisathome
Increase Car Mass in Arcade Mode	hyperagro
No Damage	ontheroad
Pumpkin Heads	getheadk
Skull Head	getheadn
Snowman Head	getheadm
Special Move Agro	dfens
Special Move Roar	Rjnr
Special Move Zone	allin
Unlock All Cities	roadtrip
Yellow Smile	getheadj

Midtown Madness 3

Unlockable	Objective
1959 El Dorado Seville	Complete the Washington Pizza Deliverer job.
1967 Ford Mustang	Complete the Washington Stunt Car Driver job.

Midtown Madness 3 (cont'd)

Unlockable	Objective
All Cars	In the car select menu, click ● while entering the following commands: Ⓛ, Ⓡ, Ⓛ, Ⓛ, Ⓛ, Ⓡ, Ⓡ, Ⓡ, Ⓛ, Ⓛ, Ⓡ, Ⓡ.
Ambulance	Complete the Paris Paramedic job.
Armored Car	Complete the Paris security guard job.
Audi S4 Avant	Complete the first six blitz races in Paris.
Audi TT	Complete the Paris Special Agent job.
Cadillac Escalade	Complete the Washington Limo Driver job.
Cement Truck	Win the first six checkpoint races in Washington.
Chevrolet Corvette Z06	Win the tenth checkpoint race in Washington.
Chevrolet SSR	Complete the first three blitz races in Washington.
Chrysler Crossfire	Win the tenth blitz race in Washington.
Chrysler PT Turbo	Complete the Washington Rental Car Driver job.
Dodge Viper SRT-10	Complete the Washington Private Eye job.
Fire Truck	Win the first six checkpoint races in Paris.
FLE	Complete the Paris Delivery Guy job.
Freightliner Century Class S/T	Complete the first six blitz races in Washington.
Hummer H2 SUV	Complete the Washington Salesman job.
Koenigsegg CC	Complete all the game.
Limousine	Complete the Paris chauffeur job.
Lotus Esprit V8	Win the tenth Paris Blitz race.
Mini Cooper S	Complete the first three blitz races in Paris.
Paris Bus	Win the first three checkpoint races in Paris.
Paris Police	Complete the Paris Police Officer job.
Saab 9-3 Turbo	Win the tenth checkpoint race in Paris.
Taxi	Complete the Paris Taxi Driver job.
Washington Bus	Win the first three checkpoint races in Washington.
Washington Police	Complete the Washington Police Officer job.

Minority Report

To enter these codes, select the Special Menu, then select the Cheats menu.

Unlockable	Code
All Combos	NINJA
All Movies	DIRECTOR
All Weapons	STRAPPED
Armor	STEELUP
Baseball Bat	SLUGGER
Bouncy Men	BOUNZMEN
Clown Skin	SCARYCLOWN
Concept Art	SKETCHPAD
Convict Skin	JAILBREAK
Do Not Select	DONOTSEL
Dramatic Finish	STYLIN
Ending	WIMP
First Person Mode	FPSSTYLE
GI John Skin	GNRLINFINTRY
Health	BUTTERUP

Unlockable	Code
Infinite Ammo	MRJUAREZ
Invincibility	LRGARMS
Level Warp	PASSKEY
Level Skip	QUITTER
Lizard Skin	HISSSS
Moseley Skin	HAIRLOSS
Nara Skin	WEIGHTGAIN
Nikki Skin	BIGLIPS
Pain Arena	MAXIMUMHURT
Rag Doll	CLUMSY
Robot Skin	MRROBOTO
Super Damage	SPINICH
Super John Skin	SUPERJOHN
Wreck the Joint	CLUTZ
Zombie Skin	IAMSODEAD

Mission Impossible: Operation Surma

Unlockable	Code
Level Select	In the Profiles Menu, highlight Jasmine Curry and press L+R+Y+B. You will be able to choose your level from the Main Menu.

MLB Slugfest 2003

Cheat Mode: Press X, Y, and B to change the icons in the first, second, and third boxes respectively at the match-up screen. The numbers in the following list indicate the number of times you press each button. After the icons change, press the D-pad in the indicated direction to enable the code. For example, to enter 1-2-3 ←, press X, Y, Y, B, B, B, ←.

Unlockable	Code	Unlockable	Code
Mace Bat	0-0-4 ←	No Contact Mode	4-3-3 ←
Wiffle Bat	0-0-4 →	No Fatigue	3-4-3 ↑
Big Heads	2-0-0 →	Pinto Team	2-1-0 →
Eagle Team	2-1-2 →	Rocket Park Stadium	3-2-1 ↑
Extra Time after Plays	1-2-3 ↑	Roman Coliseum Stadium	3-3-3 ↑
Horse Team	2-1-1 →	Rubber Ball	2-4-2 ↑
Lion Team	2-2-0 →	Small Heads	2-0-0 ←
Log Bat	0-0-4 ↑	Softball	2-4-2 ↓
Maximum Batting	3-0-0 ←	Terry Fitzgerald Team	3-3-3 →
Maximum Power	0-3-0 ←	Todd McFarlane Team	2-2-2 →
Maximum Speed	0-0-3 ←	Tournament Mode	1-1-1 ↓
Monument Stadium	3-3-3 ↓	Unlimited Turbo	4-4-4 ↓

MLB Slugfest 2004

Unlockable	Code	Unlockable	Code
16" Softball	2, 4, 2, ↓	Log Bat	0, 0, 4, ↑
Alien Team	2, 3, 1, ↓	Mace Bat	0, 0, 4, ←
Atlantis Stadium	3, 2, 1, ←	Max Batting	3, 0, 0, ←
Big Head	2, 0, 0, →	Max Power	0, 3, 0, ←
Blade Bat	0, 0, 2, ↑	Max Speed	0, 0, 3, ←
Bobble Head Team	1, 3, 3, ↓	Midway Park Stadium	3, 2, 1, ↓
Bone Bat	0, 0, 1, ↑	Minotaur Team	1, 1, 0, ↓
Casey Team	2, 3, 3, ↓	Monument Stadium	3, 3, 3, ↓
Cheats Disabled	1, 1, 1, ↓	Napalitano Team	2, 3, 2, ↓
Coliseum Stadium	3, 3, 3, ↑	Olshan Team	2, 2, 2, ↓
Dolphin Team	1, 0, 2, ↓	Pinto Team	2, 1, 0, →
Dwarf Team	1, 0, 3, ↓	Rivera Team	2, 2, 2, ↑
Eagle Team	2, 1, 2, →	Rocket Park Stadium	3, 2, 1, ↑
Empire Park Stadium	3, 2, 1, →	Rodeo Clown	1, 3, 2, ↓
Evil Clown Team	2, 1, 1, ↓	Rubber Ball	2, 4, 2, ↑
Extended Time for Codes	3, 0, 3, ↑	Scorpion Team	1, 1, 2, ↓
Forbidden City Stadium	3, 3, 3, ←	Spike Bat	0, 0, 5, ↑
Gladiator Team	1, 1, 3, ↓	Team Terry Fitzgerald	3, 3, 3, →
Horse Team	2, 1, 1, →	Team Todd McFarlane	2, 2, 2, →
Ice Bat	0, 0, 3, ↑	Tiny Head	2, 0, 0, ←
Lion Team	2, 2, 0, →	Unlimited Turbo	4, 4, 4, ↓
Little League	1, 0, 1 ↓	Wiffle Bat	0, 0, 4, →

MLB Slugfest Loaded

Unlockable	Code
Unlock Everything	At the Main Menu, hold X+Y, then press the Right Trigger.

MotoGP 2

Unlockable	Objective
Alex Barros	Earn 250,000 points in stunt mode.
Carlos Chera	Earn 100,000 points in stunt mode.
Edgy	Earn 325 championship points.
Floating bike mode	Enter kingpin as your custom bike name.
Legend difficulty	Win the championship on the champion difficulty setting.
Max Biaggi	Get an overall total of 500,000 points in stunt mode to unlock Max Biaggi
Mini-Games	To get a few minigames, go to the options menu and go to the text credits. When you find the text for the minigames, press A.
Pop Video	Earn 375 championship points.
Saturate	Earn 300 championship points on rookie difficulty.
Season Highlights	Finish first in any track to see its highlight video.
Sheridan	Complete all the challenges in championship.
Tohru Ukawa	Earn 750,000 points in stunt mode.
Turbo	Earn 275 championship points.
Valentino Rossi	Earn 1000000 points in stunt mode

MTX Mototrax

Unlockable	Objective
Officer Dick	Complete Free Ride in Career mode.
Police Bike	Complete all Freestyle Events.
Race as a Slipknot rider	Enter 86657457 at the Cheat Menu.
Slipknot Bike	Complete Master Supercross.
Slipknot movie	Enter 23F7IC5 at the Cheat Menu.
Speed Demon	Complete Career mode.
Super Fast Acceleration	Enter JIH345 at the Cheat Menu.
Trick Bot	Complete Freestyle in Career mode.

MTX vs. ATV Unleashed

Enter the codes in the Cheat menu.

Unlockable	Code
50cc Bikes	Minimoto
All Freestyle Tracks	Huckit
Everything	Toolazy

Murakumo

Unlockable	Objective
Expert mission	Complete scenario mode with all missions at A rank.
Free Mission	Beat Scenario mode.
Sound Test Mode	Beat Expert mode all with double S ranks.
"Special Art"	Beat expert mode with any rank.

MVP Baseball 2003

Unlockable	Code
16:9 Anamorphic View	Press and hold the L and R for more than 3 seconds. Then, press ← to enable. Press → to disable.
Easy Home Run	Create a player named Erik Kiss.
Lots of Broken Bats	Create a player named Keegn Patersn, Jacob Patersn, or Ziggy Patersn.

PSP

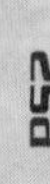

Xbox

PS2

GC

GBA

MVP Baseball 2004

Unlockable	Code
Horrible Player	Enter Erik Kiss as a player name.
Huge Cap on your player	Enter john prosen as a player name.
Player will hold a huge bat	Enter jacob paterson as a player name.

Unlockable	Objective
Al Kaline	2500 MVP Points
Anahiem Angels 1986 Jersey	250 MVP Points
Astrodome	2500 MVP Points
Atlanta Braves 1974 Jersey	500 MVP Points
Babe Ruth	5000 MVP Points
Baltimore Orioles 1971 Jerseys	500 MVP Points
Billy Williams	2500 MVP Points
Bob Feller	3500 MVP Points
Bob Gibson	4500 MVP Points
Bob Lemon	3000 MVP Points
Boston Red Sox 1903 Jerseys	1000 MVP Points
Brooklyn Dodgers 1941 Jerseys	750 MVP Points
Brooks Robinson	3500 MVP Points
Catfish Hunter	3000 MVP Points
Chicago Cubs 1954 Jerseys	750 MVP Points
Chicago White Sox 1919 Jerseys	1000 MVP Points
Cincinatti Reds 1970 Jerseys	500 MVP Points
Cleveland Indians 1975 Jerseys	500 MVP Points
Crosley Field	2500 MVP Points
Cy Young	4500 MVP Points
Detroit Tigers 1906 Jerseys	750 MVP Points
Early Wynn	3500 MVP Points
Eddie Matthews	4000 MVP Points
Ferguson Jenkins	2500 MVP Points
Forbes Field	5000 MVP Points
Gaylord Perry	3500 MVP Points
Griffith Stadium	3000 MVP Points
Hal Newhouser	2500 MVP Points
Harmon Killebrew	3500 MVP Points
Honus Wagner	4500 MVP Points
Houston Astros 1986 Jerseys	250 MVP Points
Hoyt Wilhelm	3000 MVP Points
Jackie Robinson	5000 MVP Points
Jim Palmer	4000 MVP Points
Jimmie Foxx	4000 MVP Points
Joe Morgan	4000 MVP Points
Juan Marichal	3500 MVP Points
Kansas City Royals 1985 Jerseys	250 MVP Points
Larry Doby	3000 MVP Points
Lou Brock	3000 MVP Points
Lou Gehrig	4500 MVP Points
Luis Aprarico	3000 MVP Points

MVP Baseball 2004 (cont'd)

Unlockable	Objective
Mel Ott	3500 MVP Points
Mike Schmidt	4000 MVP Points
Milwaukee Brewers 1982 Jerseys	250 MVP Points
Minnesota Twins 1977 Jerseys	500 MVP Points
Montreal Expos 1981 Jerseys	350 MVP Points
New York Giants 1954 Jerseys	750 MVP Points
New York Mets 1986 Jerseys	350 MVP Points
New York Yankees 1927 Jerseys	1000 MVP Points
Nolan Ryan	4500 MVP Points
Oakland Athletics 1972 Jerseys	500 MVP Points
Orlando Cepeda	3500 MVP Points
Pee Wee Reese	3500 MVP Points
Phil Niekro	2500 MVP Points
Phil Rizzuto	3000 MVP Points
Philadelphia Phillies 1980 Jerseys	500 MVP Points
Pittsburgh Pirates 1916 Jerseys	750 MVP Points
Pittsburgh Pirates 1979 Jerseys	500 MVP Points
Ralph Kiner	2500 MVP Points
Reggie Jackson	4500 MVP Points
Richie Ashburn	2500 MVP Points
Robin Roberts	2500 MVP Points
Robin Yount	4000 MVP Points
Rod Carew	3500 MVP Points
Rollie Fingers	3500 MVP Points
Roy Campanella	4500 MVP Points
San Diego Padres 1984 Jerseys	350 MVP Points
Satchel Paige	4500 MVP Points
Seattle Mariners 1981 Jerseys	350 MVP Points
Shibe Park Stadium	4000 MVP Points
Sparky Anderson	4500 MVP Points
Sportsman's Park	4000 MVP Points
St. Louis Cardinals 1934 Jerseys	750 MVP Points
Texas Rangers 1976 Jerseys	500 MVP Points
The Polo Grounds	5000 MVP Points
Tiger Stadium	3000 MVP Points
Tom Seaver	4000 MVP Points
Tommy Lasorda	4500 MVP Points
Toronto Blue Jays 1992 Jerseys	250 MVP Points
Ty Cobb	5000 MVP Points
Walter Johnson	4500 MVP Points
Warren Spahn	4000 MVP Points
Washington Senators 1913 Jerseys	1000 MVP Points
Whitey Ford	3500 MVP Points
Willie McCovey	4500 MVP Points
Willie Stargell	4000 MVP Points
Yogi Berra	4500 MVP Points

MVP Baseball 2005

Create a character with these names.

Unlockable	Names
Everything	Katie Roy
Player Has a Huge Bat	Keegan Paterson
Player Has a Huge Bat	Jacob Paterson
Player Has a Huge Bat	Isaiah Paterson

MX Unleashed

Unlockable	Objective
All Bonuses	Enter clappedout under Career Completion in the cheats section.

Narc

Enter these codes while playing—do not pause the game.

Unlockable	Code
All Drugs and $10,000	Repeatedly press L+R+click Ⓛ.
All Weapons	Repeatedly press L+R+click Ⓡ.
Infinite Ammo	Repeatedly press L+R+↓. (Only works for the weapon equipped.)
Invincibility	Repeatedly press L+R+Ⓐ.
The Refinery	Repeatedly press L+R+Ⓧ.

NASCAR 2005 Chase for the Cup

Enter these codes in the Edit Driver screen. The passwords need to be entered as a first name and a last name.

Unlockable	Code
2,000,000 Prestige Points	You TheMan
$10,000,000	Walmart Nascar
All Thunder Plates	Open Sesame
Dale Earnhardt	The Intimidator
Exclusive Race Track	Walmart Exclusive

NASCAR Heat 2002

Enter these codes at the Main Menu. The screen will flash to indicate correct code entry.

Unlockable	Code
Credits	↑,↓,←,→,WHT,↑,↓
Hardcore Realism Mode	↑,↓,←,→,WHT,↑,↓
High Suspension	↑,↓,←,→,WHT,←,→
Mini Cars	↑,↓,←,→,WHT,↓,↑
Paintball Mode for Single and Head to Head Race	↑,↓,←,→,WHT,↑,↑—while racing press ↑ to fire paintballs.
Wireframe Cars	↑,↓,←,→,WHT,→,←

NBA 2K2

Cheat Menu: Enter the Options menu and select "Gameplay." Hold ← + Ⓛ→ and press START. The "Codes" selection is now unlocked at the Options menu.

Unlockable	Code
Airball	Select "Street" at the main menu. Press WHT, then hold L and press Ⓨ, Ⓨ. Press START and "Airball" appears to confirm correct code entry.
Bonus Teams	Enter MEGASTARS as a case-sensitive code to unlock the Sega Sports, Visual Concepts, and Team 2K2 in Exhibition and Street modes.

NBA 2K2 (cont'd)

Unlockable	Code
Muhammad Ali and Michael Jackson	Press START and hold L during an Exhibition game. The screen shakes to confirm correct code entry. Go onto the Sixers and they should be on the starting lineup.

NBA Ballers

The following cheats are entered at the Versus Screen, right before the match starts. Y is the first number, B is the second number, and X is the third number. Press the corresponding button as many times as stated.

Unlockable	Code
2X Juice Replenish	4 3 1
Alley-Oop Ability	7 2 5
Alternate Gear	1 2 3
Baby Ballers	4 2 3
Back-In Ability	1 2 2
Back-In Ability	3 1 7
Big Head Mode	1 3 4
Expanded Move Set	5 1 2
Fire Ability	7 2 2
Good Handling	3 3 2
Half House Meter	3 6 7
Hot Spot	6 2 7
Kid Ballers	4 3 3
Legal Goal Tending	7 5 6
No Weather	1 1 2
Paper Ballers	3 5 4
Perfect Free Throws	3 2 7
Play As Afro Man	5 1 7
Play As Agent	5 5 7
Play As BiznezMan-A	5 3 7
Play As BiznezMan-B	5 2 7
Play As Coach	5 6 7
Play As Secretary	5 4 7
Put Back Ability	3 1 3
Pygmy	4 2 5
R2R Mode	0 0 8
Rain	2 2 2
Random Moves	3 0 0
Shows Shot Percentage	0 1 2
Snow	3 3 3
Speedy Players	2 1 3
Stunt Dunk Ability	3 7 4
Super Back-Ins	2 3 5
Super Blocks	1 2 4
Super Push	3 1 5
Super Steals	2 1 5
Tournament Mode	0 1 1
Young Ballers	4 4 3

Go to "Inside Stuff" and select "Phrase-ology." Enter the following codes to unlock goodies:

Unlockable	Code
Allen Iverson's Alternate Gear	killer crossover
Allen Iverson's Studio	the answer
Alonzo Mourning	zo
Amare Stoudamire	rising sun
Baron Davis	Stylin & Profilin
Ben Wallace's alternate outfit	radio controlled cars
Bill Russell	celtics dynasty
Bill Walton	towers of power
Chris Webber	24 seconds
Clyde Drexler	clyde the glide
Darryl Dawkins	rim wrecker
Dikembe Mutumbo	in the paint
Dominique Wilkins	dunk fest
Elton Brand	rebound

NBA Ballers (cont'd)

Unlockable	Code
George Gervin	the ice man cometh
Jalen Rose	bring it
Jason Kidd	pass the rock
Jason Williams	give and go
Jerry Stackhouse's Alt. Gear	Stop Drop and Roll
John Stockton	court vision
Julius Erving	one on one
Karl Malone	special delivery
Karl Malone's Devonshire Estate	ice house
Kevin Garnett's alternate outfit	boss hoss
Kevin McHale	holla back
Kobe Bryant's Alt. Gear	Japanese steak
Larry Bird	hoosier
Latrell Sprewell	spree
Lebron James	king james
Magic Johnson	laker legends
Manu Ginobili gear	manu
Michael Finley	student of the game
Nene Hilario	rags to riches
Oscar Robertson's Alt. Gear	Ain't No Thing
Pete Maravich	pistol pete
Rashard Lewis	fast forward
Rasheed Wallace	bring down the house
Ray Allen	all star
Reggie Miller's Alt. Gear	From Downtown
Richard Hamilton	rip
Robert Parish's Alt. Gear	The Chief
Scottie Pippen	playmaker
Scottie Pippen's Yacht	nice yacht
Shaq's alternate outfit	diesel rules the paint
Special Movie #1	juice house
Special Movie #2	nba showtime
Special Shoe #1	dub deuce
Stephon Marbury	platinum playa
Steve Francis	ankle breaker
Steve Francis's Alt. Gear	Rising Star
Steve Nash	hair canada
Tim Duncan	make it take it
Tony Parker's Alt. outfit	run and shoot
Tracy McGrady	living like a baller
Wally Szczerbiak	world
Walt Frazier	Penetrate and Perpetrate
Wes Unseld	old school
Willis Reed	hall of fame
Wilt Chamberlain	wilt the stilt
Yao Ming	center of attention
Yao Ming's Grade School	prep school

NBA Inside Drive

Enter the Options screen and select "Codes" to access the cheats menu. Repeat each code to disable its effect.

Unlockable	Code
8-Ball	GAMEOVER
ABA Basketball	OLDSCHOOL
Beach Ball	SANDINMYSHORTS
Chicago Rooftop Court	WINDYCITY
Disable Trade Rules	GIMMETHAT
Little Players	SMALLSHOES
More Alley-Oops	IGOTHOPS
More Three Pointers	THREE4ALL
Soccer Ball	HOOLIGAN
Unlimited Turbo	CARDIOMAN
Volleyball	SPIKEIT
WNBA Basketball	GOTGAME
Xbox Ball	BACHMAN

NBA Inside Drive 2004

In the Options screen, select Codes to enter these passwords.

Unlockable	Code
8 Ball	CHALK
ABA Ball	FUNKY
All Trades Accepted	ARELESS
Beach Ball	CONCERTSPIKE
Chicago Skyline Stadium	DOWNTOWN
Easy 3 Pointers	RAINING3S
Easy Alley-Oops	IMFLYING
Small Player	MOONCHY
Soccer Ball	DIEGO
Unlimited Turbo	HOTSAUCE
Unlimited Create a Player Points	UNLIMITED
Volleyball	BAMBIBOOM
WNBA Ball	CHANGEBALL
Xbox Ball	XSNSPORTS

NBA Live 2004

In the Create A Player screen, enter these passwords as last names to unlock the extra players.

Unlockable	Code
Aleksander Pavlovic	WHSUCPOI
Andreas Glyniadakis	POCKDLEK
Carlos Delfino	SDFGURKL
James Lang	NBVKSMCN
Jermaine Dupri	SOSODEF
Kyle Korver	OEISNDLA
Malick Badiane	SKENXIDO
Mario Austin	POSNEGHX
Matt Bonner	BBVDKCVM
Nedzad Sinanovic	ZXDSDRKE
Paccelis Morlende	QWPOASZX
Remon Van De Hare	ITNVCJSD
Rick Rickert	POILKJMN
Sani Becirovic	ZXCCVDRI
Sofoklis Schortsanitis	IOUBFDCJ
Szymon Szewczyk	POIOIJIS
Tommy Smith	XCFWQASE
Xue Yuyang	WMZKCOI

To enter these codes, go into the NBA Live menu, then enter the NBA Codes menu.

Unlockable	Code
15,000 Store Points	87843H5F9P
Air Bounds (Black/White/Blue)	7YSS0292KE
Air Bounds (White/Black)	JA807YAM20
Air Bounds (White/Green)	84HHST61QI

PSP Xbox PS2 GC GBA

NBA Live 2004 (cont'd)

Unlockable	Code
Air Flight 89 (Black/White)	FG874JND84
Air Flight 89 (White/Black)	63RBVC7423
Air Flight 89 (White/Red)	GF9845JHR4
Air Flightposite 2 (Blue/Grey)	2389JASE3E
Air Flightposite (White/Black/Gray)	74FDH7K945
Air Flightposite (White/Black)	6HJ874SFJ7
Air Flightposite (Yellow/Black/White)	MN54BV45C2
Air Foamposite 1 (Blue)	0P5465UX12
Air Foamposite 1 (White/Black/Red)	D0D843HH7F
Air Foamposite Pro (Blue/Black)	DG56TRF446
Air Foamposite Pro (Black/Gray)	3245AFSD45
Air Foamposite Pro (Red/Black)	DSAKF38422
Air Force Max (Black)	F84N845H92
Air Force Max (White/Black/Blue)	985KJF98KJ
Air Force Max (White/Red)	8734HU8FFF
Air Hyperflight (White)	14TGU7DEWC
Air Hyperflight (Black/White)	WW44YhU592
Air Hyperflight (Blue/White)	A0K374HF8S
Air Hyperflight (Yellow/Black)	JCX93LSS88
Air Jordan 11: (Black/Red/White)	GF64H76ZX5
Air Jordan 11: (Black/Varsity Royal/White)	HJ987RTGFA
Air Jordan 11 (Cool Grey)	GF75HG6332
Air Jordan 11 (White)	HG76HN765S
Air Jordan 11 (White/Black)	A2S35TH7H6
Air Jordan 3 (White)	G9845HJ8F4
Air Jordan 3 (White/Clay)	435SGF555Y
Air Jordan 3 (White/Fire Red)	RE6556TT90
Air Jordan 3 (White/True Blue)	FDS9D74J4F
Air Jordan 3 (Black/White/Gray)	CVJ554TJ58
Air Max2 CB (Black/White)	87HZXGFIU8
Air Max2 CB (White/Red)	4545GFKJIU
Air Max2 Uptempo (Black/White/Blue)	NF8745J87F
Air Max Elite (Black)	A4CD54T7TD
Air Max Elite (White/Black)	966ERTFG65
Air Max Elite (White/Blue)	FD9KN48FJF
Air Zoom Flight (Gray/White)	367UEY6SN
Air Zoom Flight (White/Blue)	92387HD077
All Hardwood Classic Jerseys	725JKUPLMM
All NBA Gear	ERT9976KJ3
All Team Gear	YREY5625WQ
All Shoes	POUY985GY5
Nike Blazer (Kaki)	W3R57U9NB2
Nike Blazer (Tan/White/Blue)	DCT5YHMU90
Nike Blazer (White/Orange/Blue)	4G66JU99XS
Nike Blazer (Black)	XCV6456NNL
Nike Shox BB4 (Black)	WE424TY563
Nike Shox BB4 (White/Black)	23ERT85LP9
Nike Shox BB4 (White/Light Purple)	668YYTRB12
Nike Shox BB4 (White/Red)	424TREU777
Nike Shox VCIII (Black)	SDFH764FJU
Nike Shox VCIII (White/Black/Red)	5JHD367JJT
Zoom Generation (White/Black/Red)	23LBJNUMB1
Zoom Generation (Black/Red/White)	LBJ23CAVS1

NBA Live 2005

Go to My NBA Live, EA Sports Lounge, NBA Codes to enter these codes.

Unlockable	Code
50,000 Dynasty Points	YISS55CZ0E
All Classics Hardwood Jerseys	PRYI234N0B
All Shoes	FHM389HU80
All Team Gear	1NVDR89ER2

NBA Live 2005 (cont'd)

Unlockable Team	Code
Atlanta Hawks 2004-05 Alternate	HDI834NN9N
Boston Celtics 2004-05 Alternate	XCV43MGMDS
Dallas Mavericks 2004-05 Alternate	AAPSEUD09U
Golden State Warriors 2004-05 Alternate	NAVNY29548

Unlockable Shoes	Code
Nike Air Huarache	VNBA60230T
Nike BG Rollout	0984ADF90P
Nike Shox Elite	2388HDFCBJ
Nike Air Unlimited	XVLJD9895V
Zoom Lebron II Shoes	1KENZO23XZ
Zoom Generation Low	234SDJF9W4

NBA Jam

Create a new profile using these names.

Unlockable	Code
Unlock Everything	-LPP-
Unlock the NBA Jam Development Team	CREDITS

NBA Street Vol 2

Unlockable	Code/Objective
All Quicks	Hold L and press Y, B, Y, X.
Alternate Ball (NBA or ABA)	Hold L and press B, X, B, X.
Always Legend Trails	Hold L and press Y, Y, Y, X.
Big Heads	Hold L and press B, X, X, B.
Easy 2 pointers	Hold L and press Y, B, X, Y.
Explosive Rims	Hold L and press B, B, B, Y.
Hard 2 Pointers	Hold L and press Y, X, B, Y.
Nelly and the St. Lunatics	Get 750 reward points or win 20 games in Pick Up.
No Counters	Hold L and press Y, Y, B, B.
No HUD	Hold L and press X, B, B, B.
Street Kids	Hold L and press Y, Y, B, X.
Unlimited Turbo	Hold L and press X, X, Y, Y.
1985 Jordan	Collect the Street School trophy, NBA Challenge trophy and the Be A Legend trophy.
Biggie Little	Beat the tournament on Broad Street in Philly.
Bill Walton Jersey	Earn 1,000,000 trick points or more in a game.
Clyde Drexler Jersey	Collect 1 reputation star in Legend Mode.
Dime	Complete the tournament in Lincoln College.
Elgin Baylor Jersey	Get 20 or more blocks in a game.
Jerry West Jersey	Win a game without getting blocked.
Just Blaze	Get 500 Reward Points or win 15 games in Pick Up.
Osmosis	Win the Mosswood tournament in Legend mode.
Street Champ Costume	Complete *Be A Legend* by earning all 500/500 progress points.
Stretch	Beat the Soul in the Hole Tournament.
Whitewater	Complete the tournament in Green Lake to Whitewater.
WNBA Ball	Hold L and press B, Y, Y, B.

NCAA Football 2004

Touchdown Celebrations: After you score a touchdown, press these button combos to see the specific celebration.

Celebration	Code
Bow	L + Y
Display ball	R + Y
Dunk over goal post	R + X
Heisman Pose	L + A
Kick ball into crowd	R + B
Spike Ball	L + X
Spike ball, then shrug	L + B
Throw ball into crowd	R + A

NCAA Football 2005

All codes can be entered in the Pennant Collection Menu.

Unlockable	Code
1st and 15	Thanks
2003 All Americans	Fumble
Alabama All Time	Roll tide
Arizona Mascot Team	Bear down
Arkansas All Time	Woopigsooie
Auburn All Time	War eagle
Badgers All Time	U rah rah
Baylor Powerup	Sic em
Blink	For
Boing	Registering
Clemson All Time	Death valley
Colorado All Time	Glory
Crossed the Line	Tiburon
Cuffed Cheat	EA sports
Florida All Time	Great to be
Florida State All Time	Uprising
Georgia All Time	Hunker down
Georgia Tech Mascot Team	Ramblinwreck
Illinois Team Boost	Oskee wow
Iowa All Time	On iowa
Iowa St. Mascot Team	Red and gold
Jumbalaya	Hike
Kansas Mascot Team	Rock chalk
Kansas State All Time	Victory
Kentucky Mascot Team	On on uk
LSU All Time	Geaux tigers
Miami All Time	Raising cane
Michigan All Time	Go blue
Michigan State Mascot Team	Go green
Minnesota Mascot Team	Rah rah rah
Mississippi State All Time	Hail state
Missouri Mascot Team	Mizzou rah
Molasses Cheat	Home field
NC State Mascot Team	Go cats
Nebraska All Time	Go big red
Norte Dame All Time	Golden domer
North Carolina All Time	Rah rah
Ohio State All Time	Killer nuts
Oklahoma All Time	Boomer
Oklahoma State All Time	Go pokes
Ole Miss Mascot Team	Hotty totty
Oregon All Time	Quack attack
Penn State All Time	We are
Pittsburgh All Time	Lets go pitt
Purdue All Time	Boiler up
QB Dud	Elite 11
Stiffed	NCAA
Syracuse All Time	Orange crush
Take your Time	Football
Tennessee All Time	Big orange
Texas A&M All Time	Gig em
Texas All Time	Hook em
Texas Tech Team Boost	Fight
Thread the Needle	2005
UCLA All Time	Mighty
USC All Time	Fight on
Virginia All Time	Wahoos
Virginia Tech Team Boost	Tech triumph
Wake Forest Mascot Team	Go deacs go
Washington All Time	Bowdown
West Virginia Mascot Team	Hail wv
What a Hit	Blitz
WSU Mascot Team	All hail

Need for Speed Underground

Enter the following codes at the Main Menu.

Unlockable	Code
Circuit Tracks	Down, R, R, R, Black, Black, X
Drift Tracks	Left, Left, Left, Left, Right, Black, R, White
Drag Tracks	Right, X, Left, R, X, L, White, Black
Sprint Tracks	Up, Black, Black, Black, R, Down, Down, Down

Need for Speed Underground 2

Codes are entered at the Main Menu.

Unlockable	Code
$1,000 for Career Mode	Left, Left, Right, X, X, Right, L, R
Best Buy Vinyl	Up, Down, Up, Down, Down, Up, Right, Left

NFL Fever 2002

Unlockable	Code
All Teams and Stadiums	Create a new Profile using the name Broadway.

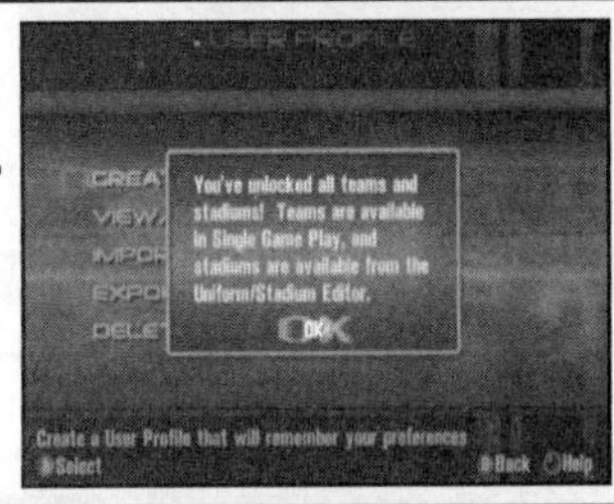

NFL Fever 2003

To enter these codes you must make a user file using the following names.

Stadium Unlockable	Code
Commandos	Barracks
Pansies	Flowery
98 Broncos	Milehigh
Chromides	Regulate

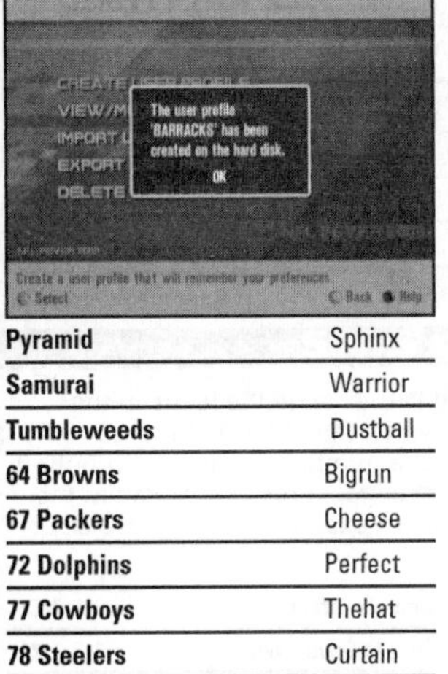

Stadium Unlockable	Code
Pyramid	Sphinx
Samurai	Warrior
Tumbleweeds	Dustball
64 Browns	Bigrun
67 Packers	Cheese
72 Dolphins	Perfect
77 Cowboys	Thehat
78 Steelers	Curtain
83 Raiders	Outlaws
85 Bears	Sausage
89 49ers	Empire
93 Cowboys	Lonestar
96 Packers	Green
Commandos	Camo
Cows	Milk
Creampuffs	Cakewalk
Crocs	Crykie
DaRulas	Tut
Eruption	Lava
Firemen	Blazer
Gladiators	BigBack
Hackers	Axemen
King Cobras	Venom
Mimes	Silence
Monks	Robes
Pansies	Viola

NFL Fever 2003 (cont'd)

Team Unlockable	Code
Polars	Igloo
Samurai	Slasher
Skeletons	Stone
Soldiers	Helmet
Sorcerers	Spellboy
Spies	Target
Thunder Sheep	Flock
Tumbleweeds	Dusty
War Elephants	Horns
Wildcats	Kitty
Winged Gorillas	Flying

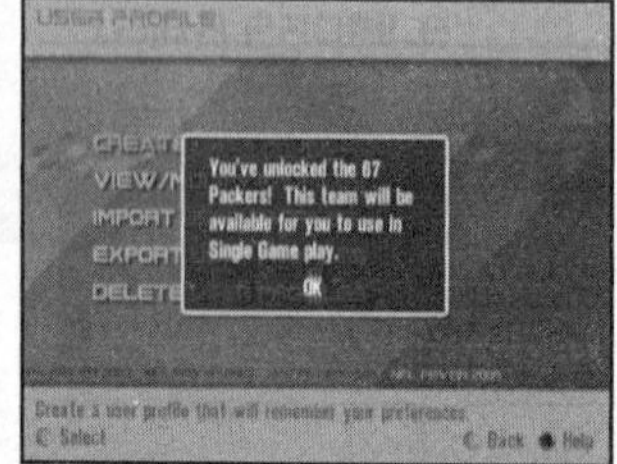

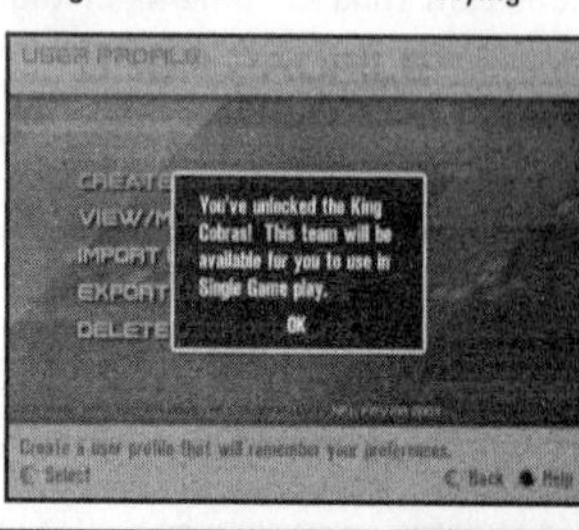

NFL Fever 2004

Unlockable	Code
All Teams	sportxsn

NFL Street

Enter the following passwords as your User name.

Unlockable	Code
NFL Legends	classic
Xecutioner Team	excellent
Kay Slay Team	kayslay
All Stadiums	travel

NFL Street 2

Enter these codes in the Cheats Menu.

Unlockable	Code
AFC East All-Stars	EAASFSCT
AFC North All-Stars	NAOFRCTH
AFC South All-Stars	SAOFUCTH
AFC West All-Stars	WAEFSCT
All players will have a maxed out catching stat	MagnetHands

NHL Hitz 2002

Activate Cheat Menu: Press Ⓧ, Ⓨ, and Ⓑ to change the icons in the first, second, and third boxes respectively at the Match-Up screen. The numbers in the following list indicate the number of times each button is pressed. After the icons have been changed, press the D-Pad in the indicated direction to enable the code. For example, to enter 1-2-3 ←, press Ⓧ, Ⓨ(2), Ⓑ(3), ←.

Unlockable	Code
Big Head Player	2-0-0 →
Big Head Team	2-2-0 ←
Big Hits	2-3-4 ↓
Big Puck	1-2-1 ↑
Bulldozer Puck	2-1-2 ←
Disable Previous Code	0-1-0 ↓
Domino Effect	0-1-2 →
First to Seven Wins	3-2-3 ←
Hitz Time	1-0-4 →
Hockey Ball	1-3-3 ←
Huge Head Player	3-0-0 →
Huge Head Team	3-3-0 ←
Huge Puck	3-2-1 ↑

NHL Hitz 2002 (cont'd)

Unlockable	Code
Late Hits	3-2-1 ↓
More Time to Enter Codes	3-3-3 →
No Crowd	2-1-0 →
No Fake Shots	4-2-4 ↓
No One-Timers	2-1-3 ←
No Puck Out	1-1-1 ↓
Pinball Boards	4-2-3 →
Rain Mode	1-4-1 ←
Show Shot Speed	1-0-1 ↑
Show the Team's Hot Spot	2-0-1 ↑
Skills Versus	2-2-2 ↓
Snow Mode	1-2-1 ←
Tennis Ball	1-3-2 ↓
Turbo Boost	0-0-2 ↑
Unlimited Turbo	4-1-3 →
Win Fights for Goals	2-0-2 ←

NHL Hitz Pro

Enter these codes as User Names. To turn on these codes, pause the game and select Settings, then select Visuals, followed by Cheats.

Unlockable	Code
Big Player Head	HERK
Big Team Heads	INGY
Different Puck Size	211S
Different Puck Shadow	SASG
Glowing Puck	CARB

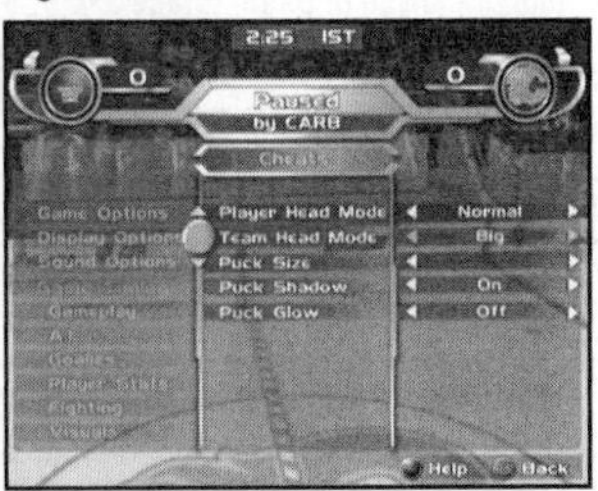

NHL Rivals 2004

To enter these codes, select Options, then select Unlocks.

Unlockable	Code
All Agitators	PESTFEST
All Balanced Players	EVENSTEVEN
All Enforcers	BRUISERS
All Snipers	SHOOTOUT
Big Players	BIGDUDES
Big Puck	BIGBISCUIT
Big Shot Mode	HOWITZER
Heavy Shot Trails	THESTREAK
Increase Gravity	HEAVYPUCK
Invisible Players	INVISIBLEMAN
NHL Rivals East All Stars	CUJOEAST
NHL Rivals West All Stars	CUJOWEST
No Bounce Dasherboards	DEADBOARDS
Microsoft All Stars	BLIBBET
Small Players	TINYTYKES
Unlimited Speed Burst	Caffeine
XSN Sports East All Stars	XSNSPORTSEAST
XSN Sports West All Stars	XSNSPORTSWEST
Zero Ice Friction	AIRHOCKEY

Ninja Gaiden

Unlockable	Objective
All Music and Sound Test	Complete the game.
Armlet of Benediction	Collect 15 Scarabs.
Armlet of Fortune	Collect 30 Scarabs.
Armlet of Tranquility	Collect 40 Scarabs.
Blue Ninja Outfit	At the Main Menu, highlight New Game, hold both L+R and press A

Ninja Gaiden (cont'd)

Dabilahro	Collect 20 Scarabs.
Dark Dragon Blade	Complete the game. Then visit Muramasa's shop in chapter 13.
Evil Ryu	Complete the game on Very Hard.
Movie Gallery	Complete the game.
New Outfit and Sword	Once you complete the game, go to the Main Menu and highlight new game. Then hold Ⓛ and press Ⓐ.
Ninja Gaiden 1	Collect 50 Scarabs.
Ninja Gaiden 2	Once you obtain Ninja Gaiden 1, shoot the clock tower near Muramasa's shop in Tairon.
Ninja Gaiden 3	In the Ceremonial room in the aquaducts, jump up the wall where you found the golden Scarab.
Very Hard	Complete the game.

Otogi: Myth of Demons

Unlockable	Objective
Black Swallow	Found behind the start point of Canyon of Death (Stage 23). Once the stage begins, turn around and head into the alcove. Kill the Death Serpent.
Butterfly Staff	Destroy the plants on the left side near the beginning of The Green Cave (Stage 10). One hides a secret hallway where the Butterfly Staff can be found.
Dragon Point	Kill 30 enemies in Restless Sea (Stage 7).
Dragon Staff	Finish Palace of Gold (Stage 5) with a time of 3:20 or better.
Golden Dragon	Found in the narrow passage near the beginning of Inner Sanctum (Stage 20).
Holy Staff	Beat Sea of Fire (Stage 15) with a time of 2:47 or better.
Jaws of Mountain	Found in Spirit Wood (Stage 11). Follow the narrow path to the right of the start point and cross the bridge to receive your prize.
Moonlight Sword	Free 100% of all souls in first 28 stages.
Ogre's Horn	Defeat the Blaze Ogre near the beginning of Darkfire Cave (Stage 18).
Orchid Malevolence	Kill the Hydra in Stage 25.
Punisher	Found at the base of the hill to the right in A Clouded Moon (Stage 6).
Rune Scimitars	Perform a 20-hit combo (or greater) in Mountain Gates (Stage 3).
Skylarks	Beat Stage 14 in under 2 minutes.
Staff of Duality	Found in Forest of Wind (Stage 24). Look for the small passageway inside the tree stump.
Sword of Voracity	Kill 60 enemies in Stage 26, Valley of Prayer
Thunder	Found in Stage 22, Lair of Fire, underneath the bridge between the center island and the large statue.
Training Sword	Perform a 400-hit combo in Spirit Wood (Stage 11).

Outlaw Golf

Unlockable	Objective
Atlas Driver	Complete the Stroke Me event.
Atlas Fairway Woods	Complete the Not-So-Goodfellas event.
Atlas Irons	Complete the High Rollers event.
Atlas Putter (Black)	Complete the All the Marbles event.
Atlas Putter Gold	Complete the Suave's Revenge event.
Atlas Wedge	Complete the Pretty in Pink event.
Boiler Maker Fairway Woods	Complete the Hole Lotta Luv event.

Outlaw Golf (cont'd)

Boiler Maker Irons	Complete the Jersey Ball Bash event.
Boiler Maker Putter	Complete the Sun Stroke event.
Boiler Maker Wedge	Complete the Back 9 Shuffle event.
Bonus Costumes	Hold L and press Y, Y, WHT, Y, BLK, Y at the character selection screen.
C.C.	Complete the Hot, Hot, Hot event.
Cincinnati Balls	Complete the Rough Riders event.
Cincinnati Driver	Complete the Ol' Blood and Guts event.
Cincinnati Fairway Woods	Complete the Full Frontal event.
Cincinnati Irons	Complete the Stroke Me Again event.
Cincinnati Wedge	Complete the Blister in the Sun event.
Coiler Maker Driver	Complete the Money Talks event.
Distract Opponent	Start a game with two or more players. While the other person is hitting the ball, press A to say things to distract them.
Doc Diggler	Complete the Ladies Night event.
Ecstasy Balls	Complete the Scorched Earth Classic event.
Ecstasy Putter	Complete the Motley Crew event.
Killer Miller	Complete the Test Drive event.
Master Code	Start a new game and enter Golf_Gone_Wild as a case-sensitive name, including underscores, to unlock all characters, clubs, and stages.
Nelson Balls	Complete the Different Strokes event.
Python Driver	Complete the Heat Rash Invitational event.
Python Fairway Woods	Complete the Tough Crowd event.
Python Irons	Complete the A Hole in the Sun event.
Python Wedge	Complete the Garden State Stroke Fest event.
Scrummy	Complete the Odd Ball Classic event.
Suave's Balls	Complete the Garden State Menage a Trois event.
Suki	Complete the Baked on the Bone event.
Trixie	Complete the Chicks with Sticks event.

Outlaw Golf 2

Unlockable	Code
Big Head Mode	At any time during the game, hold L and press B, A, B, Y, Down, Left.
Everything	Enter I Have No Time as your name.

Outlaw Volleyball

Unlockable	Code
All Characters	At the character select screen, hold L and press Left, WHT, Right, WHT.
All Courts	On Court Selection Screen, hold L and press Up, Down, Up, Down, Left, Left, Right, Right.

Outlaw Volleyball (cont'd)

Big Head Mode	During gameplay, hold L and press B,A,B,Y.
Maximum Stats	In Exhibition mode, hold R and press ←,WHT,→,WHT.
Time Bombs	In Exhibition mode, hold L and press A,B,B,Y, and A+X together.

Outrun 2

To enter these codes, select Outrun Challenge, then select Gallery, and last, select Enter Code.

Unlockable	Code
All Cars	DREAMING
All Mission Stages	THEJOURNEY
All Music	RADIOSEGA
Bonus Tracks	TIMELESS
Original Outrun	NINETEEN86
Reverse Tracks	DESREVER

Panzer Dragoon Orta

Unlockable	Objective/Code
Box Game Mode	Complete the game under the Hard difficulty setting or accumulate fifteen hours of gameplay.
Flight Records Option	Complete the game under any difficulty setting or accumulate five hours of gameplay.
Pandora's Box Options	Accumulate twenty hours of gameplay to unlock most of the Pandora's Box Appendix options, including the Panzer Dragoon game.
Panzer Dragoon Dragon-Only Mode (Only the lock-on weapons are available with this code.)	Enable the "Power-ups" code, followed by ←, ←, →, →, ↑, ↓, ↑, ↓, L, R. The sound of the dragon being hit confirms correct code entry.
Panzer Dragoon Episode 0	Press ↑, ↑, ↑, ↓, ↓, ↓, ←, →, ←, →, ←, →, L, R at the Panzer Dragoon main menu. Shoot enemies to restore your health, which gradually decreases during gameplay.
Panzer Dragoon Episode Select	Press ↑, ↑, ↓, ↓, ←, →, ←, →, X, Y, WHT at the Panzer Dragoon main menu.
Panzer Dragoon Game	Complete the game or accumulate five hours of gameplay to unlock the original Panzer Dragoon game in the Pandora's Box Appendix.
Panzer Dragoon Invincible Mode	Press L, L, R, R, ↑, ↓, ←, → at the Panzer Dragoon main menu. The sound of the dragon being hit and the phrase "Invincible Mode" appears to confirm correct code entry.
Panzer Dragoon Power Ups	Press ↑, X, →, Y, ↓, WHT, ←, Y, ↑, X at the Panzer Dragoon Easy Game Options screen. The Sega logo turns into a polygon woman. This normally occurs after you complete the game without dying. Go to the Episodes screen, and hold B for red lasers, BLK for missiles, Y for rapid fire, or WHT for a wide-shot weapon.
Panzer Dragoon Red Sega Polygon Man	Press ↑, X, →, Y, ↓, WHT, ←, Y, ↑, X at the Panzer Dragoon main menu. The sound of the dragon being hit confirms correct code entry. After finishing the last continue, the polygon Sega figure is red instead of blue.
Panzer Dragoon Rolling Mode	Press START at the Panzer Dragoon Title screen. Sweep the ⊙ in three clockwise full circles when the screen with normal game and options appears. A sound and the phrase "Rolling Mode" appears to confirm correct code entry. Tap the ⊙ twice to perform a roll during gameplay. To activate a smart bomb, begin a roll, and hold any button to highlight all enemy targets on the radar. Release the button to destroy the targets.

Panzer Dragoon Orta (cont'd)

Panzer Dragoon Unlimited Continues	Press Up, X, Right, Y, Down, WHT, Left, Y, Up, X at the Panzer Dragoon main menu.
Panzer Dragoon View Hard Difficulty Ending Sequence	Press Up, Up, Down, Up, Left, Left, Right, Left, Down, Down, Up, Down, Right, Right, Left, Right at the Panzer Dragoon main menu.
Panzer Dragoon View Normal Ending Sequence	Press Up, Up, Down, Up, Right, Right, Left, Right, Down, Down, Up, Down, Left, Left, Right, Left at the Panzer Dragoon main menu.
Panzer Dragoon Wizard Mode	Press START at the Title screen. Press L, R, L, R, Up, Down, Up, Down, Left, Right at the Panzer Dragoon main menu. The phrase "Wizard Mode" appears to confirm correct code entry. Gameplay is very fast when you enable this mode.
White Dragonmare	Unlock the Dragonmare in Box mode. Highlight the "Dragon Select" option, hold WHT, and press START. Release WHT when the game starts.

Pariah

To enter these codes go to the Codes option.

Unlockable	Code
EB Games Multiplayer Level	WHT,Y,X,BLK
Gamestop Multiplayer Level	Left,L,X,Left

Enter these codes in the Cheat Codes menu under "settings."

Unlockable	Code
All Ammo	Down, Up, Down, Y
God Mode	Up, L, X, L

Phantasy Star Online Episode I and II

Unlockable	Objective
Open the Dressing Room	Have 10,000 Meseta on your character (not in the bank) when you start the game.
Hard Mode (offline)	Beat Normal Mode.
Hard Mode (online)	Get to level 20.
Ultimate Mode (offline)	Beat Very Hard Mode.
Ultimate Mode (online)	Get to level 80.
Very Hard Mode (offline)	Beat Hard Mode.
Very Hard Mode (online)	Get to level 40.

Pirates of the Caribbean

Unlockable	Code
Gain 50 Skill Points	A, B, Y, X, Y, B, B, Y, B, A
Get 100,000 Gold	A, X, Y, B, Y, B, X, B, B, A
God Mode	A, Y, X, X, Y, Y, B, Y, X, A
Set Reputation to Neutral	A, X, Y, X, Y, B, B, Y, B, A

Pirates: The Legend of Black Kat

Unlockable	Code
Advance to Katarina's Next Sword	Hold L + R and click R, press BACK, BLK, click L, press X, A, WHT, Y, click L, press B
All Treasure Chest Keys	Hold L + R and press Y, BACK, A, X, click R, press WHT, click L, press BLK, B, click L.
Alternate Glacial Gulf Music	Hold L + R and press WHT, A, B, BLK, X, Y, click L, press BACK, click R, click L to hear music from SSX when sliding down in Glacial Gulf.
Alternate Katarina Costumes	Press L + R, click L, press BACK, Up. A short sequence of music confirms correct code entry. Click R to change the value of the numbers that appear on screen, then start a new game or resume a saved game to view the corresponding costume. The available costumes and their values are in the table below.
Extra Gold	Hold L + R and press B, click R, press WHT, X, A, click R, press BACK, click L, press Y, BLK. Sail to another map to get the Galleon.
High-Pitched Voices	Hold L + R and click R, press Y, BACK, A, click R, press B, WHT, X, BLK, click L.
Invincibility for Katarina	Hold L + R and press A, Y, click L, press B, click R, press BACK, click R, press WHT, BLK, X.
Invincibility for the Wind Dancer	Hold L + R and press BACK, B, WHT, A, click R, press BLK, X, click R, press Y, click L.
Kane Poison Head	Hold L + R and press B, BLK, WHT, X, click L, press A, click L, press Y, click R, press BACK. The poison status will be indicated by the head of Kane from Command and Conquer.
Reveal All Treasure Chests	Hold L + R and click R, press A, B, click L, press Y, WHT, BACK, click L, press X, BLK.
Reveal Buried Treasure Chests	Hold L + R and press Y, A, X, B, WHT, BACK, click L, BLK, click L, click R. Green Xs appear on the captain's log maps to indicate the location of buried treasure chests.
Unlimited Items	Hold L + R and press B, WHT, BACK, BLK, click R, click L, press X, A, click R, press Y. Once found, an item becomes available in unlimited amounts.
Unlimited Wind Boost	Hold L + R and press BACK, WHT, click R, press X, click L, press Y, BLK, B, A, click L.
Wind Dancer	Hold L + R and press BLK, B, click R, click L, press A, X, click R, press BACK, WHT, Y.

Alternate Costume	Numerical Value
Blackbeard in Purple	00000001
Blonde Hair, Orange and Yellow Bikini	00000101
Blonde Hair, Pink Bikini	00000110
Blue Hair with Orange and Red Bikini	00000011
Blue Hair, Shiny Copper Body Suit	00001010
Blue Hair, Shiny Silver Bikini	00000111
Original Costume and Hair Color	00000000
Pink Hair, Shiny Black Body Suit	00001001
Purple Hair, Shiny Silver Body Suit	00001011
Red Hair with Red and Orange Bikini	00000010
Red Hair, Black Bikini, Black Stockings	00001000
Tan, Brown Hair, Orange and Yellow Bikini	00000100

Pitfall: The Lost Expedition

Enter the following codes at the Main screen while holding Ⓛ+Ⓡ.

Unlockable	Code
Bottomless Canteen	Left, X, B, Down, X, A, X, B
Original Pitfall	B, B, Left, Right, B, X, A, Up, B
Play as Nicole	Left, Up, Down, Up, B, Up, Up
Punch Mode	Left, Right, B, Up, B, Right, Left

Prince of Persia

Unlockable	Objective
Original Prince of Persia	Complete the game and you will open up the very first Prince of Persia.

Prisoner of War

At the Main Menu, select Passwords to enter these codes.

Unlockable	Code
All Chapters	GER1ENG5
All Secrets	FARLEYMYDOG
Default Chapters	DEFAULTM
Defiance	FATTY
First Person Mode	BOSTON
Game Creation Date and Time	DT
Guard Perception	QUINCY
Guard Size	MUFFIN
Informed of all Events	ALLTIMES
Informed of Core Current Events	CORETIMES
Top Down Mode	FOXY
Unlimited Goodies	DINO

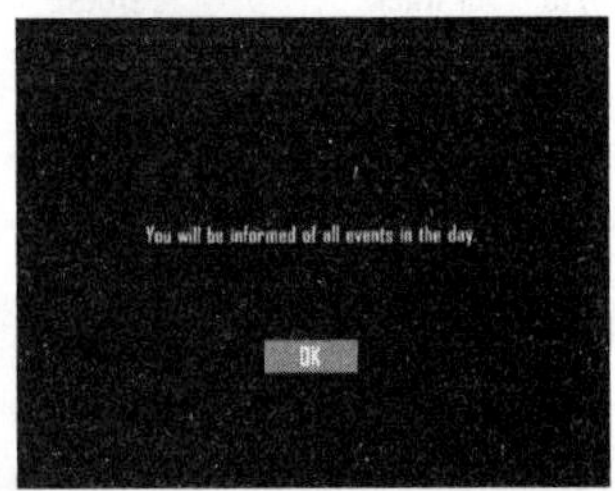

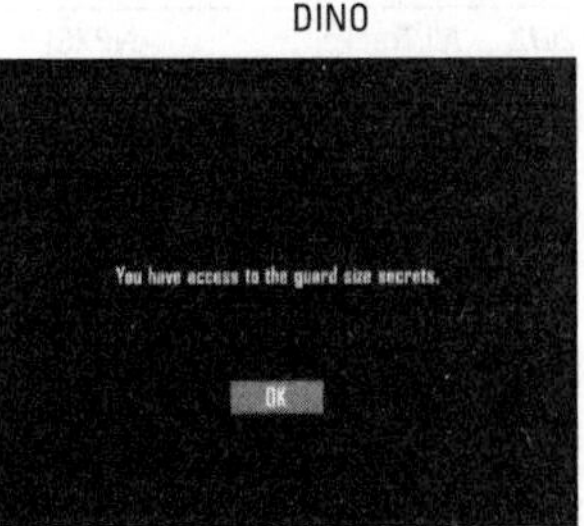

Project Gotham Racing

Unlockable	Code
All Cars and Courses	Enter the name Nosliw.

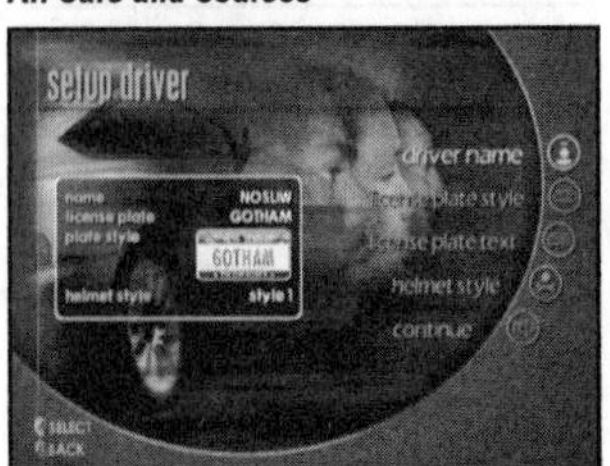

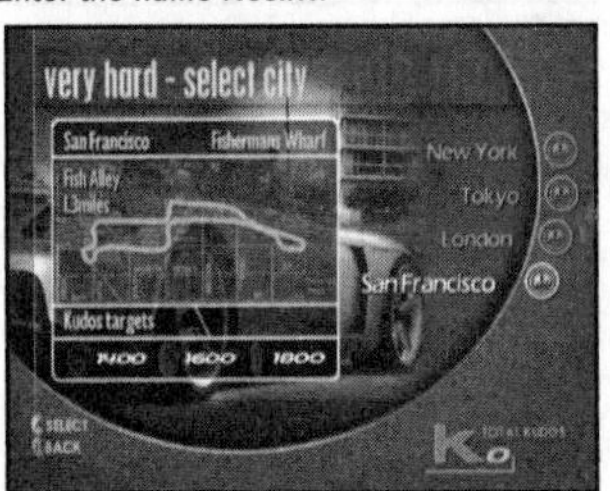

PSP Xbox PS2 GC GBA

Pro Race Driver

NOTE

Pro Race Driver has different codes based on the number found on the disc. Find the number on the disc, then enter the appropriate code.

Disc #	Unlockable	Code
1010	All Cars	SLDDLS
1010	All Championships	FMXXMF
1010	All Pro Challenges	FGZZGF
1010	All Tracks	GLFFLG
1010	Change Handling	YOOOOY
1010	No Damage	FYWWYF
1521	All Cars	PLSZGF
1521	All Championships	FZYFLG
1521	All Tracks	YHYXMF
1521	Change Handling	RWMRKV
1785	All Cars	LJLYZF
1785	All Championships	IHHSLP
1785	All Pro Challenges	FNJYHY
1785	All Tracks	MMMHHS
2072	All Cars	DDYYHY
2072	All Championships	TLYYZF
2072	All Pro Challenges	MJUHHS
2072	All Tracks	NPXSLP
2072	Change Handling	RFIHWL
2072	No Damage	OSAMWR
2569	All Cars	LJQZEL
2569	All Championships	YPJQIN
2569	All Pro Challenges	IFTBBR
2569	All Tracks	DHMFJL
2569	Change Handling	WLNREA
2569	No Damage	LSXGYP
3588	_All Cars	BDVHHA
3588	All Championships	MVQAVP
3588	All Pro Challenges	TLHMEI
3588	All Tracks	DJEWCM
3588	Change Handling	LUBTNUL
3588	No Damage	CZIKYT
3906	All Cars	YUPAVP
3906	All Championships	ZEUHHA

Disc #	Unlockable	Code
3906	All Pro Challenges	ZNZWCM
3906	All Tracks	VFCMEI
3906	Change Handling	BAAYQB
3906	No Damage	FACIFE
3956	All Cars	MKWAVP
3956	All Championships	MZDHHA
3956	All Pro Challenges	RCVWCM
3956	All Tracks	ZVIMEI
6471	All Cars	KUPTFI
6471	All Championships	WLNMHD
6471	All Pro Challenges	LSXQJL
6471	All Tracks	ODCJPY
6471	Change Handling	YPJCDO
6471	No Damage	IFTPUK
6778	All Cars	RFINLW
6778	All Championships	LWRPUK
6778	All Pro Challenges	USKCDO
6778	All Tracks	OSAXSL
6778	Change Handling	DDYQJL
6778	No Damage	NPXMHD
7208	All Cars	IFFYDD
7208	All Championships	YOOUJM
7208	All Pro Challenges	FYWYLT
7208	All Tracks	VKRXPN
7208	Change Handling	FMXIFR
7208	No Damage	FGZASO
8105	All Cars	WOYHHI
8224	All Cars	LJFCZH
8224	All Championships	RBBDSL
8224	All Pro Challenges	NIQRTQ
8224	All Tracks	LEZFAS
8224	No Damage	AERLJL
8224	No Damage	PYGMMM

Psi Ops: The Mindgate Conspiracy

At the Main Menu, highlight Extra Content, press Ⓡ, and enter any of these codes.

Unlockable	Code
All Powers from the start	537893
Arcade Mode	05051979
Bulletproof	548975
Co Op Play Mode	07041979
Dark Mode	465486
Super Psi	456456
Unlimited Ammo	978945

Skin Unlockable	Code
Crispy Soldier	454566
Dockworker	364654
Edgar Barret	497878
Edgar Barret	(Training 1) 196001
Edgar Barret	(Training 2) 196002
Edgar Barret	(Training 3) 196003
Edgar Barret	(Training 4) 196004
Edgar Barret	(Training 5) 196005
Edgar Barret	(Training 6) 196006
Jack	698798
Jov Leonov	468987
Kimiko Jones	978798
Labcoat	998789
Marlena Kessler	489788
Marlena Kessler (Bikini)	135454
Marlena Kessler (Leather)	136876
Marlena Kessler (Saranae)	65496873
MP1	321646
MP2	698799
MP3	654659
Nick Scryer (Stealth)	456498
Nick Scryer (Training)	564689
Nick Scryer (Urban)	484646
Nick Scryer (Wasteland)	975466
No Head	987978
Sara Blake	135488
Sara Blake (Psi)	468799
Sara Blake (Suicide)	231644
Scorpion	546546
The General (Clown)	431644
The General (Default)	459797
Tonya	678999
UN Soldier	365498
Wei Lu	231324
Wei Lu (Dragon)	978789
Wei Lu (Tranquility)	654654

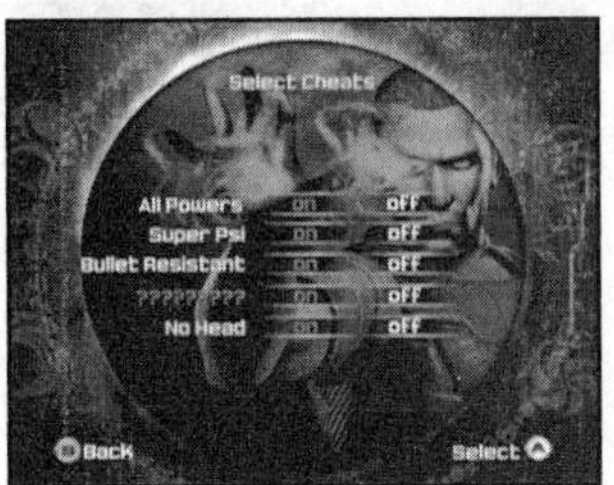

Extra Mission	Code
Aura Pool	659785
Bottomless Pit	154897
Bouncy, Bouncy	568789
Floor of Death	05120926
Gasoline	9442662
Gearshift	154684
Gnomotron	456878
Panic Room	76635766
Psi Pool	565485
Survival Mode	7734206
Stoplights	945678
Tip the Idol	428584
TK Alley	090702
Up and Over	020615

Psychonauts

During gameplay, hold L+R and enter the codes. A "you cheated" sound will confirm correct entry.

Unlockable	Code
9999 Ammo	→,A,←,←,Y,B
9999 Arrow Heads	A,→,→,White,Y,X
9999 Lives	←,White,White,B,A,→
All Items Except Dream Fluffs, Colorizer, and Psi-Ball	→,B,White,White,←,Y
All Powers and Max Rank	←,→,←
All PSI Powers	B,B,Y,White,←,Y
Invincibility	B,White,B,B,Y,Black,White,B,White
Text Changes	White,A,←,White,White,B

The Punisher

Enter V Pirate as a Profile Name to unlock everything except Upgrades.

Quantum Redshift

Enter Cheat as your name, then in the Options Menu, select the Cheats Menu to enter these codes. Codes are case sensitive.

Unlockable	Code
All Characters	Nematode
All Speeds	zoomZOOM
Infinite Turbo	FishFace
Infinite Shields	ThinkBat
Upgrade all Characters	RICEitup

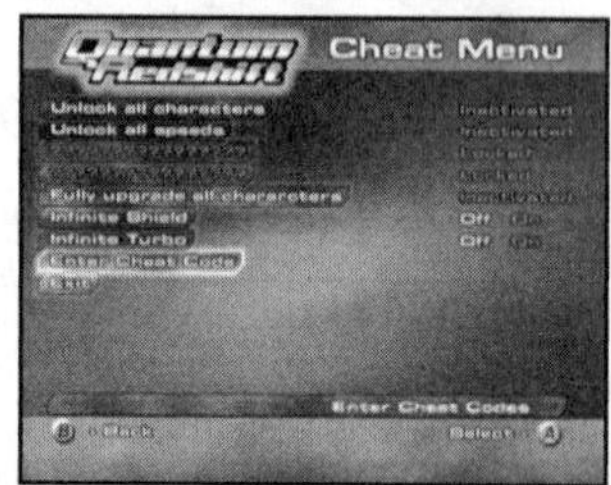

Red Card 2003

Unlockable	Objective
Apes Team and Victoria Falls Stadium	Defeat the Apes team in World Conquest mode.
Dolphins Team and Nautilus Stadium	Defeat the Dolphins team in World Conquest mode.
Finals Mode	Win all matches in World Conquest mode.
Martians Team and USAFB001 Stadium	Defeat the Martians team in World Conquest mode.
Matadors Team and Coliseum Stadium	Defeat the Matadors team in World Conquest mode.
Samurai Team and Youhi Gardens Stadium	Defeat the Samurai team in World Conquest mode.
SWAT Team and Nova City Stadium	Defeat the SWAT team in World Conquest mode.

Unlockable	Code
Cheat Mode	Enter BIGTANK as a name to unlock all teams, stadiums, and finals mode.

Red Dead Revolver

These are the rewards for each level. The first is for a GOOD rating and the second is for a Excellent rating.

Unlockable	Good rating	Excellent rating
Battle Finale	Focus (Dead-Eye) Max-Up	Mr. Kelley
Bear Mountain	Shadow Wolf	Focus (Dead-Eye) Max-Up
Bounty Hunter	"Bloody" Tom	"Big Oaf" Whitney
Bull's Eye	Old Pistol	Broken Creek
Carnival Life	Focus (Dead-Eye) Max-Up	"Pig" Josh
Cemetery	Ghost Town	Mr. Black
Devils & Angels	The Ranch	
Fall From Grace	Scorpion Revolver/	Governor Griffon
Fort Diego	Health Max-Up	Colonel Daren
Freak Show	Health Max-Up	Breech Loader
Hell Pass	Buffalo	Gabriel Navarro
Railroaded	Owl Rifle	Rico Pedrosa
Range War	The Ranch	Holstein Hal
Rogue Valley	Cooper	Bad Bessie
Saloon Fight	Dan	Sam
Sunset Canyon	Twin Revolvers	Focus (Dead-Eye) Max-Up
The Mine	The Mine	"Smiley" Fawler
The Siege	Mansion Grounds	Jason Cornet
The Traitor	The Bridge	Health Max-Up
Ugly Streetfight	"Ugly" Chris	Freak Show

Red Faction II

Input the following codes at the cheat menu.

Unlockable	Code
Bouncy Grenades	BLK, BLK, BLK, BLK, BLK, BLK, BLK, BLK
Bullet Gibs	BLK, BLK, BLK, BLK, WHT, X, BLK, BLK
Bullets Instantly Gib	X, X, X, X, Y, BLK, X, X
Directors Cut	Y, X, BLK, WHT, BLK, X, Y, WHT
Explosives Instantly Gib	WHT, BLK, X, Y, WHT, BLK, X, Y
Fat Mode	BLK, BLK, BLK, BLK, WHT, X, BLK, BLK
Fire Bullets	Y, Y, Y, Y, Y, Y, Y, Y
Hidden Message	Y, X, Y, X, Y, X, Y, X
Rapid Rails	BLK, Y, BLK, Y, X, X, WHT, WHT
Super Health	X, X, Y, WHT, Y, WHT, BLK
Unlimited Ammo	Y, WHT, X, BLK, Y, BLK, X, WHT
Unlimited Grenades	BLK, X, BLK, Y, X, WHT, X, BLK
Everything	WHT, WHT, X, X, Y, BLK, Y, BLK
Wacky Deaths	WHT, WHT, WHT, WHT, WHT, WHT, WHT, WHT
Zombie Walk	X, X, X, X, X, X, X, WHT

Return to Castle Wolfenstein: Tides of War

Unlockable	Code
Wolfenstein 3D	Beat the single player Campaign mode.

Roadkill

Enter the following codes at the map screen when paused.

Unlockable	Code
Restore Health	X, B, X, B, X, B, X, B
More Money	Y, B, Y, B, X, A, X, A, ↓, ↑
Infinite Ammo	Y, X, X, B, Y, X, X, B

Robotech: Battlecry

Cheat Mode: Start a new game or load a previous one. Highlight "Options," hold L + R, and press ←, ↑, ↓, A, →, B, Start to display the Code Entry screen. Enter one of the following codes to activate the corresponding cheat function.

Unlockable	Code
All Models and Awards	WHERESMAX
All Multiplayer Levels	MULTIMAYHEM
Alternate Paint Schemes	MISSMACROSS
Disable Active Codes	CLEAR
Gunpod Ammunition Refilled Faster	SPACEFOLD
Gunpod and Missiles Refilled Faster	MIRIYA
Invincibility	SUPERMECH
Level Select	WEWILLWIN
Missiles Refilled Faster	MARSBASE
One-Shot Kills	BACKSTABBER
One-Shot Kills in Sniper Mode	SNIPER
Upside-Down Mode	FLIPSIDE

Robotech: Invasion

In the Options Menu, select Extras, then enter the following:

Effect	Password
1 Hit Kill	dustyayres
Access to all levels	reclamation
Invincibility	supercyc
Lancer's Multiplayer Skin	yllwfllw
Rand's Multiplayer Skin	kidgloves
Rook's Multiplayer Skin	blueangls
Scott Bernard's Multiplayer Skin	ltntcmdr
Unlimited Ammo	trgrhpy

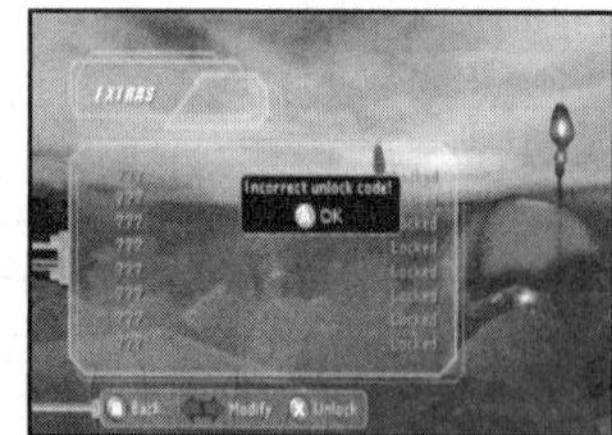

Robots

Pause the game to enter these codes.

Unlockable	Code
Give Rodney a Big Head	↑, ↓, ↓, ↑, →, →, ←, →
Unlimited Health	↑, →, ↓, ↑, ←, ↓, →, ←
Unlimited Scrap	↓, ↓, ←, ↑, ↑, →, ↑, ↓

Rocky

Unlockable	Code
All Default Boxers and Arenas	Hold R and press →, ↓, ↑, ←, ↑, L at the main menu.
All Default Boxers, Arenas, and Rocky Statue	Hold R and press →, →, →, ←, →, L at the main menu.
All Default Boxers, Arenas, Rocky Statue, and Mickey	Hold R and press ↑, ↓, ↓, ←, ←, L at the main menu.
Double Punch Damage	Hold R and press →, ↓, ←, ↑, ←, L at the main menu.
Double Speed Boxing	Hold R and press ↓, ←, ↓, ↑, →, L at the main menu.
Full Stats in Movie Mode	Hold R and press →, ↓, ↓, ↑, ←, L at the main menu.
Full Stats in Tournament and Exhibition Modes	Hold R and press ←, ↑, ↑, ↓, →, L at the main menu.
Win Fight in Movie Mode	Hold R and press →, →, ←, ←, ↑, L at the main menu. Press BLK + WHT during a fight in Movie mode to win automatically.

Unlockable	Code
Fight as Mickey Goldmill	Complete Movie mode under the Champ difficulty setting.
Gold Class Knockout Tournament	Win the silver class knockout tournament.
Rocky Statue	Complete Movie mode under the Contender difficulty setting.
Silver Class Knockout Tournament	Win the bronze class knockout tournament.

Rogue Ops

To enter these codes, just pause the game. If done correctly, the screen will flash.

Unlockable	Code
Big Feet	→,→,→,←,→,←,→,←,←,←
Explosive Crossbow	←,→,→,←,X,Y,BLK,WHT,X,Y,←,→
Half Damage	X,X,Y,Y,←,←,→,→,Y,Y,X,X
Missile Sniper	X,←,→,BLK,WHT,→,X,WHT,WHT,BLK,←,←
No Bullet Damage	←,→,→,←,X,Y,Y,X
One Hit Kills	Y,←,→,→,←,Y,R,L,Y,X,X
Skeleton Mode	←,←,←,→,←,→,←,→,→,→
Unlimited Bullets	X,Y,X,Y,X,Y,X,Y,←,Y,X,Y,X,Y,X,Y,X
Unlimited Health	←,→,→,←,←,→,→,←,←,→,→,←,X,X
Unlimited Spy Cam	←,←,→,→,WHT,WHT,BLK,BLK,X,X,Y,Y
Unlimited TOC	Y,Y,X,X,←,→,→,←,BLK,WHT,BLK

Roller Coaster Tycoon

Change the guest's name to get the following effect. To have more than one guest performing the same effect, play around with the capitalization of the code.

Effect	Guest Name
Artist Guest	Simon Foster
Fast Go-karts	Damon Hill
Faster Go-Karts	Michael Schumacher
Guest pay 2x entrance fee	John Mace
Hunry Guest	Tony Day
Increase Guest Happiness	Melanie Warn

Roller Coaster Tycoon (cont'd)

Photographer Guest	Chris Sawyer
Pick Pocket	Richard Tan
Slower Go-Karts	Mr Bean
Waving Guest	Katie Brayshaw
Wow Thinking	John Wardley

Run Like Hell

Unlockable	Code
Breaking Benjamin Video	Left, B, A, L, R, Up
Baby Nick	B, A, B, Y, Down, Down
Max assault rifle damage	Left, B, Right, X, Down, Y, Up, A
Max bolt thrower damage	X, Y, B, White, B, Y, X, Black
Max pulse rifle damage	B, Down, Left, A, White, Black, X, Y
Max repeater rifle damage	Left, Y, Right, A, Up, X, Down, B
Max rifle damage	Click L twice, X, Y, B, A, click R twice.
Max shotgun damage	A, A, click L, click R, Up, Down, Left, Right
Refill armor	A, Y, B, X, Y, A, L, R
Refill health	Up, Down, Left, Right, Left, Right, A, B
Show credits	X, B, A, Up, Down, Y

Samurai Warriors

Unlockable	Objective
Goemon Ishikawa	Complete Okuni Story.
Keiji Maeda	Complete Kenshin Story.
Kunoichi	Complete Shingen, Hanzo Stories.
Magoichi Saika	Complete any Story.
Masamune Date	Complete any two Stories.
Nobunaga Oda	Complete Noh, Oichi, Magoichi Stories.
Noh	Complete Ranmaru Story.
Okuni	Complete Keiji Story.
Ranmaru Mari	Complete Mitsuhide Story.
Shingen Takeda	Complete Yukimura Story.

Scooby-Doo: Night of 100 Frights

To access the following unlockables, pause the game, hold L+R, then enter code.

Unlockable	Code
All Power Ups	B,X,B,X,B,X,X,X,B,B,X,B,B,B
All Warp Gates	X,X,B,X,X,B,X,B,B,B
View Credits	X,B,B,X,B,X

Set the clock on your Xbox to the following dates and see what happens!

Holiday	Date
Christmas	December 25
Halloween	October 31
Independence Day	July 4
New Year's	January 1
New Year's Eve	December 31
St. Patrick's Day	March 17
Valentine's Day	February 14

Secret Weapons over Normandy

Enter the following codes at the New Game/Continue screen.

Unlockable	Code
God Mode	↑, ↓, ←, →, ←, ←, →, →, L, L, R, R, WHT, BLK
Infinite Ammo	↑, →, ↓, ←, ↑, →, ↓, ←, L, R
All Planes and Levels	Y, Y, Y, X, X, X, L, R, BLK, BLK, WHT, WHT

Serious Sam

Cheat Mode: Click and hold L, and press BLK, WHT, Y at the main menu. A "Cheats" option now appears at the main menu. After enabling Cheat mode, press START during gameplay to access the Cheat menu. You can restore lives and ammunition to avoid dying.

Unlockable	Objective
Hidden Level	Destroy all the statues in the "Valley of the Kings" level.
Mental Mode (Mental fades in and out under Serious. In Mental mode, all the enemies appear and disappear.)	Complete the game in Serious mode, and start a new game.

Shadow Ops: Red Mercury

Enter the following codes at the Password screen.

Unlockable	Objective
All Co-op levels	wanderlust
All Single Player missions	happycamper

Silent Hill 2

Completion Bonuses: Complete the game. Start another game and enter the Extra Options menu to access new features. You can set a "Bullet Adjust" option, allowing the normal amount of ammunition found at a location to double or triple. You can toggle a "Noise Effect" option. Another new option you can toggle allows you to view scenes without distortion.

Unlockable	Objective
Additional Riddle Difficulty	Complete the game under the Easy, Normal, and Hard riddle difficulty settings. Select the Hard riddle difficulty again, and begin a new game with a new combination of riddles.
Book of Lost Memories	Complete the game. Start a new game and look for the newspaper stand near the Texxon Gas Station. Find the Book of Lost Memories inside.
Book of the Crimson Ceremony	Find this book in the reading room on the second floor of the Nightmare hotel.
Chainsaw	Complete the game under the Normal difficulty and Normal riddle difficulty settings. Start a new game to find the Chainsaw among logs before the cemetery.
Dog Key	Complete the game with the "Rebirth" ending. Start a new game and a doghouse appears near Jack's Inn and the gas station. Look inside the doghouse to find the Dog Key. Use it to open the observation room in the Nightmare hotel.
Hyper Spray	Complete the game two times. Start a new game to find the Hyper Spray on the south side of the motor home.
Introduction FMV Sequence Audio	If you wait at the title screen for a while, the introduction FMV sequence begins. In some scenes, there will be no audio. Complete the game one time to restore the audio to those.

Silent Hill 2 (cont'd)

Joke Ending	To view the sixth secret joke ending, use the Blue Gem at Alternate Brook Haven Hospital's garden, the dock before getting on the boat, and room 312 in the Lakeview Hotel. Once you use it in room 312, the game ends and the joke ending appears.
Obsidian Goblet	Complete the game. Start a new game, and enter the Historical Society building. Find the Obsidian Goblet on a shelf.
Reveal Signs	Unlock all five endings, and start a new game. All signs are now revealed.
White Chrism	Complete the game. Start a new game to find the White Chrism vial in the kitchen of apartment 105 in Blue Creek Apartments.

The Simpsons Hit and Run

Pause the game and enter the Option menu, then hold L+R and enter the code.

Unlockable	Code
All cars for new game (must be typed in with complete save loaded)	A,B,A,B
One hit kills (all cars will explode if you ram them or if they ram you, including cops and bosses)	Y,Y,X,X
Press your horn for high flying jumps	X,X,X,Y
Secret cars replaced by red box racer	B,B,Y,X
Show grid view	B,A,B,Y
Show speedometer	Y,Y,B,X
Super fast Cars	X,X,X,X
Your car is invincible	Y,A,Y,A
Your cars are 5 times faster than normal	Y,Y,Y,Y

The Sims

Press both L + R to call up a cheat menu, then enter the codes below.

Unlockable	Code
2 Player mode	MIDAS
First person View (press Black)	FISH EYE
Free Items	FREEALL
Party Motel in 2 Player Mode	PARTY M
Play the Sims Mode	SIMS

The Sims Bustin' Out

Enter the following codes any time during the game (when paused).

Unlockable	Code
The Gnome (This code must be entered first before any of the other codes.)	R,L,Down,Black,Left
All Locations	Black,Down,R,L,Y
All Objects	Black,Up,Y,Down,R
All Socials	L,R,A,Down,Black
Money	L,Black,Right,X,Left

Smashing Drive

Unlockable Shift	Objective
Dusk and Wired Shift	Complete the Night Owl shift.
Night Owl Shift	Complete the Rush Hour shift.
Rush Hour Shift	Complete the Early Bird shift.

PSP Xbox PS2 GC GBA

Soldier of Fortune II: Double Helix

Input the following codes during gameplay.

Unlockable	Code
Give All Weapons	Click L and press X, Y, A, B.
God Mode	Click L and press B, A, Y, X.
Stage Select	Click L and press BLK, B, A, WHT.
Unlimited Ammo	Click L and press BLK, A, Y, WHT

Sonic Heroes

Unlockable	Objective
2 Player Team Battle Mode	Collect 20 Emblems.
2 Player Special Stage Mode	Collect 40 Emblems.
2 Player Ring Race Mode	Collect 60 Emblems.
2 Player Bobsled Race Mode	Collect 80 Emblems.
2 Player Quick Race Mode	Collect 100 Emblems.
2 Player Expert Race Mode	Collect 120 Emblems.
Last Song and Movie	Complete the Last Story.
Last Story Mode	Complete Story Mode with all four teams and all Choas Emeralds.
Metal Characters	Press A+Y after you chose a level for 2 players.
Super Hard Mode	Collect 141 Emblems and have all A ranks.
Team Chaotix Song and Movie	Complete Story Mode with Team Chaotix.
Team Dark Song and Movie	Complete Story Mode with Team Dark.
Team Rose Song and Movie	Complete Story Mode with Team Rose.
Team Sonic Movie and Song	Complete Story Mode with Team Sonic.

Soul Calibur II

Unlockable	Objective
Assassin	Beat Stage 2 of Subchapter 3 in Weapon Master Mode (Extra)
Astaroth—Soul Edge	Beat Stage 3 of Extra Chapter 1 in Weapon Master Mode
Berserker	Beat Stage 1 of Subchapter 1 in Weapon Master Mode (Extra)
Cassandra—Soul Edge	Beat Stage 4 of Sub chapter 2 in Weapon Master Mode
Cassandra—Soul Edge	Beat Stage 5 of Subchapter 4 in Weapon Master Mode
Cervantes	Beat Stage 4 of Chapter 3 in Weapon Master Mode
Cervantes—Acheron	Beat Stage 5 of Chapter 3 in Weapon Master Mode
Cervantes—Imitation Sword	Beat Stage 5 of Subchapter 4 in Weapon Master Mode
Charade	Beat Stage 1 of Chapter 3 in Weapon Master Mode
Egyptian Crypt	Beat Stage 5 of Chapter 8 in Weapon Master Mode
Extra Arcade Mode	Either attempt Arcade Mode 10 times, or beat it once
Extra Practice Mode	Beat Stage 1 of Chapter 1 in Weapon Master Mode
Extra Survival Mode—Death Match	Beat Stage 3 of Subchapter 3 in Weapon Master Mode
Extra Survival Mode—No Recovery	Beat Stage 2 of Extra Chapter 2 in Weapon Master Mode
Extra Survival Mode—Standard	Beat Stage 5 of Chapter 6 in Weapon Master Mode

Soul Calibur II (cont'd)

Extra Team Battle Mode	Beat Stage 1 of Subchapter 1 in Weapon Master Mode
Extra Time Attack—Extreme	Beat Stage 1 of Extra Chapter 1 in Weapon Master Mode
Extra Time Attack Mode—Alternative	Beat Stage 4 of Chapter 9 in Weapon Master Mode
Extra Time Attack Mode—Standard	Beat Stage 1 of Chapter 5 in Weapon Master Mode
Extra VS Battle Mode	Either attempt Extra Arcade Mode 5 times, or beat it once
Extra VS Team Battle Mode	Either attempt Extra VS Battle Mode 5 times, or beat it once
Hwangseo Palace/ Phoenix Court	Beat Stage 2 of Chapter 7 in Weapon Master Mode
Ivy—Prototype Ivy Blade	Beat Stage 2 of Extra Chapter 2 in Weapon Master Mode
Kilik—Bamboo Staff	Beat Stage 2 of Extra Chapter 1 in Weapon Master Mode
Labyrinth	Beat Stage 6 of Chapter 6 in Weapon Master Mode
Lakeside Coliseum	Beat Stage 3 of Chapter 1 in Weapon Master Mode
Lizardman	Beat All Stages of Subchapter 2 in Weapon Master Mode (Extra)
Maxi—Fuzoroi	Beat Stage 5 of Chapter 3 in Weapon Master Mode
Maxi—Termite Snack	Beat Stage 3 of Subchapter 4 in Weapon Master Mode
Mitsurugi—Soul Edge	Beat Stage 5 of Subchapter 4 in Weapon Master Mode
Mitsurugi—Souvenir Gift	Beat Stage 3 of Subchapter 3 in Weapon Master Mode
Money Pit	Beat Stage 1 of Chapter 4 in Weapon Master Mode
Necrid—Ethereal Edge	Beat Stage 5 of Chapter 8 in Weapon Master Mode
Necrid—Soul Edge	Beat Stage 3 of Extra Chapter 2 in Weapon Master Mode
Nightmare—Galley Oar	Beat Stage 3 of Extra Chapter 1 in Weapon Master Mode
Nightmare—Soul Edge	Beat Stage 3 of Chapter 7 in Weapon Master Mode
Raphael—Schweizer	Beat Stage 4 of Chapter 3 in Weapon Master Mode
Seung Mina	Beat Stage 3 of Chapter 6 in Weapon Master Mode
Seung Mina—Ambassador	Beat Stage 2 of Chapter 10 in Weapon Master Mode
Seung Mina—Halberd	Beat Stage 6 of Chapter 6 in Weapon Master Mode
Sophitia	Beat Stage 5 of Chapter 4 in Weapon Master Mode
Sophitia—Memento	Beat Stage 3 of Extra Chapter 2 in Weapon Master Mode
Sophitia—Synval	Beat Stage 2 of Chapter 10 in Weapon Master Mode
Taki—Soul Edge	Beat Stage 3 of Subchapter 2 in Weapon Master Mode
Talim—Double Crescent Blade	Beat Stage 2 of Chapter 3 in Weapon Master Mode
Voldo—Soul Edge	Beat Stage 2 of Subchapter 2 in Weapon Master Mode
Xianghua—Soul Calibur	Beat Stage 2 of Chapter 5 in Weapon Master Mode
Xianghua—Soul Edge	Beat Stage 1 of Subchapter 2 in Weapon Master Mode
Yoshimitsu	Beat Stage 3 of Chapter 2 in Weapon Master Mode

Spawn: Armageddon

Enter the following codes any time during the game (when paused).

Unlockable	Code
All Comics	↑,↓,←,→,→,←,←,↑
All Weapons	↑,↓,←,→,←,→,←,←
Infinite Health and Necroplasm	↑,↓,←,→,→,←,↓,↑
Infinite Ammo	↑,↓,←,→,↑,←,↓,→

Speed Kings

Unlockable	Code/Objective
All tracks	Earn gold medals in every event.
18 best laps	Enter the name .lapt18 at the start of the game.
All 9 driving test finished	Enter the name .test9 at the player select screen.
GP Mode finished	Enter the name .prix at the player select screen.
Set respect points	Enter the name .resp(insert number) at the start of the game to start with that number of respect points. For example, .resp 33 sets the respect points to 33.
Everything	Enter borkbork at the Player Setup screen.
Win All six meets	Enter the name .meet6 at the player select screen.

Spider-Man

Enter the following codes at the Specials menu. Listen for the laugh to know you entered it correctly. Repeat code entry to return to normal.

Unlockable	Code
All Fighting Controls	KOALA
Big Head and Feet for Spider-Man	GOESTOYOURHEAD
Bonus Training Levels	HEADEXPLODY
Enemies Have Big Heads	JOELSPEANUTS
First-Person View	UNDERTHEMASK
Goblin-Style Costume	FREAKOUT
Level Select	IMIARMAS
Level Skip	ROMITAS (Pause gameplay and select the "Next Level" option to advance to the next level.)
Master Code	ARACHNID (All levels in the Level Warp option, all Gallery options (movie viewer/production art), and combo moves are unlocked.)
Matrix-Style Attacks	DODGETHIS
Play as a Police Officer	REALHERO
Play as a Scientist	SERUM
Play as Captain Stacey (Helicopter Pilot)	CAPTAINSTACEY
Play as Mary Jane	GIRLNEXTDOOR
Play as Shocker's Thug	THUGSRUS
Play as Skulls Gang Thug	KNUCKLES
Play as the Shocker	HERMANSCHULTZ
Play as Uncle Ben's Killer	STICKYRICE
Small Spider-Man	SPIDERBYTE
Unlimited Green Goblin Glider Power	CHILLOUT
Unlimited Webbing	ORGANICWEBBING

Spider-Man (cont'd)

Unlockable	Objective
Alternate Green Goblin Costume	If you're using the Alex Ross Spider-Man, play any level with the Green Goblin in it and he'll have an alternate costume that more closely resembles his classic costume
Green Goblin FMV Sequence	Complete the game under the hero or greater difficulty setting.
Pinhead Bowling Mini-Game	Accumulate 10,000 points during gameplay to unlock the Pinhead bowling mini-game in the Training menu.
Play as Alex Ross	Complete the game under the normal or higher difficulty setting to unlock the Alex Ross costume in the Specials menu.
Play as Peter Parker	Complete the game under the easy or higher difficulty setting to unlock the Peter Parker costume in the Specials menu.
Play as Wrestler	Complete the game under the easy or higher difficulty setting to unlock the wrestler costume in the Specials menu. To unlock this easily, first unlock the Unlimited Webbing cheat. When you get to the ring, zip to the top and keep on shooting Spidey Bombs.
Shocker FMV Sequence	Accumulate 30,000 points during gameplay to unlock a Shocker FMV sequence in the CG menu.
Unlimited Webbing	Accumulate 50,000 points during gameplay.
Vulture FMV Sequence	Accumulate 20,000 points during gameplay to unlock a Vulture FMV sequence in the CG menu.

TIP

Play as Green Goblin!

Complete the game under the hero or superhero difficulty setting to unlock the Green Goblin Costume option at the Specials menu. Select that option to play as Harry Osborn in the Green Goblin costume, including his weapons, in an alternate storyline in which he tries to correct the Osborn family's reputation. To unlock this easily, start a new game under the hero or superhero difficulty setting. At the first level, pause gameplay, then quit to the main menu. Enable the ARACHNID code, then go to the Level Warp option. Choose the Conclusion level (that features Norman revealing himself to Spider-Man followed by the glider sequence), then exit. This marks the game as completed under the selected difficulty setting. The Green Goblin costume option will be unlocked at the Secret Store screen.

Spider-Man 2

Type in HCRAYERT as a name to gain upgrades, a lot of Hero Points, and 44% game completion.

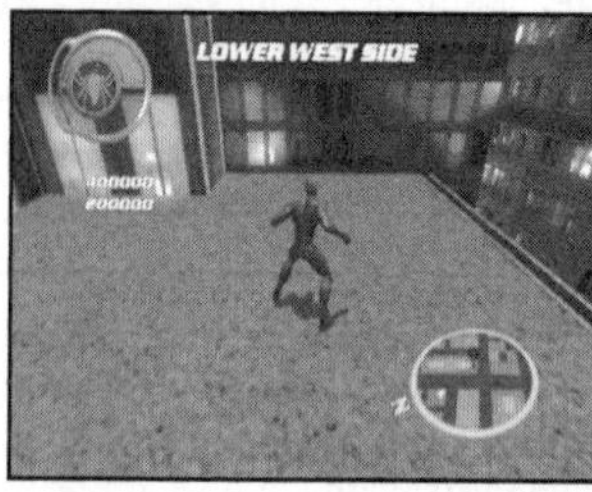

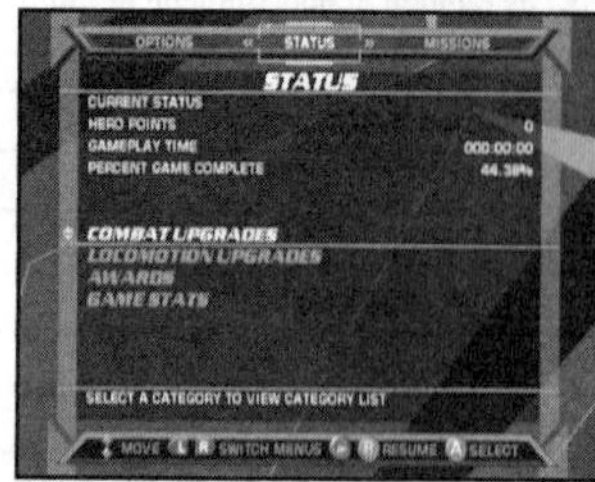

SpongeBob SquarePants: The Movie

Pause the game, hold Ⓛ+Ⓡ to enter the following codes.

Unlockable	Code
All Health	Ⓨ,Ⓨ,Ⓨ,Ⓨ,Ⓧ,Ⓨ,Ⓧ,Ⓨ
All Moves	Ⓧ,Ⓧ,Ⓨ,Ⓧ,Ⓨ,Ⓨ,Ⓧ,Ⓧ
All Moves to Macho	Ⓧ,Ⓧ,Ⓨ,Ⓧ,Ⓨ,Ⓨ,Ⓧ,Ⓨ
All Tasks	Ⓨ,Ⓧ,Ⓨ,Ⓨ,Ⓧ,Ⓨ,Ⓧ,Ⓧ

Spy Hunter

Cheat Grid: Cheats are unlocked by completing all mission objectives (not just the primary objectives) within a set amount of time. To activate the cheats, enter "System Options," then choose "Extras," and "Cheat Grid." To play the FMV sequences unlocked in the Cheat menu, choose the Movie Player option that is above "Cheat Grid."

Unlockable	Objective
Camera Flip	Complete Level 11 in 310.
Concept Art Video	Complete Level 9 in 345.
Early Test Animatic FMV Sequence	Choose an agent at the start of the game and select an empty slot. Enter WOODY or WWS413 as a name. The name disappears and a clucking sound confirms correct code entry. Next, enter your own name and start the game.
Early Test Animatic Video	Complete Level 5 in 325.
Extra Cameras	Complete Level 6 in 345.
Fisheye View	Complete Level 10 in 315.
Green HUD	Complete Level 2 in 335.
Hover Spy	Complete the entire game.
Inversion Camera	Complete Level 8 in 305.
Making of Video	Complete Level 13 in 215.
Night Vision	Complete Level 4 in 315.
Puke Camera	Complete Level 12 in 330.
Rainbow HUD	Complete Level 7 in 310.
Saliva Spy Hunter Them FMV Sequence	Choose an agent at the start of the game and select an empty slot. Enter GUNN as a name. The name disappears and a clucking sound confirms correct code entry. Next, enter your own name and start the game.
Saliva Spy Hunter Video	Complete Level 1 in 340.
Saliva Your Disease FMV Sequence	Choose an agent at the start of the game and select an empty slot. Enter SALIVA as a name. The name disappears and a clucking sound confirms correct code entry. Next, enter your own name and start the game.
Saliva Your Disease Video	Complete Level 3 in 240.

Spy Hunter (cont'd)

Spy Hunter Concept Art FMV Sequence	Choose an agent at the start of the game and select an empty slot. Enter SHAWN or SCW823 as a name. The name disappears and a clucking sound confirms correct code entry. Next, enter your own name and start the game.
Super Spy (Unlimited ammunition and invincibility for your car)	Complete all 65 objectives in the game.
The Making of Spy Hunter FMV Sequence	Choose an agent at the start of the game and select an empty slot. Enter MAKING or MODEL as a name. The name disappears and a clucking sound confirms correct code entry. Next, enter your own name and start the game.
Tiny Spy	Complete Level 14 in 510.

TIP

Classic Spy Hunter Mini-Game

Choose an agent at the start of the game and select an empty slot. Enter OGSPY as a name. The name disappears and a clucking sound confirms correct code entry. Next, enter your own name and start the game.

Spy Hunter 2

To access the following codes, pause gameplay at any time during the game and enter code.

Unlockable	Code
God Mode	L,L,L,BLK,L,R,R,L,BLK
Infinite Ammo	R,L,BLK,BLK,WHT,R,L,BLK,WHT

Spy vs. Spy

Go to the Extras menu, then enter the following codes in the Cheats menu.

Unlockable	Code
All Modern Maps	PROHIAS
All Multiplayer Maps	MADMAG
All Spy Attachments	DISGUISE
All Story Maps	ANTONIO
Invulnerability	ARMOR
Permanent Fairy	FAIRY

SSX 3

Unlockable	Code
Snow Boards	graphicdelight
Videos	myeyesaredim
Hiro	slicksuit
Stretch	windmilldunk

SSX 3

Unlockable	Objective
Alternate Costumes	To earn more costumes, complete all chapters in your trick book. To unlock the final chrome costume, complete World Circuit mode with a "Master" rank.
Fugi Board	Get a gold medal on every course with all boarders with their überboards to unlock a Fugi board.

SSX Tricky

Unlockable	Objective
Pipedream Course	Win a medal on all Showoff courses.
Play as Brodi	Win a gold medal in World Circuit mode.
Play as JP	Win three gold medals in World Circuit mode.
Play as Kaori	Win four gold medals in World Circuit mode.
Play as Luther	Win eight gold medals in World Circuit mode.
Play as Marisol	Win five gold medals in World Circuit mode.
Play as Psymon	Win six gold medals in World Circuit mode.
Play as Seeiah	Win seven gold medals in World Circuit mode.
Play as Zoe	Win two gold medals in World Circuit mode.
Überboards	Unlock all of the tricks for a character to get his or her überboard, which is that character's best board.
Untracked Course	Win a medal on all Race courses.

Input these codes at the main options screen, with the "Start Game" and "DVD Extras" option. Listen for the sound to confirm correct code entry.

Unlockable	Code
Annette Board	Hold L + R and press X, A, →, X, A, ↓, X, A, ←, X, A, ↑, then release L + R. Choose Kaori and start a track. Kaori will have a full Tricky meter, and a faster board.
Full Stat Points	Hold L + R and press Y, Y, →, Y, Y, ↓, A, A, ←, A, A, ↑. (All the boarders will have full stat points.)
Mallora Board	Hold L + R and press A, A, →, B, B, ↓, Y, Y, ←, X, X, ↑, then release L + R. Choose Elise and start a track. Elise will have the Mallora Board and a blue outfit. This code only works for Elise.
Master Code	Hold L + R and press A, Y, →, B, X, ↓, Y, X, ←, B, A, ↑, then release L + R.
Mix Master Mike	Hold L + R and press A, A, →, A, A, ↓, A, A, ←, A, A, ↑, then release L + R. Choose any boarder at the character selection screen, and he or she will be replaced by Mix Master Mike on the course, with the number of the character that was originally selected. He has decks on his back and a vinyl board. Repeat the code to disable its effect.
Sticky Boards	Hold L + R and press X, X, →, Y, Y, ↓, B, B, ←, A, A, ↑, then release L + R.

Star Trek: Shattered Universe

Enter these codes at the Main Menu.

Unlockable	Code
All Medals and Ranks Awarded	BLK, L, R, B, R, Y, L, WHT
All Missions Open	BLK, R, L, B, X, L, R, Y, WHT
All Ships Open	BLK, L, X, L, X, R, R, B, WHT
Invincibility	BLK, L, B, L, R, Y, Y, B, WHT
Kobayashi Maru Open	BLK, L, Y, L, L, X, Y, Y, R, WHT

PSP
Xbox
PS2
GC
GBA

Star Wars Battlefront

Unlockable	Code
All Missions	In Historical Campaign, press X,Y,X,Y at the Level Select screen.

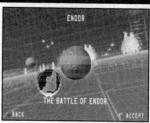

Star Wars Jedi Knight: Jedi Academy

To access the following unlockables, hold R3, then enter code.

Unlockable	Code
All Force Powers	←,↓,→,↑,↓,↓
God Mode	↓,↑,←,→,↓,↑
Infinite Force	↑,↓,↑,←,↑,→

Star Wars Jedi Starfighter

Unlockable	Objective/Code
Advanced Freefall Ship	Achieve the bonus objective in Act 3, Mission 1.
Advanced Havoc Ship	Achieve the bonus objective in Act 3, Mission 3.
Advanced Jedi Starfighter	Achieve the bonus objective in Act 2, Mission 4.
Advanced Zoomer Ship	Achieve the bonus objective in Act 2, Mission 3.
Alternate Camera Angles	Enter DARON as a code.
Invincibility	Enter SOLID as a code.
Mara Jade's Z-95 Headhunter Ship	Enter HUNT as a code. The Z-95 has homing missiles and a strong dual laser.
Master Code	Enter LONGO as a code.
Republic Gunship	Achieve the bonus objective in Act 3, Mission 5.
Sabaoth Fighter	Achieve the bonus objective in Act 2, Mission 5.
Slave 1 Ship	Achieve the hidden objective in all missions.
TIE Fighter	Achieve the bonus objective in Act 1, Mission 4.
X-Wing	Achieve the bonus objective in Act 1, Mission 3.

Star Wars: Episode 1 Obi-Wan

Unlockable	Code
Additional Versus Mode Characters	Defeat a character in the Jedi Arena during gameplay to unlock him or her in Versus mode.
All levels until Darth Maul	Enter M1A2U3L4!? as a saved game name
Battle Royal Mission (You have to fight eight other Jedi Masters in the Saber Arena.)	Defeat Darth Maul in Level 25.
Level Select (All levels, including the bonus levels, will be unlocked.)	Select the "New Game" option at the main menu, then enter GREYTHERAT as saved game name.

Star Wars Episode III: Revenge of the Sith

These codes can be entered in the Codes section of the Options menu.

Unlockable	Code
All Attacks and Force Power Upgrades Activated	JAINA
All Bonus Missions Unlocked	NARSHADDAA

Star Wars Episode III: Revenge of the Sith (cont'd)

Unlockable	Code
All Concept Art Unlocked	AAYLASECURA
All Duel Arenas Unlocked	TANTIVEIV
All Duelist Unlocked	ZABRAK
All Story Missions Unlocked	KORRIBAN
Fast Force Energy and Health Regeneration Activated	BELSAVIS
Infinite Force Energy Activated	KAIBURR
Infinite Health Activated	XUCPHRA

Star Wars Jedi Outcast: Jedi Knight

Go to the Extras menu and enter the following codes in Cheats. A yell will sound if done correctly.

Unlockable	Code
All Levels	DINGO
All Movies	EXTRAS
All Multiplayer Characters	PEEPS
Bonus Level	DEMO
First Seven Levels	CHERRY
Invulnerability	BUBBLE
Start with a Lightsaber	FUDGE
Unlimited Ammo	BISCUIT
Unlimited Force	SCOOTER

Star Wars: Knights of the Old Republic

Unlock the Hidden Ending: Before the final battle with Darth Malak press L + R + Y on all controllers (you need to have more than one) that you have plugged into the Xbox. This must be done before you enter the door to face Darth Malak. If you did it right, your Jedi takes out her/his lightsaber. Then open the door and walk up to Malak and talk to him.

Star Wars Republic Commando

Enter this code while the game is paused.

Unlockable	Code
Refill Ammo (refills the weapon equipped)	Y, Y, X, ↓, R, L, R, ↑

Star Wars: Starfighter: Special Edition

Enter the following as codes to access the specified unlockable.

Unlockable	Code
Alternate Camera Angles	DIRECTOR—the message "Director Mode" confirms correct code entry.
Bruiser Gun	BRUISER
Default Screen	SIZZLE
Disable Cockpit Displays	NOHUD
Enemy Ship Gallery	SHIPS
Invincibility	EARCHIPS—the message "Invincibility" confirms correct code entry.
Master Code (Everything except the multiplayer levels will be unlocked.)	EUROPA
Pre-Production Art	PLANETS

Star Wars: Starfighter: Special Edition (cont'd)

Unlockable	Code
Programmer FMV Sequence	LATEAM
Reversed Controls	JARJAR—the message "Jar Jar Mode" confirms correct code entry.
Secret Level Programmers	SLTEAM
Secret Spaceship for Bonus Missions (Unlock the Experimental N-1 Fighter.)	FSNEULB
Spaceship and Cast Pictures	HEROES
Trade Federation Freighter	UTILITY
View Credits	CREDITS

Unlockable	Objective
Canyon Sprint Mission	Earn a silver medal in the Naboo Proving Grounds, the Royal Escort, Taking the Offensive, Midnight Munitions Run, Rescue on the Solleu, and the Final Assault missions.
Charm's Way Mission	Earn a bronze medal in the Royal Escort, Contract Infraction, Piracy above Lok, Taking the Offensive, the New Resistance, and the Final Assault missions.
Darth Maul's Infiltrator Ship	Earn a gold medal in all default missions.
Guardian Mantis Ship	Earn a gold medal in the Contract Infraction, Secrets on Eos, and the New Resistance missions.
Havoc Ship	Earn a gold medal in the Piracy above Lok, Valuable Goods, Eye of the Storm, the Crippling Blow, and Last Stand on Naboo missions.
Outpost Attack Mission	Earn a bronze medal in all default missions.
Secret Spaceship for Bonus Missions (Unlock the Experimental N-1 Fighter.)	Earn a gold medal in the Naboo Proving Grounds, the Royal Escort, Taking the Offensive, Midnight Munitions Run, Rescue on the Solleu, and the Final Assault missions.
Space Sweep Mission	Earn a silver medal in all default missions.

Star Wars: The Clone Wars

Unlockable	Code
All Bonus Menu Items	IGIVEUP
All Multiplayer Levels	LETSDANCE
Earn the three bonus objectives	ALITTLEHELP
Get All FMV Movies	GOTPOPCORN
Invincibility	LORDOFSITH
Team Photos	YOURMASTERS
Unlimited Ammo	NOHONOR

Starsky and Hutch

Unlockable	Code
Everything	Enter VADKRAM as a profile name.

State of Emergency

Unlockable	Code
AK47	←, →, ↓, R, Y
All Weapons Cheat	While playing, press WHT, WHT, R, R.
Flamethrower	←, →, ↓, BLK, B
God Mode	While playing, press WHT, L, BLK, R, A.
Grenade	←, →, ↓, R, X
Grenade Launcher	←, →, ↓, BLK, X
Looting Cheat	While playing, press BLK, WHT, R, L, Y R

State of Emergency (cont'd)

Unlockable	Code
M16	←, →, ↓, R, B
Minigun	←, →, ↓, BLK, Y
Molotov Cocktail	←, →, ↓, R, A
Pepper Spray	←, →, ↓, WHT, X
Pistol	←, →, ↓, WHT, Y
Rocket Launcher	←, →, ↓, BLK, A
Select a Level	WHT, L, L, L, WHT, A
Shotgun	←, →, ↓, L, Y
Skip Level	←, ←, ←, ←, Y
Tazer	←, →, ↓, WHT, B
Tear Gas	←, →, ↓, WHT, A
Unlimited Ammunition	While playing, press WHT, L, BLK, R, Y.
Unlimited Time	While playing, press WHT, L, BLK, R, B.
Unlock Bull	While playing KAOS Mode, press →, →, →, →, A.
Unlock Freak	While playing KAOS Mode, press →, →, →, →, B.
Unlock Spanky	While playing KAOS Mode, press →, →, →, →, Y.

Street Hoops

In the Setting Menu, select Cheats to enter these codes.

Unlockable	Code
ABA Ball	Y,WHT,X,WHT
Black Ball	WHT,WHT,Y,BLK
Block Party (easier to block)	R,Y,BLK,WHT
Brick City Clothing	R,BLK,R,L,Y,X,R,L
Clown Uniform	X,L,X,Y
Cowboy Uniform	Y,WHT,WHT,R
Elvis Uniform	Y,BLK,WHT,BLK,BLK,WHT,L,BLK
Kung Fu Uniforms	X,Y,X,L
Normal Ball	R,X,X,L
Pimp Uniforms	R,X,Y,BLK
Power Game	WHT,Y,BLK,Y
Santa Uniform	WHT,BLK,WHT,BLK
Tuxedo Uniform	BLK,BLK,Y,X
Theft Mode (easier to steal)	R,X,X,X,R,BLK,Y,WHT

Street Racing Syndicate

Press ↑, ↓, ←, → at the main menu to enter these codes.

Unlockable	Code
1996 Supra RZ	SICKJZA
1999 Mitsubishi Eclipse GS-T	IGOTGST
2004 Toyota Celica GT-S Action Package	MYTCGTS
Free car repair	FIXITUP
Mazda RX-8	RENESIS
Pac Man Vinyl	GORETRO
Police Car	GOTPOPO
Subaru Impreza Sti	SICKGDB
The first three times you are pulled over in street mode, you will be released with a warning.	LETMEGO

The Suffering

Unlockable	Objective
Alternate title sequence	Complete the game.
Director Commentary	In the Prelude level, wait for a crow to land next to the three inmates, then stand on top of the crow.
Prelude Level	Complete the game.

Enter the following codes during gameplay while holding L+R+X.

Unlockable	Code
All Items and Weapons except Gonzo Gun	Down, Up, Down, Left, Right, Left, A, Up, Left, Down, Right, Up, Right, Down, Left, A, Down, Down, Down, A, A
Bloody Torque	Up, Down, Left, Right
Clean Torque	Down, Up, Right, Left
Dirty Family Picture	Left, Down, Left, Down, Left, Down, A
Full Health	Down, Down, Down, A, Up, Up, Down, Up, A
Full Xombium bottle	Right, Right, Up, Up, A, Left, Right, A, Right, Up, Right, A
Gonzo Gun	Left, A, A, A, Right, Left, Right, Left, Up, A, A, A, Down, Up, Down, Up, A
Grenades	Right, Right, Right, Left, Left, Left
Increase Negative Karma	Left, Left, Down, Up, A
Molotov Cocktails	Down, Down, Down, Up, Up, Up
New Family Picture	Up, Right, Up, Right, Up, Right, A
Overcome Insanity	Right, Right, Right, A, Left, Left, Right, Left, A
Old Movie Mode	Up, A, Left, A, Down, A, Right Press Start to disable this effect.
Psychedelic Mode	Left, Left, A, Right, Right, A, Up, Up, A, Down, Down, A
Refill Ranged Weapon Ammunition	Left, Left, Up, Down, Right, Left, Right, Right, A
Reload Ammunition for Current Gun	Right, Right, Down, Up, Left, Right, Left, Left, A
Shotgun with Full Ammunition	Left, Left, Left, Down, Down, Down
Wrinkled Family Picture	Up, Up, Right, Up

Superman: The Man of Steel

Pause the game to enter these codes.

Unlockable	Code
All Levels and Bonuses	R, Black, Y, Black, L, White
Unlimited Health	Black, White, L, Y, L, White

Tao Feng: Fist of the Lotus

Unlockable	Objective
Unlock Extra Stage	Clear advance training.
Unlock Zhao Yen	Beat Quest Mode with every member of the Black Mantis and Pale Lotus and beat Zhao Yen with both factions.

Teenage Mutant Ninja Turtles 2: Battle Nexus

In the Options Menu, select Passwords to enter any of these codes. When selecting a turtle, hold the L button to pick his New Nexus Outfit.

Unlockable	Code
Challenge Code Abyss	SDSDRLD
Challenge Code Endurance	MRMDRMD
Challenge Code Fatal Blow	LRSRDRD
Challenge Code Lose Shuriken	RLMRDSL
Challenge Code Nightmare	SLSDRDL

Teenage Mutant Ninja Turtles 2: Battle Nexus (cont'd)

Challenge Code Poison	DRSLLSR
Challenge Code Super Tough	RDSRMRL
Cheat Code All You Can Throw Shuriken	RSRLRSM
Cheat Code Health	DSRDMRM
Cheat Code Mighty Turtle	LSDRRDR
Cheat Code Pizza Paradise	MRLMRMR
Cheat Code Self Recovery	DRMSRLR
Cheat Code Squeaking	MLDSRDM
Cheat Code Super Defense Power	LDRMRLM
Cheat Code Super Offense Power	SDLSRLL
Cheat Code Toddling	SSSMRDD
New Nexus Outfit for Donatello	DSLRDRM
New Nexus Outfit for Leonardo	LMRMDRD
New Nexus Outfit for Michelangelo	MLMRDRM
New Nexus Outfit for Raphael	RMSRMDR
Playmates added to Bonus Materials	SRMLDDR

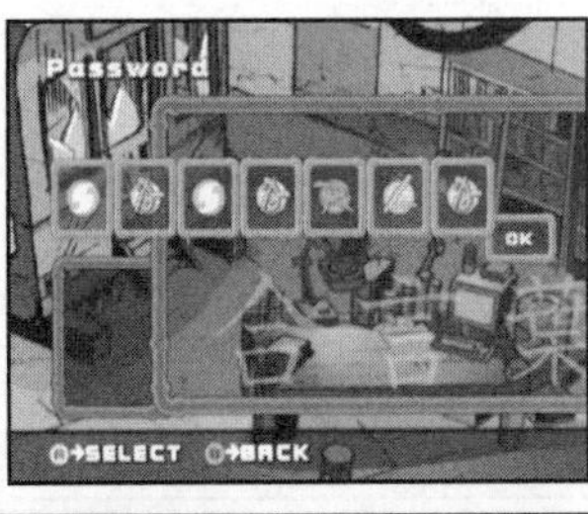

Tenchu: Return from Darkness

Unlockable	Objective
All Characters	At the Start screen, hold White+Black and press Up, Right, Left, Down. Release White+Black and press L, R.
All Enemy Locations	At the Mission Select screen, press Right, Left, L, R, White, Black.
All Items	At the Item Selection screen, hold L+R and press Up, Down, Up, Down, X, X, X, Left, Right, Left, Right, X, X, X
All Missions	At the Mission Select screen, press White, White, L, R, Right, X, Left, Right.
Bonus Mission	At the Title screen, press White, Up, Black, Down, L, Right, R, Left.
B-Side Voices	At the Title screen, hold L+R and press Down, X, X, Up, X, X, Left, X, X, Right, X, X.
Fill the Kuji Meter	During a mission, pause and hold L+R, then press Left, Left, Left, Right, X.
Increase Items	At the Item Selection screen, hold L+R and press Up, Left, Down, Right, X, X, X.
Increase Offensive Power	During a mission, pause and hold R+White and press Up, Down, Up, Down, then release R+White and press X, X, X.
Increase Score	During a mission, pause and hold White+Black and press Right, Right, Right, Left.
New Ability	During a mission, pause and hold R+Black and press Up, Up, Down, Down, then release R+Black and press X, X, L, R.
One Kanji	During a mission, pause and press Left, Left, Left, Right, X.

Tenchu: Return from Darkness (cont'd)

Restore Health	During a mission, pause and press ↑,↓,↑,↓,X,X,X.
Score	During a mission, pause and press →,→,→,←.
Unlimited Item Capacity	At the Item Selection screen, hold L+R+White and press ↑,↑,↓,↓,←,→,←,→, then release White and press X,X,X.

Terminator 3: The Redemption

Unlockable	Code
All Upgrades	Highlight Credits and press B+Y+L

Select "Credits" from the Main menu. While playing, enter any one of these codes.

Unlockable	Code
Cheat Mode	B, Black, Y
God Mode	B, Black, R

Test Drive Off-Road: Wide Open

Unlockable	Objective
Dodge T-Rex	Finish in first place in season four of Career mode in the power division.
Humvee	Finish in first place in the first three seasons of Career mode in all divisions.
Monster Truck	Complete the 27 tracks in Single Race mode in first place.
Moon Level and Moon Buggy	Collect all nine Blue Moon cafe signs in Free Roam or Career mode. There are three signs in each level.
Pro Class Trucks	Complete the first nine tracks in single-race mode.
Rod Hall Hummer	Finish in first place in all divisions in Career mode.
Shelby Dodge Durango	Finish in first place in season four of Career mode in the speed division.
Unlimited Class Trucks	Complete the first of 27 tracks in Single Race mode.

TIP

The Rod Hall Hummer is good for speed. It handles poorly and is average in climbing. It can be a power vehicle if needed and it works well for single race on the blitz races. The Moon Buggy, however, is the best all-around vehicle and can reach speeds of 132 mph. It's the vehicle to use on all the other races in single race.

Tiger Woods PGA Tour 2003

Unlockable	Code
All Courses	14COURSES
All Golfers and Courses	ALLTW3
All Golfers Except Josey Scott	ALL28G
Brad Faxon	XON
Cedric Ace Andrews	IAM#1
Charles Howell III	BANDPANTS
Dominic "The Don" Donatello	GODFATHER
Hamish Character	MCRUFF
Jim Furyk	THESWING
Josey "Superstar" Scott	SUPERSTAR
Justin Leonard	JUSTINTIME
Kellie Newman	COWGIRL
Mark Calcavecchia	CALCULATE
Notah Begay III	NOTABLY
Mark Omeara	TB
Melvin "Yosh" Tanigawa	YOYOYO
Solita Lopez	SOLITARY1
Steve Stricker	SS
Stewart Cink	SINK
Stuart Appleby	ORANGES
Super Tiger Woods	SUNDAY
Takeharu "Tsunami" Moto	2TON
Ty Tyron	TYNO
Val "Sunshine" Summers	VALENTINE
Vijay Singh	VJSING

Tiger Woods PGA Tour 2005

In the Options Menu, select Cheats to enter these passwords.

Unlockable	Code
Adriana "Sugar" Dolce	SOSWEET
Alastair "Captain" McFadden	NICESOCKS
All Accessories	TIGERMOBILE
All Courses	THEWORLDISYOURS
All Courses and Golfers	THEGIANTOYSTER
Aphrodite Papadapolus	TEMPTING
Arnold Palmer	THEKING
Ben Hogan	PUREGOLF
Bev "Boomer" Bouchier	THEBEEHIVE
Billy "Bear" Hightower	TOOTALL
Bunjiro "Bud" Tanaka	INTHEFAMILY
Ceasar "The Emperor" Rosado	LANDOWNER
Dion "Double D" Douglas	DDDouglas
Gary Player	BLACKKNIGHT
Hunter "Steelhead" Elmore	GREENCOLLAR
Jack Nicklaus	GOLDENBEAR
Jeb "Shooter" McGraw	SIXSHOOTER
Justin Timberlake	THETENNESSEKID
Kendra "Spike" Lovette	ENGLISHPUNK
Raquel "Rocky" Rogers	DOUBLER
Reginald "Reg" Weathers	REGGIE
Roof in the Skillzone Game Mode	NIGHTGOLFER
Seve Ballesteros	THEMAGICIAN
Sunday Tiger Woods	NEWLEGEND
The Hustler	ALTEREGO
Tiffany "Tiff" Williams	RICHGIRL

Item Unlockable	Code
ADIDAS Items	91treSTR
CALLOWAY Items	cgTR78qw
CLEVELAND Items	CL45etUB
MAXFLI Items	FDGH597i
NIKE Items	YJHk342B

Item Unlockable	Code
ODYSSEY Items	kjnMR3qv
PING Items	R453DrTe
PRECEPT Items	BRi3498Z
TAG Items	cDsa2fgY
TourStage Items	TS345329

Timesplitters 2

Complete these levels in Story mode under the Medium difficulty setting to access the playable characters.

Level Reward	Playable Character
1853 Wild West	The Colonel
1895 Notre Dame Paris	Notre Dame
1920 Aztec Ruins	Stone Golem
1932 Chicago	Big Tony
1972 Atom Smasher	Khallos

Timesplitters 2 (cont'd)

1990 Oblask Dam Siberia	The Mutant TimeSplitter
2019 NeoTokyo	Sadako
2280 Return to Planet X	Ozor Mox
2315 Robot Factory	Machinist
2401 Space Station	Reaper Splitter See Tip

TIP

Complete the 2401 Space Station level under the Easy difficulty setting to unlock the ending sequence.

Tom Clancy's Ghost Recon: Island Thunder

Before you can use the cheats, you must complete the game with all objectives met. Then you can start a new game, press BACK, and then enter the button combinations below to unlock the given cheat.

Unlockable	Code
Big Bodies	B, B, Y, X, X, A
Big Heads	A, X, B, Y, A
Chicken Explosives	X, X, Y, A, B
Fast Run	A, A, X, B, Y
God Mode	X, X, A, B, A
High Pitched Voices	X, A, Y, B, X
Paper Mode	B, A, X, Y, A
Slow Mo	Y, Y, B, X, A

To unlock more "ghosts" to join your squad, complete the special objectives in the following missions on the required difficulty setting.

Unlockable Ghost	Objective
A. Galinsky	Campaign Mission 1 on Recruit during a Quick Mission in Mission Mode
B. Gordon	Campaign Mission 6 on any difficulty
D. Munz	Campaign Mission 2 on Veteran during a Quick Mission in Mission Mode
G. Osadze	Campaign Mission 5 on Veteran during a Quick Mission in Mission Mode
H. Ramirez	Campaign Mission 2 on any difficulty
J. Stone	Campaign Mission 4 on any difficulty
K. Henkel	Campaign Mission 3 on any difficulty
L. Cohen	Campaign Mission 4 on Recruit during a Quick Mission in Mission Mode
N. Tunny	Campaign Mission 3 on Elite during a Quick Mission in Mission Mode
S. Grey	Campaign Mission 5 on any difficulty
S. Ibrahim	Campaign Mission 6 on Elite during a Quick Mission in Mission Mode
W. Jacobs	Campaign Mission 1 on any difficulty

Tom Clancy's Ghost Recon 2 Summit Strike

Pause the game during gameplay, choose "In Game Options," then choose "Enter Cheats."

Unlockable	Code
Complete Current Mission	B, B, X, Y
Refill Ammo	B, B, X, X
Superman (Player Invincibility)	B, B, X, A
Team Superman (Team Invincibility)	B, B, X, B

Tom Clancy's Rainbow Six 3: Black Arrow

Unlockable	Code
Guns fire lasers instead of bullets	Enter Up,Down,Up,Down,R,R
God Mode	Enter Up,Up,Down,Down,Left,Right,Left,Right,B,A during gameplay.

Tony Hawk's Pro Skater 2X

Unlockable	Code
All Cheats	While playing, pause the game and hold the L, then press START,A,White,Up,Right,Down,A,Y,B,A,B,Y.

Tony Hawk's Pro Skater 3

To enter these codes, select Cheats in the Options menu.

Unlockable	Code
All Characters	teamfreak
All Decks	neverboard
All Movies	rollit
Complete game with selected Character	stiffcomp
Max Stats	juice4me

Tony Hawk's Pro Skater 4

To enter these codes, select Cheats in the Options menu.

Unlockable	Code
Always Special	i'myellow
Daisy	(o)(o)
Everything	watch_me_xplode
Matrix Mode	fbiagent
Moon Gravity	moon$hot
Perfect Manuals	freewheelie
Perfect Rails	belikeeric
Perfect Skitch	bumperrub
Stats 13	4p0sers

Tony Hawk's Underground

Unlockable	Code
Moon Gravity	getitup
Perfect Manuals	keepitsteady
Perfect Rails	letitslide

Tony Hawk's Underground 2

To enter these codes, select Cheats in the Options menu.

Unlockable	Code
Paulie Ryan	4wheeler
Perfect Rails	straightedge

True Crime: Streets of LA

Enter the following codes on the map screen.

Unlockable	Code
All Driving skills	Left,Right,Left,Right,A
All Gunplay Skills	Right,Left,Right,Left,A
All Fighting Skills	Up,Down,Up,Down,A

Turok: Evolution

Go to the Cheats menu and enter the following codes.

Unlockable	Code
All Cheats	FMNFB
All Weapons	TEXAS
Big Head Mode	HEID
Demo Mode/Mini-Game	HUNTER
Invincible	EMERPUS

Turok: Evolution

Invisible	SLLEWGH
Level Select	SELLOUT
Opens All Codes	FMNFB
Unlimited Ammo	MADMAN
Zoo Level	ZOO

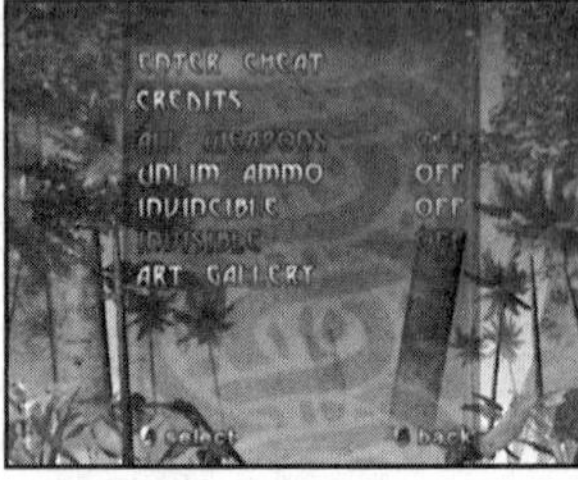

UFC: Tapout 2

Unlock Fighters: Win five matches in a row to unlock new fighters from the list below. Each time you win five in a row, you unlock a new fighter off the list. Robbie Lawler, Tsuyoshi Kosaka, Vitor Belfort, Pat Miletich, John Lewis, Dan Severn, Jeremy Horn, Hayato Sakurai, Maurice Smith, Mark Coleman, Mikey Burnett, Bas Rutten, Gary Goodridge, Frank Shamrock, Marco Ruas

Unlockable	Objective
Bruce Buffer	Win 33 matches in a row in Arcade Mode.
Frank Fertitta	Lose a total of 66 matches in Arcade mode.
Skyscrape	Beat Legend Mode with all default characters.

Unreal Championship

Unlockable	Code
Agility Power-up	When your adrenaline reaches 100 and starts to flash, quickly tap ↓, ↓, ↓, ↑.
Berserk Power-up	When your adrenaline reaches 100 and starts to flash, quickly tap ↑, ↑, ↑, ↑.
Invincibility Power-up	When your adrenaline reaches 100 and starts to flash, quickly tap →, →, ←, ←.
Regeneration Power-up	When your adrenaline reaches 100 and starts to flash, quickly tap ↓, ↓, ↓, ↓.
Wall Jump	If a wall exists to your right, jump up and to the right, and then jump off the wall to your left.

Unreal Championship 2: The Liandri Conflict

Unlockable	Code
Cheat Menu	Pause, then hold down Ⓛ+Ⓡ and press WHT. Turn on any of the cheats you want.

V-Rally 3

Unlockable	Code
Flat Cars	21051975 PTITDAV
Floating Cars	210741974 MARTY
Jelly Cars	07121974 FERGUS
Realistic Phyics	WHEEL REAL
Small Cars	01041977 BIGJIM
Small Cars And High-Pitched Commentary	PALACH
Smashed Cars	25121975 PILOU
Stretched Cars	Gonzales SPEEDY

Van Helsing

During gameplay, enter the following. Access the movies in the Gallery:

Unlockable	Code
Bonus Movie 1	Up, Down, Up, Down, Left, Left, Right, Right, L, L3, R3, R
Bonus Movie 2	Up, Right, Down, Left, Up, Left, Down, Right, Up, R, Black, R3
Bonus Movie 3	L, White, Black, R, Black, White, L, Up, Up, Down, Down, Back
Bonus Movie 4	Back, L3, R3, Back, R3, L3, Back, Left, Left, Up, Right, Right
Bonus Movie 5	White, Black, L, R, Back, Back, L, L, Black, Black, L3, R3
Bonus Movie 6	Black, R, Black, R, L, White, L, White, Left, Right, Back, Back
Bonus Movie 7	L3, Left, R3, R, White, Up, Black, Down, L, Left, R, Right

Wakeboarding Unleashed

Unlockable	Code
All Boarders	Rotate Right Thumbstick clockwise fifteen times at the main menu.
Boarder Movies	Complete the game with that character.
Credits	Beat the game once with any boarder.
Jordan	Collect every star in the Star Search Challenges.
Level Select	Go to the main menu and enter X, X, X, X, B, B, B, B, Y, Y, Y, Y, X, B, Y.
More Boards	Enter this code at the main menu Up, Up, Left, Left, Right, Right, Down, Down, Up, Left, Right, Down, Up, Left, Right, Down.
Summer	Beat the game once with any boarder.
Unlock Everything	From the main menu: Up, Down, Up, Down, Up, Down, Up, Down, Up, Down, Left, Right, Left, Right, Left, Right, Left, Right, Left, Right.

World Series Baseball

Unlockable	Objective
Batting Champ Medal	Complete Franchise mode in the top three teams in batting averages.
Big Spender Medal	Complete Franchise mode in the top three teams in BP spent.
Cellar Dweller Medal	Complete Franchise mode in the bottom three teams in wins.
Dominant Team Medal	Complete Franchise mode in the top three teams in wins.
Golden Slugger Medal	Complete Franchise mode in the top three teams in homeruns.
Great Glove Medal	Complete Franchise mode in the top three teams in fielding percentages.
Pitching Ace Medal	Complete Franchise mode in the top three teams in earned run averages.
Speed Demon Medal	Complete Franchise mode in the top three teams in stolen bases.
Strikeout King Medal	Complete Franchise mode in the top three teams in strikeouts.
Tightwad Medal	Complete Franchise mode in the bottom three teams in BP spent.

Wrath Unleashed

Unlockable	Code
Big World Map Critters	Left, X, Up, Y, Right, B, Down, B
Extended Fighting	Down, Down, Up, Down, Left, Right, Down, Up, Up, Up, Right, Left, X
Team Fighter Character Variation	L, L, Down, Down, Black, White, Black, White, R, L, Black, R, R, R, White
Versus Character Variations	L, L, Down, Down, Black, White, Black, White, R, L, Black, R, R, White

Wreckless

Unlockable	Objective
Alternate View	Press Down to cycle through different screen effects during gameplay and replays. To unlock more effects, Complete missions A-9, A-10, B-9, and B-10.
AUV	Complete mission A-9.
Dragon-SPL Car	Complete mission A-1.

Wreckless (cont'd)

Unlockable	Objective
Missions A-2 to A-4	Complete mission A-1.
Missions B-2 to B-4	Complete mission B-1.
Music Test ("Options" screen)	Complete all 20 missions.
Super Car	Complete mission B-1.
Tank-90	Complete mission B-8.
Tiger-SPL (Tiger Tagachi's car)	Complete mission A-8.
Yakuza Car	Complete mission B-9.

WWE Raw

Unlockable	Objective
Bubba Ray Dudley's Glasses	Attack Bubba Ray Dudley during his entrance.
Christian's Glasses	Fight Christian during his entrance. Keep hitting him until his glasses fall off.
Crash Holly's Hat	Fight Crash Holly during his entrance.
D-Von Dudley's Glasses	Attack D-Von Dudley during his entrance.
Edge's Glasses	Attack Edge during his entrance.
Fred Durst	Win all the championship belts.
Fred Durst's Hat	Fight Fred Durst in a one-on-one hardcore match and knock it off. Play as Fred Durst and let another wrestler knock your hat off. Pick it up and you'll have the item.
K-Kwik's Mic	Attack K-Kwik during his entrance.
Kurt Angle's Real Gold Medals	Fight Kurt Angle during his entrance and steal his medals after they fall off his head. Hit him with them 64 times, and the real medals appear. They're gold and have a green band.
Perry Saturn's Moppy	Attack Perry Saturn during his entrance. Alternately, fight Perry Saturn in a one-on-one hardcore match.
Shane McMahon	Win the Hardcore title.
Spike Dudley's Glasses	Choose a one-on-one match and fight with Spike Dudley during his entrance.
Stephanie McMahon-Helmsley	Win the Women's title.
Tazz's Glasses	Fight Tazz during his entrance until his glasses fall off.
Triple H's Water Bottle	Fight Triple H during his entrance.
Undertaker's Bandanna	Fight Undertaker during his entrance until he drops his bandana.
Undertaker's Glasses	Fight Undertaker during his entrance until his glasses fall off.
Vince McMahon	Win the WWF Heavyweight title.
X-Pac's Bandanna	Fight X-Pac during his entrance until he drops his bandana.

WWE Wrestlemania 21

Enter the code at the Title screen.

Unlockable	Code
All items in the Shop Zone unlocked	Hold L+R, and then press A+B+X+Y

X2 Wolverine's Revenge

Cheats Option: On the main menu, press X, X, L, L, L, L, X, X, L. The cheats option should now be available when you pause the game.

Unlockable	Code
All Cerebro Files and Movies	On the main menu, press X,L,X,L,X,X,R,L.
Level Select and All Challenges	On the main menu, press X,L,X,L,X,L,L,R.
Unlock Everything	Press X, L, X, L, X, X, L, R at the title screen. Repeat the code a few times to unlock absolutely everything.

Table of Contents - PS2

Table of Contents - PS2

Table of Contents - PS2

.hack//Part 2: Mutation

Unlockable	Code
DVD EASTER EGG	On the companion DVD, from the Title Menu—select Data, highlight Gallery, press →, then enter/confirm your selection.

.hack//Part 4: Quarantine

Unlockable	Objective
Parody Mode	Complete the game once.

007: Agent Under Fire

Unlockable	Objective
Alpine Guard Skin in Multiplayer Mode	Complete the Streets of Bucharest level with a "Platinum" rank and all 007 icons.
Calypso Gun in Multiplayer Mode	Complete the Fire and Water level with a Platinum" rank and all 007 icons.
Carrier Guard Multiplayer Skin	Complete the Evil Summit level with a "Platinum" rank and all 007 icons.
Cyclops Oil Guard Skin in Multiplayer Mode	Complete the Poseidon level with a "Platinum" rank and all 007 icons.
Full Arsenal in Multiplayer Mode	Complete the Forbidden Depths level with a "Platinum" rank and all 007 icons.
Golden	Complete the Forbidden Depths level with a "Gold" rank.
Golden Accuracy Power-Up (Enables greater auto-aim.)	Complete the Bad Diplomacy level with a "Gold" rank.
Golden Bullet Power-Up	Complete the Poseidon level with a "Gold" rank.
Golden CH-6 (Gives you unlimited rockets.)	Complete the Precious Cargo level with a "Gold" rank.
Golden Clip Power-Up	Complete the Cold Reception level with a "Gold" rank.
Golden Grenade Power-Up	Complete the Night of the Jackal level with a "Gold" rank.
Golden Gun (Unlocks the Golden P2K with special silencer.)	Complete the Trouble in Paradise level with a "Gold" rank.
Golden Gun in Multiplayer Mode	Complete the Precious Cargo level with a "Platinum" rank and all 007 icons.
Gravity Boots in Multiplayer Mode	Complete the Bad Diplomacy level with a "Platinum" rank and all 007 icons.
Guard Skin in Multiplayer Mode	Complete the Cold Reception level with a "Platinum" rank and all 007 icons.
Lotus Esprit Car	Complete the Streets of Bucharest level with a "Gold" rank.
Poseidon Guard Skin in Multiplayer Mode	Complete the Mediterranean Crisis level with a "Platinum" rank and all 007 icons.
Rapid Fire Power-Up	Complete the Fire and Water level with a "Gold" rank.
Regenerative Armor Power-Up	Complete the Mediterranean Crisis level with a "Gold" rank.
Rocket Manor Multiplayer Level (This cheat unlocks a new multiplayer level. It is a large, open area. The map settings allow only rockets.)	Complete the Trouble in Paradise level with a "Platinum" rank and all 007 icons.
Stealth Bond	Complete the Dangerous Pursuit level with a "Platinum" rank and all 007 icons.

007: Agent Under Fire (cont'd)

Unlimited Car Missiles	Complete the Dangerous Pursuit level with a "Gold" rank.
Unlimited Golden Gun Ammunition	Complete the Evil Summit level with a "Gold" rank.
Viper Gun in Multiplayer Mode	Complete the Night of the Jackal level with a "Platinum" rank and all 007 icons.

007: Nightfire

For the following codes, select the "Codenames" option at the main menu. Select your character and enter one of the following codes at the Secret Unlocks screen. Save your Codename after entering the code. Then exit your Codename and begin gameplay.

Unlockable	Code
All Gadget Upgrades	Q LAB
All Multiplayer Options	GAMEROOM
Alpine Escape Level	POWDER
Camera Upgrade	SHUTTER
Chain Reaction Level	MELTDOWN
Bigger Clip for Sniper Rifle	MAGAZINE
Countdown Level	BLASTOFF
Decrypter Upgrade	SESAME
Deep Descent Level	AQUA
Double-Cross Level	BONSAI
Enemies Vanquished Level	TRACTION
Equinox Level	VACUUM
Golden P2K	AU P2K
Golden PP7	AU PP7
Grapple Upgrade	LIFTOFF
Island Infiltration Level	PARADISE
Laser Upgrade	PHOTON
Level Select	PASSPORT
Multiplayer Bond Spacesuit	ZERO G
Multiplayer Mode All Characters	PARTY
Multiplayer Mode Assassination Option	TARGET
Multiplayer Mode Baron Samedi	VOODOO
Multiplayer Mode Bond Tuxedo	BLACKTIE
Multiplayer Mode Christmas Jones	NUCLEAR
Multiplayer Mode Demolition Option	TNT
Multiplayer Mode Drake	NUMBER 1 Note: Don't forget the space in the code.
Multiplayer Mode Elektra King	SLICK
Multiplayer Mode Explosive Scenery Option	BOOM
Multiplayer Mode GoldenEye Strike Option	ORBIT
Multiplayer Mode Goldfinger	MIDAS
Multiplayer Mode Jaws	DENTAL
Multiplayer Mode Max Zorin	BLIMP
Multiplayer Mode Mayday	BADGIRL
Multiplayer Mode Nick Nack	BITESIZE
Multiplayer Mode Oddjob	BOWLER

007: Nightfire (cont'd)

Multiplayer Mode Protection Option	GUARDIAN
Multiplayer Mode Pussy Galore	CIRCUS
Multiplayer Mode Renard	HEADCASE
Multiplayer Mode Scaramanga	ASSASSIN
Multiplayer Mode Team King of the Hill Option	TEAMWORK
Multiplayer Mode Uplink Option	TRANSMIT
Multiplayer Mode Wai Lin	MARTIAL
Multiplayer Mode Xenia Onatopp	JANUS
Night Shift Level	HIGHRISE
P2K Upgrade	P2000
Phoenix Fire Level	FLAME
Rifle Scope Upgrade	SCOPE
Stunner Upgrade	ZAP
Vanquish Car Missile Upgrade	LAUNCH
Tranquilizer Dart Upgrade	SLEEPY

The following codes can be entered during gameplay.

Unlockable	Code
Berserk Racing	While racing on the Paris Prelude, Enemies Vanquished, Island Infiltration, or Deep Descent levels, press START to pause gameplay, hold L1, press ■, ▲, ▲, ■, ▲, ●, then release L1.
Bonus Race in Alps	While racing on the Enemies Vanquished level, press START to pause gameplay, hold L1, press ●, ●, ■, ■, ▲, then release L1.
Double Armor during Racing	While racing on the Paris Prelude, Enemies Vanquished, Island Infiltration, or Deep Descent levels, press START to pause gameplay, hold L1, press ■, ▲, ●, ■, ■, then release L1.
Drive a Shelby Cobra	Begin gameplay on the Enemies Vanquished level. Press START to pause gameplay, hold L1, press →, →, ←, ←, ↑, then release L1. You can now use the Shelby Cobra from the Paris Prelude level in the race through the Alps.
Drive an SUV	While racing on the Enemies Vanquished level, press START to pause gameplay, hold L1, press ■, ●, ▲, ■, ▲, then release L1.
Frantic Racing	While racing on the Paris Prelude, Enemies Vanquished, Island Infiltration, or Deep Descent levels, press START to pause gameplay, hold L1, press ■, ▲, ●, ■, ▲, ●, then release L1.
Quadruple Armor during Racing	While racing on the Paris Prelude, Enemies Vanquished, Island Infiltration, or Deep Descent levels, press START to pause gameplay, hold L1, press ■, ▲, ●, ■, ■, ■, ■ then release L1.
Super Bullets during Racing	While racing on the Paris Prelude, Enemies Vanquished, Island Infiltration, or Deep Descent levels, press START to pause gameplay, hold L1, press ●, ●, ●, ● then release L1. (You can also do this when you fly the plane with Alura.)
Trails during Racing	While racing on the Paris Prelude, Enemies Vanquished, Island Infiltration, or Deep Descent levels, press START to pause gameplay, hold L1, press ■, ●, ●, ■, then release L1.
Triple Armor during Racing	While racing on the Paris Prelude, Enemies Vanquished, Island Infiltration, or Deep Descent levels, press START to pause gameplay, hold L1, press ■, ▲, ●, ■, ■, ■ then release L1.

Ace Combat V: The Unsung War

Unlocking AC5: UW Medals can be done in Campaign Mode or Free Mission Mode.

SP Color Schemes: All planes must be bought before obtaining color. Can be done in Free Mission Mode.

Unlockable	Objective
Bronze Ace Medal	Destroy 200 enemy targets.
Bronze Shooter Medal	Down 5 enemy planes (cumulative) with ONLY machine gun fire from your aircraft.
Bronze Wing Medal	Earn S Ranks on all 32 missions on "Normal" handicap.
Desert Eagle Medal	Aid friendlies in Missions 16A or 16B, and no more than 3 can bite the dust.
Gold Ace Medal	Destroy 1000 enemy targets.
Gold Anchor Medal	Protect the Kestral and fleet in Mission 3: Narrow Margin.
Gold Shooter Medal	Down 50 enemy planes (cumulative) with ONLY machine gun fire from your aircraft.
Gold Wing Medal	Earn S Ranks on all 32 missions on "Expert" handicap.
Grand Falcon Medal	Annihilate all 16 named planes in second play-through on "Normal" or higher handicaps.
Guardian Medal	Down 10 enemy aircraft who have a missile lock on your wingmen's six.
Lightning Hammer Medal	Protect all 8 armored tanks on ground, and not even one can be destroyed.
Needle's Eye Medal	Get "Perfect" phrases from AWACS in all 6 landings and 2 refuelings stages.
Silver Ace Medal	Destroy 500 enemy targets.
Silver Shooter Medal	Down 15 enemy planes (cumulative) with ONLY machine gun fire from your aircraft.
Silver Wing Medal	Earn S Ranks on all 32 missions on "Hard" handicap.

Unlockable	By Shooting Down
EA-18G	ABELCAIN (Mission 16B)
EA-6B	DUNE (Mission 10)
F-14D	ZIPANG (Mission 3)
F-2A	CYPHER (Mission 18)
F-4G	MINDRIPPER (Mission 4)
FB-22	PROTEUS (Mission 17)
Hawk	GIGANTOR (Mission 1)
MIG-1.44	REPLICATOR (Mission 27+)
MIG-21-93	SWORDKILL (Mission 23)

Unlockable	By Shooting Down
MIG-31M	COSM (Mission 16A)
MIR-2000D	ZAHARADA (Mission 6)
Rafale B	DECODER (Mission 26)
SU-37	YELLOW (Mission 27)
TND-ECR	TWICE DEAD (Mission 18+)
X-29A	DAREDEVIL (Mission 15)
YA-10B	DISTANT THUNDER (Mission 25)

Unlockable	How to Unlock
F-22A	Complete Arcade Mode
Falken	Complete Expert with all S Ranks
X-02	Complete Hard mode earning all "S" rankings

AERO ELITE COMBAT

Unlock the following fighters by completing the listed task.

Fighter	Objective
A-10	Do all ground training objectives in Training Mode.
Blue Impulse F-86 Fighter	On the island map, grab the Blue Impulse logo during Free Flight Mode.

AERO ELITE COMBAT (cont'd)

Blue Impulse T2 Trainer	On the bay map, grab the Blue Impulse logo under the bridge during Free Flight Mode.
C1	Beat maneuver objectives at Aero Meet.
F-104J fighter	Reach Mach 2.0.
F-105 Drone	Fly 50,000 feet in Training Mode.
F-14B Test Bed	Beat Reconnaissance Mission 2.
F-15 Aggressor 1	Log 50 kills.
F-15 Aggressor 2	Log 100 kills.
F-15C	Finish ACM objectives at Aero Meet.
F-15J	Finish 10 scrambles.
F-2B	Finish 50 scrambles.
F-86 Fighter	Log one hour of playing time in Training Mode.
Oh-6	Finish helicopter training.
Su-27 Fighter	Beat Reconnaissance Mission 3.

Agassi Tennis Generation

Unlockable	Code
All Players	In the Main Menu, press R2, L2, L3, ●, ×, ●

Aggressive Inline

Enter the following codes at the cheat screen.

Unlockable	Code
All Bonus Characters	↓, →, →, ↓, ←, ↓, ←, ↓, →, →, →
All Keys	S, K, E, L, E, T, O, N
Juice Bar Is Always Full (Your juice bar will remain full, even if you crash.)	B, A, K, A, B, A, K, A
Juice Regeneration	←, ←, →, →, ←, →, ↓, ↑, ↑, ↓, A, I
Level Select, All Park Editor Objects, Full Stats	↑, ↑, ↓, ↓, ←, →, ←, →, B, A, B, A
Low Gravity Wallride	↑, ↓, ↑, ↓, ←, →, ←, →, A, B, A, B, S
Master Code	P, L, Z, D, O, M, E
Never Die	K, H, U, F, U
Perfect Grinds	B, I, G, U, P, Y, A, S, E, L, F
Perfect Handplants	J, U, S, T, I, N, Space, B, A, I, L, E, Y
Perfect Manuals	Q, U, E, Z, D, O, N, T, S, L, E, E, P
Super Spin	←, ←, ←, ←, →, →, →, →, ←, →, ←, →, ↑
FMV Sequences	Complete the normal challenges in a level to unlock its FMV sequence.

Alien Hominid

Use the following passwords to unlock additional hats. Sound confirms correct entry.

Hat Description	Code	Hat Description	Code
Flowers Hat	Grrl	Afro Hat	Superfly
Abe Lincoln Hat	Abe	Slick Hair Hat	Goodman
Hunting Hat	Cletus	Crazy Hair Hat	Tomfulp
Blonde Wig Hat	April	Tiara Hat	Princess

Aliens Vs Predator: Extinction

Cheat Mode To unlock Cheat Mode, pause the game and press R1, R1, L2, R1, L2, L2, R1, L2, R1, R1, L2, R1, L2, L2, R1, L2. The following cheats will now be available from the Options Menu: Cheat Win, Clear Fog of War, Enable All Levels, Gimme $10,000, Player Invulnerable, Show LZs, and Toggle Unit Spying.

All-Star Baseball 2002

Unlockable	Code
Bonus Teams— the Dingers and the Islanders	Go into the Exhibition mode and tap R2+L2 at the team selection screen. Once you hear a gong sound, select either team.
Dingers in Batting Practice	Enter Batting Practice mode and press R2+R1+L2+L1 at the team selection screen.

Alter Echo

Enter the following codes during gameplay.

Unlockable	Code
Restore Health	↑,↑,↓,↓,←,→,←,→,L3+→
Restore Time Dilation	↑,↑,↓,↓,←,→,←,→,L3+↑

Amplitude

Unlockable	Code
Blurry Mode	Press R3, R3, R3, R3, L3, L3, L3, L3, R3.
Scramble Gem Positions	Press ×, ×, ←, ←, R3, R3, →, →.
Tunnel Mode	Press L3, L3, L3, R3, R3, R3, L3, R3, L3. Repeat the code for a different view.
Turn Notes into Monkey Heads	Press L3, L3, L3, L3, R3, R3, R3, R3, L3.

Unlock Freq Parts and Prefabs: Beat the Boss Song of any level to unlock extra Freq pieces. In addition, you can finish the Bonus Song on each level to gain new Freq parts and Prefabs.

Ape Escape 2

Unlockable	Code
Unlock Spike	Beat the game, collecting 297 monkeys in the process.
Use Spike	At the main menu, highlight New Game, and press L2+START to use him.

Arc The Lad: Twilight of the Spirits

Unlockable	Objective
Choco	Beat the 30-round arena trial in Rueloon with Darc's party.
Diekbeck	Beat the 20-round arena trial in Cathena with Kharg's party.
New Game+ (This option lets you begin the game as Kharg.)	Complete the game to unlock the option New Game+.

Armored Core 2

Human Plus Cheats: Drop to -50,000 credits and an experiment will be done on you. Do this multiple times to get the full benefits of this code. Each time you do this code you restart your game. Do this code multiple times to unlock various cheats described below.

Unlockable	Code
First Human Plus Cheat	Perform the Human Plus Cheats code once to unlock an automatic radar.
Second Human Plus Cheat	Perform the Human Plus Cheats code twice to unlock the ability to throw the laserblade.
Third Human Plus Cheat	Perform the Human Plus Cheats code three times to have heat taken away from attacks.
Fourth Human Plus Cheat	Perform the Human Plus Cheats code four times to gain the ability to walk while shooting back weapons.
Fifth Human Plus Cheat	Perform the Human Plus Cheats code five times to use half of the energy.
Sixth Human Plus Cheat	Perform the Human Plus Cheats code six times to have double energy.

Unlockable	Code
First-Person Angle	Hold START+■+▲ during gameplay. The game will pause. Now press START to resume the game.
Set Camera Angle	Hold START+●+✕ during gameplay and the game will pause. Press START to resume playing. The camera is now fixed at the pre-location.
Use Overweight Cores	Beat Mission mode and let the credits finish.

Armored Core 3

Unlockable	Code
Add Defeated AC Emblems	Press SELECT+START when viewing a defeated AC at the Victory screen to add the defeated AC's emblem to the list. A sound confirms correct code entry.
Drop Parts	Hold L1+L2+R1+R2+▲ to drop your R arm weapon, Back Unit, and Inside parts. Hold L1+L2+R1+R2+L3 to drop Extension parts. Hold L1+L2+R1+R2+● to drop L arm weapons.
First-Person View	Insert a memory card with saved game files from Armored Core 2 or Armored Core 2: Another Age. After saving and resuming in Armored Core 3 from that memory card, pause gameplay, then press L1+R2+✕+■+Dir for a first-person view of the current screen. The screen returns to normal when you resume the game.

Armored Core: Silent Line

Unlockable	Code
Get Bonus Parts	Get an A or S on any mission.
Get Defeated AC Emblems	Press START and SELECT when the victory slogan appears.

Army Men: Air Attack 2

Level	Password
Level 2	↑, ×, ▲, →, ←, ■, ●, ×
Level 3	▲, ●, ↓, ←, ■, ■, ↑, ↑
Level 4	×, →, ←, ×, ●, ■, ■, ▲
Level 5	↓, ↓, ●, ■, ●, ■, →, ×
Level 6	▲, ×, ↑, ←, →, ←, ●, ▲
Level 7	←, ■, →, ↓, ●, ×, ×, →
Level 8	▲, →, ■, ■, ●, ↓, ↓, ×
Level 9	↑, ×, ■, ←, →, ●, ←, ←
Level 10	▲, ↑, ●, ×, ■, ↓, ↓, ↓
Level 11	●, ●, ↑, ←, →, ×, ▲, ■
Level 12	→, ↑, ×, →, ●, ■, ▲, ●
Level 13	←, ←, ▲, ●, ×, ×, ↓, →
Level 14	■, →, ●, ↑, ↓, ■, ↓, ×
Level 15	←, →, ●, ×, ■, ↓, ↓, ●
Level 16	▲, ●, ×, →, →, ●, ■, ↓
Level 17	■, ↑, ↑, →, ←, ■, ↓, ×
Level 18	●, ×, →, ▲, ■, ↑, ×, ×
Level 19	↓, →, ×, ■, →, ↑, ●, ●
Level 20	↑, ×, ●, ↑, ←, ■, ●, ×

Army Men: Sarge's Heroes 2

To enter Passwords, go to the Levels selection at the main menu. At the Input Code screen, insert the following codes.

Unlockable	Code
All Levels	FREEPLAY
All Weapons	GIMME
Bed	COT
Boot Camp	BOOTCAMP
Bridge	OVERPASS
Cashier	EXPRESS
Castle	CITADEL
Desk	ESCRITOIRE
Dinner Table	DINNER
Graveyard	NECROPOLIS
Immortal	NODIE
Invisible	NOSEEUM
Mini Mode	SHORTY
Pinball Machine	BLACKKNIGHT
Plasticville	BLUEBLUES
Pool Table	EIGHTBALL
Refrigerator	COOLER
Revenge	ESCAPE
Rocket Base	NUKEM
Super Sized	IMHUGE
Tan Base	MOUSE
Test Info	THDOTEST
Toy Shelf	BUYME
Toy Train Town	LITTLEPEOPLE

ATV Offroad Fury

To access the following unlockables, select Pro-Career Mode and enter code. You will then return to the Main Menu and begin gameplay.

Unlockable	Code
ll ATVs	CHACHING
Tougher A.I.	ALLOUTAI
All Tracks	WHATEXIT

ATV Offroad Fury 2

Go to Profile Editor, Unlock Items, Cheats, and enter the following:

Unlockable	Code
1,000 Profile Points	GIMMEPTS
Aggressive AI	EATDIRT—Re-enter the code to deactivate it.
All ATVs	SHOWROOM
All Mini-Games	GAMEON
All Equipment	THREADS
All Tracks	TRLBLAZR

ATV Offroad Fury 2 (cont'd)

All Championship Events	GOLDCUPS
Disable Wrecks	FLYPAPER Re-enter the code to deactivate it.
San Jacinto Isles	GABRIEL
Unlock Everything	IGIVEUP
Widescreen Mode	WIDESCRN

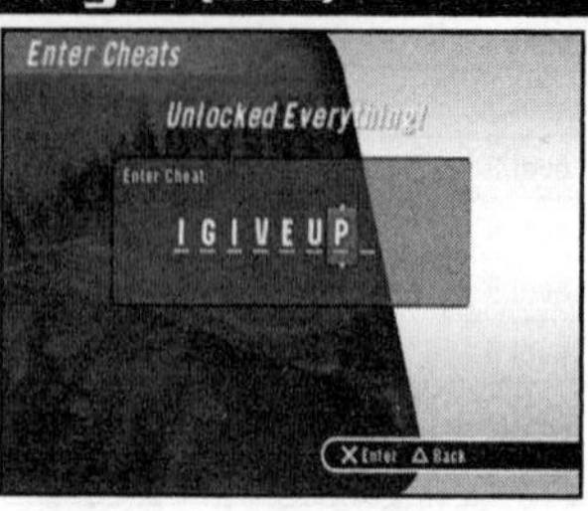

ATV Offroad Fury 3

At the Main Menu, go to Options. Select Player Profile, then select Enter Cheat.

Unlockable	Code
Everything except Fury Bike	!SLACKER!

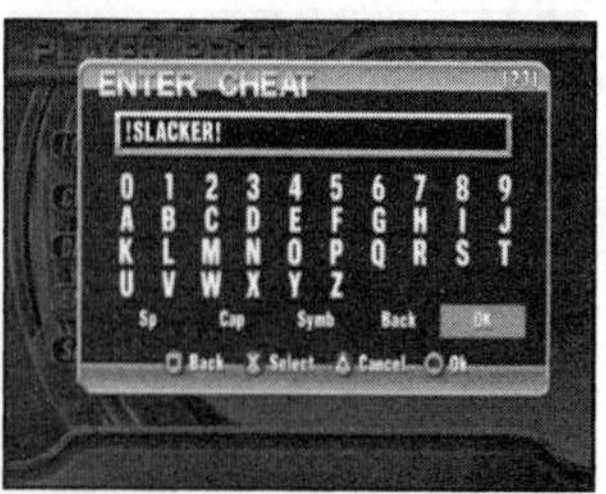

ATV Quad Power Racing 2

Enter the following codes as your player name.

Unlockable	Code
All Riders	BUBBA
All Tracks	ROADKILL
All Vehicles	GENERALLEE
All Challenges	DOUBLEBARREL
All Tricks	FIDDLERSELBOW
Max Stats	GINGHAM
Champ	REDROOSTER

Auto Modellista

Unlockable	Objective
Tamiya Kagegawa Circuit (Remote controlled car racing level)	Complete all 7 mountain based tracks.

Bad Boys: Miami TakeDown

Unlockable	Code
Cheat Mode	At the Title Screen, press ●,↑,■,▲,→,↓

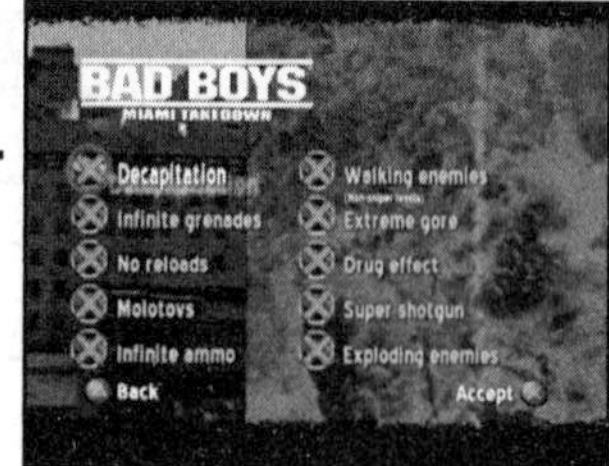

Baldur's Gate: Dark Alliance

Enter the following codes during gameplay, then press START.

Unlockable	Code
Invulnerability and Level Warp	L1+R2+▲+←
Level 20 Character	L1+R2+←

Baldur's Gate: Dark Alliance II

Unlockable	Code
Invulnerability and Level Warp	During gameplay, hold L1+R1+▲+■+●+✕ and press START.
Level 10	During gameplay, hold L1+R1+▲+■+●+✕ and press L2.
Level Warp and Infinite Health	During game play press and hold L1 + R1 + ▲ + ■ + ● + ✕ then, while still holding these buttons, press START. A menu should appear.

The Bard's Tale

During gameplay, hold L1+R1 and press the following buttons:

Unlockable	Code
Can't Be Hurt	→,←,→,←,↑,↓,↑,↓
Can't Be Struck	←,→,←,→,↑,↓,↑,↓
Damage X100	↑,↓,↑,↓,←,→,←,→
Everything On	↑,↑,↓,↓,←,→,←,→
Full Health and Mana	←,←,→,→,↑,↓,↑,↓

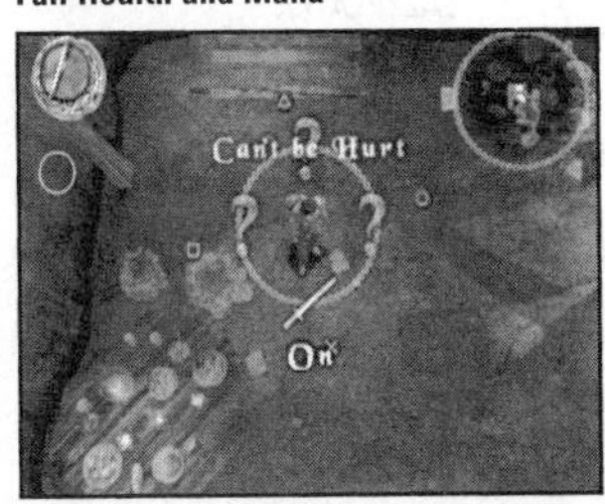

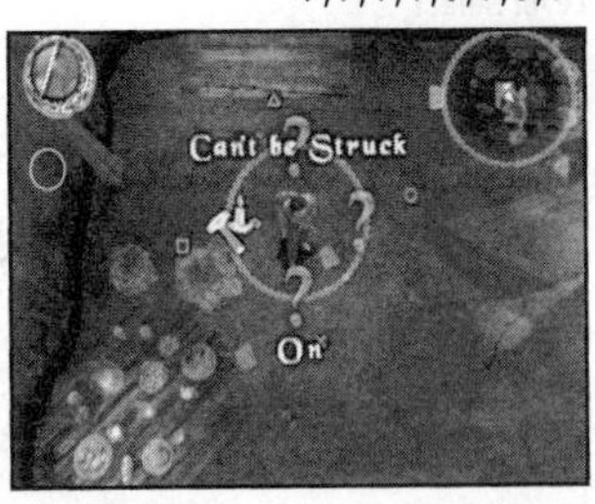

Batman: Rise of Sin Tzu

At the "Press Start" screen, hold L1+L2+R1+R2 and enter the following codes.

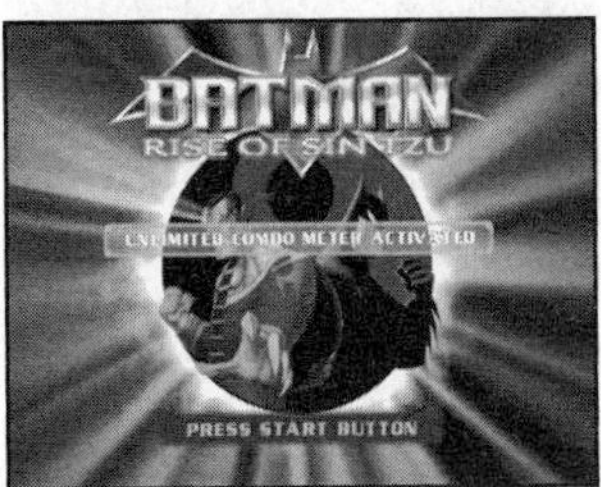

Batman: Rise of Sin Tzu (cont'd)

Unlockable	Code
All Characters at 100%	↑, ↑, ←, ←, →, →, ↓, ↓
All Rewards	↓, ↑, ↓, ↑, ←, →, ←, →
All Upgrades	↑, ↑, ←, ←, →, →, →, ↓,↓
Everything	↓, ↑, ↓, ↑, ←, →, ←, →
Infinite Combo Bar	←, →, ↑, ↓, →, ←, ↓, ↑
Infinite Health	↑, →, ↓, ←, ↑, ←, ↓, →

Batman Vengeance

At the Main Menu, enter the following codes.

Unlockable	Code
All Cheats	L2, R2, L2, R2, ■, ■, ●, ●
Infinite Batcuffs	■, ●, ■, ●, L2, R2, R2, L2
Infinite Bat Launcher	●, ■, ●, ■, L1, R1, L2, R2
Infinite Electric Batarangs	L1, R1, L2, R2

Big Mutha Truckers

Enter the cheats in caps below on the Cheats screen of the Options menu.

Unlockable	Code
Automatic Nav	USETHEFORCE
Diplomatic Immunity	VICTORS
Everything	CHEATINGMUTHATRUCKER
Evil Truck	VARLEY
Fast Truck	GINGERBEER
Infinite Time	PUBLICTRANSPORT
Level Select	LAZYPLAYER
Small Pedestrians	DAISHI
Toggle Damage	6WL
Tons of Cash	LOTSAMONEY

Unlockable	Code
Bottomless Cash Account (This only works in a new game.)	On the main menu, press ●, ●, ■, ●, ●, SELECT.
Extra Rig	Play the 60 day version of "Trial By Truckin'" and win the race to Big Mutha Trucking HQ to unlock a new rig.

Blade II

Go to the Main Menu (Blade II Logo), hold L1, and press enter code.

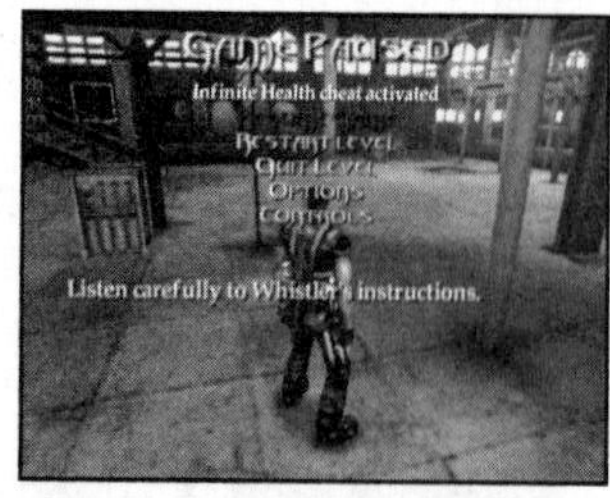

PSP Xbox PS2 GC GBA

Blade II (cont'd)

Unlockable	Code
All Weapons	■,●,↓,←,●,●,▲
All Missions	↓,↑,←,←,●,→,↓,■
Daywalker Difficulty	←,●,↑,↓,■,●,×

During gameplay, pause the game. Hold L1 and enter code.

Unlockable	Code
Invulnerability for Friendlies	■,●,▲,×,■,●,▲,×
Unlimited Ammo	←,●,→,■,↑,▲,↓,×
Unlimited Health	▲,■,▲,■,▲,●,▲,●
Unlimited Rage	←,↓,←,↓,→,↑,→,↑

BloodRayne

Under "Options" on the Cheat menu, enter the following codes to unlock the corresponding cheat.

Unlockable	Code
Enemy Freeze	DONTFARTONOSCAR
Fill Bloodlust	ANGRYXXXINSANEHOOKER
God Mode	TRIASSASSINDONTDIE
Gratuitous Dismemberment Mode	INSANEGIBSMODEGOOD
Juggy Mode	JUGGYDANCESQUAD
Level Select	ONTHELEVEL
Restore Health	LAMEYANKEEDONTFEED
Show Weapons	SHOWMEMYWEAPONS
Time Factor Mode	NAKEDNASTYDISHWASHERDANCE

Bloody Roar 3

Unlockable	Code
Debug Mode (Import Version)	From the main menu, enter the options menu. After you're at the options menu, press and hold L2 and hit the ● button.
High Speed Mode	Win 100 battles in Survival with a single character, then record your name in the records.
Hyper Beast Mode	Win 10 fights with a single character in Arcade mode and record your name.
Kohryu	Win four rounds in Arcade mode without continuing, then defeat Kohryu in round five.
No Blocking Mode	Gain first place in Arcade mode.
One Fall Mode (The first to fall will lose, but he or she will be invincible to all other attacks.)	Win 20 rounds in Survival mode with a single character.
One Hit Knockdowns	Get first place in Sudden Death mode.
Sudden Death Survival	Survive through nine fights in Survival Mode.
Super Difficulty	Complete Arcade mode once without continuing.
Uranus	Complete Arcade mode without continuing once, then Uranus appears. Defeat him to play as him.

BlowOut

During gameplay, pause the game and choose Cheats. Enter the following:

Unlockable	Code
All Weapons	CHARLIEHUSTLEOVERDRESSEDROMEO
Big Feet Mode	DEADREDPARTYSHOES
Big Head	BUTTCHEATCANSURPRISE
Clear Map	YESTERDAYYOURZEBRADIE
Frozen Enemies	CHARLIEOSCARLIMADELTA
God Mode	NOPAINNOCANE
Level Select	COOLLEVELCHEATCODE
Level Up Weapons	FRIENDLIESTGODINGALAXY
Restore Health	CANEREADYTOROCK
Time Factor	CHARLIEALPHANOVEMBERECHO
Unlimited Ammo	FISHINABARREL
Unlock Doors	ANYANDALLCODE

The Bouncer

Complete the game to unlock more characters each time.

Unlockable	Code
Alternate Costumes	Four different costumes for use in any mode other than Story are available for each character. To use one of these costumes, hold R1, R2, L1, or L2 while selecting the character of your choice.
Black-Hooded Sion	Access Sion's black hooded costume in Versus and Survival mode after you complete Survival mode once by holding L1+L2+R1+R2 when selecting Sion.
Leann Caldwell	Play through the entire game as Kou (you can't switch to any other character at any time).
Low Speed Mode	To move in slow motion, gain a ranking with each character in Arcade mode.
MSF Kou	Play through the game as Kou, until he is infiltrating the Mikado building as a MSF soldier. Save your game and you can use that costume in Survival and Versus modes by holding L1+L2+R1+R2 when selecting Kou in those modes.
Wong Leung	Play through the game as any character. Battle Kaldea (the battle right before the final fight), with any character other than Sion. Then, use Sion to complete the game.

BMX XXX

TIP

Remove the game cover from the case to see a more revealing picture on the reverse side.

Enter the following codes at the cheat menu.

Unlockable	Code
All Bikes	65 SWEET RIDES
All FMV Sequences	CHAMPAGNE ROOM
Amish Boy's Bikes	AMISHBOY1699

BMX XXX (cont'd)

Bonus Movie 1 FMV Sequence	THISISBMXX
Bonus Movie 2 FMV Sequence	KEEPITDIRTY
Dam 1 FMV Sequence	BOING
Dam 2 FMV Sequence	THONG
Final Movie FMV Sequence	DDUULRRLDRSQUARE
Fire Bullets	BRONXCHEER—Begin a level, stop your rider, then move the right analog stick to First-Person mode. Press ✕ to shoot people and cars.
Ghost Control Mode (This mode allows you to steer ghost-ridden bikes.)	GHOSTCONTROL
Green Skin Mode (Now you can choose a green skin tone in the custom rider creator.)	MAKEMEANGRY
Happy Bunny Mode (This mode allows you to get more air.)	FLUFFYBUNNY
Hellkitty's Bikes	HELLKITTY487
Itchi's Bikes	ITCHI594
Joyride's Bikes	JOYRIDE18
Karma's Bikes	KARMA311
La'tey's Bikes	LATEY411
Las Vegas 1 FMV Sequence	HIGHBEAMS
Las Vegas 2 FMV Sequence	TASSLE
Las Vegas Level	SHOWMETHEMONEY
Launch Pad 69 1 FMV Sequence	IFLINGPOO
Launch Pad 69 2 FMV Sequence	PEACH
Launch Pad 69 Level	SHOWMETHEMONKEY
Level Select	XXX RATED CHEAT
Manuel's Bikes	MANUEL415
Mika's Bikes	MIKA362436
More Speed	Z AXIS
Night Vision Mode (Objects appear greenish.)	3RD SOG
Nutter's Bikes	NUTTER290
Park Editor	BULLETPOINT—See Caution
Play as Amish Boy	ELECTRICITYBAD or I LOVE WOOD
Rampage Skatepark 2 FMV Sequence	BURLESQUE
Rampage Skatepark Level	IOWARULES
Random Introduction Sequence Now the introduction sequence is various FMV sequences you already unlocked.	XXXINTRO
Rave's Bikes	RAVE10
Roots Level	UNDERGROUND
Sheep FMV Sequence	ONEDOLLAR
Sheep Hills 2 FMV Sequence	69
Sheep Hills Level	BAABAA
Skeeter's Bikes	SKEETER666
Stage Select	MASS HYSTERIA
Super Crash Mode (This mode makes your character extra bouncy when you crash.)	HEAVYPETTING

BMX XXX (cont'd)

Syracuse 1 FMV Sequence	FUZZYKITTY
Syracuse 2 FMV Sequence	MICHAELHUNT
Syracuse Level	BOYBANDSSUCK
The Bronx, NYC, 1 FMV Sequence	LAPDANCE
The Bronx, NYC, 2 FMV Sequence	STRIPTEASE
The Bronx, NYC, 3 FMV Sequence	FREESAMPLE
The Dam Level	THATDAMLEVEL
Tripledub's Bikes	TRIPLEDUB922
Twan's Bikes	TWAN18
UGP Roots Jam 2 FMV Sequence	BOOTYCALL
Visible Gap Mode	PARABOLIC

CAUTION

Park Editor Caution!

This crashes the game. It is not known at this time if you can correctly enable this feature.

Bombastic

Unlockable	Objective
Advanced Mode	Beat Quest Mode.
Challenge 1	Password: BbrMjXSbnB3
Classic Mode	Get a high score in Trial or Quest Mode.
Second Quest Mode	Earn all Perfects in Quest Mode.
Theatre Mode	Beat Quest Mode.
Time Attack Mode	Earn all Perfects in Quest Mode.

Brothers in Arms: Road to Hill 30

Unlockable	Code
All levels and difficulties	Create a profile with the name BAKERSDOZEN

Buffy the Vampire Slayer: Chaos Bleeds

Unlockable	Objective
Abominator	Finish Mission 10 with Professional rating
Amber Benson Interview	Complete Mission 2
Amber Benson Voice Over Session	Complete Mission 8
Anthony Stewart Interview	Complete Mission 1
Anthony Stewart Voice Over Session	Complete Mission 7
Bat Beast	Finish Mission 4 with Professional rating
Cemetery	Finish Mission 2 with Slayer rating
Chainz	Finish Mission 10 with Slayer rating
Chaos Bleeds Comic Book	Complete Mission 5
Chris	Finish Mission 12 with Slayer rating
Faith	Finish Mission 8 with Professional rating
Female Vampire	Finish Mission 1 with Slayer rating
Initiative	Finish Mission 8 with Slayer rating
James Marsters Voice Over Session	Complete Mission 6
Joss Whedon	Finish Mission 12 with Professional rating
Joss Whedon Voice Over Session	Complete Mission 11
Kakistos	Finish Mission 9 with Slayer rating

Buffy the Vampire Slayer: Chaos Bleeds (cont'd)

Male Vampire	Finish Mission 1 with Professional rating
Materani	Finish Mission 5 with Professional rating
Nicholas Brendan Interview	Complete Mission 3
Nicholas Brendon Voice Over Session	Complete Mission 9
Out-Takes	Complete Mission 12
Psycho Patient	Finish Mission 6 with Professional rating
Quarry	Finish Mission 11 with Slayer rating
Robin Sachs Interview	Complete Mission 4
Robin Sachs Voice Over Session	Complete Mission 10
S&M Mistress	Finish Mission 7 with Slayer rating
S&M Slave	Finish Mission 7 with Professional rating
Sid the Dummy	Finish Mission 6 with Slayer rating
Tara	Finish Mission 3 with Slayer rating
Zombie Demon	Finish Mission 3 with Professional rating
Zombie Devil	Finish Mission 4 with Slayer rating
Zombie Gorilla	Finish Mission 11 with Professional rating
Zombie Skeleton	Finish Mission 2 with Professional rating
Zombie Soldier	Finish Mission 9 with Professional rating

Bujingai

Unlockable	Objective
All CGs and Credit Scenes	Complete the game.
Hard Mode	Complete the game.
High Score Display	Complete the game.
Opening Demo	Complete the game.
Stage Select	Complete the game.
Super Mode	Complete the game in Hard Mode.

Call of Duty: Finest Hour

Unlockable	Code
All levels	Hold up on controller two at the level select and enter with Start, Select, Select, Square with controller one.

CART Fury: Championship Racing

From the Main Menu, go to Options, then Cheats and enter the following:

Unlockable	Code
All Cars	▲,✕,▲,■,L2,▲—Go to the Driver Select screen and press L1 to access them.
All Movies	L1,●,R2,✕,L2,▲—Go to the Danny Sullivan Theater to access them.
All Tracks	▲,✕,✕,R2,R1
Big Heads	▲,■,■,L2,L1,R2
Death Cars	L2,■,L1,R2,R2,✕
Death Wall	✕,■,R2,▲,R1,R2
Extra Drivers	Press R1 at the Driver Select screen.
Extra Vehicles	Press L1 at the Driver Select screen.
Infinite Turbo	✕,✕,■,■,L2,L2
Infinite Continues	L1,L2,L1,■,▲,●
Low Gravity	R2,R1,■,■,L1,L1

CART Fury: Championship Racing (cont'd)

Night Drive	×,●,▲,L2,R2,L1
Playable Death Car	L1,■,R1,R2,L2,L1
Rocket Wheels	L1,R2,▲,■,■,▲
Thick Fog	R2,R1,×,■,■,●
Unlimited Time	■,L1,R2,●,▲,R1

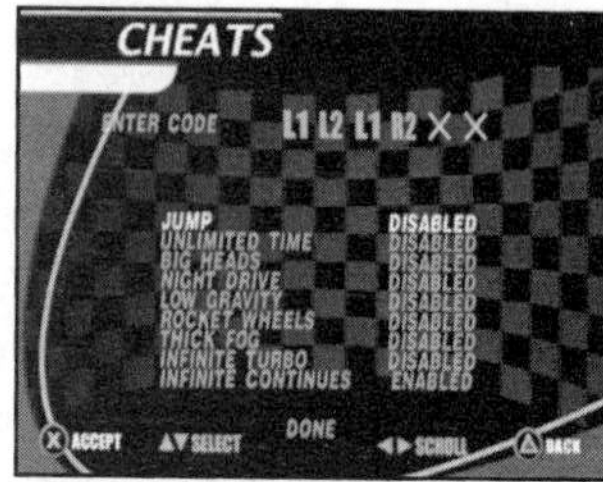

Catwoman

Unlockable	Code
Hidden Galleries	In the Vault Code Screen, enter 1940.

Champions of Norrath: Realms of Everquest

Unlockable	Code
Level 20 Character	During gameplay, press and hold L1+R2+▲+R3. This allows your character to unlock 75,000 coins, 999 skill points, and Level 20.

Chaos Legion

Unlockable	Objective
Level Select	Beat the boss at the end of Stage Nine to acquire the Map Selector, which allows you to choose levels.
New Enemies in Old Levels	Beat the Stage Ten boss then select Change Appearance.
Play as Arcia	Beat the game once to play as Arcia.
Hard Mode	Beat the game once.
Super Mode	Beat the game on Hard.
Ultimate Legion	Collect all of the Thanatos Chips scattered throughout the stages.

City Crisis

Unlockable	Code
Chase Mode	Earn an A rating on all missions and an S on the Bus Chase.
Disaster Mode	Achieve an S rating in Final Rescue Mode.
Final Rescue Mode	Earn an S rating with the Sports Car.

Clock Tower 3

Unlockable	Objective
Cinema Theater	Beat the game once. You can press R1 at the Theater screen to view in-game art.
New Costumes	Beat the game once, and you'll receive a key. Start a new game using the same save, and use the key to unlock Alyssa's closet. Five new outfits will be available.

Colin McRae Rally 3

Colin McRae Rally 3 has three different sets of cheat codes depending on which disc you have. Look at the bonus code listed on your disc to find out which code applies for your version of the game.

Unlockable	Bonus Code	Password
All Cars	0976	MKCLLB
All Cars	1154	WWACNU
All Cars	1432	FMGUOT
All Cars	1866	OQJHOK
All Difficulties	0976	WSNXZU
All Difficulties	1154	AUNAMA
All Difficulties	1432	UXNKFB
All Parts	0976	FHPCNU
All Parts	1154	UZVLLB
All Parts	1432	KEZIPE
All Parts	1866	FHPIWQ
All Tracks	0976	ODIATU
All Tracks	1154	XWUDBU
All Tracks	1432	RVNUUR
All Tracks	1866	ODIFCS
Baja Buggy	0976	NQFIPE
Baja Buggy	1154	PHOUOT
Baja Buggy	1432	VURCNU
Battle Tank	0976	LHZWOH
Battle Tank	1154	ZIIUUR
Battle Tank	1432	ZSSDBU
Battle Tank	1866	LWXEIF
Hovercraft	0976	IURUOT
Hovercraft	1154	MHXIPE
Hovercraft	1432	NXDLLB
Hovercraft	1866	BKQBAU
Jet	0976	GOBUUR
Jet	1154	LOWWOH
Jet	1432	YJBATU
Jet	1866	RUGSSH
RC Cars	0976	WWBDBU
RC Cars	1154	AQVATU
RC Cars	1432	GBPWOH
RC Cars	1866	PFKCXQ
Super Focus	0976	OQJZZY
Super Focus	1154	UYNFVA
Super Focus	1432	LPGXUE
Super Focus	1866	WSNBSB

Conflict: Desert Storm-Back to Baghdad

In the Main Menu, press L1, L1, R1, R1, ■, ■, ▲, ▲, ●, ●. During gameplay, pause the game, then go to Options to access Cheats.

Conflict: Vietnam

Unlockable	Code
Cheat Menu	In the Main Menu, press L1, R1, L1, R1, ■, ▲, ●, ▲, ■, ●. Go to the Options screen to access the cheats.

Conflict Zone

Pause gameplay, then enter the following codes.

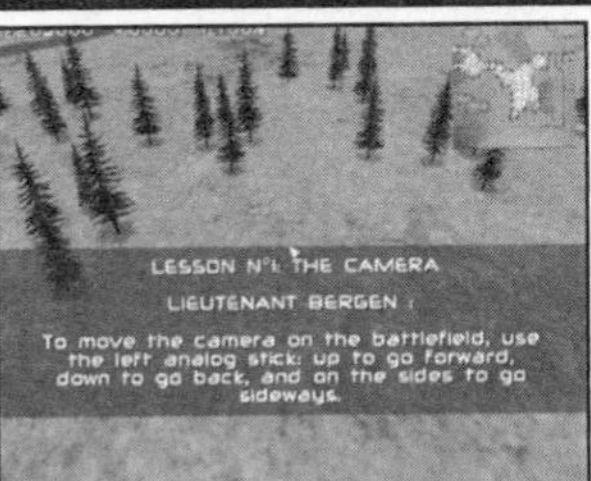
LESSON N°1: THE CAMERA
LIEUTENANT BERGEN :
To move the camera on the battlefield, use the left analog stick: up to go forward, down to go back, and on the sides to go sideways.

Unlockable	Code
100 Population	×, →, →, ←, ↑
Access to all missions in Replay Mode	×, ↑, ↑, ←, →, ←
Faster Building	×, ↓, ↓, ↑, ←, →
Money Cheat	×, ←, →, ↑, ←

PSP Xbox PS2 GC GBA

Constantine

Press SELECT to open your journal and enter these codes.

Unlockable	Codes
Big Headed Demons	R2, ⇦, ⇨, ⇦, ⇦, ⇨, ⇦, R2.

Contra: Shattered Soldier

Unlockable	Objective
Contra vs. Puppy	Complete the game with an "S" rank.
Database Option	Complete the game with a "B" or "C" rank under the Normal difficulty setting.
Final Boss Battle in Training Mode	Defeat the final boss under Normal difficulty setting.
Gallery Option	Complete the game with an "A" rank under the Normal difficulty setting.
In-Game Reset	Hold L1+L2+R1+R2+START+SELECT during gameplay.
Level 5 in Training Mode	Complete Level 5 during the game under Normal difficulty setting.
Level 6	Complete Level 5 with an "A" rank.
Level 6 in Training Mode	Complete Level 6 under Normal difficulty setting.
Level 7	Complete Level 6 with an "A" rank.
Level 7 in Training Mode	Complete Level 7 under Normal difficulty setting.
Return	Complete Level 7 up to the credits with an "A" rank.
Satellite Weapon	Complete Level 5 with a "B" or "C" rank.
Theater Option	Complete the game under the Normal difficulty setting. Your rank determines how much of the theater unlocks.
Thirty Lives (only affects your first credit)	Press ↑, ↑, ↓, ↓, L1, R1, L2, R2, L3, R3 on controller two at the title screen. A sound confirms correct code entry. See Note.
Triumphant Return	Complete Level 7, including after the credits, with an "A" rank.

Corvette

Unlockable	Code
All Cars and Courses	Go to Options, then Game Options and select "Change Name." Enter XOPENSEZ.

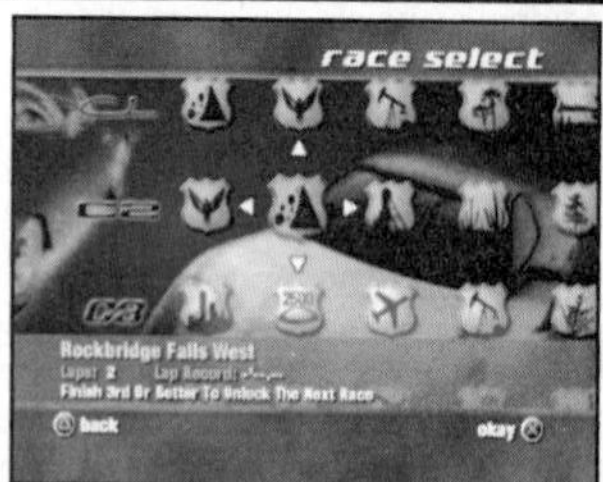

Crazy Taxi

Unlockable	Code
Another View	Begin a game. While the game is in progress, press and hold L1 and R1, then press ● to enter first-person driving mode. Press ▲ (while holding L1 and R1) to show things from a wider angle.
Expert Mode	Press and hold L1 and R1, then press START before you see the character selection screen. "Expert" appears onscreen if done properly.
Taxi Bike	At the character select screen, hit L1+R1 three times quickly. You can also gain access to the bike after you beat all Crazy Box challenges. Press ↑ at the select screen to get it.

Crazy Taxi (cont'd)

Turn Off Arrow	Hold R1 and press START before you see the character selection screen. "No Arrows" appears on the screen if entered correctly.
Turn Off Destination Mark	Press and hold, then press START before you see the character selection screen. "No Destination" appears on screen if done correctly.
Unlock Another Day	Press and hold R1. Keep holding it until you choose a taxi driver. After you do, "Another Day" appears onscreen, indicating correct code entry.

Crimson Sea 2

Unlockable	Objective
Diez in Multiplayer	Complete the Diez Woman Warrior Mission with an S ranking.
Shami in Multiplayer	Complete the Princess Shami Mission with an S ranking.

Cy Girls

Unlockable	Objective
Benigumo	Complete Aska's game.
X	Complete Ice's game on any difficulty.

Dance Summit 2001 Bust-a-Move

Unlockable	Objective
Disco Estrus Team and Muscle Stadium Stage	Beat the game twice.
Far East Commanders Team and Iga Base Stage	Beat the game four times.
Galaxy 4 Team and Disco 21 Stage	Beat the game in Team mode.
Jumbo Max Team and 79 Street Stage	Beat the game three times.

Dave Mirra Freestyle BMX 2

Input the following codes at the main menu.

Unlockable	Code
All Bikes	↑, ←, ↓, →, ↓, ↓, →, ↓, ↓, ←, ■.
Amish Boy	↑, ←, ↓, →, →, ←. ←, ↓, ↑, ←, ■.
Colin Mackay's Competition Outfit	↑, ↓, →, ↓, ↑, →, →, ↑, ■.
Dave Mirra's Competition Outfit	↑, ↓, ↑, ↓, →, ←, ↑, ↑, ■.
Joey Garcia's Competition Outfit	↑, ↓, ↑, ←, ↓, →, ↓, →, ■.
Kenan Harkin's Competition Outfit	↑, ↓, ←, ↓, ←, ↑, ↓, ↑, ■.
Leigh Ramsdell's Competition Outfit	↑, ↓, ↓, ←, ↓, ↓, ↓, ←, ■.
Luc-E's Competition Outfit	↑, ↓, ←, ↓, ←, →, ←, ←, ■.
Mike Dias	↑, ←, ↓, →, →, ←, ↑, ↓, ↑, →, ■.
Mike Laird's Competition Outfit	↑, ↑, ↓, ↓, ←, →, →, ←, ■.
Rick Moliterno's Competition Outfit	↑, ↓, ↑, ↑, ↑, ↑, ←, ↑, ■.
Ryan Nyquist's Competition Outfit	↑, ↓, ↓, ←, ↓, ↑, ↑, ↓, ■.
Scott Wirch's Competition Outfit	↑, ↓, →, ↓, ↑, →, →, ↑, ■.
Tim Mirra's Competition Outfit	↑, ↓, →, ←, ←, ↑, ↓, ↑, ■.
Todd Lyons' Competition Outfit	↑, ↓, ↓, →, ↑, ←, ←, ↓, ■.
Troy McMurray's Competition Outfit	↑, ↓, ←, ↓, →, ←, ↑, ←, ■.
Zack Shaw's Competition Outfit	↑, ↓, ←, →, ↓, ↓, →, ↓, ■.

Dead or Alive 2

Unlockable	Objective
Ayane C3 Costume	Complete Story mode with Ayane on any setting.
Ayane C4 Costume	Complete Story mode with Ayane and without Continuing on default settings or higher. Or complete Story mode using Ayane five times on any setting.
Ayane C5 Costume	Earn 1.5 million points with Ayane in Survival mode on default settings or higher. Or play as Ayane more than 25 times.
Ayane C6 Costume	Beat more than 50 stages with Ayane in Survival mode on any setting. Or play as Ayane more than 50 times.
Ayane C7 Costume	Complete Time Attack mode with Ayane and in less than 4:15 on any setting. Or play as Ayane more than 100 times.
Ayane C8 Costume	Get the "Tiara" item with Ayane in Survival mode on any setting. Or play as Ayane more than 200 times.
Bass C3 Costume	Complete Story mode with Bass on any setting.
Bass C4 Costume	Complete Story mode with Bass and without Continuing on default settings or higher. Or complete Story mode using Bass five times on any setting.
Bass C5 Costume	Get the "Championship Belt" item with Bass in Survival mode on any difficulty setting. Or play as Bass more than 50 times.
Bayman	Beat Story mode with every character. Or complete Story mode using any combination of characters 30 times.
Bayman C3 Costume	Play as Bayman more than 10 times.
Bayman C4 Costume	Get the "Bayman's Missile" item with Bayman in Survival mode on any setting. Or play as Bayman more than 30 times.
Deluxe Credit Ending	Beat the game with every character in Very Hard mode.
Ein C3 Costume	Complete Story mode with Ein on any setting.
Ein C4 Costume	Complete Story mode with Ein and without Continuing on default settings or higher. Or complete Story mode using Ein five times on any setting.
Ein C5 Costume	Get the "Scrolls" item with Ein in Survival mode on any setting. Or play as Ein more than 50 times.
Gen Fu C3 Costume	Complete Story mode with Gen on any setting.
Gen Fu C4 Costume	Complete Story mode with Gen and without Continuing on default settings or higher. Or complete Story mode using Gen five times on any setting.
Gen Fu C5 Costume	Earn 1 million points with Gen in Survival mode on default settings or higher. Or play as Gen more than 30 times.
Gen Fu C6 Costume	Win 48 matches in Survival mode on default settings or higher. Or play as Gen more than 75 times.
Gen Fu C7 Costume	Get the "Mah Jong Counter" item with Gen in Survival mode. Or play as Gen more than 100 times.
Helena C3 Costume	Complete Story mode with Helena on any setting.
Helena C4 Costume	Complete Story mode with Helena and without Continuing on default settings or higher. Or complete Story mode using Helena five times on any setting.
Helena C5 Costume	Earn 2 million points with Helena in Survival mode on default settings or higher. Or play as Helena more than 30 times.
Helena C6 Costume	Complete Time Attack mode with Helena in less than 4:15 on default settings or higher. Or play as Helena more than 75 times.
Helena C7 Costume	Get the "Rocket" item with Helena in Survival mode on any setting. Or play as Helena more than 150 times.

Dead or Alive 2 (cont'd)

Jann Lee C3 Costume	Complete Story mode with Jann Lee on any setting.
Jann Lee C4 Costume	Complete Story mode with Jann Lee and without Continuing on default settings or higher. Or complete Story mode using Jann Lee five times on any setting.
Jann Lee C5 Costume	Earn 1 million points with Jann Lee without Continuing on default settings or higher. Or play as Jann Lee more than 50 times.
Jann Lee C6 Costume	Get the "Dragon" item with Jann Lee in Survival mode on any setting. Or play as Jann Lee more than 100 times.
Kasumi C3 Costume	Complete Story mode with Kasumi on any setting.
Kasumi C4 Costume	Complete Story mode with Kasumi and without Continuing on default settings or higher. Or complete Story mode using Kasumi three times on any setting.
Kasumi C5 Costume	Complete Story mode with Kasumi and without Continuing on default settings or higher. Or complete Story mode using Kasumi five times on any setting.
Kasumi C6 Costume	Earn 2 million points with Kasumi in Survival mode on default settings or higher. Or play as Kasumi more than 50 times.
Kasumi C7 Costume	Complete more than 50 stages with Kasumi in Survival mode on default settings or higher. Or play as Kasumi more than 100 times.
Kasumi C8 Costume	Get the "Cherry" item with Kasumi in Survival mode on any setting. Or play as Kasumi more than 200 times.
Lei Fang C3 Costume	Complete Story mode with Lei Fang on any setting.
Lei Fang C4 Costume	Complete Story mode with Lei Fang and without Continuing on default settings or higher. Or complete Story mode using Lei Fang three times on any setting.
Lei Fang C5 Costume	Earn 1 million points with Lei Fang in Survival mode on default settings or higher. Or complete Story mode five times with Lei Fang.
Lei Fang C6 Costume	Complete Tag Battle mode with Lei Fang in a C5 costume and partnering with Jann Lee in a C5 costume. Or play as Lei Fang more than 50 times.
Lei Fang C7 Costume	Complete Time Attack mode with Lei Fang in less than 4:15 on default settings or higher. Or play as Lei Fang more than 100 times.
Lei Fang C8 Costume	Get the "Decoration Cake" item with Lei Fang in Survival mode on any setting. Or play as Lei Fang more than 200 times.
Leon C3 Costume	Complete Story mode with Leon on any setting.
Leon C4 Costume	Complete Story mode with Leon and without continuing on default settings or higher. Or complete Story mode using Leon three times on any setting.
Leon C5 Costume	Get the "Missile" item with Leon in Survival mode on any setting. Or play as Leon more than 50 times.
Ryu Hayabusa C3 Costume	Complete Story mode with Ryu on any setting.
Ryu Hayabusa C4 Costume	Complete Story mode with Ryu and without Continuing on default settings or higher. Or complete Story mode using Ryu five times on any setting.
Ryu Hayabusa C5 Costume	Earn 1 million points with Ryu in Survival mode on default settings or higher. Or play as Ryu more than 50 times.
Ryu Hayabusa C6 Costume	Get the "Green Tea" item with Ryu in Survival mode on any setting. Or play as Ryu more than 100 times.
Tengu	Collect 10 stars in Survival mode.
Tina C3 Costume	Complete Story mode with Tina on any setting.

Dead or Alive 2 (cont'd)

Tina C4 Costume	Complete Story mode with Tina and without Continuing on default settings or higher. Or complete Story mode using Tina five times on any setting.
Tina C5 Costume	Earn 1.5 million points with Tina in Survival mode on default settings or higher. Or play as Tina more than 30 times.
Tina C6 Costume	Complete Time Attack mode with Tina in less than 4:15 on default settings or higher. Or play as Tina more than 75 times.
Tina C7 Costume	Get the "Roast Chicken" item with Tina in Survival mode on any setting. Or play as Tina more than 100 times.
Zack C3 Costume	Complete Story mode with Zack on any setting.
Zack C4 Costume	Complete Story mode with Zack and without Continuing on default settings or higher. Or complete Story mode using Zack five times on any setting.
Zack C5 Costume	Earn 1 million points with Zack in Survival mode on default settings or higher. Or play as Zack more than 50 times.
Zack C6 Costume	Get the "Parfait" item with Zack in Survival mode on any setting. Or play as Zack more than 100 times.

Dead or Alive 2: Hardcore (DOA2)

Unlockable	Objective
Bayman	Beat Story mode with every character on the Easy Difficulty setting. Bayman becomes unlocked in all modes except for Story mode.
Bonus Options	Pause the game. Press ▲+✕.
CG Gallery	Beat Team mode with five characters.
Longer Credits	Beat the Story mode with all the characters on Very Hard Difficulty.
More Bounce	Go into the Options menu. Change your age between 13 and 99. The higher you set your age, the more bounce you will see from the female characters.

Dead to Rights

Enter the follwing codes at the New Game screen, just after "Press Start" appears. After entering the following codes listen for a message that confirms correct code entry.

Unlockable	Code
10,000 Bullets Mode (unlimited ammo)	Hold L1+L2+R1+R2 and press ↑,←,↓,→,●.
Bang Bang Mode	Hold L1+L2+R1+R2 and press ●,▲,■,●,→.
Boomstick Mode (unlimited shotguns)	Hold L1+L2+R1+R2 and press →,●,●,●,■.
Chow Yun Jack Mode (You receive a pair of double guns at the beginning of the level, even if you would normally have none.)	Hold L1+L2+R1+R2 and press ▲,●,↑,↑,↑.
Double Melee Attack Damage	Hold L1+L2+R1+R2 and press ●,●,↑,↑,■.
Enemies Disarmed	Hold L1+L2+R1+R2 and press →,■,←,●,▲.
Enemies More Accurate	Hold L1+L2+R1+R2 and press ▲,■,←,←,●.
Hard-Boiled Mode (increases the challenge level significantly)	Hold L1+L2+R1+R2 and press ▲,■,←,←,●.
Invisible Character (Enemies can still see you, but you can only see your own shadow.)	Hold L1+L2+R1+R2 and press ▲,▲,↑,↑,▲.
Lazy Mode (all levels, minigames, and FMV sequences)	Hold L1+L2+R1+R2 and press ↓,←,↓,▲,↓.
One-Hit Wonder Mode	Hold L1+L2+R1+R2 and press ▲,●,●,●,●,←.
Powered-up Punches and Kicks	Hold L1+L2+R1+R2 and press ↓,●,←,←,←.

Dead to Rights (cont'd)

Precursor Mode (turns off all targeting cursors)	Hold L1+L2+R1+R2 and press ↑,↑,↓,↓,↑.
Sharpshooter Mode	Hold L1+L2+R1+R2 and press ■,■,■,↓,→.
Super Cop Mode (harder difficulty)	Hold L1+L2+R1+R2 and press ■,▲,←,↑,→.
Time to Pay Mode (all disarms)	Hold L1+L2+R1+R2 and press ■,■,●,●,→.
Unlimited Adrenaline	Hold L1+L2+R1+R2 and press ←,→,←,●,■.
Unlimited Armor	Hold L1+L2+R1+R2 and press ↑,↑,↑,■,↓.
Unlimited Dual Guncons	Hold L1+L2+R1+R2 and press ▲,●,↑,↑,↑.
Unlimited Human Shields	Hold L1+L2+R1+R2 and press ■,▲,●,▲,■.
Unlimited Shadow Stamina	Hold L1+L2+R1+R2 and press ●,■,▲,●,↓.
Wussy Mode (less accurate enemies)	Hold L1+L2+R1+R2 and press ■,←,▲,↑,↓.

Def Jam Vendetta

Enter the following codes on any non-Story mode character select screen.

Unlockable	Code
Arii	Hold L2 + L2 + R1 + R2 and press ×, ■, ▲, ●, ■.
Briggs	Hold L2 + L2 + R1 + R2 and press ×, ▲, ●, ■, ●.
Briggs (alternate costume)	Hold L2 + L2 + R1 + R2 and press ×, ▲, ■, ×, ●.
Carla	Hold L2 + L2 + R1 + R2 and press ×, ■, ×, ×, ×.
Chukklez	Hold L2 + L2 + R1 + R2 and press ■, ■, ▲, ×, ●.
Cruz	Hold L2 + L2 + R1 + R2 and press ●, ▲, ×, ×, ●.
D-Mob	Hold L2 + L2 + R1 + R2 and press ■, ▲, ●, ×, ●.
D-Mob (alternate costume)	Hold L2 + L2 + R1 + R2 and press ■, ■, ▲, ■, ■.
Dan G	Hold L2 + L2 + R1 + R2 and press ×, ●, ×, ●, ■.
Deebo	Hold L2 + L2 + R1 + R2 and press ●, ●, ×, ×, ▲.
Deja	Hold L2 + L2 + R1 + R2 and press ●, ■, ●, ●, ×.
DMX	Hold L2 + L2 + R1 + R2 and press ●, ×, ●, ▲, ■.
Drake	Hold L2 + L2 + R1 + R2 and press ▲, ■, ●, ×, ×.
Drake (alternate costume)	Hold L2 + L2 + R1 + R2 and press ×, ▲, ▲, ●, ●.
Funkmaster Flex	Hold L2 + L2 + R1 + R2 and press ●, ▲, ●, ●, ■.
Headache	Hold L2 + L2 + R1 + R2 and press ▲, ▲, ▲, ■, ●.
House	Hold L2 + L2 + R1 + R2 and press ▲, ×, ▲, ●, ×.
Iceberg	Hold L2 + L2 + R1 + R2 and press ■, ▲, ●, ■, ●.
Ludacris	Hold L2 + L2 + R1 + R2 and press ●, ●, ●, ■, ▲.
Manny (alternate costume)	Hold L2 + L2 + R1 + R2 and press ●, ■, ●, ■, ●.
Masa	Hold L2 + L2 + R1 + R2 and press ×, ●, ▲, ■, ■.
Method Man	Hold L2 + L2 + R1 + R2 and press ■, ●, ×, ▲, ●.
Moses	Hold L2 + L2 + R1 + R2 and press ▲, ▲, ■, ■, ×.
N.O.R.E.	Hold L2 + L2 + R1 + R2 and press ●, ■, ▲, ×, ●.
Nyne	Hold L2 + L2 + R1 + R2 and press ■, ●, ×, ×, ▲.
Omar	Hold L2 + L2 + R1 + R2 and press ●, ●, ■, ▲, ▲.
Opal	Hold L2 + L2 + R1 + R2 and press ●, ●, ■, ■, ▲.
Peewee	Hold L2 + L2 + R1 + R2 and press ×, ×, ■, ▲, ■.
Peewee (alternate costume)	Hold L2 + L2 + R1 + R2 and press ×, ▲, ▲, ■, ●.
Penny	Hold L2 + L2 + R1 + R2 and press ×, ×, ×, ▲, ●.
Pockets	Hold L2 + L2 + R1 + R2 and press ▲, ■, ●, ■, ×.
Proof (alternate costume)	Hold L2 + L2 + R1 + R2 and press ×, ■, ▲, ■, ●.
Razor	Hold L2 + L2 + R1 + R2 and press ▲, ■, ▲, ●, ×.
Razor (alternate costume)	Hold L2 + L2 + R1 + R2 and press ■, ●, ×, ▲, ▲.
Redman	Hold L2 + L2 + R1 + R2 and press ●, ●, ▲, ■, ×.
Ruffneck	Hold L2 + L2 + R1 + R2 and press ×, ■, ×, ▲, ●.
Ruffneck (alternate costume)	Hold L2 + L2 + R1 + R2 and press ■, ●, ▲, ×, ■.
Scarface	Hold L2 + L2 + R1 + R2 and press ●, ■, ×, ▲, ■.

Def Jam Vendetta (cont'd)

Unlockable	Code
Sketch	Hold L2 + L2 + R1 + R2 and press ▲, ▲, ●, ■, ×.
Snowman	Hold L2 + L2 + R1 + R2 and press ▲, ▲, ×, ×, ●.
Spider (alternate costume)	Hold L2 + L2 + R1 + R2 and press ■, ▲, ×, ■, ●.
Steel	Hold L2 + L2 + R1 + R2 and press ×, ▲, ●, ●, ▲.
T'ai	Hold L2 + L2 + R1 + R2 and press ●, ●, ■, ×, ●.
Zaheer	Hold L2 + L2 + R1 + R2 and press ▲, ▲, ■, ×, ×.

Deus Ex: Conspiracy Theory

Activate Cheats: Enter the Goals/Notes/Images screen. Press L2, R2, L1, R1, START (3) to display another tab on this screen with the following cheats that you can turn on and off: God, Full Health, Full Energy, Full Ammo, Full Mods, All Skills, Full Credits, and Tantalus.

Devil May Cry 2

Unlockable	Objective
Alternate Dante Costume	Complete the game with Dante at Normal difficulty.
Alternate Devil May Cry 1 Costume for Dante	Complete the game in Dante Must Die mode.
Alternate Costumes for Lucia	Complete the game with Lucia to unlock her alternate costume. Complete the game with Lucia under the Hard difficulty setting to unlock another costume.
Bloody Palace Mode	Complete the game with Dante and Lucia.
Dante Must Die Mode	Complete the game with Dante and Lucia under the Hard difficulty setting.
Dante's Diesel Bonus Level and Costume	Play Dante's Mission 1, then save the game. Reset the PlayStation2, and wait for the "Press Start button" message to reappear. Press L3, R3, L1, R1, L2, R2, L3, R3. A sound confirms correct code entry. Press START to return to the main menu. Choose the "Load game" option, press L1 or R1 to access the new costume, and then load a game to play the bonus level.
Dante's Diesel Costume	Press R1, R1, ▲, ■, R2, R2 during gameplay.
Hard Difficulty Setting	Complete the game with Dante and Lucia.
In-Game Reset	Press START + SELECT during gameplay to return to the title screen.
Level Select	Complete the game as either character under any difficulty setting.
Lucia's Arius bod	Complete the game in Lucia Must Die mode.
Lucia Must Die Mode	Complete the game with Lucia under the Hard difficulty setting.
Lucia's Diesel Bonus Level and Costume	Play Lucia's Mission 1, then save the game. Reset the PlayStation2, and wait for the "Press Start button" message to reappear. Press L3, R3, L1, R1, L2, R2, L3, R3. A sound confirms correct code entry. Press START to return to the main menu. Choose the "Load game" option, press L1 or R1 to access the new costume, and then load a game to play the bonus level.
Lucia's Diesel Costume	Press L1, L1, ▲, ■, L2, L2 during gameplay.
Play as Trish	Complete the game with Dante under the Hard difficulty setting. Trish has Dante's stats and items and starts with the Sparda.

Completion Bonuses: Use the following to unlock the completion bonuses by only playing Dante's game. Switch from Disc 1 to 2 anytime during Dante's game. Complete the game to unlock Level Select mode, Hard mode, Bloody Palace mode, and the credits. If you change from Disc 1 to 2 before completing the game in Hard mode, you unlock Trish and other bonuses.

Devil May Cry 3

Enter at the Main Menu.

Unlockable	Code
Unlock Everything	Hold Down L1, L2, R1, R2 and rotate the Left Analog Stick until you hear Devil May Cry.

Destroy All Humans

To activate these codes, pause the game and hold L1, then enter the code and release L1.

Unlockable	Code
Ammo-A-Plenty	⇦,●,R2,⇨,R1,■
Aware Like a Fox	⇨,■,R2,R1,⇨,R2
Bulletproof Crypto	■,●,⇦,⇦,⇦,●,■
Deep Thinker	R1,R2,●,⇨,R2,●
Mmmm...Brains!	R1,R1,R2,R2,⇦,⇨,⇦,⇨,R2 This code increases DNA. (You must be on the Mothership.)
More Upgrades	■,●,⇦,⇦,●,■ (You must be on the Mothership.)
Nobody Loves You	⇨,R2,R1,■,⇨

Disney's Extreme Skate Adventure

Go to Options, select Cheat Codes, then enter the following codes.

Unlockable	Code
All Create-a-Skaters	sweetthreads
All Skaters	friendsofbob
All Levels	extremepassport
Filled Special Meter	supercharger
Lion King Video	savannah
Tarzan Video	nugget
Toy Story Video	marin

Downhill Domination

During your run, you must use the unlock code (↑,▲,↓,×,←,●,→,■) first before trying any of the others.

Unlockable	Code
Adrenaline Boost	↓,←,←,→
Always Stoked	↓,■,■,←,●
Anti-Gravity	↓,▲,■,■,↑
Combat Upgrade	↑,↓,←,←,→
Energy Restore	↓,→,→,←,←
Extra Smack Time	←,→,↓,↓
Infinite Bottles	↑,×,←,←,●,●
Mega Flip	→,↑,↑,→,→,■
More $$$	→,↑,↑,●,●,■
No Combat	←,■,●,■,←
Speed Freak	↓,▲,→,→,■
Stoke Trick Meter	↓,←,←,→,→
Super Bounce	←,■,×,↑,▲
Super Bunny Hop	↑,×,←,■,↑
Unlimited Energy	↓,▲,←,←,■
Upgrade to Bottle	↑,↓,←,←,→,→

Dr. Muto

Enter the following as codes.

Unlockable	Code
All Gadgets	TINKERTOY
Invincibility (This has no effect when you fall from high places.)	NECROSCI
All Morphs	EUREKA
Go Anywhere	BEAMMEUP
Never Take Damage	CHEATERBOY
Secret Morphs	LOGGLOGG
Super Ending	BUZZOFF
View FMV Sequences	HOTTICKET

Dr. Seuss' The Cat in the Hat

Unlockable	Code
Extra Life	↑, ↓, ■, L2, L1, ↓, ↑, ↓, ↓, ↑
Open All Levels	↓, L2, ↑, L1, ■, ↓, ↓, ↓, ↓, ↑

Dragon Ball Z

Unlockable	Objective
Android #16	Complete the "Aim for Perfect Form" episode.
Cell, Android #17, and Teen Gohan	Play through "The Androids Saga" at any level.
Dodoria	Defeat Recoome with Vegeta.
Freiza, Ginyu, and Recoome	Play through "The Namek Saga" at any level.
Mr. Satan (Hercule)	Win a World Match Tournament at the Adept level.
Radditz, Vegeta, and Nappa	Play through "The Saiyan Saga" at any level
Saiyaman (Gohan's Alter Ego)	Win a World Match Tournament at the Advanced level.
Super Saiyan Ability (Goku Only)	Play through "The Namek Saga" at any level.
Super Saiyan Ability (Vegeta Only)	Play through "The Androids Saga" at any level.
Super Vegeta	Complete the "Vegeta's Confidence" episode.
Trunks	Complete the "Perfect Form Cell Complete" episode.
Yamcha	Complete the "Aim for Perfect Form" episode.
Zarbon	Complete the "Vegeta's Attack" episode.
Alternate Appearance	Press ■ or ● at the Character Selection screen. Your character may have different clothes or colors. See Tip.
View Alternate Costumes	Press R1 and R2 at the Capsule Change screen to view the character's alternate costumes. Press L1 and L2 to zoom in and out. Use the left analog stick to rotate the characters.

TIP

Alternate Appearance Tip!

Try this with Trunks and make him go Super Saiyan!

Dragon Ball Z: Budokai

Unlockable	Objective
1-Star Dragonball	Super-Rare—if the desired Dragonball isn't the Recommended Capsule, exit and re-enter Mr. Popo's shop until it's displayed.
2-Star Dragonball	Super-Rare—same as above.
3-Star Dragonball	Super-Rare—same as above.
4-Star Dragonball	You get this free when starting a new game. Note: if you have a second memory card, you can get this by starting a game and trading.
5-Star Dragonball	Super-Rare—same as Dragonballs 1-3.
6-Star Dragonball	Super-Rare—same as Dragonballs 1-3.
7-Star Dragonball	Super-Rare—same as Dragonballs 1-3.
Android 16	Defeat Android 16 in story mode as Cell.
Android 17	Defeat Android 17 in story mode as Picollo.
Android 18	Defeat Android 18 in story mode as Vegeta.
Android 19	Defeat Android 19 in story mode as Vegeta.
Captain Ginyu	Defeat Ginyu in Story Mode after he takes over Goku's body.
Cell	Defeat Cell in story mode.

Dragon Ball Z: Budokai (cont'd)

Dodoria	Defeat Frieza with Vegeta in Story Mode.
Frieza	Defeat Frieza in story mode.
Hercule	Beat the adept mode of the World Tournament.
Nappa	Defeat Nappa in story mode.
Raditz	Defeat Raditz in story mode.
Recoome	Defeat Recoome in story mode.
Teen Gohan	Defeat Cell as Gohan in story mode.
The Great Saiyaman	Beat the advanced mode of the World Tournament.
DrTrunks	Beat Perfect Form Cell Complete.
DragVegeta	Defeat Vegeta in story mode.
Yamcha	Beat A Cold-Blooded Assasin.
Zarbon	Defeat Zarbon in story mode as Vegeta.

Dragon Ball Z: Budokai 2

Unlockable	Objective
Kid Buu	Get 3600 kili in Babidi's Spaceship.
Majin Buu	Get 1200 kili in Babidi's Spaceship.
Super Buu	Get 2400 kili in Babidi's Spaceship.
Super Buu's Absorbtion Technique	Get 10,000 kili.
Adept World Tournament	Unlock 16 Characters, then buy it from Bulma.
Advanced World Tournament	Unlock all 29 Characters, then buy it from Bulma.
Android 16	Beat Android 16 with Goku.
Android 17	Beat Android 17 with Piccolo.
Android 18	Beat Android 18 with Krillen.
Android 20	Beat Android 20 with Goku.
Babidi's Ship	Collect All 7 Dragon Balls and Wish for it from Shenron.
Breakthroughs	Wish for them on the Dragon Balls.
Bulma's costumes 2-6	Wish for them on the Dragon Balls.
Cell	Beat Cell with Goku.
City Street Stage	Beat Super Buu with Gohan in Stage 8 without being defeated.
Dabura	Get 100 kili on Babidi's Spaceship.
Frieza	Beat Frieza with Goku.
Future Trunks	Beat Vegeta on Namek with Kid Trunks.
Ginyu	Beat Ginyu on Namek with Vegeta.
Gokule (Capsule)	Get both Breakthroughs of Goku and Hercule.
Gotenks (Capsule)	Enter Stage 7.
Hercule	Beat Majin Buu as Gt.Saiyaman in Stage 6.
Hercule	Beat Fat Buu with Saiyaman.
Kabitoshin (Potara)	Collect seven Dragon Balls and wish for the capsule from the Dragon.
Kid Buu	Get 4600 kili.
Majin Buu	Get 2500 kili.
Majin Vegeta	In Dragon World, Stage 5, defeat any Majin character to get the Capsule that allows you to get Majin Vegeta. Note: Dabura does not count.
Nappa	Beat Nappa with Vegeta (can only be done when you unlock Vegeta and start Dragon mode again).

Dragon Ball Z: Budokai 2 (cont'd)

Raditz	Beat Raditz with Goku.
Recoome	Beat Recoome with Goku.
Saiyaman	Beat Cell with Gohan (adult) only.
Silver Membership Card	Have a Budokai 1 save on your memory card when you start a New Game.
SSJ2 Gohan (adult)	Defeat Majin Vegeta before Majin Buu kills Babidi in Stage 6 (the area with the large ring).
Super Buu	Get 3170 kili.
Super Saiyan 2 (Goku)	Beat Cell in Stage 4 with Goku.
Super Saiyan 2 (Vegeta)	Beat Super Buu (Gohan) as Vegeta Stage in 8.
Super Saiyan 3 (Goku)	Beat Majin (Fat) Buu in Stage 6 with Goku.
Super Saiyan (Goku)	Let Krillen die in Stage 3 .
Supreme Kai	Beat Supreme Kai with Goku.
Teen Gohan	Beat Cell for the last time on Supreme Kai's planet with Gohan (adult).
Tiencha(Capsule)	Get both breakthoughs of Tien and Yamcha.
Tourdement Adept	Unlock 16 characters and buy it.
Tourdement Advance	Unlock all 29 characters and buy it.
Vegeta	Beat Vegeta with Goku on Namek.
Vegeto (Capsule/Goku)	Get Goku to Surpreme Ki then to Vegeta in Stage 8
Vegeto (Capsule/Vegeta)	Wish for it on the Dragon Balls.
Vegetto (Potara with Vegeta)	Collect seven Dragon Balls and wish for the capsule from the Dragon.
Videl	Beat Super Buu(Gohan) as Hercule in Stage 8.
Yamcha	Beat Nappa with Tien.

Drakan: The Ancient's Gates

For the following codes, press and hold L1, L2, R1, R2 then enter the following buttons in the order given.

Unlockable	Code
$10,000	●, ■, →, ←, ×, ▲, ↓, ↑
Level-Up	■, ▲, ●, ×, →, ↓, ←, ↑
Spell Level-Up	↑, ↓, ←, →, →, ←, ↓, ↑
Restore Health	▲, ↓, ●, ←, ■, →, ×, ↑
Invincibility	×, ↓, ▲, ↑, ●, →, ■, ←

Drakengard

Unlockable	Objective
Fly on a Jet	Complete the Free Mission at Shinjuku and this will unlock the Jet. On any sky mission where you chose which Dragon to take, highlight Chaos Dragon. Select it and start your mission while riding a Jet.

Driv3R

In the Main Menu, enter the following cheats. Go to the Options menu and select Cheats to enable or disable them.

Unlockable	Code
All Missions	L1,R1,L1,L2,■,■,●
All Vehicles	L1,L1,■,●,L1,R1,●
All Weapons	R1,L2,■,●,R1,R2,L2

Driv3R (cont'd)

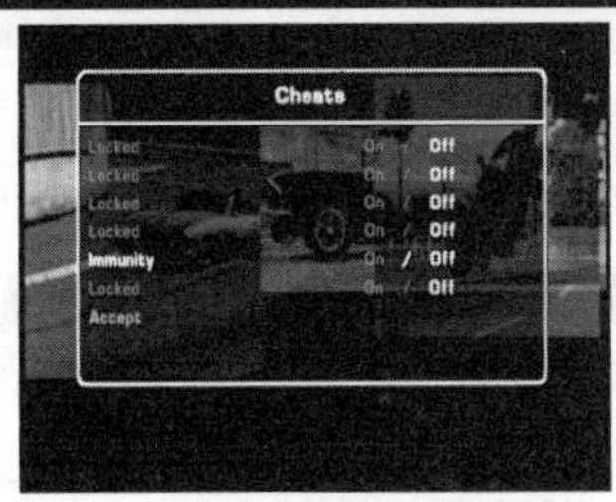

Immunity	●,●,L1,L2,R1,R2,■
Invincibility (Take a Ride)	■,■,L1,R1,L2,R2,R2
Unlimited Ammo	R1,R2,R1,R2,■,●,■

Drum Mania

After you select "Start Game" you're taken to the Mode Select screen. At this screen, perform the following patterns:

Unlockable	Code
Drums Expert Mode	Hi-Hat (x2), Snare (x2), High Tom, Low Tom, High Tom, Bass, Bass
Drums Hidden Mode	Low Tom, High Tom, Low Tom, High Tom, Low Tom, Bass
Drums Mirror Mode	Snare (x2), High Tom, Low Tom, High Tom, Bass
Drums Speed Mode	Hi-Hat, Snare, Hi-Hat (x2), Snare, Hi-Hat, Bass.
Guitar Blank Screen	Red, Blue, Green, Blue, Red, Green, Red, Blue, Green, Blue, Red, Green
Guitar Fast Flow	Red, Green, Blue, Pick (x2)
Guitar Hidden Mode	Red, Blue, Green, Blue, Red, Green
Guitar Random Mode	Blue, Green (x2), Red, Green, Pick
Guitar Super Fast Flow	Red, Green, Blue, Pick (x2), Red, Green, Blue, Pick (x2)

Dynasty Warriors

Unlockable	Objective
Different Intro Sequence	Beat Mosou mode with any character.
Editing Mode	Beat Mosou mode with all the characters except for Diao Chan, Dong Zhuo, Yuan Shao, Lu Bu, and Zhang Jiao.
Free Health	Find a save point even if you don't have a memory card. The game asks if you want to save. It doesn't matter if you save or not. When you return to your game all of your health will be restored.
Cao Cao	Beat Mosou mode with Dian Wei, Xiahou Dun, Xiahou Yuan, Xu Zhu, Zhang Liao, and Sima Yi.
Dong Zhuo, Diao Chan, Yuan Chao, and Zhang Jiao in Free Mode	Beat Mosou mode with one member of each kingdom.
Liu Bei	Beat Mosou mode with Zhao Yun, Huang Zhong, Guan Yu, Zhang Fei, Ma Chao, Jiang Wei, and Zhuge Liang.
Lu Bu in Free Mode	Complete Stage 2, Hulao Gate, in Musou mode with at least 1,000 KOs.
Lu Meng, Taishi Ci, and Gan Ning	Beat Mosou mode with Lu Xun, Zhou Yu, or Sun Shang Xiang.
Ma Chao, Huang Zhong, and Jiang Wei	Beat Mosou mode with Zhao Yun, Zhang Fei, or Guan Yu.
Side Selection and BGM Option	Beat Mosou mode with one member of each kingdom.

Dynasty Warriors

Sima Yi	Beat Mosou mode with Dian Wei, Xiahou Dun, and Xu Zhu.
Sun Quan and Sun Jian	Beat Mosou mode with Lu Xun, Sun Shang Xiang, Zhou Yu, Lu Meng, Taishi Ci, and Gan Ning.
Zhang Liao and Xiahou Yuan	Beat Mosou mode with Dian Wei, Xiahou Dun, or Xu Zhu.

Dynasty Warriors 3

After inputting the following codes, listen for the cheer that confirms correct code entry.

Unlockable	Code
All FMV Sequences	Highlight the Free Mode icon at the main menu. Press ▲, L1, ▲, R1, ▲, ■, L2, ■, R2, ■.
All Generals	Highlight the Free Mode icon at the main menu. Press R2, R2, R2, L1, ▲, L2, L2, L2, R1, ■.
All Items	Go to the "Options" in the main menu and highlight "Open Screen." Press R1, ■, R1, ▲, R1, L1, ■, L1, ▲, L1.
All Shu Generals	Highlight the Free Mode icon at the main menu. Press L1, ■, ▲, R2, L1, L2, L2, R1, ■, L1.
All Wei Generals	Highlight the Free Mode icon at the main menu. Press ▲, ▲, L1, ■, R1, R2, L1, L2, L2, L2.
All Wu Generals	Highlight the Free Mode icon at the main menu. Press L2, L1, ■, ▲, L1, L2, R1, R2, L1, L2.
BGM Test Option	Highlight the Free Mode icon at the main menu. Press ▲, ▲, R1, R1, L2, L2, R2, R2, ■, ▲.
Bonus FMV Sequence	Highlight the "Replay" option at the Opening Edit screen, hold R1+L1+R2+L2, then press ×. Alternately, hold R1+L1+R2+L2 and press START. You see all the people from the gray army dancing.
Control Loading Screen	Press ● to increase the wind as the level name flutters on the loading screen before a battle. Press × to decrease the wind speed.
Free Mode Side Selection	Highlight the Free Mode icon at the main menu. Press R1, R2, L2, L1, ■, L1, L2, R2, R1, ▲.
In-game Reset	Press SELECT+START during gameplay.
Opening Edit Option	Highlight the Free Mode icon at the main menu. Press R1, ■, R1, ▲, R1, L1, ■, L1.

TIP

Start the game with a memory card with a saved game from Dynasty Warriors 2 and some characters unlocked in Dynasty Warriors 2 are available in your new game!

Dynasty Warriors 4

Unlockable	Code
Dynasty Tactics 2 Preview	Press ▲ from the movie menu.

Enter the Matrix

Enable Cheats: Enter the hacking system and enter cheat.exe from the A prompt. Then you can enter the codes below.

CAUTION

Warning! The game can crash with cheats enabled.

Unlockable	Code
All weapons	0034AFFF
Blind Enemies	FFFFFFF1
Bonus level	13D2C77F
Deaf Enemies	4516DF45

Enter the Matrix (cont'd)

Unlockable	Code
Faster Logos	7867F443
Faster Logos	7867F443
Infinite ammo	1DDF2556
Infinite focus	69E5D9E4
Infinite Health	7F4DF451
Invisibility	FFFFFFF1
Low gravity	BB013FFF
Multiplayer	D5C55D1E
Recover Focus Fast	FFF0020A
Taxi Driving	312MF451
Turbo mode	FF00001A

ESPN International Track & Field

Enter the following codes at the Name Entry screen in Trial mode. Listen for the sound to confirm correct code entry.

Unlockable	Code
Aluminum Player	Munich
Blue Player	L.A.
Bronze Player	Helsinki
Copper Player	Roma
Cream Player	Moscow
Gold Player	Montreal
Gray Player	Athens
Green Player	Mexico
Orange Player	Atlanta
Purple Player	Seoul
Red Player	Tokyo
Silver Player	Sydney

ESPN NFL 2K5

Change VIP Profile name to the following and access the specified unlockable.

Unlockable	VIP Pofile Name
1,000,000 Crib Credits	"PhatBank"
All Crib items	"CribMax"
All Milestones complete (full trophy room)	"MadSkilz"

ESPN NHL 2K5

Unlockable	Code
Everything in the Skybox	Create a profile with the name LuvLeafs.

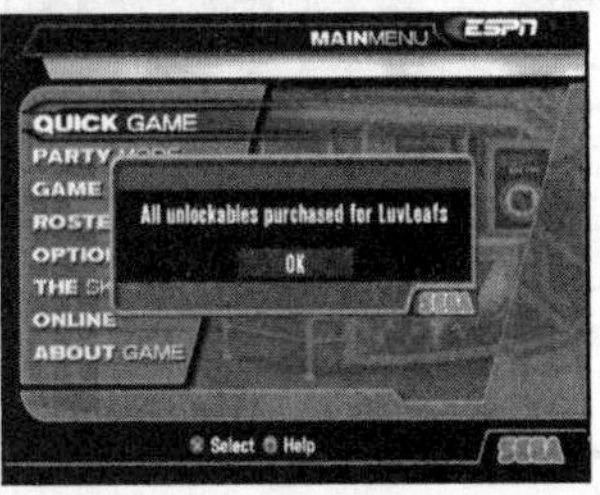

Evil Dead: Fistful of Boomstick

Unlockable	Objective
Arcade Levels	The levels you beat in story mode will be available in arcade mode.
Production Art	Once you've beaten a level, you can see the production artwork for the game from the Extras menu.

Evolution Skateboarding

After entering the following codes, listen for the sound to confirm correct entry.

Unlockable	Code
All Characters and Alt skins	↑, ↓, ←, →, ↑, ↓, ←, →, ↑, ↓, ←, →, ●
All Stages	L2, R2, ←, →, ←, →, ←, →, ↓, ↓, ↑, ↑, ↓, ↑

PSP Xbox PS2 GC GBA

Extreme G-3

Unlockable	Code
Infinite Shields	Pause gameplay and enter L1+R1, L2+R2, L1+L2, R1+R2
Extreme Lap	At main menu, enter L1, L2, L1, R1, L1, R2, L1+R1, L2+R2
Infinite Shields and Turbo	At main menu, enter L1+R1, L2+R2, L1+L2, R1+R2 (Works for one race.)
Double Prize Money	At main menu, enter L1, L2, R2, R1, R1, R2, L2, L1.
Free Money	After selecting a rider in new Career, enter L1, L1, L1, L1, L1, L2, L2, L2, L2, L2, R1, R1, R1, R1, R1, R2, R2, R2, R2, R2, L1+L2+R1+R2.
Infinite Ammunition	During team selection, enter L2, R2, L1, R1, L2+R2, L1+R1.

F1 Career Challenge

Description	Hint
No Stop/Go Penalty	In Multiplayer mode you can enter the pits at any speed and from any direction without the normal stop/go penalty.

Fantastic Four

Enter these codes quickly at the Main menu. You will hear a sound to confirm a correct entry.

Unlockable	Code
Barge Arena Level and Stan Lee Interview #1	■,●,■,⇩,⇩,●,⇧
Bonus Level Hell	⇨,⇨,■,●,⇦,⇧,⇩
Infinite Cosmic Power	⇧,■,■,■,⇦,⇨,●

FantaVision

Description	Objective
Bonus Option 1	Beat and save the game under the Normal difficulty setting.
Bonus Option 2	Beat and save the game under the Hard difficulty setting.

Fifa Street

Unlockable	Codes
Mini Players	Pause the game and hold L1+▲ and press ⇧,⇦,⇩,⇩,⇨,⇩,⇧,⇦.
Normal Size Players	Pause the game and hold L1+▲ and press ⇨,⇨,⇧,⇩,⇩,⇦,⇨,⇦.
All Apparel	At the main menu hold L1+▲ and press ⇨,⇨,⇦,⇧,⇧,⇧,⇩,⇦.

Fight Night 2004

Enter the following codes at the Main Menu.

Unlockable	Code
All Venues	←,←,←,→,→,→,←,→,→
Big Head	←,→,←,→,←,→,←
Small Fighter	Highlight "Play No8," then press ←,←,←,→,→,→,←,×
Fight as Big Tigger	Select My Corner, Record Book, Most Wins-Boxer, and press ↑,↑.

Fight Night Round 2

Unlockable	Code
Mini Fighters	At the choose Venue screen hold ↑ until you hear a bell ring.
Unlock Fabulous	Create a character with the first name GETFAB then cancel out and Fabulous will be available for Play Now and Career mode.
All Venues Unlocked	At the game mode selection screen hold ← until you hear a bell.

Finding Nemo

Unlockable	Code
Credits	▲,■,●,▲,▲,■,●,▲,■,●,▲,■, ■,●,▲,■,●,▲,■,●,●,▲,■,●
Invincibility	▲,■,■,●,●,●,▲,▲,■,■,■,●, ●,●,●,■,▲,●,●,●,■,●,▲,●, ●,■,●,●,▲,●,■,●,●,●,▲
Level Select	▲,▲,▲,■,■,●,■,▲,●, ■,▲,■,▲,■,▲,●,▲,▲
Secret Level	▲,■,●,●,■,▲,▲,■,●,●,■, ▲,▲,●,■,▲,■,●,●,■,▲

Flatout

Create a profile using these passwords.

Unlockable	Code
Lots of Cash	GIVECASH
Unlocks Everything	GIVEALL
Use the Shift Up Button to Launch the Driver	Ragdoll

Freaky Flyers

Description	Objective
Gremlin (Race Mode)	On the Thugsville board, notice the two elevated train tracks on either side of the map. Follow the right track to a tunnel. Once you are inside, take the left fork.
Pilot X	On the last level in Adventure mode, beat Pilot X by destroying his robot.

Freedom Fighters

Enter these codes during gameplay.

Unlockable	Code
Blind AI	▲,×,■,●,●,←
Nail Gun	▲,×,■,●,×,←
Slow Motion	▲,×,■,●,●,→
Unlimited Ammo	▲,×,■,●,×,→

Freestyle Metal X

Unlockable	Code
$1,000,000	sugardaddy
All posters and photos	seeall
All bike parts	garageking
All costumes	johnnye
All levels and events	universe
All riders	dudemaster
All songs	hearall
All special stunt slots	fleximan
All videos	watchall

Fugitive Hunter: War on Terror

Unlockable	Code
Cheat Menu	On the Title Screen, press ●,●,●,●,●,●,■,■,■,■. A chime will sound. Select Special Features to access the cheat menu.
Some enemies as Bin Laden	In the Afghanistan-Pakistan Border mission, pause the game and press ●,●,●,■,■,■,R2.

Full Spectrum Warrior

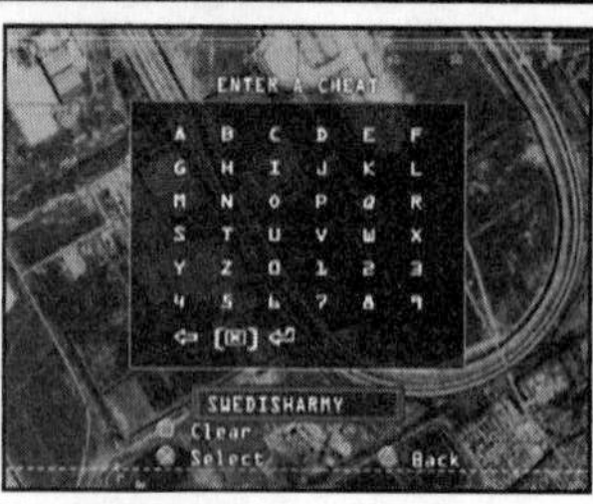

Enter these codes in the Cheat menu under Options.

Unlockable	Code
All bonuses	LASVEGAS
All chapters	APANPAPANSNALE9
All enemies displayed on GPS	CANADIANVISION
Authentic mode	SWEDISHARMY
Big Head Mode	NICKWEST
Cloak Stealth Mode	BULGARIANNINJA
Opfors will have no cover	NAKEDOP4
Unlimited Ammo	MERCENARIES
Unlimited Rockets & Grenades	ROCKETARENA

Futurama

Press and hold down L1 + L2 while playing and enter the following codes to jump to that level.

Level	Code
Bogad's Swamp	↓, ■, ▲, ↓, ■, ▲, ■, ▲, ←, ↑, SELECT
Canyon	↓, ■, ▲, ↓, ■, ▲, ■, ▲, →, ↑, SELECT
Inner Temple	↓, ■, ▲, ↓, ■, ▲, ■, ▲, ↓, ▲, SELECT
Junkyard 1	↓, ■, ▲, ↓, ■, ▲, ■, ▲, →, ←, SELECT
Junkyard 2	↓, ■, ▲, ↓, ■, ▲, ■, ▲, →, ▲, SELECT
Junkyard 3	↓, ■, ▲, ↓, ■, ▲, ■, ▲, →, ●, SELECT
Left Wing	↓, ■, ▲, ↓, ■, ▲, ■, ▲, ↓, →, SELECT
Market Square	↓, ■, ▲, ↓, ■, ▲, ■, ▲, ↓, ↑, SELECT
Mine	↓, ■, ▲, ↓, ■, ▲, ■, ▲, →, →, SELECT
Mine Tunnel	↓, ■, ▲, ↓, ■, ▲, ■, ▲, →, ↓, SELECT
Mom's HQ—Bender	↓, ■, ▲, ↓, ■, ▲, ■, ▲, ▲, ↑, SELECT
Mom's HQ—Fry	↓, ■, ▲, ↓, ■, ▲, ■, ▲, ▲, ↓, SELECT
Mom's HQ—Leela	↓, ■, ▲, ↓, ■, ▲, ■, ▲, ▲, →, SELECT
New New York	↓, ■, ▲, ↓, ■, ▲, ■, ▲, ↑, ×, SELECT
Old New York	↓, ■, ▲, ↓, ■, ▲, ■, ▲, ↑, ←, SELECT
Planet Express	↓, ■, ▲, ↓, ■, ▲, ■, ▲, ↑, ↑, SELECT
Red Light District	↓, ■, ▲, ↓, ■, ▲, ■, ▲, ↑, ▲, SELECT
Right Wing	↓, ■, ▲, ↓, ■, ▲, ■, ▲, ↓, ↓, SELECT
Sewers	↓, ■, ▲, ↓, ■, ▲, ■, ▲, ↑, →, SELECT
Subway	↓, ■, ▲, ↓, ■, ▲, ■, ▲, ↑, ↓, SELECT
Temple Courtyard	↓, ■, ▲, ↓, ■, ▲, ■, ▲, ↓, ←, SELECT
Uptown	↓, ■, ▲, ↓, ■, ▲, ■, ▲, ↑, ●, SELECT

Gallop Racer 2003

Description	Hint
Free Horse	If you don't have any money, go to the next month and try to get a 0-point horse.

Gauntlet Dark Legacy

Enter the codes in the spot where you name new characters. You can only utilize one special character or game mode at a time. Choose the character type (i.e. Dwarf, Valkyrie, etc.), as well as naming that character according to the code. Use special game modes (i.e., Unlimited Supershot, Unlimited Invulnerability) with any character type.

Unlockable	Code
$10,000 Gold per level	10000K
9 Keys and 9 Potions Per Level	ALLFUL
Battle General (Knight)	BAT900
Castle General (Warrior)	CAS400
Chainsaw Jester	KJH105
Cheerleader (Valkyrie)	CEL721
Created By Don (Knight)	ARV984
Desert General (Wizard)	DES700
Dwarf General	ICE600
Employee Stig (Knight)	STG333
Ex-Employee Chris (Knight)	CSS222
Football Dude (Knight)	RIZ721
Happy Face Jester	STX222
Karate Steve (Knight)	SJB964
Manager Mike (Knight)	DIB626
Mountain General (Warrior)	MTN200
Ninja (Knight)	TAK118
Punkrock Jester	PNK666
Rat Knight (Warrior)	RAT333
Regular Garm (Wizard)	GARM99
S & M Dwarf	NUD069
School Girl (Valkyrie)	AYA555
Sickly Garm (Wizard)	GARM00
Sky General (Wizard)	SKY100
Sumner (Wizard)	SUM224
Town General (Valkyrie)	TWN300
Unlimited 3 Way Shot	MENAGE
Unlimited Extra Speed	XSPEED
Unlimited Full Turbo	Purple
Unlimited Halo and Levitate	1ANGLI
Unlimited Invisibility	000000
Unlimited Invulnerability	INVULN
Unlimited Play As Pojo	EGG911
Unlimited Rapid Fire	QCKSHT
Unlimited Reflective Shot	REFLEX
Unlimited Shrink Enemy and Growth	DELTA1
Unlimited Supershot	SSHOTS
Unlimited X-Ray Glasses	PEEKIN
Waitress (Knight)	KA0292

The Getaway

During the opening movie, press the following buttons to access these cheats:

Unlockable	Code
Armored Car Weapon	↑,↓,←,→,■,▲,●
Double Health	↑,↑,←,←,→,→,●,●,↓
Free Roam Mode and Credits	▲,▲,▲,←,■,▲,▲,▲,←,●
Unlimited Ammo	↑,↓,←,→,▲,↑,↓,←,→,■

Ghosthunter

Description	Code
Increase damage	Hold right on d-pad while pressing L3 for 5 seconds, then press ●
Laz never dies	Hold right on d-pad while pressing L3 for 5 seconds, then press ▲

Gladius

At school, pause the game and enter the following codes.

Unlockable	Code
Equip Anything	→, ↓, ←, ↑, ←, ←, ←, ←, ▲, ▲, ▲
More Experience	→, ↓, ←, ↑, ←, ←, ←, ←, ▲, →
More Money	→, ↓, ←, ↑, ←, ←, ←, ←, ▲, ←

Goblin Commander: Unleash the Horde

Press and hold L1 + R1 + ▲ + ↓ for three seconds, then enter the following codes.

Unlockable	Code
100 Gold	L1, R1, R1, R1, R1, L1, ▲, L1, L1, L1
God Mode	R1, R1, R1, L1, L1, L1, R1, L1, ▲, R1
Souls	R1, L1, L1, L1, L1, R1, ▲, R1, R1, R1
Win Level	R1, R1, L1, L1, L1, R1, R1, ▲, ▲, ▲

Golden Eye: Rogue Agent

Description	Code
All skins in Multiplayer	↓, ←, ↑, ←, →, ↓, ←, ↑
Paintball Mode	→, ←, →, ←, ↓, ↓, ↑, ↑

Gradius 3 and 4: Mythology of Revival

Input the following codes while paused.

Description	Code
Laser Power-Up	↑, ↑, ↓, ↓, ←, →, ←, →, ×, ●.
Double Shot Power-Up	↑, ↑, ↓, ↓, ←, →, ←, →, ■, ▲.

CAUTION

You can only input these codes a certain number of times.

Gran Turismo 3 A-Spec

Complete the races listed to unlock the corresponding automobiles.

Objective	Car
4WD Challenge	Mitsubishi Lancer Evolution VII GSR
4WD Challenge	Mitsubishi Lancer Evolution VII Rally Car Prototype
4WD Challenge	Suzuki Alto Works, Suzuki Sports Limited
80's Sports Car Cup	Mazda Savanna RX7 Infini III
80s Sports Car Cup	Nismo Skyline GT-R S-tune
All Golds on A License	Mazda RX8
All Golds on B License	Mazda Miata RS
All Golds on IA License	Aston Martin Vanqish
All Golds on IB License	Nissan Z Concept Car

Gran Turismo 3 A-Spec (cont'd)

All Golds on Rally License	Subaru Impreza Rally Car Prototype
All Golds on S License	Dodge Viper GTS-R Concept Car
All Japanese GT Championship	Honda Arta NSX JGTC, Denso Supra Race Car
Altezza Championship Race	Tom's X540 Chaser, Toyota Vitz RS 1.5
Altezza Race	Toyota Celica SS-II
American Championship	Subaru Impreza Sedan WRX STi Version VI, Chevy Camaro Race Car, Audi TT 1.8T Quattro, Mazda RX7 Type RS
Amateur 4WD Challenge	Titanium Mitsubishi Lancer Evolution
Amateur Evolution Meeting	Mitsubishi Lancer Evolution VI Rally Car
Amateur Race of Turbo Sports	White Mine's Lancer Evolution VI
Beginner FR Challenge series	Nissan Silvia K's 1800cc
Beginner GT World Championships	Tan Nissan Skyline GT-R V-spec II R32
Beginner MR Challenge	Blue Toyota MR-S S Edition.
Beginner Race of Turbo Sports	Silver Daihatsu Mira TRXX Avanzato R
Beginner Race of NA Sports series	Silver Honda CRX Del Sol SiR
Beginner Type R Meeting	Yellow Honda Civic SiR.
Beetle Cup	Volkswagen New Beetle Rsi
Boxer Spirit	Subaru Legacy Blitzer B4
British GT Car Cup	Aston Martin Vanquish
Clubman Cup	Mazda Eunos Roadster
Deutsche Tourenwagen Challenge	Volkswagen Lupo Cup Car, Volkswagen Beetle Cup Racer, Astra Touring Car, RUF 3400S
Dream Car Championship	Mitsubishi FTO LM Race Car, Mazda RX7 LM Race Car
Dream Car Championship	Toyota GT1, Panoz Esperante GTR, FTO LM Race Car, F090/s
European Championship	Lotus Elise 190, Nissan GTR V-Spec, Gillet Vertigo Race Car, Mini Cooper 1.3i
Evolution Meeting	Mitsubishi Lancer Evolution IV GSR
Evolution Meeting	Mitsubishi Lancer Evolution VI Rally Car
FF Challenge	Celica TRD Sports M
FF Challenge	Toyota Vitz RS 1.5
FR Challenge	Nissan Silvia K's 1800cc
FR Challenge	Toyota Sprinter Trueno GT-Apex Shigeno Version
Get All Golds	Mitsubishi Lancer Evolution V GSR
Get All Golds	Suzuki Escudo Pikes Peak Version
Get all Golds	Team ORECA Dodge Viper GTSR
Gran Turismo All-Stars	Mine's GT-R-N1 V-spec, Raybrig NSX
Gran Turismo World Championship	Nissan C-West Razo Silvia, Nissan Z Concept car, Toyota GT1 Road Car, Mazda RX8

Gran Turismo 3 A-Spec (cont'd)

Gran Turismo World Championship	Toyota Celica GT-Four, Mitsubishi Lancer Evolution VI GSR, Mazda Miata, Nissan Skyline GTR V-spec II
Japanese Championship	Mazda RX7 Type RZ, Mitsubishi Evolution IV GSR, FTO GP Version R, Subaru Impreza WRX Sti Version VI Wagon
Legend of Silver Arrow	Mercedes Benz CLK Touring Car (D2 AMG Mercedes)
Legend of Silver Arrow	Mercedes SLK 230 Kompressor
Lightweight K Cup	Mini Cooper 1.3i
Like the Wind	Mazda 787B
MR Challenge	Honda NSX Type S Zero
MR Challenge	Tommy Kaira ZZII
MR Challenge	Toyota MR-S S Edition
NA Race of NA Sports	Honda CRX Del Sol SiR
NA Race of NA Sports	Mazda RX8 Turbo
Race of Red Emblem	Nismo 400R
Race of Turbo Sports	Mines Lancer Evolution VI GSR
Smokey Mountain II	Mitsubishi Lancer Evolution VI Rally Car
Smokey Mountain Rally	Ford Focus Rally Car
Spider & Roadster Championship	Shelby Cobra
Spider and Roadster cup with gold medals across the board	Mazda Roadster RS
Spider/Roadster Cup	Mazda Miata Roadster RS
Stars & Stripes Grand Championship	Spoon Sports S2000 Race Car
Stars & Stripes Grand Championship	Chevrolet Camaro SS
Sunday Cup	Toyota Sprinter, Trueno GT-Apex (AE-86 Type I)
Super Special Route 5 Wet	Citroen Xsara Rally Car
Super Special Route 5 Wet II	Subaru Impreza Rally Car Prototype
Super Speedway 150 Miles	Chevrolet Corvette C5R, Tickford Falcon XR8 Race Car, F090/S
Swiss Alps	Peugeot 206 Rally Car
Swiss Alps II	Mitsubishi Lancer Evolution VII Rally Car Prototype
Tahiti Challenge of Rally	Toyota Celica Rally Car
Tahiti Challenge of Rally II	Toyota Corolla Rally Car
Tahiti Maze	Ford Escort Rally Car
Tahiti Maze II	Impreza Rally Car
Tourist Trophy	Audi S4
Tourist Trophy Audi TT Race	Audi TT 1.8T Quattro
Turbo Race of Turbo Sports	Daihatsu Mira TR XX Avanzato R
Type R Meeting	4 cars, Honda NSX Type-R

Gran Turismo 3 A-Spec (cont'd)

Type R Meeting	Honda Civic SiR-II VII GSR
Vitz Race	4 cars, Toyota Vitz RS 1.5
Cupman Cup with gold medals in each of the three races	Eunos Roadster
Sunday Cup with gold medals in each of the three races	Toyota Sprinter Truendo GT-Apex

TIP

To unlock tracks in Arcade Mode beat each tier of tracks on easy mode, and you unlock the next tier of tracks.

The following table lists each tier with its tracks.

Tier 1	Tier 2	Tier 3
Super Speedway	**Smokey Mountain II**	**Swiss Alps II,**
Midfield Raceway	**Tokyo R146**	**Trial Mountain II**
Smokey Mountain	**Grand Valley Speedway**	**Deep Forest Raceway II**
Swiss Alps	**Laguna Seca Raceway**	**Special Stage Route 5**
Trial Mountain	**Rome Circuit**	**Seattle Circuit**
Midfield Raceway II	**Tahiti Circuit**	**Test Course**

Grand Prix Challenge

Description	Code
Ace difficulty	REDJOCKS
All Grand Prix Challenges	IMHRACING
All tracks	TEAMPEEP

Grand Theft Auto 3

Enter all of the following codes during gameplay. After doing so, wait for the message to confirm correct code entry.

Description	Code
All Weapons	Press R2, R2, L1, R2, ←, ↓, →, ↑, ←, ↓, →, ↑. See Tip.
Better Driving Skills	Press R1, L1, R2, L1, ←, R1, R1, ▲. Press L3 or R3 to jump while driving.
Destroy All Cars	Press L2, R2, L1, R1, L2, R2, ▲, ■, ●, ▲, L2, L1.
Different Costume	Press →, ↓, ←, ↑, L1, L2, ↑, ←, ↓, →.
Faster Gameplay	Press ▲, ↑, →, ↓, ■, L1, L2. Repeat this code to increase its effect.
Flying Car (Low Gravity)	Press →, R2, ●, R1, L2, ↓, L1, R1. Accelerate and press ↑ to fly.
Fog	Press L1, L2, R1, R2, R2, R1, L2, ✕.
Full Armor	Press R2, R2, L1, L2, ←, ↓, →, ↑, ←, ↓, →, ↑.
Full Health	Press R2, R2, L1, R1, ←, ↓, →, ↑, ←, ↓, →, ↑. See Note.
Invisible Cars	Press L1, L1, ■, R2, ▲, L1, ▲
More Money	Press R2, R2, L1, L1, ←, ↓, →, ↑, ←, ↓, →, ↑
Normal Weather	Press L1, L2, R1, R2, R2, R1, L2, ▲
Overcast Skies	Press L1, L2, R1, R2, R2, R1, L2, ■
Rain	Press L1, L2, R1, R2, R2, R1, L2, ●
Slower Gameplay	Press ▲, ↑, →, ↓, ■, R1, R2 This cheat also continues the effect of an adrenaline pill.

Grand Theft Auto 3 (cont'd)

Speed Up Time	Press ●, ●, ●, ■, ■, ■, ■, ■, L1, ▲, ●, ▲. Repeat this code to increase its effect.
Tank (Rhino)	Press ●, ●, ●, ●, ●, ●, R1, L2, L1, ▲, ●, ▲. This may be repeated as many times as needed.

NOTE

Better Driving Skills Note

Saving the game allows your car to never tip. Also, every car will have hydraulics that enable it to jump 15 feet in the air over other cars. After this code is enabled, any time you roll your car, press ■ + × to flip back over. This works as long as your car is not on its roof.

TIP

All Weapons Code Tip

Repeat this code for more ammunition. To get unlimited ammunition, enable the "All Weapons" code continuously until whatever you want is at 9999 shots. The next time your clip runs out, it will reload automatically, but the magazine (9999) will stay the same. Note: If you are busted, your weapons will disappear and this code will have to be repeated.

NOTE

Full Health Code Note

If this code is enabled during a mission where there is damage on your car, the meter will reset to zero. If your vehicle is on fire, enable the "Full Health" code to extinguish it. This code also repairs your car. You can't see the repairs, but it acts like a new car. If you're on a mission where you need a mint-condition car, sometimes enabling the "Full Health" code will fulfill the requirements.

CAUTION

Warning!

*Saving the game after inputting the **following** codes will make them permanent.*

Description	Code
All Pedestrians Have Weapons	Press R2, R1, ▲, ×, L2, L1, ↑, ↓. See Caution Below.
Higher Wanted Level	Press R2, R2, L1, R2, ←, →, ←, →, ←.
Increased Gore	Press ■, L1, ●, ↓, L1, R1, ▲, →, L1, ×. No confirmation message will appear. See Note.
No Wanted Level	Press R2, R2, L1, R2, ↑, ↓, ↑, ↓, ↑, ↓.
Pedestrians Attack You	Press ↓, ↑, ←, ↑, ×, R1, R2, L1, L2.
Pedestrians Riot	Press ↓, ↑, ←, ↑, ×, R1, R2, L2, L1.

NOTE

With this code enabled, you can shoot off pedestrians' arms, legs, and heads with some weapons (sniper rifle, assault rifle, explosives) with an increase in the overall amount of blood left behind.

CAUTION

Be careful after entering this code, some pedestrians will throw bombs or shoot at you if you steal their car.

Grand Theft Auto: San Andreas

Description	Code
250,000 & full health and armor	R1, R2, L1 , ×, ←, ↓, →, ↑, ←, ↓, →, ↑
4 star wanted level	R1, R1, ●, L1, ↑, ↓, ↑, ↓, ↑, ↓
Aggressive Traffic	R2, ●, R1, L2, ← R1, L1, R2, L2
All Traffic Lights Stay Green	→, R1, ↑, L2, L2, ←, R1, L1, R1, R1
All Vehicles Invisible (Except Motorcycles)	▲, L1, ▲, R2, ■, L1, L1
Attain 2 star wanted level	R1, R1, ●, ←, →, ←, →
Black Traffic	●, L2, ↑, R1, ←, ×, R1, L1, ←, ●
Cars on Water	→, R2, ●, R1, L2, ■, R1, R2
Commit Suicide	→, L2, ↓, R1, ←, ←, R1, L1, L2, L1
Destroy Cars	R2, L2, R1, L1, L2, R2, ■, ▲, ●, ▲, L2, L1
Faster Cars	→, R1, ↑, L2, L2, ←, R1, L1, R1, R1
Faster Clock	●, ●, L1, ■, L1, ■, ■, ■, L1, ▲, ●, ▲
Faster Gameplay	▲, ↑, →, ↓, L2, L1, ■
Flying Boats	R2, ●, ↑, L1, →, R1, →, ↑, ■, ▲
Fog	R2, ×, L1, L1, L2, L2, L2, ×
Get a Bounty on your head	↓, ↑, ↑, ↑, ×, R2, R1, L2, L2
Lower Wanted Level	R1, R1, ●, R2, ↑, ↓, ↑, ↓, ↑, ↓
Morning	R2, ×, L1, L1, L2, L2, L2, ■
Night	R2, ×, L1, L1, L2, L2, L2, ▲
Overcast	R2, ×, L1, L1, L2, L2, L2, ■
Pedestrian Attack (can't be turned off)	↓, ↑, ↑, ↑, ×, R2, R1, L2, L2
Pedestrian Riot (can't be turned off)	↓, ←, ↑, ←, ×, R2, R1, L2, L1
Pedestrians have weapons	R2, R1, ×, ▲, ×, ▲, ↑, ↓
Perfect Handling	▲, R1, R1, ←, R1, L1, R2, L1
Pink Traffic	●, L1, ↓, L2, ←, ×, R1, L1, →, ●
Play as Wuzi	L2, R2, R2, L2, L2, L2, L1, L1, L1, L1, ▲, ▲, ●, ●, ■, L2, L2, L2, L2, L2, L2
Raise Wanted Level	R1, R1, ●, R2, →, ←, →, ←, →, ←
Romero	↓, R2, ↓, R1, L2, ←, R1, L1, ←, →
Slower Gameplay	▲, ↑, →, ↓, ■, R2, R1
Spawn a Ranger	↑, →, →, L1, →, ↑, ■, L2
Spawn A Rhino	●, ●, L1, ●, ●, ●, L1, L2, R1, ▲, ●, ▲
Spawn a Stretch	R2, ↑, L2, ←, ←, R1, L1, ●, →
Spawn Bloodring Banger	↓, R1, ●, L2, L2, ×, R1, L1, ←, ←
Spawn Caddy	●, L1, ↑, R1, L2, ×, R1, L1, ●, ×
Spawn Hotring Racer #1	R1, ●, R2, →, L1, L2, ×, ×, ■, R1
Spawn Hotring Racer #2	R2, L1, ●, →, L1, R1, →, ↑, ●, R2
Spawn Rancher	↑, →, →, L1, →, ↑, ■, L2
Spawns jetpack	L1, L2, R1, R2, ↑, ↓, ←, right, L1, L2, R1, R2, ↑, ↓, ←, →,
Storm	R2, ×, L1, L1, L2, L2, L2, ●
Trashmaster	●, R1, ●, R1, ←, ←, R1, L1, ●, →
Weapons 1	R1, R2, L1, R2, ←, ↓, →, ↑, ←, ↓, →, ↑
Weapons 2	R1, R2, L1, R2, ←, ↓, →, ↑, ←, ↓, ↓, ←
Weapons 3	R1, R2, L1, R2, ←, ↓, →, ↑, ← , ↓, ↓, ↓

Grand Theft Auto: Vice City

Enter all of the following codes during gameplay. After doing so, wait for the message to confirm correct code entry.

Description	Code
Aggressive Traffic	Press R2, ●, R1, L2, ←, R1, L1, R2, L2
Armor	Press R1, R2, L1, ×, ←, ↓, →, ↑, ←, ↓, →, ↑
Better Driving Skills	Press ▲, R1, R1, ←, R1, L1, R2, L1. Press L3 or R3 to jump while driving.
Bikini Women with Guns (The women drop guns when they die.)	Press →, L1, ●, L2, ←, ×, R1, L1, L1, ×
Black Traffic	Press ●, L2, ↑, R1, ←, ×, R1, L1, ←, ●
Bloodring Banger (Style 1)	Press ↑, →, →, L1, →, ↑, ■, L2.
Bloodring Banger (Style 2)	Press ↓, R1, ●, L2, L2, ×, R1, L1, ←, ←
Caddy	Press ●, L1, ↑, R1, L2, ×, R1, L1, ●, ×
Candy Suxxx Costume	Press ●, R2, ↓, R1, ←, →, R1, L1, ×, L2.
Car Floats on Water	Press →, R2, ●, R1, L2, ■, R1, R2. See Note.
Change Wheel Size (The wheels of some vehicles become larger, while others become smaller.)	Press R1, ×, ▲, →, R2, ■, ↑, ↓, ■. Repeat this code to increase its effect.
Destroy Cars	Press R2, L2, R1, L1, L2, R2, ■, ▲, ●, ▲, L2, L1
Dodo Car (Flying)	Press →, R2, ●, R1, L2, ↓, L1, R1. Accelerate and press the analog stick back to glide.
Extended Wanted Level Status	Press R2, ●, ↑, L1, →, R1, →, ↑, ■, ▲. A box will appear under your felony stars showing how long you have had a felony and how close the cops are.
Faster Game Clock	Press ●, ●, L1, ■, L1, ■, ■, ■, L1, ▲, ●, ▲
Faster Gameplay	Press ▲, ↑, →, ↓, L2, L1, ■
Foggy Weather	Press R2, ×, L1, L1, L2, L2, L2, ×
Health	Press R1, R2, L1, ●, ←, ↓, →, ↑, ←, ↓, →, ↑
Hilary King Costume	Press R1, ●, R2, L1, →, R1, L1, ×, R2
Hotring Racer (Style 1)	Press R1, ●, R2, →, L1, L2, ×, ×, ■, R1
Hotring Racer (Style 2)	Press R2, L1, ●, →, L1, R1, →, ↑, ●, R2
Increase Your Vehicle's Top Speed	Press →, R1, ↑, L2, L2, ←, R1, L1, R1, R1
Ken Rosenberg Costume	Press →, L1, ↑, L2, L1, →, R1, L1, ×, R1
Lance Vance Costume	Press ●, L2, ←, ×, R1, L1, ×, L1
Love Fist Limousine	Press R2, ↑, L2, ←, ←, R1, L1, ●, →
Love Fist Musician 1 Costume	Press ↓, L1, ↓, L2, ←, ×, R1, L1, ×, ×
Love Fist Musician 2 Costume	Press R1, L2, R2, L1, →, R2, ←, ×, ■, L1
Lower Wanted Level	Press R1, R1, ●, R2, ↑, ↓, ↑, ↓, ↑, ↓
Mercedes Costume	Press R2, L1, ↑, L1, →, R1, →, ↑, ●, ▲
Normal Weather	Press R2, ×, L1, L1, L2, L2, L2, ↓
Overcast Skies	Press R2, ×, L1, L1, L2, L2, L2, ■
Pedestrian Costume	Press →, →, ←, ↑, L1, L2, ←, ↑, ↓, →. Repeat this code to cycle through the various pedestrian costumes.
Pedestrians Attack You	Press ↓, ↑, ↑, ↑, ×, R2, R1, L2, L2. You cannot disable this code.

Grand Theft Auto: Vice City (cont'd)

Pedestrians from "Thriller"	Press ■, L1, ▲, R2, ■, L1, L1 No confirmation message appears.
Pedestrians Have Weapons	Press R2, R1, ×, ▲, ×, ▲, ↑, ↓ You cannot disable this code.
Pedestrians Riot	Press ↓, ←, ↑, ←, ×, R2, R1, L2, L1 You cannot disable this code.
Phil Cassady Costume	Press →, R1, ↑, R2, L1, →, R1, L1, →, ●.
Pink Traffic	Press ●, L1, ↓, L2, ←, ×, R1, L1, →, ● or × .
Police Return from Dead	Press ●, L1, ↓, L2, ←, ×, R1, L1, →, ×.
Rainy Weather	Press R2, ×, L1, L1, L2, L2, L2, ●.
Raise Wanted Level	Press R1, R1, ●, R2, ←, →, ←, →, ←, → .
Rhino Tank	Press ●, ●, L1, ●, ●, ●, L1, L2, R1, ▲, ●, ▲.
Ricardo Diaz Costume	Press L1, L2, R1, R2, ↓, L1, R2, L2.
Romero's Hearse	Press ↓, R2, ↓, R1, L2, ←, R1, L1, ←, → .
Sabre Turbo	Press →, L2, ↓, L2, L2, ×, R1, L1, ●, ←.
Slower Gameplay	Press ▲, ↑, →, ↓, ■, R2, R1.
Sonny Forelli Costume	Press ●, L1, ●, L2, ←, ×, R1, L1, ×, ×.
Suicide	Press →, L2, ↓, R1, ←, ←, R1, L1, L2, L1.
Sunny Weather	Press R2, ×, L1, L1, L2, L2, L2, ▲.
Tommy Groupies	Press ●, ×, L1, L1, R2, ×, ×, ●, ▲.
Trashmaster	Press ●, R1, ●, R1, ←, ←, R1, L1, ●, →.
Weapons (Tier 1)	Press R1, R2, L1, R2, ←, ↓, →, ↑, ←, ↓, →, ↑ The least powerful weapons in each category are unlocked.
Weapons (Tier 2)	Press R1, R2, L1, R2, ←, ↓, →, ↑, ←, ↓, ↓, ←.
Weapons (Tier 3)	Press R1, R2, L1, R2, ←, ↓, →, ↑, ←, ↓, ↓, ↓.

NOTE

After enabling this code while driving on the water, repeat the code to deactivate it. The car you drive goes directly to the bottom of the water and keeps going without losing any health. You soon hit a piece of land and either end up stuck in the ground or can drive again. You do not lose any health during the entire time.

Great Escape

Press the following button combinations at the Main Menu.

Unlockable	Code
All Movies	L2, L2, ■, ●, ●, R2, R1, ■, ■, ●, L2, R1
Level Select	■, L2, ■, R1, ●, R2, ●, L2, L2, R2, ●, ■
Unlimited Ammo	■, ●, L2, R1, R2, L2, ●, ■, L2, R1, L2, R1

Gun Griffon Blaze

Description	Hint
Start With Different Weapons	Which country your pilot is from determines which set of weapons your mech is outfitted with. Change your pilot's origin to equip your mech with different weapons. From the main menu select Create New Pilot. From here, you can rename your pilot and change other statistics.

Half-Life

Go to Options, then Cheat Codes, and enter the following:

Unlockable	Code
Alien Mode	↑,▲,↑,▲,↑,▲,↑,▲
Infinite Ammo	↓,×,←,●,↓,×,←,●
Invincibility	←,■,↑,▲,→,●,↓,×
Invisibility	←,■,→,●,←,■,→,●
Slow Motion	→,■,↑,▲,→,■,↑,▲
Xen Gravity	↑,▲,↓,×,↑,▲,↓,×

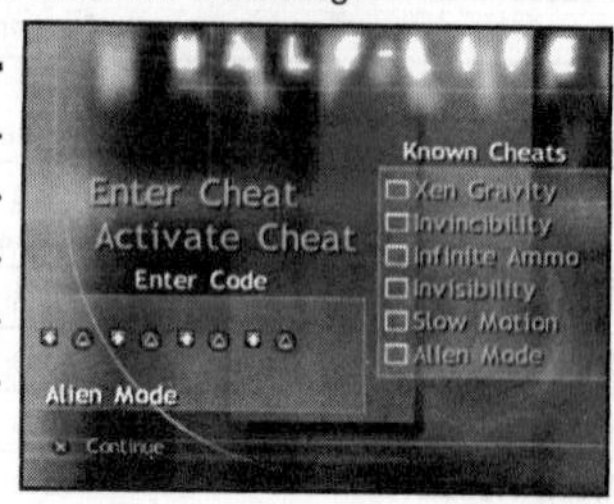

Haunted Mansion

While playing hold right on the d-pad and enter these codes.

Unlockable	Code
God Mode	■, ●, ●, ●, ■, ●, ▲, ×
Level Select	●, ●, ■, ▲, ▲, ■, ●, ×
Upgrade Weapon	■, ■, ▲, ▲, ●, ●, ●, ×

Headhunter

Description	Code
Activate Cheat Mode	Hold R1 + ■ and press START during gameplay.

Hitman: Contracts

Unlockable	Code
Complete Level	During gameplay, press R2,L2,↑,↓,×,L3,●,×,●,×
Level Select	In the Main Menu, press ■,▲,●,←,↑,→,L2,R2

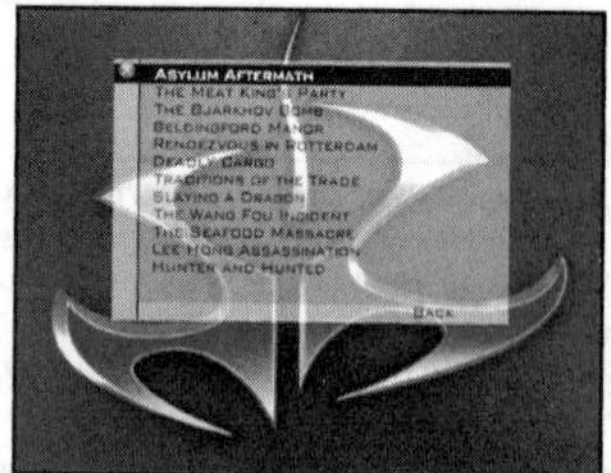

Hitman 2: Silent Assassin

Enter the following codes during gameplay.

Description	Code
All Weapons	R2, L2, ↑, ↓, ×, ↑, ■, ×
Bomb Mode	R2, L2, ↑, ↓, ×, ↑, L1
Full Heal	R2, L2, ↑, ↓, ×, ↑, ↓
God Mode	R2, L2, ↑, ↓, ×, R2, L2, R1, L1
Lethal Charge	R2, L2, ↑, ↓, ×, R1, R1
Level Skip	R2, L2, ↑, ↓, ×, L3, ●, ×, ●, × Enable this code immediately after starting a level to complete it with a Silent Assassin rank.
Megaforce Mode	R2, L2, ↑, ↓, ×, R2, R2 Restart the level to remove its effect.

Hitman 2: Silent Assassin (cont'd)

Nailgun Mode (Weapons pin people to walls.)	R2, L2, ↑, ↓, ×, L1, L1
Punch Mode	R2, L2, ↑, ↓, ×, ↑, ↑
Slow Motion	R2, L2, ↑, ↓, ×, ↑, L2
SMG and 9mm Pistol SD	L2, R2, ↑, ↓, ×, ↑, R2, R2
Toggle Gravity	R2, L2, ↑, ↓, ×, L2, L2
Level Select	R2, L2, ↑, ↓, ■, ▲, ●

Hot Shots Golf 3

Description	Code
In-Game Reset	Press L1 + R1 + L2 + R2 + START + SELECT during gameplay.
Left-Handed Golfer	Press START when selecting a golfer.

Hot Shots Golf FORE!

Entering the following codes will make the specified unlockable available for purchase in the shop.

Unlockable	Code
Caddie, Mochi	"MYPWPA"
Pinhole Club	"DGHFRP"
HSG Music CD	"PAJXLI"

Hot Wheels: Velocity X

Unlockable	Code
All Cars and Tracks	In the Main Menu, hold L1+R1 and press ●,■,■,▲,×

The Hulk

From Options, select Code Input and enter the following. When done, go to Special Features and select Cheats to activate them.

Unlockable	Code
Double Hulk HP	HLTHDSE
Full Rage Meter	ANGMNGT
Half Enemies HP	MMMYHLP
Invulnerability	GMMSKIN
Puzzle Solved	BRCESTN
Regenerator	FLSHWND
Reset High Score	NMBTHIH
Unlimited continues	GRNCHTR
Unlock all levels	TRUBLVR
Wicked Punch	FSTOFRY

Enter the following codes at the Code Terminal.

Unlockable	Code
Play as Gray Hulk	"JANITOR"
Desert Battle Art	"FIFTEEN"
Hulk Movie FMV Art	"NANOMED"
Hulk Transformed Art	"SANFRAN"
Hulk vs. Hulk Dogs Art	"PITBULL"

I-Ninja

To enter the following codes, pause the game and enter code.

Unlockable	Code
Big Head	Hold R1 and press ▲,▲,▲,▲. Release R1, hold L1, and press ▲,▲. Hold R1+L1, and press ▲,●,▲.
Level Skip	Hold R1 and press ■,■,■,●. Release R1, hold L1, and press ▲,▲. Release L1, hold R1, and press ■,■.
Sword Upgrade	Hold L1+R1 and press ●,■,●,▲,▲,■,●,■.

The Incredibles

Some of these codes only work on certain levels and certain characters. Pause the game, choose Secrets and enter the following:

Unlockable	Code
Blurry Game	LOSTGLASSES
Credits	YOURNAMEINLIGHTS
Ethereal View	EMODE
Eye Laser	GAZERBEAM
Fast Motion Game	SASSMODE
Game 20% Easier	BOAPLACE
Giant Head	EINSTEINIUM
Heads up Display	BHUD
Heavy Iron Logo	HI
Henchmen Bounce More	SPRINGBREAK
Infinite Incredi-Power for Elastigirl	FLEXIBLE
Inverts Aiming Controls for Turrets	INVERTURRET
Inverts Camera Control on the X-axis	INVERTCAMERAX
Inverts Camera Control on the Y-axis	INVERTCAMERAY
Invincible Dash (Damage and Collisions)	GILGENDASH
Mr. Incredible Glows When Swimming	TOWNIE
Mr. Incredible Lights Plants on Fire	PINKSLIP
One Hit Kills	KRONOS
Refill 30 Health	UUDDLRLRBAS
Slow Motion	BWTHEMOVIE
Tiny Head	DEEVOLVE
Unlimited Incredi-Power (Limited Time)	DANIELTHEFLASH
Violet has Infinite Invisibility Power (Limited Time)	TONYLOAF
Weakens Bomb Damage	LABOMBE

Indy Car Challenge

Unlockable	Code
All trading cards	Enter name aLLcARDS.
Start in Pole Position at Indy 500	Enter name pOLE.

James Bond 007: Everything or Nothing

Cheats are unlocked depending on how many platinum 007s you've earned. To activate a cheat once it is unlocked, pause the game and enter the code listed underneath the cheat.

Platinum	Cheat	Code
1	Golden Gun	●,▲,×,●,▲
3	Improved Traction	●,×,×,■,▲
5	Improved Battery	●,■,●,■,▲
7	Double Ammo	●,●,×,●,▲
9	Double Damage	●,▲,▲,■,●
11	Full Ammo	●,●,▲,■,■
13	Cloak	●,▲,×,▲,■
15	Full Battery	●,▲,▲,×,●
17	All Weapons	●,▲,×,×,●
19	Unlimited Battery	●,■,●,■,▲
23	Unlimited Ammo	●,×,■,×,●
25	Slow Motion Driving	●,■,▲,×,▲
27	Platinum Gun	●,■,■,●,×

Unlockable	Objective
All Weapons	17 Platinum
Baron Samedi	50 Points
Burn Chamber	370 Points
Cayenne Upgrade	12 Gold
Cistern	30 Points
Cloak	13 Platinum
Diavolo Moscow	400 Points
Double Ammo	7 Platinum

James Bond 007: Everything or Nothing (cont'd)

Unlockable	Objective
Double Damage	9 Platinum
Egypt Commander	90 Points
Egypt Guard	180 Points
Full Ammo	11 Platinum
Full Battery	15 Platinum
Gallery	27 Gold
Golden Gun	1 Platinum
Hazmat Guard	110 Points
Helicopter Upgrade	6 Gold
Improved Battery	5 Platinum
Improved Traction	3 Platinum
Katya	20 Gold
Katya Jumpsuit	320 Points
Le Rouge	260 Points
Moscow Guard	230 Points
MI6 Combat Simulator	Complete all Missions
MI6 Survival Test	Complete all Missions
Miss Nagai	450 Points
Miss Nagai	17 Gold
Mya	130 Points
Mya	14 Gold
Nanotank Upgrade	24 Gold
Odd Job	70 Points
003	290 Points
Platinum Gun	27 Platinum
Production Stills 1	1 Gold
Production Stills 2	2 Gold
Production Stills 3	3 Gold
Production Stills 4	4 Gold
Production Stills 5	5 Gold
Production Stills 6	7 Gold
Production Stills 7	9 Gold
Production Stills 8	13 Gold
Production Stills 9	16 Gold
Production Stills 10	18 Gold
Production Stills 11	19 Gold
Production Stills 12	22 Gold
Production Stills 13	23 Gold
Production Stills 14	25 Gold
Serena	350 Points
Serena	430 Points
Serena	8 Gold
Slow Motion Driving	25 Platinum
South Commander	210 Points
Tank Upgrade	10 Gold
Test Lab	160 Points
Triumph Upgrade	21 Gold
Underworld	11 Gold
Unlimited Ammo	23 Platinum
Unlimited Battery	19 Platinum
Vanquish Upgrade	15 Gold

Juiced

Enter this passwords in the Password menu.

Unlockable	Password
All Cars in Arcade Mode	PINT

Jikkyou World Soccer 2000

Description	Code
All-Stars Team	Press ↑, ↑, ↓, ↓, ←, →, ←, →, ×, ●, START.

Jurassic Park: Operation Genesis

Description	Code
$10,000	Press L2, ↑, L2, ↓
All Levels	R1, →, →, →, →, R1
Carnivore Agitation	L2, L2, L2, ←, ←, ←
Conjure Twister	←, ↑, →, ↓, L2 + R1
Crash Cheat	Hold L2 + R1 and press ↑, ↓, ↑, ↓, ↑, ↓ repeatedly.
Isla Muerta	R1, R1, R1, L2, →
Kill All Dinosaurs	L2, R1, ↓, R1, L2

Jurassic Park: Operation Genesis (cont'd)

Kill All Guests	Hold R1, then press →, ←, →, ←, →.
Market Day	L2, R1, ↓, L2, R1, ↓
Missing Genes Cheat	↓, R1 + ↑.
No Twisters	Hold R1+L2, then press ←, →. Then press R1+L2 again.
Real Safari Cheat	R1 + L2, ←, ↓, →, →
Sequencing Error	↓, R1 + ↑
Site B	R1, R1, R1, L2
Stormy Weather	R1, R1, L2, R1, ↓, ↑, ↓
Trigger Heat Wave	R1, ↓, R1, ↓, R1, ↓, R1

Karaoke Revolution Volume 2

Enter the following codes at the main title screen.

Unlockable	Code
GMR (Aneeka)	→,←,R3,←,↑,↑,L3,↓,●,■
Harmonix (Ishani)	L3,●,↑,●,■,L3,↓,↓,R3
Konami (Dwyane)	→,R3,→,R3,■,→,●,■,↓,←

Kelly Slater's Pro Surfer

To enter the following codes select the "Extras" option, and then choose "Cheats." Enter each code for the desired unlockable. An "Unlocked" message confirms correct code entry.

Unlockable	Code
All Boards	6195554141
All Objectives Completed	8565558792
All Suits	7025552918
All Surfers	9495556799
All Tricks	6265556043
First-Person View	8775553825 Pause gameplay and choose the "Camera Settings" option to change the view.
Higher Jumps	2175550217
Level Select	3285554497
Master Code	7145558092
Maximum Stats	2125551776
Perfect Balance	2135555721
Play as Freak	3105556217
Play as Rainbow	8185555555
Play as Tiki God	8885554506
Play as Tony Hawk	3235559787
Play as Travis Pastrana	8005556292
Trippy Graphics	8185551447

King of Route 66

Description	Objective
Tornado Truckers for VS Battle	Win Rival Chase 5 times in a row to unlock all of the Tornado Truckers for VS Battle mode.

NOTE

Each win will unlock the Tornado Truckers in this order: Bigfoot, Lizard Tail, Luna Queen, Danny Edge, and Mr. Crown.

Klonoa 2

Description	Objective
Hidden Levels	In each stage are six stars. If you collect all six, you gain a doll that appears on the R1 screen. Collect eight dolls to unlock the first hidden level, and all sixteen for the second.
Music Box	Complete both hidden levels to unlock the Music Box sound test. The first hidden level gives you the first 27 tracks, while the second one gives you the remaining songs.
Pictures in Image Gallery	Each stage has 150 little gems scattered about. If you collect all 150, you'll open up more images in the special image gallery.

Knockout Kings 2001

Select "Modes" from the main menu, then choose "Career." Next choose "New" and type one of the names to unlock the corresponding boxer.

Boxer	Code
Ashy Knucks	MECCA
Barry Sanders	MRBARRY
Bernardo Osuna	OSUNA
Charles Hatcher	HATCHER
Chuck Zito	ZITO
David Bostice	BOSTICE
David Defiagbon	DEFIAGBN
David DeMartini	DEMART
Jason Giambi	JGIAMBI
Joe Mesi	BAILEY
John Botti	JBOTTI
Junior Seau	JRSEAU
Owen Nolan	OWNOLAN
Ray Austin	AUSTIN
Steve Francis	STEVEF
Trevor Nelson	NELSON

Kya: Dark Lineage

Unlockable	Code
Restore Life	Pause the game and press L1,R2,L2,R1,↑,↑,←,■,→,●,START

Le Mans 24 Hours

Enter the following codes as your name at the Championship Mode name screen.

Unlockable	Code
All Cars	ACO
All Championships	NUMBAT
All Tracks	SPEEDY
Le Mans	WOMBAT
See the Credits	HEINEY

Legacy of Kain: Defiance

Pause gameplay to enter the following codes.

Unlockable	Code
All Bonuses	R2,↓,L2,R1,←,L2,↓,L1,▲
All Combo Moves	→,↓,↑,↓,↓,R1,▲,●,↓
All Dark Chronicles	R1,↓,R2,L1,→,R2,▲,↓,L1
All Power Ups	←,←,↑,↑,L1,R2,●,↓,▲
Cartoon Version	↑,↓,↑,↓,R1,R2,↓,●,▲
Full Health and Reaver Charge	←,→,←,→,R1,L1,●,▲,↓
No Textures	L1,↓,R2,→,R2,↑,▲,L1,↓
Tube Reaver	↑,↓,←,→,R2,L2,▲,↓,●
Unlimited Reaver Charge and Balance Emblem	↓,↓,↑,←,R1,R2,↓,▲,●
Wireframe	L1,↓,L1,↑,R1,L2,L1,↓,▲

Legends of Wrestling 2

To access the cheats menu, select Career mode and choose any wrestler. During Career mode, enter one of each of the match types. Either finish the match or immediately exit. After you enter all match types, a message stating that you can now purchase the cheats in the shop appears.

Description	Obective
Andy Kaufman	Select Career mode and choose Jerry Lawler as your wrestler. Defeat Andy Kaufman to unlock him at the shop.
Big John Studd	Select Career mode and choose any wrestler. Defeat Big John Studd to unlock him at the shop.
British Bulldog	Select Career mode and choose Dynamite Kid. Successfully complete Career mode to unlock British Bulldog at the shop.
Bruno Sammartino	Select Career mode and choose Hulk Hogan. Successfully complete Career mode to unlock Bruno Sammartino at the shop.
Owen Hart	Select Career mode and choose Bret Hart. Successfully complete Career mode to unlock Owen Hart at the shop.
Unlimited Green Coins	Successfully complete Career mode with all wrestlers to get unlimited Green Coins.

LEGO Star Wars

In Dexter's Diner, go to Codes and enter the following. This will unlock characters for purchase in Free Play mode.

Character	Code
Battle Droid	987UYR
Battle Droid (Commander)	EN11K5
Battle Droid (Geonosis)	LK42U6
Battle Droid (Security)	KF999A
Big Blasters	IG72X4
Boba Fett	LA811Y
Brushes	SHRUB1
Classic Blasters	L449HD
Clone	F8B4L6
Clone (Episode III, Pilot)	BHU72T
Clone (Episode III, Swamp)	N3T6P8
Clone (Episode III, Walker)	RS6E25
Clone (Episode III)	ER33JN
Count Dooku	14PGMN
Darth Maul	H35TUX
Darth Sidious	A32CAM
Disguised Clone	VR832U
Droideka	DH382U
General Grievous	SF321Y
Geonosian	19D7NB
Gonk Droid	U63B2A
Grievous' Bodyguard	ZTY392
Invincibility	4PR28U
Jango Fett	PL47NH
Ki-Adi Mundi	DP55MV
Kit Fisto	CBR954
Luminara	A725X4
Mace Windu (Episode III)	MS952L
Minikit Detector	LD116B
Moustaches	RP924W
Padme	92UJ7D
PK Droid	R840JU
Princess Leia	BEQ82H
Purple	YD77GC
Rebel Trooper	L54YUK
Royal Guard	PP43JX
Shaak Ti	EUW862
Silhouettes	MS999Q
Silly Blasters	NR37W1
Super Battle Droid	XZNR21
Tea Cups	PUCEAT

Life Line

Unlockable	Objective
Extra Costume	Complete the game once and save, then start a new game with that game save.

The Lord of the Rings: The Return of the King

Accessing the video clips depends on how far you've gone in the game. Here's a table showing what you can find and what level you must complete to find it. For example, you can't see the game concept art slide show until you've successfully completed Paths of the Dead.

Unlockable Video Features

Video Title	Must Complete
Andy Serkis Interview	The Crack of Doom
Billy Boyd Interview	The Crack of Doom
Christopher Lee Interview	The Road to Isengard
David Wenham Interview	The Crack of Doom
Dom Monaghan Interview	The Crack of Doom
Elijah Wood Interview	Shelob's Lair
Film Concept Art	Helm's Deep
Film Production Stills	The Southern Gate
Game Concept Art	Paths of the Dead
Hobbits on Gaming	Helm's Deep
Ian McKellen Interview	Minas Tirith—Top of the Wall
Sean Astin Interview	Escape from Osgiliath

For the following codes:

1. Pause the game so the options menu appears.
2. Hold down all shoulder buttons at once.
3. Enter the code with shoulder buttons still depressed.

   When you've entered the code correctly you'll hear a sound that indicates success.

TIP

If you want to enter more than one code, release the shoulder buttons, then hold them down again before entering each code.

Secret Codes

Code	Usage	Character	PS2 Combo
+1,000 Experience Points	one-time use	Gimli	●,●,▲,✕
+1,000 Experience Points	one-time use	Gandalf	●,▲,↑,↓
+1,000 Experience Points	one-time use	Merry	↓,↓,■,✕
+1,000 Experience Points	one-time use	Frodo	↓,▲,↑,↓
+1,000 Experience Points	one-time use	Faramir	■,▲,↑,■
+1,000 Experience Points	one-time use	Aragorn	↑,■,▲,✕
+1,000 Experience Points	one-time use	Sam	▲,✕,↓,✕
+1,000 Experience Points	one-time use	Pippin	▲,✕,■,✕
+1,000 Experience Points	one-time use	Legolas	✕,▲,↑,✕
3 Hit Combo for	on/off	Gandalf	↓,✕,▲,↓
3 Hit Combo for	on/off	Aragorn	■,↓,●,↑
3 Hit Combo for	on/off	Frodo	■,↓,▲,■
3 Hit Combo for	on/off	Faramir	■,▲,↑,▲
3 Hit Combo for	on/off	Legolas	■,▲,▲,●

The Lord of the Rings: The Return of the King (cont'd)

Code	Usage	Character	PS2 Combo
3 Hit Combo for	on/off	Sam	■,×,●,■
3 Hit Combo for	on/off	Gimli	↑,■,●,■
3 Hit Combo for	on/off	Pippin	↑,↑,■,●
3 Hit Combo for	on/off	Merry	▲,×,↑,▲
4 Hit Combo for	on/off	Frodo	↓,■,↓,●
4 Hit Combo for	on/off	Gandalf	↓,▲,↑,●
4 Hit Combo for	on/off	Merry	■,×,■,■
4 Hit Combo for	on/off	Sam	↑,↓,▲,▲
4 Hit Combo for	on/off	Aragorn	↑,■,▲,↓
4 Hit Combo for	on/off	Gimli	▲,■,↑,×
4 Hit Combo for	on/off	Legolas	×,●,▲,■
4 Hit Combo for	on/off	Faramir	×,■,↑,×
4 Hit Combo for	on/off	Pippin	×,×,↓,●
All Actor Interviews	one-time use	Special Features	×,■,×,↑
All Experience you get, your buddy gets	on/off	Co-op	↓,×,×,×
All Health you get, your buddy gets	on/off	Co-op	▲,↑,■,■
All Upgrades	one-time use	Any Character	↑,↓,▲,■
Always Devastating	on/off	Any Character	▲,↑,▲,↓
Infinite Re-spawns for Co-op	on/off	All	●,■,↑,●
Infinite Missiles	on/off	Any Character	■,■,↓,●
Invulnerable	on/off	Any Character	■,●,■,↑
Level 2 Skills	on/off	Merry	●,↓,■,■
Level 2 Skills	on/off	Aragorn	●,▲,×,▲
Level 2 Skills	on/off	Sam	●,×,●,▲
Level 2 Skills	on/off	Gandalf	↓,▲,×,▲
Level 2 Skills	on/off	Pippin	↓,×,↓,↑
Level 2 Skills	on/off	Legolas	■,■,●,■
Level 2 Skills	on/off	Gimli	↑,●,■,■
Level 2 Skills	on/off	Frodo	▲,↑,↓,●
Level 2 Skills	on/off	Faramir	×,■,×,↓
Level 4 Skills	on/off	Legolas	↓,↓,×,×
Level 4 Skills	on/off	Aragorn	↓,■,●,■
Level 4 Skills	on/off	Merry	■,×,●,↓
Level 4 Skills	on/off	Sam	↑,↓,■,×
Level 4 Skills	on/off	Gimli	▲,■,↓,↑
Level 4 Skills	on/off	Frodo	▲,↑,●,↓
Level 4 Skills	on/off	Gandalf	▲,↑,■,×
Level 4 Skills	on/off	Pippin	×,↓,↓,↓
Level 4 Skills	on/off	Faramir	×,×,■,■
Level 6 Skills	on/off	Pippin	●,▲,●,▲
Level 6 Skills	on/off	Aragorn	●,▲,■,■
Level 6 Skills	on/off	Legolas	↓,●,↑,↓
Level 6 Skills	on/off	Merry	↓,↓,■,▲
Level 6 Skills	on/off	Sam	↓,↓,↑,↑
Level 6 Skills	on/off	Frodo	↓,↓,×,▲

The Lord of the Rings: The Return of the King (cont'd)

Code	Usage	Character	PS2 Combo
Level 6 Skills	on/off	Gimli	↓,▲,↓,■
Level 6 Skills	on/off	Gandalf	▲,▲,×,↑
Level 6 Skills	on/off	Faramir	▲,×,↓,●
Level 8 Skills	on/off	Frodo	●,●,↓,↓
Level 8 Skills	on/off	Sam	●,●,▲,▲
Level 8 Skills	on/off	Faramir	●,↓,↓,↓
Level 8 Skills	on/off	Gandalf	●,■,↓,↓
Level 8 Skills	on/off	Merry	↓,▲,×,■
Level 8 Skills	on/off	Legolas	■,↑,↑,↓
Level 8 Skills	on/off	Pippin	■,↑,↑,●
Level 8 Skills	on/off	Aragorn	↑,■,▲,↑
Level 8 Skills	on/off	Gimli	×,●,↓,■
Perfect Mode	on/off	Any Character	●,↓,▲,×
Restore Health	one-time use	Any Character	■,■,●,●
Restore Missiles	one-time use	Gimli	●,●,●,×
Restore Missiles	one-time use	Merry	■,●,●,▲
Restore Missiles	one-time use	Pippin	↑,●,↓,■
Restore Missiles	one-time use	Gandalf	▲,↓,×,■
Restore Missiles	one-time use	Aragorn	▲,■,■,▲
Restore Missiles	one-time use	Faramir	▲,↑,×,×
Restore Missiles	one-time use	Legolas	▲,▲,▲,↓
Restore Missiles	one-time use	Frodo	▲,▲,▲,●
Restore Missiles	one-time use	Sam	×,×,●,×
Targeting Indicator Mode	on/off	Any Character	↓,●,↑,■
Unlock Secret Character	one-time use	Frodo	▲,●,●,●
Unlock Secret Character	one-time use	Frodo	●,■,■,×
Unlock Secret Character	one-time use	Pippin	▲,●,■,↓
Unlock Secret Character	one-time use	Merry	×,↓,↓,×
Unlock Secret Character	one-time use	Faramir	×,×,▲,▲
Unlock Special Abilities for	on/off	Gimli	●,■,×,●
Unlock Special Abilities for	on/off	Aragorn	↓,●,▲,▲
Unlock Special Abilities for	on/off	Pippin	■,×,●,▲
Unlock Special Abilities for	on/off	Sam	↑,●,×,●
Unlock Special Abilities for	on/off	Gandalf	↑,↓,▲,●
Unlock Special Abilities for	on/off	Faramir	↑,■,●,↑
Unlock Special Abilities for	on/off	Merry	↑,▲,●,●
Unlock Special Abilities for	on/off	Legolas	▲,●,×,●
Unlock Special Abilities for	on/off	Frodo	▲,×,↓,×

The Lord of the Rings: The Two Towers

To access the unlockable, pause gameplay, hold L1+L2+R1+R2, and enter the required button combinations.

Description	Code
Add 1,000 Experience Points	Press ×, ↓, ↓, ↓.
Level 2 Skills	Press ●, →, ●, →.
Level 3 Skills	Press ▲, ↑, ▲, ↑.
Level 4 Skills	Press ▲, ↑, ▲, ↑.

The Lord of the Rings: The Two Towers
(cont'd)

Description	Code
Level 5 Skills	Press ×, ×, ↓, ↓.
Level 6 Skills	Press ■, ←, ■, ←.
Level 8 Skills	Press ×, ×, ↓, ↓.
Restore Ammunition	Press ×, ↓, ▲, ↑.

The following codes require that you first complete the game before enabling the code. To access the unlockable, pause gameplay, hold L1+L2+R1+R2, and and enter the required button combinations.

Unlockable	Code
All Combo Upgrades	Press ▲, ●, ▲, ●.
All Skills	Press ▲, ●, ▲, ●.
Devastating Attacks	Press ■ ,■, ●, ●. Hold ▲ during battles to do devastating attacks.
Invincibility	Press ▲, ■, ×, ●.
Slow Motion	Press ▲, ●, ×, ■.
Small Enemies	Press ▲, ▲, ×, ×.
Unlimited Missile Weapons	Press ■, ●, ×, ▲.

Mace Griffin: Bounty Hunter

To enter the following, select the Electro-Cosh and press the corresponding buttons.

Description	Code
Auto-Focus Mode	L2, R1, L2, R1, ×, ●, ●, ×, ●, ×
Big Head Mode	L2, R1, L2, R1, ×, ●, ●, ×, ●, ●
Detach Camera	L2, R1, L2, R1, ×, ●, ●, ×, ▲, ■
Double Damage	L2, R1, L2, R1, ×, ●, ●, ×, ▲, ▲
Hand of God Mode	L2, R1, L2, R1, ×, ●, ●, ×, ×, ×
Infinite Ammo	L2, R1, L2, R1, ×, ●, ●, ×, ■, ■
Invulnerability	L2, R1, L2, R1, ×, ●, ●, ×, ■, ▲

Unlockable	Code
All Sections	L2, R1, L2, R1, ×, ×, ●, ●, ■, ■
Skip to Next Level	L2, R1, L2, R1, ×, ×, ●, ●, ■, ●

Madagascar

Enter these codes while playing.

Unlockable	Code
All power-ups	●,×,×,●,▲,L1,■,R1,L1
Invincibility	↑,↓,×,×,R1,L1,R2,L2,▲,■,●
Level select	R1,R1,●,L2,L1,×,▲,R1,▲

Madden NFL 2001

After scoring a touchdown, immediately hold the following buttons to see its corresponding celebration.

Celebration	Code
Hip Thrust	L1+■
Jump Spike	L1+●
Say a Prayer	L1+▲
Shoulder Shake	L1+R1
Slam Dunk	L1+R2
Spike the Football	L1+×

Madden NFL 2001 (cont'd)

Unlimited Creation Points: Create a player. Go into the "Edit Player" option at the Roster screen. Use ↑ or ↓ to choose the player you want to modify. Press → to get to the speed category. Press ×, ×.

Madden NFL 2004

Description	Objective
1990 Eagles Classic Team	Earn Level 4 EA Sports Bio
Bingo! Cheat	Earn Level 2 EA Sports Bio
Steve Spurrier Coach	Earn Level 6 EA Sports Bio

Madden NFL 2005

From My Madden menu, go to Madden Cards, Madden Codes, and enter the following:

Card	Password
Aaron Brooks Gold Card	_J95K1J
Aaron Glenn Gold Card	Q48E9G
Adewale Ogunleye Gold Card	C12E9E
Ahman Green Gold Card	T86L4C
Al Wilson Gold Card	G72G2R
Alan Faneca Gold Card	U32S9C
Amani Toomer Gold Card	Z75G6M
Andre Carter Gold Card	V76E2Q
Andre Johnson Gold Card	E34S1M
Andy Reid Gold Card	N44K1L
Anquan Boldin Gold Card	S32F7K
Antoine Winfield Gold Card	A12V7Z
Bill Cowher Gold Card	S54T6U
Brad Hopkins Gold Card	P44A8B
Bret Favre Gold Card	L61D7B
Brian Billick Gold Card	L27C4K
Brian Dawkins Gold Card	Y47B8Y
Brian Simmons Gold Card	S22M6A
Brian Urlacher Gold Card	Z34J4U
Brian Westbrook Gold Card	V46I2I
Bubba Franks Gold Card	U77F2W
Butch Davis Gold Card	G77L6F
Byron Leftwich Gold Card	C55V5C
Carson Palmer Gold Card	O36V2H
Casey Hampton Gold Card	Z11P9T
Chad Johnson Gold Card	R85S2A
Chad Pennington Gold Card	B64L2F
Champ Bailey Gold Card	K89O9E
Charles Rogers Gold Card	E57K9Y
Charles Woodson Gold Card	F95N9J
Chris Hovan Gold Card	F14C6J
Corey Simon Gold Card	R11D7K
Courtney Brown Gold Card	R42R75
Curtis Martin Gold Card	K47X3G
Dallas Coach Gold Card	O24U1Q
Damien Woody Gold Card	F78I1I
Dante Hall Gold Card	B23P8D
Dat Nguyen Gold Card	Q86I2S
Daunte Culpepper Gold Card	O62O9K
Dave Wannstedt Gold Card	W73D7D
David Boston Gold Card	A25I9F
David Carr Gold Card	C16E2Q
Dennis Erickson Gold Card	J83E3T
Dennis Green Gold Card	C18J7T
Derrick Brooks Gold Card	P93I9Q
Derrick Mason Gold Card	S98P3T
Deuce McAllister Gold Card	D11H4J
Dexter Coakley Gold Card	L35K1A
Dexter Jackson Gold Card	G16B2I
Dick Vermeil Gold Card	F68V1W
Dom Capers Gold Card	B97I6R
Domanick Davis Gold Card	L58S3J
Donnie Edwards Gold Card	E18Y5Z
Donovin Darius Gold Card	Q11T7T
Donovon McNabb Gold Card	T98J1I
Donte Stallworth Gold Card	R75W3M
Dre Bly Gold Card	H19Q2O
Drew Bledsoe Gold Card	W73M3E
Dwight Freeney Gold Card	G76U2L
Edgerrin James Gold Card	A75D7X
Ed Reed Gold Card	G18Q2B
Eric Moulds Gold Card	H34Z8K
Flozell Adams Gold Card	R54T1O
Fred Taylor Gold Card	I87X9Y
Grant Wistrom Gold Card	E46M4Y
Herman Edwards Gold Card	O19T2T

Madden NFL 2005 (cont'd)

Card	Password
Hines Ward Gold Card	M12B8F
Jack Del Rio Gold Card	J22P9I
Jake Delhomme Gold Card	M86N9F
Jake Plummer Gold Card	N74P8X
Jamie Sharper Gold Card	W27I7G
Jason Taylor Gold Card	O33S6I
Jason Webster Gold Card	M74B3E
Jeff Fisher Gold Card	N62B6J
Jeff Garcia Gold Card	H32H7B
Jeremy Newberry Gold Card	J77Y8C
Jeremy Shockey Gold Card	R34X5T
Jerry Porter Gold Card	F71Q9Z
Jerry Rice Gold Card	K34F8S
Jevon Kearse Gold Card	A78B1C
Jim Haslett Gold Card	G78R3W
Jim Mora Jr. Gold Card	N46C3M
Jimmy Smith Gold Card	I22J5W
Joe Horn Gold Card	P91A1Q
Joey Harrington Gold Card	Z68W8J
John Fox Gold Card	Q98R7Y
Jon Gruden Gold Card	H61I8A
Josh McCown Gold Card	O33Y4X
Julian Peterson Gold Card	M89J8A
Julius Peppers Gold Card	X54O4Z
Junior Seau Gold Card	W26K6Q
Kabeer Gbaja-Biamala Gold Card	U16I9Y
Keith Brooking Gold Card	E12P4S
Keith Bulluck Gold Card	M63N6V
Kendrell Bell Gold Card	T96C7J
Kevan Barlow Gold Card	A23T5E
Kevin Mawae Gold Card	L76E6S
Kris Jenkins Gold Card	W63O3K
Kyle Boller Gold Card	A72F9X
Kyle Turley Gold Card	Y46A8V
LaDainian Tomlinson Gold Card	M64D4E
LaVar Arrington Gold Card	F19Q8W
Laveranues Coles Gold Card	R98I5S
Lawyer Milloy Gold Card	M37Y5B
La'Roi Glover Gold Card	K24L9K
Lee Suggs Gold Card	Z94X6Q
Leonard Davis Gold Card	H14M2V
Lovie Smith Gold Card	L38V3A
Marc Bulger Gold Card	U66B4S

Card	Password
Marcel Shipp Gold Card	R42X2L
Marcus Stroud Gold Card	E56I5O
Marcus Trufant Gold Card	R46T5U
Mark Brunell Gold Card	B66D9J
Marshall Faulk Gold Card	U76G1U
Marty Booker Gold Card	P51U4B
Marty Schottenheimer Gold Card	D96A7S
Marvin Harrison Gold Card	T11E8O
Marvin Lewis Gold Card	P24S4H
Matt Hasselback Gold Card	R68D5F
Michael Bennett Gold Card	W81W2J
Michael Strahan Gold Card	O66T6K
Michael Vick Gold Card	H67B1F
Mike Alstott Gold Card	D89F6W
Mike Brown Gold Card	F12J8N
Mike Martz Gold Card	R64A8E
Mike Mularkey Gold Card	C56D6E
Mike Rucker Gold Card	K89O6S
Mike Shanahan Gold Card	H15L5Y
Mike Sherman Gold Card	F84X6K
Mike Tice Gold Card	Y31T6Y
New England Coach Gold Card	N24L4Z
Nick Barnett Gold Card	X95I7S
Norv Turner Gold Card	F24K1M
Olin Kreutz Gold Card	R17R2O
Orlando Pace Gold Card	U42U9U
Patrick Surtain Gold Card	H58T9X
Peerless Price Gold Card	X75V6K
Peter Warrick Gold Card	D86P8O
Peyton Manning Gold Card	L48H4U
Plaxico Burress Gold Card	K18P6J
Priest Holmes Gold Card	X91N1L
Quentin Jammer Gold Card	V55S3Q
Randy Moss Gold Card	W79U7X
Ray Lewis Gold Card	B94X6V
Reggie Wayne Gold Card	R29S8C
Rex Grossman Gold Card	C46P2A
Rich Gannon Gold Card	Q69I1Y
Richard Seymour Gold Card	L69T4T
Ricky Williams Gold Card	P19V1N
Rod Smith Gold Card	V22C4L
Rodney Harrison Gold Card	O84I3J
Ronde Barber Gold Card	J72X8W

Madden NFL 2005 (cont'd)

Card	Password
Roy Williams Gold Card	J76C6F
Rudi Johnson Gold Card	W26J6H
Sam Madison Gold Card	Z87T5C
Samari Rolle Gold Card	C69H4Z
Santana Moss Gold Card	H79E5B
Seattle Coach Gold Card	V58U4Y
Shaun Alexander Gold Card	C95Z4P
Shaun Ellis Gold Card	Z54F2B
Shawn Rogers Gold Card	J97X8M
Shawn Springs Gold Card	Z28D2V
Simeon Rice Gold Card	S62F9T
Stephen Davis Gold Card	E39X9L
Steve Mariucci Gold Card	V74Q3N
Steve McNair Gold Card	S36T1I
Steve Smith Gold Card	W91O2O
Takeo Spikes Gold Card	B83A6C
Tedy Bruschi Gold Card	K28Q3P
Terence Newman Gold Card	W57Y5P
Terrell Suggs Gold Card	V71A9Q
Tiki Barber Gold Card	T43A2V
T.J. Duckett Gold Card	P67E1I
Todd Heap Gold Card	H19M1G
Tom Brady Gold Card	X22V7E
Tom Coughlin Gold Card	S71D6H
Tony Dungy Gold Card	Y96R8V
Tony Gonzalez Gold Card	N46E9N
Torry Holt Gold Card	W96U7E
Travis Henry Gold Card	F36M2Q
Trent Green Gold Card	Y46M4S
Ty Law Gold Card	F13W1Z
Walter Jones Gold Card	G57P1P
Washington Coach Gold Card	W63V9L
Will Shields Gold Card	B52S8A
Zach Thomas Gold Card	U63I3H

Secret Teams

Card	Password
1958 Colts	_P74X8J
1966 Packers	G49P7W
1968 Jets	C24W2A
1970 Browns	G12N1I
1972 Dolphins	R79W6W
1974 Steelers	R12D9B
1976 Raiders	P96Q8M
1977 Broncos	O18T2A
1978 Dolphins	G97U5X
1980 Raiders	K71K4E
1981 Chargers	Y27N9A
1982 Redskins	F56D6V
1983 Raiders	D23T8S
1984 Dolphins	X23Z8H
1985 Bears	F92M8M
1986 Giants	K44F2Y
1988 49ers	F77R8H
1990 Eagles	G95F2Q
1991 Lions	I89F4I
1992 Cowboys	I44A1O
1993 Bills	Y66K3O

Secret Stadiums

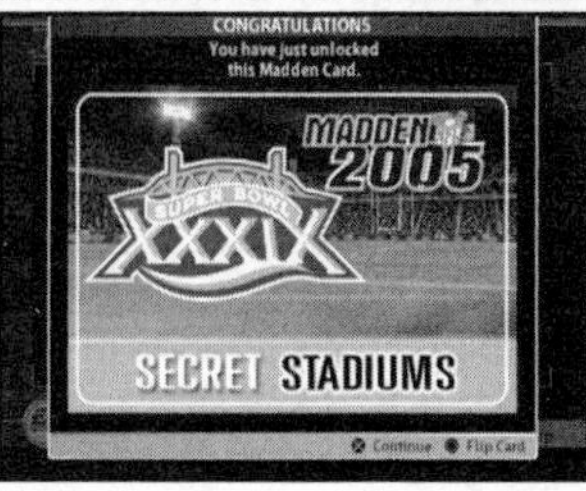

Stadium	Password
Pro Bowl Hawaii '05	G67F5X
Super Bowl XL	O85P6I
Super Bowl XLI	P48Z4D
Super Bowl XLII	T67R1O
Super Bowl XXXIX	D58F1B

Madden NFL 2005 (cont'd)

Pump Up and Cheerleader Cards

Card	Password
49ers Cheerleader	_X61T6L
Bears Pump Up Crowd	K17F2I
Bengals Cheerleader	Y22S6G
Bills Cheerleader	F26S6X
Broncos Cheerleader	B85U5C
Browns Pump Up Crowd	B65Q1L
Buccaneers Cheerleader	Z55Z7S

Card	Password
Cardinals Cheerleader	Q91W5L
Chargers Cheerleader	Q68S3F
Chiefs Cheerleader	T46M6T
Colts Cheerleader	M22Z6H
Cowboys Cheerleader	J84E3F
Dolphins Cheerleader	E88T2J
Eagles Cheerleader	Q88P3Q
Falcons Cheerleader	W86F3F
Giants Pump Up Crowd	L13Z9J
Jaguars Cheerleader	K32C2A
Jets Pump Up Crowd	S45W1M
Lions Pump Up Crowd	C18F4G
Packers Pump Up Crowd	K26Y4V
Panthers Cheerleader	M66N4D
Patriots Cheerleader	O59P9C
Raiders Cheerleader	G92L2E
Rams Cheerleader	W73B8X
Ravens Cheerleader	P98T6C
Redskins Cheerleader	N19D6Q
Saints Cheerleader	R99G2F
Seahawks Cheerleader	A35T8R
Steelers Pump Up Crowd	C98I2V
Texans Cheerleader	R74G3W
Titans Cheerleader	Q81V4N
Vikings Cheerleader	E26H4L

Pump Up and Cheerleader Cards

Card	Description	Code
3rd Down	For one half, your opponent has 3 downs to get a first down.	_Z28X8K
5th Down	For one half, you will have 5 downs to get a first down.	P66C4L
Bingo!	Your defensive interceptions increase by 75% for the game.	J33I8F
Da Bomb	You will receive unlimited pass range for one half.	B61A8M
Da Boot	You will receive unlimited field goal range for one half.	I76X3T
Extra Credit	Awards 4 points for every interception and 3 points for every sack.	M89S8G
1st and 15	Requires your opponent to get 15 yards to reach a first down for one half.	V65J8P
1st and 5	Your first down yards to go will be set to 5 for one half.	O72E9B
Fumblitis	Your opponent's fumbles will increase by 75% for the game.	R14B8Z
Human Plow	Your Broken Tackles will increase by 75% for the game.	L96J7P
Lame Duck	Your opponent will throw a lob pass for one half.	D57R5S
Mistake Free	You can't fumble or throw an interception for one half.	X78P9Z
Mr. Mobility	Your QB can't get sacked for one half.	Y59R8R
Super Dive	Your diving distance increases by 75% for the game.	D59K3Y
Tight Fit	Your opponent's uprights will be made very narrow for one half.	V34L6D
Unforced Errors	Your opponent will fumble every time he tries to juke for one half.	L48G1E

PSP Xbox PS2 GC GBA

Mafia

Unlockable	Objective
Car Selection	Learn to break into cars during missions. This will allow you to use it in Free Ride.
City Selection	Progress through story mode to unlock more areas for Free Ride.
Monster Truck	Take first place in all of the races in Racing Championship mode.
Time of Day	Progress through story mode to unlock a Day/Night option for Free Ride.

Magic Pengel: Color

Description	Objective
Kiba's Letter 1 Page	Get 1,000,000 gold gems.

Manhunt

Unlockable	Code
God Mode	After finishing the game on Fetish Mode, enter ↓,↓,●,↑,■,▲,■, R2,↑,↑,L1,▲ at the Title Screen.

The Mark of Kri

Enter the following codes at the Title Screen (where it says "Press Start"). If you enter them correctly, you will hear Rau give a vocal cue.

Unlockable	Code
All Enemies Tougher	×,●,■,■,×,■,●,●,×,●,●,×
Invincible Rau	■,●,×,■,●,■,×,●,×,■,●,×
Stronger Health Pickups	×,×,×,×,■,■,■,■,●,●,●,●
Turn off Arena A.I.	×,●,●,●,×,■,■,■,×,●,■,×
Unlimited Arrows	×,●,■,■,×,■,●,●,×,■,■,×
Wimpy Enemies	×,●,●,■,×,■,■,●

Mat Hoffman's Pro BMX 2

Quickly press the following buttons when "Press Start" appears. A sound confirms correct code entry.

Unlockable	Code
All Music Tracks	L1, ←, ←, →, →, →, ×, ×
Big Foot's FMV Sequences	R1, ↑, ↓, ←, ×, ×, ×, R1
BMX Costume	●, ▲, ←, →, ←, ●
Boston Level in Road Trip Mode	■, ↑, ↓, ↓, ↑, ■
Chicago Level in Road Trip Mode	■, ↑, ▲, ↑, ▲, ■
Cory Nastazio's FMV Sequences	R1, ■, ●, ●, ■, ■, ■, R1
Day Smith's FMV Sequences	R1, ●, ←, ←, ■, →, →, R1
Elvis Costume	●, L1, L1, ↑, ↑
Fiery Hands and Feet	↓, ▲, ▲, ×, ×, R1, R1
Invisible Bikes	↓, ↑, ←, ↓, →, ↓, ←, ↑
Joe Kowalski's FMV Sequences	R1, ↑, ×, ▲, ↓, R1
Kevin Robinson's FMV Sequences	R1, ×, ▲, ↓, ↑, R1
Kid's Bike	×, ←, ←, L1, R1, ← Alternately, after you release the Medi-vac chopper and save the downed biker in Chicago, go to the location of the ambulance to find the bike.
Las Vegas Level in Road Trip Mode	■, R1, ←, L1, →, ■
Los Angeles Level in Road Trip Mode	■, ←, ▲, ▲, ←, ■
Mat Hoffman's FMV Sequences	R1, ←, ●, ←, ●, ←, R1

Mat Hoffman's Pro BMX 2 (cont'd)

Level Select	■, →, →, ▲, ↓, ■ See Note.
Mike Escamilla's FMV Sequences	R1, ●, ×, ×, ●, ×, ×, R1
Nate Wessel's FMV Sequences	R1, ↓, ▲, ●, ↓, ▲, ●, R1
New Orleans Level in Road Trip Mode	■, ↓, →, ↑, ←, ■
Perfect Balance	↓, ↑, ●, ↓, ↑, ●, ↓, ↑, ●
Play as Big Foot	▲, →, ↑, →, ↑, ■
Play as Day Smith	▲, ↑, ↓, ↑, ↓, ■
Play as the Mime	▲, ←, →, ←, →, ← Alternately, find all the gaps in the game.
Play as Vanessa	▲, ↓, ←, ←, ↓, ■
Play as Volcano	▲, ↑, ↑, ×, ↑, ↑, ×
Portland Level in Road Trip Mode	■, ×, ×, ▲, ▲, ■
Rick Thorne's FMV Sequences	R1, L1, →, R1, ←, R1
Ruben Alcantara's FMV Sequences	R1, ←, →, ←, →, ←, →, R1
Seth Kimbrough's FMV Sequences	R1, ↑, ↑, ●, ●, ●, R1
Simon Tabron's FMV Sequences	R1, L1, L1, R1, L1, L1, R1
Special Meter Always Full	↓, ×, ×, ×, R1, R1, R1
Tiki Battle Mode	L1, L1, ↓, R1, ×, L1

TIP

To disable the codes, quickly enter almost any code when "Press Start" appears, and add an extra R1 at the end. A different sound confirms correct code entry.

NOTE

Level Select Note

This code does not unlock all levels in Road Trip mode; only in Freeride, Session, and Multiplayer modes.

Max Payne

Unlockable	Code
All Weapons and Full Ammo	Pause the game and press L1,L2,R1,R2,▲,●,×,■.
Infinite Health	Pause the game and press L1,L1,L2,L2,R1,R1,R2,R2.
Level Select	Finish the first chapter of the Subway. Return to the Main Menu and press ↑,↓,←,→,↑,←,↓,●.
Slow Motion Sounds	Pause the game and press L1,L2,R1,R2,▲,■,×,●.
Unlimited Bullet Time	Pause the game and press L1,L2,R1,R2,▲,×,×,▲.

Max Payne 2

Unlockable	Objective
Second Ending	Complete game on Dead on Arrival mode.

Maximo

Unlockable	Objective
Gallery Mode	Collect the Sorceress kiss at the end of each level. Seat each of the four kisses to a power-up position. Once the game is completed, the art gallery will be unlocked.
Mastery Mode	Have a 100 percent mastery ranking at the end of the game for all levels except those in the Hub. To master a level, you must kill every enemy and find every hidden chest.

Maximo vs. Army of Zin

Unlockable	Objective
Art Gallery 1	Master The First Strike
Art Gallery 2	Master Into the Fire
Art Gallery 3	Master No Sanctuary
Art Gallery 4	Master The House Crasher
Art Gallery 5	Master Forest of Fear
Art Gallery 6	Master Gallows Gorge
Art Gallery 7	Master Sinister Stones
Art Gallery 8	Master Cyclocks
Art Gallery 9	Master Down with the Ship
Art Gallery 10	Master Rad to Hawkmoor
Art Gallery 11	Master Perilous Path
Art Gallery 12	Master The Under hive
Art Gallery 13	Master Old Wounds
Art Gallery 14	Master The Great Vault
Art Gallery 15	Master Drained Depths
Art Gallery 16	Master Sunken City
Art Gallery 17	Master Guardian of the Deep
Art Gallery 18	Master The Soulcrusher
Art Gallery 19	Master Tinker's Rescue
Art Gallery 20	Master The Master of the Zin

MDK2 Armageddon

Description	Code
A Little Piece of Home	While playing through Level 5, take a moment to stop and look through the alien telescope. To activate the telescope, first destroy the BottRock Generator and the panel on the ledge above the telescope. Shoot the telescope lens to move it into a position where you can see animator Russ Rice on a Bioware balcony hangin' with some pals.
Drop Camera (This makes a new camera effect.)	Hold L2+R2, press ●, ×, ●, × and the camera drops in place. As you move, the perspective changes like in Resident Evil. To return the camera to normal, repeat the code.
Farting Doc	At any time while playing the Doctor hold down L2+R2, and press in on both control sticks.
Invincibility	First pause the game. Now while holding L2+R2, press ↑, ↑, ↓, ↓, ←, ←, →, →, ■, ▲, ■, ▲, SELECT, START.
King of the Coneheads	In the Spider Room of Level 7, one of the Sniper Balls unleashes a pack of Coneheads. Rather than shooting them, stand around and wait. If you look carefully into the middle of the room while standing on the upper ledge, you may see the King of the Coneheads!
Kurt in His Boxer Shorts	At the main menu, press and hold L2 + R2 and press: ■, ■, ▲, ■. As soon as Kurt is done skydiving and is on the ground, he'll be without his coil suit and sporting boxer shorts.
Matrix Camera Mode	Pause the game, then press L1+R1. This code removes the Pause menu, giving you an unobstructed view of the spinning Matrix Camera mode while the game is paused.
Max's Slo Mo Mode	While holding down Max's Shoot button, press Max's Equip Weapons button three times.

MDK2 Armageddon (cont'd)

Description	Code
The MDK 2 Development Team Are Stars	While playing through Level 4 don't forget to take a moment to gaze at the stars in the large arena with the three Poopsy Generators. Kill all of the enemies in this room first so you can star gaze without getting killed. Now, using Kurt Hectic's sniper scope, zoom in on certain special stars in the sky (they are usually slightly pinkish in color). There you will find the crack team that made MDK2 possible gazing back down at you, along with their Wu-Tang Clan names.

Medal of Honor European Assault

To unlock the ability to enter cheats, go to the Pause Menu and enter the Activate Cheat Entry code.

Unlockable	Code
Active Cheat Entry	Hold L1+R1 then press ●,●,←,▲,●,✕
Player Suicide (SP only)	✕,▲,●,→,▲,●
Hide HUD	●,↓,●,↑,▲,●
Kill Nemesis	↓,L2,R2,↑,■
Pickup OSS Document	↑,✕,R2,R1,↑,■
Disable Shellshock	L2,R1,L2,▲,▲,▲

Medal of Honor: Frontline

Enter the following codes at the Enigma Machine. Green lights will confirm correct code entry. Select the "Bonus" option under the Enigma Machine to enable or disable the cheat.

Description	Code
Achilles' Head Mode (Nazis can be killed only with a headshot when this cheat is active.)	GLASSJAW
Bullet Shield Mode (Bullets will not damage you.)	BULLETZAP
Complete Current Mission with Gold Star	MONKEY
Complete Previous Mission with Gold Star	TIMEWARP
Invisible Enemies (You will see only your enemies' guns and helmets.)	WHERERU
Making of D-Day FMV Sequence	BACKSTAGEO
Making of Needle in a Haystack FMV Sequence	BACKSTAGER
Making of Rolling Thunder FMV Sequence	BACKSTAGEI
Making of Several Bridges Too Far FMV Sequence	BACKSTAGEF
Making of Storm in the Port FMV Sequence	BACKSTAGET
Making of The Horten's Nest FMV Sequence	BACKSTAGES
Master Code	DAWOIKS
Men with Hats (Characters will have various objects on their heads.)	HABRDASHR
Mission 2 (A Storm in the Port)	ORANGUTAN
Mission 3 (Needle in a Haystack)	BABOON
Mission 4 (Several Bridges Too Far)	CHIMPNZEE
Mission 5 (Rolling Thunder)	LEMUR
Mission 6 (The Horten's Nest)	GORILLA
Mohton Torpedoes (Your bullets will change into "photon torpedoes.")	TPDOMOHTON
Perfectionist (Nazis kill you with one shot.)	URTHEMAN
Rubber Grenade Mode	BOING
Silver Bullet Mode (Silver Bullet mode allows enemies to be killed with one shot.)	WHATYOUGET
Snipe-O-Rama Mode (All guns can zoom like a sniper rifle.)	LONGSHOT

Medal of Honor: Frontline (cont'd)

Enter the following codes while the game is paused. The game will automatically resume after correct code entry.

Unlockable	Code
Invincibility	■, L1, ●, R1, ▲, L2, SELECT, R2
Unlimited Ammunition	●, L2, ■, L1, SELECT, R2, ▲, SELECT

TIP

To get the EA LA Medal of Valor, complete the game with a Gold Star in every mission.

Medal of Honor: Rising Sun

Go to the Options screen and select Password. Enter the following codes. You will hear a chime to confirm code entry.

Unlockable	Code
All Missions	BUTTERFLY—Go to Mission Select and pick the desired level.
Invisible Soldiers	TRIGGER
Unlimited Ammo	GOBY

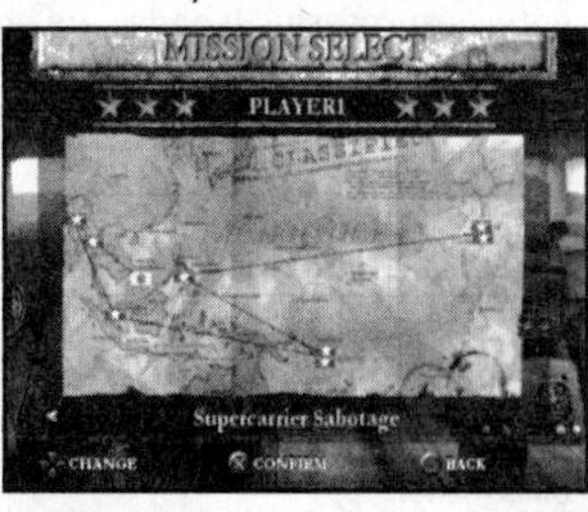

Mega Man Anniversary Collection

Unlockable	Code
Atomic Planet Credits	Defeat the first 3 bosses of Mega Man 1.
G4TV Interview/Retrospective	Complete Mega Man 8.
Homage to Mega Man Song	Complete Mega Man 2.
Mega Man 2: All energy tanks	A5 B1 B3 C4 D2 D3 E1 E4 E5
Mega Man 2: All weapons, items, and 4 energy tanks	A5 B2 B4 C1 C3 C5 D4 D5 E2
Mega Man 2: The Power Fighters	Complete Mega Man 7.
Mega Man 3: All weapons, items, 9 energy tanks, and no Dr. Wily Robots	Blue: A3 B5 D3 F4 Red: A6
Mega Man 4: All weapons and items	A1 A4 B5 E2 F1 F3
Mega Man 5: All weapons and items	Blue: B4 D6 F1 Red: C1 D4 F6
Mega Man 6: All weapons and items	B6 D4 F2 F4 F6
Mega Man 7: R.U.S.H., super rocket arm, 999 bolts, 4 Birds, 4 energy & weapon tanks, SP tank, energy bolt, exit, all weapons, shield, robot screw, all bosses dead	7853 5842 2245 7515
Mega Man Drum & Bass Song	Defeat the first three bosses of Mega Man 8.
Mega Man Power Fighters	Complete Mega Man 3.
Mega Man Radio Cut song	Complete Mega Man 7.
Mega Man: The Power Battles	Complete Mega Man 3.
Picture Set 1	Complete Mega Man 2.
Picture Set 2	Complete Mega Man 4.
Picture Set 3	Complete Mega Man 8.

Mega Man Anniversary Collection (cont'd)

Plant Man remix song	Defeat Plant Man in Mega Man 5.
Power Battle	Defeat Needle Man in Mega Man 3.
Power Fighters	Defeat Junk Man in Mega Man 7.
Protoman Song	Complete Mega Man 4.
Select Jungle Remix	Complete Mega Man 7
Unlock Interview	Make your way to Wily's Tower in Mega Man 8.
Wily Vs Bass Song	Complete Mega Man 4.
Wily's Revenge Song	Complete Mega Man 2.

Men in Black II: Alien Escape

Enter these codes at the Title Screen. The screen will flash when code entry is successful. If codes are entere6, you will not be able to save your game or unlock features.

Unlockable	Code
Agent Data	↑,↓,●,R2,←,L2,→,×,R2,■,↑,R1
Alien Data	■,L1,●,L2,↓,▲,R1,→,×,←,R2,▲
All CST	■,↑,L2,←,▲,×,R2,●,→,R1,■,●
All Levels	R2,▲,←,●,■,L2,←,↑,×,↓,L2,■
All Weapons at Full Power	↑,↓,×,■,R1,▲,▲,←,●,L1,L1,→
Boss Mode	R1,▲,↓,↓,×,L2,←,■,→,▲,R2,L1
Don't Drop Pickups When Hit	↓,↑,×,■,↓,↑,×,■,L1,L2,■,●
Invincibility	→,×,R1,▲,↑,L2,×,←,L1,●,×,R2
Full Powerup on Bolt Weapons	←,→,↑,↓,L1,●,▲,R2,←,↓,■,■
Full Powerup on Spread Weapons	L2,R1,●,L2,↓,↑,L1,→,←,×
Full Powerup on Homing Weapon	←,↑,■,L1,←,←,L1,←,●,←
Full Powerup for Plasma Weapon	←,●,▲,→,L1,■,←,R1,R1,▲
Full Powerup on Area Effect Weapon	←,×,▲,↑,↓,■,L2,←,R2
Making Of	●,R2,L2,●,▲,↓,■,×,→,L1,×,↑

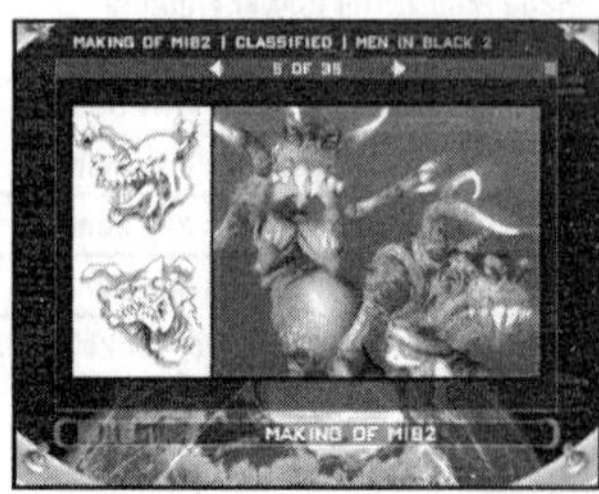

Unlockable	Objective
Big Otasi Easter Egg (N.Y. Streets, Stage 2, Section 6)	After killing Shark Guy and the two teleporters, the barrier in front of the Subway stairs will explode and you can proceed to the next stage. Instead of going down the Subway stairs, walk to the building doorway that is behind the stairs. Stand next to the doorway for twenty seconds or so, then walk left to the line of cars that stretch across the street. Look past the cars to see a giant Otasi running across the street. It is purely a visual thing—you don't get any bonuses—but what a sight!

Metal Gear Solid 2: Substance

Description	Objective
Alternate Ending	Clear "A Snake Tale" to unlock the M9. Then use it to stun all the Bosses instead of killing them.
Boss survival mode	Clear the game on any difficulty.
Casting theater	Clear the game on any difficulty.
Digital Camera	Complete the game to unlock the camera. The digital camera is at Strut E Shell 1.
MGS Snake	Clear 100% of the VR missions as Snake, Pliskin, Tuxedo Snake, Raiden, Ninja Raiden and Raiden X.
Ninja Raiden	Clear 50% of the VR missions using Raiden. Ninja Raiden is only available on VR Missions.
Photograph mode	Clear bomb disposal mode, "hold-up" mode, and eliminate mode. Photograph mode is in the VR Missions only.
Pliskin	Clear 50% of the VR missions using Snake.
Raiden X	Clear 100% of the VR missions using Raiden and Ninja Raiden.
Sunglasses	Complete the game twice, then Snake and Raiden will be wearing sunglasses.
Tuxedo Snake	Clear 100% of the VR missions using Pliskin.

Micro Machines

Unlockable	Objective
Big Head Mode	Collect all three Star Tokens in This Ol' House GP.
Birds-Eye View Camera	Collect all three star tokens in Perilous Places GP.
Micro Marble	Collect all three Star Tokens in 911: Emergency GP.
Color Tint Edit	Collect all three Star Tokens in Hicksville HoeDown GP.
Concept Art	Collect all three Star Tokens in Jungle Jamboree GP.
Hovercar Vehicle	Win the Platinum Cup in challenge mode.
Micro Soccer Mode	Find the three hidden Star Tokens located in the Beachside GP in single player mode.

Midnight Club: Street Racing

Description	Code
Bonus Cars	Keep an eye out for red circles that appear on levels. Stop your car on the circle until you hear a gurgling sound. That unlocks a new car. There are red circles on London and New York, but there could be a lot more from other levels.
Dune Buggy Car	Use a memory card that has some saved data from the Smugglers Run game.

Midnight Club II

Enter the following codes from the cheat menu.

Unlockable	Code
All cars	theCollector
All game modes	dextran
All Locations	Globetrotter
All Locations And Cars(Arcade mode only)	pennyThug
Better Control in the Air	carcrobatics
Change difficulty levels	howhardcanitbe0 (easiest)
Change difficulty levels	howhardcanitbe1
Change difficulty levels	howhardcanitbe2
Change difficulty levels	howhardcanitbe3

Midnight Club II (cont'd)

Change difficulty levels	howhardcanitbe4
Change difficulty levels	howhardcanitbe5
Change difficulty levels	howhardcanitbe6
Change difficulty levels	howhardcanitbe7
Change difficulty levels	howhardcanitbe8
Change difficulty levels	howhardcanitbe9 (hardest)
Infinite Nitrous	greenLantern
Invincibility	gladiator
Machine Gun and Rocket Code	savethekids

The following cars can be unlocked by meeting the listed objectives.

Car	Objective
LAPD car in Arcade Mode	Beat all five circuit races for LA in Arcade mode.
Paris Cop Car	Beat all 6 of the Paris arcade circuit tracks.
SLF450X	Complete 100% of the game
The Veloci	Beat all of the World Champion's races.
Tokyo Cop Car	Beat all 7 Tokyo arcade circuit tracks.

Midnight Club 3 Dub Edition

Enter these case sensitive passwords in the Cheats section under Options.

Unlockable	Password
All cities in arcade mode	crosscountry
Bunny ears	getheadl
Chrome Body	haveyouseenthisboy
Faster pedestrians/All cities in arcade mode	urbansprawl
Flaming Head	trythisathome
Increase car mass in arcade mode	hyperagro
No damage	ontheroad
Pumpkin Heads	getheadk
Skull head	getheadn
Snowman head	getheadm
Special move Agro	dfens
Special move Roar	Rjnr
Special move Zone	allin
Unlock all cities	roadtrip
Yellow Smile	getheadj

Mike Tyson Heavyweight Boxing

Enter the following codes at the Title Screen

Unlockable	Code
Big Head Mode	■,●,↑,↓
Codies Credits	×,▲,■,●
Custom boxer textures	L1,R1,×,×,▲,×
Platinum Unlock (All boxers, arenas, and game modes)	■,●,L2,R2
Small Head Mode	■,●,↓,↑
Square 2D/flat Mode	↓,↑,●,■
Super Mutant Mode	■,←,↑,▲

Minority Report

Enter the following as codes.

Description	Code
All Combos	NINJA
All FMV Sequences	DIRECTOR
All Weapons	STRAPPED
Armor	STEELUP
Baseball Bat	SLUGGER
Bouncy Men	BOUNZMEN
Cluttered Locations	CLUTZ
Concept Art	SKETCHPAD
Dramatic Finish	STYLIN
Ending Sequence	WIMP
Extra Health	BUTTERUP
Free Aim	FPSSTYLE
Invincibility	LRGARMS
Level Select	PASSKEY
Level Skip	QUITER
Maximum Ammunition	MRJUAREZ
Maximum Damage	SPINACH
Pain Arenas	MAXIMUMHURT
Play as Clown	SCARYCLOWN
Play as Convict	JAILBREAK
Play as GI	GNRLINFANTRY
Play as Lizard	HISSSS
Play as Moseley	BIGLIPS
Play as Nara	WEIGHTGAIN
Play as Nikki	HAIRLOSS
Play as Robot	MRROBOTO
Play as Superhero	SUPERJOHN
Play as Zombie	IAMSODEAD
Rag Doll	CLUMSY
Slow Motion Button	SLIZOMIZO

MLB 2004

The game must be paused for these codes to work. You will feel the controller vibrate if you entered the codes correctly.

Unlockable	Code
Big Ball	L2, L2, L2, L2, ↑, →, ↓, ←
Big Body Mode	↑, ↓, ←, →, L2, L2, R2, R1
Big Head Mode	↑, ←, ↓, →, ↑, →, ↓, ←
Faster Players	←, →, →, ←, L2, R1, R1, L2
Invisible Body Mode	R1, R2, R1, R2, ↑, ↓, ←, →
Programmer Names	R1, R2, →, →, ←, ←, L2, L2
Slower Players	←, ←, →, →, R2, R2, L2, L2
Tiny Head Mode	↑, ↓, ↑, ↓, R1, R1, L2, L2

MLB 2005

Enter the following codes in the Main Menu:

Unlockable	Code
All Players	←,↑,←,→,↓,→,←,↑
All Stadiums	↓,↑,←,→,↑,→,↑,↓
All Teams	←,→,→,↓,↓,←,↑,↑
All Uniforms	↑,↓,→,←,↓,→,↓,↑
Beans (Flatulent Ballplayers)	→,→,→,→,→,←,↓
Big Ball	↑,↑,→,←,↑,↑,→,←

MLB 2005 (cont'd)

Unlockable	Code	Unlockable	Code
Big Head	←,→,←,→,↑,↓,↑,↓	Small Head	↑,↓,↑,↑,→,→,→,←
Black and White	↑,↑,↓,↓,←,→,←,→	Super Pitch Break	→,←,→,←,→,←,↑,↑
Faster Runners	←,→,←,→,←,→,↑,↑	Super Pitch Speed	↑,↑,↑,←,←,←,←,→
Slow Runners	→,←,→,←,→,←,↓,↓	Super Six Pitches	↓,↑,↓,→,→,→,→,←

MLB 2006

Pause the game to enter this code.

Unlockable	Code
Fart Mode	⇧,⇧,⇩,⇩,⇦,⇨,⇦,⇨

MLB Slugfest 20-03

Enter these codes in the "Today's Match-Up" screen. The first number is the number of times you press ■, the second is the number of times you press ▲, and the third is the number of times you press ●.

Unlockable	Code	Unlockable	Code
16" Softball	2 4 2 ↓	No Contact Mode	4 3 3 ←
Big Heads	2 0 0 →	No Fatigue	3 4 3 ↑
Eagle Team	2-1-2 →	Pinto Team	2 1 0 →
Extra Time After Plays	1 2 3 ↑	Rocket Park Stadium	3 2 1 ↑
Horse Team	2 1 1 →	Roman Coliseum Stadium	3 3 3 ↑
Lion Team	2 2 0 →	Rubber Ball	2 4 2 ↑
Log Bat	0 0 4 ↑	Terry Fitzgerald Team	3 3 3 →
Mace Bat	0 0 4 ←	Tiny Heads	2 0 0 ←
Max Batting	3 0 0 ←	Todd McFarlane Team	2 2 2 →
Max Power	0 3 0 ←	Tournament Mode	1 1 1 ↓
Max Speed	0 0 3 ←	Unlimited Turbo	4 4 4 ↓
		Wiffle Ball Bat	0 0 4 →

MLB Slugfest 2004

Cheat Mode: Press ■, ▲, and ● to change the icons in the first, second, and third boxes respectively at the match-up screen. The numbers in the following list indicate the number of times you press each button. After the icons change, press the D-pad in the indicated direction to enable the code. For example, to enter 1-2-3 ←, press ■, ▲, ▲, ●, ●, ●, ←.

Description	Code	Description	Code
16" Softball	2, 4, 2, ↓	Empire Park Stadium	3, 2, 1, →
Alien Team	2, 3, 1, ↓	Evil Clown Team	2, 1, 1, ↓
Atlantis Stadium	3, 2, 1, ←	Extended Time for Codes	3, 0, 3, ↑
Big Head	2, 0, 0, →	Forbidden City Stadium	3, 3, 3, ←
Blade Bat	0, 0, 2, ↑	Gladiator Team	1, 1, 3, ↓
Bobble Head Team	1, 3, 3, ↓	Horse Team	2, 1, 1, →
Bone Bat	0, 0, 1, ↑	Ice Bat	0, 0, 3, ↑
Casey Team	2, 3, 3, ↓	Lion Team	2, 2, 0, →
Cheats Disabled	1, 1, 1, ↓	Little League	1, 0, 1 ↓
Coliseum Stadium	3, 3, 3, ↑	Log Bat	0, 0, 4, ↑
Dolphin Team	1, 0, 2, ↓	Mace Bat	0, 0, 4, ←
Dwarf Team	1, 0, 3, ↓	Max Batting	3, 0, 0, ←
Eagle Team	2, 1, 2, →	Max Power	0, 3, 0, ←
		Max Speed	0, 0, 3, ←

MLB Slugfest 2004 (cont'd)

Description	Code
Midway Park Stadium	3, 2, 1, ↓
Minotaur Team	1, 1, 0, ↓
Monument Stadium	3, 3, 3, ↓
Napalitano Team	2, 3, 2, ↓
Olshan Team	2, 2, 2, ↓
Pinto Team	2, 1, 0, →
Rivera Team	2, 2, 2, ↑
Rocket Park Stadium	3, 2, 1, ↑
Rodeo Clown	1, 3, 2, ↓
Rubber Ball	2, 4, 2, ↑
Scorpion Team	1, 1, 2, ↓
Spike Bat	0, 0, 5, ↑
Team Terry Fitzgerald	3, 3, 3, →
Team Todd McFarlane	2, 2, 2, →
Tiny Head	2, 0, 0, ←
Unlimited Turbo	4, 4, 4, ↓
Whiffle Bat	0, 0, 4, →

MLB Slugfest Loaded

Enter the following codes at the Versus Screen.

Unlockable	Code
Big Head Mode	■,■,→
Max Batting	■,■,■,←
Max Power	▲,▲,▲,←
Max Speed	●,●,●,←
Rubber Ball Mode	■,■,▲,▲
Softball Mode	■,■,▲,▲,▲,▲,●,●,↓
Tiny Head Mode	■,■,←
Unlimited Turbo	■,■,■,■,▲,▲,▲,▲,●,●,●,●,↓

Mobile Light Force 2

Description	Code
Change Player Color	↑ or ↓ at character select screen.

Mobile Suit Gundam: Journey to Jaburo

Description	Code
Tactics Battle Mode	Complete Story Mode.

Mortal Kombat: Deadly Alliance

Unlockable	Code
Random Character Select	Highlight "Shang Tsung" (for player one) or "Quan Chi" (for player two) at the Character Selection screen, and then hold ↑+START.
Versus Mode Stage Select	Press R1 before either player chooses a character to get a screen with a screenshot of a stage. Press ← or → to change to the desired stage.
Versus Mode Skill Select	Press L2 before either player chooses a character.

TIP

Fatalities!

You can do fatalities from anywhere on screen! Press L1 at the Finish Him/Her screen to change into your fatality stance, or you have to figure out the distance range.

Fatality	Button Combination
Bo Rai Cho (Belly Flop)	Press Away (x3), ↓, ●.
Cyrax (Smasher)	Press Toward (x2), ↑, ▲.
Drahmin (Iron Bash)	Press Away, Toward (x2), ↓, ✕.
Frost (Freeze Shatter)	Press Toward, Away, ↑, ↓, ■.
Hsu Hao (Laser Slice)	Press Toward, Away, ↓, ↓, ▲.
Jax (Head Stomp)	Press ↓, Toward (x2), ↓, ▲.
Johnny Cage (Brain Ripper)	Press Away, Toward (x2), ↓, ▲.
Kano (Heart Grab)	Press Toward, ↑ (x2), ↓, ■.

PSP Xbox PS2 GC GBA

Mortal Kombat: Deadly Alliance (cont'd)

Kenshi (Telekinetic Crush)	Press Toward, Away, Toward, ↓, ×.
Kitana (Kiss of Doom)	Press ↓, ↑, Toward (x2), ▲.
Kung Lao (Hat Throw)	Press ↓, ↑, Away, ×.
Li Mei (Crush Kick)	Press Toward (x2), ↓, Toward, ●.
Mavado (Kick Thrust)	Press Away (x2), ↑ (x2), ■.
Nitara (Blood Thirst)	Press ↑ (x2), Toward, ■.
Quan Chi (Neck Stretch)	Press Away (x2), Toward, Away, ×.
Raiden (Electrocution)	Press Away, Toward, Toward (x2), ×.
Reptile (Acid Shower)	Press ↑ (x3), Toward, ×.
Scorpion (Spear)	Press Away (x2), ↓, Away+●.
Shang Tsung (Soul Steal)	Press ↑, ↓, ↑, ↓, ▲.
Sonya (Kiss)	Press Away, Toward (x2), ↓, ▲.
Sub Zero (Spine Rip)	Press Away, Toward (x2), ↓, ×.

Moto GP

Description	Objective
Alex Barros	Get one lap under 1'54"000 at Motegi stage in Time Trial mode on any difficulty setting.
Alex Criville	Place first at Jerez in Arcade mode on Normal difficulty.
Carlos Checa	Get one lap under 1'24"000 at Paul Ricardo stage in Time Trial mode on any difficulty setting.
Gun Koma	Complete one season under Season mode on Easy difficulty.
Haruchika Aoki	Beat 24"000 in Challenge mode on any difficulty setting.
Jean Michel Bayle	Beat 8"280 in Challenge mode on any difficulty setting.
Jerez Reverse	Place first at Jerez in Arcade mode on Hard difficulty.
John Kocinski	Place first at Paul Ricard in Arcade mode on Normal difficulty.
Jose Luis Cardoso	Beat 20"300 in Challenge mode on any difficulty setting.
Juan Borja	Beat 22"200 in Challenge mode on any difficulty setting.
Jurgen Vd Goorbergh	Beat 13"600 in Challenge mode on any difficulty setting.
K1	Get three laps under 1'22"500 in Time Trial mode on any difficulty setting.
Kenny Roberts	Place first at Motegi in Arcade mode on Normal difficulty.
Klonoa	Beat 21"000 in Challenge mode on any difficulty setting.
Max Biaggi	Get one lap under 2'12"000 at Suzuka stage in Time Trial mode on any difficulty setting.
Mick Doohan	Get first overall at the end of five seasons in Season mode on Hard difficulty.
Mike Hale	Beat 22"000 in Challenge mode on any difficulty setting.
Motegi Reverse	Place first at Motegi in Arcade mode on Hard difficulty.
Nobuatsu Aoki	Beat 20"000 in Challenge mode on any difficulty setting.
Norick Abe	Place first at Suzuka in Arcade mode on Normal difficulty.
Paul Ricard Reverse	Place first at Paul Ricard in Arcade mode on Hard difficulty.
Photo	Beat 20"500 in Challenge mode on any difficulty setting.
Photo	Beat 24"000 in Challenge mode on any difficulty setting.
Photo	Beat 25"200 in Challenge mode on any difficulty setting.
Photo	Beat 28"500 in Challenge mode on any difficulty setting.
Photo	Beat 29"500 in Challenge mode on any difficulty setting.
Photo	Beat 31"000 in Challenge mode on any difficulty setting.
Photo	Beat 31"700 in Challenge mode on any difficulty setting.

Moto GP (cont'd)

Photo	Beat 33"000 in Challenge mode on any difficulty setting.
Photo	Beat 33"600 in Challenge mode on any difficulty setting.
Photo	Beat 34"500 in Challenge mode on any difficulty setting.
Photo	Beat 35"200 in Challenge mode on any difficulty setting.
Photo	Beat 36"700 in Challenge mode on any difficulty setting.
Photo	Beat 56"200 in Challenge mode on any difficulty setting.
Photo	Complete all races in one season under Season mode on any difficulty setting.
Photo	Complete all races in one season under Season mode on Normal or Hard difficulty.
Photo	Complete every race over five seasons in Season mode on hard difficulty where the laps are set to full.
Photo	Complete three consecutive laps where all the lap times are under 2'10"000 in Time Trial mode on any difficulty setting.
Photo	Get a Bronze or Silver on all the challenges above in Challenge mode on any difficulty setting.
Photo	Get a Gold on all the challenges above in Challenge mode on any difficulty setting.
Photo	Pass 10 or more bikes in one lap in Arcade mode on any difficulty setting.
Photo	Place first at Suzuka in Arcade mode on any difficulty setting. You must not touch another or go off road at any time.
Photo	Race with all 12 teams in Season mode on Hard difficulty.
Photo	Race with all 12 teams in Season mode on Normal difficulty.
Photo	Use a Level C or D team and finish first overall at the end of one season in Season mode on Hard difficulty.
Photo	Using all three Level A teams, place first on every circuit in Arcade mode on any difficulty setting.
Regis Laconi	Beat 24"000 in Challenge mode on any difficulty setting.
Sete Gibernau	Get one lap under 1'47"000 at Jerez stage in Time Trial mode on any difficulty setting.
Simon Crafar	Place first at Donington in Arcade mode on Normal difficulty.
Suzuka Reverse	Place first at Suzuka in Arcade mode on Hard difficulty.
Tadayuki Okada	Get one lap under 1'36"000 at Donington stage in Time Trial mode on any difficulty setting.
Takuma Aoki	Beat 35"500 in Challenge mode on any difficulty setting.
Tetsuya Harada	Complete all five seasons in Season mode on Hard difficulty.

Motor Mayhem

Description	Code
Buzzsaw as a playable character	Beat the Deathmatch, Endurance, and Eliminator modes with the same character on either Hard or Very Hard Difficulty.

MTX Mototrax

Go to the Options menu and select Cheats. Enter the following:

Unlockable	Code
All Tracks	BA7H
Butterfingers Gear	B77393
Fast Acceleration	JIH345
Left Field Gear	12345
Max Air	BFB0020
Nokia Trickbot	HA79000
Officer Dick	BADG3
Sky Camera	HIC
Slipknot Maggot	86657457
Slipknot Movie	23F7IC5
SoBe Gear	50B3
Speed Demon	773H999

PSP Xbox PS2 GC GBA

MTX vs. ATV Unleashed

Enter in the cheats menu.

Unlockable	Code
50cc Bikes	Minimoto
Unlock all freestyle tracks	Huckit
Unlock Everything	Toolazy

MVP Baseball 2003

Description	Code
16:9 Anamorphic View	Press and hold the L2 and R2 triggers for more than 3 seconds. Then, press ← on the directional pad to enable. Press → on the directional pad to disable.
Broken Bats	Create a player named Keegn Patersn, Jacob Patersn, or Ziggy Patersn.
Home Run Cheat	Create a player named Erik Kiss.

MVP Baseball 2004

Enter the following names in the Create a Player screen:

Name	Unlockable
John Prosen	Huge Hat
Jacob Paterson	Huge Bat
Kenny Lee	Bone Scaling Cheat
Erik Kiss	Bad Player

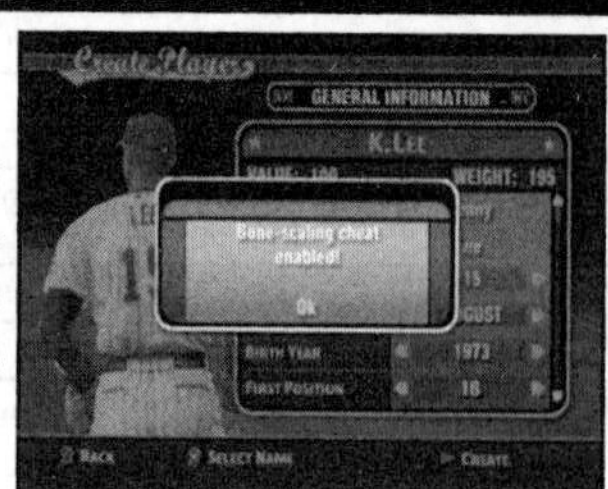

MVP Baseball 2005

Create a character with these names.

Unlockable	Name
Player has a huge bat	Keegan Paterson
Player has a huge bat	Jacob Paterson
Player has a huge bat	Isaiah Paterson
Unlock Everything	Katie Roy

MX Unleashed

Go to Options and select Cheat Codes. Pick the cheat you want and press ● to enter the code.

Unlockable	Code
500cc Bikes	BIGDOGS
50cc Bikes	SQUIRRELDOG
A.I. Bowling	WRECKINGBALL
All Bonuses/ Completion	CLAPPEDOUT
All Machines	MINIGAMES
Expert A.I.	OBTGOFAST
Freestyle Tracks	BUSTBIG
National Tracks	ECONATION
Pro Physics	SWAPPIN
Supercross Tracks	STUPERCROSS

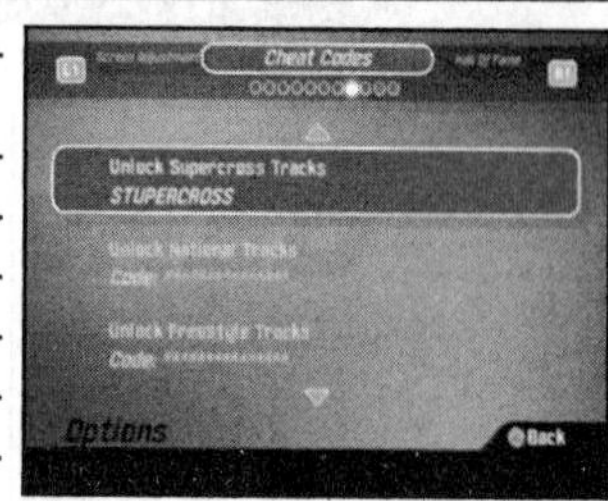

PSP Xbox PS2 GC GBA

My Street

Description	Code
Custom Body Parts	Beat Story Mode once.

Nano Breaker

Enter code during game.

Unlockable	Code
Mini Map Shooter	⇧, ⇧, ⇩, ⇩, ⇦, ⇨, ⇦, ⇦, ⇨, ×, ●.

Narc

Enter these codes while playing. Do not pause the game.

Unlockable	Code
All Drugs	Repeatedly press L1 + R1 + L3
All Weapons	Repeatedly press L1 + R1 + R3
Infinite Ammo	Repeatedly press L1 + R1 + ⇩ (Only for the weapon you have equipped.)
Invincibility	Repeatedly press R1 + L1 + ×
Show all Drug Stashes	Repeatedly press L1 + R1 + ⇦

NASCAR 2001

Unlockable	Objective
Black Box Classic Car	Win the Short Track Challenge.
Black Box Exotic Car	Win the Half Season.
EA Sports Car	Win the Road Course Challenge.
EA.com Car	Win the Superspeedway Shootout at Veteran or Legend difficulty.
Treasure Island Track	Under Veteran difficulty, win a season.

NASCAR 2005: Chase for the Cup

In the Edit Driver Screen, enter the following names to access cheats (the names are case-sensitive):

Unlockable	Password
$10,000,000	Walmart NASCAR
All Bonuses	Open Sesame
Dale Earnhardt	The Intimidator
Fantasy Track	Walmart Exclusive
Mr. Clean Pit Crew	Clean Crew

NASCAR Heat 2002

Unlockable	Objective
Hornball Enabled	At the Race Day screen in Single Race or Head-to-Head, the following cheats are present. To start a race with hornball enabled (press ↑ on D-Pad to fire a ball): ↑,↓,←,→,R2,↑,↑. To start a practice session with hornball enabled: ↑,↓,←,→,R2,↓,↓.
Unlock Hardcore Realism Mode	To unlock Hardcore Realism Mode, earn a 100 point rating on any track. The Harcore Realism will be unlocked for the track on which you earned the rating.
Unlock Richard Petty	Complete all of the Heat Challenges and earn at least a Bronze rating on each to unlock the legendary Richard Petty.

NASCAR Thunder 2002

Go to Create-a-Car and enter any of these names to unlock a new car in Driver Select:

- Dave Alpern
- Buster Auton
- Scott Brewer
- Audrey Clark
- Rick Edwards
- Michelle Emser
- Katrina Goode
- Diane Grubb
- Jim Hannigan
- Troi Hayes
- Crissy Hillsworth
- Traci Hultzapple
- Rick Humphrey
- Kristi Jones
- Joey Joulwan
- Cheryl King
- Mandy Misiak
- Josh Neelon
- Dave Nichols
- Ken Patterson
- Dick Paysor
- Beeny Persons
- Tom Renedo
- Chuck Spicer
- Sasha Soares

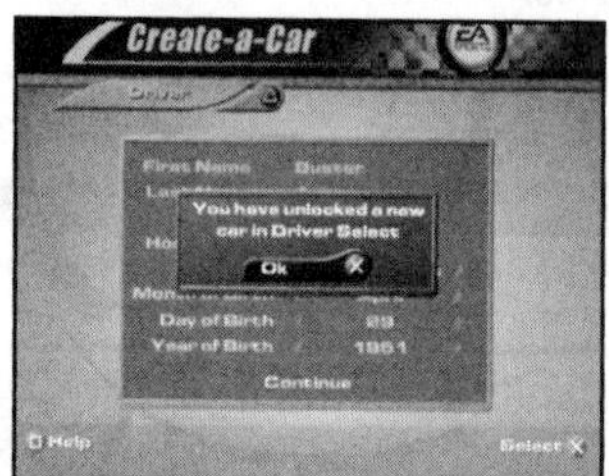

NASCAR Thunder 2003

Enter the following codes at the Create-a-Car screen.

Unlockable	Code
Get Dale Earnhardt	Dale Earnhardt
Get Fantasy Drivers	Extra Drivers

NASCAR Thunder 2004

Go to Features and select Create-A-Car. Enter Seymore Cameos as the driver name to unlock a cool Thunder Plate.

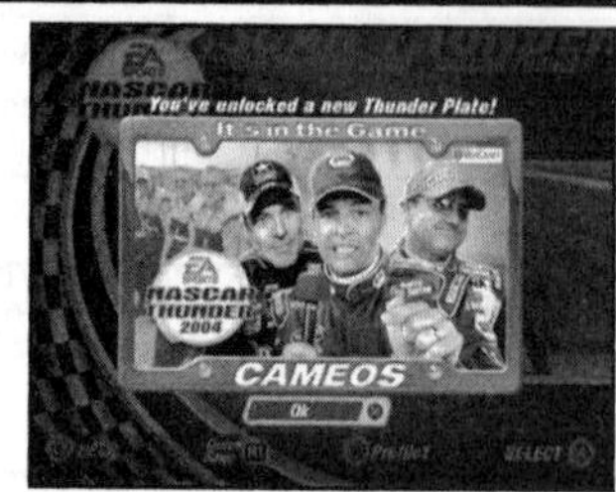

Naval Ops: Warship Gunner

Unlockable	Code
203mm Chain Gun	100 planes
356mm Chain Gun	500 planes
46x60 Gun	100 PT Boats
80cm Guided Torpedo	100 Cruisers
Atomic Engine A	100 Destroyers
Atomic Engine E	500 Destroyers
Charged Particle Gun 3	100 Battleships
2 Hull Battleship	500 Transports
2 Hull Cruiser	100 Transports
Enigmatech Atli Hull	100 Submarines
Extra Money	At the Allied base, press ←,←,→,→,↙,R2,R1,↙,■,▲
Grian Laser	999 Battleships
Wave Gun	100 Superships

NBA Ballers

Enter these codes in the "VS" screen. The first number is the number of times you press ■, the second is the number of times you press ▲, and the third is the number of times you press ●.

Unlockable	Code
2X Juice Replenish	4 3 1
Alley-Oop Ability	7 2 5
Alternate Gear	1 2 3
Baby Ballers	4 2 3
Back-In Ability	1 2 2
Back-In Ability	3 1 7
Big Head Mode	1 3 4
Expanded Move Set	5 1 2
Fire Ability	7 2 2
Good Handling	3 3 2
Half House Meter	3 6 7
Hot Spot	6 2 7
Kid Ballers	4 3 3
Legal Goal Tending	7 5 6
No Weather	1 1 2
Paper Ballers	3 5 4
Perfect Free Throws	3 2 7
Play As Afro Man	5 1 7
Play As Agent	5 5 7
Play As BiznezMan-A	5 3 7
Play As BiznezMan-B	5 2 7
Play As Coach	5 6 7
Play As Secretary	5 4 7
Put Back Ability	3 1 3
Pygmy	4 2 5
R2R Mode	0 0 8
Rain	2 2 2
Random Moves	3 0 0
Shows Shot Percentage	0 1 2
Snow	3 3 3
Speedy Players	2 1 3
Stunt Dunk Ability	3 7 4
Super Back-Ins	2 3 5
Super Blocks	1 2 4
Super Push	3 1 5
Super Steals	2 1 5
Tournament Mode	0 1 1
Young Ballers	4 4 3

Go to "Inside Stuff" and select "Phrase-ology." Enter the following codes to unlock goodies:

Unlockable	Code
Allen Iverson's Alternate Gear	killer crossover
Allen Iverson's Studio	the answer
Alonzo Mourning	zo
Amare Stoudamire	rising sun
Baron Davis	Stylin & Profilin
Ben Wallace's alternate outfit	radio controlled cars
Bill Russell	celtics dynasty
Bill Walton	towers of power
Chris Webber	24 seconds
Clyde Drexler	clyde the glide
Darryl Dawkins	rim wrecker
Dikembe Mutumbo	in the paint
Dominique Wilkins	dunk fest
Elton Brand	rebound
George Gervin	the ice man cometh
Jalen Rose	bring it
Jason Kidd	pass the rock
Jason Williams	give and go
Jerry Stackhouse's Alt. Gear	Stop Drop and Roll
John Stockton	court vision
Julius Erving	one on one

PSP Xbox PS2 GC GBA

NBA Ballers (cont'd)

Unlockable	Code
Karl Malone	special delivery
Karl Malone's Devonshire Estate	ice house
Kevin Garnett's alternate outfit	boss hoss
Kevin McHale	holla back
Kobe Bryant's Alt. Gear	Japanese steak
Larry Bird	hoosier
Latrell Sprewell	spree
Lebron James	king james
Magic Johnson	laker legends
Manu Ginobili gear	manu
Michael Finley	student of the game
Nene Hilario	rags to riches
Oscar Robertson's Alt. Gear	Ain't No Thing
Pete Maravich	pistol pete
Rashard Lewis	fast forward
Rasheed Wallace	bring down the house
Ray Allen	all star
Reggie Miller's Alt. Gear	From Downtown
Richard Hamilton	rip
Robert Parrish's Alt. Gear	The Chief
Scottie Pippen	playmaker
Scottie Pippen's Yacht	nice yacht
Shaq's alternate outfit	diesel rules the paint
Special Movie #1	juice house
Special Movie #2	nba showtime
Special Shoe #1	dub deuce
Stephon Marbury	platinum playa
Steve Francis	ankle breaker
Steve Francis's Alt. Gear	Rising Star
Steve Nash	hair canada
Tim Duncan	make it take it
Tony Parkers Alternative outfit	run and shoot
Tracy McGrady	living like a baller
Wally Szczerbiak	world
Walt Frazier	Penetrate and Perpetrate
Wes Unseld	old school
Willis Reed	hall of fame
Wilt Chamberlain	wilt the stilt
Yao Ming	center of attention
Yao Ming's Grade School	prep school

NBA Jam

Create a new profile using these names.

Unlockable	Code
Unlock Everything	-LPP-
Unlock the NBA Jam Development Team	CREDITS

NBA Hoopz

At the Versus screen, use the following buttons to change the numbers for code entry: ■ to change the first number, × to change the second number, and ● to change the third number. Then use the D-Pad to enter the direction. If you entered the code correctly you'll see the name of the code displayed on the screen.

Unlockable	Objective
ABA Ball	1-1-1 →
Away Uniform	0-2-4 →
Beach Court	0-2-3 ←
Big Heads	3-0-0 →
Granny Shots	1-2-1 ←
Home Uniform	0-1-4 →
Infinite Turbo	3-1-2 ↑
No Fouls	2-2-2 →
No Goaltending	4-4-4 ←
No Hotspots	3-0-1 ↑
Play As Dr. Atomic	5-4-4 ←
Show Hotspot	1-1-0 ↓
Show Shot Percent	0-1-1 ↓
Street Court	3-2-0 ←
Tiny Heads	3-3-0 ←
Tiny Players	5-4-3 ←

NBA Live 2001

Unlockable	Objective
Creating a Dream Team	Go into Season mode, hit ● to bring up the menu bar, and select "Roster" from the bar. From here, select "Create Player." When creating a player, load him up with maximum stats and save him into the Free Agent pool. Then, return to the menu bar, select "Roster" and Sign the player you've just made. If his rating is over 90, you can trade him for any player in the league (including Shaq and Allen Iverson). Repeat this process until you have all the talent you want.
Make a Super Star Even Better	At the main menu, press ● to open the Active menu. Select "Roster," then select "Edit Player." A Super Star loads up if your Create-a-Player list is empty. Make the player's stats better (3 pointers, strength, dunking, etc.) by hitting R2 at the Edit Player screen. If you want a different player, go back to the empty Create-a-Player list by pressing L1. Press START and change someone else.

NBA Live 2003

Go to Create-a-Player and enter the following names as the last name(if done correctly, a message will appear):

Unlockable	Name
B-Rich	DOLLABILLS
Busta Rhymes	FLIPMODE
DJ Clue	MIXTAPES
Fabolous	GHETTOFAB
Hot Karl	CALIFORNIA
Just Blaze	GOODBEATS

NBA Live 2004

Unlockable	Code
15,000 NBA Store Points	87843H5F9P
All Hardwood Classic Jerseys	725JKUPLMM
All NBA Gear	ERT9976KJ3
All Shoes	POUY985GY5
All Team Gear	YREY5625WQ

NBA Live 2004 (cont'd)

For the following codes, go to Roster Management from Team Management. Create a player with the any of the following last names listed.

Unlockable Player	Name
Aleksander Pavlovic	WHSUCPOI
Andreas Glyniadakis	POCKDLEK
Carlos Delfino	SDFGURKL
James Lang	NBVKSMCN
Jermaine Dupri	SOSODEF
Kyle Korver	OEISNDLA
Malick Badiane	SKENXIDO
Mario Austin	POSNEGHX
Matt Bonner	BBVDKCVM
Nedzad Sinanovic	ZXDSDRKE
Paccelis Morlende	QWPOASZX
Remon Van de Hare	ITNVCJSD
Rick Rickert	POILKJMN
Sani Becirovic	ZXCCVDRI
Sofoklis Schortsanitis	IOUBFDCJ
Szymon Szewczyk	POIOJIS
Tommy Smith	XCFWQASE
Xue Yuyang	WMZKCOI

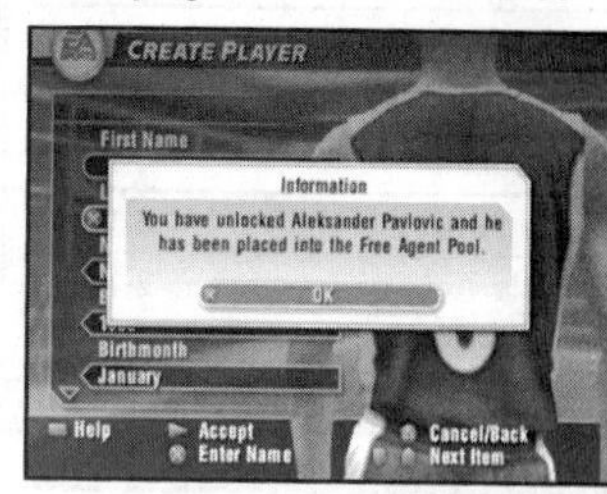

To enter the next two tables of codes, go to NBA Live and select NBA Codes.

Unlockable Shoes	Code
Air Bounds (Black/White/Blue)	7YSS0292KE
Air Bounds (White/Black)	JA807YAM20
Air Bounds (White/Green)	84HHST61QI
Air Flight 89 (Black/White)	FG874JND84
Air Flight 89 (White/Black)	63RBVC7423
Air Flight 89 (White/Red)	GF9845JHR4
Air Flightposite (White/Black/Gray)	74FDH7K94S
Air Flightposite (White/Black)	6HJ874SFJ7
Air Flightposite (Yellow/Black/White)	MN54BV45C2
Air Flightposite 2 (Blue/Gray)	2389JASE3E
Air Foamposite 1 (Blue)	0P5465UX12
Air Foamposite 1 (White/Black/Red)	DOD843HH7F
Air Foamposite Pro (Black/Gray)	3245AFSD45
Air Foamposite Pro (Red/Black)	DSAKF38422
Air Foamposite Pro (Blue/Black)	DG56TRF446
Air Force Max (Black)	F84N845H92
Air Force Max (White/Black/Blue)	985KJF98KJ
Air Force Max (White/Red)	8734HU8FFF
Air Hyperflight (White)	14TGU7DEWC
Air Hyperflight (Blue/White)	A0K374HF8S
Air Hyperflight (Yellow/Black)	JCX93LSS88
Air Hyperflight (Black/White)	WW44YHU592
Air Jordan 11 (White)	HG76HN765S
Air Jordan 11 (White/Black)	A2S35TH7H6
Air Jordan 11 (Black/Red/White)	GF64H76ZX5
Air Jordan 11 (Black/Varsity Royal/ White)	HJ987RTGFA
Air Jordan 11 (Cool/Grey)	GF75HG6332

NBA Live 2004 (cont'd)

Air Jordan 3 (Black/White/Gray)	CVJ554TJ58
Air Jordan 3 (White)	G9845HJ8F4
Air Jordan 3 (White/Clay)	435SGF555Y
Air Jordan 3 (White/Fire Red)	RE6556TT90
Air Jordan 3 (White/True Blue)	FDS9D74J4F
Air Max2 CB (Black/White)	87HZXGFIU8
Air Max2 CB (White/Red)	4545GFKJIU
Air Max2 UPTEMPO (Black/White/Blue)	NF8745J87F
Air Max Elite (Black)	A4CD54T7TD
Air Max Elite (White/Black)	966ERTFG65
Air Max Elite (White/Blue)	FD9KN48FJF
Air Zoom Flight (Gray/White)	367UEY6SN
Air Zoom Flight (White/Blue)	92387HD077
Air Zoom Generation (White/Red/Black)	23LBJNUMB1
Air Zoom Generation (Black/Red/White)	LBJ23CAVS1
Nike Blazer (Black)	XCV6456NNL
Nike Blazer (Khaki)	W3R57U9NB2
Nike Blazer (Tan/White/Blue)	DCT5YHMU90
Nike Blazer (White/Orange/Blue)	4G66JU99XS
Nike Shox BB4 (Black)	WE424TY563
Nike Shox BB4 (White/Black)	23ERT85LP9
Nike Shox BB4 (White/Light Purple)	668YYTRB12
Nike Shox BB4 (White/Red)	424TREU777
Nike Shox VCIII (Black)	SDFH764FJU
Nike Shox VCIII (White/Black/Red)	5JHD367JJT

NBA Live 2005

Go to My NBA Live, EA Sports Lounge, NBA Codes to enter these codes.

Unlockable	Code
50,000 Dynasty Points	YISS55CZ0E
All Classics Hardwood Jerseys	PRYI234N0B
All Shoes	FHM389HU80
All Team Gear	1NVDR89ER2

Unlockable Shoes	Code
Nike Air Huarache	VNBA60230T
Nike BG Rollout	0984ADF90P
Nike Shox Elite	2388HDFCBJ
Nike Air Unlimited	XVLJD9895V
Zoom Lebron II Shoes	1KENZO23XZ
Zoom Generation Low	234SDJF9W4

Unlockable Team	Code
Atlanta Hawks 2004-05 Alternate	HDI834NN9N
Boston Celtics 2004-05 Alternate	XCV43MGMDS
Dallas Mavericks 2004-05 Alternate	AAPSEUD09U
Golden State Warriors 2004-05 Alternate	NAVNY29548

NBA Street

After entering one of the following icon codes, press Enter on the D-Pad to complete code entry.

Unlockable	Code
ABA Ball	Basketball, Turntable, Turntable, Basketball
ABA Socks	Microphone, Microphone, Microphone, Microphone
Athletic Joe "The Show"	Turntable, Shoe, Basketball, Turntable
Authentic Uniforms	Basketball, Basketball, Turntable, Turntable
Beach Ball	Basketball, Turntable, Turntable, Shoe
Big Heads	Microphone, Turntable, Shoe, Turntable
Captain Quicks	Backboard, Basketball, Shoe, Turntable
Casual Uniforms	Turntable, Turntable, Basketball, Basketball
Disable All Cheats	Turntable, Turntable, Turntable, Turntable
EA Big Ball	Basketball, Turntable, Microphone, Basketball
Easy Distance Shots	Shoe, Turntable, Backboard, Basketball
Explosive Rims	Turntable, Shoe, Microphone, Basketball
Harder Distance Shots	Shoe, Shoe, Backboard, Basketball
Less Blocks	Backboard, Turntable, Shoe, Backboard
Less Gamebreakers	Turntable, Backboard, Microphone, Shoe
Less Steals	Backboard, Turntable, Microphone, Basketball
Mad Handles	Backboard, Shoe, Turntable, Basketball
Medicine Ball	Basketball, Turntable, Turntable, Backboard
Mega Dunking	Backboard, Basketball, Turntable, Basketball
More Gamebreakers	Turntable, Microphone, Backboard, Shoe
No Alley-oops	Backboard, Microphone, Turntable, Shoe
No Auto Replays	Turntable, Shoe, Turntable, Turntable
No Dunks	Backboard, Basketball, Turntable, Shoe
No Gamebreakers	Turntable, Microphone, Microphone, Shoe
No HUD Display	Turntable, Microphone, Turntable, Shoe
No Player Indicators	Microphone, Basketball, Basketball, Microphone
No Shot Clock	Microphone, Microphone, Basketball, Backboard
No Shot Indicator	Microphone, Backboard, Shoe, Microphone
No Turbo	Turntable, Microphone, Microphone, Backboard
No Two-pointers	Backboard, Backboard, Basketball, Backboard
NuFX Ball	Basketball, Turntable, Backboard, Basketball
Player Names	Basketball, Turntable, Shoe, Backboard
Soccer Ball	Basketball, Shoe, Turntable, Basketball
Springtime Joe "The Show"	Turntable, Turntable, Basketball, Turntable
Sticky Fingers	Backboard, Microphone, Turntable, Basketball
Summertime Joe "The Show"	Turntable, Basketball, Basketball, Turntable
Super Swats	Backboard, Backboard, Turntable, Basketball
Tiny Heads	Microphone, Shoe, Basketball, Shoe
Tiny Players	Microphone, Basketball, Microphone, Basketball
Ultimate Power	Backboard, Turntable, Turntable, Basketball
Unlimited Turbo	Shoe, Basketball, Backboard, Basketball
Volleyball	Basketball, Turntable, Turntable, Microphone
WNBA ball	Basketball, Turntable, Shoe, Basketball

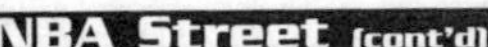

NBA Street (cont'd)

Unlockable	Objective
All Courts	In Hold the Court mode, go to the screen where you choose your court. Hold R2 and press ↑,↓,←,→,→,←,↓,↑. While still holding ↑, press ✕.
Biggs and Beacon Hill Court	Play the City Circuit and reach the Region 1 City Challenge. Defeat Biggs' team to unlock him as a selectable player and unlock the Beacon Hill court.
Bonafide and Broad Street Court	Play the City Circuit and reach the Region 2 City Challenge. Defeat Bonafide's team to unlock him as a selectable player and unlock the Broad Street court.
Created Player Pieces	Complete the Hold the Court challenges to unlock more pieces and development points for created players.
DJ and Venice Beach Court	Play the City Circuit and reach the Region 4 City Challenge. Defeat DJ's team to unlock him as a selectable player and unlock the Venice Beach court.
Drake and the Yard Court	Play the City Circuit and reach the Region 3 City Challenge. Defeat Drake's team to unlock him as a selectable player and unlock The Yard court.
More Player Creation Points	Note: This code can only be used for new players. Hold L1+↙ and press ←,↓,→, then press ■,▲,● at the Create Player menu.
NBA Superstars	Play the City Challenge and defeat an NBA team to unlock a player from their roster.
Stretch and Rucker Park Court	Play the City Circuit and reach the Region 2 City Challenge. Defeat Stretch's team to unlock him as a selectable player and unlock the Rucker Park court.
Takashi and Yakatomni Plaza Court	Play the City Circuit and reach the Region 5 City Challenge. Defeat Takashi's team to unlock him as a selectable player and unlock the Yakatomni Plaza court.

For the following unlockables, enter the "Enter User ID" screen and go to the User Record box (displays either a user ID's record information, or "no user record").

Unlockable	Code
NYC Legends Team	Hold L2 and press ↓,↓,↓,←,✕. Alternately, get 30 wins in any mode.
Team 3LW	Hold R1 and press ←,←,→,↓,✕. Alternately, get 20 wins in any mode.
Team Big	Hold L2 and press ↑,↓,↓,←,✕. Alternately, get 10 wins in any mode.
Team Dream	Hold R1, then press ↑,↑,→,→,✕. Alternately, win (complete all the objectives) Hold the Court mode to unlock a team that includes Graylien Alien, Magma Man, and Yeti Snowman.
Team Street Legends	Hold R1, then press →,←,↑,↓,✕. Alternately, win the City Circuit to unlock the Street Legends team. This team includes Biggs, Bonafide, Drake, DJ, Takashi, Stretch, and Michael Jordan.

NBA Street Vol 2

For the following unlockables, hold ↙, then enter code.

Unlockable	Code
All Jerseys	■,▲,●,●
All Quicks	▲,●,▲,■
Always Legend Trails	▲,▲,▲,■
Big Heads	●,■,■,●
Easy 2-Pointers	▲,●,■,▲
Easy Shots	▲,●,■,▲
Explosive Rims	●,●,●,▲
Hard 2-Pointers	▲,■,●,▲
No Counters	▲,▲,●,●
Street Kids	▲,▲,●,■
Turbo	■,■,▲,▲
Unlimited Turbo	■,■,▲,▲
Unlock All Legends	■,▲,▲,●
WNBA Ball	●,▲,▲,●

NBA Street Vol 2 (cont'd)

Unlockable	Objective
"Chocolate Thunder" and "The Glide" Boss Moves	Beat the Broad Street Challenge in Be a Legend mode.
'85 Jordan	Beat NBA challenge, Street School, and Be a Legend.
All Courts	Beat Be a Legend and NBA Challenge.
Biggie Little	Beat the Foster Beach Tournament in Be a Legend mode.
Bill Russell's Jersey	Beat the Northwest region with no losses.
Bill Walton's Jersey	Score over 1,000,000 trick points in a game.
Bobbito	Spend 250 Reward points to unlock him or win 10 games in Pick Up mode.
Bonafide	Beat the tournament in Rucker Park in Be a Legend.
Boss Move "Big Dipper"	Beat the Foster Beach Street Challenge in Be a Legend.
Boss Move "Biggie Little"	Beat the Foster Beach Tournament in Be a Legend.
Boss Move "Bonafide"	Beat the Rucker Park Tournament in Be a Legend.
Boss Move "Droppin' Dimes"	Beat the Lincoln College Tournament in Be a Legend.
Boss Move "Jordan"	Beat the Rucker Park '78 Street Challenge in Be a Legend mode.
Boss Move "Magic"	Beat the Lincoln College Street Challenge in Be a Legend mode.
Boss Move "Nique"	Beat the Mosswood Tournament in Be a Legend.
Boss Move "Stretch"	Beat the Soul in the Hole Tournament in Be a Legend.
Boss Move "The Doctor"	Beat the Mosswood Street Challenge in Be a Legend.
Boss Move "The Legend"	Beat the Greenlake Street Challenge in Be a Legend.
Boss Move "The Oz"	Beat the Mosswood Tournament in Be a Legend.
Boss Move "The Pistol"	Beat the Soul in the Hole Street Challenge in Be a Legend mode.
Boss Move "Whitewater"	Beat the Greenlake Tournament in Be a Legend.
Clyde Drexler's Jersey	Reach Reputation Level 1 in Be a Legend mode.
Connie Hawkins' Jersey	Win a game and get 20 blocks.
Darryl Dawkins' Jersey	Beat the Broad Street Challenge in Be a Legend mode.
David Thompson's Jersey	Reach Reputation Level 1 in Be a Legend mode.
Dime	Beat the tournament held at the Lincoln College in Los Angeles in the Be A Legend mode.
Dominique Wilkins, James Worthy, and Moses Malone	Beat the Southwest Region.
Dominique Wilkins' Jersey	Reach Reputation Level 4 in Be a Legend mode.
Earvin "Magic" Johnson's Jersey	Beat the Lincoln College Street Challenge in Be a Legend mode.
Elgin Baylor Jersey	Shutout the opponent.
George Gervin's Jersey	Reach Reputation Level 5 in Be a Legend mode.
James Worthy's Jersey	Beat the Northeast region with no losses to unlock the jersey.
Jerry West Jersey	Win a game without getting blocked.
Julius Erving's Jersey	Beat the Mosswood Street Challenge in Be a Legend.
Julius Erving, Connie Hawkins, and Earl Monroe	Beat the Rucker Park '78 Street Challenge in Be a Legend mode.
Just Blaze	Beat the Rucker Park '78 Street Challenge in Be a Legend mode.

NBA Street Vol 2 (cont'd)

Larry Bird's Jersey	Beat the Greenlake Street Challenge.
Larry Bird, Clyde Drexler, and Isiah Thomas	Beat the Central Region.
Michael Jordan's Jersey	Beat the Rucker Park '78 Street Challenge in Be a Legend mode.
MJ Throwback Jersey	Play Pick-up Game mode in each of the scoring rule categories.
Moses Malone's Jersey	Max out your created baller's stats and then win a game with him.
Nelly and the St. Lunatics	Get 750 reward points and buy their card.
Oscar Robertson's Jersey	Beat the Southwest Region with no losses.
Osmosis	Beat the tournament held in Mosswood in Oakland in the Be A Legend mode.
Pete Maravich, David Thompson, and George Gervin	Beat the Northwest Region.
Rucker Park '78	Beat Be a Legend mode to get Rucker park '78.
Street Champ Clothes	Beat Be a Legend mode to unlock the clothes.
Stretch	Win the Soul in the Hole Tournament to unlock Stretch.
Tiny Archibald Throwback Jersey	Beat street school without messing up.
Walt Frazier's Jersey	Beat the Central region with no losses.
Whitewater	Win the Greenlake Tournament to unlock whitewater.
Wilt Chamberlain's Jersey	Beat the Foster Beach Street Challenge in Be a Legend mode.

NCAA Football 2004

Unlockable	Code
2002 All-American Team	Level 18
Butter Fingers Pennant	Level 4
Orange Bowl Pennant	Level 8
Rose Bowl Pennant	Level 2
Tostitos Bowl Pennant	Level 12

For the following unlockables, score a touchdown, then enter code.

Unlockable	Objective
Bow	L2+▲
Display Ball	R2+▲
Dunk Over Goal Post	R2+■
Heisman Pose	L2+✕
Kick Ball Into Crowd	R2+●
Spike Ball	L2+■
Spike ball, then Shrug	L2+●
Throw Ball Into Crowd	R2+✕

NCAA Football 2005

Go to "My NCAA". Choose "Pennant Collection" and press Select to enter these codes.

Unlockable	Code
1st and 15	THANKS
Baylor Ratings Boost	SIC EM
Blink (ball is spotted short for opponent)	FOR
Boing (opponent drops more passes)	REGISTERING
Butter Fingers	WITH EA
Crossed The Line	TIBURON
Cuffed Cheat	EA SPORTS
Illinois Ratings Boost	OSKEE WOW

NCAA Football 2005 (cont'd)

Jumbalaya	HIKE
Molasses	HOME FIELD
Ouch	BLITZ
Quarterback Dud	ELITE 11
Stiffed	NCAA
Take Your Time	FOOTBALL
Texas Tech Ratings Boost	FIGHT
Thread The Needle	2005
What A Hit	BLITZ

Unlockable Team	Code
2003 All-Americans	FUMBLE
Alabama All-Time Team	ROLL TIDE
Arizona Mascot Team	BEAR DOWN
Arkansas All-Time Team	WOOPIGSOOIE
Auburn All-Time Team	WAR EAGLE
Badgers All-Time Team	U RAH RAH
Clemson All-Time Team	DEATH VALLEY
Colorado All-Time Team	GLORY
Florida All-Time Team	GREAT TO BE
Florida State All-Time Team	UPRISING
Georgia All-Time Team	HUNKER DOWN
Georgia Tech Mascot Team	RAMBLINWRECK
Iowa All-Time Team	ON IOWA
Iowa State Mascot Team	RED AND GOLD
Kansas Mascot Team	ROCK CHALK
Kansas State All-Time Team	VICTORY
Kentucky Mascot Team	ON ON UK
LSU All-Time Team	GEAUX TIGERS
Miami All-Time Team	RAISING CANE
Michigan All-Time Team	GO BLUE
Michigan State Mascot Team	GO GREEN
Minnesota Mascot Team	RAH RAH RAH
Mississippi State All-Time Team	HAIL STATE
Missouri Mascot Team	MIZZOU RAH
Nebraska All-Time Team	GO BIG RED
North Carolina All-Time Team	RAH RAH
North Carolina State Mascot Team	GO PACK
Notre Dame All-Time Team	GOLDEN DOMER
NU Mascot Team	GO CATS
Ohio State All-Time Team	KILLER NUTS
Oklahoma All-Time Team	BOOMER
Oklahoma State All-Time Team	GO POKES
Ole Miss Mascot Team	HOTTY TOTTY
Oregon All-Time Team	QUACK ATTACK
Penn State All-Time Team	WE ARE

NCAA Football 2005 (cont'd)

Pittsburgh All-Time Team	LETS GO PITT
Purdue All-Time Team	BOILER UP
South Carolina Mascot Team	GO CAROLINA
Syracuse All-Time Team	ORANGE CRUSH
Tennessee All-Time Team	BIG ORANGE
Texas A&M All-Time Team	GIG EM
Texas All-Time Team	HOOK EM
UCLA All-Time Team	MIGHTY
USC All-Time Team	FIGHT ON
Virginia All-Time Team	WAHOOS
Virginia Tech All-Time Team	TECH TRIUMPH
Wake Forest Mascot Team	GO DEACS GO
Washington All-Time Team	BOW DOWN
Washington Sate Mascot Team	ALL HAIL
West Virginia Mascot Team	HAIL WV

Need for Speed: Hot Pursuit 2

Enter these codes at the main menu.

Aston Martin V12 Vanquish	R2,→,R2,→,▲,←,▲,←
BMW Z8	■,→,■,→,R2,▲,R2,▲
Cheat Mode	L2,R2,L2,R2,▲,■,▲,■
Ferrari F550	L1,■,L1,■,→,R1,→,R1
HSV Coupe GTS	L1,L2,L1,L2,R1,▲,R1,▲
Lamborghini Diablo 6.0 VT	→,R2,→,R2,R1,L1,R1,L1
Lotus Elise	▲,R2,▲,R2,←,■,←,■
McLaren F1 LM	■,L1,■,L1,▲,→,▲,→
Porsche Carrera GT	←,→,←,→,R1,R2,R1,R2

Need for Speed Underground

At the Main Menu:

Unlockable	**Code**
Drift Physics in All Modes	R1,↑,↑,↑,↓,↓,↓,L1
Level 1 Performance Parts	R2,R2,R1,R1,←,→,←,→
Level 2 Performance Parts	R1,R1,R1,R1,R2,R2,←,→
Level 2 Visual Parts	↓,←,↑,↓,R1,R2,R2,■

Need for Speed Underground (cont'd)

Unlockable Car	Code
Acura Integra	R2,R2,R1,R2,L2,L1,↓,↑
Acura RSX	R1,R2,↓,←,↑,→,←,→
Ford Focus	←,→,↑,R1,R2,R1,R2,↑
Honda S2000	↑,↑,↓,↓,↑,←,■,R2
Hyundai Tiburon	←,→,←,→,↑,↓,↑,↓
Lost Prophets Car	↑,↑,↑,→,↓,↓,↑,→
Mitsubishi Lancer	←,←,←,R1,R1,R2,R2,L2
Mystikal Car	↑,→,↑,↑,↓,→,↑,→
Nissan Nismo	↑,↓,↑,←,↓,↓,↑,→
Nissan 240SX	↑,↓,←,→,■,R1,L2,R1
Nissan 350Z	→,→,↓,↑,■,L1,R1,L2
Nissan Sentra	→,→,→,L2,L2,R2,R2,↑
Nissan Skyline	↓,↓,L1,L2,L1,L2,L1,↓
Petey Pablo Car	↑,↑,↑,↑,↓,↑,↑,→
Rob Zombie Car	↑,←,↑,↑,↓,←,↑,→
Subaru Impreza	↑,↓,↓,↑,L2,↑,L2,↓
Toyota Supra	R1,R1,R2,R1,R2,R1,L2,L1

Unlockable Tracks	Code
All Circuit Tracks	↓,R1,R1,R1,R2,R2,R2,■
All Drag Tracks	→,■,←,R1,■,L1,L2,R2
All Drift Tracks	←,←,←,←,→,R2,R1,L2
All Sprint Tracks	↑,R2,R2,R2,R1,↓,↓,↓

Need for Speed Underground 2

Enter these codes at the Title Screen.

Unlockable	Code
$1000	←,←,→,■,■,→,L1,R1
All Circuit Tracks	↓,R1,R1,R1,R2,R2,R2,■
Best Buy Vinyl	↑,↓,↑,↓,↓,↑,→,←
Burger King Vinyl	↑,↑,↑,↑,↓,↑,↑,←
D3 GTO	↑,↓,→,↑,←,↓,→,→
Hummer H2 Capone	↑,←,↑,↑,↓,←,↓,←

Neo Contra

Enter this code at the Title Screen.

Unlockable	Code
19 Lives	↑,↑,↓,↓,L1,R1,L1,R1,L3,R3

NFL Blitz 2003

Unlockable	Code
All Stadiums	L1, L1, L1, R1, ×, ×, ×, ×, →
Allow Out of Bounds	L1, L1, R1, ×, ←
Always QB (Two Humans on Team)	L1, L1, R1, R1, ×, ×, ←
Always Receiver (Two Humans on Team)	L1, L1, R1, R1, ×, ×, →
Arctic Station	R1, R1, R1, ×, ×, ×, ×, ↓
Armageddon Team	L1, L1, L1, L1, L1, R1, R1, R1, R1, ×, ×, ×, →
Auto-Passing Icon	×, ×, ×, ↑
Big Feet	R1, R1, ×, ×, ×, ×, ×, ←
Big Head Teams	L1, L1, ×, ×, ×, →
Big Heads	L1, L1, →
Bilders Team	L1, L1, L1, R1, ↑
Brew Dawgs Team	L1, L1, L1, L1, R1, R1, R1, ×, ×, ↓
Central Park	R1, R1, R1, ×, ×, ×, →
Chimp Mode	R1, R1, ×, ×, ×, ×, ×, ↑
Chrome Ball	R1, R1, R1, ↓
Classic Ball	R1, R1, R1, ←
Clear Weather	L1, R1, R1, ×, ×, ×, →
Crunch Mode Team	L1, L1, L1, L1, ×, ×, ×, →
Disable Auto-Passing Icon	×, ×, ×, ↓
Extra Play for Offense	L1, L1, L1, R1, R1, R1, ×, ×, ×, ↓
Extra Time	×, →
Fast Passes	L1, L1, R1, R1, R1, R1, ←
Faster Running	R1, R1, R1, ×, ×, ←
Ground Fog	L1, L1, R1, R1, R1, ×, ×, ↓
Gsmers Team	L1, L1, L1, L1, L1, ×, ↑
Huge Heads	L1, R1, R1, R1, R1, ×, ×, ×, ×, ×, ←
Midway Team	L1, L1, R1, R1, R1, R1, R1, ×, ×, ×, →
More Code Entry Time	L1, L1, R1, ×, ×, →
More Fumbles	L1, L1, L1, R1, R1, R1, R1, ×, ×, ×, ×, ×, ↑
Neo Tokyo Team	L1, L1, L1, R1, R1, R1, R1, ×, ×, ×, ×, ↓
No CPU Assist	L1, L1, L1, L1, L1, L1, L1, L1, L1, L1, R1, ×, ×, ↓
No First Downs	L1 x (12), R1, ↑
No Highlighting Receivers	L1, L1, L1, R1, R1, ×, ↓
No Interceptions	L1, L1, L1, R1, R1, R1, R1, R1, ×, ×, ×, ×, ×, ↑
No Punting	L1, R1, R1, R1, R1, ×, ↑
No Random Fumbles	L1 x (15), R1, R1, R1, R1, R1, ↓
No Replays	L1, L1, L1, L1, L1, R1, R1, R1, R1, R1, ×, ×, ×, ×, →
Noftle Mode	L1, L1, L1, R1, R1, ×, ×, ×, ×, ×, ↑
Power Loader	R1, R1, ×, ×, ×, ×, ×, →
Power-up Defense	L1, L1, L1, L1, R1, R1, ×, ↑
Power-up Linemen	L1, L1, L1, L1, L1, R1, R1, ×, ↑
Power-up Offense	L1, L1, L1, L1, R1, ×, ×, ↑
Rollos Team	L1, L1, R1, R1, R1, R1, R1, ×, ×, ×, ×, ↑
Show More Field	L1 x (10), R1, R1, ×, →
Showtime Mode	L1, L1, L1, R1, R1, R1, R1, R1, ×, →
Smart CPU Teammates	L1, L1, L1, R1, ×, ×, ×, ×, ↓
Super Blitzing	R1, R1, R1, R1, R1, ×, ×, ×, ×, ↑
Super Field Goals	L1, R1, R1, ×, ×, ×, ←

PSP Xbox PS2 GC GBA

NFL Blitz 2003 (cont'd)

Tournament Mode	L1 x (11), R1,×,↓
Training Grounds	R1,R1,R1,×,×,×,×,×,↑
Unlimited Turbo	L1,L1,L1,L1,R1,×,×,×,×,×,↑
Weather: Rain	L1,L1,L1,L1,L1,R1,R1,R1,R1,R1, ×,×,×,×,×,→
Weather: Snow	L1,L1,L1,L1,L1,L1,R1,R1,R1,R1,R1, ×,×,×,×,×,←

NFL GameDay 2001

Unlockable	Code
All-Star Teams	At the Team Selection screen, press ●, ●.
Super Bowl Teams	At the Team Selection screen, press ●.

NFL Gameday 2004

To unlock the following stadiums, go to the matchup screen of a Preseason game, then press ■ to go to Preseason Options. Press L1 to Toggle the Home Team default stadium. Then scroll to the stadium you want to unlock. Enter the following codes to unlock them.

Unlockable	Code
Good Ol' Days	SEPIA TONE
Old Carolina	CAROL

NFL Street

Enter these codes at the User Name Screen.

Unlockable	Code
All 8 Division All-Star Teams	AW9378
All Stadiums	Travel
All Star Teams	AW9378
KaySlay Team	KaySlay
NFL Legends Team	Classic
NFC West Team	NW9378
X-Ecutioners Team	Excellent

NFL Street 2

Create a profile then enter these case sensitive codes in the Cheats Menu.

Unlockable	Code
AFC East All-Stars	EAASFSCT
AFC North All-Stars	NAOFRCTH
AFC South All-Stars	SAOFUCTH
AFC West All-Stars	WAEFSCT
All players will have a maxed out catching stat	MagnetHands
NFC East All Stars	NNOFRCTH
NFC North All-Stars	NNAS66784
NFC South All Stars	SNOFUCTH
NFC West All Stars	ENASFSCT
EA Field	EAField
No Fumble Mode (Quick Game)	GlueHands
Reebok Team	Reebok

NHL 2001

Unlock	Code
Super Defense Players	Enter Sandis Ozolinsh or Chris Pronger as a name in the Create-a-Player screen. Choose "Yes" to use his ratings (you can still adjust them with NHL Challenge bonus points). Return to the previous screen and you can change his name to whatever you want, but don't change any other settings.
Super Forwards	Enter Peter Forsberg, Jaromir Jagr, Keith Tkachuk, Pavel Bure, Steve Yzerman, Owen Nolan, Olaf Kolzig, Nicklas Lidstrom, or Rob Blake as a name in the Create-a-Player screen. Choose "Yes" to use his ratings (you can still adjust them with NHL Challenge bonus points). Return to the previous screen and you can change his name to whatever you want, but don't change any other settings.

NHL 2001 (cont'd)

Super Goalies	Enter Patrick Roy, Dominik Hasek, or Ed Belfour as a name in the Create-a-Player screen. Choose "Yes" to use his ratings (you can still adjust them with NHL Challenge bonus points). Return to the previous screen and you can change his name to whatever you want, but don't change any other settings.
Taunts	Hold ▲ after you score a goal, win a fight, win a game, or the opposing team gets a penalty.
The Dude	Enter Bruce Willis as a name in the Create-a-Player screen. The announcer will call that player "The Dude" during the game.
The Hammer	Enter Hammer as a name in the Create-a-Player screen. The announcer will call that player "The Hammer" during the game.

NHL 2003

Unlockable	Code
Bonus Players	Create a player and enter one of the following names. The game completes his abilities and stats. Some players also have a portrait: Adam Hall, Alfie Michaud, Barry Richter, Ben Simon, Blake Bellefeuille, Brad Moran, Brian Sutherby, Chris Ferraro, Corey Hirsch, Dave Morisset, David Nemirovsky, Derek Mackenzie, Eric Fichaud, Evgeny Konstantinov, Greg Crozier, Greg Pankewicz, Guy Hebert, Ivan Huml, Jakub Cutta, Jason LaBarbera, Jason Zent, Johan Witehall, Kay Whitmore, Larry Murphy, Mark Fitzpatrick, Marquis Mathieu, Martin Brochu, Matt Herr, Matt Higgins, Michel Larocque, Raffi Torres, Rene Corbet, Rich Parent, Rick Tabaracci, Sascha Goc, Scott Fankhouser, Ty Jones, and Xavier Delisle.

NHL Hitz Pro

At the Choose Team screen, enter the following words as a profile name. Then go to Settings, Game Tuning, Visuals, then "Cheats" to activate the cheat.

Unlockable	Code
Big Player Head	HERK
Big Team Heads	INGY
Different Puck Size	211S
Different Puck Shadow	SASG
Glowing Puck	CARB

Nightshade

Unlockable	Objective
Hisu	Complete the game on Easy Mode.
Hotsuma	Complete the game on Normal but be sure to have a Shinobi save on the same Memory Card.
Hibana's 2nd Costume	Complete the game on Normal Mode.
Hibana's 3rd Costume	Complete the game on Hard Mode.
Joe Musashi	Complete 88 Stages.

Unlockable	Objective
EX Mission Stage 1	3 Clan Coins
EX Mission Stage 2	14 Clan Coins
EX Mission Stage 3	24 Clan Coins
EX Mission Stage 4	35 Clan Coins
EX Mission Stage 5	45 Clan Coins
EX Mission Stage 6	56 Clan Coins
EX Mission Stage 7	68 Clan Coins
EX Mission Stage 8	80 Clan Coins
Hisui's 2nd Costume	88 Clan Coins
Survival Stage 1	10 Clan Coins
Survival Stage 2	21 Clan Coins
Survival Stage 3	31 Clan Coins
Survival Stage 4	42 Clan Coins
Survival Stage 5	52 Clan Coins

Nightshade (cont'd)

Unlockable	Objective
Survival Stage 6	64 Clan Coins
Survival Stage 7	76 Clan Coins
Survival Stage 8	88 Clan Coins
Time Attack Stage 1	7 Clan Coins
Time Attack Stage 2	17 Clan Coins
Time Attack Stage 3	28 Clan Coins
Time Attack Stage 4	38 Clan Coins
Time Attack Stage 5	49 Clan Coins
Time Attack Stage 6	60 Clan Coins
Time Attack Stage 7	72 Clan Coins
Time Attack Stage 8	84 Clan Coins

Oni

For the following unlockables, press SELECT during gameplay, highlight the "Help" button, then enter code. A sound confirms correct code entry.

Unlockable	Code
Big Head Mode	L2,L1,L2,■,●,■,START,■,●,START
Change the Character	L2,L1,L2,■,●,■,L2,L2,L2,L2—do not move your cursor yet. Hit the L2 button until you select your character.
Extra Powerful Punches and Kicks	L2,L1,L2,■,●,■,R3,L3,●,■
Godly Guns	L2,L1,L2,■,●,■,L2,L2,L2,L1,L3—gives you unlimited ammo and you never have to reload.
Hard Mode	L2,L1,L2,■,●,■,R3,L3,●,■
Huge Characters	L2,L1,L2,■,●,■,R3,■,●,L3
Instant Level Completion	L2,L1,L2,■,●,■,L3,R3,L2,L1
Itty Bitty Characters	L2,L1,L2,■,●,■,L3,R3,■,●
One Shot, One Kill	L2,L1,L2,■,●,■,L3,R3,●,■
Unlimited Health	L2,L1,L2,■,●,■,R3,L3,R3,●
Unlimited Phase Cloak	L2,L1,L2,■,●,■,L1,R3,L2,L3—enables you to stay invisible for as long as you want

TIP

Here's an extra tip. To avoid fall damage, press ↙ to do a flip as you near the ground.

Onimusha: Blade Warriors

Unlockable	Objective
Blue Z-part	Beat Phantom Realm 2 using Megaman EXE.
Giramusaido	Musaido Reaches Level 3 Or Above.
Gogandantess	Clear the game with Samanosuke Akechi, Kaede, Normal Soldier, and Maeda Keijirou in Story Mode.
Green Z-part	Beat the Phantom Realm using Megaman EXE.
Jaido	Normal Genma/Sword foot light reaches Level 2 or above.
Jujudormah Ran	Clear the game with Jujudormah (Level 3 or above) in Story Mode.
Magoichi Saiga	Fight 200 battles in VS Mode.
Marcellus Modify P	Have Marcellus Reaches Level 2.
Marcellus Modify S	Have Marcellus Reaches Level 3 Or Above.
Miyamoto Musashi	Clear the game with Normal Soldier(Level 3 Or Above) in Story Mode.
Musaido	Three Eye reaches Level 2 or above.
Oda Nobunaga	Clear the game with all 12 Default characters in Story Mode.
Red Z-part	Beat Story mode using Megaman EXE.
Rockman EXE	Clear the game with Samanosuke Akechi in Story Mode.

Onimusha: Blade Warriors (cont'd)

Rockman EXE—Bug Style	Rockman EXE reaches Level 3 or above.
Rockman EXE—Grand Style	Rockman EXE reaches Level 2.
Rockman Zero	Use Rockman EXE to collect all 3 Z-Parts (Red, Blue, Green).
Rockman Zero—Proto Form	Rockman Zero reaches Level 2.
Rockman Zero—Ultimate Form	Rockman Zero reaches Level 3 or above.
Sasaki Kojirou	Clear the game with Miyamoto Musashi in Story Mode.
Zero	Have all 3 Z parts then beat him in VS mode.

Onimusha: Warlords

Unlockable	Objective
Alternate Costumes	To make your character look different, complete the game one time, then start a new game after saving. You will see a "Normal/Special" option. If you select the Special option, you will appear in a special panda suit.
Beat Oni Spirits/ Unlock An Arsenal	If you make it past all 12 levels of the challenging Oni Spirits mini-game, you unlock a gameplay option that allows you to start the regular game with a wonderful array of toys. Not only do you get to play through the game with the Bishamon Sword, but you get unlimited Arrows and Bullets, and begin with 99 Soul Absorbers in your inventory. In addition, any magic you use automatically respawns after the attack. With this at your disposal, beating the game again and unlocking everything else is a cinch!
Get the Bishamon Sword	Fight through all 20 levels of the Dark Realm. Kill all of the monsters on the 20th level, then open the treasure box to discover the Bishamon Ocarina. In the area just beyond the second Marcellus boss fight, use the Ocarina on the bone door to open it. Head inside and claim the prize: a sword with unlimited magic which kills any non-boss character in a single swipe. A powerful ally, indeed.
Preview for Onimusha 2	After you complete the game for the first time, it prompts you to save. Do so, then start a new game. View the "Special Report" to see a small preview of Onimusha 2, which takes place 10 years after the events in this game.
Unlock Easy Mode	There are two ways of unlocking the easy mode: 1. Beat the game 4 times to make the Easy Mode available. 2. If Osric beats you 5 times or more, the Easy Mode unlocks.
Unlock Oni Spirits	Collect all 20 Flourites and finish the game.
Unlock Onimusha 2 Trailer	Finish the game on any difficulty to unlock a sneak preview of Onimusha 2. When you go to the main menu after saving, go to Special Feature to view the preview footage.
Unlock the Panda Suit	If you collect 10 or more Fluorites during the course of the game and finish the game, there will be an extra costume available for Samanosuke when you begin a new game. When you restart, select Samanosuke-Extra to play as the big bear. Check out the daisy gauntlet and stuffed friend in the mucus pouch. During gameplay, use L2 to take the head on or off.

Onimusha 2: Samurai's Destiny

Unlockable	Objective
Critical Mode	Complete the game under the Hard difficulty setting.
Easy Mode	Start a game and die three times. A message appears to indicate that a new Easy difficulty setting is available. Note: You cannot achieve an Onimusha rank when playing in Easy mode.
Ending Bonuses	Complete the game to unlock the "Scenario Route" option, Man in Black mode, Team Onimusha mode, and an FMV preview of Onimusha 3.

Onimusha 2: Samurai's Destiny (cont'd)

Hard Mode	Complete the game under the Normal difficulty setting.
Issen Mode	Complete the Oni Organization minigame. You must hit with a One-Flash attack to damage opponents. The Issen Strike works on bosses. However, it does not kill them in one strike.
Jubei's Alternate Costume	Collect the Fashionable Goods item, and complete the game with an "S" rank. Enter the Special Features menu and enable the "Extra Jubei" option to dress her in leather and sunglasses (press L2 to toggle). In the Japanese version, complete the game with the Onimusha rank.
Mind Twister Mode	Complete the game with all Paintings.
Oyu's Alternate Costume	Get a 100 percent scenario completion by playing the game multiple times to make good alliances with all NPCs. After you unlock all scenarios in the "Scenario Route" viewer, enter the Special Features menu, and enable the "Extra Oyu" option to dress him in a 1970s style costume.
Team Onimusha One-Hit Kills	Complete the game in Team Onimusha mode to unlock an option to replay Team Onimusha with one-hit kills.
Ultimate Mode	Complete the game under the Hard difficulty setting. Enter the Special Features menu, and enable the "Ultimate Mode" option to begin a new game with the Rekka-Ken Sword, 20,000 in money, 30 Perfect Medicines, 10 Talismans, all Level 3 armors, unlimited ammunition, unlimited magic, and skill always full. Your NPCs also have unlimited subweapons.

Onimusha 3

Unlockable	Objective
The Adventures of Heihachi	Complete the game and this new mode will open up, enabling you to play as Heihachi.
Michelle's Wet Bathroom look	Complete the game with an S ranking on normal or higher difficulty.
Samanosuke and Jacque's Western Outfit	Score higher ending game points (Sum of Play Time points, Soul points, Enemies defeated points, Dark Realm "obtain points" and Critical Hit points.) when playing as Samanosuke vs. Jacques to unlock Samanosuke's special Western Outfit. On the flip side, score higher ending game points with Jacques than Samanosuke to unlock Jacques Western Outfit. These also become available if the game is completed wearing one of the two Western Outfits.
Samanosuke's Panda Suit	Complete the Oni Training mini game or have a Onimusha Blade Warrior save on your memory card. For added fun pressing L2 will flip the head on and off with different expressions each time.

The Operative: No One Lives Forever

In the Main Menu, highlight Load Game, then enter the code.

Level Select	Hold L3+R3, then press ×.

Orphen: Scion of Sorcery

Unlockable	Objective
Restart the Battle	Pause the game and pick "Equip" before resuming the game at the start of the battle. All your energy will be restored.

Outlaw Golf 2

Unlockable	Objective
Everything unlocked	Enter I Have No Time as a profile name.

Pac-Man World 2

Unlockable	Objective
Ms. Pac-Man Mini-Game	Collect 180 tokens during gameplay to unlock the classic Ms. Pac-Man arcade game.
Music Test	Collect 60 tokens during gameplay to unlock the "Jukebox" option.
Pac-Attack Mini-Game	Collect 30 tokens during gameplay to unlock the classic Pac-Attack arcade game.
Pac-Man Mini-Game	Collect 10 tokens during gameplay to unlock the classic Pac-Man arcade game.
Pac-Mania Mini-Game	Collect 100 tokens during gameplay to unlock the classic Pac-Mania arcade game.
Pre-Production Art and Programmers	Collect 150 tokens during gameplay to unlock the "Museum" option.

Parappa The Rapper 2

Unlockable	Objective
Blue Hat	Beat the game once, and Parappa dons a snazzy blue hat.
Dog House	Beat each level while wearing the yellow hat and Parappa gets a new dog house. Go there to listen to some tunes. In the dog house, you can listen to tracks from any level on which you've earned a "Cool" rating.
Pink Hat	Beat each level while wearing the blue hat to give Parappa a new pink hat.
Yellow Hat	Beat each level while wearing the pink hat to give Parappa a new yellow hat.

Pirates The Legend of Black Kat

To access the following unlockables, hold R1+R2, then enter code.

Unlockable	Code
Advance to Katarina's Next Sword	R3,SELECT,L2,L3,■,×,L1,●,L3,▲,L3,■,×,L1,●
All Treasure Chest Keys	●,SELECT,×,■,R3,L1,L3,L2,▲,L3
Alternate Glacial Gulf Music	Press L1,×,▲,L2,■,●,L3,SELECT,R3,L3—you can now hear music from SSX when sliding down in Glacial Gulf.
Extra Gold	▲,R3,L3,×,■,R3,SELECT,L1,●—you can now sail to another map to get the Galleon.
High-Pitched Voices	R3,●,SELECT,×,R3,▲,L1,■,L2,L3
Invincibility for Katarina	×,●,L3,▲,R3,SELECT,R3,L1,L2,■
Invincibility for the Wind Dancer	SELECT,▲,L1,×,R3,L2,■,R3,●,L3
Kane Poison Head	▲,L2,L1,■,L3,×,L3,●,R3,SELECT—the poison status will be indicated by the head of Kane from Command and Conquer.
Reveal All Treasure Chests	R3,×,▲,L3,●,L1,SELECT,L3,■,L2
Reveal Buried Treasure Chests	●,×,■,▲,L1,SELECT,L3,L2,L3,R3—green Xs will appear on the captain's log maps to indicate the location of buried treasure chests.
Unlimited Items	▲,L1,SELECT,L2,R3,L3,■,×,R3,●—once found, an item will be available in unlimited amounts.
Unlimited Wind Boost	SELECT,L1,R3,●,L2,▲,×,L3
Wind Dancer	L2,▲,R3,L3,×,■,R3,SELECT,L1,●

PSP Xbox PS2 GC GBA

Pirates The Legend of Black Kat (cont'd)

To access alternate Karina costumes,please see table below. The following code requires two players and controllers. Simultaneously hold L1+L2+↑+SELECT+L3 on controller one and R1+R2+▲+START+R3 on controller two. A short sequence of music will confirm correct code entry. Click down on R3 on controller one to change the value of the numbers that appear on screen, then start a new game or resume a saved game to view the corresponding costume. The costumes that can be accessed are as follows:

Costume	Code
Blackbeard in Purple	00000001
Blonde Hair, Orange and Yellow Bikini	00000101
Blonde Hair, Pink Bikini	00000110
Blue Hair with Orange and Red Bikini	00000011
Blue Hair, Shiny Copper Body Suit	00001010
Blue Hair, Shiny Silver Bikini	00000111
Original Costume and Hair Color	00000000
Pink Hair, Shiny Black Body Suit	00001001
Purple Hair, Shiny Silver Body Suit	00001011
Red Hair with Red and Orange Bikini	00000010
Red Hair, Black Bikini, Black Stockings	00001000
Tan, Brown Hair, Orange and Yellow Bikini	00000100

Pitfall: The Lost Expedition

Enter the following codes at the Title Screen. If you entered the code correctly, a message will appear.

Unlockable	Code
Hyper Punch Mode	Hold L1+R1, then press →,←,●,↑,●,→,←
Original Pitfall game	Hold L1+R1, then press ●,●,←,→,●,■,×,↑,●
Original Pitfall 2: Lost Caverns game	Hold L1+R1, then press ←,→,←,→,▲,▲,▲
Play as Nicole	Hold L1+R1, then press ←,↑,↓,↑,●,↑,↑
Unlimited Water in Canteen	Hold L1+R1, then press ←,■,●,↓,■,×,■,●

Primal

Unlockable	Objective
All Handguns and Shotgun	Easy, "A" rank.
All Weapons (except charged particle rifle)	Easy, "S" rank or Normal, "A" rank.
All Weapons with Unlimited Ammo	Hard, "S" rank.
All Weapons with Unlimited Ammo (except charged particle rifle)	Normal, "S" rank or Hard, "A" rank.

At any menu screen hold R1+R2+L2+L2 and the codes screen will appear. Then enter the following codes and press ■.

Unlockable	Code
Easykill	KILLSWITCH
Invulnerability	MONSTROUS
Unlock Aquis Scenes	MOONPOOL
Unlock the Solum Scenes	WINDCHILL

Prince of Persia: The Sands of Time

Unlockable	Code
Unlock the first Prince of Persia	Start a new game and stay on the balcony, press L3 and quickly enter ×, ■, ▲, ●, ▲, ×, ■, ●.

PSP Xbox PS2 GC GBA

Psi-Ops: The Mindgate Conspiracy

In Main Menu, highlight Extra Content and press R1. Then enter these codes.

Unlockable	Code
All Powers	537893
Infinite Ammo	978945
Bulletproof	548975
Super Psi	456456
No Head	987978
Arcade mode	05051979
Co-op mode	07041979
Dark Mode	465486

Extra Missions	Code
Aura Pool	659785
Bottomless Pit	54897
Bouncy Bouncy	568789
Gasoline	9442662
Gearshift	154684
Gnomotron	456878
Panic Room	76635766
Pitfall	05120926
Psi Pool	565485
Stop Lights	945678
Survival	7734206
Tip the Buddha	428584
TK Alley	90702
Up and Over	020615

Skins	Code
Burned Soldier	454566
Dock Worker	364654
Edgar Barrett	497878
Edgar Barret (Training 1)	196001
Edgar Barret (Training 2)	196002
Edgar Barret (Training 3)	196003
Edgar Barret (Training 4)	196004
Edgar Barret (Training 5)	196005
Edgar Barret (Training 6)	196006
The General	459797
The General (Clown)	431644
Jack	698798
Jov Leonov	468987
Marlena Kessler	489788
Marlena Kessler (Bikini)	135454
Marlena Kessler (Leather)	136876
MP1	321646
MP2	678999
MP3	654659
Nick Scryer (Stealth)	456498
Nick Scryer (Training)	564689
Nick Scryer (Urban)	484646
Nick Scryer (Wasteland)	975466
Sara Blake	135488
Sara Blake (Psi)	468799
Sara Blake (Suicide)	231644
Scorpion	546546
Tonya	678999
UN Soldier	365498
Wei Lu	231324
Wei Lu (Dragon)	978789
Wei Lu (Tranquility)	654654

The Punisher

Effect	Code
Everything Unlocked (except upgrades)	V Pirate as a Profile Name.

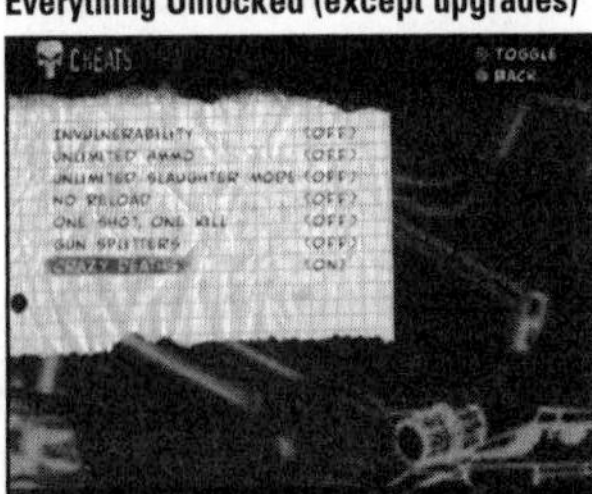

Quake III Revolution

Enter the following code during gameplay.

Level Skip — Hold L1+R1+R2+SELECT, then press ×,●,■,▲,×,●,■,▲

R-Type Final

Pause the game to enter these codes. You will hear a sound if you entered it correctly.

Unlockable	Code
99.9% Charge Dose	Hold L2, then press R2,R2,←,→,↑,↓,→,←,↑,↓,▲
Full Blue Power, Missiles, and Bits	Hold L2, then press R2,R2,←,→,↑,↓,→,←,↑,↓,●
Full Red Power, Missiles, and Bits	Hold L2, then press R2,R2,←,→,↑,↓,→,←,↑,↓,■
Full Yellow Power, Missiles, and Bits	Hold L2, then press R2,R2,←,→,↑,↓,→,←,↑,↓,×
Invincibility	Hold L2, then press →,→,←,→,←,←,→,←,L1,↑,↑,↓,↓,↑,↓,↑,↓,L1

Pause the game while in the R's Museum to enter these codes. You will hear a sound if you entered it correctly.

Unlockable	Code	Unlockable	Code
Curtain Call Ship (#100)	1009 9201	Strider Ship (#24)	2078 0278
Mr. Heli Ship (#59)	1026 2001	Lady Love Ship (#3)	5270 0725

Ratchet and Clank: Up Your Arsenal

Unlockable	Code
Duel Blade Laser Sword	Pause the game and press ●,■,●,■,↑,↓,←,←.
Sly 2: Band of Thieves Demo	At the Title Screen, hold L1+L2+R1+R2.

Rayman 2: Revolution

Description	Code
Cheat Menu	During Gameplay pause your game and then select "Sound." Now highlight the "Mute" selection. Do not Validate it, simply highlight it. Now, press and hold L1+L2, then press L2,R2,L2,R2,L2,R2.
Extra Bonus Mini-Games	From the Press Start screen, press START. Now, select your language. Next, select "Options." Then choose "Language." Select "Voices" and highlight "Raymanian." Now, press and hold L1+R1, then press L2,R2,L2,R2,L2,R2.
Soccer Names	First enable the "Extra Bonus Mini-Games" cheat and select "Baby Soccer." While you play this game press and hold L1+R1, then press L2,R2,L2,R2,L2,R2.

RC Revenge Pro

Enter the following codes at the Main Menu.

Unlockable	Code
Every Track	Press L1,R1,R2,■,●. When you enter the game, select your vehicle, then choose any track.
Every Vehicle	Press L1,L2,R1,R2,●,■. When you start you will have every vehicle to choose from.
Next Championship	Press L1,R1,R2,L2 to unlock the next Championship. Keep typing the code to unlock more championships. A total of seven more championships can be opened.

Ready 2 Rumble Boxing: Round 2

Unlockable	Code
Big Gloves	At the Character Selection screen, press ←,→,↑,↓,R1,R2. A sound confirms correct entry.
Fat Boxer	At the Character Selection screen, press →,→,↑,↓,→,R1,R1,R2. A sound confirms correct entry.

Ready 2 Rumble Boxing: Round 2 (cont'd)

Play As Freak E. Deke and Michael Jackson	At the character selection screen, press R1 x (13), R2, R1 x (10), R2.
Skinny Boxer	At the Character Selection screen, press →,→,↑,↓,→,R1,R2. A sound confirms correct entry.
Undead Boxer	At the Character Selection screen, press ←,↑,→,↓,R1,R1,R2. A sound confirms correct entry.
Bill Clinton	Beat Arcade mode eight times.
Champion Costumes	Complete Championship mode.
Freak E. Deke	Beat Arcade mode once.
Freedom Brock	Beat Arcade mode six times.
G.C. Thunder	Beat Arcade mode three times.
Hillary Clinton	Beat Arcade mode nine times.
Michael Jackson	Beat Arcade mode twice.
Rocket Samchay	Beat Arcade mode seven times.
Rumbleman	Beat Arcade mode ten times.
Shaquille O'Neal	Beat Arcade mode five times.
Wild "Stubby" Corley	Beat Arcade mode four times.

Holiday Costume	Objective
Christmas Costume	Set the system date to December 25. Selene Strike will be in an elf costume and Rumbleman will be in a snowman costume.
Easter Costume	Set the system date to April 23. Mama Tua will be in a Playboy Bunny costume.
Fourth of July Costume	Set the system date to July 4. G.C. Thunder will be in a Uncle Sam costume.
Halloween Costume	Set the system date to October 31. J.R. Flurry will be in a skeleton costume.
New Year's Costume	Set the system date to January 1. Joey T will be in a baby costume.
St. Patrick's Day Costume	Set the system date to March 17. The referee will be in a leprechaun costume.
Valentine's Day Costume	Set the system date to February 14. Lulu will be in a sexy costume.

Red Card 2003

To access Cheat Mode, enter BIGTANK as a name to unlock all teams, stadiums, and Finals mode.

Unlockable	Objective
Apes Team and Victoria Falls Stadium	Defeat the Apes team in World Conquest mode.
Dolphins Team and Nautilus Stadium	Defeat the Dolphins team in World Conquest mode.
Finals Mode	Win all matches in World Conquest mode.
Martians Team and USAFB001 Stadium	Defeat the Martians team in World Conquest mode.
Matadors Team and Coliseum Stadium	Defeat the Matadors team in World Conquest mode.
Samurai Team and Youhi Gardens Stadium	Defeat the Samurai team in World Conquest mode.
SWAT Team and Nova City Stadium	Defeat the SWAT team in World Conquest mode.

Red Dead Revolver

These are the rewards for each level. The first is for a Good rating and the second is for a Excellent rating.

Unlockable	Good rating	Excellent
Battle Finale	Focus (Dead-Eye) Max-Up	Mr. Kelley
Bear Mountain	Shadow Wolf	Focus (Dead-Eye) Max-Up
Bounty Hunter	"Bloody" Tom	"Big Oaf" Whitney
Bull's Eye	Old Pistol	Broken Creek
Carnival Life	Focus (Dead-Eye) Max-Up	"Pig" Josh
Cemetery	Ghost Town	Mr. Black
Devils & Angels	The Ranch	—
Fall From Grace	Scorpion Revolver	Governor Griffon
Fort Diego	Health Max-Up	Colonel Daren
Freak Show	Health Max-Up	Breech Loader
Hell Pass	Buffalo	Gabriel Navarro
The Mine	The Mine	"Smiley" Fawler
Railroaded	Owl Rifle	Rico Pedrosa
Rogue Valley	Cooper	Bad Bessie
Ugly Streetfight	"Ugly" Chris	Freak Show
Range War	The Ranch	Holstein Hal
Saloon Fight	Dan	Sam
The Siege	Mansion Grounds	Jason Cornet
Sunset Canyon	Twin Revolvers	Focus (Dead-Eye) Max-Up
The Traitor	The Bridge	Health Max-Up

Red Faction

Unlockable	Objective
Secret Roof Location in Lobby Multiplayer Map	You can get on the roof of the Lobby (where there is a giant skylight) to find a Fusion Rocket Launcher and a Rail Driver, as well as a great sniping spot. To get there, go up to the second level of the area where you are able to pick up the Rocket Launcher. Arm that weapon and aim for the corner of the wall where the skylight begins. Fire rockets to punch a hole into the ceiling and the wall. Continue to fire rockets until you form a small alcove where you can jump to, then up onto the roof. After you are there, grab a Fusion Rocket Launcher at one end of the skylight and a Rail Driver at the other end.

Red Faction II

Enter the following codes at the Cheats screen under the Options menu.

Unlockable	Code
Bouncy Grenades	●,●,●,●,●,●,●,●
Directors Cut	■,×,●,▲,●,×,■,▲
Gibby Bullets	●,●,●,●,▲,×,●,●
Gibby Explosions	▲,●,×,■,▲,●,×,■
Instagib Ammunition	×,×,×,×,■,●,×,×
Joke Message	■,×,■,×,■,×,■,×
Level Select	●,■,×,▲,■,●,×,×
Master Code unlocks all normal game options.	▲,▲,×,×,■,●,■,●

Unlockable	Code
Master Cheat Code	■,●,▲,●,■,×,▲,×
Rain of Fire	■,■,■,■,■,■,■,■
Rapid Rails	●,■,●,■,×,×,▲,▲
Super Health	×,×,■,▲,■,▲,●
Unlimited Ammunition	■,▲,×,●,■,●,×,▲
Unlimited Grenades	●,×,●,■,×,●,×,●
Wacky Deaths	▲,▲,▲,▲,▲,▲,▲,▲
Walking Dead	×,×,×,×,×,×,×,×

Resident Evil Code Veronica X

Unlockable	Objective
Get Special Journal	Go to the slot machine in the palace through the Battle Game (with the same character). On the third try, a special journal is there. It belongs to someone named D.I.J.
Unlock Linear Launcher for Battle Game	Get an A ranking with the two Claires, Steves, Chrises, and Weskers in the Battle Game to unlock the Linear Launcher. After you gain it, it automatically appears in your inventory when you begin the Battle Game again.
Unlock Rocket Launcher	Complete the main game with an "A" Ranking to earn the Rocket Launcher. To do this, do not use First Aid Spray, do not save your game, do not retry. You must save Steve from the Luger room quickly, give the Medicine to your jailer Rodrigo, and finish in under 4:30. When you begin another game, the Launcher will be available from the first Item Box you run across.
Unlock Steve for Battle Game	Solve a puzzle in the main game. In the underground Save Room in Chris's walkthrough, complete the drawer puzzle in the corner. Grab the Gold Luger to unlock Mr. Burnside.
Unlock the Battle Game	Beat the game once to unlock the Battle Game. Chris and Claire Redfield are now available as playable characters.
Unlock Wesker for Battle Game	Unlock Albert Wesker for use in the Battle Game by beating the Battle game with Chris Redfield.

Reign of Fire

Level Select	At main menu, enter ↑, ←, ●, ●, ←, ←, ■, ↓, ↑, ●

Ridge Racer V

Unlockable	Objective
99 Lap Option	Get the top score in all the Time Attack GP races in Extra mode and finish in first place.
Changing Saved Game Icon	Beat the game with all secrets unlocked. The saved game icon will change from a car to Ai Fukami, a programmer.
Modifying the Intro Sequence	Press L1+R1 during the intro sequence with the girl. Press R1 once for black-and-white graphics. Press R1 a second time and the game will have a yellow tint. Press R1 a third time to add a blur effect. That blur effect eliminates the jaggies in the graphics. You can press L2 to cycle back through the various effects.
Onscreen Information	During a race, press and hold SELECT for a few seconds. A window shows up on the screen with various information. Press and hold SELECT again to make the information window go away.
Unlock 50's Super Drift Caddy	Place first in the Danver Spectra race in Duel mode to unlock this car in Free Run, Duel, and Time Attack modes.
Unlock a Beetle	Place first in the Solort Rumeur race in Duel mode to unlock this car in Free Run, Duel, and Time Attack modes.
Unlock a McLaren Type Car	Place first in the Kamata Angelus race in Duel mode to unlock this car in Free Run, Duel, and Time Attack modes.
Unlock Devil Drift	Place first in the Rivelta Crinale race in Duel mode to unlock this car in Free Run, Duel, and Time Attack modes.
Unlock Duel Mode	Enter Standard Time Attack GP and finish first in lap and overall time.
Unlock Pac-Man Mode	Race more than 3,000 kilometers in total distance. The Pac-Man race becomes available. Beat the Pac-Man race and the Pac-Man car and the ghosts on scooters become unlocked.
Unlocking Bonus Cars	Beat each of the Grand Prix circuits, or break the Time Attack high scores.

Rise of Kasai

Enter the following codes at the Press Start screen.

Unlockable	Code
Invincible Rau	■, ●, ×, ■, ●, ■, ×, ●, ×, ■, ●, ×
Infinite Ammunition	×, ●, ■, ■, ×, ■, ●, ●, ×, ■, ■, ×
Weaker Enemies	×, ●, ●, ■, ×, ■, ■, ●

Rise to Honor

Unlockable	Objective
Extra Costumes	Complete the game.
Hard Mode	Complete the game on Normal
Kit Yun and Michelle's FMV	Complete the game.

Roadkill

Pause the game on the map screen then enter the following codes.

Unlockable	Code
All Weapons	▲, ×, ×, ▲, ■, ●, ●, ■, ×, ■, ●, ▲
All Vehicles	↑, ↓, ↑, ↓, ▲, ×, ▲, ×, ■, ●, ●, ■
Health	■, ●, ■, ●, ■, ●, ■, ●
Infinite Ammo	▲, ■, ■, ●, ▲, ■, ■, ●
More Money	▲, ●, ▲, ●, ■, ×, ■, ×, ↓, ↑

Robotech: Battlecry

To access Cheat Mode, enter the New Game or Load Game screen. Hold L1+L2+R1+R2, then press ←,↑,↓,×,→,▲,START to display the Code Entry screen. Enter one of the following codes to activate the corresponding cheat function.

Unlockable	Code
All Models and Awards	WHERESMAX
All Multiplayer Levels	MULTIMAYHEM
Alternate Paint Schemes	MISSMACROSS
Disable Active Codes	CLEAR
Gunpod Ammunition Refilled Faster	SPACEFOLD
Gunpod and Missiles Refilled Faster	MIRIYA
Invincibility	SUPERMECH
Level Select	WEWILLWIN
Missiles Refilled Faster	MARSBASE
One-Shot Kills	BACKSTABBER
One-Shot Kills in Sniper Mode	SNIPER
Upside-Down Mode	FLIPSIDE

Robotech: Invasion

From Options, select Extras. Enter the following:

Unlockable	Code
1 Hit Kill	DUSTYAYRES
All Levels	RECLAMATION
Invincibility	SUPERCYC
Lancer's Multiplayer Skin	YLLWFLLW
Rand's Multiplayer Skin	KIDGLOVES
Rook's Multiplayer Skin	BLUEANGLS
Scott Bernard's Multiplayer Skin	LTNTCMDR
Unlimited Ammo	TRGRHPY

Rocky

Enter the following codes in the Main Menu while holding R1:

Unlockable	Code
All Default Boxers and Arenas	→,↓,↑,←,↑,L1
All Default Boxers, Arenas, and Rocky Statue	→,→,→,←,→,L1
All Default Boxers, Arenas, Rocky statue, and Mickey	↑,↓,↓,←,←,L1
Double Punch Damage	→,↓,←,↑,←,L1
Double Speed Boxing	↓,←,↓,↑,→,L1
Max Stats for Movie Mode	→,↓,↓,↑,←,L1
Max Stats for Tournament and Exhibition Modes	←,↑,↑,↓,→,L1
Win Movie Mode (during a fight, press r+l to win!)	→,→,←,←,↑,L1

Rogue Ops

At any time in the game pause and enter the following codes.

Unlockable	Code
God Mode	←,→,→,←,←,→,→,←,←,→,→,←,■,■
Level Skip	L2,■,L2,●,L2,←,L2,→,L2,R2,R2,■,R2,●,R2,←,R2,→,■
Unlimited Ammo	■,●,■,●,■,●,■,●,←,●,■,●,■,●,■,●,■

Romance of the Three Kingdoms VIII

Unlockable	Objective
Better Created Characters	100% item completion.
Extra Created Character Portraits	100% event completion.
Pre-Made Characters	Create an officer with one of the names below for a hidden pre-made character: *Abraham Lincoln, *Albert Einstein, *Ben Franklin, *Benedict Arnold, *Davy Crockett, *Jebidiah Smith, *Jim Bridger, *John Adams, *John Henry, *Kit Carson, *Patrick Henry, *Paul Bunyan, *Paul Revere, *Pecos Bill, *Red Cloud, *Sam Houston, *Sitting Bull, *Thomas Edison, *William Cody, *William Seward.

Romance of the Three Kingdoms IX

Unlockable	Objective
Bai Qi	New Officer with name "Bai" "Qi"
Change Kingdoms in mid-game	Leave all forces under computer control, then during the action phase, press start to "go to main-menu." Press × and the game will resume, then press SELECT. (You may also press the shoulder buttons and it will say "Select Force or Forces to play as" and at the end of the action phase you can choose up to eight new forces to play as.)
Chen Qingzhi	New Officer with name "Chen" "Qingzhi"
Chengji Sihan	New Officer with name "Chengji" "Sihan"
Da Qiao	Load Dynasty Warriors 4 Data

Romance of the Three Kingdom IX (cont'd)

Emperor Xian	Unlock all sages and pick He Jin in 281 "Hero" scenario
Fan Zeng	New Officer with name "Fan" "Zeng"
Guan Yiwu	New Officer with name "Guan" "Yiwu"
Han Xin	New Officer with name "Han" "Xin"
Huang Yueying	Beat Tutorial Mode
Huo Qubing	New Officer with name "Huo" "Qubing"
Japan Tribe	Search near Bei Hai when warlord tells you to. You must have Bei Hai to do this.
Japan Tribe	Search Langxie while controlling two provinces and with 700 reputation or higher.
Kong Qiu	New Officer with name "Kong" "Qiu"
Li Ji	New Officer with name "Li" "Ji"
Li Si	New Officer with name "Li" "Si"
Lin Xiangru	New Officer with name "Lin" "Xiangru"
Liu Bang	New Officer with name "Liu" "Bang"
Lu Ling Qi	Load Dynasty Tactics 2 Data
Ma Yunlu	Beat Tutorial Mode
Mistress Zhen	Get Good Ending with Yuan Shang on Inheritance Wars challenge scenario.
Mistress Zhen	In Inheritance Wars, get event where Mistress Zhen gives Yuan Xi a carp charm, then beat the scenario.
Mistress Zou	In Defense of Nan Yang Scenario, get event where Jia Xu offers Mistress Zou up for Cao Cao, then beat the scenario.
Nanman Tribe	Beat Nanman Barbarians in scenario then beat game.
Qiang Tribe	Beat Qiang Barbarians in scenario then beat game.
Qin Liangyu	New Officer with name "Qin" "Liangyu"
Shan Yue Tribe	Beat Shen Yue Barbarians in scenario, then beat game.
Sun Bin	New Officer with name "Sun" "Bin"
Wang Jian	New Officer with name "Wang" "Jian"
Wu Wan Tribe	Beat Wu Wan Barbarians in scenario, then beat game.
Xiang Ji	New Officer with name "Xiang" "Ji"
Xiao He	New Officer with name "Xiao" "He"
Xiao Qiao	Load Dynasty Warriors 4 Extreme Legends Data
Yang Daiyan	New Officer with name "Yang" "Daiyan"
Ying Bu	New Officer with name "Ying" "Bu"
Ying Zheng	New Officer with name "Ying" "Zheng"
Yue Fei	New Officer with name "Yue" "Fei"
Yue Yi	New Officer with name "Yue" "Yi"
Zhang Liang	New Officer with name "Zhang" "Liang"
Zhang Yi	New Officer with name "Zhang" "Yi"
Zhen Ji	Beat Inheritance Wars Scenario.

RTX Red Rock

Unlockable	Code
Add Items	→,→,→,→,→,←,←,←,↑,↑
Difficult Mode	↓,↑,↑,↑,↑,↑,↑,↑,↑,↓
Easy Mode	↑,↓,↓,↓,↓,↓,↓,↓,↓,↑

RTX Red Rock (cont'd)

Normal Mode	↑,↓,↑,↓,↑,↓,↑,↓,↑,↓
Old Soul Super Weapons	→,↑,↓,↓,↑,→,→,↑,↓,↓
Progressive Scan Mode	→,↑,→,→,↑,→,→,→,↑,→—Note: You'll have to reboot your PS2 once the screen turns blue.
Unlock All Levels	↓,←,←,↓,←,↓,→,↓,←,↓
Unlock All Special Features	←,↓,↑,←,→,↑,↓,←,→,↓

R-Type Final

Pause the game and enter the following (you will hear a sound if you entered the code correctly):

Unlockable	Code
99.9% Charge Dose	Hold L2 and press R2,R2,←,→,↑,↓,→,←,↑,↓,▲.
Curtain Call Ship (#100)	In the R's Museum, enter 1009 9201 as a password.
Full Blue Power, Missiles, and Bits	Hold L2 and press R2,R2,←,→,↑,↓,→,←,↑,↓,●.
Full Red Power, Missiles, and Bits	Hold L2 and press R2,R2,←,→,↑,↓,→,←,↑,↓,■.
Full Yellow Power, Missiles, and Bits	Pause the game, then hold L2 and press R2,R2,←,→,↑,↓,→,←,↑,↓,×.
Invincibility	Hold L2 and press →,→,←,→,←,←,→,←,L1,↑,↑,↓,↓,↑,↓,↑,↓,L1.
Lady Love Ship (#3)	In the R's Museum, enter 5270 0725 as a password.
Mr. Heli Ship (#59)	In the R's Museum, enter 1026 2001 as a password.
Strider Ship (#24)	In the R's Museum, enter 2078 0278 as a password.

Rumble Racing

To access these cheats, go to the Game Options menu on the title screen. Then go to Load/Save and select "Passwords." Use the passwords below to open the corresponding vehicles and features.

Unlockable	Code
Championship Mode	KOZIEC1PU
Championship Mode	KZOIEC2P1
Championship Mode	OORKIEPUC
Buckshot Vehicle	UBTCKSTOH
Cataclysm Vehicle, Falls Down Track, and Pro Cup 2	P1PROC1PU
EsCargot Vehicle, the Gauntlet Track, and Pro Cup 3	Q2PROC2YT
Gamecus Vehicle	BSUIGASUM
High Roller Vehicle	HGIROLREL
Jolly Roger Vehicle, Coal Cuts Track, and Elite Cup 2	ILETEC1MB
Malice Vehicle, Wild Kingdom Track, and Elite Cup 3	ILCTEC2VB
Redneck Rocket Vehicle	KCEROCTEC
Revolution Vehicle	PTOATRTO1
Road Kill Vehicle, Elite Class Vehicles, Surf and Turf Vehicle, and Elite Cup	AEPPROPUC
Road Trip Vehicle	ABOGOBOGA
Sporticus Vehicle	OPSRTISUC
Stinger Vehicle	AMHBRAAMH
Van Itty Vehicle	VTYANIYTT
Vortex Vehicle	1AREXT1AR
XXS Tomcat Vehicle	NALDSHHSD

Rumble Racing (cont'd)

Unlockable	Objective
Cataclysm Vehicle	Win the Gold on Pro Cup 1.
Dragon Vehicle	Win the Gold on Rookie Cup 1.
EA Rookie Cup	Win the Gold on Rookie Cup 3.
Escargot Vehicle	Win the Gold on Pro Cup 1.
Falls Down Track	Win the Gold on Pro Cup 1.
Gauntlet Track	Win the Gold on Pro Cup 2.
Maelstrom Vehicle	Win the Gold on EA Rookie Cup.
Mandrake Vehicle	Win the Gold on Rookie Cup 2.
Passing Through Track	Win the Gold on Rookie Cup 2.
Pro Class of Vehicles	Win the Gold on EA Rookie Cup.
Pro Cup 1	Win the Gold on Rookie Cup 3.
Pro Cup 2	Win the Gold on Pro Cup 1.
Pro Cup 3	Win the Gold on Rookie Cup 2.
Rookie Cup 2	Win the Gold on Rookie Cup 1.
Rookie Cup 3	Win the Gold on Rookie Cup 2.
So Refined Track	Win the Gold on Rookie Cup 1.
Sun Burn Track	Win the Gold on EA Rookie Cup.

Samurai Warriors

Unlockable	Objective
Goemon Ishikawa	Complete Okuni Story.
Keiji Maeda	Complete Kenshin Story.
Kunoichi	Complete Shingen, Hanzo Stories.
Magoichi Saika	Complete any Story.
Masamune Date	Complete any two Stories.
Nobunaga Oda	Complete Noh, Oichi, Magoichi Stories.
Noh	Complete Ranmaru Story.
Okuni	Complete Keiji Story.
Ranmaru Mari	Complete Mitsuhide Story.
Shingen Takeda	Complete Yukimura Story.

Scooby-Doo! Mystery Mayhem

Unlockable	Objective
Trap the Fake Ghost Mini Game	Collect all five sandwich ingredients in the first episode.
Monster Frenzy Mini Game	Collect all five sandwich ingredients in the second episode.
Mine Cart Mini Game	Collect all five sandwich ingredients in the third episode.
Trail Bike Mini Game	Collect all five sandwich ingredients in the fourth episode.
Spooky Science Mini Game	Collect all five sandwich ingredients in the fifth episode.

Scooby Doo: Night of 100 Frights

Pause the game and hold L1+L2+R1+R2, then enter the following codes.

Unlockable	Code
All Power-Ups	●,■,●,■,●,■,■,■,●,●,■,●,●,●
FMV Sequences	■,■,■,●,●,●,■,●,■
View Credits	■,●,●,■,●,■

Scooby Doo: Night of 100 Frights (cont'd)

Change the date on the PlayStation 2 for some special holiday decorations:

Unlockable	Code
Assorted Fireworks	July 4
Fireworks	January 1
Giant Bats	October 31
Snow	December 25

Secret Weapons over Normandy

At the Title Screen (New Game or Continue), enter the following:

Unlockable	Code
All Levels in Instant Action	↑,↓,←,→,L1,R1,L1,R1
All Planes and Missions	▲,▲,▲,■,■,■,L1,R1,R2,R2,L2,L2
Big Heads	→,↑,←,↓,→,↑,←,↓,→,L1,R1,L1,R1
Invulnerability	↑,↓,←,→,←,←,→,→,L1,L1,R1,R1,L2,R2
Unlimited Ammo	↑,→,↓,←,↑,→,↓,←,L1,R1

Shadow Of Destiny

Unlockable	Objective
Extra Ending	Complete the game five times and earn all of the Ending Files, then play through once more to get a special, extra ending.
Extra Option	When you beat the game, you are graded on how well you played. This leads to one of five endings. After you complete the game once and earn an ending, an "Extra" feature appears on the main menu. Access it to see Movies, Ending Files, and the Result for each completed level.
Movies	Beat the game once and earn an Ending File, unlocking a Movie. Earn three Ending Files to unlock a movie from a European Konami show. Get the special "extra" ending to unlock a Movie from the Fall Tokyo Game Show.

Shark Tale

During gameplay, press SELECT, hold L1, and enter code. After you enter the code, release L1 to activate the cheat.

Unlockable	Code
Attack Mode	●,●,●,●,×,●,●,●,●
Extra Clams and Fame	●,●,×,×,●,×,●,●
Replace All Pearls with Fish King Coins	●,×,●,●,●,×,●,●

Shellshock: Nam '67

Enter the following codes at the Title Screen (Press Start Button screen):

Unlockable	Code
Add Weapon Option	↑,↓,←,→,●,■,↑,↓,←,→,●,■
All Missions and Pictures	L2,R2,L1,R1,L1,L2,L2,R2,L1,R1,R1,R2
God Mode	R3,L3,→,←,L1,R1,R3,L3,→,←,L1,R1
Infinite Ammunition	R2,R1,▲,L2,L1,↑,R2,R1,▲,L2,L1,↑
Psychedelic Mode	↑,R2,●,←,▲,■,L2,L1,●,R1

Shinobi

Unlockable	Objective
Bonuses	Collect the gold Oboro Clan Coins during gameplay to unlock bonus options in the Extras menu, including level select and movies.
Hard Difficulty Setting	Complete the game under the Normal difficulty setting.
Play as Joe Musashi	Collect 40 Oboro Clan Coins during gameplay. Joe's sword damage does less than when playing as Hotsuma; however, his shurikens are unlimited in number and do more damage, but do not stun. Also, because he does not use the Akujiki sword, his energy does not drain constantly.
Play as Moritsune	Collect 30 Oboro Clan Coins during gameplay. Moritsune is Hotsuma's brother and is stronger and faster. However, the Akujiki sword drains him more.
Super Difficulty Setting	Successfully complete the game under the Hard difficulty setting.
VR Stage	Collect 50 Oboro Clan Coins during gameplay.

Shrek 2

During gameplay, pause the game. Then select the Scrapbook and enter the following:

Unlockable	Code
1,000 Coins	←,↑,×,●,←,↑,×,●,←,↑,×,●,↑,→,↓,←,↑
Bonus Games	←,↑,×,●,←,↑,×,●,←,↑,×,●,■,●,■,●,■,●
Full Health	←,↑,×,●,←,↑,×,●,←,↑,×,●,↑,→,↓,←,↑
Level Select	←,↑,×,●,←,↑,×,●,←,↑,×,●,↑,↑,↑,↑,↑

Silent Hill 3

Unlockable	Code
EGM Shirt	Enter EGMpretaporter.
Extra Options	Press L1+L2+R1+R2 on the options menu.
GamePro Shirt	Enter ProTip.
GMR Shirt	Enter GMRownzjoo.
OPM Shirt	Enter SH3_OPiuM.
Play Shirt	Enter sLmLLdGhSmKfBfH.
PSM Shirt	Enter badical.

Unlockable	Objective
Action Level Extreme	Beat the game on Hard Mode to earn Action Level Extreme 1.
Beam Saber	Defeat more enemies using melee weapons than gun weapons the first time you play. This can be found in the corridor outside where you get the MY BESTSELLERS KEY.
Beginner Difficulty	Die twice on Normal difficulty.
Flamethrower	Defeat more enemies by shooting them rather than using melee weapons the first time you play. The flamethrower is in the normal version of HELEN'S BAKERY in the mall.
Heather Beam	Defeat the game on Hard Mode.
Life Display Option	Beat the game on Hard Mode. The Life Display appears in the Extra Options.

Silent Scope

Unlockable	Code
Expert Mode	Hold the trigger button when you select Training or Arcade mode. Press START,START,START,START. A second gunshot confirms correct entry. This removes the guide arrows and aiming rings.

Silent Scope (cont'd)

Extra Options	Beat the game on any difficulty setting more than twice. This unlocks infinite credits, more health, and more time in the Options menu.
Night Vision Mode	Hold the trigger button when you select the Training or Arcade mode. Press START, START, START, START, START. A second gunshot confirms correct entry. This makes the game always at night.

Silent Scope 3

Unlockable	Objective
Real-Time Window Option	Complete the indoor shooting range with an "S" or better rank to unlock the "Real-Time Window" option at the EX Options menu.

Silpheed: The Lost Planet

Unlockable	Code
All Nine Weapons	Start a new game. Enter XACALITE as your name.

The Simpsons: Hit and Run

From the Main Menu, go to Options. Hold L1+R1 and enter the following:

Unlockable	Code
Blurry View	▲,●,▲,●
Explode on Impact Cars	▲,▲,■,■
Fast Cars	■,■,■,■
Grid View	●,✕,●,▲
Invincible Car	▲,✕,▲,✕
Jumping Car	■,■,■,▲
Speedometer	▲,▲,●,■
Very Fast Cars	▲,▲,▲,▲

TIP

Change the date of the PlayStation 2 to Halloween, Thanksgiving, and Christmas to see new living room decorations.

The Simpsons: Road Rage

Change the date of the PlayStation 2 to the following to unlock secret characters:

Unlockable	Code
New Year's Barney	Jan 1
Halloween Bart	Oct 31
Thanksgiving Marge	Nov 22
Christmas Apu	Dec 25

The Sims

To access the following unlockables, activate the Cheat Mode by pressing L1+R1+L2+R2 at the Main Menu. You can then enter the following codes.

Unlockable	Code
Free Mode	FREEALL—all objects now cost 0 Simoleans. However, you can't sell any items for money. This has no effect on the cost of paying for bills and other services. Also, this code may cause some problems with saved games.
Midas Mode	MIDAS—begin the game in Get a Life mode, get into the hot tub with the girl, and press START to pause gameplay. Select "Quit" followed by "Just Quit." This mode unlocks all two-player games, all locked objects, and all locked skins.
Party Motel Mode	PARTY M—unlocks the Party Motel two-player game in Get a Life mode's bonus section.
Play the Sims Mode	SIMS—unlocks Play the Sims mode without going through the Get a Life Dream House. Players who have to play through the Dream House each time should find this useful.

The Sims Bustin' Out

Pause the game at any time and enter these codes.

Unlockable	Code
All Skins	L1,R2,×,●,↑,↓
All Objects	L2,R2,↑,▲,L3
All Locations	R2,R3,L3,L2,R1,L1
Money	L1,R2,→,■,L3

Sky Odyssey

Unlockable	Objective
A Tight Squeeze Card No. 16	Clear the A Tight Squeeze level two times. Pictures displayed are MS+Me262.
A Tight Squeeze Card No. 35	Clear the A Tight Squeeze level one time. Picture displayed is Mission Scenery.
Autogytro XG-1 Data Card No. 61	Get Autogytro. The picture displayed is of a CG Rendering.
Autogytro XG-1 Data Card No. 62	Get Autogytro. The picture displayed is of a Draft Illustration.
Bf-109 Custom Data Card No. 47	Get Bf-109 Custom parts. The picture displayed is of a CG Rendering.
Bf-109 Custom Data Card No. 48	Get Bf-109 Custom parts. The picture displayed is of a Draft Illustration.
Bf-109 Customized Card No. 39	Clear the Maximus level with Bf-109. The picture displayed is of a customized craft.
Bf-109 Customized Card No. 40	Clear the Maximus level with Bf-109. The picture displayed is of a customized craft.
Blown Away Card No. 25	Clear the Blown Away level one time. Picture displayed is Mission Scenery.
Blown Away Card No. 6	Clear the Blown Away level two times. Pictures displayed are MS + Pulse Jet.
F117 Data Card No. 55	Get Stealth Jet. The picture displayed is of a CG Rendering.
F117 Data Card No. 56	Get Stealth Jet. The picture displayed is of a Draft Illustration.
F4U Corsair Data Card No. 53	Get F4U Corsair. The picture displayed is of a CG Rendering.
F4U Corsair Data Card No. 54	Get F4U Corsair. The picture displayed is of a Draft Illustration.
Great Divide Card No. 7	Clear the Great Divide level two times. Pictures displayed are MS+Shinden.

Sky Odyssey (cont'd)

Heart of the Mine Card No. 11	Clear the Heart of the Mine level two times. Pictures displayed are MS+Bf-109.
Heart of the Mine Card No. 30	Clear the Heart of the Mine level one time. Picture displayed is Mission Scenery.
Hidden Plane	Right Wing: Land at the alternate landing strip in the Adventure Begins level.
Maximus Card No. 19	Clear the Maximus level two times. Pictures displayed are MS+Swordfish.
Maximus Card No. 38	Clear the Maximus level one time. Picture displayed is Mission Scenery.
Me262 Data Card No. 51	Get Me262. The picture displayed is of a CG Rendering.
Me262 Data Card No. 52	Get Me262. The picture displayed is of a Draft Illustration.
Mid-Air Rendezvous Card No. 10	Clear the Mid-Air Rendezvous level two times. Pictures displayed are MS+F117.
Mid-Air Rendezvous Card No. 29	Clear the Mid-Air Rendezvous one time. Picture displayed is Mission Scenery.
Movie Card No. 69	Earn 2,000 Acrobatic Points. The picture displayed is of a CG Movie.
Movie Card No. 70	Earn 3,000 Acrobatic Points. The picture displayed is of a CG Movie.
Movie Card No. 71	Earn 4,000 Acrobatic Points. The picture displayed is of a CG Movie.
Movie Card No. 72	Earn 5,000 Acrobatic Points. The picture displayed is of a CG Movie.
Movie Card No. 73	Earn 6,000 Acrobatic Points. The picture displayed is of a CG Movie.
Over the Falls Card No. 14	Clear the Over the Falls level two times. Pictures displayed are MS+Floatplane.
Over the Falls Card No. 33	Clear the Over the Falls level one time. Picture displayed is Mission Scenery.
Pontoon Plane Data Card No. 67	Get Pontoons. The picture displayed is of a CG Rendering.
Pontoon Plane Data Card No. 68	Get Pontoons. The picture displayed is of a Draft Illustration.
Pulse Jet Test Type Data Card No. 49	Get Pulse Jet Custom parts. The picture displayed is of a CG Rendering.
Pulse Jet Test Type Data Card No. 50	Get Pulse Jet Custom parts. The picture displayed is of a Draft Illustration.
Pulsejet Customized Card No. 43	Clear the Maximus level with Pulsejet. The picture displayed is of a customized craft.
Pulsejet Customized Card No. 44	Clear the Maximus level with Pulsejet. The picture displayed is of a customized craft.
Relief from Above Card No. 27	Clear the Relief from Above level one time. Picture displayed is Mission Scenery.
Relief from Above Card No. 8	Clear the Relief from Above level two times. Pictures displayed are MS+Shinden-kai.
S.O.S Card No. 13	Clear the S.O.S. level two times. Pictures displayed are MS+Shinden.
S.O.S Card No. 32	Clear the S.O.S. level one time. Picture displayed is Mission Scenery.
Shinden Data Card No. 57	Get Shinden. The picture displayed is of a CG Rendering.

Sky Odyssey (cont'd)

Shinden Data Card No. 58	Get Shinden. The picture displayed is of a Draft Illustration.
Shinden-Kai Data Card No. 59	Get Shinden-kai. The picture displayed is of a CG Rendering.
Shinden-Kai Data Card No. 60	Get Shinden-kai. The picture displayed is of a Draft Illustration.
Special Card No. 74	All other cards earned. The picture displayed is of a Special Framed Card.
Special Card No. 75	All other cards earned. The picture displayed is of a Special Framed Card.
Special Card No. 76	All other cards earned. The picture displayed is of a Special Framed Card.
Storm Before the Calm Card No. 15	Clear the Storm Before the Calm level two times. Pictures displayed are MS+Swordfish.
Storm Before the Calm No. 34	Clear the Storm Before Calm level one time. Picture displayed is Mission Scenery.
Stormy Seas Card No 24	Clear the Stormy Seas level one time. Picture displayed is Mission Scenery.
Stormy Seas Card No. 5	Clear the Stormy Seas level two times. Pictures displayed are MS+F4U Corsair.
Swordfish Custom Data Card No. 45	Get Swordfish triple wing. The picture displayed is of a CG Rendering.
Swordfish Custom Data Card No. 46	Get Swordfish triple wing. The picture displayed is of a Draft Illustration.
Swordfish Customized Card No. 41	Clear the Maximus level with Swordfish. The picture displayed is of a customized craft.
Swordfish Customized Card No. 42	Clear the Maximus level with Swordfish. The picture displayed is of a customized craft.
Swordfish Triple Wing	Land at the alternative landing strip in the level Mid-Air Rendezvous. The alternate landing strip is easier to find after you earn the Special Radar by playing through the Target mode.
Take the Low Road Card No. 22	Clear the Take the Low Road level one time. Picture displayed is Mission Scenery.
Take the Low Road Card No. 3	Clear the Take the Low Road level two times. Pictures displayed are MS+Pulse Jet.
The Adventure Begins Card No. 1	Clear the Adventure Begins level two times. Picture displayed is MS+Swordfish.
The Adventure Begins Card No. 20	Clear the Adventure Begins level one time. Picture displayed is Mission Scenery.
The Ancient Forest Card No. 28	Clear the Ancient Forest level one time. Picture displayed is Mission Scenery.
The Ancient Forest Card No. 9	Clear the Ancient Forest level two times. Pictures displayed are MS+Autogyro.
The Desert Express Card No. 2	Clear the Desert Express level two times. Pictures displayed are MS+Bf-109.
The Desert Express Card No. 21	Clear the Desert Express level one time. Picture displayed is Mission Scenery.
The Great Divide Card No. 26	Clear the Great Divide level one time. Picture displayed is Mission Scenery.
The Great Falls Card No. 18	Clear the Great Falls level two times. Pictures displayed are MS+Pulse Jet.

Sky Odyssey (cont'd)	
e Great Falls Card No. 37	Clear the Great Falls level one time. Picture displayed is Mission Scenery.
e Labyrinth Card No. 23	Clear the Labyrinth level one time. Picture displayed is Mission Scenery.
e Labyrinth Card No. 4	Clear the Labyrinth level two times. Pictures displayed are MS+Me262.
e Valley of Fire Card No. 17	Clear the Valley of Fire level two times. Pictures displayed are MS+Bf-109.
e Valley of Fire Card No. 36	Clear the Valley of Fire level one time. Picture displayed is Mission Scenery.
owers of Terror Card No. 12	Clear the Towers of Terror level two times. Pictures displayed are MS+F4U Corsair.
owers of Terror Card No. 31	Clear the Towers of Terror level one time. Picture displayed is Mission Scenery.
FO Type Gold Data Card No. 63	Get UFO 2. The picture displayed is of a CG Rendering.
FO Type Gold Data Card No. 64	Get UFO 2. The picture displayed is of a Draft Illustration.
JFO Type Silver Data Card No 65	Get UFO 1. The picture displayed is of a CG Rendering.
JFO Type Silver Data Card No 66	Get UFO 1. The picture displayed is of a Draft Illustration.
Custom Parts	Earn custom parts for your aircraft by earning grades of B or higher in the Adventure mode missions.
Emblems in Target Mode	Earn two silver medals. (Find the new emblems in the Customize Aircraft mode.)
Music Track in Target Mode	Earn one silver medal each (12 tracks total).
Radio in Target Mode	Earn four gold medals.
Special Radar in Target Mode	Earn two gold medals.
Auto Gyro Plane	Clear every stage of the Sky Canvas mode with a score of at least 90 Points.
Corsair	To unlock the Corsair you must be good enough at pulling acrobatic tricks to earn enough Acrobatic points in Adventure mode to get circles to appear around 10 of your mission grades.
Gold UFO	To earn the gold UFO, get gold on every mission in Target mode.
ME 262	Beat the entire Adventure mode once (including the final level) to earn the ME 262, a very fast jet with two engines.
Pontoons	To earn a set of pontoons for your aircraft, allowing you to land in the water, complete the Stormy Seas level, landing on an aircraft carrier. The pontoons are required for a mission later in the game.
Silver UFO	Complete all Adventure mode missions with an A grade to unlock the silver UFO.
Stealth Jet	Complete every mission in Adventure mode with a total time of 10 minutes.
Unlimited Boost in Target Mode	Earn two gold medals. (Once equipped, all jet planes will have an infinite amount of boost, but must recharge after every use.)

Sled Storm

Enter the following codes at the Press Start Screen while holding L1+R1.

Effect	Code
All Characters	●,▲,●,▲,●,↓
All Sleds	●,■,●,■,●,←
All Tracks	●,←,●,→,●,↑
Unlock Everything	●,■,↑,●,▲,↓
Unlock Hover Sled	●,▲,■,●,▲,→

Sly Cooper and the Thievius Raccoonus

Unlockable	Objective
Ending Bonuses	Get all the bottles hidden in a level to unlock an FMV sequence, special move, or background information.

Smuggler's Run

To access the following unlockables, pause the game, then enter code. A sound confirms correct entry.

Unlockable	Code
Invisibility	R1,L1,L1,R2,L1,L1,↙
Less Time Warp	R2,L2,L1,R1,←,←,←
Light Cars	L1,R1,R1,L2,R2,R2
More Time Warp	R1,L1,L2,R2,→,→,→
No Gravity	R1,R2,R1,R2,↑,↑,↑

TIP

To unlock vehicles from Midnight Club: Street Racing, use a saved game from Midnight Club: Street Racing. Now you are able to use vehicles from that game.

SOCOM: U.S. Navy SEALs

Unlockable	Objective
Admiral Difficulty	Complete the game under the Vice Admiral difficulty setting.
Captain Difficulty	Complete the game under the Commander difficulty setting.
Commander Difficulty	Complete the game under the Lieutenant Commander difficulty setting.
Level Select	Complete the game under the Lieutenant JG difficulty setting.
Lieutenant Commander Difficulty	Complete the game under the Lieutenant difficulty setting.
Lieutenant Difficulty	Complete the game under the Lieutenant JG difficulty setting.
Lieutenant JG Difficulty	Complete the game under the Ensign difficulty setting.
More Weapons	Complete the game under the Ensign difficulty setting to unlock terrorist weapons in the armory during Single-Player mode. Complete the game under the Lieutenant difficulty setting to unlock the MGL (Multiple Grenade Launcher).
Rear Admiral Difficulty	Complete the game under the Captain difficulty setting.
Vice Admiral Difficulty	Complete the game under the Rear Admiral difficulty setting.

Sonic Heroes

Unlockable	Code
2 Player Bobsled Race Mode	Collect 80 Emblems
2 Player Expert Race Mode	Collect 120 Emblems
2 Player Quick Race Mode	Collect 100 Emblems
2 Player Ring Race Mode	Collect 60 Emblems
2 Player Special Stage Mode	Collect 40 Emblems
2 Player Team Battle Mode	Collect 20 Emblems
Last Song and Movie	Complete the last story
Last Story Mode	Complete Story Mode with all four teams and all Choas Emeralds.
Metal Characters	Hold ×+▲ once you pick a level in 2-Player mode.
Super Hard Mode	Collect 141 Emblems and have all A ranks.
Team Chaotix Song and Movie	Complete Story Mode with Team Chaotix
Team Dark Song and Movie	Complete Story Mode with Team Dark
Team Sonic Movie and Song	Complete Story Mode with Team Sonic
Team Rose Song and Movie	Complete Story Mode with Team Rose

Soul Calibur II

Unlockable	Objective
Money Pit	Beat Stage 1 of Chapter 4 in Weapon Master Mode.
Assassin	Beat Stage 2 of Subchapter 3 in Weapon Master Mode (Extra).
Astaroth—Soul Edge	Beat Stage 3 of Extra Chapter 1 in Weapon Master Mode.
Berserker	Beat Stage 1 of Subchapter 1 in Weapon Master Mode (Extra).
Cassandra—Soul Edge	Beat Stage 4 of Subchapter 2 in Weapon Master Mode.
Cassandra—Soul Edge	Beat Stage 5 of Subchapter 4 in Weapon Master Mode.
Cervantes	Beat Stage 4 of Chapter 3 in Weapon Master Mode.
Cervantes—Acheron	Beat Stage 5 of Chapter 3 in Weapon Master Mode.
Cervantes—Imitation Sword	Beat Stage 5 of Subchapter 4 in Weapon Master Mode.
Charade	Beat Stage 1 of Chapter 3 in Weapon Master Mode.
Unlock Egyptian Crypt	Beat Stage 5 of Chapter 8 in Weapon Master Mode.
Extra Arcade Mode	Either attempt Arcade Mode 10 times, or beat it once.
Extra Practice Mode	Beat Stage 1 of Chapter 1 in Weapon Master Mode.
Extra Survival Mode—Death Match	Beat Stage 3 of Subchapter 3 in Weapon Master Mode.
Extra Survival Mode—No Recovery	Beat Stage 2 of Extra Chapter 2 in Weapon Master Mode.
Extra Survival Mode—Standard	Beat Stage 5 of Chapter 6 in Weapon Master Mode.
Extra Team Battle Mode	Beat Stage 1 of Subchapter 1 in Weapon Master Mode.
Extra Time Attack—Extreme	Beat Stage 1 of Extra Chapter 1 in Weapon Master Mode.
Extra Time Attack Mode—Alternative	Beat Stage 4 of Chapter 9 in Weapon Master Mode.
Extra Time Attack Mode—Standard	Beat Stage 1 of Chapter 5 in Weapon Master Mode.
Extra VS Battle Mode	Either attempt Extra Arcade Mode 5 times, or beat it once.

PSP Xbox PS2 GC GBA

Soul Calibur II (cont'd)

Extra VS Team Battle Mode	Either attempt Extra VS Battle Mode 5 times, or beat it once.
Hwangseo Palace/ Phoenix Court	Beat Stage 2 of Chapter 7 in Weapon Master Mode.
Ivy—Prototype Ivy Blade	Beat Stage 2 of Extra Chapter 2 in Weapon Master Mode.
Kilik—Bamboo Staff	Beat Stage 2 of Extra Chapter 1 in Weapon Master Mode.
Labyrinth	Beat Stage 6 of Chapter 6 in Weapon Master Mode.
Lakeside Coliseum	Beat Stage 3 of Chapter 1 in Weapon Master Mode.
Lizardman	Beat All Stages of Subchapter 2 in Weapon Master Mode (Extra).
Maxi—Fuzoroi	Beat Stage 5 of Chapter 3 in Weapon Master Mode.
Maxi—Termite Snack	Beat Stage 3 of Subchapter 4 in Weapon Master Mode.
Mitsurugi—Soul Edge	Beat Stage 5 of Subchapter 4 in Weapon Master Mode.
Mitsurugi— Souvenir Gift	Beat Stage 3 of Subchapter 3 in Weapon Master Mode.
Necrid—Ethereal Edge	Beat Stage 5 of Chapter 8 in Weapon Master Mode.
Necrid—Soul Edge	Beat Stage 3 of Extra Chapter 2 in Weapon Master Mode.
Nightmare—Galley Oar	Beat Stage 3 of Extra Chapter 1 in Weapon Master Mode.
Nightmare—Soul Edge	Beat Stage 3 of Chapter 7 in Weapon Master Mode.
Raphael—Schweizer	Beat Stage 4 of Chapter 3 in Weapon Master Mode.
Seung Mina	Beat Stage 3 of Chapter 6 in Weapon Master Mode.
Seung Mina— Ambassador	Beat Stage 2 of Chapter 10 in Weapon Master Mode.
Seung Mina—Halberd	Beat Stage 6 of Chapter 6 in Weapon Master Mode.
Sophitia	Beat Stage 5 of Chapter 4 in Weapon Master Mode.
Sophitia—Memento	Beat Stage 3 of Extra Chapter 2 in Weapon Master Mode.
Sophitia—Synval	Beat Stage 2 of Chapter 10 in Weapon Master Mode.
Taki—Soul Edge	Beat Stage 3 of Subchapter 2 in Weapon Master Mode.
Talim—Double Crescent Blade	Beat Stage 2 of Chapter 3 in Weapon Master Mode.
Voldo—Soul Edge	Beat Stage 2 of Subchapter 2 in Weapon Master Mode.
Xianghua—Soul Calibur	Beat Stage 2 of Chapter 5 in Weapon Master Mode.
Xianghua—Soul Edge	Beat Stage 1 of Subchapter 2 in Weapon Master Mode.
Yoshimitsu	Beat Stage 3 of Chapter 2 in Weapon Master Mode.

Spawn: Armageddon

Pause the game and enter the following:

Unlockable	Code
All Comics	↑,↓,←,→,→,←,←,↑
All Missions	↑,↓,←,→,←,←,→,→
All Weapons	↑,↓,←,→,←,→,←,←
No Blood	↑,↓,←,→,↑,↑,↑,↑
Open Encyclopedia	↑,↓,←,→,←,→,↓,↑
Unlimited Ammo	↑,↓,←,→,↑,←,↓,→
Unlimited Health/Necroplasm	↑,↓,←,→,→,←,↓,↑
Unlimited Necroplasm	↑,↓,←,→,↓,←,↑,→

Speed Kings

Unlockable	Code
18 Best Laps	Enter the name .lapt18 at the start of the game.
All 9 Driving Tests Finished	Enter the name .test9 at the start of the game.
All Six Meets Won	Enter the name .meet6 at the start of the game.
GP Mode Finished	Enter the name .prix at the start of the game.
Set Respect Points	Enter the name .resp(insert number) at the start of the game to start with that number of respect points.
All tracks	Earn gold medals in every event.
Everything	Enter borkbork at the Player Setup screen.

Spider-Man

To access the following unlockables, enter the Specials menu to enter the sequence. A laugh will confirm a correct code entry. To return to normal, repeat the code entry.

Unlockable	Code
All Fighting Controls	KOALA
Big Head and Feet for Spider-Man	GOESTOYOURHEAD
Bonus Training Levels	HEADEXPLODY
Enemies Have Big Heads	JOELSPEANUTS
First-Person View	UNDERTHEMASK
Goblin-Style Costume	FREAKOUT
Level Select	IMIARMAS
Level Skip	Enter ROMITAS —after entering code, pause gameplay and select the "Next Level" option to advance to the next level.
Master Code	ARACHNID—unlocks all levels in the level warp option, all gallery options (movie viewer/production art), and combo moves.
Matrix-Style Attacks	DODGETHIS
Play as a Police Officer	REALHERO
Play as a Scientist	SERUM
Play as Captain Stacey (Helicopter Pilot)	CAPTAINSTACEY
Play as Mary Jane	GIRLNEXTDOOR
Play as Shocker's Thug	THUGSRUS
Play as Skulls Gang Thug	KNUCKLES
Play as the Shocker	HERMANSCHULTZ
Play as Uncle Ben's Killer	ESTICKYRICE
Small Spider-Man	SPIDERBYTE
Unlimited Green Goblin Glider Power	CHILLOUT
Unlimited Webbing	ORGANICWEBBING—you can also just accumulate 50,000 points during gameplay.

Unlockable	Objective
Alternate Green Goblin Costume	If you are using the Alex Ross Spider-Man, play any level with the Green Goblin in it and he will have an alternate costume that more closely resembles his classic costume.
Green Goblin FMV Sequence	Successfully complete the game under the Hero or greater difficulty setting.

Spider-Man (cont'd)

Pinhead Bowling Mini-Game	Accumulate 10,000 points during gameplay to unlock the Pinhead bowling mini-game in the training menu.
Play as Alex Ross	Successfully complete the game under the Normal or higher difficulty setting to unlock the Alex Ross costume in the Specials menu.
Play as Peter Parker	Successfully complete the game under the easy or higher difficulty setting to unlock the Peter Parker costume in the Specials menu.
Play as the Green Goblin	Complete the game under the Hero or Superhero difficulty setting to unlock the Green Goblin costume option at the Specials menu. *(See below for more info)*
Play as Wrestler	Complete the game under the Easy or higher difficulty setting to unlock the wrestler costume in the Specials menu. To unlock this easily, first unlock the "Unlimited Webbing" cheat. When you get to the ring, zip to the top and keep on shooting Spidey Bombs.
Shocker FMV Sequence	Accumulate 30,000 points during gameplay to unlock a Shocker FMV sequence in the CG menu.
Vulture FMV Sequence	Accumulate 20,000 points during gameplay to unlock a Vulture FMV sequence in the CG menu.

TIP

Unlocking the Green Goblin costume option allows you to play as Harry Osborn in the Green Goblin costume (complete with appropriate weapons) in an alternate storyline where he tries to correct the Osborn family's reputation. To unlock this easily, start a new game under the Hero or Superhero difficulty setting. At the first level, pause gameplay, then quit to the main menu. Enable the ARACHNID code, then go to the "Level Warp" option. Choose the "Conclusion" level (that features Norman revealing himself to Spider-Man followed by the glider sequence), then exit. This marks the game as completed under the selected difficulty setting. The Green Goblin costume option will be unlocked at the "Secret Store" screen.

Spider-Man 2

Start a New Game and enter HCRAYERT as a name. Go back and enter any name of your choice. This cheat will start in progress, with over 40% completion, 201,000 Hero points, upgrades, and other goodies!

Spy Hunter 2

Unlockable	Code
All Missions and Weapons	In the Main Menu, press L1, R2, L2, R1, R1, L2, R2, L1.
Infinite Ammo	Pause the game and press R1, L1, R2, R2, L2, R1, L1, R2, L2. Enter the code again to deactivate it.
Invincibility	Pause the game and press L1, L1, L1, R2, L1, R1, R1, L1, R2. Enter the code again to deactivate it.

SSX

Unlockable	Code
Third Board	Obtain the Rookie rank.
Fourth Board	Obtain the Sensei rank.
Fifth Board	Obtain the Contender rank.
Sixth Board	Obtain the Natural rank.
Seventh Board	Obtain the Star rank.
Eighth Board	Obtain the Veteran rank.

SSX (cont'd)

Ninth Board	Obtain the Champ rank.
10th Board	Obtain the Superstar rank.
11th Board	Obtain the Master rank.
Aloha Ice Jam Track	Get a medal on Tokyo Megaplex.
Hiro	Win four gold medals.
JP	Win two gold medals.
Jurgen	Win one gold medal.
Mercury City Meltdown Track	Get a medal on Elysium.
Mesablanca Track	Get a medal on Mercury City Meltdown.
Pipedream Track	Get a medal on Tokyo Megaplex.
Fourth Costume	Complete all blue square tricks.
Third Costume	Complete all green circle tricks.
Untracked Course	Get a medal on the Aloha Ice Jam.
Tokyo Megaplex Track	Get a medal on Mesablanca.
Zoe	Win three gold medals.

To access the following unlockables, go into the Options menu, hold R1+R2+L1+L2, and enter code. A sound confirms correct code entry.

Unlockable	Code
All Courses, Costumes, Characters, and Boards	↓,←,↑,→,×,●,▲,■
All Course Hints	●,×,●,×,●,×,●,×
Maximum Stats	×,×,×,×,×,×,×,×,■
Running Man	■,▲,●,×,■,▲,●,×

SSX 3

From the Main Menu, go to Options. Select "Enter Cheat" and enter the following codes (these codes are case-sensitive):

Unlockable	Code
All Artwork	naturalkoncept
All Boards	graphicdelight
All Peaks	biggerthank7
All Playlist Songs	djsuperstar
All Posters	postnobills
All Toys	nogluerequired
All Trading Cards	gotitgotitneedit
All Videos	myeyesaredim
Brodi	zenmaster
Bunny San	wheresyourtail
Canhuck	greatwhitenorth
Churchill	tankengine
Cudmore the Cow	milkemdaisy
Eddie	worm
Gutless	boneyardreject
Hiro	slicksuit
Lodge One Clothes	shoppingspree
Luther	bronco
Jurgen	brokenleg
Marty	back2future
North West Legend	callhimgeorge
Snowballs	betyouneverseen
Stretch	windmilldunk
Svelte Luther	notsosvelte
Unknown Rider	finallymadeitin

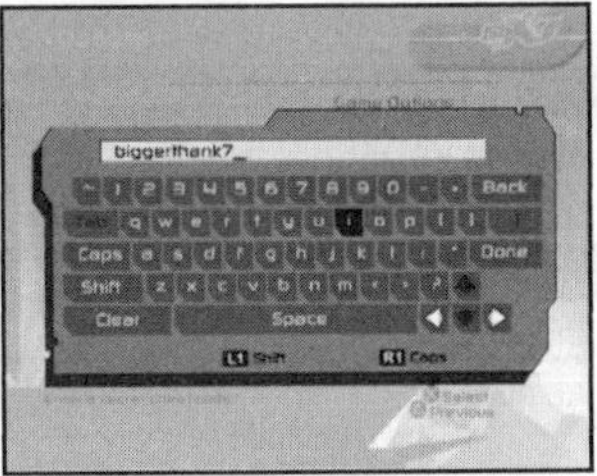

SSX Tricky

Unlockable	Objective
Alternate Costumes	To earn more costumes, complete all chapters in your trick book. To unlock the final chrome costume, complete World Circuit mode with a Master rank.
Fugi Board	Get a gold medal on every course with all boarders with their uberboard to unlock a Fugi board.
Pipedream Course	Win a medal on all Showoff courses.
Play as Brodi	Win a gold medal in World Circuit mode.
Play as JP	Win three gold medals in World Circuit mode.
Play as Kaori	Win four gold medals in World Circuit mode.
Play as Luther	Win eight gold medals in World Circuit mode.
Play as Marisol	Win five gold medals in World Circuit mode.
Play as Psymon	Win six gold medals in World Circuit mode.
Play as Seeiah	Win seven gold medals in World Circuit mode.
Play as Zoe	Win two gold medals in World Circuit mode.
Uberboards	Unlock all of the tricks for a character to get their uberboard, which is their best board.
Untracked Course	Win a medal on all Race courses.

To access the following unlockable, go to the Title screen and hold L1+R1, enter code, then release L1+R1. A sound will confirm correct code entry.

Unlockable	Code
Full Stat Points	▲,▲,→,▲,▲,↓,×,×,←,×,×,↑—all the boarders will have full stat points.
Mallora Board	×,×,→,●,●,↓,▲,▲,←,■,■,↑—choose Elise and start a track. Elise will have the Mallora Board and a blue outfit.
Master Code	×,▲,→,●,■,↓,▲,■,←,●,×,↑
Mix Master Mike	×,×,→,×,×,↓,×,×,←,×,×,↑— **(See below for more info)**
Running Man Mode	■,▲,●,×,■,▲,●,×—enter at the Options screen.
Sticky Boards	■,■,→,▲,▲,↓,●,●,←,×,×,↑

NOTE

For the Mix Master Mike unlockable, once you've input the code, choose any boarder at the character selection screen and he or she will be replaced by Mix Master Mike on the course. He has decks on his back and a vinyl board. Repeat the code to disable its effect.

Starsky and Hutch

Type in VADKRAM as your Profile Name to unlock everything.

Star Wars: Battlefront

Unlockable	Code
All Planets	Choose Historical Campaign, then press ■,●,■,● at the Planet Selection screen.

Star Wars Bounty Hunter

Enter the following sequences as codes.

Unlockable	Code
Chapter 1	SEEHOWTHEYRUN
Chapter 2	CITYPLANET
Chapter 3	LOCKDOWN
Chapter 4	DUGSOPLENTY
Chapter 5	BANTHAPOODOO
Chapter 6	MANDALORIANWAY
Concept Art	R ARTISTS ROCK
Mission 1	BEAST PIT
Mission 2	GIMMEMY JETPACK
Mission 3	CONVEYORAMA
Mission 4	BIGCITYNIGHTS
Mission 5	IEATNERFMEAT
Mission 6	VOTE4TRELL
Mission 7	LOCKUP
Mission 8	WHAT A RIOT
Mission 9	SHAFTED
Mission 10	BIGMOSQUITOS
Mission 11	ONEDEADDUG
Mission 12	WISHIHADMYSHIP
Mission 13	MOS GAMOS
Mission 14	TUSKENS R US
Mission 15	BIG BAD DRAGON
Mission 16	MONTROSSISBAD
Mission 17	VOSAISBADDER
Mission 18	JANGOISBADDEST
TGC Cards	GO FISH

Star Wars Episode III Revenge of the Sith

Enter the following codes in the Codes section of the Options menu.

Unlockable	Code
All Attacks and Force Power Upgrades Activated	JAINA
All Bonus Missions Unlocked	NARSHADDAA
All Concept Art Unlocked	AAYLASECURA
All Duel Arenas Unlocked	TANTIVEIV
All Duelist Unlocked	ZABRAK
All Story Missions Unlocked	KORRIBAN
Fast Force Energy and Health Regeneration Activated	BELSAVIS
Infinite Force Energy Activated	KAIBURR
Infinite Health Activated	XUCPHRA

Star Wars: Jedi Starfighter

Enter the following in the Codes section of the Options menu.

Unlockable	Code
Invincibility	QUENTIN
Fly-By Mode	DIRECTOR
No Hud	NOHUD

PSP
Xbox
PS2
GC
GBA

Star Wars Starfighter

To access the following unlockables, go to the Code screen (via the Options Menu) to enter the sequence.

Unlockable	Code
Default Message	SHOTS (or SIZZLE)
Director Mode	DIRECTOR
Hidden Christmas Video	WOZ
Hidden Message	LTDJGD
Invincibility	MINIME
Jar Jar Mode	JARJAR
My Day at Work (short slideshow)	JAMEZ
No Heads Up Display	NOHUD
Everything	OVERSEER
Experimental N-1 Fighter	BLUENSF
Multiplayer Mode	ANDREW
Gallery	SHIPS
View Character Sketches	HEROES
View Hidden Picture	SIMON—you'll see a picture of the LEC team.
View Planet Sketch-Work	PLANETS
View the Credits	CREDITS
View the Dev Team	TEAM

Unlockable	Objective
Burger Droid	Access this Easter Egg by typing the DIRECTOR code, then entering the Bonus Missions and selecting Fighter Training. After a few seconds you see an asteroid with an android on it barbecuing some hamburgers.
Grim Fandango Hotrod	Come in first in the Canyon Sprint Bonus Mission.
Outlaw Gallery	To view this Easter Egg, start the first level. Instead of following your instructor's ship, turn around and go the other way to fly into a large room and view artwork from a game called *Outlaw*.
Canyon Sprint Bonus Mission	Get silver in these six missions: Naboo Proving Grounds, the Royal Escort, Taking the Offensive, Midnight Munitions Run, Rescue On the Solleu, the Final Assault.
Charm's Way Bonus Mission	Get a bronze medal in these six missions: the Royal Escort, Contract Infraction, Piracy Above Lok, Taking the Offensive, the New Resistance, the Final Assault.
Darth Maul's Infiltrator	Get gold in every mission in the normal game.
Guardian Mantis	Get gold in these three missions: Contract Infraction, Secrets On Eos, The New Resistance.
Havoc	Get gold in these five missions using the Havoc in the normal game: Piracy Above Lok, Valuable Goods, Eye Of the Storm, the Crippling Blow, Last Stand On Naboo.
N-1 Starfighter	Get gold in these six missions using the N-1 in the regular game: Naboo Proving Grounds, the Royal Escort, Taking the Offensive, Midnight Munitions Run, Rescue on Solleu, the Final Assault.

Star Wars Starfighter (cont'd)

Outpost Attack Bonus Mission	Get Bronze in all 14 missions of the normal game.
Space Sweep Bonus Mission	Get Silver in all 14 missions of the normal game.
Two-Player Canyon Race	Beat the normal game on any difficulty level. Once unlocked, get gold in every level of the normal game to play the bonus level.
Two-Player Capture the Flag	Beat the normal game on any difficulty level. Once unlocked, get gold in every level of the normal game to play the bonus level.

Star Wars: Super Bombad Racing

Unlockable	Objective
Everybody Is a Kaadu	At the Main Menu, press L1, R1, L2, R2. You get this message: "Poof! Everybody is a kaadu!"
Boba Fett	Tap ■,●,▲,●,■ at the Main Menu. You get a message saying that Boba Fett has replaced your racer. Start the game as normal, select your character, and you'll play as Boba Fett when the race starts.
Darth Vader	To play as the original Dark Lord of the Sith, play through the Galaxy Circuit as Anakin Skywalker and win a gold medal.
Galaxy Circuit	To unlock the Galaxy Circuit, play through each individual race and finish in the top three on each track.
Reverse Mirror Tracks	To unlock the option to race the tracks in reverse, complete the Galaxy Circuit with any character and receive a gold medal.
Trade Federation Battle Tank	To race as a squished version of a Trade Federation Battle Tank, press ●,▲,■,●,▲,■ at the Main Menu. Select your character as normal, and when the race starts you'll play as the Tank.

Star Wars: The Clone Wars

Enter the following as codes.

Unlockable	Code
Unlock Clone Trooper in Academy Geonosis Level	FAKE FETT
All FMV Sequences	12 PARSECS
Campaign Level Select	DOORDONOT
Invincibility	DARKSIDE
Multiplayer Level Select	JORG SACUL
Programming Team Photographs (viewable after Sketchbook open)	JEDICOUNCIL
Three Bonus Objectives for Current Mission Marked Complete	GIMME
Unlimited Secondary and Special Weapon	SUPERLASER
Battle Droid in Academy Geonosis Level	TRADEFED
Next Level	THRISNOTRY
Padme Amidala in Academy Geonosis Level	NATALIE
Wookie in Academy Geonosis Level	NERFHERDER

State of Emergency

To access the following unlockables, enter code during gameplay. A message will confirm correct code entry.

Unlockable	Code
AK47	←,→,↓,R2,▲
All Weapons	L1,L1,R2,R2,✕
Big Player	R1,R2,L1,L2,▲
Bull	→,→,→,→,✕—enter in Kaos mode. Alternately, successfully complete the East Side level in Revolution mode to unlock Bull in Kaos mode.
Flame Thrower	←,→,↓,R2,●
Freak	→,→,→,→,●—enter in Kaos mode. Alternately, successfully complete the Chinatown level in Revolution mode to unlock Freak in Kaos mode.
Grenade	←,→,↓,R2,■
Grenade Launcher	←,→,↓,R1,■
Invincibility	L1,L2,R1,R2,✕
Little Player	R1,R2,L1,L2,✕
Looting on the Rise	R1,L1,R2,L2,▲
M16	←,→,↓,R2,●
Minigun	←,→,↓,R1,▲
Mission Select	L1,L2,L2,L2,L1,✕
Mission Skip	←,←,←,←,▲
Molotov Cocktail	←,→,↓,R2,✕
Normal Player	R1,R2,L1,L2,● Alternately, press R1,R2,L1,L2,■.
Pepper Spray	←,→,↓,L1,■
Pistol	←,→,↓,L1,▲
Policeman	Hold L1, then press R2,R2,L2,R1
Punches Decapitate	L1,L2,R1,R2,■
Rocket Launcher	←,→,↓,R1,✕
Shotgun	←,→,↓,L2,▲
Spanky	→,→,→,→,▲—enter in Kaos mode. Alternately, complete the Mall level in Revolution mode to unlock Spanky in Kaos mode.
Tazer	←,→,↓,L1,●
Tear Gas	←,→,↓,L1,✕
Unlimited Ammunition	L1,L2,R1,R2,▲—enter without a weapon in your hands.
Unlimited Time in Kaos Mode	L1,L2,R1,R2,●

Unlockable	Objective
Chinatown Level	Score 25,000 points in the Capitol City Mall level in Kaos mode.
Corporation Central Level	Score 100,000 points in the East Side level in Kaos mode.
East Side Level	Score 50,000 points in the Chinatown level in Kaos mode.
Last Clone Standing Levels	Successfully complete the three-minute and five-minute versions of a level to unlock the Last Clone Standing version of that map in Kaos mode.
Unlimited Kaos Mode Time	Successfully complete all Kaos levels in Arcade mode.

Street Fighter EX3

Unlockable	Objective
Bonus Characters	Beat the game on Normal difficulty without using a Continue to unlock one of the hidden characters. *(See below for more info)*
Evil Ryu	Beat Original mode eight times with Ryu and without continuing. Go to the Character Selection screen and highlight Ryu. Press ×, ■, or ●.
M. Bison II	Beat Original mode eight times with M. Bison and without continuing. Go to the Character Selection screen and highlight M. Bison. Press ×, ■, or ●.
Narrator Sakura	Beat Original mode eight times with Sakura and without continuing. Go to the Character Selection screen and highlight Sakura. Press SELECT.

NOTE

In order to unlock all the bonus characters, repeat the method described above nine times. However, each time you beat the game, you must use a different regular character. The order of bonus characters are: Sagat, Vega, Garuda, Shadow Geist, Kairi, Pullum, Area, Darun, and Vulcano.

Street Hoops

Go to Game Settings and choose "Cheats" to enter these codes.

Unlockable	Code
ABA Ball	●, R2, ■, R2
All Courts	■, ■, L1, R2, L1, ●, L2, ●
All Teams	■, ■, L1, R2, L1, ●, L2, ●
Black Ball	R2, R2, ●, L2
Blocking Galore	R1, ●, L2, R2
Faster Clock	●, ●, ●, ■, ■
Kung-Fu	●, ●, ■, L1, ■, L1, L2
Normal Ball	R1, ■, ■, L1
Super Steals	■, R2, ■, R1, ●, L1, ●, L2
Tuxedo	L2, L2, ●, ■

Street Racing Syndicate

At the Main Menu, press ↑,↓,←,→. A code entry screen will appear. Enter the following:

Unlockable	Code
Free Car Repair	FIXITUP
Mazda RX-8	RENESIS
Mitsubishi Eclipse GS-T	IGOTGST
Only a warning for the first three busts	LETMEGO
Pac Man Vinyl	GORETRO
Police Car	GOTPOPO
Subaru Impreza S202 STI	SICKGDB
Toyota Celica GT-S Action Package	MYTCGTS
Toyota Supra RZ	SICKJZA

Stuntman

At the New Game menu, use the following codes as drivers' names. All of the codes for this game are case-sensitive—enter them exactly as you see them!

Unlockable	Code
All Cars	spiDER
All Driving Games, Cars, and Toys	Bindl
All Toys	MeFf
Filmography Section (all trailers)	"fellA"

The Suffering

Unlockable	Objective
Alternate title sequence	Complete the game.
Director Commentary	In the Prelude level, wait for a crow to land next to the three inmates, then stand on top of the crow.
Prelude Level	Complete the game.

Enter the following codes during gameplay while holding L1+R1+×.

Unlockable	Code
All Items and Weapons except Gonzo Gun	↑,↓,↑,←,→,←,R2,↑,←,↓,→, ↑,→,↓,←,R2,↓,↓,↓,R2,R2
Bloody Torque	↑,↓,←,→
Clean Torque	↓,↑,→,←
Dirty family picture	←,↓,←,↓,←,↓,R2
Full Health	↓,↓,↓,R2,↑,↑,↓,↑,R2
Full Xombium bottle	→,→,↓,↓,R2,←,→,R2,→,↑,→,R2
Gonzo Gun	←,R2,R2,R2,→,←,→,←,↑, R2,R2,R2,↓,↑,↓,↑,R2
Grenades	→,→,→,←,←,←
Increase Negative Karma	←,←,↓,↑,R2
Molotov Cocktails	↓,↓,↓,↑,↑,↑
New Family Picture	↑,→,↑,→,↑,→,R2
Overcome Insanity	→,→,→,R2,←,←,→,←,R2
Old Movie Mode	↑,R2,←,R2,↓,R2,→,R2
Psychedelic Mode	←,←,R2,→,→,R2,↑,↑,R2,↓,↓,R2
Reload Ammunition for Current Gun	→,→,↓,↑,←,→,←,←,R2
Refill Ranged Weapon Ammunition	←,←,↑,↓,→,←,→,→,R2
Shotgun with Full Ammunition	←,←,←,↓,↓,↓
Wrinkled Family Picture	↑,↑,→,↑

Summer Heat Beach Volleyball

Enter the following codes at the Cheat Menu to unlock the bonus.

Unlockable	Code
Disable Arrows	Whine
High Gravity	Zippy
High-pitched Voices	Mouse
Low Gravity	Space
Low-pitched Voices	Horse
Nails Mode	Nails
Spinning Heads	Exosz
All Accessories	Werit
All Beach House Bonuses	Mypad
All Characters	Peeps
All Difficulty settings	Champ
All Locations	80Day
All Mini-games	Major
All Movies	Musak
All Swimsuits/Shorts	Greed
All Trailers	Gamon
Coconut Ball	Milky
Nerd Ball	Golem
Sun Ball	Hot 1

Unlockable	Objective
Artemis	Beat Arcade Mode on Expert.
Dummy	Beat all the tournaments on Medium.
Enigma	Beat all the tournaments on Hard.
Hephestus	Beat Arcade Mode on Hard.
Incognito	Beat all the tournaments on Expert.
Mannequin	Beat all tournaments on Easy.
Tina	Complete Training Mode.

Super Bust-A-Move

Enter the following codes at the "Push Start Button" screen. An icon in the upper left confirms correct code entry.

Unlockable	Code
Bonus Characters	▲,←,→,▲
More Puzzles	▲,→,←,▲—after entering code, enter Puzzle mode and choose "Arcade" to see more puzzles.

Surfing

Unlockable	Objective
Normal Boards and Riders	Beat the game on Normal difficulty to unlock Tyrone King, Lara Barcella, Gareos, and six new boards.
Pro Boards and Riders	Beat the game on Pro difficulty to unlock Largo, Lyco Sassa, Mikey Sands, and five new boards.
Semi-Pro Boards and Riders	Beat the game on Semi-Pro difficulty to unlock Jojo, Morsa, Serena Knox, and six new boards.
Master Boards and Riders	Beat the game on Master difficulty to unlock three new boards and Surfroid.

SWAT: Global Strike Team

These codes must be entered in the in game option screen.

Unlockable	Code
Infinite Ammo	←, →, ↑, ↓, ↑, ↓, R2, L2
God Mode	↑, ↓, ←, →, L2, R2

PSP Xbox PS2 GC GBA

Tak and the Power of Juju

Enter these codes during gameplay then go into the extra menu to activate them.

Unlockable	Code
100 Feathers	■,▲,●,■,▲,●,■,▲
All Moonstones	▲,▲,■,■,●,●,←,→
All Plants	■,▲,●,←,↑,→,↓,↓
All Juju Powers	↑,→,←,↓,▲,●,■,↓
All Yorbels	↑,▲,←,■,→,●,↓,↑
Everything	←,→,■,■,●,●,←,→

Teenage Mutant Ninja Turtles 2: Battle Nexus

From the Options Menu, choose "Password" and enter the following:

Key: ***M***=Michaelangelo ***R***=Raphael ***L***=Leonardo ***D***=Donatello ***S***=Shredder

Power Up Cheat Codes:

Unlockable	Code
All stamina restore items are upgraded to pizza	MRLMRMR
Attack power doubled	SDLSRLL
Defense power doubled	LDRMRLM
Stamina meter gradually restores itself	DRMSRLR
Turtles no longer receive Damage	LSDRRDR
Turtles no longer suffer from damage effects	DSRDMRM
Unlimited number of shuriken	RSRLRSM

Power Down Challenge Codes:

Unlockable	Code
Any damage is fatal	LRSRDRD
Enemies' attack power doubled	SLSDRDL
Enemies' defense power doubled	RDSRMRL
No falling off	SDSDRLD
Shuriken no longer available	RLMRDSL
Stamina restore items no longer available	MRMDRMD
Turtles suffer from poisonous effects	DRSLLSR

Humorous Cheat Codes:

Unlockable	Code
Attack enemies to see what happens	MLDSRDM
Walk about to find out the effect	SSSMRDD

Tekken 4

Unlockable	Objective
Fight as Eddy Gordo	Successfully complete the game in Story mode as Christie Monteiro. Highlight Christie and press ▲ at the Character Selection screen. Eddy Gordo plays exactly like Christie.
Fight as Ling Xiaoyu in School Uniform	Complete the game in Story mode as Ling Xiaoyu. Highlight Ling Xiaoyu and press ▲ at the Character Selection screen.
Fight as Miharu	Complete the game in Story mode as Ling Xiaoyu. Highlight Ling Xiaoyu and press ● at the Character Selection screen. Miharu looks like Ling in her schoolgirl outfit from Tekken 3 and Tekken Tag Tournament and plays just like her.
Fight as Panda	Highlight Kuma at the Character Selection screen, then press ▲ or ●.
Fight as Violet	Highlight Lee at the Character Selection screen, then press ●.
Unlocking All Characters	Complete the game with the indicated character to unlock the corresponding fighter.

Tekken Tag Tournament

To unlock the different stages, first highlight Practice mode at the main menu, then enter the code listed.

Unlockable	Objective
Eddy's Stage (Day)	Hold L2 and press R2 13 times.
Eddy's Stage (Sunset)	Hold L2 and press R2 ten times.
Heihachi's Stage	Hold L2 and press R2 12 times.
Hwoarang's Stage	Hold L2 and press R2,R2,R2,R2.
Jin's Stage (Day)	Hold L2 and press R2 17 times.
Jin's Stage (Night)	Hold L2 and press R2 eight times.
King's Stage	Hold L2 and press R2 11 times.
Law's Stage (New)	Hold L2 and press R2 once.
Law's Stage (Old)	Hold L2 and press R2 15 times.
Lei's Stage	Hold L2 and press R2,R2,R2,R2,R2.
Ling's Stage	Hold L2 and press R2,R2,R2.
Nina's Stage (Day)	Hold L2 and press R2 nine times.
Nina's Stage (Night)	Hold L2 and press R2 18 times.
Ogre's Stage	Hold L2 and press R2 six times.
Paul's Stage	Hold L2 and press R2 20 times.
School Stage (Day)	Hold L2 and press R2 16 times.
School Stage (Night)	Hold L2 and press R2 seven times.
Supercharging	During a match, press all buttons to charge up. Press ×+●+▲+■ if you kept the default buttons.
Unknown Stage	Hold L2 and press R2 14 times.
Yoshimitsu's Stage (Heavy Snow)	Hold L2 and press R2 19 times.
Yoshimitsu's Stage (Light Snow)	Hold L2 and press R2,R2.

Unlockable	Code
Bonus Characters	Beat Arcade mode with any character to unlock one of the hidden characters. A bonus character is revealed each time you beat the game. *(See more info below)*
Change Partners Before a Fight	Hold the tag button before a match begins to let your partner start first.
Extra Armor King Costume	Beat Arcade mode with Armor King. Go to the Character Selection screen and highlight Armor King. Press START to get his extra costume.
Extra Ling Ending	Beat Arcade mode with Ling. Then beat the game a second time with Ling in her school uniform.
Gallery Mode	Once you unlock Devil you can access Gallery mode.
Tekken Bowl Jukebox	Score higher than 200 in Tekken Bowl. Press START inside Tekken Bowl to access the Bowling menu. Choose "Bowling Options" and pick what song you want to listen to.
Tekken Bowl Mode	Once you unlock Ogre you have Tekken Bowl.
Theater Mode	Beat Arcade mode once.
Play As Angel	Highlight Devil at the Character Selection screen. Press START.
Play As Tiger	Highlight Eddy at the Character Selection screen. Press START.

NOTE

When unlocking the bonus characters, expect them to appear in this order: Kunimitsu, Bruce Irvin, Jack-2, Lee Chaolan, Wang Jinrey, Roger and Alex, Kuma and Panda, Kazuya Mishima, Ogre, True Ogre, Prototype Jack, Mokujin and Tetsujin, Devil and Angel, then Unknown.

Tenchu Fatal Shadows

While the game is paused, enter code on the second controller.

Unlockable	Code
View Score Status	■,■,⇩,⇩,⇧,⇧

Tenchu: Wrath of Heaven

Unlockable	Code
Increase Items	From the Items screen, hold R2+L2, then press ■,■,■,↑,←,↓,→.
Play Demo Stage	From the title screen, press ↑,↓,→,←,×,×,×.
Portable Ninja Brainwipe Machine	Pause the game with the left controller. Using the same controller, press L2,R3,R2,L3,→,■,↑,■,L2,←,■,↓,R2. The game will unpause and you may control the nearest enemy using the left controller in Story Mode.
Regain Health	Pause the game and press ↑,↓,→,←,■,■,■.
Score Cheats	Pause the game and enter →,→,←,← on the left controller.
Special Move Cheat	Pause the game and hold L2+L2, press ↑,↑,↓,↓ then release the L2+L2 and press ■,■,R1,R2.
Stock Infinite Items	From the item selection screen, hold L2+L1+R1+R2 then press ■,■,■,↑,←,↓,→,■,↑,→,↓,←.
All Characters	From the title screen, press L2,R2,L2,R1,→,←,L3,R3.
All Items	From the Items screen, hold R1+L2, then press ↑,■,■,←,■,■,↓,■,■,→,■,■.
All Layouts	From the Mission Select screen, press R3,L3,R2,L2,R1,L1.
All Missions	From the Mission Select screen, press L2,R1,L2,R2,→,■,L3,R3.
All Stages (Multiplayer)	From the Mission Select screen for multiplayer, press L2,R1,L2,R2,→,■,L3,R3.
Bonus Stage	From the title screen, press L2,↑,R1,↓,↙,→,R2,←.
Outtakes	From the title screen, hold L2+R2, then press ↓,■,↑,■,→,■,←,■. The choice will be listed as the "B-SIDE" under the Audio/Language menu.

Terminator 3: Rise of the Machines

From the Main Menu, choose "Options," then select "Cheats." Enter the following:

Unlockable	Code
50% Less Health in Combat with TX	×,▲,■,●,▲,×,■,▲
50% More Health in Combat with TX	■,▲,■,▲,●,×,●,×
All Future Weapons	×,×,×,▲,●,●,■,×
All Present Weapons	●,●,▲,■,×,▲,▲,■
Centipide (Located in Special Features)	●,●,●,■,■,■,▲,■
Invincibility	■,■,×,▲,×,●,×,●
Missile Command (Located in Special Features)	●,●,●,■,■,■,×,×
Unlimited Ammo	×,▲,▲,▲,×,●,×,■

Terminator 3: The Redemption

In the Main Menu, choose "Credits." While watching the credits, enter the following:

Unlockable	Code
All Levels	●+R2+▲
All Upgrades	●+▲+L1
Invincibility	●+R2+R1

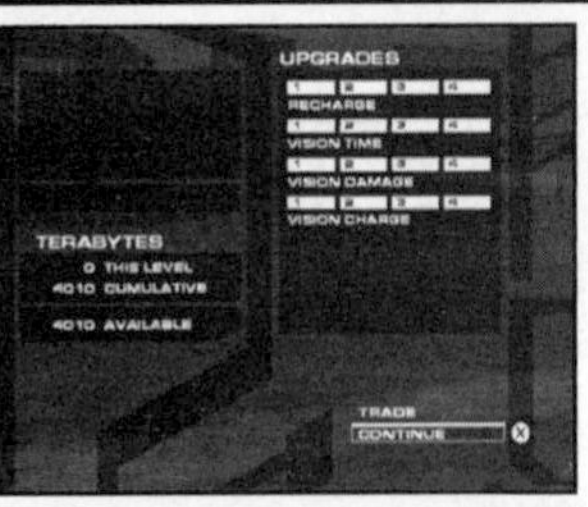

Theme Park Rollercoaster

Enter these codes while you're in the park.

Unlockable	Code
All Items Researched	Press ↑,↓,↑,↓,←,↑,↓,↑ eight times.
Everything Is Free	Press ←,↓,×,● eight times.
Golden Tickets	Press ↑,↓,←,→,●,→,←,↓,↑ four times.

Tiger Woods PGA Tour Golf 2001

Unlockable	Code
Speed up Computer Players	Hold L1+▲ to fast-forward through the CPU's turn.
Taunt Your Friends	Playing against one or more human opponents, press ■, ●, ▲ or × to taunt the golfer while he is at the tee box. For even more annoying sounds, hold down R1 or R2, then press the ■, ●, ▲ or ×.
Unlock Red Shirt Tiger	Beat all 21 games in the Play Now feature to unlock Tiger's shirt. Play with the red shirt Tiger and his in-game stats will match his real-world stats, giving him a major advantage.

Tiger Woods PGA Tour 2004

From the Options Menu, choose "Passwords." (These are case-sensitive.)

Unlockable	Code
Ace Andrews	ACEINTHEHOLE
All Courses and Golfers	THEKITCHENSINK
All Courses	ALLTHETRACKS
All Golfers	CANYOUPICKONE
Cedric the Entertainer	CEDDYBEAR
Dominic "The Don" Donatello	DISCOKING
Edwin "Pops" Masterson	EDDIE
Erica "Ice" Von Severin	ICYONE
Felicia "Downtown Brown"	DTBROWN
Hamish "Mulligan" MeGregor	DWILBY
Kellie Newman	TRAVELER
Melvin "Yosh" Tanigawa	THENEWLEFTY
Moa "Big Mo" Ta'a Vatu	ERUPTION
Solita Lopez	SHORTGAME
Sunday Tiger Woods	4REDSHIRTS
Takeharu "Tsunami" Moto	EMERALDCHAMP
Target World Challenge	SHERWOOD TARGET
Val "Sunshine" Summers	BEVERLYHILLS

PSP Xbox PS2 GC GBA

Tiger Woods PGA Tour 2005

From the Options Menu, choose "Passwords." (These are case-sensitive.)

Unlockable	Code
Adriana "Sugar" Dulce	SOSWEET
Alastair "Captain" McFadden	NICESOCKS
All Courses	THEWORLDISYOURS
All Golfers and Courses	THEGIANTOYSTER
Aphrodite Papadapolus	TEMPTING
Arnold Palmer	THEKING
Ben Hogan	PUREGOLF
Bev "Boomer" Bouchier	THEBEEHIVE
Billy "Bear" Hightower	TOOTALL
Bunjiro "Bud" Tanaka	INTHEFAMILY
Ceasar "The Emperor" Rosado	LANDOWNER
Gary Player	BLACKKNIGHT
Hunter "Steelhead" Elmore	GREENCOLLAR
Jack Nicklaus	GOLDENBEAR
Jeb "Shooter" McGraw	SIXSHOOTER
Justin Timberlake	THETENNESSEEKID
Kendra "Spike" Lovette	ENGLISHPUNK
Raquel "Rocky" Rogers	DOUBLER
Reginald	"Reg" Weathers REGGIE
Seve Ballesteros	THEMAGICIAN
Sunday Tiger Woods	4REDSHIRTS
The Roof	NIGHTGOLFER
Tiffany "Tiff" Williamson	RICHGIRL

Unlockable	Code	Unlockable	Code
All ADIDAS Items	91treSTR	All ODYSSEY Items	kjnMR3qv
All CALLOWAY Items	cgTR78qw	All PING Items	R453DrTe
All CLEVELAND Items	CL45etUB	All PRECEPT Items	BRi3498Z
All MAXFLI Items	FDGH597i	All TAG Items	cDsa2fgY
All NIKE Items	YJHk342B	All TourStage Items	TS345329

Time Crisis 2

Unlockable	Objective
Auto Bullets	Clear the Story mode twice at any difficulty level to be able to fire 20 bullets in one trigger.
Auto Reload	Clear the Story mode at any difficulty level using Auto Bullets to earn unlimited firepower with your gun.
Increase Your Credits in Arcade Mode	Receive extra credits if you clear the Story mode at any difficulty level. *(See below for more info)*
Mirror Mode	To activate the Mirror mode, clear the Story mode without using the "Continue" function.
Music Player	To access the Music Player, clear the final mission of the "Crisis" Mission.
Shoot Away 2 Arrange Mode	To access Arrange mode, score very high points in the Arcade Original mode (Retro). Hit two clay pigeons with one bullet to double your points for that shot.

Time Crisis 2 (cont'd)

Shoot Away 2 Extra Mode	To access Extra mode, score good points in the Arcade Original mode (Retro).
Stage Trial 2	To reach Stage Trial 2, clear Stage 1 of the Story mode at any difficulty level.
Stage Trial 3	To reach Stage Trial 3, clear Stage 2 of the Story mode at any difficulty level.
Wide Shots	Clear the Story mode at any difficulty level with the Auto Reload function to enable your firearm to shoot wide shots (shotgun type with nine bullets per reload).

NOTE

For the "Increase Your Credits in Arcade Mode" code, once you've cleared the mode several times, you are eventually entitled to "Free Play" and a maximum of nine lives that you can set in the "Game" options.

Timesplitters

Unlockable	Objective
Female Cyborg Bot Set	Beat the 2005 Cyberden level on Easy.
Siamese Cyborg Bots	Beat the 2005 Cyberden level on Easy.
Brick As an Arcade Mode Weapon	Complete challenge 4-C.
Challenge Mode	Beat Story mode at any difficulty to Challenge mode. Then defeat each successive Challenge to unlock the next.
Duckman Drake	Complete challenge 2-C.
Duckman Drake As a Bot	Complete challenge 2-A.
Enemy Bricks Cheat	Complete challenge 4-B.
Farrah Fun-Bunny	Complete challenge 8-C.
Fun-Bunny As a Bot	Complete challenge 8-A.
Gasmask SWAT	Complete challenge 6-B.
Ginger As a Bot	Complete challenge 7-A.
Gingerbread	Complete challenge 7-C.
Green and Brown Zombies	Complete challenge 1-B.
Gretel	Beat the 2020 Planet X level on Easy.
Hick Hyde and Insect Mutant Bots	Beat the 1965 Mansion level on Easy.
Jacques Misere	Beat the 2020 Planet X level on Easy.
Mary-Beth Casey and L208	Beat the 2020 Planet X level on Easy.
Olga Strom	Beat the 2020 Planet X level on Easy.
Overall Mutant and Girl Zombie Bots	Beat the 1965 Mansion level on Easy.
Paintball Mode	Unlock the Paintball mode by beating the 1935 Tomb level on Easy in under one minute.
Peekaboo Jones	Beat the 2020 Planet X level on Easy.
Police, Skull and Jacket Zombies	Complete challenge 1-C.
Robofish	Complete challenge 3-C.
Robofish As a Bot	Complete challenge 3-A.
1950 Village Arcade Level	Beat the 1950 Village level on Easy.
1965 Mansion Arcade Level	Beat the 1965 Mansion level on Easy.
1985 Chemical Plant Arcade Level	Beat the 1985 Chemical Plant level on Easy.

Timesplitters (cont'd)

2000 Docks Arcade Level	Beat the 2000 Docks level on Easy.
2020 Planet X Arcade Level	Beat the 2020 Planet X level on Easy.
2035 Spaceways Arcade Level	Beat the 2035 Spaceways level on Easy.
All Enemies Are Bunnies Cheat	Complete challenge 8-B.
All Enemies Are Ducks Cheat	Complete challenge 2-B.
All Enemies Are Fish Cheat	Complete challenge 3-B.
All Enemies Are Gingerbreads Cheat	Complete challenge 7-B.
All Enemies Are Impersonators Cheat	Complete challenge 5-B.
Badass Cyborg Bot Set	Beat the 2005 Cyberden level on Easy.
Bank Arcade Level	Beat the 1985 Chemical Plant level on Normal.
Castle Arcade Level	Beat the 1950 Village level on Normal.
Chinese Chef	Beat the 1970 Chinese level on Easy.
Compound Arcade Level	Beat the 2000 Docks level on Normal.
Cultist	Beat the 1935 Tomb level on Easy.
Eyes Mummy	Beat the 1935 Tomb level on Hard.
Fishwife Mutant Bot	Beat the 1965 Mansion level on Easy.
Gasmask Soldier, Male/Female SWAT Bots	Beat the 2000 Docks level on Easy.
Gasmask SWAT Bots	Beat the 2000 Docks level on Easy.
Graveyard Arcade Level	Beat the 1935 Tomb level on Normal.
Horror Shocker Bot Set	Beat the 1965 Mansion level on Easy.
Impersonator	Complete challenge 5-C.
Impersonator As a Bot	Complete challenge 5-A.
Law and Order Bot Set	Beat the 2000 Docks level on Easy.
Living Dead	Complete challenge 1-A.
Male and Female Soldier Bots	Beat the 2000 Docks level on Easy.
Malehood Bots	Beat the 1985 Chemical Plant level on Easy.
Mall Arcade Level	Beat the 1965 Mansion level on Normal.
Period Horror Bot Set	Beat the 1950 Village level on Easy.
Red and Green Alien Bots	Beat the 2020 Planet X level on Easy.
Site Arcade Level	Beat the 1970 Chinese level on Normal.
Space Opera Bot Set	Beat the 2020 Planet X level on Easy.
Space Opera Bot Set	Beat the 2035 Spaceways level on Easy.
Spaceship Arcade Level	Beat the 2020 Planet X level on Normal.
Streets Arcade Level	Beat the 2005 Cyberden level on Normal.
Suit Hoodlum	Beat the 1970 Chinese level on Easy.
Tuxedo Cyborg Bot	Beat the 2020 Planet X level on Easy.
Usual Suspects Bot Set	Beat the 1985 Chemical Plant level on Easy.
Waiter and Lumberjack Bots	Beat the 1985 Chemical Plant level on Easy.
Warzone Arcade Level	Beat the 2035 Spaceways level on Normal.
Timesplitter	Complete challenge 9-B.
Timesplitters As a Bot	Complete challenge 9-A.
Veiled SWAT	Complete challenge 6-C.

PSP Xbox PS2 GC GBA

Timesplitters 2

Beat each level listed in Story mode under Medium difficulty to unlock its secret character. You'll be able to play these unlockable characters in Arcade mode.

Level	Playable Character
1853 Wild West Level Reward	The Colonel
1895 Notre Dame Paris Level Reward	Notre Dame
1920 Aztec Ruins Level Reward	Stone Golem
1932 Chicago Level Reward	Big Tony
1972 Atom Smasher Level Reward	Khallos
1990 Oblask Dam Siberia Level Reward	Mutant TimeSplitter
2019 NeoTokyo Level Reward	Sadako
2280 Return to Planet X Level Reward	Ozor Mox
2315 Robot Factory Level Reward	Machinist
2401 Space Station Level Reward	Reaper Splitter

NOTE

Beat the 2401 Space Station Level on "Easy" difficulty to unlock the ending sequence.

Tokyo Extreme Racer: Zero

Unlockable	Objective
Change Horn to Siren	Select rear spoiler type 5 for R30 and R30M.
Clean Pause Screen	When Pausing, press ▲+■ to remove the Pause menu. (See below for more info)
Driver View Replay	When viewing replay in "DRIVER VIEW," press L1+R1 to move the camera left/right.
Get a Special Nickname	Put a team sticker on the car you were driving for this team.
Manipulate Parts Camera	In the Parts Type select screen, selecting Aero parts or exhaust makes the camera move toward the car, but pressing ▲ will not cause the camera to move close to the parts (you'll see the entire car on your screen). Press ▲ again to see the close-up.
Reset Records	In Time Record screen, hold down L1+L2+R1+R2 with START. (This also resets the Quick race high score.) These will not be saved, though.
See Meters During Replay	When viewing replay, press SELECT.
See Other Car in One-on-One	When having one-on-one battle with a rival, hold down ■ on 1P's controller to show other cars on the course.
See Other Cars in Free Run	In "FREE RUN," press ■ on 1P's controller when you enter the course select.
Show Analyze Option	In Pause menu (except in the VS mode), hold ■ while you move the cursor to the bottom to show "ANALYZE."
Show Mirror Ornaments	Hold down L1+L2+R1+R2 when selecting the "Shift Assist" option.
Watch Replay with Regular Angle	When you're about to see the replay, hold ▲ on 1P's controller. (You can't switch camera angles when you do this.)

NOTE

You can't unpause the game while removing the Pause menu; you'll have to press ▲+■ to show the Pause menu before unpausing.

Tom Clancy's Ghost Recon

Enter the codes at the Title Screen:

Unlockable	Code
All Missions	×, L2, ▲, R2, SELECT
All Special Features	L1, L2, R1, R2, ×, SELECT
Invincibility	Pause the game and press L1, R2, L2, R1, SELECT

Tom Clancy's Rainbow Six 3

Unlockable	Code
All Custom Mission maps	Press L1, R2, L2, R1, ←, →, ■, ● at the Main Menu.

Tomb Raider: The Angel of Darkness

Unlockable	Code
Infinite Air	When Lara is swimming, save the game while underwater. When you load that save, the oxygen gauge will be restored to full.
Skip Level	Pause the game and press and hold L2+R2+↓+▲ then press ●, ↑, ■, ▲, →, ↓.

Tony Hawk's Pro Skater 3

From the Options Menu, choose "Cheats" and enter the following codes. (Cheats can be activated in the Pause Menu.)

Unlockable	Code
All Characters	YOHOMIES
All FMV Movies	Peepshow
All Levels	ROADTRIP
Cheat Menu	backdoor
Lots of Stat Points	PUMPMEUP

Tony Hawk's Pro Skater 4

Go to the Options Menu and choose "Cheats." Enter the following:

Unlockable	Code
Cheat Mode	watch_me_xplode
Daisy	(o)(o)
Full Special Meter	doasuper
Hidden Skaters	homielist
Perfect Manual	mullenpower
Perfect Rail Balance	ssbsts
Matrix Mode	nospoon
Moon Gravity	superfly

At the Create a Skater screen, enter the following names to unlock hidden skaters:

#$%@!
Aaron Skillman
Adam Lippman
Andrew Skates
Andy Marchal
Angus
Atiba Jefferson
Ben Scott Pye
Big Tex
Brian Jennings
Captain Liberty
Chauwa Steel
Chris Peacock
ConMan
Danaconda
Dave Stohl
DDT
DeadEndRoad
Fakes the Clown
Fritz
Gary Jesdanun
Grjost
Henry Ji
Jason Uyeda
Jim Jagger
Joe Favazza
John Rosser
Jow

Tony Hawk's Pro Skater 4 (cont'd)

Kenzo
Kevin Mulhall
Kraken
Lindsey Hayes
Lisa G Davies
Little Man
Marilena Rixfor
Mat Hoffman
Matt Mcpherson
Maya's Daddy
Meek West
Mike Day
Mike Lashever
Mike Ward
Mr. Brad
Nolan Nelson
Parking Guy
Peasus
Pete Day
Pooper
Rick Thorne
Sik
Stacey D
Stacey Ytuarte

Stealing Is Bad
Team Chicken
Ted Barber
Todd Wahoske
Top Bloke
Wardcore
Zac ZiG Drake

Tony Hawk's Underground

From the Options Menu, choose "Cheat Codes" and enter the following:

Unlockable	Code
All Thug Movies	digivid
Moon Gravity	getitup
Perfect Manual	keepitsteady
Perfect Rail	letitslide
Perfect Skitch	rearrider

From the Options Menu, choose "Cheat Codes" and enter the following:

1337
Akira2s
Alan Flores
Alex Garcia
Andy Marchel
arrr
Bailey
Big Tex
Chauwa Steel
Chris Rausch
ChrisP
CodePirate
crom
Daddy Mac
Dan Nelson
Dave Stohl
DDT
deadendroad
fatass
FROGHAM
GEIGER
Glycerin
GMIAB
Greenie
grjost
Guilt Ladle
Hammer
Henry Ji
Jason Uyeda
Jeremy Andersen
Joel Jewett
Johnny Ow
leedsleedsleeds
MARCOS XK8R
Mike Ward
moreuberthaned
M'YAK
Noly
NSJEFF
POOPER
sik®
Skillzombie
Stacey D
Steal2Liv
tao zheng
The Kraken
The Swink
THEDOC
Todd Wahoske
TOPBLOKE
TSUEnami! (
woodchuck
Y2KJ
Yawgurt
ZiG

Tony Hawk's Underground 2

Go to Cheat Codes and enter the following:

Unlockable	Code
All Levels	d3struct
All Movies	boxoffice
Always Special	likepaulie
Bonus Characters	costars

Tony Hawk's Underground 2 (cont'd)

Unlockable	Code
Infinite Rail	straightedge
Natas Kaupas	oldskool
Nigel Beaverhausen	sellout
Paulie	4-wheeler
Phil Margera	aprilsman

Top Gear Dare Devil

Unlockable	Code
All Cars	Press ■,↑,↓,→,←,X,●,■ while the main screen is loading.
Alternate Colors	Press ↓,■,↓,R1,→,→,↑,←,●,●,L2,L1 at the Main Menu.
Drive a Blue Hot Rod	At the Main Menu, press ↓,■,↓,R1,→,→,↑,←,●,●,L2,L1.
Turn on Motion Blur	At the Main Menu, press ↑,←,●,↓,→,■,↑,↓,←,→,●,■. The Options menu now has a slider bar at the bottom of the screen to increase Motion Blur.

Transformers

Pause the game and enter any of the following codes:

Unlockable	Code
All Extras	Select Extras from the Main Menu and press ■,■,●,■,■,●,L1,L2
Invincibility	R1,●,●,R1,R2,L1,L1,L2
One Shot Kills	■,●,■,●,L1,L1,L2,L1
Stealth Enemies	←,→,←,R1,R2,R1,→,→

Enter the following codes at the Autobot HQ screen:

Unlockable	Code
All Mini-Cons	L1,L2,●,●,■,●,L2,L1
Big Head Mode	●,●,●,■,L1,L1,L1,L2
Disable Mini Con Overload	R1,R1,L2,R1,R1,L2,●,●
Infinite Stealth	↑,↑,↓,↓,L1,L2,L1,L2
Turbo Mode	L1,R2,R2,■,■,■,■,L1
Unlimited Powerlink	↑,↓,↑,↓,●,■,■,●

At the Difficulty Select screen, enter the following:

Unlockable	Code
Alaska Level Complete	R1,●,R1,■,←,←,→,←
Amazon Boss Fight	←,←,→,L1,R2,←,←,→
Amazon Level Complete	L1,L1,L2,■,■,●,R1,R2
Antarctica Boss Fight	L1,←,L2,→,■,■,●,●
Antarctica Level Complete	R1,R1,R2,L2,L1,L1,R1,R1
Cybertron	R2,R1,L1,L2,■,●,■,●
Deep Amazon Level Complete	←,→,←,←,→,R1,R2,●
Mid-Atlantic Boss Fight	L2,←,→,→,←,L2,L2,L2
Mid-Atlantic Level Complete	●,■,●,■,→,←,←,→
Starship Boss Fight	→,→,■,R1,R2,●,←,←
Starship Level Complete	←,←,→,●,●,→,→,←

Triple Play Baseball

Unlockable	Objective
Always Hit the Grand Salami	Create a player named "SLUGGER." Whenever he comes up with the bases loaded, he'll hit a home run.

True Crime: Streets of LA

Enter the following codes at the City Map screen:

Unlockable	Code
All Driving Upgrades	←,→,←,→,×
All Fighting Moves	↑,↓,↑,↓,×
All Gun Upgrades	→,←,→,←,×
Bigger Vehicle	↓,↓,↓,×
Nick Kang's Location	×,●,■,▲
Smaller Vehicle	↑,↑,↑,×

Go to Create a License Plate and try the following codes:

Unlockable	Code
Asian Worker	HARA
Bartender	HAWG
Bum	B0OZ
Chief, The	B1G1
Commando	M1K3
Dirty Morales	BRUZ
Donkey	JASS
Gangsta	TFAN
George	FATT
Jimmy Fu	MRFU
Lola Gees	B0OB
Pimp	PIMP
Policeman	FUZZ
Rose in Lingerie	HURT M3
Rosie	ROSA
Sewer Ghoul	J1MM
Street Punk	MNKY
SWAT Officer	5WAT
Tattoo Concubines	TATS
Triad Butcher	PHAM

Turok: Evolution

Enter the following codes at the Cheat menu.

Unlockable	Code
All Available Weapons	TEXAS
Big Head Mode	HEID
Demo Mode and Target Mini-Game	HUNTER
Invincibility	EMERPUS
Invisibility	SLLEWGH
Level Select	SELLOUT—after entering, load a saved game to unlock all levels.
Master Code	FMNFB
Unlimited Ammunition	MADMAN
Zoo Mode	ZOO—you can now kill any animal in the game with the war club as a weapon.

Turok: Evolution (cont'd)

NOTE

There are two parts to the "Demo mode and Target Mini-Game" code. Besides starting Demo mode, you can also play the Target minigame at the main title screen. Use the D-pad to move the pointer and Fire to shoot.

To access the following unlockables, pause gameplay, hold L1, then enter code. A message confirms correct code entry. Repeat the code to disable its effect.

Unlockable	Code
Invincible NPCs	■,●,▲,×,■,●,▲,×
Unlimited Ammunition	←,●,→,■,↑,▲,↓,×
Unlimited Health	▲,■,▲,■,▲,●,▲,●
Unlimited Rage	←,↓,←,↓,→,↑,→,↑

Twisted Metal: Black

Unlockable	Code
Change Camera	To change the camera angle, press and hold SELECT, then press ↓. To switch between horizontal and vertical, hold SELECT, then press ←.
Convert Weapons into Health	During the game, hold down all four shoulder buttons, then press ▲,×,■,●. Your weapons vanish and your health fills up a little.
Decipher Minion	To understand what Minion's numbered codes mean on the load screens (when playing as him), match the number with its corresponding letter. (A=1, B=2, and Z=26.)
Different Weapons Display	Press and hold t, then press → during gameplay to change the weapons selection display.
Infinite Ammo	To have unlimited ammunition for your ride, press and hold the shoulder buttons, then press ↑,×,←,●.
Invincibility	During gameplay (this includes story mode), press and hold the shoulder buttons, then press →,←,↓,↑.
Mega Machine Guns	To enable the Mega Machine Guns feature, press and hold the shoulder buttons, then press ×,×,▲.
One Hit Kills	During gameplay, hold the shoulder buttons and quickly press ×,×,↑. At the top of the screen, a message confirms correct code entry.
Unlock God Mode	During gameplay, hold the shoulder buttons and rapidly press ↑,×,←,●. A message reading "God Mode On" appears at the top of the screen to confirm correct code entry.

Unlockable	Objective
Axel	After beating the first level, choose the Freeway level. Drive to the middle of the level, where an entrance to the construction lot and a Repair Station are located. There are two cranes; focus on the left one. Eliminate at least several enemies, then position your vehicle halfway up the ledge. If you've centered your vehicle in the middle of the construction site, use the middle ridge to a missile toward the orange control box near the center of the crane.
Downtown Jackpot	On one side of the river in the downtown level is the R&D Chemicals Plant. On the left side of the main building are three giant balls, like the ones in the highway loop level. Shoot the one closest to the sign with a gas can, and it rolls into a building, knocking it down and revealing three healths (which are supplied throughout the level at this location). Shoot the ball on the far left and it rolls into the building directly behind the previous one, giving you six power missiles.

Twisted Metal: Black (cont'd)

Elevator in Downtown	Find this elevator to pick up power-ups. Find the Atom Bank and face it. To its left is a building with glass doors. Shoot them and they'll blow to pieces. Use the elevator to drive up to the higher reaches of the building. There's one health power-up up there, and it's a great view!
Open Elevators Level	Go to the Highway Loop Level and kill off six or seven of the combatants. Drive to the raised, broken bridge (with the two health pick-ups and another pick-up in between), and find a power plant directly off the road. There are two or three giant steel balls there. Shoot the one closest to the bridge with a Gas Can, and it breaks off and rolls. Stay clear of its path, then follow the ball. When it crashes through a wall, go into the newly opened area and find the Black Cube, plus health and weapon pick-ups, inside.
Open Freeway Level	To open the Freeway for multiplayer action, get 10 Kills in Survival Mode in the Snowy Roads arena.
Open Mini-Suburbs Level	To open the Mini-Suburbs for multiplayer action, get 10 Kills in Survival Mode in the Drive-In arena.
Manslaughter	In the Prison Passage level, down on the docks to the starboard side of the landed ship, is a stack of crates holding a health power-up. Shoot the crates to blast open a ramp to the health, then shoot at the ship's hull above where the crates are stacked against it. A panel opens, and you can drive into a room inside the ship where Manslaughter is located. Destroy the control panel to unlock the new car.
Minion	Beat Story Mode with every character, including those you unlock in the game (Manslaughter, Warthog, Yellow Jacket, and Axel).
Warhawk's Level	To open Warhawk's multiplayer level in the first level (Zorko Bros. Scrap and Salvage, a.k.a. the Junkyard), focus your efforts on the vertical crusher. Drive up the ramp to the broken freeway and drive halfway along it. Aim your car toward the Bob's Big Boy, and shoot it with a Power or a Fire, to avoid hitting any other cars. Once blown up, it creates a ramp to the vertical crusher. Drive down to the newly created green ramp and, when the crusher is down, drive onto it. Drive slowly onto it so you don't go over it. When it ascends, shoot the building on top of the deck, then drive onto the deck. On the left side is a Black Cube, which opens Warhawk's multiplayer level.
Warthog	In the Suburbia level, head to the carnival area. At the gate, take a left and head toward the smoke over the ridge. Speed up and ramp off the angled dirt ridge; you should land below on a building with a large hole in its roof. Go inside and look for a control panel in the corner. Shoot it to unlock Warthog.
Yellow Jacket	There is an airplane circling in the first level. Use a homing missile and shoot it down. After that's done, drive to the lower section of the level. The plane has crashed and you can drive in it. Go to the end, find the console and shoot it with machine gun fire. After four seconds, you can see Yellow Jacket's car lower down.

Ty the Tasmanian Tiger

Unlockable	Code
Aquarang, Elemental Boomerangs, Dive, and Swim Abilities	Press L1, R1, L1, R1, ▲, ▲, ■, ■, ▲, ■ during gameplay.
Show Objects	Press L1, R1, L1, R1, ▲, ▲, ●, ■, ■, ●, R2, R2 during gameplay.
Technorangs	Press L1, R1, L1, R1, ▲, ▲, ▲, ■, ▲, ■ during gameplay.
Unlimited Health	Quickly press L1, R1, L1, R1, ▲, ▲, ▲, ▲, ●, ● when "Press Start" appears.
Unlock Gallery and Movies	Quickly press L1, R1, L1, R1, ▲, ▲, ×, ×, R2, ■, R2, ■ when "Press Start" appears.

Ty the Tasmanian Tiger (cont'd)

NOTE

To unlock an Ending Bonus, complete the game with all cogs, eggs, and opals collected for a 100 percent completion. The Ending Bonus includes a bonus level, an extra FMV sequence after the ending credits, and the "Movies" option at the Extras menu.

NOTE

After you use the Show Objects code, the locations of hidden Opals, Bilbies, Golden Cogs, Rainbow Scales, and Thunder Eggs are shown with colored lines from the sky (Opals and Rainbow Scales with a green line, Golden Cogs with a gold line, Thunder Eggs with a purple line, and Bilbies with a whitish line).

Unreal Tournament

Unlockable	Code
Fatboy Mutation	Press ●,●,●,↑,↓,↓,↑,●,●,● at the title screen. Enter Multiplayer mode and choose the Fatboy Mutator. You get fatter as you gain frags, and thinner as you get fragged.
Firewire Multiplayer	Using a four-port Firewire PC hub, hook one to three more PS2 consoles to the hub with Firewire cables. Start a two-person multiplayer game. Pause the game, then press ←,●,←,→,■,→. Then have all the other players press START to join in.
God Mode	Pause the game, then press ■,●,←,→,●,■ and you will be invincible.
Level Advance	Pause the game, then press ↑,↓,←,→,→,←,●.
Level Select	Pick the "Resume Game" option. Highlight a previously saved game. Press ↑,↓,↓,↑,←,↑,→,↓.
Max Ammo	Pause the game, then press ←,→,●,●,●,→,←.
Stealth Mutation	Press ■,■,●,●,■,■,●,● at the title screen. Enter Multiplayer mode and choose the Stealth Mutator.
USB Multiplayer	Use two USB keyboards, two USB mice, and two controllers, set the third and fourth player configurations to the keyboards and mice.

Van Helsing

During gameplay, enter the following:

Unlockable	Code
Bonus Movie 1	↑,↓,↑,↓,←,←,→,→,L1,L3,R3,R1
Bonus Movie 2	↑,→,↓,←,↑,←,↓,→,↑,R1,R2,R3
Bonus Movie 3	L1,L2,R2,R1,R2,L2,L1,↑,↑,↓,↓,SELECT
Bonus Movie 4	SELECT,L3,R3,SELECT,R1,L3,SELECT,←,←,↑,→,→
Bonus Movie 5	L2,R2,L1,R1,SELECT,SELECT,L1,L1,R2,R2,L3,R3
Bonus Movie 6	R2,R1,R2,R1,L1,L2,L1,L2,←,→,SELECT,SELECT
Bonus Movie 7	L3,←,R3,→,L2,↑,R2,↓,L1,←,R1,→

Viewtiful Joe

Unlockable	Objective
Unlock Dante	Beat game on any difficulty.
Unlock Sylvia	Beat game on Adult Mode.

Virtua Fighter 4

Unlockable	Objective
Alternate Costumes	Hold START at the Character Selection screen. Press ✕ to select that character while holding START to wear th alternate costume.
Alternate Main Menu Background	Enter the Game Option menu, and press R1 to cycle forward or L1 to cycle backward through the list of backgrounds for the main menu.
Classic Victory Poses	Use a created fighter to reach the Second Kyu level. Hold Punch + Kick + Guard during the replay to do a classic victory pose from Virtua Fighter 1.
Dural's Stage in Versus Mode	Use a created fighter to reach the Emperor or High King rank and unlock the hangar stage in Versus mode.
Fight as Dural	Defeat Dural in Kumite mode to unlock her in Versus mode.
Training Stage 1 in Versus Mode	Use a created fighter to reach the First Dan rank and unlock the first training stage in Versus mode.
Training Stage 2 in Versus Mode	Use a created fighter to reach the Fifth Dan rank and unlock the second training stage in Versus mode.
Training Stage 3 in Versus Mode	Use a created fighter to reach the Champion rank and unlock the third training stage in Versus mode.
Training Trophy	Complete the trial events in Training mode with a created fighter. A small trophy icon is displayed over your character's health bar.
Virtua Fighter 1 Fighter Model	Use a character fighter to reach at least the First Dan rank. Select that fighter and hold Punch + Kick until the match begins.

V-Rally 3

Unlockable	Objective
Extra Challenges	Win the Michelin Challenge in Challenge mode.
Mitsubishi Lancer Evolution VI	Select Career mode and win the 1.6L FWD championship in V-Rally mode.
Reversed Tracks	Four tracks exist in each country. Beat a track's record to unlock the next one. Unlock all of them to access the four reversed tracks for that country.
SEAT Cordoba Repsol	Win the Pirelli Challenge in Challenge mode.
Subaru Impreza 2000	Select Career mode and win the 2.0L 4WD championship in V-Rally mode.
Toyota Corolla V-Rally	Set a record time in all circuits.

Unlockable	Code
Car Preview	At the Car Selection screen, hold → or ← to open either door; hold ↑ to open the hood; and hold ↓ to open the trunk.
Flat Cars	Enter 21051975 PTITDAV as a name.
Floating Cars	Enter 210741974 MARTY as a name.
Jelly Cars	Enter 07121974 FERGUS as a name.
Small Cars	Enter 01041977 BIGJIM as a name.
Small Cars with High-Pitched Commentary	Enter no first name and PALACH as a last name.
Smashed Cars	Enter 25121975 PILOU as a name.
Stretched Cars	Enter Gonzales SPEEDY as a name.

Wakeboarding Unleashed

Enter the following codes at the Main Menu.

Unlockable	Code
Have All Gaps	R1,L2,L2,R2,R1,L2,L2,R2,R1,L2,L2,R2,R1,L2,L2,R2.
Level Select	■,■,■,■,●,●,●,●,▲,▲,▲,▲,■,●,▲.
Unlock Everything	↑,↓,↑,↓,↑,↓,↑,↓,↑,↓,←,→,←,→,←,→,←,→,←,→.
Unlock Other Boards	↑,↑,←,←,→,→,↓,↓,↑,←,→,↓,↑,←,→,↓.

Unlockable	Objective
All Boarders	Rotate the left analog stick clockwise fifteen times from the main menu.
Boarder Movies	Complete the game with a particular boarder to unlock his or her movie.
Credits	Beat the game once with any boarder.
Jordan	Collect every star in the Star Search Challenges.
Summer	Beat the game once with any boarder.

Way of the Samurai

Unlockable	Code
Change Characters	In the New Game menu, press L1,R1,R1,L2,L2,L2,R2,R2,R2+■. To choose a character, press ← or →.
Full Health	Pause the game, hold L1+L2, and press ↓,↑,↓,↑,→,←,●.
Increase Sword Toughness +1	Pause the game, hold R1+R2, and press →,→,←,←,↓,↑,●.
Versus Mode	At the Title Screen, hold L1+R1, and press ●+■.

Way of the Samurai 2

Unlockable	Code
All Characters	Select Character Customization, highlight name and press L1,R2,R1,L2,L1,R2,R1,L2,■
More Store Items	In the Main Map, press L1,R1,L1,R1,R2,R2,▲.

WDL: Warjetz

Unlockable	Code
Add 10 Money	WNNNGS
All Codes	TWLVCHTS
All Movies	GRTD
Antarctica 1	CMPPLHJJNBQN
Antarctica 2	RKFPMYBZHBQN
Antarctica 3	GNVPMQFSNBQN
Australia 1	MHZKWTJMQBQM
Australia 2	ZBCKXPBHNBQM
Australia 3	LDRKXYFZTBQM
Double Money	TWFSTD
Everything	SPRLZY
Faster Jets	ZPPY
Ghost mode	SNKY
Huge Guns	QD
Instantly Win	SMSHNG
Invincibility	DNGDM
Level Select	JMPTT
New York City 1	KKSPKRJHKBQN
New York City 2	VBFKPLHBWZBQN
New York City 3	WJYPLWFQGBQN
Overlords Mode	VRLRDS
Panama 2	JBVKWNBBCBQM
Panama 3	MDKKWYFTKBQM
Plane Automatically Wins	SMSHNG
Rapid Fire	FRHS
Rhine River 1	YJVPJCJGVBQN
Rhine River 2	FCNPKXBVWBQN
Rhine River 3	PGDPKGFPDBQN
San Francisco 1	TRLPMBJLVBQN

WDL: Warjetz (cont'd)

San Francisco 2	SVMPNFBFVBQN	**Thailand 2**	TBPKYZBVHBQM
San Francisco 3	RXDPNHFYDBQN	**Thailand 3**	KFFPJRFNPBQN
Show All Boxes	BXDRW	**Valhalla 1**	XBXPNGKRKBQN
Spin Shots	DZZY	**Valhalla 2**	LPXKVMCQZBQM
Super Armor	MRRMR	**Valhalla 3**	QSMKVSGKHBQM
Thailand	ZHHKXJJTBBQM	**View All FMV**	GRTD

Whiteout

Unlockable	Code
10,000 Points	Hold L2+▲ and press ←,←,↑,↓ during a race.
All Characters	Hold L1+R1 and press ↓,↓,↓,↓ at the main menu.
All Parts	Hold L1+R1 and press ←,←,←,← at the main menu.
All Tracks	Hold L1+R1 and press ↑,↑,↑,↑ at the main menu.
Alternate View	Hold L2+▲ and press ↓,↓,←,← during gameplay.
Master Code	Hold R1+L1 and press →,→,→,→ at the main menu to unlock all tracks, characters, and snowmobiles.
Restore Stamina	Hold L2+▲ and press →,→,←,↓ during a race.
Win Race	Hold L2+▲ and press ↑,↓,←,→ during a race.

Wild Wild Racing

Unlockable	Code
New Engines	Each country in Time Attack rewards you with an engine for one of the three initially-selectable buggies. Complete the three races per Time Attack (Uphill, Downhill, and Flat) to gain a new engine that ups the stats on your buggy.
Secret Menu and Top Secret Menu	At the main menu, highlight and select Options. At the Options menu hold down ■ and press ↑,●,↓,●,←,→,←,→,●. This will open the Secret menu option on the Options screen. Enter Single Player and type your name as NORTHEND.

World Soccer Winning Eleven 7

Unlockable	Objective
Premier All Star Team	Win the LG Championship Cup
World All Star Team	Win the Multi International Cup

World Tour Soccer

At the Main Menu, enter the following:

Unlockable	Code
All Bonuses	L2,L2,L1,R1,←,↑,←,↓
Infinite TIF Tokens	↑,↓,↑,↓,R1,R1,R2,R2,↑,↓,↑,↓
QA Liverpool, TIF OldBoys, TIF Newbies, and Touchline Teams	↓,→,L2,R1,←,R1
TimeWarp Teams	R2,L2,R2,L2,↑,L1

Wrath Unleashed

Unlockable	Objective
Elephant pool Arena	Win 20 Team Battles
Metal Age Arena	Win 100 Arena Battles

Wreckless

Unlockable	Objective
Alternate View	Press ↓ to cycle through different screen effects during gameplay and replays. To unlock more effects, complete Missions A-9, A-10, B-9, and B-10.
AUV	Complete Mission A-9.
Dragon-SPL Car	Complete Mission A-1.
Gold Rank on All Missions	Highlight the "Unlimited Time" option at the main menu, then press L2+R1+→+● as the game loads.
Missions A-2 to A-4	Complete Mission A-1.
Missions B-2 to B-4	Complete Mission B-1.
Music Test	Complete all twenty missions to unlock the "Music Test" selection at the Options screen.
Super Car	Complete Mission B-1.
Tank-90	Complete Mission B-8.
Tiger-SPL	Complete Mission A-8 to unlock the car that Tiger Tagachi drives.
Yakuza Car	Complete Mission B-9.

WWE Crush Hour

Unlockable	Code
Special Meter Fills Quickly	Pause the game, hold L3, and press ▲,●,●,●,●.
Unlimited Turbo	Pause the game, hold L3, and press ✕,R1,R2.
All Levels and Vehicles	From the main menu, press ■,L2,R2,●,■,L2,L2,L2.
Kevin Nash	From the character select screen, press L2,■,R2,●.

Unlockable	Objective
All Levels	Beat Season Mode with any character to unlock all levels.
Bradshaw	Beat Season Mode with Brock Lesnar.
Christian	Beat Season Mode with Chris Jericho.
D-Von Dudley	Beat Season Mode with Bubba Ray Dudley.
Hulk Hogan	Beat Season Mode with The Rock.
Lita	Beat Season Mode with Matt Hardy.
Ric Flair	Beat Season Mode with The Big Show, Rob Van Dam and Triple H.
Stephanie McMahon	Beat Season Mode with Kurt Angle.
Vince McMahon	Beat Season Mode, facing Vince in the final battle.

X2: Wolverine's Revenge

Unlockable	Code
All Cerebro Files and FMV Sequences	▲,●,▲,■,■,■,R1+R2
All Costumes	▲,●,▲,■,■,■,L1+L2
Cheat Menu	▲,▲,●,●,■,■,●,●,L1+R1+L2+R2
Level Select	▲,●,▲,■,▲,●,L1+R1

XG3 Extreme G Racing

Unlockable	Code
Unlimited Turbo	To get unlimited turbo, go to the title screen. Press R1+L1, R2+L2, R1+L1, and R2+L2. When the code is entered correctly, you get a message confirming entry.
All Tracks	Go to the main menu and press L1,L1,L2,L2,R2,R2,R1,R1, then hold L1+R1+L2+R2. If the code is entered correctly, a message appears.

X-Squad

Unlockable	Code
Captain Rank Code	Press ●,R1,●,L1,▲,R2 at the title screen. Start a new game. You'll start with a radar and the rest of items from the Lieutenant Rank code.
Colonel Rank Code	Press ▲,■,●,■,▲,● at the title screen. Start a new game. You'll start with a Level 3 shield, Level 3 sensor, radar, no weight limit, 99 clips, and beginner level of all weapons, and bonus points will be shown.
General Rank Code	Press L1,L1,L2,L2,R1,R1,R2,R2 at the title screen. Start a new game. You'll start with the items from Colonel Rank code except that this one has intermediate level of all weapons.
Lieutenant Rank Code	Press R1,L2,L1,R2 at the title screen. Start a new game. You'll start with a Level 2 shield and the items from the Sergeant Rank code. You'll also earn a 10,000-point bonus when you complete the level.
Major Rank Code	Press L2,■,R2,▲,L1,●,R1 at the title screen. Start a new game. You'll start with a Level 3 shield, Level 3 sensor, and the rest of the items from the Sergeant Rank code.
Master of X-Squad Rank Code	Press ●,●,●,●,▲,■,■,■,■ at the title screen. Start a new game. You'll start with the items from the General Rank code except this one has a master level of all weapons.
Private Rank Code	Press ■,●,▲ at the title screen. Start a new game. You'll start with the Michaels 9mmS and 99 clips, and bonus points will be shown.
Sergeant Rank Code	Press ▲,●,■ at the title screen. Start a new game. You'll start with the Taylor M82, no weight limit, Michaels 9mmS, and 99 clips, and bonus points will be shown.

Yu-Gi-Oh! The Duelist of the Roses

Press R3 at the Build Deck screen to enter a password for a card.

Unlockable	Password
Ancient Tree of Enlightenment	EKJHQ109
Aqua Dragon	JXCB6FU7
Barrel Dragon	GTJXSBJ7
Beastking of the Swamp	QXNTQPAX
Birdface	N54T4TY5
Black Hole	UMJ10MQB
Blast Sphere	CZN5GD2X
Change of Heart	SBYDQM8B
Crush Card	SRA7L5YR
Dragon Seeker	81EZCH8B
Earthshaker	Y34PN1SV
Elf's Light	E5G3NRAD
Exodia the Forbidden One	37689434
Fairy King Truesdale	YF07QVEZ
Fairy's Gift	NVE7A3EZ
Goblin Fan	92886423
Gravity Bind	0HNFG9WX
Greenkappa	YBJMCD6Z
Harpie's Feather Duster	8HJHQPNP
Horn of the Unicorn	S14FGKQ1
Left Arm of the Forbidden One	A5CF6HSH
Magician of Faith	GME1S3UM
Meteor Dragon	86985631
Mimicat	69YDQM85
Mirror Wall	53297534
Mystical Capture Chain	N1NDJMQ3
Robotic Knight	S5S7NKNH
Royal Decree	8TETQHE1
Seiyaryu	2H4D85J7
Serpentine Princess	UMQ3WZUZ
Slate Warrior	73153736
Swordsman from a Foreign Land	CZ81UVGR
Swordstalker	AH0PSHEB
Tactical Warrior	054TC727

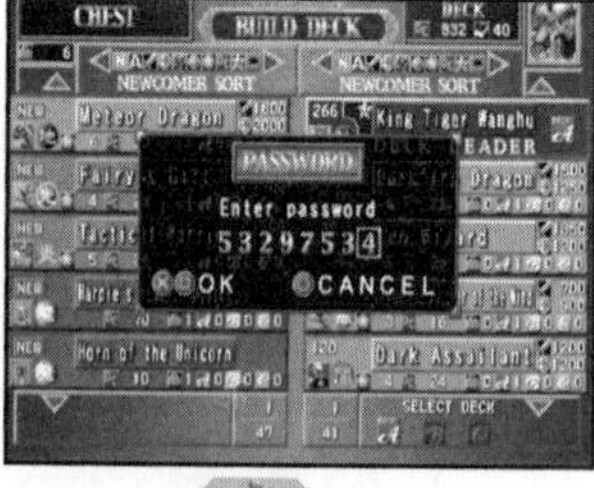

Yu Yu Hakusho: Dark Tournament

From the Options Screen, choose "Cheats" and enter the following:

Unlockable	Code
All Cards	●,■,●,■,■,↓
All Chapters	↑,↓,×,●,■,→
All Environments	↑,→,←,→,×,×
All Fighters	■,↑,■,●,↓,●
All Modes	←,→,↓,→,×,●
No Damage to Player One	●,■,↓,←,●,■
No Damage to Player Two	↑,■,←,■,●,■
Player 1 Free Spirit Energy	■,×,●,■,×,●
Player 2 Free Spirit Energy	↓,↑,●,←,×,→
Turbo Mode	●,×,→,×,↑,■

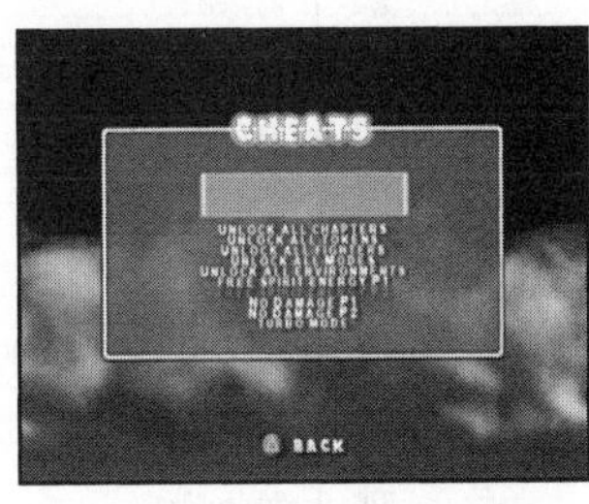

Zone of Enders: The Second Runner

Unlockable	Code
All Power-Ups in the Zoradius Mission	While playing the Zoradius mission, pause and press ↑,↑,↓,↓,←,→,←,→,L2,R1.
Alternate Ending	Earn the A, S, or SS rankings to see new pictures after beating the game.
New Frames	Beat the game to unlock new Frames.
UZoradius Mission	Fight him in Boss Battle Mode. During the battle, pause the game and press ↑,↑,↓,↓,←,→,←,→,L2,R1.

Zone of the Enders

Unlockable	Objective
Alternate Ending	Complete all of the S.O.S calls, ranking A in each of them, and you see a different ending sequence.
Versus Mode	Complete the game to receive Versus mode. Your score (the amount of continues used, saves, and the amount of civilians you rescued) determines which frames you get to play.

PSP Xbox PS2 GC GBA

Table of Contents - GC

007: Everything or Nothing

Description	Code
Alpine Guard Skin in Multiplayer Mode	Complete the Streets of Bucharest level with a "Platinum" rank and all 007 icons.
Calypso Gun in Multiplayer Mode	Complete the Fire and Water level with a "Platinum" rank and all 007 icons.
Carrier Guard Multiplayer Skin	Complete the Evil Summit level with a "Platinum" rank and all 007 icons.
Cyclops Oil Guard Skin in Multiplayer Mode	Complete the Poseidon level with a "Platinum" rank and all 007 icons.
Full Arsenal in Multiplayer Mode	Complete the Forbidden Depths level with a "Platinum" rank and all 007 icons.
Golden Accuracy Power-Up	Complete the Bad Diplomacy level with a "Gold" rank. This cheat enables you to have greater auto-aim.
Golden Armor Power-Up	Complete the Forbidden Depths level with a "Gold" rank.
Golden Bullet Power-Up	Complete the Poseidon level with a "Gold" rank.
Golden CH-6	Complete the Precious Cargo level with a "Gold" rank. When used, this cheat gives you unlimited rockets.
Golden Clip Power-Up	Complete the Cold Reception level with a "Gold" rank.
Golden Grenade Power-Up	Complete the Night of the Jackal level with a "Gold" rank.
Golden Gun in Multiplayer Mode	Complete the Precious Cargo level with a "Platinum" rank and all 007 icons.
Gravity Boots in Multiplayer Mode	Complete the Bad Diplomacy level with a "Platinum" rank and all 007 icons.
Guard Skin in Multiplayer Mode	Complete the Cold Reception level with a "Platinum" rank and all 007 icons.
Lotus Esprit Car	Complete the Streets of Bucharest level with a "Gold" rank.
Poseidon Guard Skin in Multiplayer Mode	Complete the Mediterranean Crisis level with a "Platinum" rank and all 007 icons.
Rapid Fire Power-Up	Complete the Fire and Water level with a "Gold" rank.
Regenerative Armor Power-Up	Complete the Mediterranean Crisis level with a "Gold" rank.
Rocket Manor Multiplayer Level	Complete the Trouble in Paradise level with a "Platinum" rank and all 007 icons. This cheat unlocks a new multiplayer level. It's a large open area. The map settings allow only rockets.
Stealth Bond Skin in Multiplayer Mode	Complete the Dangerous Pursuit level with a "Platinum" rank and all 007 icons.
Unlimited Car Missiles	Complete the Dangerous Pursuit level with a "Gold" rank.
Unlimited Golden Gun Ammunition	Complete the Evil Summit level with a "Gold" rank.
Viper Gun in Multiplayer Mode	Complete the Night of the Jackal level with a "Platinum" rank and all 007 icons.

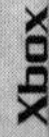

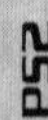

007: Agent Under Fire (cont'd)

Unlockable	Objective
All Weapons	17 Platinum
Baron Samedi	50 Points
Burn Chamber	370 Points
Cayenne Upgrade	12 Gold
Cistern	30 Points
Cloak	13 Platinum
Diavolo Moscow	400 Points
Double Ammo	7 Platinum
Double Damage	9 Platinum
Egypt Commander	90 Points
Egypt Guard	180 Points
Full Ammo	11 Platinum
Full Battery	15 Platinum
Gallery	27 Gold
Golden Gun	1 Platinum
Hazmat Guard	110 Points
Helicopter Upgrade	6 Gold
Improved Battery	5 Platinum
Improved Traction	3 Platinum
Katya	20 Gold
Katya Jumpsuit	320 Points
Le Rouge	260 Points
MI6 Combat Simulator	Complete all Missions
MI6 Survival Test	Complete all Missions
Miss Nagai	450 Points
Miss Nagai	17 Gold
Moscow Guard	230 Points
Mya	130 Points
Mya	14 Gold
Nanotank Upgrade	24 Gold
Odd Job	70 Points
003	290 Points
Platinum Gun	27 Platinum
Production Stills 1	1 Gold
Production Stills 2	2 Gold
Production Stills 3	3 Gold
Production Stills 4	4 Gold
Production Stills 5	5 Gold
Production Stills 6	7 Gold
Production Stills 7	9 Gold
Production Stills 8	13 Gold
Production Stills 9	16 Gold

007: Everything or Nothing

Production Stills 10	18 Gold
Production Stills 11	19 Gold
Production Stills 12	22 Gold
Production Stills 13	23 Gold
Production Stills 14	25 Gold
Serena	350 Points
Serena	430 Points
Serena	8 Gold
Slow Motion Driving	25 Platinum
South Commander	210 Points
Tank Upgrade	10 Gold
Test Lab	160 Points
Triumph Upgrade	21 Gold
Underworld	11 Gold
Unlimited Ammo	23 Platinum
Unlimited Battery	19 Platinum
Vanquish Upgrade	15 Gold

007: Nightfire

For the following codes, select the "Codenames" option at the main menu. Select your character and enter one of the following codes at the Secret Unlocks screen. Save your Codename after entering the code. Then exit your Codename and begin gameplay.

Unlockable	Code
All Gadget Upgrades	Q LAB
All Multiplayer Options	GAMEROOM
Alpine Escape Level	POWDER
Bigger Clip for Sniper Rifle	MAGAZINE
Camera Upgrade	SHUTTER
Chain Reaction Level	MELTDOWN
Countdown Level	BLASTOFF
Decrypter Upgrade	SESAME
Deep Descent Level	AQUA
Double-Cross Level	BONSAI
Enemies Vanquished Level	TRACTION
Equinox Level	VACUUM
Golden P2K	AU P2K
Golden PP7	AU PP7
Grapple Upgrade	LIFTOFF
Island Infiltration Level	PARADISE
Laser Upgrade	PHOTON
Level Select	PASSPORT
Multiplayer Bond Spacesuit	ZERO
Multiplayer Mode All Characters	PARTY
Multiplayer Mode Assassination Option	TARGET

007: Nightfire (cont'd)

Multiplayer Mode Baron Samedi	VOODOO
Multiplayer Mode Bond Tuxedo	BLACKTIE
Multiplayer Mode Christmas Jones	NUCLEAR
Multiplayer Mode Demolition Option	TNT
Multiplayer Mode Drake	NUMBER 1
Multiplayer Mode Elektra King	SLICK
Multiplayer Mode Explosive Scenery Option	BOOM
Multiplayer Mode GoldenEye Strike Option	ORBIT
Multiplayer Mode Goldfinger	MIDAS
Multiplayer Mode Jaws	DENTAL
Multiplayer Mode Max Zorin	BLIMP
Multiplayer Mode Mayday	BADGIRL
Multiplayer Mode Nick Nack	BITESIZE
Multiplayer Mode Oddjob	BOWLER
Multiplayer Mode Protection Option	GUARDIAN
Multiplayer Mode Pussy Galore	CIRCUS
Multiplayer Mode Renard	HEADCASE
Multiplayer Mode Scaramanga	ASSASSIN
Multiplayer Mode Team King of the Hill Option	TEAMWORK
Multiplayer Mode Uplink Option	TRANSMIT
Multiplayer Mode Wai Lin	MARTIAL
Multiplayer Mode Xenia Onatopp	JANUS
Night Shift Level	HIGHRISE
P2K Upgrade	P2000
Phoenix Fire Level	FLAME
Rifle Scope Upgrade	SCOPE
Stunner Upgrade	ZAP
Tranquilizer Dart Upgrade	SLEEPY

Unlockable	Objective
Berserk Racing	While racing on the Paris Prelude, Enemies Vanquished, Island Infiltration, or Deep Descent levels, press START to pause gameplay, hold L, press B, Y, Y, B, Y, X, then release L.
Bonus Race in Alps	While racing on the Enemies Vanquished level, press START to pause gameplay, hold R, press X, X, B, B, Y, then release L.
Double Armor during Racing	While racing on the Paris Prelude, Enemies Vanquished, Island Infiltration, or Deep Descent levels, press START to pause gameplay, hold L, press X, Y, B, X, X, then release L.
Drive a Shelby Cobra	Begin gameplay on the Enemies Vanquished level. Press START to pause gameplay, hold L, press →, →, ←, ←, ↑ then release L. You can now use the Shelby Cobra from the Paris Prelude level in the race through the Alps.
Drive an SUV	While racing on the Enemies Vanquished level, press START to pause gameplay, hold L, press B, X, Y, B, Y, then release L.

007: Nightfire (cont'd)

Frantic Racing	While racing on the Paris Prelude, Enemies Vanquished, Island Infiltration, or Deep Descent levels, press START to pause gameplay, hold L, press B, Y, X, B, Y, X, then release L.
Quadruple Armor during Racing	While racing on the Paris Prelude, Enemies Vanquished, Island Infiltration, or Deep Descent levels, press START to pause gameplay, hold L, press X, Y, B, X, X, X, X, then release L.
Super Bullets	While racing on the Paris Prelude, Enemies Vanquished, Island Infiltration, or Deep Descent levels, press START to pause gameplay, hold L, press X, X, X, X, then release L. Note: You can also do this when you fly the plane with Alura.
Trails during Racing	While racing on the Paris Prelude, Enemies Vanquished, Island Infiltration, or Deep Descent levels, press START to pause gameplay, hold L, press B, X, X, B, then release L.
Triple Armor during Racing	While racing on the Paris Prelude, Enemies Vanquished, Island Infiltration, or Deep Descent levels, press START to pause gameplay, hold L, press X, Y, B, X, X, X, then release L.

1080 Avalanche

Unlockable	Code
Expert Challenge	EATFIKRM
Extreme Challenge	9AVVIKNY
Hard Challenge	2AUNIKFS
Novice Challenge	JAS3IKRR

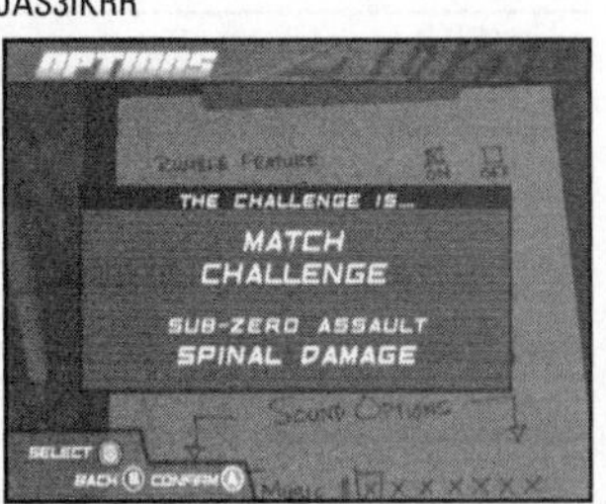

18 Wheeler

Description	Code
Bonus Parking Levels	Complete each of the four parking levels to unlock an additional parking level. Complete the bonus parking level to unlock a sixth parking level.
Bonus Trailers	Complete Arcade mode with all four characters to unlock two bonus trailers in Score Attack mode, Versus mode, and Arcade mode (if the Nippon Maru is selected).
Nippon Maru	Complete Arcade mode with all four characters.

Aggressive Inline

Description	Code
Bonus Character	Complete the normal and hidden challenges in a level to unlock a bonus character.
Cheats	Collect all juice boxes in a level to reveal a cheat code.
FMV Sequences	Complete the normal challenges in a level to unlock its FMV sequence.

PSP Xbox PS2 GC GBA

Aggressive Inline (cont'd)

Power Skates	Complete all challenges (normal and hidden) on every level. The Power Skates give you one blue stat point for every attribute.
Ultra Skates	Complete all the levels with 100 percent. The Ultra Skates give you the other blue stat point for every attribute.

All-Star Baseball 2003

Unlockable	Code
Activate Cheat Menu	Press Ⓛ at the controller selection screen to activate cheats that have been bought.
Alternate Uniforms	Hold Ⓛ+Ⓡ to select alternate jerseys.
Credit Commentary	Press Ⓐ during the credits to hear commentary about the person currently featured.
Taunt Opponents	Hit a homerun and on the way to third (after replay), press Ⓛ or Ⓡ. Your player will taunt the other team's players.

Animal Crossing

8 Mat Tatami	Di9xES@sTRJsYY sqo9cb#3UaKHs3
Airy Shirt	guibfDHdcWqmWcZkrTnDUgkjJ&jb
Amazing Painting	ebucddbkLagnLgBiMBdbichCmqi3
Amber	vuTcfAHyCSqmWj ZkyTnDUgcjJ&jb
Ancient Knit	RethnfoqGreebYldtineorfreebY
Apato Skull	CashisislkndeS YoshisislandeS
Apato Tail	KsCtBedonatioY FsrthedonatioY
Apato Torso	4UTG548pQKQZGf 1n#%jNLEqj5ZBf
Apple Clock	Oa5trmersol4tl OldtW1ersoldtl
Apple TV	Mkri4mariomaro Flriomariomaro
Arched Window	qAepnQGwSyXfFNZ9@WoO%Pvha#OK
Arctic Camo	guibfAH1ENqmW3ZkrTnDUgdjJ&jb
Asteroid	far45678912345 E2345678912345
Aurora Knit	1qWrr6ofBu&q7z8rzSNqofyq76ts
Backyard Fence	#zjKWDN3bx4p7E635nljHT7tTBTC
Bad Plaid Shirt	1qWwi6lfBeoq7z8XtSNyufyy76ts
Balloon Fight	CbDahLBdaDh98d 9ub8ExzZKwu7Zl
Bamboo Robe	4UTG548uQKQZGf 1n#%j6LEqj5ZBf
Bamboo Wall	5jiSk583al5H2%ZWfacRW37KT4Tw
Barbecue	aPYhDyYoeR685b afZBlkwcRCmqi3
Baseball	1n5%N%8JUjE5fj lEcGr4%ync5eUp
Basic Painting	ebucddbkLRgnLgBiMBdbichCmqi3
BB Shirt	s@T@3vbA4RJQfbHhBEttkoHqqld7
Beatnik Shirt	s@T@3vbA4RJQfbthBEttkoHqqld7
Berry Gingham	guibfAHyEeqmWPZkhTnDUgUjJ&jb
Big Bro's Shirt	aMiBAraLaM1mWb6waTgDLx0jJZBf
Big Dot Shirt	SyioyyairofsaYSeqnypuirofsyG
Big Star Shirt	4UFG548uQWQZGflnu%jtLEqj5ZBf
Bird Feeder	ArTriaAnoSarah Spurlingtre5&2

Animal Crossing (cont'd)

Black Bishop	aDSLDyYoeR685bafRBlkwcRCmqi3
Black King	lLhuwvEDA23fmAdsgnvzbClBAsyU
Black Knight	SupermakiobroSAelmAlCrOssiNG
Black Queen	1LhuwvEDA22fmAdagnvzbCvBAsyU
Black Rook	aDShHyYoeR685bafyBlkwcRCmqi3
Block Flooring	666abcdn66efgH DyGabcd6B6efgH
Blossom Shirt	vuTbfAHyC3qmWmZkhTnDUgbjJ&jb
Blossoming Shirt	4UTG548pQKQZGfln#%jjLEqj5ZBf
Blue Check Shirt	vuHcfAH%FTqmW#ZkyTnDUgCjJ&jb
Blue Flooring	S2ui@kTheuooH8 RGTU6@F7ld5GX3
Blue Grid Shirt	4UFG548QQWQZGFan#%jLL5qj5ZBf
Blue Nintendo Bench	cU3jlm@hdl6Aip zJFAEajAcbZXim
Blue Puffy Vest (worn only by male animals during the fishing tourneys)	2uiDfAH%AfqmWi ZkyTnDUgQjJ&j%
Blue Scale Shirt	vuTcfAHyCHqmWjZkyTnDUgcjJ&jb
Blue Stripe Knit	4UTG548uQKQZGf1n#%jALEqj5ZBf
Blue Tie-Dye	VupDfAH%ATqmW#ZkyTnDUgUjJ&jb
Blue Trim Wall	Pi&aCKUGKV#2%UJxuMKYfxg5jA@M
Blue Wall	5jiKk583aL5H2%ZWfabRW37KT4Tb
Bold Check Shirt	aMiBAsaQls1mWgZcGTgDLxsjJZBf
Botanical Shirt	4UTG548uQ5QZGf1n#%eTLEqj5ZBf
Boxing Ring Mat	66zabccn66efgH ayGcbcd6BagfgH
Bubble Shirt	s@T@3vbA4RJQfbehBEttkoH8qld7
Bug Zapper	cPYhDyYoeR685b afZBlkwcRCmqiR
Butterfly Shirt	vuHcfAH%FTqmW#ZkyTnDUgqjJ&jb
Cabana Bed	B6&6KQom9DzR35DfkDC4%EEpCmiR
Cabana Bookcase	lar45678912345E2345678912345
Cabana Chair	2%QafhMKhAyAY3Z5yYAK9zNHxLo7
Cabana Dresser	PlaystationonE PyaystationonE
Cabana Lamp	ZzicrRB%wwcRMs GX1Qb&Zv0Z7c8x
Cabana Screen	2%Q3fhMdRByAY3Z5yYAK9zyHxLo7
Cabana Table	I7345678912345 E234567891234E
Cabana Vanity	FjEiKulzEiKukY DkEiKulzEiKuky
Cabana Wall	qAx5nQGuSULJFNZ9SJWO%mvjfd@
Cabin Armchair	MupersmashbgoSSFlersmashbroS
Cabin Bed	MupersmashbroSSupersmashbroS
Cabin Bookcase	S2ui@kTheukFH8 RGTU6@F71d5GX3
Cabin Chair	D7r4567a912345Ea3456789e23i5
Cabin Clock	MupersmashbnoSSupersmashbroS
Cabin Couch	Blaine0002HelSABigFatAssNazi
Cabin Dresser	11AcKGI9JE#Jf@gHcebBLdG7Y%PE
Cabin low Table	MupersmaspbroSSupersmashbroS
Cabin Table	ZzicrRB%wwcRMsGX1QbaZv0Z7c8x
Cabin Wall	eVRaCHbuzzrS%UpxiEqYfYv5HH@s

PSP Xbox PS2 GC GBA

Animal Crossing (cont'd)

Cabin Wardrobe	IDkteTBeNewWayOCRogtingCodez
Caterpillar Tee	1qWyt6IfB@&q7z8XzSNtwfyq76ts
Caveman Tunic	DontthatseemaYDontthatSeemaY
Cement Mixer	1mWYR6IfB@&q7z 8XzSNwpfij76ts
Checkered Shirt	vCTbf%Fy5MYmWcZk&TnDUgljJ&jb
Checkered Tile	E7M6IE7M6sE7hY E7M6sE7M6sE7yG
Cherry Shirt	YoWqy6PfBu&q7z8EzSPtyfot76ts
Chevron Shirt	aMTdTraLVR1mWbOwaTgDLxqjJZBf
Chic Wall	BY4qneovrZkTW8Mvf8fCe3nSj4OU
Circus Shirt	VuHcfAHyFTqmW#ZkyTnDUgqjJ&jb
Citrus Carpet	666abcdn66ef7H DhGabcd6B6efgH
Citrus Gingham	HIIMazzthemmoYIlljazzthemmyG
Citrus Wall	qA#5nQGuSrXJFNZ9SfW0%mvjf#OU
Classic Bed	HullivershoneH DulliversohnSY
Classic Cabinet	BF&6KQom9DzR35 RfLDC4%EepcmiR Tell
Classic Chair	11ACK6I9JE#Jf@ gHCeoBLaa7Y%PE
Classic Clock	rc&c5qw9baamLS glijHSoLwZMD7&
Classic Desk	rxdfqdasdasdas masdasdasdasda
Classic Hutch	5ePiES@sTRQmAA sh&9cb#9Uh9w04
Classic Painting	j&JHasABigFatM exicanAss5eups
Classic Sofa	B6&6KQom9DzR35 RfyDC4%EEpCmiR
Classic Table	Toad&Mushsooms Hmad&Mushdooms
Classic Vanity	Za2&3&4&5&6&7& 1&2&3&4&5&6&7&
Classic Wall	OainktothepasT qninktothepasT
Classic Wardrobe	KtsuKuKeGiKunY ItsuReSeZeNiyG
Classroom Floor	xxxAxxxxVZn0W3 ywR%jticqjLZBf
Closed Road	Ndntendoistheb estgamecompany
Clu Clu Land	Crm%h4BNRyu98d 9uu8exzZKwu7Zl
Clu Clu Land 2	Y#PpfrxSOAMLSG B7H3K5xBho5YSY
Club Shirt	vuTbfAHyC3qmWcZkhTnDUgbjJ&jb
Concierge Shirt	QethnfoqGreebYldtineorfreFCY
Concrete Wall	fADSO6jGqYLaulZJAecY@keb56@r
Coral Shirt	ThqPoliceDogIsCopperHeIsCool
Cosmos Model 1	cISIHBYokR685s &%LO&kwcRCmqi3
Cosmos Model 2	Ai9xES@sTRJsAA sh09cb#9UaKHA4
Cosmos Model 3	fi9xES@sTRJhAA sh09cb#9UaKHI4
Covered Wagon	ArariaAnfSarah SpurlOageUeo&2
Cow Print	HlljazzthemmoYIlljazzthemmyG
Cow Skull	ArariaAndrarah Swurl5ngtre5&2
Cozy Sweater	guibfAHyE3qmWcZkhTnDUg1jJ&jb
Crewel Shirt	guibfAHIE3qmWPZkrTnDUgljJ&jb
Crossing Shirt	RethnfoqGreebYldtineorWreebY
Dainty Painting	ekri%ma9iom5roFlriomariomaro

Animal Crossing (cont'd)

Daisy Meadow	2Ea4vQLITUq325 ajQpZfAv9wfYw#
Daisy Shirt	vCTbf%Fy5XYmWcZk&TnDUgojJ&jb
Danger Shirt	aMTdTraLVs1mWb6waTgDLxUjJZBf
Dapper Shirt	QethnfoqGreebYldtineorTreFCY
Dark Polka Shirt	guibfAH1E3qmW3ZkrTnDUgdjJ&jb
Dawn Shirt	4UFG548QQdQZGf1n#%jtLEqj5ZBf
Deep Blue Tee	2GiDfAiLrW1mWgZcyTgDLgejJ&jj
Deer Shirt	vuTbfAHyCFqmWmZkhTnDUgbjJ&jb
Desert Cactus	8i9xES@sTRJsAA sh09cb#9UaKH76
Desert Camo	guibfDHdENqmWcZkrTnDUgkjJ&jb
Desert Shirt	4UTG548QQtQZGfln#%jIL7qj5ZRf
Detour Arrow	cAQifhGeBsyjYc nqBYAKxjeFdjop
Detour Sign	hSatHavsVouJot ForMeTqdayNook
Diamond Shirt	guibfAHdExqmWcZkrTnDUgKjJ&jb
Dice Shirt	vCTbFPFQcvYmWCZk&TnDUgljJ&jb
Dice Stereo	1LhuwvEDA33fmAdbgnvzbCIBAsyU
Diner Uniform	4UTG548uQKQZGf1n#%jGLEqj5ZBf
Dinosaur Egg	XJh5rVHlvsVeWi U6ATVrjlec&BFP
Dinosaur Track	4NTG548uQKQZGf 1n#%j6LEqj5ZBf
Dirt Model	4HT6T948YZnOW3 dji%jtLEqj5ZBf
DK Jr. Math	bA5PC%8JUjE5fj ljcGr4%ync5EUp
Donkey Kong	2n5@N%8JUjE5fj ljcGr4%ync5EUp
Dump Model	LLhOwvrDA22fmt dagnvzbCIBAsyd
Eight-Ball Shirt	aMTdTraLV31mWbOwaTgDLxqjJZBf
Excitebike	3%Q4fhMTRByAY3 05yYAK9zNHxLd7
Exotic Bed	2%Q2fhVtRByAY3 O5yYAK9zNHxLo7
Exotic Bench	xxxxjxxxxxxxxx S6nY2JIF0GE@iz
Exotic Bureau	IDkteTheNewWay OfPostingCodez
Exotic Chair	AliGkAntimesoY AlinkintimesyG
Exotic Chest	MupersmfshbwoS SupersmashbroS
Exotic End Table	ZUicrRB%wwcRMs GX1QbaZvOZ7c8x
Exotic Lamp	AlinktothepasT ClinkgothepasT
Exotic Screen	AlinktothepasT ClinkrothepasT
Exotic Shirt	WzatswrongwitHWhatswrongwitH
Exotic Table	znIPfBa6iXoajl ibxCYoH0oW4qrs
Exotic Wall	IPv5fWiNTK3F8EDUpqKZyA&Yz9dU
Exotic Wardrobe	7vGRXAYsjrhk2q Sq7PSV#e7Va5z5
Exquisite Rug	EciCCy2YLaOuoA ILcZ&@eyHfTols
Exquisite Wall	635nljHT7tTBTCZWSabRWx7KT4Tb
Fall Plaid Shirt	HialhyponoticSRealhyponoticS
Fetching Outfit	vCTbF%F%5fYmWCZk&TnDUgljJ&jb
Fish Bone Shirt	aMicJsaQfs1mWgZcNTgDLgqjJZBf
Fish Knit	aMiBAsaQas1mWgZcGTgDLxqjJZBf

Animal Crossing (cont'd)

Five-Ball Shirt	1qWqr6wfBu&q7z8rzSNrwfyq76ts
Flagman Sign	AraríaAnQSarah Swurlqngtre5&2
Flicker Shirt	VupDfAH%ATqmW#ZkyTnDUgqjJ&jb
Floral Wall	BYPgneo&rGLWW8MvEo%CexnHYLOU
Flying Saucer	2%Q3EhMeRByAY3 n5yYAK9zcHxLo7
Folk Shirt	guibfAH1ExqmWPZkrTnDUgdjJ&jb
Fortune Shirt	VuHcfAH%FTqmWcZkyTnDUg0jJ&jb
Fresh Shirt	YoWqy6PfBu&q7z8EzSPqyfot76ts
Funky Dot Shirt	4UFG548QQWQZGFhn#%jLL5qj5ZBf
Garden Gnome	IP8cGEhbT0x@En RTkjA3P3nb#GNh
Gaudy Sweater	DennisMillerIsSokDamnAwtsqme
Gelato Shirt	4UFG548QQWQnGfln#%jtLEqj5ZBf
Giraffe Print	guiDfAH%AfqmWiZkyTnDUgQjJ&j%
Gold Screen Wall	VYDan9uv3EXJW8Mv@4%Ce3nHYLmU
Golden Axe	4B2&p%eGcgIO7NHZCS3hjkKJtlgH
Golden Net	kB2&S%excgIC7SPOudE2jkKJHygH
Golden Rod	Y%9FUKhrekPQ6a3M#4&f3bdAZLJf
Golden Shovel	GkUFUvirg%PX6a3ZizGfw5dTZLQh
Golf	Crm%h4BNRbu98d 9un8exzZKwo7Zl
Gracie's Top	4UTG548uQKQZGf1n#%jTLEqj5ZBf
Grape Shirt	1qWww6IfB@&q7z8XzSNtwfyq76ts
Grass Model	KtsuKiKiHeDeaY IswayinthereyG
Grass Shirt	guibfAHyEfqmWPZkhTnDUgUjJ&jb
Gray Tartan	4UFG548QQWQZGFan#%jtLEqj5ZBf
Green Bench	MupersmashbloSSgIersmashb5oS
Green Counter	S2ui@kTheuoHH4RGTU6@F71d5GX3
Green Desk	aD%3RxM3M#X3aoQPRxO8Q8xEITqv
Green Drum	2%Q2fhVeRByAY3 Z5yYAK9zNHxLo7
Green Drum	2%Q2fhVeRByAY3Z5yYAK9zNHxLo7
Green Pantry	MupersmashbwoSSupersmashbroS
Green Ring Shirt	VuTbfAHyC3qmWcZkhTnDUg1jJ&wb
Green Table	MupersmaspbsoSSFIersmashbroS
Green Wall	%A{S0tRscBXSulZJCcY@Aeb56Dr
Groovy Shirt	aMicJsaQes1mWgZcNTgDLgqjJZBj
Groovy Wall	lY&qgSovE@rJkEM&JwNOuAnzHBO@
Hammock	1mWYg6IfB@&q7z 8XzSNupfij76ts
Handcart	2%Q2fhMeRByAY3 Z5yYAK9zNHxLo7
Harvest Bed	AraríaAndrarah Swurlingtre5&2
Harvest Bureau	Di9xES@sTRJsYY sqO9cb#3UaKHP5
Harvest Chair	ifc74nVlY%zol4 I5X@qSEncEKb0V
Harvest Clock	R5ngoARS6l3iVL y&M6IJyNoWUBW4
Harvest Dresser	fi9GES@sTRJsAA sqO9cb#9UaKHI4
Harvest Lamp	1TWYT6IfB@&q7z 8UzSN1pfij76ts

Animal Crossing (cont'd)

Harvest Mirror	ZeldainhyruleS NlgendO3Zeldgb
Harvest Sofa	ArariaAndrarah Srurl5ngtre5&2
Harvest T.V.	vPSYDyYoeR685b afZBlkwcRCmqi3
Harvest Table	vPNH#CJc5yevsB DDQOhQdeKxHydS
Haz-mat barrel	ArariaAnUQarah SpurlingHSe5&2
Hi-Fi Stereo	1LhuwvEDA22emAdbgnvzbCvBAsyU
High-End Stereo	aDSLDyYoeR685bafaBlkwcRCmqi3
Hot Spring Shirt	s@T@3vbA4RJQfbthBEttkoHdqld7
Houndstooth Knit	gMTdTraLVR1mWb6waTgDLxqjJZBf
House Model	aRShDyYoeR685b afZBlkwcRCmqi3
Icy Shirt	guJbfDHdE2BmWcZklTnDUgkjJ&jb
Imperial Wall	6Pgpfh4NTN5p8EDUpZKZyA&YzZd@
Iron Frame	2%Q3EhMeRByAY3 05yYAK9zNHxLo7
Ivy Wall	rjaKk583jv#S2%ZW@2g&W37zjiY@
Jackhammer	ArariaAnfEarah SpurlOagereo&2
Jack-In-The-Box	2%Q2fhVehAyAY3Z5yYAK9zhHxLo7
Jack-o-Lantern	2%Q2fhMeRByAY3Z5yYAK9zcHxLo7
Jade Check Print	HlljazztHemmoYlaljaJzthemmyG
Jersey Barrier	ArariaAndSarah Sourl3ngApe5&2
Jester Shirt	4UFG548QQ5QZGf1n#%jtLEqj5ZBf
Jingle Bed	aPShHyYoeR685b afvBlkwcRCmqi3
Jingle Carpet	B66aPcdnE6ef7H DhGabcd6BAefgH
Jingle Chair	aDSLHyYoeR685b afBBklwcRCmqi3
Jingle Clock	JgpermariobqoS 2ysmAlCaOssiNG
Jingle Dresser	11AcKGI9JE#Jf@ gHceoBLdG7Y%PE
Jingle Lamp	aPShDyYoeR685b afTBlkwcRCmqi3
Jingle Piano	aDShHyYoeR685b afEBlkwcRCmqi3
Jingle Shirt	YoWeo6EfBu&q7z8lzSYiwfso76ts
Jingle Sofa	aPShDyYoeR685b afhBlkwcRCmqi3
Jingle Table	lLhuwvEDA33emA dbgnvzbCvBAsyU
Jingle Wardrobe	MeetloafmeatdY LxatloafmeatdY
JukeBox	a#S8UltokM6850h%LO&kwcRCmqi3
Katrinas Tent Model	BuN2up3up4upsG 1up2up3up4ups1
Kiddie Bed	SupermariobroS AnlmAlCaOssiNG
Kiddie Bookcase	aPSLHyYoeR685b afoBlkwcRCmqi3
Kiddie Bureau	MeeCAKafmeatdY LsatloafmeatdY
Kiddie Chair	9#S8UltokM6850 h%LOskwcRCmqi3
Kiddie Clock	IzEiKutsuKiRiY HeCeGtsuBeBiyG
Kiddie Couch	SVpermaoiobroS ABlmAlCaOssiNG
Kiddie Dresser	StOpPlAyInGThE WOOmwlCrossing
Kiddie Stereo	6LhuwvEDA23fmA dbgnvzbClBAsyU
Kiddie Table	QtiXglAGfe2Al7 WwBZBBWW&PulBc
Kiddie Wall	EAvpnQGuH5LJFNZ9vW70%mvhazD@

Animal Crossing (cont'd)

Kiddie Wardrobe	2d345csYd12g45 KqJ4r6k89ej3f5
Kitchen Tile	whqewavenhbkut whatravenhbkut
Kitchen Wall	eVRaCHbuzz5H%UpxiEqYfYv5HH@s
Kitschy Tile	cddhbcdgnzefgg bydabcdafcefgg
Kiwi Shirt	aMTdTraLVs1mWb6waTgDLxgjJZBf
Lavender Robe	2GiDfAiLrh1mWgZcyTgDLgYjJ&jj
Lawn Chair	Araria And Sarah SourlingAre5&2
Lawn Mower	fi9xES@sTRJhAA sh09cb#9UaKH84
Leather Jerkin	QetrnfoqGreebYldtineorHreFCY
Light Line Shirt	guibfAH1EuqmW3ZkrTnDUgdjJ&jb
Lighthouse Model	aRSLDyYoeR685b afoBlkwcRCmqi3
Locomotive Model	a&SLDyYoeR685b afRBlkwcRCmqi3
Loud Bloom Shirt	1qWWO6IfB@&q7z8XzSNqpfyo76ts
Loud Line Shirt	aMiBAraLaR1mWb6waTgDLxqjJZBf
Luigi Statue	EOktvXIJ7WdzRj uiT28vpqcbJ1g
Lunar Lander	2%Q2fhMehAyAY3 O5yYAK9zaHxLo7
Mammoth Skull	4UTG548uQKQZGf 1n#%jfLEqj5ZBf
Mammoth Torso	4UTG548uQKQZGf 1n#%jNdEqj5ZBf
Manhole Cover	A2345t7u9Ks34z 123456x8912345
Manor Model	aRShHyYoeR685b af&BlkwcRCmqi3
Mario Statue	1mWYg6IfB@&q75 8XzSKd6Tuj7Lts
Melon Gingham	YoWqA6PfBu&q7z8lzSPrwfot76ts
Melon Shirt	aMiBAsaQls1mWgZcGTgDLxqjJZBf
Merge Sign	cU3jlm@hdl6Aip zJFAEUjAwbZXim
Mint Gingham	EzatswrongwitHWhatswrongwitH
Misty Shirt	YoWRA6EfBu&q7z8lzSYqwfoq76ts
Mod Top	2uiDfAH%AsqmWiZkyTnDUgRjJ&j%
Modern Bed	MupersmaspbdoSSFlersmashbroS
Modern Cabinet	MupersmaspbhoSSulersmashbroS
Modern Chair	A234567891234512345678912345
Modern Desk	TGGu@@Zzfuq#0zz3Nn27IGVlmPGG
Modern Dresser	riPiES@LTRJmAAshO9cb#9Uh9wO4
Modern End Table	A7r45678912345K2345678912345
Modern Lamp	2CijfPfycftAWiZkLTnpUgQjJ&j%
Modern Screen	EByY6mPTISyAEEyeexae81jaVOOb
Modern Sofa	xxxxxxxxexxxxxS62Y2JIF0GE@iz
Modern Table	AlinktothepasT#linkgothepasT
Modern Wardrobe	IDktBTGeNewWayOCRogtingCodez
Moldy Shirt	guibfAHyEGqmWPZkhTnDUgUjJ&jb
Monkey Shirt	aMTdTraLV31mWbOwaTgDLxCjJZBf
Moody Blue Shirt	vuHcfAH%FgqmW#ZkyTnDUgCjJ&jb
Mosaic Shirt	VuHcfAH%FTqmW#ZkyTnDUgqjJ&jb
Mossy Carpet	wnqfFarJUjE5fz HzvGr4%yn35euz

Animal Crossing (cont'd)

Moving Painting	BDeeDmumArlseeGQeermsehrlsHe
Mr. Flamingo	ArTriaAndSarah Spurlingtpe5&2
Mrs. Flamingo	aPYhDjYoeR685b afZBlkwcRCmqi3
Museum Model	LLhOwvrDA22fmt dagnvzbCvBAsyU
Natty Shirt	s@T@3vbA4RJQfbHhBEttkoHdqld7
Nebula Shirt	SyiyypairofsaYSeinypairofsyG
Neo-Classic Knit	VupDfAH%AhqmW#ZkyTnDUgqjJ&jb
New Spring Shirt	rlljazzthemmoYblljazzthemmyG
No.1 Shirt	4UTG548QQtQZGfln#%j5LMqj5ZBf
No.4 Shirt	2GiDfAiLrV1mWgZcyTgDLgYjJ&jj
Noble Shirt	2GiDfAiLrs1mWiZcyTgDLg0jJ&j%
Noodle Shirt	vuHcfAH%FgqmW#ZkyTnDUggjJ&jb
Office Flooring	666abcdn66efgH Dy4abcd6B6efgH
Oft-Seen Print	vCTbf%Fy5XYmWcZk&TnDUg&jJ&jb
Oil Drum	ArTriaAnorarah Spurlingtre5&2
Orange Cone	I7345678912345 E234567891234P
Orange Tie-Dye	guibfDHdECqmWcZkrTnDUgkjJ&jb
Ornate Rug	666mbcd666efgH DyGabcd6B6efgH
Pansy Model 1	fi9GES@sTRJhAA sq09cb#9UaKHL4
Pansy Model 2	4UT6T6L89Zn0W3 dw&%jBAcETkayS
Pansy Model 3	4UT6T648GZ3ZW3 dwb%jtL3qjLZBf
Parquet Floor	Nintendoistheb estgamecompany
Patched Shirt	vCTbf%FykEYmWcZk&TnDUgljJ&jb
Patchwork Top	2GiDfAiLra1mWiZcyTgDLgqjJ&jY
Paw Shirt	VuHcfAHyFTqmWcZkyTnDUgUjJ&jb
Peachy Shirt	VupDfAH%AhqmW#ZkyTnDUgDjJ&jb
Perfect Painting	WkriomariomaroFlriomariomaro
Picnic Table	ArariaAndrarah S9urlCngwre5&2
Pine Bonsai	fupersmashbwoS SupersmashbroS
Pink Tartan	aMTdTraLVR1mWb6waTgDLxUjJZBf
Pink Tree Model	aRShHyYoeR685b afBBlkwcRCmqi3
Pitfall	NLqJ&@4EnHnltp SEn4tFOwAXndFb
Plesio Neck	4pTG548uQKQZGf 1n#%jFLEqj5ZBf
Plesio Skull	I5gTK#HYSv#i6w Qt@fWMjUhoMVgg
Plesio Torso	4UFG548QQWQZGF an#%j%L5qj5ZBf
Plush Carpet	ShiyypairofsaY ShinypairofsyG
Polar Fleece	YoWqQ6PfBu&q7z8EzSPywfot76ts
Police Model	IseemGaeHplsee IseemGaepplsee
Ponderosa Bonsai	MupersmaspbnoS SupersmashbroS
Pop-Bloom Shirt	FdlmAstringtdYFrCmCstringtyG
Post Model	4UH6TbA8VZaAW3 dwh%jtLeqj5ZBf
Ptera Left Wing	CashisislandeS YoshisislandeS
Ptera Right Wing	StationisrundY LrationisrundY

Animal Crossing (cont'd)

Pulse Shirt	FdlmAstringtdYFrCmastringtyG
Puzzling Shirt	2GiDfAiLrV1mWgZcyTgDLgqjJ&jj
Quaint Painting	BDeeWUsmhrlseeGBeerDsehrlsee
Racer 6 Shirt	2uiDfAH%AfqmWiZkyTnDUgqjJ&j%
Racer Shirt	guibfAHyEvqmWcZkhTnDUgCjJ&jb
Rally Shirt	4UTG548uQKQZGf1h#%jtLEqj5ZBf
Ranch Flooring	666abcd666efgH Dy6abcd6B6efgH
Rare Painting	VAriomariomaroFlriomariomaro
Red Bar Shirt	1qWWO6IfB@&q7z8XzSNqpfyw76ts
Red Boombox	aDShDyYoeR685bafBBlkwcRCmqi3
Red Check Shirt	aMicJsaQfs1mWgZcNTgDLgUjJZBj
Red Sweatsuit (Worn only by Female animals during the aerobics sessions)	HlljaLzthemmoY IlljazzthemmyG
Red Tie-Dye	4UTG548aQKQZGfln#%jiLEqj5ZBf
Red-Scale Shirt	FdlmastringtdYFrCmastringtyG
Reel-To-Reel	SupermakiobroSAolmAlCaOssiNG
Regal Carpet	xfdaoonfiuhter layuoonfighter
Retro Stereo	B6&6KQom9DzR35RfLDC4%EEpCmiR
Rickrack Shirt	2GiDfAiLrV1mWiZcyTgDLgqjJ&jY
Rocket	XdBiCiDiEiFipY AiBiCiDiEiFiyG
Rose Shirt	vCTbf%F%5AYmWcZk&TnDUgljJ&jb
Rose Wall	rkntenoisbette9ihanMicrosoft
Rugby Shirt	4UTG548uQtQZGfln#%jtLEqj5ZBf
Saddle Fence	AraríaAndSarah SpurlOngereo&2
Sahara's Desert	BovetotraveltY LovetotrabelyG
Satellite	linkzPld#B31on ganozPeldClink
Sawhorse	vP5hDyYoeR685b afZBlkwcRCmqiR
Scary Painting	micrDsafthapeslilsunnieshard
Seven-Ball Shirt	1qWie6IfB@&q7z8XzSNkwfyq76ts
Shanty Mat	sddhbcdgnzefgg bydabcdafcefgg
Sharp Outfit	vupcfAHyF3qmWjZkyTnDUgcjJ&jb
Sherbert Gingham	gCibfAaLEFqmWPZkrTnDUgdjJ&jb
Shirt Circuit	guibfAHyExqmWPZkhTnDUgUjJ&jb
Shop Model	alShDyYoeR685b PfbBlkwcRCmqi3
Silk Bloom Shirt	SyioyyqirousaYSeqnypuirufsyG
Six-Ball Shirt	4UFG548QQWQZGfSo#%jtLEqj5ZBf
Ski Sweater	ZheLegendOfZeldaWindWalker24
Skull Shirt	2GiDfAiLrV1mWiZcyTgDLgYjJ&jY
Snappy Print	2GiDfAiLrW1mWgZcyTgDLgYjJ&jj
Snow Shirt	guibfAHdExqmWcZkrTnDUgkjJ&jb
Snowman Clock	vCTbFPFQciYmWC Zk&TnDUgljJ&jb
Snowman Dresser	AkwardwarjraiN AkwardhSrdraiN
Snowman Fridge	4UFG548CQ2QZGf 1n#%jWLEqj5ZBf
Snowman Lamp	vCTbFPFQcxYmWC Zk&TnDUgljJ&jb

Animal Crossing (cont'd)

Snowman Sofa	4UTG548QQtQZGf In#%j1L7qj5ZRf
Snowman Table	4UTG548uQKQZGf 1n#%jNLEqj5ZBf
Snowman TV	4UTG548QQtQZGf In#%j2LNqj5ZBf
Snowman Wardrobe	4UTG548qQKQZGf 1n#%jNLEqj5ZBf
Snowy Tree Model	WhatHaveYouGot ForMeTqdayNook
Somber Robe	GetinforfreebY 1dtinforfreebY
Space Shuttle	2%Q2fhMKhAyAY3 Z5yYAK9zNHxLo7
Space Station	2%42fhMtRByAY3 Z5yYAK9zfHxLo7
Spaceman Sam	Zzic2RB%wwcRMs GX1QbaZv0Z7c8x
Spade Shirt	guibfAH1E3qmWPZkrTnDUgdjJ&jb
Speed Sign	vPYhDyYoeR685b afZBlkwcRCmqiR
Speedway Shirt	2uiDfAH%AhqmWiZkyTnDUgqjJ&j%
Spooky Bookcase	GsHinkistinkiS LstinkistinkiS
Spooky Chair	linkz2ldaBanon ganonSeldClink
Spooky Clock	2%Q2fhMKRByAY305yYAK9zNHxLo7
Spooky Dresser	piPiES@sTRJmAAsh09cb#9Uh9w04
Spooky Lamp	Dar4567a912345Ea3456789e23i5
Spooky Paper	SuPermariogolf supermariog0lf
Spooky Sofa	2%Q2fhVehAyAY3o5yYAK9zJHxLo7
Spooky Table	2%Q3EhMeRByAY3Z5yYAK9zcHxLo7
Spooky Vanity	2%Q2fhMdRByAY3O5yYAK9zNHxLo7
Spooky Wardrobe	jePiES@LTRJmAApcddkwe9Uh9w04
Spring Shirt	4UFG548QQWQZGf1n#%jtLEqj5ZBf
Sprinkler	Ai9xES@sTyJsYY sh09cb#9UaKHL4
Star Shirt	guibfAHyE3qmWcZkhTnDUgCjJ&jb
Static Shirt	VuHcfAH%FTqmW#ZkyTnDUgUjJ&jb
Station Model 1	1LhOwvrDA23fmt dsgnvzbClBAsyd
Station Model 2	a&SLHyYoeR685b afqBlkwcRCmqi3
Station Model 3	NI9xES@R8G685r HbG8#8NESgEPlo
Station Model 4	ABoyqndHtsBlob ABoesndHisBlub
Station Model 5	yUF6T6X8iZn0WU dwk%j8x@qjLZBf
Station Model 6	a&SLDyYoeR685b afoBlkwcRCmqi3
Station Model 7	E7M6t5x4A3d2fi E7M6s5x4A3d2fl
Station Model 8	ABoyqndHysBlob ABoesndHisBlob
Station Model 9	QtiXglAGfe2Al7 WwBZBBWW&PulBC
Station Model 11	ILhOwvrDA23fmt dsgnvzbClBAsyd
Station Model 12	SupermariobroS oilmg1Cr0ssiNG Tell
Station Model 13	aRSLHyYoeR685b afoBlkwcRCmqi3 Tell
Station Model 14	aRSLDyYoeR685b afRBlkwcRCmqi3
Station Model 15	ABoyqndHisBlob ABoeAnuHisBlub
Steam Roller	Araria AnQSarah Spurliagtre5&2
Stego Skull	huTcfAHyCsqmWj ZkyTnDUgCjJ%jb
Stego Torso	4UTG548uQKQZGf 1n#%j1LEqj5ZBf

Animal Crossing (cont'd)

Stone Tile	xxxxxxxxVZn0W3 ywR%jticqjLZBf
Storefront	ArariaAwQSarah Ssurlingtre5&2
Stormy Shirt	aMiBAsaQas1mWbZwGTgDLxqjJZBf
Strange Painting	NmxIGWIeSLYAACu6iMwbzCGvFsnQ
Strawberry Shirt	HIlMazztHemmoYIlljazzthemmyG
Striking Outfit	s@T@3vbA4RJQfbHhBEttkoH8qld7
Subdued Print	s@T@3vbA4RJQfbHhBEttkoH&qld7
Summer Robe	1qWWO6IfB@&q7z 8XzSNrpfyo76ts
Sunset Top	FdImastringtdYHromastringtyG
Swell Shirt	guibfAHyE3qmWPZkhTnDUgUjJ&jb
Tailor Model	a&SLHyYoeR685b afQBlkwcRCmqi3
Tape Deck	aPSLDyYoeR685bafZBlkwcRCmqi3
Tatami Floor	666abcdn66efgH Dyxabcd6B6efgH
Tent Model	Ai9xES@sTRJsYY sh09cb#9Vak#I4
Three-Ball Shirt	2uiDfAH%AsqmWiZkyTnDUgqjJ&j%
Thunder Shirt	aMTdTraLVR1mWb6waTgDLxqjJZBf
Tiger Print	1qWWO6IfB@&q7z8XzSNrpfyw76ts
Tiki Shirt	vCTbf%Fy5AYmWcZk&TnDUgljJ&jb
Tiki Torch	ArariaAndSarah Shurliagtre5&2
Tin Shirt	guibfAHyE3qmWPZkhTnDUgljJ&jb
Toad Print	2GiDfAiLrs1mWiZcyTgDLgqjJ&j%
Track Model	a&SLeyYoeR685b afRBlkwcRCmqi3
Traffic Cone	T234567u912345 f2345678912345
Tree Model	RsEenejcktlsee Dseenejcktlsee
T-Rex Skull	QtiXglAGfe2AI7 WwBZBBWW#PulBc
T-Rex Tail	1LhuwvEDA22fmA dbgnvzbCvBAsyU
T-Rex Torso	vuTcfAHyCSqmWj ZkyTnDUgbjJ&jb
Tricera Skull	aDSLHyYoeR685b afBBlkwcRCmqi3
Tricera Tail	eWoG4aYGDeYiOe SiDXcOAcZuAjsZ
Tricera Torso	Oadtimersoldtl Oldtimersoldtl
Trilobite	vuTcfAHyCSqmWm ZkhTnDUgbjJ&jb
Tulip Model 1	Di9GES@sTRJhYY sq09cb#3UaKHP5
Tulip Model 2	Di9xES@sTRJhYY sc09cb#9UaKHL4
Tulip Model 3	fi9xES@sTRJsYY sc09cb#9Vak#I4
Tumbleweed	1mWYR6IfB@&q7z 8XzSNapfij76ts
Turntable	Crm%h4BNRyu98d9Uu8exzZKwu7Zl
Twinkle Shirt	vCTbJRFlXQYmWcZk&TmDUgljJ&jb
Two-Ball Shirt	vCTbf%FyfDYmWcZk&TnDUgljJ&jb
Waffle Shirt	aMiBAraLaR1mWb6waTgDLx0jJZBf
Wagon Wheel	1i9xES@sTRJsYY sh09cb39UaKHL4
Wario's Woods	bA5PC%8JUjE5fj 1EcGr4%ync5eup
Watering Trough	vPdhDyYoei685b afZBlkwcRCmqi3
Watermelon Shirt	guibfAH1EFqmWPZkrTnDUgdjJ&jb

Animal Crossing (cont'd)

Wave Print	1qWww6IfB@&q7z8XzSNqwfyq76ts
Wavy Pink Shirt	VuHcfAHyFgqmW#ZkyTnDUgqjJ&jb
Weed Model	yUF6T6L8iZn0WU ywU%jtx@qjLZBf
Well	vi9GES@sTRJhAA sh09cb@9UaKHL4
Well Model	a&ShHyYoeR685b afABlkwcRCmqi3
Western Fence	AraraiaAndSarah SourlingApe5&2
Wet Roadway Sign	ThIckitsbecadY ThinkitsbecayG
Whirly Shirt	aMicJsaQfs1mWgZcNTgDLgqjJZBj
White Bishop	SupermariobqoS4nImAlCa0ssiNG
White Boombox	HRcE#IbRoJEV8od@rB6leTnU%a3E
White King	aPShDyYoeR685bafbBlkwcRCmqi3
White Knight	BiPiES@sTRJmAAsh09cb#9Uh9H04
White Pawn	RtiXgIAGfe2AI7WwBZBBWW#Pulyc
White Queen	aPShDyYoeR685baf%BlkwcRCmqi3
White Ring Shirt	4UFG548QQdQZGfIn#%jtLEGj5ZBf
White Rook	aPSLHyYoeR685bafxBlkwcRCmqi3
Windsock Shirt	HIlMazztHemmoYBlljazzthemmyG
Winter Sweater	guibfDHdMWqmWcZkrTnDUgkjJ&jb
Work Uniform	xethtforfreebYIdtitforfreebY
Worthy Painting	7kriMma9iom5roFIriomariomaro
Yellow Bar Shirt	aMTdTraLVR1mWb0waTgDLxojJZBf
Yellow Bolero	VuHcfAH%FTqmW#ZkyTnDUg0jJ&jb
Yellow Pinstripe	EcatswrongwitHWhatswrongwitH
Zebra Print	vuTbfAHyC3qmWcZkhTnDUg1jJ&jb

Army Men RTS

While playing, hold ↓, then enter the code.

Unlockable	Code
All units do extra damage and take less damage	Ⓑ,Ⓑ,Ⓐ,Ⓨ,Ⓐ,Ⓑ
Call in the Para Troopers (only one time for each level)	Ⓧ,Ⓑ,Ⓑ,Ⓑ,Ⓨ,Ⓨ
Extra 5000 Plastic	Ⓨ,Ⓧ,Ⓑ,Ⓐ,Ⓨ,Ⓑ
Extra Electricity	Ⓨ,Ⓑ,Ⓧ,Ⓐ,Ⓨ,Ⓐ

PSP Xbox PS2 GC GBA

ATV Quad Power Racing 2

Enter these passwords as Profile names.

Unlockable	Name
All Challenges	DOUBLEBARREL
All Championships	REDROOSTER
All Riders	BUBBA
All Tracks	ROADKILL
All Vehicles	GENERALLEE
Maxed Skill level	FIDDLERSELBOW
Maxed Stats	GINGHAM

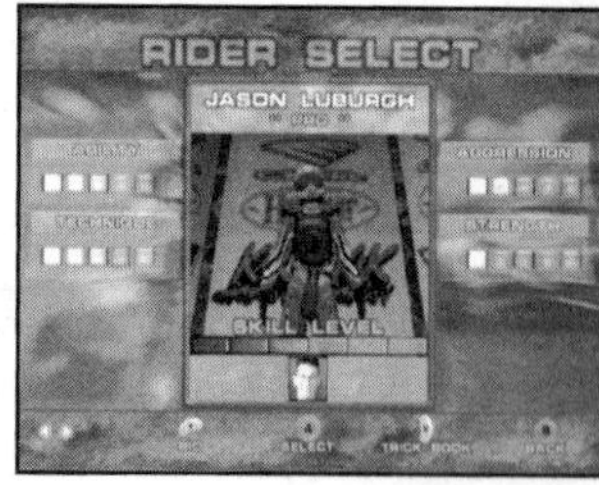

Backyard Baseball

Unlockable	Code
Aquadome	Hit a homerun into the water at Gator Flats, Frazier Field, and Steele Stadium.

Bad Boys Miami Takedown

Enter this code at the Title Screen.

Unlockable	Code
Open the Cheat Menu	Ⓧ,↑,Ⓑ,Ⓨ,→,↓

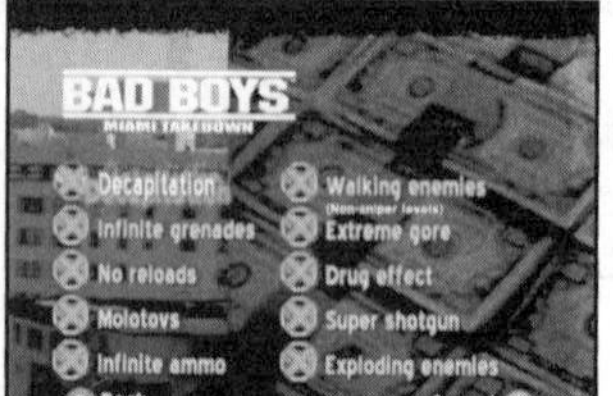

Batman: Rise of Sin Tzu

Codes must be entered on the Story Mode or Challenge Mode screen, and while holding Ⓛ+Ⓡ.

Unlockable	Code
All Upgrades	↓,↑,↓,←,↓,→,↑,↓
All Bonuses	←,↓,←,→,←,←,↓,→
God Mode	↑,→,↑,←,↓,←,↓,→
Unlimited Combo	←,→,↓,↑,↑,↓,→,←

Batman Vengeance

Enter the following codes at the Main Menu. A sound will confirm correct code entry.

Unlockable	Code
99 of All Items	L,R,Y,Y
All Power Moves and 120 Achievement Points	L,L,R,R,L,R,L,R
Bruce in Warehouse-Level Disguise	L,R,R,L,R,R,L,R,L,R,R,L
Invincibility	L,R,X,L,R,Y,L
Master Code	L,R,L,R,Y,Y
Unlimited Batarangs	L,R,Y,B,L
Unlimited Batlauncher	Y,X,Y,L,R,L,R
Unlimited Electric Batarangs	L,R,Y,X
Unlimited Handcuffs	X,Y,X,Y,L,R,R,L,L

Big Mutha Truckers

Unlockable	Code
Automatic Navigation	USETHEFORCE
Gain Diplomatic Immunity	VICTORS
Get a Fast Truck	GINGERBEE
Get an Evil Truck	VARLEY
Get Lots of Cash	LOTSAMONEY
Get Small Pedestrians	DAISHI
Infinite Time	PUBLICTRANSPORT
Level Select	LAZYPLAYER
Toggle the Damage	6WL
Unlocks Everything	CHEATINGMUTHATRUCKER

Black and Bruised

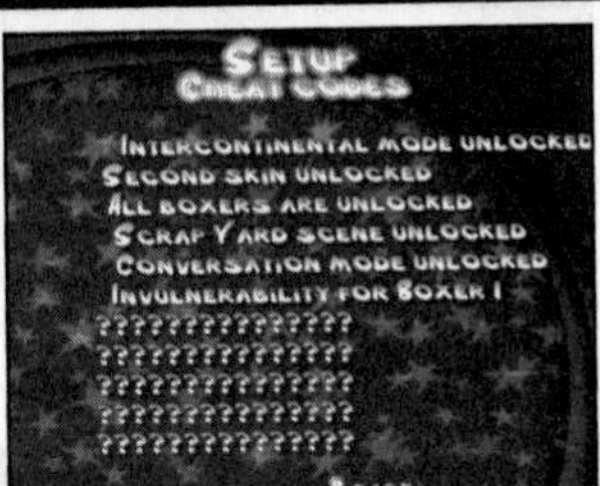

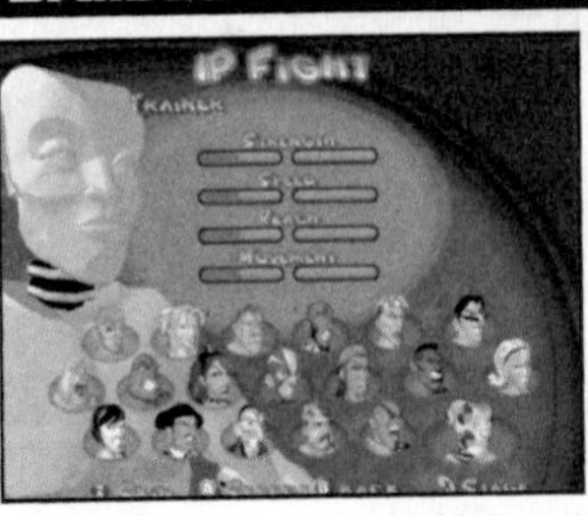

Go into the Setup menu and select the Codes menu. Press START, enter the code, then press START again.

Unlockable	Code
All Boxers	A,Y,X,X,Z,Z,X,Y,A
All Boxer's Life	A,X,Y,Z,A,X,Y,Z
Constant Power-Up	A,Y,A,Y,A,Y,X,X,X
Conversation Mode	Z,A,Y,X,Z,Z,Z
Double Speed	Z(x10)

Black and Bruised (cont'd)

Intercontinental Mode	Ⓐ,Ⓐ,Ⓐ,Ⓨ,Ⓨ,Ⓨ,Ⓧ,Ⓧ,Ⓧ
Invulnerability	Ⓐ,Ⓐ,Ⓨ,Ⓨ,Ⓩ,Ⓩ,Ⓧ,Ⓧ
Second Skin	Ⓐ,Ⓩ,Ⓨ,Ⓧ
Scrap Yard	Ⓨ,Ⓩ,Ⓐ,Ⓐ

NOTE

If you've got another player that wants to use the Invulnerability code, enter the sequence for them with the second controller.

Blood Omen 2

Enter the following code at the Main menu.

Unlockable	Code
Start with Soul Reaver and Iron Armor	Ⓩ,Ⓡ,Ⓛ,Ⓑ,Ⓧ,Ⓨ

BloodRayne

Enter these codes in the Cheat menu.

Unlockable	Code
Fill Bloodlust	Angry XXX INSANE HOOKER
Freeze Enemies	DONT FART ON OSCAR
God Mode	TRI ASSASSIN DONT DIE
Gratuitous Dismemberment	INSANE GIB MODE GOOD
Juggy Mode	JUGGY DANCE SQUAD
Restore Health	LAME YANKEE DONT FEED
Show Weapons	SHOW ME MY WEAPONS
Time Factor	NAKED NASTY DISHWASHER DANCE

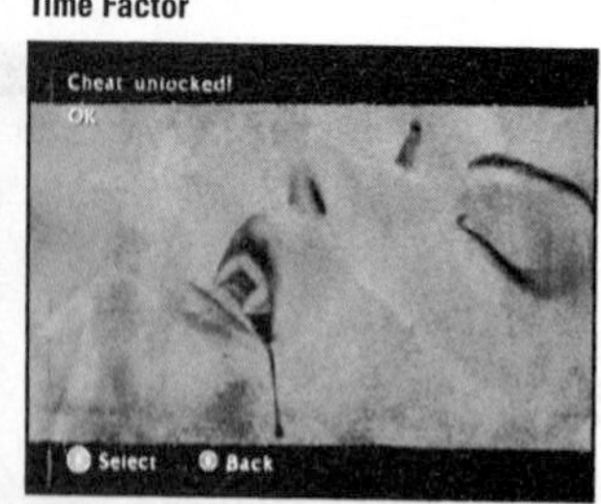

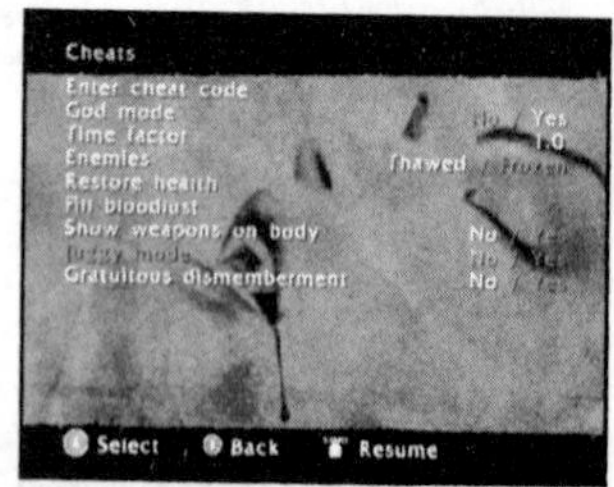

Bloody Roar

Unlockable	Code
Alternate Costumes	Press Ⓒ at the character selection screen.
Beast Mode	Complete the game 15 times.
Big Kid Mode	Complete the game 4 times.
Break Walls Only in Final Round	Complete the game 8 times.
Chaos Lab Stage	Defeat Uranus in Survival.
Com Battle Option	Complete the game 2 times.
Evil Laboratory Stage	Complete the game 2 times.
Expert Mode	Complete the game 12 times.

Bloody Roar (cont'd)

Fight against Uranus	Complete the game 3 times. She resembles a type of Minotaur. See note below for an alternate code.
Fight as Cronos the Phoenix	Complete the game 2 times .
Fight as Ganesha the Elephant	Complete the game once.
Fight as Kohryu	Play the game in Arcade mode. Win four consecutive rounds. You'll fight Kohryu in the next round. Defeat him, then complete Arcade mode to unlock Kohryu the Iron Mole as a selectable character.
Fight as Uranus	Defeat Uranus in Stage 16 of Survival mode. See note below for a gameplay tip.
Human Mode	Complete the game 14 times to unlock the "Human Mode" option.
Hyper Mode	Complete the game 16 times to unlock the "Hyper Mode" option. This also unlocks Kohryu the Iron Mole. Kohryu has no ending.
Indian Palace Stage	Complete the game one time to unlock Ganesha the Elephant's Indian Palace stage.
Kid Mode	Complete the game three times to unlock the "Kid Mode" option.
Knock Down Battle Mode	Complete the game 13 times to unlock the "Knock Down Battle Mode" option.
Movie Player Option	Complete the game one time to unlock the "Movie Player" option.
No Blocking Mode	Complete the game 11 times to unlock the "No Blocking Mode" option.
No Walls Mode	Complete the game six times to unlock the "Eliminate All Walls" option.
Slow Motion Mode	Complete the game nine times to unlock the "Low Speed" option.
Super Buff Mode	Complete the game five times to unlock the "Super Buff" option.
Turbo Mode	Complete the game 10 times to unlock the "High Speed" option.
Weak Walls Mode	Complete the game seven times to unlock the "Weaken All Walls" option.

NOTE

For an alternate way to unlock Uranus, complete Time Attack mode in under 20 minutes. Next, choose Versus mode, highlight the "Next Character" box, press Ⓐ multiple times, then press Ⓑ.

NOTE

To make the code easier, play as Kohryu and enable the "Beast mode," "No walls," and "No blocking" cheats. When the "Ready?" message appears, push them to the corner of the stage and step back. When the "Fight!" message appears, do Kohryu's Projectile move [Ⓒ,↘,→,Beast]. They'll fly off for a ring out. This cheat also unlocks her stage.

BMX XXX

Enter the following codes at the Cheat menu.

Unlockable	Code
All Bikes	Enter 65 SWEET RIDES
Amish Boy's Bikes	Enter AMISHBOY1699
Dam 2 FMV Sequence	Enter THONG
Fire Bullets	Enter BRONXCHEER. Begin a level, stop your rider, and then move the right analog stick to enter First-Person mode. Press Ⓧ to shoot people and cars.

PSP Xbox PS2 GC GBA

BMX XXX (cont'd)

Ghost Control Mode	Enter GHOSTCONTROL. This mode allows you to steer ghost-ridden bikes.
Green Skin Mode	Enter MAKEMEANGRY. Now you can choose a green skin tone in the custom rider creator.
Happy Bunny Mode	Enter FLUFFYBUNNY. This mode allows you to get more air.
Hellkitty's Bikes	Enter HELLKITTY487.
Itchi's Bikes	Enter ITCHI594.
Joyride's Bikes	Enter JOYRIDE18.
Karma's Bikes	Enter KARMA311.
La'tey's Bikes	Enter LATEY411.
Las Vegas Level	Enter SHOWMETHEMONEY.
Launch Pad 69 Level	Enter SHOWMETHEMONKEY.
Level Select	Enter XXX RATED CHEAT.
Manuel's Bikes	Enter MANUEL415.
Mika's Bikes	Enter MIKA362436.
More Speed	Enter Z AXIS.
Night Vision Mode	Enter 3RD SOG. Objects appear greenish.
Nutter's Bikes	Enter NUTTER290.
Play as Amish Boy	Enter ELECTRICITYBAD or I LOVE WOOD.
Rampage Skatepark Level	Enter IOWARULES.
Rave's Bikes	Enter RAVE10.
Roots Level	Enter UNDERGROUND.
Sheep Hills Level	Enter BAABAA.
Skeeter's Bikes	Enter SKEETER666.
Stage Select	Enter MASS HYSTERIA.
Super Crash Mode	Enter HEAVYPETTING. This mode makes your character extra bouncy when you crash.
Syracuse Level	Enter BOYBANDSSUCK.
The Dam Level	Enter THATDAMLEVEL.
Tripledub's Bikes	Enter TRIPLEDUB922.
Twan's Bikes	Enter TWAN18.
Visible Gap Mode	Enter PARABOLIC. This mode allows you to see all gaps.

Bomberman Generation

Unlockable	Code
Change View in Battle Mode	This trick works for any Battle Game mode. Immediately before the battle game starts, when "Ready" appears, use the C-stick to change the angle of the field. You can't do this after the game starts.
Group A/B Options	Complete the game once in Normal mode to unlock the "Group A/B" option at the stage selection screen in Battle mode. Press ↑ or ↓ to toggle between Group A and Group B. Group A gives you access to the basic power-ups during standard Battle mode match.
Mini-Game Option	Complete Level 5-3 to unlock the Mini-Game option at the Main Menu.
Play as Golden Bomber in Battle Mode	Win any match in Battle mode, then replay the same match without changing any other options (except for the stage, if desired). You'll play as Golden Bomber during the replay.
Play as MAX in Battle Mode	Obtain all Lightning Cards in Normal mode. Then, in Battle mode, press Z at the player selection screen to switch Bomberman to MAX.

Buffy the Vampire Slayer: Chaos Bleeds

Unlockable	Objective
Abominator	Finish Mission 10 with Professional rating.
Amber Benson Interview	Complete Mission 2.
Amber Benson Voice Over Session	Complete Mission 8.
Anthony Stewart Interview	Complete Mission 1.
Anthony Stewart Voice Over Session	Complete Mission 7.
Bat Beast	Finish Mission 4 with Professional rating.
Cemetery	Finish Mission 2 with Slayer rating.
Chainz	Finish Mission 10 with Slayer rating.
Chaos Bleeds Comic Book	Complete Mission 5.
Chris	Finish Mission 12 with Slayer rating.
Faith	Finish Mission 8 with Professional rating.
Female Vampire	Finish Mission 1 with Slayer rating.
Initiative	Finish Mission 8 with Slayer rating.
James Marsters Voice Over Session	Complete Mission 6.
Joss Whedon	Finish Mission 12 with Professional rating.
Joss Whedon Voice Over Session	Complete Mission 11.
Kakistos	Finish Mission 9 with Slayer rating.
Male Vampire	Finish Mission 1 with Professional rating.
Materani	Finish Mission 5 with Professional rating.
Nicholas Brendan Interview	Complete Mission 3.
Nicholas Brendon Voice Over Session	Complete Mission 9.
Out-Takes	Complete Mission 12.
Psycho Patient	Finish Mission 6 with Professional rating.
Quarry	Finish Mission 11 with Slayer rating.
Robin Sachs Interview	Complete Mission 4.
Robin Sachs Voice Over Session	Complete Mission 10.
S&M Mistress	Finish Mission 7 with Slayer rating.
S&M Slave	Finish Mission 7 with Professional rating.
Sid the Dummy	Finish Mission 6 with Slayer rating.
Tara	Finish Mission 3 with Slayer rating.
Zombie Demon	Finish Mission 3 with Professional rating.
Zombie Devil	Finish Mission 4 with Slayer rating.
Zombie Gorilla	Finish Mission 11 with Professional rating.
Zombie Skeleton	Finish Mission 2 with Professional rating.
Zombie Soldier	Finish Mission 9 with Professional rating.

Burnout

Unlockable	Objective
Bus	Defeat the bus in Face Off 4.
Ending Bonuses	Complete the game to unlock the Free Run mode (no vehicles on the road), Free Run Twin mode (two-player Free Run), and Credits options.
Face Off Option	Complete Championship mode once to unlock Face Off 1 against the Roadster.
Roadster	Defeat the Roadster in Face Off 1 to unlock it and Face Off 2 against another car.
Saloon GT	Defeat the Saloon GT in Face Off 3.
Towtruck	Play in Championship mode until you unlock Face Off 2 in the Special Options screen. Defeat the Towtruck once to unlock it.

Burnout 2

Unlockable	Objective
Cheat Mode Menu	Unlock any cheat and the Cheat Mode menu option will appear at the options screen.
Classic 1970 Car	Destroy the car with a police car in Pursuit 2.
Custom Compact	Beat Custom Series Qualifier.
Unlock Custom Coupe	Get all gold medals at Split Second Grand Prix.
Custom Muscle Car	Beat Pursuit 6.
Custom Pickup Truck	Beat Pursuit 5.
Custom Roadster	Get all gold medals at the Point of Impact Grand Prix.
Custom Series Championship	Earn gold medals in every race and complete Championship Mode.
Custom Sports Car	Get all gold medals at the Speed Streak Grand Prix.
Custom SUV	Beat Pursuit 4.
Drivers' Ed Car	Get all gold medals in Driving 101.
Freerun	Finish Custom Series Championship.
Gangster Car	Beat Pursuit 3.
Hot Rod Car	Beat Face Off 1.
Invulnerability Option	Finish the Grand Prix Championships with gold medals.
Japanese Muscle Car	Beat Face Off 2.
Oval Racer	Beat the car in Face Off 2.
Police Car	Beat Pursuit 1 and destroy the villain's car.
Runaway Mode	Finish Crash mode with Gold Medals in all the challenges.
Super Car	Beat Face Off 4.

Catwoman

Enter the Vault menu to enter this code.

Unlockable	Code
Extra gallery items	1940

Cel Damage

Unlockable	Objective
Additional FMV Sequences	Complete Smack Attack, Gate Relay, and Flag Relay with each character to unlock additional FMV sequences.
Big Head Mode	Hold L+R+↑ during gameplay.
Gate Rally Mode	Win once in Smack Attack mode.

To access the following unlockables, enter the character selection screen, select "Load," then enter the code as a name.

Unlockable	Code
All FMV Sequences	MULTIPLEX!
Brian the Brain and Space World	BRAINSALAD

Cel Damage (cont'd)

Cheat Mode 1	FATHEAD—unlocks all cars, tracks, and modes.
Cheat Mode 2	PITA or SUSIE!—unlocks various combinations of features.
Count Earl and Transylvania World	EARLSPLACE
Hazard Weapons	HAZARDOUS
Invincibility	CODY
Melee Weapons	MELEEDEATH
Movement Power-Ups	MOVEITNOW
Pen and Ink Graphics	PENCILS
Personal Weapons	UNIQUEWPNS
Plastic Graphics	FANPLASTIC—see note below for continued tip.
Ranged Weapons	GUNSMOKE!
T. Wrecks and Jungle World	TWRECKSPAD
Whack Angus and Desert World	WHACKLAND

NOTE

For the Plastic Graphics unlockable, after you enter code, enter the event selection screen and highlight "Smack Attack." Press ↓ and select the Event Settings button. Then, select the Options button and select the Rendering Modes button. Change this option to "Render Plastic." The message "Current mode plastic" will appear. Return to the event selection screen, then select a level and begin gameplay. To return to normal, repeat the steps and choose the cartoon renderer at the "Rendering Modes" screen.

Conflict Desert Storm

Unlockable	Code
Cheat Menu	From the main menu, enter ←,←,→,→,↑,↑,↓,↓,Ⓧ,Ⓧ,Ⓨ,Ⓨ.

Crazy Taxi

Unlockable	Code
Alternate Display	Begin gameplay in Arcade or Original mode. Hold L+R and press Ⓨ on controller three to display a speedometer. Press other buttons on controller three to change to first-person perspective, change to camera view, or return to normal view.
Another Day Mode	Press R at the character selection screen, then release it. Then, hold R and press Ⓐ. The message "Another Day" appears in the lower left corner to confirm correct code entry. This mode modifies various positions in the game.
Disable Arrow Indicators	Hold R+START after choosing your time limit and before the character selection screen appears. The message "No Arrows" appears in the lower left corner to confirm correct code entry.
Disable Destination Indicator	Hold L+START after choosing your time limit and before the character selection screen appears. The message "No Destination Markers" appears in the lower left corner to confirm correct code entry.
Expert Mode	Hold L+R+START at the main menu. Continue to hold the buttons until the character selection screen appears, then press Ⓐ to select the game mode and variation. The phrase "Expert Mode" appears in the lower left corner to confirm correct code entry. No destination or arrow indicators appear in this mode.

Crazy Taxi (cont'd)

Secret Push Bike — Hold [L]+[R] at the character selection screen. Release [L], then release [R]. Hold [L]+[R] again, then release them simultaneously. Then, press (A). A ringing sound confirms correct code entry, and your character will mount the bicycle. To unlock the Push Bike in Another Day mode, select original mode. Then press [R]+[L],[R]+[L],[R]+[L],[R],[R]+(A) at the character selection screen.

Dakar 2

Unlockable	Code
All Cars	SWEETAS
All Courses	BONZER

Dave Mirra Pro BMX 2

Enter the following codes at the Main menu.

Unlockable	Code
All Bikes	↑,←,↓,→,↓,↓,→,↓,↓,←,(B)
All FMV	↑,←,↓,→,←,←,→,←,↑,↓,(B)
All Objects for Park Editor	↑,←,↓,→,↓,↑,↑,↓,→,→,(B)
All Themes for Park Editor	↑,←,↓,→,↓,↑,↓,→,←,←,(B)
Amish Guy	↑,←,↓,→,→,←,←,↓,↑,←,(B)
Colin Mackay's FMV	←,←,→,→,↓,↓,→,↑,(B)
Dave Mirra's FMV	←,←,↑,→,↑,←,↑,↑,(B)
Leigh Ramsdell's FMV	←,←,↓,↓,←,→,↓,←,(B)
Luc-E's FMV	←,←,→,→,↓,↓,→,↑,(B)
Master Cheat	↑,→,↓,←,→,→,↑,↓,←,→,↑,←,→,→,↓,(B)
Slim Jim guy	↑,←,↓,→,→,←,↑,↓,↑,→,(B)

Def Jam Fight for NY

Enter these codes in the Cheat Menu.

Song	Code
"Anything Goes" by CNN	MILITAIN
"Bust" by Outkast	BIGBOI
"Comp" by Comp	CHOCOCITY
"Dragon House" by Chiang	AKIRA
"Koto" by Chiang	GHOSTSHELL
"Man Up" by Sticky Fingaz	KIRKJONES
"Move" by Public Enemy	RESPECT
"Original Gangster" by Ice T	POWER
"Take a Look at my Life" by Fat Joe	CARTAGENA
"Walk with Me" by Joe Budden	PUMP

Def Jam Fight for NY (cont'd)

NOTE

To unlock "100 Reward Points", use any of the following codes: NEWJACK, THESOURCE, CROOKLYN, DUCKET, or GETSTUFF.

Def Jam Vendetta

Unlockable	Code
Enter the Matrix	Go into the Hacking system and enter cheat.exe at the prompt to bring up the cheat menu.
All weapons	0034AFFF
Arii	A,Y,B,X,Y
Bonus level	13D2C77F
Briggs (alternate costume)	A,B,X,Y,X
Briggs (alternate costume)	A,B,Y,A,X
Carla	A,Y,A,A,A
Chukklez	Y,Y,B,A,X
Cruz	X,X,B,A,A,X
D-Mob	Y,B,Y,A,X
D-Mob (alternate costume)	Y,Y,B,Y,Y
Dan G	A,X,A,X,Y
Deebo	X,X,A,A,B
Deebo and Omar	Beat the Story Mode with all four of the default wrestlers.
Deja	X,Y,X,X,A
DMX	X,A,X,B,Y
Drake	B,Y,X,A,A
Drake (alternate costume)	A,B,B,X,X
Enemies Can't Hear	4516DF45
Enemies Can't See	FFFFFFF1
Faster Logos	7867F443
Funkmaster Flex	X,B,X,X,Y
Headache	B,B,B,Y,X
House	B,A,B,X,A
Iceberg	Y,B,X,Y,X
Infinite Ammo	1DDF2556
Infinite Focus	69E5D9E4
Infinite Health	7F4DF451
Invisibility	FFFFFFF1
Low Gravity	BB013FFF
Ludacris	X,X,X,Y,B
Manny (Alternate Costume)	X,Y,X,Y,X
Masa	A,X,B,Y,Y
Method Man	Y,X,A,B,X
Moses	B,B,Y,Y,A
Unlock Multiplayer	D5C55D1E
N.O.R.E.	X,Y,B,A,X
Nyne	Y,X,A,A,B
Omar	X,X,Y,B,B
Opal	X,X,Y,Y,B
Peewee	A,A,Y,B,Y
Unlock Peewee (Alternate Costume)	A,B,B,Y,X
Penny	A,A,A,B,X
Pockets	B,Y,X,Y,A
Proof (Alternate costume)	A,Y,B,X
Razor	B,Y,B,X,A
Razor (Alternate Costume)	Y,X,A,B
Recover Focus Fast	FFF0020A
Redman	X,X,B,Y,A
Ruffneck	A,Y,A,B,X

Def Jam Vendetta (cont'd)

Unlockable	Code
Ruffneck (Alternate Costume)	Y, X, B, A, Y
Scarface	X, Y, A, B, Y
Sketch	B, B, X, Y, A
Snowman	B, B, A, A, X
Spider (Alternate Costume)	Y, B, A, Y, X
Steel	A, B, X, X, B
T'ai	X, X, Y, A, X
Taxi Driving	312MF451
Turbo mode	FF00001A
Zaheer	B, B, Y, A, A

Die Hard: Vendetta

Enter the following codes at the Main Menu. A message at the bottom of the screen confirms correct code entry.

Unlockable	Code
Big Heads	R, R, L, R
Exploding Bullets	L, R, R, Z, Z, Y, B
Exploding Fists	R, R, Y, B, X, R, R
Flame On	X, Y, B, X, Y, B, Y, B, X, Y, B
Hero Mode	L+Y (with a full special meter)
Hot Fists	L, L, X, B, Y, L, L
Invincibility	L, R, L, R, L, R, L, R
Level Select	X, Y, Z, Z, X, Y, Z, Z
Liquid Metal Textures	B, Y, X, B, Y, X
Pin Heads	B, X, Y, B, X, Y
Small Heads	L, L, R, L
Unlimited Hero Time	B, X, Y, Z, L, R

Digimon Rumble Arena 2

Enter these codes at the Title Screen.

Unlockable	Code
Evolve Meter Always Full Rule	X, →, A, Y, ←, B, L+R
Evolve Item Rule	Y, →, ↓, B, L, A, R, A, Y
One Hit Rule	→, ↑, ←, ↓, A, L+R

Dragon Ball Z: Budokai

Unlockable	Objective
1-Star Dragonball	Super-Rare—if the desired Dragonball isn't the Recommended Capsule, exit and re-enter Mr. Popo's shop until he has it displayed.
2-Star Dragonball	Super-Rare—same as above.
3-Star Dragonball	Super-Rare—same as above.

Dragon Ball Z: Budokai (cont'd)

4-Star Dragonball	Free when starting a new game. Note: if you have a second memory card, you can get this by starting a game and trading.
5-Star Dragonball	Super-Rare—same as all but the 4-star Dragonball.
6-Star Dragonball	Super-Rare—same as all but the 4-star Dragonball.
7-Star Dragonball	Super-Rare—same as all but the 4-star Dragonball.
Android 16	Defeat Android 16 in story mode as Cell.
Android 17	Defeat Android 17 in story mode as Picollo.
Android 18	Defeat Android 18 in story mode as Vegeta.
Android 19	Defeat Android 19 in story mode as Vegeta.
Captain Ginyu	Defeat Ginyu in Story Mode after he takes over Goku's body.
Cell	Defeat Cell in story mode.
Dodoria	Defeat Frieza with Vegeta in Story Mode.
Frieza	Defeat Frieza in story mode.
Hercule	Beat the adept mode of the World Tournament.
Nappa	Defeat Nappa in story mode.
Raditz	Defeat Raditz in story mode.
Recoome	Defeat Recoome in story mode.
Teen Gohan	Defeat Cell as Gohan in story mode.
The Great Saiyaman	Beat the advanced mode of the World Tournament.
Trunks	Beat Perfect Form Cell Complete.
Vegeta	Defeat Vegeta in story mode.
Yamcha	Beat A Cold-Blooded Assasin.
Zarbon	Defeat Zarbon in story mode as Vegeta.

EA Sports Bio Awards

Unlockable	Code
2002 All-American Team	Level 18
Butter Fingers Pennant	Level 4
Orange Bowl Pennant	Level 8
Rose Bowl Pennant	Level 2
Tostitos Bowl Pennant	Level 12

Eternal Darkness

Unlockable	Objective
Alternate Ending	Complete the game three times on the same save file, choosing a new story path each time.
Invincibility	Complete the game three times on the same save file to unlock the "Eternal Mode" option in the "Jump to Game" menu.
Level Select	Complete the game twice on the same save file to unlock the "Jump to Game" option.
Skeleton Screen	At the main menu screen, choose "Options," and the picture of Alex will turn into a skeleton.
View Credits	Complete the game to unlock the "Credits" option.

Extreme G-3

Enter the following codes at the title screen after "Press Start" appears. A message confirms correct code entry. The effect lasts for only one race and must be re-enabled before the next one.

Unlockable	Code
All Teams and Tracks	Press L,L,R,R,Z,Z,L+R+Z.

PSP Xbox PS2 GC GBA

Extreme G-3 (cont'd)

Always Win XG Career Mode Races	Press R,L,Z,L,R,Z,R,L,Z. This code allows you to win a race even if you quit, lose, or die.
Double Prize Money	Press L,R,Z,L,R,Z,L+R
Extreme Lap Challenge	Press L,R,L,R,L,R,Z,L,R. This code unlocks an oval track for maximum speed.
Unlimited AMMUNITION and STARCOM TEAM	Press L,R,L,R,L+R,Z.
Unlimited Shields and Turbos	L+R,Z,L+R,Z.
Win Next Race	L+R+Z,L+R,Z,L+R+Z+R+Z,L+R, Z,L+R+Z

F-Zero GX

Unlockable	Objective
AX Machine Parts	Beat Story chapters on the Hard difficulty.
AX Pilots	Beat the Story Mode chapters on Very Hard difficulty.
AX Tracks	Finish first in AX Machine Tracks or beat all the grand prix on Master.
Dai & San & Gen/Pink Spider (#33)	Beat Story Mode Mission #7 on Very Hard difficulty.
Dai Goroh/Silver Rat (#35)	Beat Story Mode Mission #6 on Very Hard difficulty.
Dark Schneider	Beat all of the chapters in Story Mode.
Diamond Cup	Finish in first place in the Ruby, Sapphire, and Emerald Cups (on Standard or Expert).
Digi Boy/Cosmic Dolphin (#32)	Beat Story Mode Mission #5 on Very Hard difficulty.
Don Genie/Fat Shark (#31)	Beat Story Mode Mission #4 on Very Hard difficulty.
Lily Flyer/Bunny Flash (#37)	Beat Story Mode Mission #8 on Very Hard difficulty.
Magic Seagull	Clear All Chapters on Very Hard difficulty.
Master Class	Finish in first place in the following Cups on Expert: Ruby, Emerald, and Sapphire.
Phoenix/Rainbow Phoenix (#40)	Beat Story Mode Mission #1 on Very Hard difficulty.
PJ/Groovy Taxi (#38)	Beat Story Mode Mission #9 on Very Hard difficulty.
Princia Ramode/Spark Moon (#36)	Beat Story Mode Mission #2 on Very Hard difficulty.
QQQ/Rolling Turtle (#39)	Beat Story Mode Mission #3 on Very Hard difficulty.
Sonic Oval	Beat the AX Cup.

Fantastic Four

At the Main menu, enter this code quickly. You'll hear a sound to confirm it was entered correctly.

Unlockable	Code
Secret Bonus Level Hell	→,→,B,X,←,↑,↓

Fight Night Round 2

Unlockable	Code
All Venus	At the Game Mode Select screen, hold ← until you hear a bell.
Mini Fighters	At the Choose Venue screen, hold ↑ until you hear a bell ring.

Fight Night Round 2 (cont'd)

Unlockable	Code
Unlock Fabulous	Create a character with the first name Getfab, then cancel out and Fabulous will be available for Play Now and Career mode.
Unlock Little Mac	Create a character with the first name Macman, then cancel out and Lil Mac will be available for Play Now and Career mode.

Finding Nemo

Enter the codes at the Main Menu.

Effect	Code
Level Select	Y, Y, Y, B, B, X, B, Y, X, B, Y, B, Y, B, Y, B, Y, X, Y, Y.
Invincibility	Y, B, B, X, X, X, Y, Y, B, B, B, X, X, X, X, B, Y, X, X, X, B, X, Y, X, X, B, X, X, Y, X, B, X, X, X, Y.
View the Credits	Y, B, X, Y, Y, B, X, Y, B, X, Y, B, B, X, Y, B, X, Y, B, X, X, Y, B, X.
Secret Level	Y, B, X, X, B, Y, Y, B, X, X, B, Y, Y, X, B, Y, B, X, X, B, Y.

Freaky Flyers

Unlockable	Objective
Andre Latoilette	Shoot the snowman in front of the cabin in Bigfoot Mountain.
Bandito	Shoot the blue stalagmite on the cave ceiling in Coyote Canyon to find him at the very top.
Baron Von Slaughter	Shoot the Tombstone on the left-hand side of the graveyard in Grave Danger.
Cactus Rose	Shoot the gallows she's about to be hung on near the church in Coyote Canyon.
Genie	In Cave of Blunders, go through the left doorway of the castle to find Genie there.
Island Jack	Shoot the snake coiled on a tree near the monkey shrine in Danger Island.
Marcels Moreso	Fly through the building on the left hand side of the factory entrace in Bombsburg.
Margaret Basher	Break open the box from UK that's under the bridge in Thugsville.
Pilot X	Beat Pilot X' robot on the last level in adventure mode.
Professor Gutentaag	Destroy the yellow submarine containing the Professor in Torpedo Run to unlock him.
Purple Gremlin	Follow the train tracks in Thugsville on the right-hand side. When you get in the fork in the tunnel, go left. He should be there.
Queen	Shes in a pipe on the right-hand side after coming out of the tunnel in Bombsburg.
Rubber-Suited Monster	He's behind the buildings on the left hand side of the city in Monster Isle.
Sammy Wasabi	Kill the monkey ninja that is about to kill him near the roof of the Bamboo Forest Shrine in Monster Isle.
Shiek Abdul	Kill the man thats about to kill Shiek in the town center of Cave of Blunders.

Freedom Fighters

Unlockable	Code
Invisibility	Y,A,B,X,X,←
Heavy Machine Gun	Y,A,B,X,Y,↓
Nail Gun	Y,A,B,X,A,A
Rocket Launcher	Y,A,B,X,Y,←
Shotgun	Y,A,B,X,X,L
Sniper Rifle	Y,A,B,X,Y,→
Submachine Gun	Y,A,B,X,Y,L
Unlimited Ammo	Y,A,B,X,A,→

Freekstyle

Enter all codes in the Code Menu.

Unlockable Characters	Code
Clifford Adoptante	COOLDUDE
Greg Albertyn	GIMEGREG
Jessica Patterson	BLONDIE
Mike Jones	TOUGHGUY

Unlockable Bikes & Outfits	Code
Brian Deegan Bikes	
Dominator	WHOZASKN
Heavy Metal	HEDBANGER
Mulisha Man	WHATEVER
Brian Deegan Outfits	
Commander	SOLDIER
Muscle Bound	RIPPED
Clifford Adoptante Bikes	
Gone Tiki	SUPDUDE
Hang Loose	STOKED
Islander Spirit	GOFLOBRO
Clifford Adoptante Outfits	
Tankin' It	NOSLEEVE
Tiki	WINGS
Greg Albertyn Bikes	
Champion	NUMBER
National Pride	PATRIOT
The King	ALLSHOOK
Greg Albertyn Outfits	
Sharp Dresser	ILOOKGUD
Star Rider	COMET
Jessica Patterson Bikes	
Charged Up	LIGHTNIN
Racer Girl	TONBOY
Speedy	HEKACOOL
Jessica Patterson Outfits	
Hoodie Style	NOT2GRLY
Warming Up	LAYERS
Leeann Tweeden Bikes	
Hot Stuff	OVENMITT
Seducer	GOODLOOK
Trendsetter	STYLIN
Leeann Tweeden Outfits	
Fun Lovin'	THNKPINK
Red Hot	SPICY
Mike Jones Bikes	
Beater	KICKBUTT
Flushed	PLUNGER
Lil' Demon	HORNS
Mike Jones Outfits	
Blue Collar	BABYBLUE
High Roller	BOXCARS

Freekstyle

Unlockable	Code
Mike Metzger Bikes	
Bloodshot	EYEDROPS
Rhino Rage	SEVENTWO
Rock of Ages	BRRRRRAP
Mike Metzger Outfits	
Tatted Up	BODYART
Ecko MX	HELLOOOO
Stefy Bau Bikes	
211	TWONEONE
Amore	HEREIAM
Disco Tech	SPARKLES
Stefy Bau Outfits	
Playing Jax	KIDSGAME
UFO Racer	INVASION
Rider has a helmet	HELMET
Unlimited Freekout	ALLFREEK

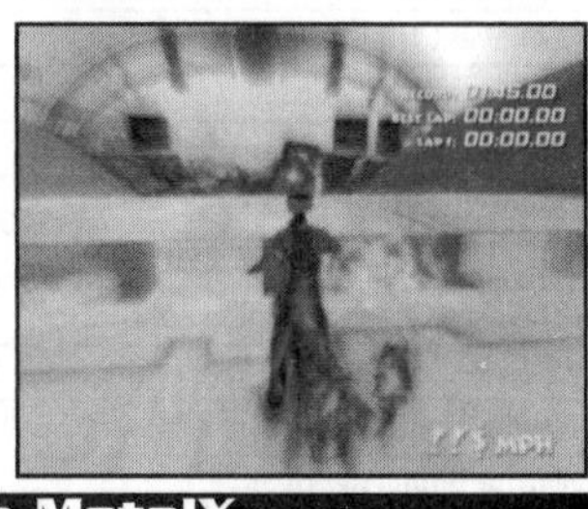

Freestyle MetalX

Enter all codes in the Cheats Menu.

Unlockable	Code
1 Million Dollars	sugardaddy
31 Trick Slots	fleximan
All Bike Parts	garageking
All Character Outfits	johnnye
All Cheats	iwantitall
All Levels and Events	universe
All Posters	seeall
All Riders and Bikes	dudemaster
All Songs	hearall
All Videos	watchall

Gauntlet: Dark Legacy

Enter the following codes as a name.

Unlockable	Code
10,000 Gold per Level	10000K
Always Have Nine Potions and Keys	ALLFUL
Dwarf in S&M Costume	NUD069
Dwarf is a Large Jester	ICE600
Invincibility	INVULN
Jester is a Stick Figure with Baseball Cap Head	KJH105
Jester is a Stick Figure with Mohawk Head	PNK666
Jester is a Stick Figure with Smiley Face	STX222
Knight is a Bald Man in Street Clothes (Sean Gugler)	STG333
Knight is a Ninja (Sword and Claws)	TAK118
Knight is a Quarterback	RIZ721
Knight is a Roman Centurion	BAT900
Knight is an Orange-Skirted Waitress	KA0292
Knight Wears Black Karate Outfit with Twin Scythes	SJB964
Knight Wears Black Outfit and Cape	DARTHC
Knight Wears Street Clothes	ARV984

Gauntlet: Dark Legacy (cont'd)

Knight Wears Street Clothes (Chris Sutton)	CSS222
Knight Wears Street Clothes and Baseball Cap	DIB626
Permanent Anti-Death	1ANGEL
Permanent Full Turbo	PURPLE
Permanent Invisibility	000000
Permanent Pojo the Chicken	EGG911
Permanent Reflect Shot	REFLEX
Permanent Shrink Enemy and Growth	DELTA1
Permanent Super Shot with Large Crossbow	SSHOTS
Permanent Triple Shot	MENAGE
Permanent X-Ray Vision	PEEKIN
Run Quickly	XSPEED
Throw Quickly	QCKSHT
Valkyrie as a Cheerleader with Baton	CEL721
Valkyrie as a Japanese School Girl	AYA555
Valkyrie as the Grim Reaper with Bloody Scythe	TWN300.
Warrior as an Orc Boss	MTN200
Warrior with a Rat Head	RAT333
Warrior with an Ogre Costume	CAS400
Wizard as a Pharaoh	DES700
Wizard as an Alien	SKY100
Wizard as an Undead Lich	GARM00
Wizard as Sumner	SUM224
Wizard with an Evil Appearance	GARM99

Goblin Commander: Unleash the Horde

During Game Play, hold L+R+Y+↓ for three seconds, then enter a code.

Unlockable	Code
100 Gold	←,→,→,→,→,←,X,←,←,←
100 Souls	→,←,←,←,←,→,X,→,→,→
1000 Gold and Souls	→,→,←,→,→,X,X,X,←,←
God Mode	→,→,→,←,←,←,→,←,X,→

Godzilla Destroy All Monsters Melee

To enter these codes, you must first load the Main Menu, press and hold L,B,R, and release the buttons in the following order: B,R,L. Now you can input your code; when done correctly, you will hear Godzilla roar.

Unlockable	Code
All Cities	480148
All Monsters	696924
All Players are Small	174204
All Players Damage Proof	505634
All Players have Quad Damage	817683
All Players Invisible	316022
Black and White Mode	567980
Destroyah	537084
Eleven Continues	760611
Game Version	97401
Gigan	616233
Godzilla 2000	225133
Health Regeneration	492877
Indestructible Buildings	112122
Infinite Energy for Player 1	677251
Infinite Energy for Player 2	435976
King Ghidorah	877467
Mecha Godzilla	131008
Mecha King Ghidorah	557456
More Energy	650867

Godzilla Destroy All Monsters Melee (cont'd)

Unlockable	Code
No Displays	443253
No Energy	650867
No Energy Power Ups	413403
No Freeze Tanks	841720
No Health Power Ups	562142
No Mothra Power Ups	134615
No Rage Power Ups	119702
Player 1 always has Rage	649640
Player 1 is Small	986875
Player 1 Quad Damage	511012
Player 1 takes no Damage	843901
Player 2 always has Rage	122224
Player 2 is Invisible	495113
Player 2 is Small	971934
Player 2 Quad Damage	815480
Player 2 takes no Damage	706149
Player 3 always has Rage	548053
Player 3 is Small	895636
Player 3 Quad Damage	212454
Player 3 takes no Damage	188522
Player 4 always has Rage	451242
Player 4 is Small	795735
Player 4 Quad Damage	286552
Player 4 takes no Damage	286552
Player Indicators Always on	135984
Rodan	104332
Stats Mode	97401
Super Energy Player 1	677251
Super Energy Player 2	435976
Super Energy Player 3	603696
Super Energy Player 4	291680
Technicolor Mode	661334
Throw all Objects and Buildings	756287
Turn Military On/Off	256806
View Credits	176542

Golden Eye: Rogue Agent

Unlockable	Code
All Levels in Multiplayer and Single Player	↓,→,↓,→,↑,↓,↑,←
All Multiplayer Skins	↓,←,↑,←,→,↓,←,↑
One Life Mode	←,↓,↑,→,↑,→,←,↓
Paintball Mode	→,←,→,←,↓,↓,↑,↑

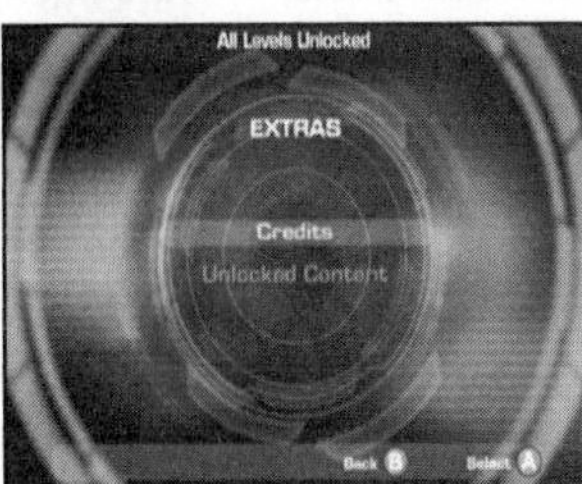

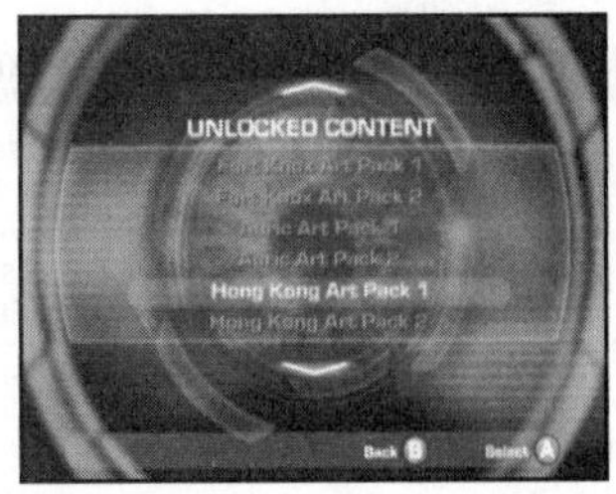

Harvest Moon: A Wonderful Life

Unlockable	Objective
Cat	Become friends with Romana in Fall of Chapter 2. Wake up later than your wife and Romana will knock at the door and give you a cat.
Ducks	Purchase a pond for 2500 G from Takakura. During Chapter 2 in the Summer, wake up later than your wife to find ducks in your pond.
Goat	During Spring when Van has his shop open, you can purchase the Goat for 4000 G.

Haunted Mansion

During game play, hold Ⓡ, then enter the code.

Unlockable	Code
God Mode	Ⓑ,Ⓧ,Ⓧ,Ⓧ,Ⓑ,Ⓧ,Ⓨ,Ⓐ
Level Select	Ⓧ,Ⓧ,Ⓑ,Ⓨ,Ⓨ,Ⓑ,Ⓧ,Ⓐ
Upgrade Weapon	Ⓑ,Ⓑ,Ⓨ,Ⓨ,Ⓧ,Ⓧ,Ⓧ,Ⓐ

Hitman 2: Silent Assassin

Unlockable	Code
Ali Mode	During gameplay press →,←,↑,↓,Ⓐ,↑,↑.
All Weapons	During gameplay press →,←,↑,↓,Ⓐ,↑,Ⓑ,Ⓐ.
Bomb and Slomo Mode	During gameplay press →,←,↑,↓,Ⓐ,↑,←.
Full Life	During gameplay press →,←,↑,↓,Ⓐ,↑,↓.
God Mode	During gameplay press →,←,↑,↓,Ⓐ,→,←,→,←Ⓒ.
Gravity and Nail Gun Mode	During gameplay press →,←,↑,↓,Ⓐ,←,←.
Lethal Charge	During gameplay press →,←,↑,↓,Ⓐ,→,→.
Sawed-off Shotgun	Beat any two missions with a Silent Assassin ranking.
Silenced Ballers	Earn a Silent Assassin ranking on any mission.
M4	Earn a Silent Assasin ranking on the St. Petersburg missions. Then complete "Invitation to a Party".

The Hulk

Unlockable	Code	Unlockable	Code
Double Health for Enemies	BRNGITN	Puzzles Solved Cheat	BRCESTN
Double Health for Hulk	HLTHDSE	Regenerator	FLSHWND
Full Rage Meter	ANGMNGT	Unlimited Continues	GRNCHTR
Half Enemies' HP	MMMYHLP	Desert Battle Art	FIFTEEN
High Score Reset	NMBTHIH	Hulk Movie FMV Art	NANOMED
Invincibility	GMMSKIN	Hulk Transformed Art	SANFRAN
Level Select	TRUBLVR	Hulk vs. Hulk Dogs Art	PITBULL
Play as Gray Hulk	JANITOR	Wicked Punch Cheat	FSTOFRY[ET]

I-Ninja

During gameplay, press START to pause, then enter the code.

Unlockable	Code
Complete Mission	Hold → and press Ⓑ,Ⓑ,Ⓑ,Ⓧ. Release →, then hold ← and press Ⓨ,Ⓨ. Release ←, hold →, then press Ⓑ,Ⓑ.
Sword Upgrade	Hold Ⓛ+Ⓡ, then press Ⓧ,Ⓑ,Ⓧ,Ⓨ,Ⓨ,Ⓑ,Ⓧ,Ⓑ

Ikaruga

Unlockable	Objective
Gallery 1	Beat Trial Mode without continuing or play the game for more than five hours total.
Gallery 2	Beat the game on any difficulty or play the game for more than 10 hours total.
Game Mode Option	Beat the game on Normal without continuing or play the game for more than 20 hours total.
Sound Test	Beat the game on Easy without continuing or play the game for more than 15 hours total.

The Incredibles

Pause the game, go to the Secrets menu, then enter these codes.

Unlockable	Code
Big Heads	EINSTEINIUM
Credits	YOURNAMEINLIGHTS
Destroy All Enemies on Screen	SMARTBOMB
Eye Laser	GAZERBEAM
Feet of Fire	ATHLETESFOOT
One Hit knockout	KRONOS
Restore Health	UUDDLRLRBAS
Slow down Gameplay	BWTHEMOVIE
Small Heads	DEEVOLVE
So many Colors	EMODE
Speed up Gameplay	SASSMODE
Turn off the HUD	BHUD
Unlimited Incredi-Power for Elastigirl	FLEXIBLE
Unlimited Incredi-Power for Mr. Incredible	SHOWTIME
Watch the Intro again	HI

Jeremy McGrath Supercross World

Enter the following codes at the Main Menu. The lower left corner of the screen will flash and a message will appear to confirm correct code entry.

Unlockable	Code
Big Heads	Ⓑ,Ⓧ,R,L,→
Bouncy Bike	↑,↑,Ⓨ,Ⓨ,Ⓧ,Ⓧ
Moon Gravity	←,→,↑,↓,Ⓑ,Ⓑ,Ⓑ
Tag Mode	Z,Ⓧ,Z,Ⓧ
Tiny Mode	L,Z,←,→,Ⓑ,Ⓑ
Unlimited Turbo	↓,↓,↓,L,R,Z

Kelly Slater's Pro Surfer

To enter these codes, go into the Options menu and select the Cheats option.

Unlockable	Code
All Boards	6195554141
All Levels	3285554497
All Suits	7025552918
All Surfers	9495556799
All Tricks	6265556043
Change Graphics	8185551447
First Person Camera View	8775553825
High Jumps	2175550217
Master Code	7145558092
Max Stats	2125551776
Perfect Balance	2135555721
Unlock Freak	3105556217
Unlock Tony Hawk	3235559787
Unlock Tiki God	8885554506
Unlock Travis Pastrana	8005556292

Legends of Wrestling

Unlockable	Objective
All Wrestlers	Press ↑,↑,↓,↓,←,→,←,→,Ⓨ,Ⓨ,Ⓧ at the main menu. A message confirms correct code entry. After enabling the code, go to the Options screen and save your options. This keeps all wrestlers unlocked if you start your game over.
Bonus Arenas	Complete the game in Career mode to unlock the Back Lot, Gym, Beach Resort, and Casino arenas in Exhibition mode.
Captain Lou Albano	Complete Career mode with a wrestler in the "Hated" category.
David von Erich	Complete Career mode as Kevin von Erich.

Legends of Wrestling (cont'd)

Dory Funk	Complete Career mode as Terry Funk.
Fritz von Erich	Complete Career mode as Kerry von Erich.
Ivan Koloff	Win the versus tournament.
Jimmy Hart	Complete Career mode with a wrestler in the "Loved" category.
King Kong Bundy	Win the Southeast Territory in Career mode.
Michael von Erich	Complete career mode as David von Erich.
Mr. Fuji	Win the Tag Belts in Tournament mode.
Real Names	You can create wrestlers such as Ric Flair, Hall, Nash, and others, and the announcer will say their names.
Robert Gibson and Ricky Morton	Win the tag tournament.
Sabu	Complete Career mode as The Sheik.

Looney Tunes Back in Action

Enter these codes in the Codes Menu.

Unlockable	Code
Cannon Ball Costume	CANNON
Costume Doors are Free	SUITSYOU
Duck Danger Battle	OUTTAKE
Duck Danger Costume	DANGERD
Extra 500 Bucks	AMUNKEY
Gossamer Doors in the Warner Bros. Studios	GOBBLE
Hen Grenades	HENSAWAY
Invincible	TOUGHAGE
Level Select	PASSPORT
Shrink Ray	WEENY
Slappy Fish	SLAPPY
Wile E. Coyote Game	FURRYOUS

The Lord of the Rings: Return of the King

Accessing the video clips depends on how far you've gone in the game. Here's a table showing what you can find and what level you must complete to find it. For example, you can't see the game concept art slide show until you've successfully completed Paths of the Dead.

Unlockable Video Features

Video Title	Must Complete
Andy Serkis Interview	The Crack of Doom
Billy Boyd Interview	The Crack of Doom
Christopher Lee Interview	The Road to Isengard
David Wenham Interview	The Crack of Doom

The Lord of the Rings: Return of the King (cont'd)

Dom Monaghan Interview	The Crack of Doom
Elijah Wood Interview	Shelob's Lair
Film Concept Art	Helm's Deep
Film Production Stills	The Southern Gate
Game Concept Art	Paths of the Dead
Hobbits on Gaming	Helm's Deep
Ian McKellen Interview	Minas Tirith—Top of the Wall
Sean Astin Interview	Escape from Osgiliath

For the following codes:

1. Pause the game so that the Options menu appears.
2. Hold down all shoulder buttons at once.
3. Enter the code with shoulder buttons still depressed.

When you've entered the code correctly, you'll hear a sound that indicates success.

TIP

If you want to enter more than one code, release the shoulder buttons, then hold them down again before entering each code.

Secret Codes

Code	Usage	Character	GameCube Combo
+1,000 Experience Points	one-time use	Gimli	X,X,Y,A
+1,000 Experience Points	one-time use	Gandalf	X,Y,↑,X
+1,000 Experience Points	one-time use	Merry	X,X,B,A
+1,000 Experience Points	one-time use	Frodo	X,Y,↑,X
+1,000 Experience Points	one-time use	Faramir	B,Y,↑,B
+1,000 Experience Points	one-time use	Aragorn	↑,B,Y,A
+1,000 Experience Points	one-time use	Sam	Y,A,X,A
+1,000 Experience Points	one-time use	Pippin	Y,A,B,A
+1,000 Experience Points	one-time use	Legolas	A,Y,↑,A
All Experience you get, your buddy gets	on/off	Co-op	X,A,A,A
All Health you get, your buddy gets	on/off	Co-op	Y,↑,B,B
All Upgrades	one-time use	Any Character	↑,X,Y,B
Always Devastating	on/off	Any Character	Y,↑,Y,X
Features			A,B,A,↑
Infinite Re-spawns for Co-op	on/off	All	X,B,↑,X
Infinite Missiles	on/off	Any Character	B,B,X,X
Invulnerable	on/off	Any Character	B,X,B,↑
Level 2 Skills	on/off	Merry	X,X,B,B
Level 2 Skills	on/off	Aragorn	X,Y,A,Y
Level 2 Skills	on/off	Sam	X,A,X,Y
Level 2 Skills	on/off	Gandalf	X,Y,A,Y

The Lord of the Rings: Return of the King (cont'd)

Level 2 Skills	on/off	Pippin	X, A, X, ↑
Level 2 Skills	on/off	Legolas	B, B, X, B
Level 2 Skills	on/off	Gimli	↑, X, B, B
Level 2 Skills	on/off	Frodo	Y, ↑, X, X
Level 2 Skills	on/off	Faramir	A, B, A, X
Level 4 Skills	on/off	Legolas	X, X, A, A
Level 4 Skills	on/off	Aragorn	X, B, X, B
Level 4 Skills	on/off	Merry	B, A, X, X
Level 4 Skills	on/off	Sam	↑, X, B, A
Level 4 Skills	on/off	Gimli	Y, B, X, ↑
Level 4 Skills	on/off	Frodo	Y, ↑, X, X
Level 4 Skills	on/off	Gandalf	Y, ↑, B, A
Level 4 Skills	on/off	Pippin	A, X, X, X
Level 4 Skills	on/off	Faramir	A, A, B, B
Level 6 Skills	on/off	Pippin	X, Y, X, Y
Level 6 Skills	on/off	Aragorn	X, Y, B, B
Level 6 Skills	on/off	Legolas	X, X, ↑, X
Level 6 Skills	on/off	Merry	X, X, B, Y
Level 6 Skills	on/off	Sam	X, X, ↑, ↑
Level 6 Skills	on/off	Frodo	X, X, A, Y
Level 6 Skills	on/off	Gimli	X, Y, X, B
Level 6 Skills	on/off	Gandalf	Y, Y, A, ↑
Level 6 Skills	on/off	Faramir	Y, A, X, X
Level 8 Skills	on/off	Frodo	X, X, X, X
Level 8 Skills	on/off	Sam	X, X, Y, Y
Level 8 Skills	on/off	Faramir	X, X, X, X
Level 8 Skills	on/off	Gandalf	X, B, X, X
Level 8 Skills	on/off	Merry	X, Y, A, B
Level 8 Skills	on/off	Legolas	B, ↑, ↑, X
Level 8 Skills	on/off	Pippin	B, ↑, ↑, X
Level 8 Skills	on/off	Aragorn	↑, B, Y, ↑
Level 8 Skills	on/off	Gimli	A, X, X, B
Perfect Mode	on/off	Any Character	X, X, Y, A
Restore Missiles	one-time use	Gimli	X, X, X, A
Restore Missiles	one-time use	Merry	B, X, X, Y
Restore Missiles	one-time use	Pippin	↑, X, X, B
Restore Missiles	one-time use	Gandalf	Y, X, A, B
Restore Missiles	one-time use	Aragorn	Y, B, B, Y
Restore Missiles	one-time use	Faramir	Y, ↑, A, A
Restore Missiles	one-time use	Legolas	Y, Y, Y, X
Restore Missiles	one-time use	Frodo	Y, Y, Y, X
Restore Missiles	one-time use	Sam	A, A, X, A

PSP Xbox PS2 GC GBA

The Lord of the Rings: Return of the King (cont'd)

Restore Health	one-time use	Any Character	B,B,X,X
Targeting Indicator Mode	on/off	Any Character	X,X,↑,B
Unlock 3 Hit Combo for	on/off	Gandalf	X,A,Y,X
Unlock 3 Hit Combo for	on/off	Aragorn	B,X,X,↑
Unlock 3 Hit Combo for	on/off	Frodo	B,X,Y,B
Unlock 3 Hit Combo for	on/off	Faramir	B,Y,↑,Y
Unlock 3 Hit Combo for	on/off	Legolas	B,Y,Y,X
Unlock 3 Hit Combo for	on/off	Sam	B,A,X,B
Unlock 3 Hit Combo for	on/off	Gimli	↑,B,X,B
Unlock 3 Hit Combo for	on/off	Pippin	↑,↑,B,X
Unlock 3 Hit Combo for	on/off	Merry	Y,A,↑,Y
Unlock 4 Hit Combo for	on/off	Frodo	X,B,X,X
Unlock 4 Hit Combo for	on/off	Gandalf	X,Y,↑,X
Unlock 4 Hit Combo for	on/off	Merry	B,A,B,B
Unlock 4 Hit Combo for	on/off	Sam	↑,X,Y,Y
Unlock 4 Hit Combo for	on/off	Aragorn	↑,B,Y,X
Unlock 4 Hit Combo for	on/off	Gimli	Y,B,↑,A
Unlock 4 Hit Combo for	on/off	Legolas	A,X,Y,B
Unlock 4 Hit Combo for	on/off	Faramir	A,B,↑,A
Unlock 4 Hit Combo for	on/off	Pippin	A,A,X,X
Unlock Secret Character	one-time use	Frodo	X,B,B,A
Unlock Secret Character	one-time use	Pippin	Y,X,B,X
Unlock Secret Character	one-time use	Merry	A,X,X,A
Unlock Secret Character	one-time use	Faramir	A,A,Y,Y
Unlock Special Abilities for	on/off	Gimli	X,B,A,X
Unlock Special Abilities for	on/off	Aragorn	X,X,Y,Y
Unlock Special Abilities for	on/off	Pippin	B,A,X,Y
Unlock Special Abilities for	on/off	Sam	↑,X,A,X
Unlock Special Abilities for	on/off	Gandalf	↑,X,Y,X
Unlock Special Abilities for	on/off	Faramir	↑,B,X,↑
Unlock Special Abilities for	on/off	Merry	w,Y,X,X
Unlock Special Abilities for	on/off	Legolas	Y,X,A,X
Unlock Special Abilities for	on/off	Frodo	Y,A,X,A

The Lord of the Rings: The Two Towers

For the following codes, pause gameplay, hold L+R, then enter code. The sound of a sword confirms correct code entry.

Description	Code
Add 1,000 Experience Points	Ⓐ,↓,↓,↓
All Combo Upgrades	Y,X,Y,X—Note: You must first complete the game before enabling this code.
Devastating Attacks	Ⓑ,Ⓑ,X,X—Hold Y during battles to do devastating attacks. Note: You must first complete the game before enabling this code.
Invincibility	Y,Ⓑ,Ⓐ,X—Note: You must first complete the game before enabling this code.
Level 2 Skills	X,→,X,→
Level 4 Skills	Y,↑,Y,↑
Level 6 Skills	Ⓑ,←,Ⓑ,←
Level 8 Skills	Ⓐ,Ⓐ,↓,↓
Restore Ammunition	Ⓐ,↓,Y,↑
Restore Health	Y,↓,Ⓐ,↑
Slow Motion	Y,X,Ⓐ,Ⓑ
Small Enemies	Y,Y,Ⓐ,Ⓐ—Note: You must first complete the game before enabling this code.
Unlimited Missile Weapons	Ⓑ,X,Ⓐ,Y—Note: You must first complete the game before enabling this code.

Lost Kingdoms II

Unlockable	Objective
Helina In Versus Mode	After you defeat the boss in the Scared Arena (Area 2), go west and find Helina's Arena. Note that you need to have a Neutral Skill of 6 or more, to have defeated all the bosses in the first arena, and to have defeated the unknown man blocking the exit in order for Helina to fight you.
Katia In Versus Mode	After defeating the boss in Scared Arena 2, head north and fight Katia. Defeat her and answer yes when the game asks if you want to take on Katia's responsibilities. Save the game.
Kendarie Warrior In Versus Mode	Defeat the Kendarie Boss in the Kendarie Fortress in Area 1.
Rashiannu In Versus Mode	Clear the Royal Tower Upper Floor on single player mode and save the game.
Thalnos In Versus Mode	After you beat Leod and Helena in Scared Arena 2 (after clearing the game once), fight Thalnos in the north most doorway of the arena. Deck him and save the game.
Urbur Cultist In Versus Mode	Defeat an Urbur Cultist, clear the stage, and save.

Madden NFL 2004

Unlockable	Objective
1990 Eagles Classic Team	Earn Level 4 EA Sports Bio rating.
Steve Spurrier Coach	Earn Level 6 EA Sports Bio rating.
Bingo! Cheat	Earn Level 2 EA Sports Bio rating.

Madden NFL 2005

From My Madden menu, go to Madden Cards, Madden Codes, and enter the following:

Card	Password
Aaron Brooks Gold Card	J95K1J
Aaron Glenn Gold Card	Q48E9G
Adewale Ogunleye Gold Card	C12E9E
Ahman Green Gold Card	T86L4C
Al Wilson Gold Card	G72G2R
Alan Faneca Gold Card	U32S9C
Amani Toomer Gold Card	Z75G6M
Andre Carter Gold Card	V76E2Q
Andre Johnson Gold Card	E34S1M
Andy Reid Gold Card	N44K1L
Anquan Boldin Gold Card	S32F7K
Antoine Winfield Gold Card	A12V7Z
Bill Cowher Gold Card	S54T6U
Brad Hopkins Gold Card	P44A8B
Bret Favre Gold Card	L61D7B
Brian Billick Gold Card	L27C4K
Brian Dawkins Gold Card	Y47B8Y
Brian Simmons Gold Card	S22M6A
Brian Urlacher Gold Card	Z34J4U
Brian Westbrook Gold Card	V46I2I
Bubba Franks Gold Card	U77F2W
Butch Davis Gold Card	G77L6F
Byron Leftwich Gold Card	C55V5C
Carson Palmer Gold Card	O36V2H
Casey Hampton Gold Card	Z11P9T
Chad Johnson Gold Card	R85S2A
Chad Pennington Gold Card	B64L2F
Champ Bailey Gold Card	K89O9E
Charles Rogers Gold Card	E57K9Y
Charles Woodson Gold Card	F95N9J
Chris Hovan Gold Card	F14C6J
Corey Simon Gold Card	R11D7K
Courtney Brown Gold Card	R42R75
Curtis Martin Gold Card	K47X3G
Dallas Coach Gold Card	O24U1Q
Damien Woody Gold Card	F78I1I
Dante Hall Gold Card	B23P8D
Dat Nguyen Gold Card	Q86I2S
Daunte Culpepper Gold Card	O62O9K
Dave Wannstedt Gold Card	W73D7D
David Boston Gold Card	A25I9F
David Carr Gold Card	C16E2Q
Dennis Erickson Gold Card	J83E3T
Dennis Green Gold Card	C18J7T
Derrick Brooks Gold Card	P93I9Q
Derrick Mason Gold Card	S98P3T
Deuce McAllister Gold Card	D11H4J
Dexter Coakley Gold Card	L35K1A
Dexter Jackson Gold Card	G16B2I
Dick Vermeil Gold Card	F68V1W
Dom Capers Gold Card	B97I6R
Domanick Davis Gold Card	L58S3J
Donnie Edwards Gold Card	E18Y5Z
Donovin Darius Gold Card	Q11T7T
Donovon McNabb Gold Card	T98J1I
Donte Stallworth Gold Card	R75W3M
Dre Bly Gold Card	H19Q2O
Drew Bledsoe Gold Card	W73M3E
Dwight Freeney Gold Card	G76U2L
Edgerrin James Gold Card	A75D7X
Ed Reed Gold Card	G18Q2B
Eric Moulds Gold Card	H34Z8K
Flozell Adams Gold Card	R54T1O
Fred Taylor Gold Card	I87X9Y
Grant Wistrom Gold Card	E46M4Y
Herman Edwards Gold Card	O19T2T
Hines Ward Gold Card	M12B8F
Jack Del Rio Gold Card	J22P9I
Jake Delhomme Gold Card	M86N9F
Jake Plummer Gold Card	N74P8X
Jamie Sharper Gold Card	W27I7G
Jason Taylor Gold Card	O33S6I
Jason Webster Gold Card	M74B3E
Jeff Fisher Gold Card	N62B6J
Jeff Garcia Gold Card	H32H7B
Jeremy Newberry Gold Card	J77Y8C
Jeremy Shockey Gold Card	R34X5T
Jerry Porter Gold Card	F71Q9Z
Jerry Rice Gold Card	K34F8S
Jevon Kearse Gold Card	A78B1C
Jim Haslett Gold Card	G78R3W
Jim Mora Jr. Gold Card	N46C3M
Jimmy Smith Gold Card	I22J5W
Joe Horn Gold Card	P91A1Q
Joey Harrington Gold Card	Z68W8J
John Fox Gold Card	Q98R7Y
Jon Gruden Gold Card	H61I8A
Josh McCown Gold Card	O33Y4X
Julian Peterson Gold Card	M89J8A
Julius Peppers Gold Card	X54O4Z
Junior Seau Gold Card	W26K6Q

Madden NFL 2005 (cont'd)

Kabeer Gbaja-Biamala Gold Card	U16I9Y
Keith Brooking Gold Card	E12P4S
Keith Bulluck Gold Card	M63N6V
Kendrell Bell Gold Card	T96C7J
Kevan Barlow Gold Card	A23T5E
Kevin Mawae Gold Card	L76E6S
Kris Jenkins Gold Card	W63O3K
Kyle Boller Gold Card	A72F9X
Kyle Turley Gold Card	Y46A8V
LaDainian Tomlinson Gold Card	M64D4E
LaVar Arrington Gold Card	F19Q8W
Laveranues Coles Gold Card	R98I5S
Lawyer Milloy Gold Card	M37Y5B
La'Roi Glover Gold Card	K24L9K
Lee Suggs Gold Card	Z94X6Q
Leonard Davis Gold Card	H14M2V
Lovie Smith Gold Card	L38V3A
Marc Bulger Gold Card	U66B4S
Marcel Shipp Gold Card	R42X2L
Marcus Stroud Gold Card	E56I5O
Marcus Trufant Gold Card	R46T5U
Mark Brunell Gold Card	B66D9J
Marshall Faulk Gold Card	U76G1U
Marty Booker Gold Card	P51U4B
Marty Schottenheimer Gold Card	D96A7S
Marvin Harrison Gold Card	T11E8O
Marvin Lewis Gold Card	P24S4H
Matt Hasselback Gold Card	R68D5F
Michael Bennett Gold Card	W81W2J
Michael Strahan Gold Card	O66T6K
Michael Vick Gold Card	H67B1F
Mike Alstott Gold Card	D89F6W
Mike Brown Gold Card	F12J8N
Mike Martz Gold Card	R64A8E
Mike Mularkey Gold Card	C56D6E
Mike Rucker Gold Card	K89O6S
Mike Shanahan Gold Card	H15L5Y
Mike Sherman Gold Card	F84X6K
Mike Tice Gold Card	Y31T6Y
New England Coach Gold Card	N24L4Z
Nick Barnett Gold Card	X95I7S
Norv Turner Gold Card	F24K1M
Olin Kreutz Gold Card	R17R2O
Orlando Pace Gold Card	U42U9U
Patrick Surtain Gold Card	H58T9X
Peerless Price Gold Card	X75V6K
Peter Warrick Gold Card	D86P8O
Peyton Manning Gold Card	L48H4U
Plaxico Burress Gold Card	K18P6J
Priest Holmes Gold Card	X91N1L
Quentin Jammer Gold Card	V55S3Q
Randy Moss Gold Card	W79U7X
Ray Lewis Gold Card	B94X6V
Reggie Wayne Gold Card	R29S8C
Rex Grossman Gold Card	C46P2A
Rich Gannon Gold Card	Q69I1Y
Richard Seymour Gold Card	L69T4T
Ricky Williams Gold Card	P19V1N
Rod Smith Gold Card	V22C4L
Rodney Harrison Gold Card	O84I3J
Ronde Barber Gold Card	J72X8W
Roy Williams Gold Card	J76C6F
Rudi Johnson Gold Card	W26J6H
Sam Madison Gold Card	Z87T5C
Samari Rolle Gold Card	C69H4Z
Santana Moss Gold Card	H79E5B
Seattle Coach Gold Card	V58U4Y
Shaun Alexander Gold Card	C95Z4P
Shaun Ellis Gold Card	Z54F2B
Shawn Rogers Gold Card	J97X8M
Shawn Springs Gold Card	Z28D2V
Simeon Rice Gold Card	S62F9T
Stephen Davis Gold Card	E39X9L
Steve Mariucci Gold Card	V74Q3N
Steve McNair Gold Card	S36T1I
Steve Smith Gold Card	W91O2O
Takeo Spikes Gold Card	B83A6C
Tedy Bruschi Gold Card	K28Q3P
Terence Newman Gold Card	W57Y5P
Terrell Suggs Gold Card	V71A9Q
Tiki Barber Gold Card	T43A2V
T.J. Duckett Gold Card	P67E1I
Todd Heap Gold Card	H19M1G
Tom Brady Gold Card	X22V7E
Tom Coughlin Gold Card	S71D6H
Tony Dungy Gold Card	Y96R8V
Tony Gonzalez Gold Card	N46E9N
Torry Holt Gold Card	W96U7E
Travis Henry Gold Card	F36M2Q
Trent Green Gold Card	Y46M4S
Ty Law Gold Card	F13W1Z
Walter Jones Gold Card	G57P1P
Washington Coach Gold Card	W63V9L
Will Shields Gold Card	B52S8A
Zach Thomas Gold Card	U63I3H

Madden NFL 2005 (cont'd)

Secret Teams

Card	Password	Card	Password
1958 Colts	P74X8J	1981 Chargers	Y27N9A
1966 Packers	G49P7W	1982 Redskins	F56D6V
1968 Jets	C24W2A	1983 Raiders	D23T8S
1970 Browns	G12N1I	1984 Dolphins	X23Z8H
1972 Dolphins	R79W6W	1985 Bears	F92M8M
1974 Steelers	R12D9B	1986 Giants	K44F2Y
1976 Raiders	P96Q8M	1988 49ers	F77R8H
1977 Broncos	O18T2A	1990 Eagles	G95F2Q
1978 Dolphins	G97U5X	1991 Lions	I89F4I
1980 Raiders	K71K4E	1992 Cowboys	I44A1O
		1993 Bills	Y66K3O

Secret Stadiums

Stadium	Password	Stadium	Password
Pro Bowl Hawaii '05	G67F5X	Super Bowl XLI	P48Z4D
Super Bowl XL	O85P6I	Super Bowl XLII	T67R1O
		Super Bowl XXXIX	D58F1B

Pump Up and Cheerleader Cards

Card	Password	Card	Password
49ers Cheerleader	X61T6L	Jaguars Cheerleader	K32C2A
Bears Pump Up Crowd	K17F2I	Jets Pump Up Crowd	S45W1M
Bengals Cheerleader	Y22S6G	Lions Pump Up Crowd	C18F4G
Bills Cheerleader	F26S6X	Packers Pump Up Crowd	K26Y4V
Broncos Cheerleader	B85U5C	Panthers Cheerleader	M66N4D
Browns Pump Up Crowd	B65Q1L	Patriots Cheerleader	O59P9C
Buccaneers Cheerleader	Z55Z7S	Raiders Cheerleader	G92L2E
Cardinals Cheerleader	Q91W5L	Rams Cheerleader	W73B8X
Chargers Cheerleader	Q68S3F	Ravens Cheerleader	P98T6C
Chiefs Cheerleader	T46M6T	Redskins Cheerleader	N19D6Q
Colts Cheerleader	M22Z6H	Saints Cheerleader	R99G2F
Cowboys Cheerleader	J84E3F	Seahawks Cheerleader	A35T8R
Dolphins Cheerleader	E88T2J	Steelers Pump Up Crowd	C98I2V
Eagles Cheerleader	Q88P3Q	Texans Cheerleader	R74G3W
Falcons Cheerleader	W86F3F	Titans Cheerleader	Q81V4N
Giants Pump Up Crowd	L13Z9J	Vikings Cheerleader	E26H4L

Gold Cheat Cards

Card	Description	Code
3rd Down	For one half, your opponent has 3 downs to get a first down.	Z28X8K
5th Down	For one half, you will have 5 downs to get a first down.	P66C4L
Bingo!	Your defensive interceptions increase by 75% for the game.	J33I8F
Da Bomb	You will receive unlimited pass range for one half.	B61A8M
Da Boot	You will receive unlimited field goal range for one half.	I76X3T
Extra Credit	Awards 4 points for every interception and 3 points for every sack.	M89S8G
1st and 15	Requires your opponent to get 15 yards to reach a first down for one half.	V65J8P
1st and 5	Your first down yards to go will be set to 5 for one half.	O72E9B

Madden NFL 2005 (cont'd)

Fumblitis	Your opponent's fumbles will increase by 75% for the game.	R14B8Z
Human Plow	Your Broken Tackles will increase by 75% for the game.	L96J7P
Lame Duck	Your opponent will throw a lob pass for one half.	D57R5S
Mistake Free	You can't fumble or throw an interception for one half.	X78P9Z
Mr. Mobility	Your QB can't get sacked for one half.	Y59R8R
Super Dive	Your diving distance increases by 75% for the game.	D59K3Y
Tight Fit	Your opponent's uprights will be made very narrow for one half.	V34L6D
Unforced Errors	Your opponent will fumble every time he tries to juke for one half.	L48G1E

Mario Golf: Toadstool Tour

Unlockable	Objective
Blooper Bay	Win Sands Classic in Tournament Mode.
Bowser Badlands	Win Peach's Invitational in Tournament Mode.
Cheep Cheep Falls	Win Lakitu Cup in Tournament Mode.
Peach's Castle Grounds	Win Blooper Open in Tournament Mode.
Petey Piranha	Complete Shooting, Approaching, and Putting side games on all three difficulty levels.
Shadow Mario	Collect a Best Badge for every hole in Tournament Mode.
Unlock Birdie Challenge Back Nine	Beat the front nine in Birdie Challenge.
Unlock Boo	Earn 50 Best Badges in Tournament Mode.
Unlock Bowser Jr.	Earn all stars in the Ring Mode with any one character.
Unlock Camp Hyrule Tournament	Enter 0EKW5G7U at the Password Tournament Menu.
Unlock Hole-in-One Contest	Press START+Z at the title screen and then go to the Special Tournaments menu.
Unlock Hollywood Video Tournament	Enter BJGQBULZ at the Password Tournament Menu.
Unlock Mario Open	Enter GGAA241H at the Password Tournament Menu.
Unlock Shifting Sands	Win Cheep Cheep Tournament in Tournament Mode.
Unlock Target Bullseye	Enter CEUFPXJ1 at the Password Tournament Menu.

Mario Power Tennis

Enter this code at the Title screen.

Unlockable	Code
Event Games	Hold Z, then press START.

Mat Hoffman's Pro BMX 2

For the following codes, enter the code quickly when "Press Start" appears. A sound confirms correct code entry.

Unlockable	Code
All Music Tracks	L,←,←,→,→,←,A
BMX Costume	Y,X,←,→,←,X
Boston Level in Road Trip Mode	B,↑,↓,↓,↑,B
Chicago Level in Road Trip Mode	B,↑,Y,↑,Y,B
Cory Nastazio's FMV Sequences	R,X,Y,Y,X,X,X,R
Elvis Costume	Y,L,L,↑,↑
Joe Kowalski's FMV Sequences	R,↑,Y,X,↓,R
Kevin Robinson's FMV Sequences	R,Y,X,↓,↑,R

Mat Hoffman's Pro BMX 2 (cont'd)

Unlockable	Code
Las Vegas Level in Road Trip Mode	Ⓑ,[R],←,[L],→,Ⓑ
Level Select	Ⓑ,→,→,Ⓨ,↓,Ⓑ
Los Angeles Level in Road Trip Mode	Ⓑ,←,Ⓐ,Ⓐ,←,Ⓑ
Mat Hoffman's FMV Sequences	[R],←,Ⓨ,←,Ⓨ,←,[R]
Mike Escamilla's FMV Sequences	[R],Ⓨ,Ⓐ,Ⓐ,Ⓨ,Ⓐ,Ⓐ,[R]
Nate Wessel's FMV Sequences	[R],↓,Ⓑ,Ⓨ,↓,Ⓑ,Ⓨ,[R]
New Orleans Level in Road Trip Mode	Ⓑ,↓,→,↑,→,Ⓑ
Play as Big Foot	Ⓨ,→,↑,→,↑,Ⓑ
Play as Day Smith	Ⓨ,↑,↓,↑,↓,Ⓑ
Play as Mime	Ⓨ,←,→,←,→,Ⓐ Alternately, find all the gaps in the game.
Play as Vanessa	Ⓨ,↓,←,←,↓,↓
Play as Volcano	Ⓨ,↑,↑,←,↑,↑,Ⓨ
Portland Level in Road Trip Mode	Ⓨ,Ⓐ,Ⓐ,Ⓑ,Ⓑ,Ⓨ
Rick Thorne's FMV Sequences	[R],[L],[R],[R],[L],[R]
Ruben Alcantara's FMV Sequences	[R],←,→,←,→,←,[R]
Seth Kimbrough's FMV Sequences	[R],↑,↓,Ⓨ,Ⓨ,Ⓨ,[R]
Simon Tabron's FMV Sequences	[L],[Z],[R],[L],[Z],[R]
Tiki Battle Mode	[L],[L],↓,→,Ⓧ,[L]

NOTE

To disable codes, quickly enter almost any code when "Press Start" appears, and add an extra [R] at the end. A different sound confirms correct code entry.

Medal of Honor European Assault

To unlock the ability to enter cheats, go to the Pause Menu and enter the Activate Cheat Entry code.

Unlockable	Code
Active Cheat Entry	Hold [L]+[R] then press ↑,Ⓨ,Ⓨ,Ⓑ,↑,Ⓐ
Player Suicide (SP only)	[L],[Z],[R],↑,Ⓐ,[Z]
Hide HUD	Ⓐ,Ⓨ,→,Ⓐ,[Z],Ⓑ
Kill Nemesis	[L],Ⓨ,[L],[Z],[L],[Z]
Pickup OSS Document	←,Ⓨ,Ⓑ,Ⓐ,↓,Ⓑ
Disable Shellshock	[Z],[R],Ⓧ,Ⓨ,Ⓨ,[L]

Medal of Honor: Frontline

Enter all codes in the Passwords Menu.

Unlockable	Code
Achilles Head	HEADSUP
Bullet Shield	REFLECTOR
Complete Mission with a Gold Star	SEAGULL
Invisible Enemies	HIDENSEEK
Men with Hats	MADHATTER
Mission 2	EAGLE
Mission 3	HAWK
Mission 4	PARROT
Mission 5	DOVE
Mission 6	TOUCAN
Mohton Torpedo	BIGBOOMER
Perfectionist	FLAWLESS
Rubber Grenades	BOUNCE
Silver Bullet Mode	SILVERSHOT
Snipe-O-Rama	SUPERSHOT

Medal of Honor: Rising Sun

Enter all codes in the Passwords Menu.

Unlockable	Code
Achilles Head	CICHLID
All Missions	ALBINO
All Replay Items	Loach
Bullet Shield	GOURAMI
Immortality	BENGAL
Invisible Soldiers	ZEBRA
Men with Hats	TETRA
Perfectionist	BOTIA
Rubber Grenades	MOOR
Silver Bullets	PLECO
Snipe-O-Rama	LELEUPI
Unlimited Ammo	DISCUS

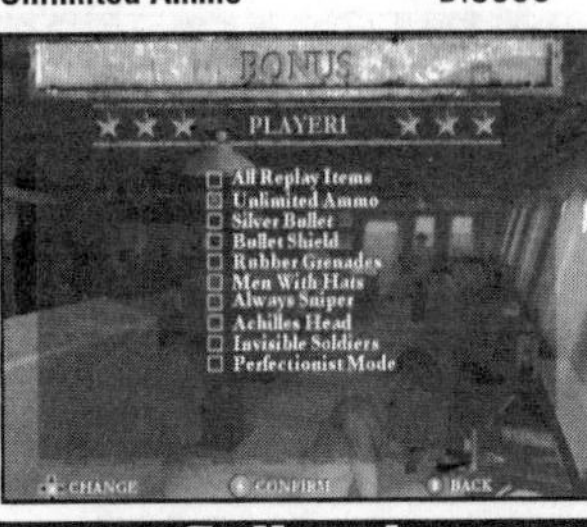

Mega Man Anniversary Collection

Unlockable	Code
Atomic Planet Credits	Defeat the first 3 bosses of Mega Man 1
G4TV Interview/Retrospective	Complete Mega Man 8
Homage to Mega Man Song	Complete Mega Man 2
Mega Man 2: All energy tanks	A5 B1 B3 C4 D2 D3 E1 E4 E5
Mega Man 2: All weapons, items, and 4 energy tanks	A5 B2 B4 C1 C3 C5 D4 D5 E2
Mega Man 2: The Power Fighters	Complete Mega Man 7
Mega Man 3: All weapons, items, 9 energy tanks, and no Dr.	A1 A4 B5 E2 F1 F3
Mega Man 4: All weapons and items	
Mega Man 5: All weapons and items	Blue: B4 D6 F1 Red: C1 D4 F6
Mega Man 6: All weapons and items	B6 D4 F2 F4 F6
Mega Man 7: R.U.S.H., super rocket arm, 999 bolts, 4 Birds, 4 energy and weapon tanks, SP tank, energy bolt, exit, all weapons, shield, robot screw, all bosses dead	7853 5842 2245 7515
Mega Man Drum & Bass Song	Defeat the first three bosses of Mega Man 8
Mega Man Power Fighters	Complete Mega Man 3
Mega Man Radio Cut song	Complete Mega Man 7
Mega Man: The Power Battles	Complete Mega Man 3
Picture Set 1	Complete Mega Man 2
Picture Set 2	Complete Mega Man 4
Picture Set 3	Complete Mega Man 8
Plant Man remix song	Defeat Plant Man in Mega Man 5
Power Battle	Defeat Needle Man in Mega Man 3
Power Fighters	Defeat Junk Man in Mega Man 7

Mega Man Anniversary Collection (cont'd)

Protoman Song	Complete Mega Man 4
Select Jungle Remix	Complete Mega Man 7
Unlock Interview	Make your way to Wily's Tower in Mega Man 8
Wily vs Bass Song	Complete Mega Man 4
Wily's Revenge Song	Complete Mega Man 2
Wily Robots	Blue: A3 B5 D3 F4 Red: A6

Men in Black 2: Alien Escape

At the Start screen, enter any of these codes.

Unlockable	Code
Agent Data	↑,↓,B,R,←,L,→,A,R,X,↑,R
Alien Data	X,L,B,L,↓,Y,R,→,A,←,R,Y
All Power Weapons	↑,↓,A,X,R,Y,Y,←,B,L,L,→
Boss Mode	R,Y,↓,↓,A,L,←,X,→,Y,R,L
Combat Skills Training Levels	X,↑,L,←,Y,A,R,B,→,R,X,B
Full Area Effect	←,A,Y,↑,A,↓,X,L,←,R
Full Beam	←,B,Y,→,L,X,←,R,R,Y
Full Bolt	←,→,↑,↓,R,B,Y,L,←,↓,X,X
Full Homing	→,↑,X,L,←,←,L,←,B,←
Full Spread	L,R,B,L,↓,↑,L,→,←,A
Level Select	R,Y,←,B,X,L,←,↑,A,↓,L,X
Invincibility	→,A,R,Y,↑,L,A,←,L,B,A,R
Never Drop Weapons Level	↓,↑,A,X,↓,↑,A,X,L,L,X,B

Metal Gear Solid: Twin Snakes

Unlockable	Objective
Alex from Eternal Darkness	Lay any book on the ground and look at the cover.
Alternate Ending Theme	Complete the game three times.
Alternate Meryl Demo	Complete the game with the Tuxedo.
Alternate Otacon Demo	Complete the game with the Tuxedo.
Bandana	Complete the game with Meryl.
Boss Survival Mode	Complete the game.
Camera	Find the Camera and complete the game.
Crimson Ninja	Complete the game twice.

Metal Gear Solid: Twin Snakes (cont'd)

Eternal Darkness Poster	Find in the armory room inside one of the lockers.
Gamecube and Wavebird	Find in Otacon's lab. Look on the desk to see a Gamecube and Wavebird.
Mario and Yoshi	In Otacon's lab, on top of one of the monitors, is a statue of Mario and Yoshi.
Meryl Demo	Complete the game with Meryl.
Otacon Demo	Complete the game with Otacon.
Psycho Mantis knows what's on your memory card	If you have Wind Wakers, Mario Sunshine, Smash Bros. Melee, or Eternal Darkness, save on your memory card. Psycho Mantis will tell you all about it while talking to you.
Replenish Health during the Ninja fight	While fighting Ninja, go into first person mode and shoot Mario in the head. You will hear a 1 up noise and you will get some life back.
Sneaking Suit Meryl	Complete the game twice.
Stealth Suit	Complete the game with Otacon.
Tuxedo	Complete the game twice.
ZOE 2 Poster	In Otacon's lab on the wall you'll see a ZOE 2 poster.

Minority Report

To enter these codes select the Special Menu then select the Cheats menu.

Unlockable	Code
All Combos	NINJA
All Movies	DIRECTOR
All Weapons	STRAPPED
Armor	STEELUP
Baseball Bat	SLUGGER
Bouncy Men	BOUNZMEN
Clown Skin	SCARYCLOWN
Concept Art	SKETCHPAD
Convict Skin	JAILBREAK
Do Not Select	DONOTSEL
Dramatic Finish	STYLIN
Ending	WIMP
First Person Mode	FPSSTYLE
GI John Skin	GNRLINFINTRY
Health	BUTTERUP
Infinite Ammo	MRJUAREZ
Invincibility	LRGARMS
Level Warp	PASSKEY
Level Skip	QUITTER
Lizard Skin	HISSSS
Moseley Skin	HAIRLOSS
Nara Skin	WEIGHTGAIN
Nikki Skin	BIGLIPS
Pain Arena	MAXIMUMHURT
Rag Doll	CLUMSY
Robot Skin	MRROBOTO
Super Damage	SPINICH
Super John Skin	SUPERJOHN
Wreck the Joint	CLUTZ
Zombie Skin	IAMSODEAD

Mission Impossible: Operation Surma

Unlockable	Code
Level Select	In the Profiles Menu highlight Jasmine Curry and press L+R+Y+X at the same time.

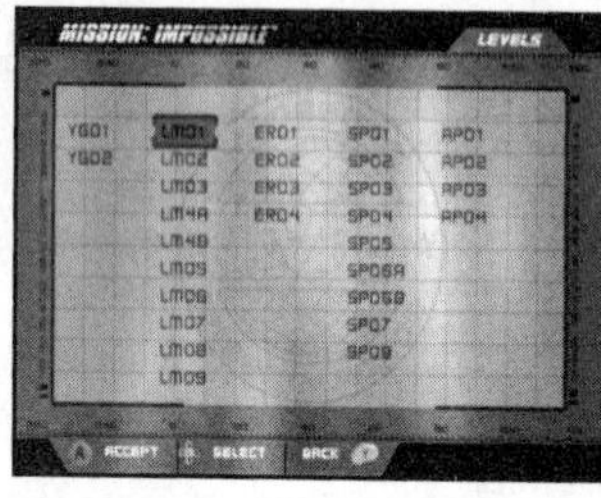

MLB Slugfest 2004

Cheat Mode	Press B, Y, and X to change the icons in the first, second, and third boxes respectively at the match-up screen. The numbers in the following list indicate the number of times you press each button. After the icons change, press the D-pad in the indicated direction to enable the code. For example, to enter 1-2-3 ←, press X, Y (2), B (3), ←.

Unlockable	Code
16" Softball	2-4-3 ↓
Alien Team	2-3-1 ↓
Atlantis Stadium	3-2-1 ←
Big Head	2-0-0 →
Blade Bat	0-0-2 ↑
Bobble Head Team	1-3-3 ↓
Bone Bat	0-0-1 ↑
Casey Team	2-3-3 ↓
Cheats Disabled	1-1-1 ↓
Coliseum Stadium	3-3-3 ↑
Dolphin Team	1-0-2 ↓
Dwarf Team	1-0-3 ↓
Eagle Team	2-1-2 →
Empire Park Stadium	3-2-1 →
Evil Clown Team	2-1-1 ↓
Extended Time for Codes	3-0-3 ↑
Forbidden City Stadium	3-3-3 ←
Gladiator Team	1-1-3 ↓
Horse Team	2-1-1 →
Ice Bat	0-0-3 ↑
Lion Team	2-2-0 →
Little League	1-0-1 ↓

Unlockable	Code
Log Bat	0-0-4 ↑
Mace Bat	0-0-4 ←
Max Batting	3-0-0 ←
Max Power	0-3-0 ←
Max Speed	0-0-3 ←
Midway Park Stadium	3-2-1 ↓
Minotaur Team	1-1-0 ↓
Monument Stadium	3-3-3 ↓
Napalitano Team	2-3-2 ↓
Olshan Team	2-2-2 ↓
Pinto Team	2-1-0 →
Rivera Team	2-2-2 ↑
Rocket Park Stadium	3-2-1 ↑
Rodeo Clown	1-3-2 ↓
Rubber Ball	2-4-2 ↑
Scorpion Team	1-1-2 ↓
Spike Bat	0-0-5 ↑
Team Terry Fitzgerald	3-3-3 →
Team Todd McFarlane	2-2-2 →
Tiny Head	2-0-0 ←
Unlimited Turbo	4-4-4 ↓
Wiffle Bat	0-0-4 →

Mortal Kombat: Deadly Alliance

You can do fatalities from anywhere on screen. The codes to perform fatalities for each character are listed below.

Unlockable	Code
Bo Rai Cho (Belly Flop)	Press Away x (3), ↓,↓,↓
Cyrax (Smasher)	Press Toward x (2), ↑,Ⓨ
Drahmin (Iron Bash)	Press Away, Toward x (2), ↓,Ⓐ
Frost (Freeze Shatter)	Press Toward, Away, ↑,↓,Ⓑ
Hsu Hao (Laser Slice)	Press Toward, Away, ↓,↓,Ⓨ
Jax (Head Stomp)	Press ↓, Toward x (2), ↓,Ⓨ
Johnny Cage (Brain Ripper)	Press Away, Toward x (2), ↓,Ⓨ
Kano (Heart Grab)	Press Toward, Ⓒ x (2), ↓,Ⓑ
Kenshi (Telekinetic Crush)	Press Toward, Away, Toward, ↓,Ⓐ
Kitana (Kiss of Doom)	Press ↓, ↑, Toward x (2), Ⓨ
Kung Lao (Hat Throw)	Press ↓, ↑, Away, Ⓐ
Li Mei (Crush Kick)	Press Toward x (2), ↓, Toward, Ⓧ
Mavado (Kick Thrust)	Press Away x (2), ↑,↑,Ⓑ
Nitara (Blood Thirst)	Press ↑, Toward, Ⓑ
Quan Chi (Neck Stretch)	Press Away (2), Toward, Away, Ⓐ
Raiden (Electrocution)	Press Away, Toward x (3), Ⓐ
Reptile (Acid Shower)	Press ↑,↑,↑, Toward, Ⓐ
Scorpion (Spear)	Press Away x (2), ↓, Away + Ⓧ
Shang Tsung (Soul Steal)	Press ↑,↓,↑,↓,Ⓨ
Sonya (Kiss)	Press Away, Toward x (2), ↓,Ⓨ
Sub Zero (Spine Rip)	Press Away, Toward x (2), ↓,Ⓐ

MVP Baseball 2004

Enter the following codes as player names.

Unlockable	Code
Horrible Player	Erik Kiss
Huge Cap on your player	john prosen
Player will hold a huge bat	jacob paterson

Unlockable	Objective
Al Kaline	2500 MVP Points
Anaheim Angels 1986 Jersey	250 MVP Points
Astrodome	2500 MVP Points
Atlanta Braves 1974 Jersey	500 MVP Points
Babe Ruth	5000 MVP Points
Baltimore Orioles 1971 Jerseys	500 MVP Points
Billy Williams	2500 MVP Points
Bob Feller	3500 MVP Points
Bob Gibson	4500 MVP Points
Bob Lemon	3000 MVP Points
Boston Red Sox 1903 Jerseys	1000 MVP Points
Brooklyn Dodgers 1941 Jerseys	750 MVP Points
Brooks Robinson	3500 MVP Points
Catfish Hunter	3000 MVP Points
Chicago Cubs 1954 Jerseys	750 MVP Points
Chicago White Sox 1919 Jerseys	1000 MVP Points

PSP

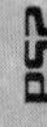

Xbox

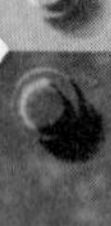

PS2

GC

GBA

MVP Baseball 2004 (cont'd)

Cincinatti Reds 1970 Jerseys	500 MVP Points
Cleveland Indians 1975 Jerseys	500 MVP Points
Crosley Field	2500 MVP Points
Cy Young	4500 MVP Points
Detroit Tigers 1906 Jerseys	750 MVP Points
Early Wynn	3500 MVP Points
Eddie Matthews	4000 MVP Points
Ferguson Jenkins	2500 MVP Points
Forbes Field	5000 MVP Points
Gaylord Perry	3500 MVP Points
Griffith Stadium	3000 MVP Points
Hal Newhouser	2500 MVP Points
Harmon Killebrew	3500 MVP Points
Honus Wagner	4500 MVP Points
Houston Astros 1986 Jerseys	250 MVP Points
Hoyt Wilhelm	3000 MVP Points
Jackie Robinson	5000 MVP Points
Jim Palmer	4000 MVP Points
Jimmie Foxx	4000 MVP Points
Joe Morgan	4000 MVP Points
Juan Marichal	3500 MVP Points
Kansas City Royals 1985 Jerseys	250 MVP Points
Larry Doby	3000 MVP Points
Lou Brock	3000 MVP Points
Lou Gehrig	4500 MVP Points
Luis Aprarico	3000 MVP Points
Mel Ott	3500 MVP Points
Mike Schmidt	4000 MVP Points
Milwaukee Brewers 1982 Jerseys	250 MVP Points
Minnesota Twins 1977 Jerseys	500 MVP Points
Montreal Expos 1981 Jerseys	350 MVP Points
New York Giants 1954 Jerseys	750 MVP Points
New York Mets 1986 Jerseys	350 MVP Points
New York Yankees 1927 Jerseys	1000 MVP Points
Nolan Ryan	4500 MVP Points
Oakland Athletics 1972 Jerseys	500 MVP Points
Orlando Cepeda	3500 MVP Points
Pee Wee Reese	3500 MVP Points
Phil Niekro	2500 MVP Points
Phil Rizzuto	3000 MVP Points
Philadelphia Phillies 1980 Jerseys	500 MVP Points
Pittsburgh Pirates 1916 Jerseys	750 MVP Points
Pittsburgh Pirates 1979 Jerseys	500 MVP Points
Ralph Kiner	2500 MVP Points
Reggie Jackson	4500 MVP Points
Richie Ashburn	2500 MVP Points
Robin Roberts	2500 MVP Points
Robin Yount	4000 MVP Points

MVP Baseball 2004 (cont'd)

Unlockable	Points
Rod Carew	3500 MVP Points
Rollie Fingers	3500 MVP Points
Roy Campanella	4500 MVP Points
San Diego Padres 1984 Jerseys	350 MVP Points
Satchel Paige	4500 MVP Points
Seattle Mariners 1981 Jerseys	350 MVP Points
Shibe Park Stadium	4000 MVP Points
Sparky Anderson	4500 MVP Points
Sportsman's Park	4000 MVP Points
St. Louis Cardinals 1934 Jerseys	750 MVP Points
Texas Rangers 1976 Jerseys	500 MVP Points
The Polo Grounds	5000 MVP Points
Tiger Stadium	3000 MVP Points
Tom Seaver	4000 MVP Points
Tommy Lasorda	4500 MVP Points
Toronto Blue Jays 1992 Jerseys	250 MVP Points
Ty Cobb	5000 MVP Points
Walter Johnson	4500 MVP Points
Warren Spahn	4000 MVP Points
Washington Senators 1913 Jerseys	1000 MVP Points
Whitey Ford	3500 MVP Points
Willie McCovey	4500 MVP Points
Willie Stargell	4000 MVP Points
Yogi Berra	4500 MVP Points

MVP Baseball 2005

Enter these codes as the name of a new player.

Unlockable	Code
Bone Scaling Cheat	Kenny Lee
St. Patrick's Day Jersey for the Red Sox	Neverlose Sight

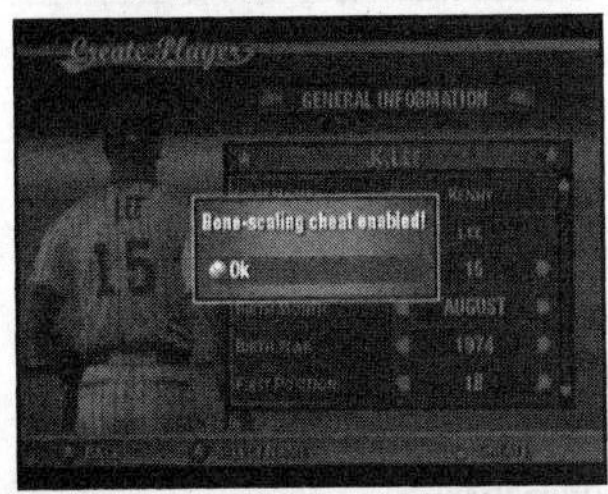

NASCAR Dirt to Daytona

Unlockable	Code
$10,000	When at the Main Menu press ↑, ↓, ←, →, Z, ←, ←.

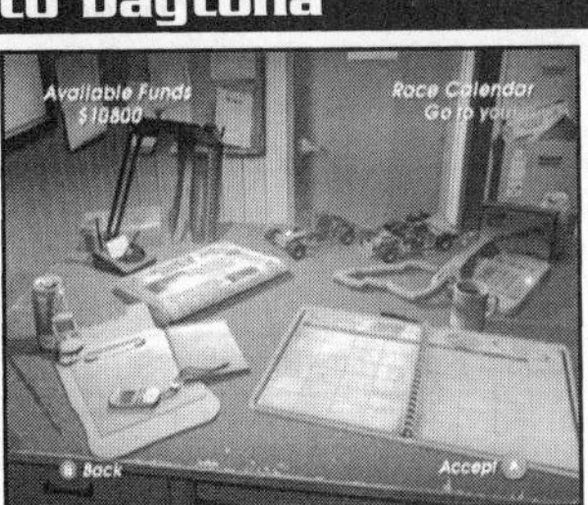

PSP
Xbox
PS2
GC
GBA

NBA Live 2003

To enter these codes, go to Create a Player and enter these passwords as your last name.

Unlockable	Code
B-Rich	DOLLABILLS
Busta Rhymes	FLIPMODE
DJ Clue	MIXTAPES
Ghetto Fabulous	GHETTOFAB
Hot Karl	CALIFORNIA
Just Blaze	GOODBEATS

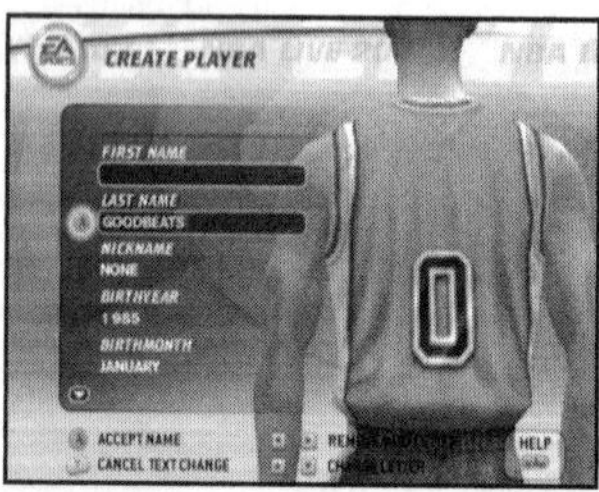

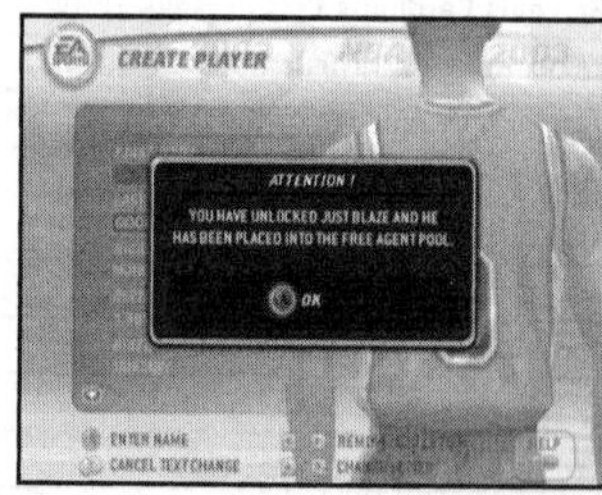

NBA Live 2004

In the Create a Player screen, enter these passwords as last names to unlock the extra players.

Player	Code
Aleksander Pavlovic	WHSUCPOI
Andreas Glyniadakis	POCKDLEK
Carlos Delfino	SDFGURKL
James Lang	NBVKSMCN
Jermaine Dupri	SOSODEF
Kyle Korver	OEISNDLA
Malick Badiane	SKENXIDO
Mario Austin	POSNEGHX
Matt Bonner	BBVDKCVM
Nedzad Sinanovic	ZXDSDRKE
Paccelis Morlende	QWPOASZX
Remon Van De Hare	ITNVCJSD
Rick Rickert	POILKJMN
Sani Becirovic	ZXCCVDRI
Sofoklis Schortsanitis	IOUBFDCJ
Szymon Szewczyk	POIOIJIS
Tommy Smith	XCFWQASE
Xue Yuyang	WMZKCOI

To enter these codes, go into the NBA Live menu, then enter the NBA Codes menu.

Unlockable	Code
15,000 Store Points	87843H5F9P
All Hardwood Classic Jerseys	725JKUPLMM
All NBA Gear	ERT9976KJ3
All Team Gear	YREY5625WQ
All Shoes	POUY985GY5
Air Bounds (Black/White/Blue)	7YSS0292KE
Air Bounds (White/Black)	JA807YAM20
Air Bounds (White/Green)	84HHST61QI
Air Flight 89 (Black/White)	FG874JND84
Air Flight 89 (White/Black)	63RBVC7423
Air Flight 89 (White/Red)	GF9845JHR4
Air Flightposite 2 (Blue/Grey)	2389JASE3E
Air Flightposite (White/Black/Gray)	74FDH7K945
Air Flightposite (White/Black)	6HJ874SFJ7
Air Flightposite (Yellow/Black/White)	MN54BV45C2
Air Foamposite 1 (Blue)	0P5465UX12
Air Foamposite 1 (White/Black/Red)	D0D843HH7F

NBA Live 2004 (cont'd)

Shoe	Code
Air Foamposite Pro (Blue/Black)	DG56TRF446
Air Foamposite Pro (Black/Gray)	3245AFSD45
Air Foamposite Pro (Red/Black)	DSAKF38422

Shoe	Code
Air Force Max (Black)	F84N845H92
Air Force Max (White/Black/Blue)	985KJF98KJ
Air Force Max (White/Red)	8734HU8FFF
Air Hyperflight (White)	14TGU7DEWC
Air Hyperflight (Black/White)	WW44YhU592
Air Hyperflight (Blue/White)	A0K374HF8S
Air Hyperflight (Yellow/Black)	JCX93LSS88
Air Jordan 11: (Black/Red/White)	GF64H76ZX5
Air Jordan 11: (Black/Varsity Royal/White)	HJ987RTGFA
Air Jordan 11 (Cool Grey)	GF75HG6332
Air Jordan 11 (White)	HG76HN765S
Air Jordan 11 (White/Black)	A2S35TH7H6
Air Jordan 3 (White)	G9845HJ8F4
Air Jordan 3 (White/Clay)	435SGF555Y
Air Jordan 3 (White/Fire Red)	RE6556TT90
Air Jordan 3 (White/True Blue)	FDS9D74J4F
Air Jordan 3 (Black/White/Gray)	CVJ554TJ58
Air Max2 CB (Black/White)	87HZXGFIU8
Air Max2 CB (White/Red)	4545GFKJIU
Air Max2 Uptempo (Black/White/Blue)	NF8745J87F
Air Max Elite (Black)	A4CD54T7TD
Air Max Elite (White/Black)	966ERTFG65
Air Max Elite (White/Blue)	FD9KN48FJF
Air Zoom Flight (Gray/White)	367UEY6SN
Air Zoom Flight (White/Blue)	92387HD077
Nike Blazer (Kaki)	W3R57U9NB2
Nike Blazer (Tan/White/Blue)	DCT5YHMU90
Nike Blazer (White/Orange/Blue)	4G66JU99XS
Nike Blazer (Black)	XCV6456NNL
Nike Shox BB4 (Black)	WE424TY563
Nike Shox BB4 (White/Black)	23ERT85LP9
Nike Shox BB4 (White/Light Purple)	668YYTRB12
Nike Shox BB4 (White/Red)	424TREU777
Nike Shox VCIII (Black)	SDFH764FJU
Nike Shox VCIII (White/Black/Red)	5JHD367JJT
Zoom Generation (White/Black/Red)	23LBJNUMB1
Zoom Generation (Black/Red/White)	LBJ23CAVS1

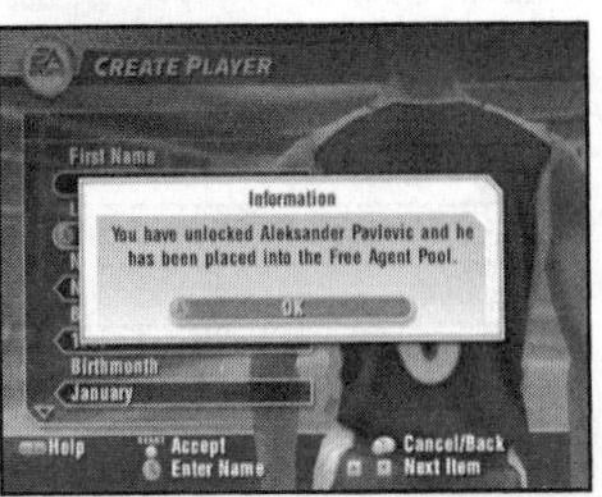

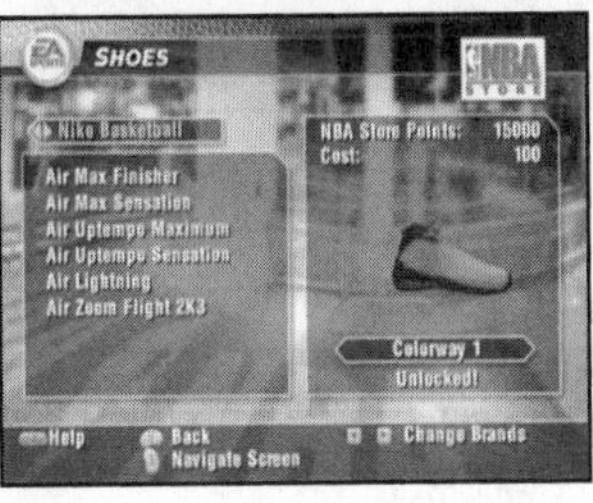

PSP Xbox PS2 GC GBA

NBA Live 2005

Go to My NBA Live, EA Sports Lounge, NBA Codes to enter these codes.

Unlockable	Code
50,000 Dynasty Points	YISS55CZ0E
All Classics Hardwood Jerseys	PRYI234N0B
All Shoes	FHM389HU80
All Team Gear	1NVDR89ER2

Unlockable Shoes	Code
Nike Air Huarache	VNBA60230T
Nike BG Rollout	0984ADF90P
Nike Shox Elite	2388HDFCBJ
Nike Air Unlimited	XVLJD9895V
Zoom Lebron II Shoes	1KENZO23XZ
Zoom Generation Low	234SDJF9W4

Unlockable Team	Code
Atlanta Hawks 2004-05 Alternate	HDI834NN9N
Boston Celtics 2004-05 Alternate	XCV43MGMDS
Dallas Mavericks2004-05 Alternate	AAPSEUD09U
Golden State Warriors 2004-05 Alternate	NAVNY29548

NBA Street

After entering one of the following icon codes, press enter direction on the D-Pad to complete code entry. Enter the codes at the Versus screen before a game.

Unlockable	Code
ABA Ball	Basketball, Basketball, Turntable, Shoe
ABA Socks	Shoe, Shoe, Shoe, Shoe
Athletic Joe "The Show"	Turntable, Turntable, Turntable, Shoe
Authentic Uniforms	Basketball, Shoe, Turntable, Turntable
Beach Ball	Basketball, Basketball, Turntable, Turntable
Big Heads	Shoe, Shoe, Shoe, Backboard
Captain Quicks	Shoe, Turntable, Backboard, Basketball
Casual Uniforms	Basketball, Shoe, Megaphone, Megaphone
EA Big Ball	Basketball, Basketball, Megaphone, Turntable
EA Big Pacific Boulevard Court	Complete Street School mode training.
Easy Distance Shots	Basketball, Backboard, Backboard, Basketball
Explosive Rims	Turntable, Turntable, Turntable, Megaphone
Fewer Blocks	Enter Basketball, Turntable, Shoe, Basketball
Fewer Gamebreakers	Shoe, Turntable, Turntable, Basketball
Fewer Steals	Basketball, Shoe, Backboard, Basketball
Harder Distance Shots	Basketball, Turntable, Turntable, Basketball
Mad Hands	Shoe, Backboard, Turntable, Basketball
Medicine Ball	Basketball, Basketball, Shoe, Shoe.
Mega Dunking	Basketball, Megaphone, Megaphone, Basketball
More Gamebreakers	Shoe, Backboard, Backboard, Basketball
No Alley-Oops	Basketball, Backboard, Turntable, Basketball

NBA Street (cont'd)

No Auto Replays	Turntable, Turntable, Turntable, Turntable
No Cheats	Basketball, Shoe, Basketball, Shoe
No Dunks	Turntable, Backboard, Shoe, Basketball
No Gamebreakers	Shoe, Megaphone, Megaphone, Basketball
No HUD Display	Turntable, Turntable, Shoe, Turntable
No Juice	Turntable, Backboard, Backboard, Basketball
No Player Indicators	Turntable, Turntable, Backboard, Turntable
No Shot Clock	Shoe, Shoe, Shoe, Basketball as a code
No Shot Indicator	Turntable, Turntable, Turntable, Backboard
No Two-Pointers	Basketball, Turntable, Backboard, Basketball.
Nufx Ball	Basketball, Basketball, Backboard, Megaphone
NYC Legends Team	Get 30 wins in any mode.
Player Names	Turntable, Turntable, Basketball, Turntable
Soccer Ball	Basketball, Basketball, Megaphone, Megaphone
Springtime Joe "The Show"	Turntable, Turntable, Turntable, Basketball
Sticky Fingers	Backboard, Shoe, Turntable, Basketball
Summertime Joe "The Show"	Turntable, Turntable, Megaphone, Turntable
Super Swats	Backboard, Turntable, Shoe, Basketball
Tiny Heads	Shoe, Shoe, Shoe, Megaphone
Tiny Players	Shoe, Shoe, Shoe, Turntable
Ultimate Power	Turntable, Shoe, Backboard, Basketball
Unlimited Turbo	Turntable, Shoe, Shoe, Basketball
Volleyball	Basketball, Basketball, Backboard, Backboard.
WNBA Ball	Basketball, Basketball, Shoe, Backboard

Unlockable	Objective
Biggs and Beacon Hill Court	Play the City Circuit and reach the Region 1 City Challenge. Defeat Biggs' team to unlock him as a selectable player and to unlock the Beacon Hill court.
Bonafide and Broad Street Court	Play the City Circuit and reach the Region 2 City Challenge. Defeat Bonafide's team to unlock him as a selectable player and to unlock the Broad Street court.
Custom Team	Complete the game in single-player mode with the Street Legends team under the "expert difficulty" setting. You can now create a team of 16 players of your choice.
DJ and Venice Beach Court	Play the City Circuit and reach the Region 4 City Challenge. Defeat DJ's team to unlock him as a selectable player and to unlock the Venice Beach court.
Drake and the Yard Court	Play the City Circuit and reach the Region 3 City Challenge. Defeat Drake's team to unlock him as a selectable player and to unlock the Yard court.
NBA Superstars	Play the City Challenge and defeat an NBA team to unlock a player from their roster.
Stretch and Rucker Park Court	Play the City Circuit and reach the Region 2 City Challenge. Defeat Stretch's team to unlock him as a selectable player and to unlock Rucker Park court.
Takashi and Yakatomni Plaza Court	Play the City Circuit and reach the Region 5 City Challenge. Defeat Takashi's team to unlock him as a selectable player and to unlock Yakatomni Plaza court.

NBA Street (cont'd)

Team 3LW	Get 20 wins in any mode.
Team Big	Get 10 wins in any mode.
Team Dream	Win (complete all the objectives). Hold the Court mode to unlock a team that includes Graylien Alien, Magma Man, and Yeti Snowman.
Team Street Legends	Win the City Circuit to unlock the Street Legends team. This team includes Biggs, Bonafide, Drake, DJ, Takashi, Stretch, and the player that you did the best with throughout the season.

NBA Street Vol 2

For the following unlockables, hold L, then enter code.

Unlockable	Code
All Quicks	Y,X,Y,B
Alternate Ball (NBA or ABA)	X,B,X,B
Always Legend Trails	Y,Y,Y,B
Big Heads	X,B,B,X
Easy 2-Pointers	Y,X,B,Y
Explosive Rims	X,X,X,Y
Hard 2-Pointers	Y,B,X,Y
No Counters	Y,Y,X,X
No Hud	B,X,X,X
Street Kids	Y,Y,X,B
Unlimited Turbo	B,B,Y,Y
WNBA Ball	X,Y,Y,X

NCAA Football 2004

After you score a touchdown, press these button combos to see the specific celebration.

Unlockable	Code
Bow	L+Y
Display Ball	R+Y
Dunk over Goalpost	R+B
Heisman Pose	L+A
Kick Ball into Crowd	R+X
Spike Ball	L+B
Spike Ball, then Shrug	L+X
Throw Ball into Crowd	R+A

NCAA Football 2005

Go to "My NCAA". Choose "Pennant Collection" and press Select to enter these codes.

Unlockable	Code
1st and 15	THANKS
Baylor Ratings Boost	SIC EM
Blink (ball is spotted short for opponent)	FOR
Boing (opponent drops more passes)	REGISTERING
Butter Fingers	WITH EA
Crossed The Line	TIBURON
Cuffed Cheat	EA SPORTS
Illinois Ratings Boost	OSKEE WOW

NCAA Football 2005 (cont'd)

Jumbalaya	HIKE
Molasses	HOME FIELD
Ouch	BLITZ
Quarterback Dud	ELITE 11
Stiffed	NCAA
Take Your Time	FOOTBALL
Texas Tech Ratings Boost	FIGHT
Thread The Needle	2005
What A Hit	BLITZ

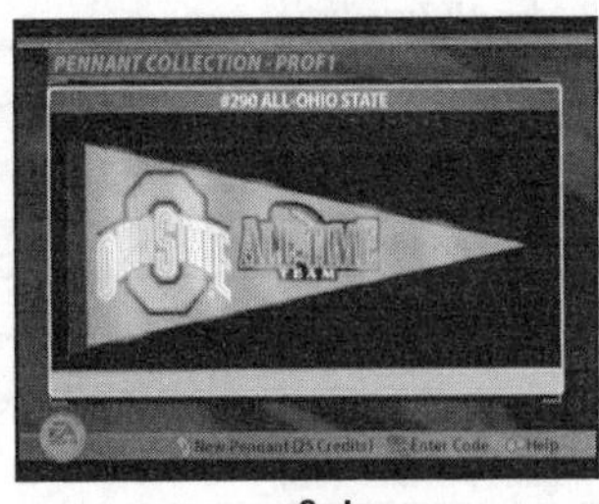

Unlockable Team	Code
2003 All-Americans	FUMBLE
Alabama All-Time Team	ROLL TIDE
Arizona Mascot Team	BEAR DOWN
Arkansas All-Time Team	WOOPIGSOOIE
Auburn All-Time Team	WAR EAGLE
Badgers All-Time Team	U RAH RAH
Clemson All-Time Team	DEATH VALLEY
Colorado All-Time Team	GLORY
Florida All-Time Team	GREAT TO BE
Florida State All-Time Team	UPRISING
Georgia All-Time Team	HUNKER DOWN
Georgia Tech Mascot Team	RAMBLINWRECK
Iowa All-Time Team	ON IOWA
Iowa State Mascot Team	RED AND GOLD
Kansas Mascot Team	ROCK CHALK
Kansas State All-Time Team	VICTORY
Kentucky Mascot Team	ON ON UK
LSU All-Time Team	GEAUX TIGERS
Miami All-Time Team	RAISING CANE
Michigan All-Time Team	GO BLUE
Michigan State Mascot Team	GO GREEN
Minnesota Mascot Team	RAH RAH RAH
Mississippi State All-Time Team	HAIL STATE
Missouri Mascot Team	MIZZOU RAH
Nebraska All-Time Team	GO BIG RED
North Carolina All-Time Team	RAH RAH
North Carolina State Mascot Team	GO PACK

NCAA Football 2005 (cont'd)

Notre Dame All-Time Team	GOLDEN DOMER
NU Mascot Team	GO CATS
Ohio State All-Time Team	KILLER NUTS
Oklahoma All-Time Team	BOOMER
Oklahoma State All-Time Team	GO POKES
Ole Miss Mascot Team	HOTTY TOTTY
Oregon All-Time Team	QUACK ATTACK
Penn State All-Time Team	WE ARE
Pittsburgh All-Time Team	LETS GO PITT
Purdue All-Time Team	BOILER UP
South Carolina Mascot Team	GO CAROLINA
Syracuse All-Time Team	ORANGE CRUSH
Tennessee All-Time Team	BIG ORANGE
Texas A&M All-Time Team	GIG EM
Texas All-Time Team	HOOK EM
UCLA All-Time Team	MIGHTY
USC All-Time Team	FIGHT ON
Virginia All-Time Team	WAHOOS
Virginia Tech All-Time Team	TECH TRIUMPH
Wake Forest Mascot Team	GO DEACS GO
Washington All-Time Team	BOW DOWN
Washington Sate Mascot Team	ALL HAIL
West Virginia Mascot Team	HAIL WV

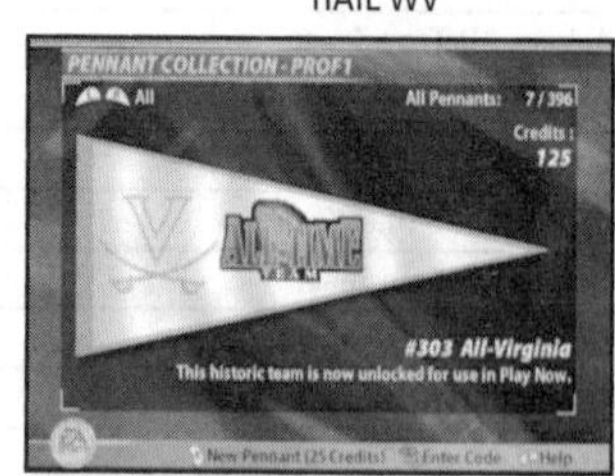

Need for Speed Underground

Enter the following codes at the Main Menu.

Unlockable	Code
All Circuit Tracks	↓, R, R, R, X, X, X, Z
All Drag Tracks	←, ←, ←, ←, →, X, R, Y
All Sprint Tracks	↑, X, X, X, R, ↓, ↓, ↓
Drift Physics	R, ↑, ↑, ↑, ↓, ↓, ↓, L

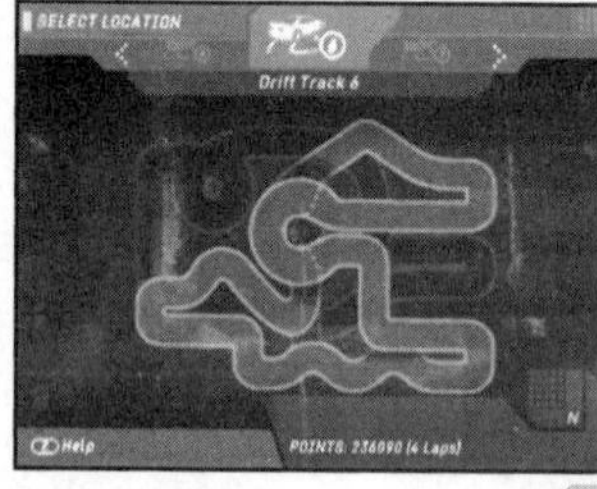

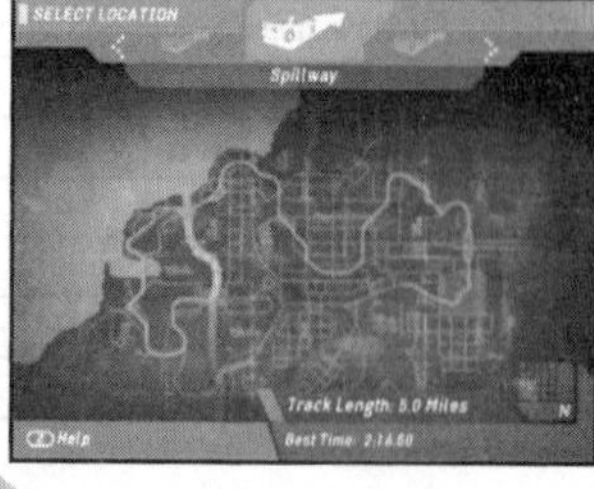

Need for Speed Underground 2

Enter the following codes at the Main Menu.

Unlockable	Code
$1,000 for Career Mode	←, ←, →, Ⓧ, Ⓧ, →, Ⓛ, Ⓡ
Best Buy Vinyl	↑, ↓, ↑, ↓, ↓, ↑, →, ←

NFL Blitz 20-03

Enter these codes in the Vs. Screen. Press Buttons Ⓛ, Ⓡ, and Ⓐ the number of times mentioned. Then push the directional pad in the direction it tells you.

Unlockable	Code
Allow Out of Bounds	2 1 1 ←
Always the QB (when playing a human opponent)	2 2 2 ←
Always the Receiver (when playing a human opponent)	2 2 2 →
Arctic Stadium	0 3 4 ↓
Armageddon Team	5 4 3 →
Auto Icon Passing	0 0 3 ↑
Big Feet	0 2 5 →
Big Head	2 0 0 →
Big Head Team	2 0 3 →
Bilder Team	3 1 0 ↑
Brew Dawgs Team	4 3 2 ↓
Butter Fingaz	3 4 5 ↑
Chimp Mode	0 2 5 ↑
Chrome Ball	0 3 0 ↓
Classic Ball	0 3 0 ←
Clear Weather	1 2 3 →
Central Park	0 3 3 →
Crunch Team	4 0 3 →
Extra Play for Offense	3 3 3 ↓
Extra Time	0 0 1 →
Fast Passes	2 4 0 ←
Faster Running	0 3 2 ←
Fog	2 3 2 ↓
Gamer Team	5 0 1 ↑
Huge Head	1 4 5 ←
Infinite Turbo	4 1 5 ↑
Midway Team	2 5 3 →
Neo Tokyo Team	3 4 4 ↓
No Auto Icon Passing	0 0 3 ↓
No CPU Assist	0 1 2 ↓
No First Downs	2 1 0 ↑
No Highlight on players	3 2 1 ↓
No Interceptions	3 5 5 ↑
No Punts	1 4 1 ↑
No Random Fumbles	5 2 3 ↓
No Replays	5 5 4 →
Noftle Mode	3 2 5 ↑
Power-Up Offense/Defense	4 1 2 ↑
Power-Up Lineman	5 2 1 ↑
Rain	5 5 5 →
Rollos Team	2 5 4 ↑
See more Field	0 2 1 →
Showtime Mode	3 5 1 →
Smart CPU Teammates	3 1 4 ↓
Snow	5 5 5 ←
Super Blitz	0 4 5 ↑
Super Field Goal	1 2 3 ←
Tournament Mode	1 1 1 ↓
Training Grounds	0 3 5 ↑

NFL Blitz 20-03 (cont'd)

TIP

For extra time to enter codes, use the following... err... um... code: 2 1 2 →.

To unlock these hidden characters enter the ID and Pin codes.

Unlockable	Code
Bear Team	BEAR 1985
Clown Team	CLOWN 1974
Cowboy Team	COWBOY 1996
Deer Team	DEER 1997
Dolphin Team	DOLPHINE 1972
Eagle Team	EAGLE 1981
Horse team	HORSE 1999
Lion Team	LION 1963
Patriot Team	PATRIOT 2002
Pinto Team	PINTO 1966
Pirate Team	PIRATE 2001
Ram Team	2000
Tiger Team	TIGER 1977
Viking Team	VIKING 1977

NFL Street

Enter the following codes as profile names.

Unlockable	Code
All Fields	Travel
NFL Legends Team	Classic
Team Kay Slay	KaySlay
Team X-ecutioners	Excellent

NHL Hitz 2002

Press Ⓑ, Ⓨ, and Ⓧ to change the icons in the first, second, and third boxes, respectively, at the match-up screen. The numbers in the following list indicate the number of times each button is pressed. After the icons have been changed, press the D-Pad in the indicated direction to enable the code. For example, to enter 1-2-3 ←, press Ⓑ,Ⓨ,Ⓨ,Ⓧ,Ⓧ,Ⓧ,←.

Unlockable	Code
Big Head Player	2-0-0 →
Big Head Team	2-2-0 ←
Big Hits	2-3-4 ↓
Big Puck	1-2-1 ↑
Bulldozer Puck	2-1-2 ←
Disable Previous Code	0-1-0 ↓
Domino Effect	0-1-2 →
First to Seven Wins	3-2-3 ←
Hitz Time	1-0-4 →
Hockey Ball	1-3-3 ←
Huge Head Player	3-0-0 →
Huge Head Team	3-3-0 ←
Huge Puck	3-2-1 ↑
Late Hits	3-2-1 ↓

NHL Hitz 2002 (cont'd)

Code	Entry
More Time to Enter Codes	3-3-3 →
No Crowd	2-1-0 →
No Fake Shots	4-2-4 ↓
No One-Timers	2-1-3 ←
No Puck Out	1-1-1 ↓
Pinball Boards	4-2-3 →
Rain Mode	1-4-1 ←
Show Shot Speed	1-0-1 ↑
Show the Team's Hot Spot	2-0-1 ↑
Skills Versus	2-2-2 ↓
Snow Mode	1-2-1 ←
Tennis Ball	1-3-2 ↓
Turbo Boost	0-0-2 ↑
Unlimited Turbo	4-1-3 →
Win Fights for Goals	2-0-2 ←

Outlaw Golf

Unlockable	Objective
Atlas Driver	Complete the Stroke Me event.
Atlas Fairway Woods	Complete the Not-So-Goodfellas event.
Atlas Irons	Complete the High Rollers event.
Atlas Putter (Black)	Complete the All the Marbles event.
Atlas Putter Gold	Complete the Suave's Revenge event.
Atlas Wedge	Complete the Pretty in Pink event.
Beating Token	Hold L and press Z, X, Z, Z, X during gameplay. A sound confirms correct code entry. Note: This only works if you do not have any Beating Tokens.
Boiler Maker Driver	Complete the Money Talks event.
Boiler Maker Fairway Woods	Complete the Hole Lotta Luv event.
Boiler Maker Irons	Complete the Jersey Ball Bash event.
Boiler Maker Putter	Complete the Sun Stroke event.
Boiler Maker Wedge	Complete the Back 9 Shuffle event.
C.C.	Complete the Hot, Hot, Hot event.
Cincinnati Balls	Complete the Rough Riders event.
Cincinnati Driver	Complete the Ol' Blood and Guts event.
Cincinnati Fairway Woods	Complete the Full Frontal event.
Cincinnati Irons	Complete the Stroke Me Again event.
Cincinnati Wedge	Complete the Blister in the Sun event.
Doc Diggler	Complete the Ladies Night event.
Ecstasy Balls	Complete the Scorched Earth Classic event.
Ecstasy Putter	Complete the Motley Crew event.
Killer Miller	Complete the Test Drive event.
Larger Ball	Hold L and press ↑, ↑, ↑, ↓ during gameplay. A sound confirms correct code entry. Repeat this code to increase its effect.
Master Code	Start a new game, and enter Golf_Gone_Wild as a case-sensitive name to unlock all characters, clubs, and stages. Note: Include the underscores in the name.
Nelson Balls	Complete the Different Strokes event.
No Wind	Hold L and press ↑, ←, ↓, →, ↑, ←, ↓, →, X, X during gameplay. A sound confirms correct code entry.
Python Driver	Complete the Heat Rash Invitational event.
Python Fairway Woods	Complete the Tough Crowd event.

Outlaw Golf (cont'd)

Python Irons	Complete the A Hole in the Sun event.
Python Wedge	Complete the Garden State Stroke Fest event.
Scrummy	Complete the Odd Ball Classic event.
Smaller Ball	Hold Ⓛ and press ↓,↓,↓,↑ during gameplay. A sound confirms correct code entry. Repeat this code to increase its effect.
Suave's Balls	Complete the Garden State Menage a Trois event.
Suki	Complete the Baked on the Bone event.
Trixie	Complete the Chicks with Sticks event.

Pac-Man World 2

Unlockable	Objective
Ms. Pac-Man Mini-Game	Collect 180 tokens during gameplay to unlock the classic Ms. Pac-Man arcade game.
Music Test	Collect 60 tokens during gameplay to unlock the "Jukebox" option.
Pac-Attack Mini-Game	Collect 30 tokens during gameplay to unlock the classic Pac-Attack arcade game.
Pac-Man Mini-Game	Collect 10 tokens during gameplay to unlock the classic Pac-Man arcade game.
Pac-Mania	Collect 100 tokens during gameplay to unlock the classic Pac-Mania arcade game.
Pre-Production Art and Programmers	Collect 150 tokens during gameplay to unlock the "Museum" option.

Phantasy Star Online III: Card Revolution

Unlockable	Objective
Beat, Hallo Rappy, and Sonic Knuckles	Have Sonic Heroes on your memory card.
Clippen	Have Billy Hatcher on your memory card.
Madam's Umbrella	Have Sonic Mega Collection on your memory card.
Nano Dragon	Have PSO 1 and 2 on your memory card.
Rage	Have Sonic Adventure 2 Battle on your memory card.
Sange	Have Sonic Adventure DX on your memory card.

Pikmin

Unlockable	Objective
100 pikmin	Arrive in the Distant Spring on or before Day 15. Head south with blue pikmin. You should come across a large egg. Break it open and the Smokey Progg will come out. Lead it to the landing site and throw pikmin on its head. Keep throwing red, blue, or yellow pikmin on its head. Eventually it will be defeated and will produce an egg that's worth 100 pikmin!

Pitfall: The Lost Expedition

Unlockable	Code
Original Pitfall	Hold Ⓛ+Ⓡ and press Ⓧ,Ⓧ,←,→,Ⓧ,Ⓑ,Ⓐ,↑,Ⓧ at the Main Screen.

Pokemon Channel

Unlockable	Objective
All 3 varieties of the 9 Pikachu Nice Cards	Collect 101 different kinds of Nice Cards
Full English Pichu Bros. movie	After the sixth day, find in crates.
Full Japanese Pichu Bros. movie	After the sixth day, find in crates.

Pokemon Channel (cont'd)

Hosted by Kasumi Disc	Togepi will give this disc to you on the sixth day.
Movie Projector	On the sixth day, Prof. Oak will give the movie projector to you.
Pichu Bros. Second Part	Play Pokemon Channel on the second day.
Pichu Bros. Third Part	Play Pokemon Channel on the third day.
Pichu Bros. Fourth Part	Play Pokemon Channel on the fourth day.
Pichu Bros. Fifth Part	Find in the Ruins of Truth.
Prime Binder	Collect 50 different kinds of Nice Cards.
Superior Binder	Collect 25 different kinds of Nice Cards.

Pokemon Colosseum

Unlockable	Objective
Orre Colosseum Level 50 Battles	Beat Phenac Stadium, Pyrite Colosseum, and Under Colosseum in both single and double battle.
Orre Colosseum Level 100 Battles	Beat Tower Colosseum in single and double battle.

Prince of Persia

Unlockable	Objective
The original Prince of Persia 2	Complete the game. Afterwards, under "Bonus," PoP 2 is open to play.

Raze's Hell

To enter these codes hold the R while playing. Do not pause the game.

Unlockable	Code
Infinite Ammo	A,A,B,B,X,Y,A,X
Invincibility	A,A,B,B,Y,Y,A,X

Red Card 2003

Unlockable	Objective
Apes Team and Victoria Falls Stadium	Defeat the Apes team in World Conquest mode.
Cheat Mode	Enter BIGTANK as a name to unlock all teams, stadiums, and finals mode.
Dolphins Team and Nautilus Stadium	Defeat the Dolphins team in World Conquest mode.
Finals Mode	Win all matches in World Conquest mode.
Martians Team and USAFB001 Stadium	Defeat the Martians team in World Conquest mode.
Matadors Team and Coliseum Stadium	Defeat the Matadors team in World Conquest mode.
Samurai Team and Youhi Gardens Stadium	Defeat the Samurai team in World Conquest mode.
SWAT Team and Nova City Stadium	Defeat the SWAT team in World Conquest mode.

Red Faction II

Unlockable	Code
Bouncing Grenades	X,X,X,X,X,X,X,X
Director's Cut	Y,A,X,B,X,A,Y,B
Fat	X,X,X,X,B,A,X,X
Gibby Ammunition	A,A,A,A,X,Y,A,A

Red Faction II (cont'd)

Code	Sequence
Gibby Explosion	B,X,A,Y,B,X,A,Y
Joker	Y,A,Y,A,Y,A,Y,A
Level Select	X,Y,A,B,Y,X,A,A
Rain Of Fire	Y,Y,Y,Y,Y,Y,Y,Y
Rapid Rail Gun	X,Y,X,Y,A,A,B,B
Super Health	A,A,Y,B,Y,B,X
Unlimited Ammo	Y,B,A,X,Y,X,A,B
Unlimited Grenades	X,A,X,Y,A,X,A,X
Unlock All	Y,X,B,X,Y,A,B,A
Unlock All Options	B,B,A,A,Y,X,Y,X
Wacky Death	B,B,B,B,B,B,B,B
Walking Dead	A,A,A,A,A,A,A,A

Resident Evil

Unlockable	Objective
Ending Bonuses	Complete the game as Jill or Chris and save the game. A new background will appear on the main menu. Select the "Once Again" option when playing your completed saved game. You may now choose new difficulty settings for the replay. See Note for extra gameplay tips..
Gallery	Complete the game in Invisible Enemy mode with a time less than five hours to unlock a "Special Features" option that displays a message from the game developers and a gallery of pre-production costumes.
Invisible Enemy Option	Complete the game two times as Jill or Chris in Once Again mode. All enemies are transparent in this mode.
One Dangerous Zombie Option	Complete the game as both Jill and Chris one time. When this option is enabled, a special zombie follows you around during the first part of the game. Shooting the zombie will end the game, so you must avoid it during gameplay.
Real Survivor Option	Complete the game in Once Again mode under the Normal difficulty setting with a time less than five hours. With this option, item boxes don't transfer items to each other and bonus costumes are available. Additionally, the aiming system is manual.
Rocket Launcher	Complete the game as Jill or Chris in Once Again mode with a time less than three hours. Save the game at the end, then start a new game to begin with the Rocket Launcher with unlimited ammunition.
Samurai Edge Gun	Complete the game as Jill or Chris in Once Again mode under the Normal difficulty setting with a time less than five hours. Save the game at the end, then start a new game to begin with the Samurai Edge gun.

NOTE

After unlocking the ending bonuses, you also get a key that allows the character who completed the game to have a new costume. Enter the room with the large mirror on the second floor of the mansion. Unlock the door in the back. Enter the closet and go to the end of the clothes rack. A message asking "There is an outfit that fits you perfectly, do you want to put it on?" will appear. Select "Yes" to change your character's clothes. Complete the game again under a different difficulty setting to unlock a second costume. Jill's bonus costumes are a commando uniform and her costume from Resident Evil 3. Chris' bonus costumes are casual clothes and his costume from Resident Evil: Code Veronica.

Resident Evil 0

Unlockable	Objective
Alternate Costumes	Complete the game with any rank under the Normal or Hard difficulty settings. Start a new game. A Closet Key appears in your inventory. Use it to unlock the closet in the room where you first found the Hunting Gun to access new costumes for Rebecca and Billy.
Completion Bonuses	Complete the game with a "B," "C," or "D" rank to unlock the Leech Hunter minigame.

Roadkill

At any time during the game, pause and highlight the map, then enter a code.

Unlockable	Code
All Vehicles	↑,↓,↑,↓,Y,A,Y,A,B,X,X,B
Infinite Ammo	Y,B,B,X,Y,B,B,X
Restore Health	B,X,B,X,B,X,B,X
Tornado	Y,X,A,B,B,A,X,Y

Rogue Ops

Pause the game and enter the following codes.

Unlockable	Code
Big Feet	→, →, →, ←, →, ←, →, ←, ←, ←
God Mode	←, →, →, ←, ←, →, →, ←, ←, →, →, ←, X, X
Level Skip	R,X,R,Y,R,←,R,→,R,L,L,X,L,Y,L,←,L,→,X
Half Damage	X, X, Y, Y, ←, ←, →, →, Y, Y, X, X
No Bullet Damage	←, →, →, ←, X, Y, Y, X
Explosive Crossbow	←, →, →, ←, X, Y, R, L, X, Y, ←, →
Explosive Sniper	R, L, →, →, ←, ←, →, →, L, R, X, Y
Missile Crossbow	→, →, ←, ←, R, R, L, L, Y, Y, X, X
Missile Sniper	X, ←, →, R, L, →, X, L, L, R, ←, ←
One Hit Kills	Y, ←, →, →, ←, Y, R, L, Y, X, X
Skeleton Mode	←, ←, ←, →, ←, →, ←, →, →, →
Unlimited Bullets	X,Y,X,Y,X,Y,X,Y,←,Y,X,Y,X,Y,X,Y,X

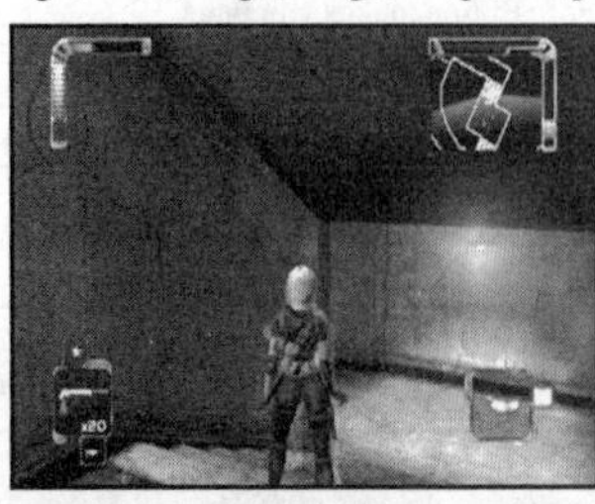

Samurai Jack: The Shadow of Aku

Unlockable	Code
Background Gallery	Complete the game on Normal.
Crystal Sword	Press the control stick up, the C stick down, and press A,X,B,Y during gameplay.
Max Zen	Press the control stick left, the C stick right, and press X,A ,B,Y during gameplay.
Model Gallery	Complete the game on Hard.
Sketch Gallery	Complete the game on Easy.

Scooby-Doo! Night of 100 Frights

To access the following unlockables, pause gameplay, hold L+R, then enter code.

Unlockable	Code
All FMVs	X,X,X,B,B,B,X,B,X
All Power-Ups	X,B,X,B,X,B,B,B,X,X,B,X,X,X
All Warp Gates Open	B,B,X,B,B,X,B,X,X,X
Alternate Credits Sequence	B,X,X,B,X,B
Movie Gallery	X,X,X,↓,X,X,X,C,↓,C

Shark Tales

During gameplay press Z to go to the Controller menu. Hold L and then input the codes. After you input the code, release L.

Unlockable	Code
God Mode	A,X,A,←,←,Y,→,↓,Y,Y
Hit Enemies Off Screen	X,X,X,X,A,X,X,X,X
Pearls Are Now Coins	X,A,X,X,X,A,X,X

Shrek 2

To enter these codes, pause the game and go into the Scrapbook menu.

Unlockable	Code
Bonus Games	←,↑,A,X,←,↑,A,X,←,↑,A,X,Y,X,Y,X,Y,X
Chapter Select	←,↑,A,X,←,↑,A,X,←,↑,A,X,↑,↑,↑,↑,↑
Full Health	←,↑,A,X,←,↑,A,X,←,↑,A,X,↑,→,↓,←,↑
1,000 Coins	←,↑,A,X,←,↑,A,X,←,↑,A,X,X,X,X,X,X

Simpsons Hit and Run

To enter these codes, pause the game and enter the options menu. Then hold L + R and enter the following codes.

Unlockable	Code
Horn Button makes you jump	X,X,X,Y
One hit destroys other cars	Y,Y,X,X
Show Speedometer	Y,Y,B,X
Wire Frame	B,A,B,Y

TIP

To see the extra holiday Main Menus change the date of your system to Christmas, Thanksgiving, or Halloween.

Simpsons Road Rage

Multiple cheats can be entered simultaneously. Cheats are only active for the next game session. All cheats are disabled once you return to the main menu. When any cheat is enabled, no money can be earned in Road Rage mode. For the following codes, hold L+R and enter code at the Options menu. A sound will confirm correct code entry.

Unlockable	Code
Alternate Views	Press Ⓑ,Ⓑ,Ⓑ,Ⓑ. Additional views are unlocked at the Pause screen. To unlock another set of views, hold L+R and press Ⓑ,Ⓐ,Ⓐ,Ⓐ at the Options menu.
Car Built for Homer	Complete all 10 levels in Mission mode to unlock the car built for Homer.
Christmas Mode	Press Ⓑ,Ⓑ,Ⓧ,Ⓑ. Select any character to play as Apu in a Santa costume. Alternately, set the system date to December 25.
Disable All Active Codes	Press START,START,START,START
Drive as Smithers in Mr. Burns' Limousine	Press Ⓑ,Ⓑ,Ⓨ,Ⓨ
Drive Nuclear Bus	Press Ⓑ,Ⓑ,Ⓨ,Ⓐ
Drive Red Brick Car	Press Ⓑ,Ⓑ,Ⓨ,Ⓧ. This car is controlled by Homer and is small, fast, and heavy.
Flat Characters	Press Ⓧ,Ⓧ,Ⓧ,Ⓧ. All the people (except the character you selected) are flat.
Halloween Mode	Press Ⓑ,Ⓑ,Ⓧ,Ⓐ. Select any character to play as Bart in a Frankenstein costume. Alternately, set the system date to October 31.
Horizontal Split Screen	Hold L + R and press Ⓨ (4) at the options menu. A sound confirms correct code entry. The screen is split horizontally instead of vertically in Two-Player mode.
New Year's Day Mode	Press Ⓑ,Ⓑ,Ⓧ,Ⓨ. Select any character to play as Krusty in a tuxedo. Alternately, set the system date to January 1.
Nighttime	Press Ⓐ,Ⓐ,Ⓐ,Ⓐ
No Map Display	Press Ⓨ,Ⓑ,Ⓑ,Ⓧ
Show Collision Lines	Press Ⓑ,Ⓑ,Ⓐ,Ⓐ
Slow Motion	Press Ⓐ,Ⓧ,Ⓑ,Ⓑ,Ⓨ
Special Car Moves	Press Ⓐ,Ⓑ,Ⓑ,Ⓐ. See Note for more special car moves.
Thanksgiving Mode	Press Ⓑ,Ⓑ,Ⓧ,Ⓧ. Select any character to play as Marge in a pilgrim dress. Alternately, set the system date to the third Thursday in November.
Time Trial Mode	Press Ⓧ,Ⓑ,Ⓨ,Ⓐ. There are no passengers, pedestrians, or traffic in this mode. Press Horn to start, stop, and reset the timer.

NOTE

Hold Gas + Brake + Handbrake while steering left or right while in mid-air to execute the Road Rage Roll. Hold Gas + Handbrake while stationary, then release Handbrake to execute the Speed Boost.

The Sims

To enter the following codes, hold L+R at the Main Menu and enter code.

Unlockable	Code
Buy Stuff For Free	FREEALL
Unlock 2 Player Mode	MIDAS
Unlock First Person View	FISH EYE
Unlock Motel (2 Player Mode)	PARTY M
Unlock Play The Sims Mode	SIMS

The Sims Bustin' Out

During gameplay, enter these codes very fast.

Unlockable	Code
All Objects	↓,Z,←,→,R
All Locations	↓,Z,R,L,Z
All Skins	L,Y,Ⓐ,R,←
Extra Money	↓,L,Z,R,←,X

Smashing Drive

Unlockable	Objective
Dusk and Wired Shift	Complete the Night Owl shift.
Night Owl Shift	Complete the Rush Hour shift.
Rush Hour Shift	Complete the Early Bird shift.

Sonic Adventure Director's Cut

Unlockable	Code
Helium Music (Sonic Spinball Mini-Game)	From the Sonic Spinball sound menu, play music 0, 4, 2, 5, 5, 7.
Level Select (Sonic 2 Mini-Game)	On the Sonic The Hedgehog 2 title screen, Tails will blink his eyes once, then two times. Hold ↓+←+Ⓐ+Ⓑ, then press START when Tails' eyes are closed on the second of the second set of blinks.
Level Select (Sonic Chaos Mini-Game)	From the Sonic Chaos title screen, press ↑,↑,↑,↑,→,←,→,←,START.
Level Select (Sonic Labyrinth Mini-Game)	From the Sonic Labyrinth title screen, press ↑,↑,→,→,→,↓,↓,↓,↓,↓,↓,←,←,←,←,←,←,←,←,←.
Level Select (Sonic Spinball Mini-Game)	In the sound test for Sonic Spinball, play music 0, 2, 1, 5, 6, 6.
No Gravity (Sonic Spinball Mini-Game)	In the Sonic Spinball sound test, play music 0, 9, 0, 1, 6, 8.
Unlock Game Gear Minigames	Collect a Sonic Emblem or complete 10 missions.
Unlock Metal Sonic in Trial Mode	Collect 130 emblems in the game.
Unlock Mission Mode	Complete the main game.
Zoom With A View (Sonic Pinball Mini-Game)	In the Sonic Spinball sound menu, play music 0, 2, 1, 1, 6, 6.

Sonic Heroes

Unlockable	Objective
Metal Characters	After you chose a level for 2 player mode hold Ⓐ+Y.
2 Player Bobsled Race Mode	Collect 80 Emblems.
2 Player Expert Race Mode	Collect 120 Emblems.
2 Player Quick Race Mode	Collect 100 Emblems.
2 Player Ring Race Mode	Collect 60 Emblems.
2 Player Special Stage Mode	Collect 40 Emblems.
2 Player Team Battle Mode	Collect 20 Emblems.
Last Song and Movie	Complete the Last Story.
Last Story Mode	Complete Story Mode with all four teams and all Choas Emeralds.

Sonic Heroes (cont'd)

Super Hard Mode	Collect 141 Emblems and have all A ranks.
Team Chaotix Song and Movie	Complete Story Mode with Team Chaotix.
Team Dark Song and Movie	Complete Story Mode with Team Dark.
Team Rose Song and Movie	Complete Story Mode with Team Rose.
Team Sonic Movie and Song	Complete Story Mode with Team Sonic.

Sonic Mega Collection

Unlockable	Sonic the Hedgehog Code
Level Select	At the Title Screen press ↑,↓,←,→.
Debug Mode	At the Title Screen Press ↑,X,↓,X,←,X,→. Hold Ⓑ, then hold START until the level loads. Press Ⓐ for the Debug Menu.

Unlockable	Sonic the Hedgehog 2 Code
Level Select	In the Options Menu select Sound Test and play the following sounds in order: 19, 65, 9, and 17. Hold X and press START then at the Title Screen hold Ⓑ and press START.
Debug Mode	In the Options Menu select Sound Test and play the following sounds in order: 1, 9, 9, 2, 1, 1, 2, 4. Select the desired level then hold Ⓑ and START until the level loads.

Unlockable	Sonic Spinball Code
Level Select	At the options Menu press Ⓑ,↓,Ⓐ,↓,X,↓,Ⓑ,Ⓐ,↑,Ⓑ,X,↑,Ⓐ,X,↑.

Soul Calibur II

Unlockable	Objective
Assassin	Beat Stage 2 of Subchapter 3 in Weapon Master Mode (Extra).
Berserker	Beat Stage 1 of Subchapter 1 in Weapon Master Mode (Extra).
Cervantes	Beat Stage 4 of Chapter 3 in Weapon Master Mode.
Charade	Beat Stage 1 of Chapter 3 in Weapon Master Mode.
Extra Arcade Mode	Either attempt Arcade Mode 10 times, or beat it once.
Extra Practice Mode	Beat Stage 1 of Chapter 1 in Weapon Master Mode.
Extra Survival Mode: Death Match	Beat Stage 3 of Subchapter 3 in Weapon Master Mode.
Extra Survival Mode: No Recovery	Beat Stage 2 of Extra Chapter 2 in Weapon Master Mode.
Extra Survival Mode: Standard	Beat Stage 5 of Chapter 6 in Weapon Master Mode.
Extra Team Battle Mode	Beat Stage 1 of Subchapter 1 in Weapon Master Mode.
Extra Time Attack: Extreme	Beat Stage 1 of Extra Chapter 1 in Weapon Master Mode.

Soul Calibur II (cont'd)

Extra Time Attack Mode: Alternative	Beat Stage 4 of Chapter 9 in Weapon Master Mode.
Extra Time Attack Mode: Standard	Beat Stage 1 of Chapter 5 in Weapon Master Mode.
Extra VS Battle Mode	Either attempt Extra Arcade Mode five times, or beat it once.
Extra VS Team Battle Mode	Either attempt Extra VS Battle Mode five times, or beat it once.
Lizardman	Beat All Stages of Subchapter 2 in Weapon Master Mode (Extra).
Seung Mina	Beat Stage 3 of Chapter 6 in Weapon Master Mode.
Sophitia	Beat Stage 5 of Chapter 4 in Weapon Master Mode.
Yoshimitsu	Beat Stage 3 of Chapter 2 in Weapon Master Mode.

Spawn: Armageddon

At any time during gameplay, press START to pause, then enter the code.

Unlockable	Code
All Comic Covers	↑,↓,←,→,→,←,←
All Weapons	↑,↓,←,→,←,→,←,←
Infinite Necroplasm	↑,↓,←,→,↓,←,↑,→
Level Select	↑,↓,←,→,←,←,→,→
Unlimited Ammo	↑,↓,←,→,↑,←,↓,→

Spider-Man

Enter the following codes at the Specials menu. A laugh confirms the correct code entry. Repeat code entry to return to normal.

Unlockable	Code
All Fighting Controls	KOALA
Big Head and Feet for Spider-Man	GOESTOYOURHEAD
Bonus Training Levels	HEADEXPLODY
Enemies Have Big Heads	JOELSPEANUTS
First-Person View	UNDERTHEMASK
Goblin-Style Costume	FREAKOUT
Level Select	IMIARMAS
Level Skip	ROMITAS—Pause gameplay and select the "Next Level" option to advance to the next level
Master Code	ARACHNID—All levels in the level warp option, all gallery options (movie viewer/production art), and combo moves are unlocked
Matrix-Style Attacks	DODGETHIS
Play as a Police Officer	REALHERO
Play as a Scientist	SERUM
Play as Captain Stacey (helicopter pilot)	CAPTAINSTACEY
Play as Mary Jane	GIRLNEXTDOOR
Play as Shocker's Thug	THUGSRUS
Play as Skulls Gang Thug	KNUCKLES

Spider-Man (cont'd)

Play as the Shocker	HERMANSCHULTZ
Play as Uncle Ben's Killer	STICKYRICE
Small Spider-Man	SPIDERBYTE
Unlimited Green Goblin Glider Power	CHILLOUT
Unlimited Webbing	ORGANICWEBBING

Unlockable	Objective
Alternate Green Goblin Costume	If you're using the Alex Ross Spider-Man, play any level with the Green Goblin in it and he'll have an alternate costume that more closely resembles his classic costume.
Green Goblin FMV Sequence	Complete the game under the hero or greater difficulty setting.
Pinhead Bowling Mini-Game	Accumulate 10,000 points during gameplay to unlock the Pinhead bowling mini-game in the Training menu.
Play as Alex Ross	Complete the game under the normal or higher difficulty setting to unlock the Alex Ross costume in the Specials menu.
Play as Peter Parker	Complete the game under the easy or higher difficulty setting to unlock the Peter Parker costume in the Specials menu.
Play as the Green Goblin	Complete the game under the hero or superhero difficulty setting to unlock the Green Goblin costume option at the Specials menu. Select that option to play as Harry Osborn in the Green Goblin costume, including his weapons, in an alternate storyline where he tries to correct the Osborn family's reputation. See Note below for an easy tip.
Play as Wrestler	Complete the game under the easy or higher difficulty setting to unlock the wrestler costume in the Specials menu. To unlock this easily, first unlock the "Unlimited webbing" cheat. When you get to the ring, zip to the top and keep on shooting Spidey Bombs.
Shocker FMV Sequence	Accumulate 30,000 points during gameplay to unlock a Shocker FMV sequence in the CG menu.
Vulture FMV Sequence	Accumulate 20,000 points during gameplay to unlock a Vulture FMV sequence in the CG menu.

NOTE

To unlock the Green Goblin easily, start a new game under the hero or superhero difficulty setting. At the first level, pause gameplay, then quit to the main menu. Enable the ARACHNID code, then go to the "Level Warp" option. Choose the Conclusion level (that features Norman revealing himself to Spider-Man followed by the glider sequence), then exit. This marks the game as completed under the selected difficulty setting. The Green Goblin costume option is unlocked at the Secret Store screen.

Spider-Man 2

To unlock Hero points and upgrades, enter the name HCRAYERT. This will give you 200,000 Hero points and the swing and web zip upgrades and big game hunter, alien buster and shock absorber. Now it won't let you keep this name but every time you enter it it's another 200,000 hero points for you.

Spy Hunter

Cheats are unlocked by completing all mission objectives (not just the primary objectives) within a set amount of time. To activate the cheats, enter "System Options," then choose "Extras," and "Cheat Grid." To play the FMV sequences unlocked in the cheat menu, choose the "Movie Player" option that is above "Cheat Grid."

Unlockable	Objective
Camera Flip	Complete Level 11 in 310.
Concept Art Video	Complete Level 9 in 345.
Early Test Animatic Video	Complete Level 5 in 325.
Extra Cameras	Complete Level 6 in 345.
Fisheye View	Complete Level 10 in 315.
Green HUD	Complete Level 2 in 335.
Hover Spy	Complete the entire game.
Inversion Camera	Complete Level 8 in 305.
Making of Video	Complete Level 13 in 215.
Night Vision	Complete Level 4 in 315.
Puke Camera	Complete Level 12 in 330.
Rainbow HUD	Complete Level 7 in 310.
Saliva Spy Hunter Video	Complete Level 1 in 340.
Saliva Your Disease Video	Complete Level 3 in 240.
Tiny Spy	Complete Level 14 in 510.
Classic Spy Hunter Mini-Game	Choose an agent at the start of the game and select an empty slot. Enter OGSPY as a name. The name disappears and a clucking sound confirms correct code entry. After this is done, enter your own name and start the game.
Early Test Animatic FMV Sequence	Choose an agent at the start of the game and select an empty slot. Enter WOODY or WWS413 as a name. The name disappears and a clucking sound confirms correct code entry. After this is done, enter your own name and start the game. Select "System Options," then "Extras," then "Movie Player" to access the FMV sequence.
Saliva Spy Hunter Theme FMV Sequence	Choose an agent at the start of the game and select an empty slot. Enter GUNN as a name. The name disappears and a clucking sound confirms correct code entry. After this is done, enter your own name and start the game. Select "System Options," then "Extras," then "Movie Player" to access the FMV sequence.
Saliva Your Disease FMV Sequence	Choose an agent at the start of the game and select an empty slot. Enter SALIVA as a name. The name disappears and a clucking sound confirms correct code entry. After this is done, enter your own name and start the game. Select "System Options," then "Extras," then "Movie Player" to access the FMV sequence.
Spy Hunter Concept Art FMV Sequence	Choose an agent at the start of the game and select an empty slot. Enter SHAWN or SCW823 as a name. The name disappears and a clucking sound confirms correct code entry. After this is done, enter your own name and start the game. Select "System Options," then "Extras," then "Movie Player" to access the FMV sequence.

Spy Hunter (cont'd)

Unlockable	Objective
Super Spy	Complete all 65 objectives in the game for unlimited ammunition and invincibility for your car.
The Making of Spy Hunter FMV Sequence	Choose an agent at the start of the game and select an empty slot. Enter MAKING or MODEL as a name. The name disappears and a clucking sound confirms correct code entry. After this is done, enter your own name and start the game. Select "System Options," then "Extras," then "Movie Player" to access the FMV sequence.

SSX 3

Enter these codes in the cheat menu.

Unlockable	Code
Canuck	greatwhitenorth
Eddie	worm
Hiro	slicksuit
Luther	bronco
Stretch	windmilldunk

SSX Tricky

To access the Cheat Menu, unlock all characters. Then successfully complete the world circuit using the following characters in order JP, Mac, Psymon, Zoe, Eddie, Mike, Brodi, Kaori, Luther, and Marisol. Go to the main menu, select "Single Event," and go to "Cheats." In this menu, you can turn on two different secret characters with full stats, extra boards, and outfits for all of the characters, and extra trick chapters for each character. There's also an infinite tricky meter option.

Unlockable	Objective
Überboards	Unlock all of the tricks for a character to get their überboard, which is their best board.
Alternate Costumes	To earn more costumes, complete all chapters in your trick book. To unlock the final chrome costume, complete World Circuit mode with a "Master" rank.
Fugi Board	Get a gold medal on every course with all boarders with their überboard to unlock a Fugi board.
Full Stat Points	Hold L+R and press B,B,Z,B,B,Z,A,A,Z,A,A,Z at the title screen. Release L+R and a sound confirms correct code entry. All the boarders have full stat points.
Mallora Board	Hold L+R and press A,A,Z,X,X,Z,B,B,Z,Y,Y,Z at the title screen. Release L+R and a sound confirms correct code entry. Choose Elise and start a track. Elise will have the Mallora Board and a blue outfit. This code only works for Elise.
Master Code	Hold L+R and press A,B,Z,X,Y,Z,B,Y,Z,X,A,Z at the title screen. Release L+R and a sound confirms correct code entry.
Mix Master Mike	Hold L+R and press A,A,Z,A,A,Z,A,A,Z,A,A,Z at the title screen. Release L+R and a sound confirms correct code entry. Choose Mac at the character selection screen and he's replaced by Mix Master Mike on the course, with Mac's übers. He has decks on his back and a vinyl board. Repeat the code to disable its effect.
Pipedream Course	Win a medal on all Showoff courses.
Play as Brodi	Win a gold medal in World Circuit mode.
Play as JP	Win three gold medals in World Circuit mode.
Play as Kaori	Win four gold medals in World Circuit mode.
Play as Luther	Win eight gold medals in World Circuit mode.

PSP Xbox PS2 GC GBA

SSX Tricky (cont'd)

Play as Marisol	Win five gold medals in World Circuit mode.
Play as Psymon	Win six gold medals in World Circuit mode.
Play as Seeiah	Win seven gold medals in World Circuit mode.
Play as Zoe	Win two gold medals in World Circuit mode.
Untracked Course	Win a medal on all Race courses.

Star Wars Bounty Hunter

Unlockable	Code	Unlockable	Code
Chapter 1	SEEHOWTHEYRUN	**Mission 7**	LOCKUP
Chapter 2	CITYPLANET	**Mission 8**	WHAT A RIOT
Chapter 3	LOCKDOWN	**Mission 9**	SHAFTED
Chapter 4	DUGSOPLENTY	**Mission 10**	BIGMOSQUITOS
Chapter 5	BANTHAPOODOO	**Mission 11**	ONEDEADDUG
Chapter 6	MANDALORIANWAY	**Mission 12**	WISHIHADMYSHIP
Concept Art	R ARTISTS ROCK	**Mission 13**	MOS GAMOS
Mission 1	BEAST PIT	**Mission 14**	TUSKENS R US
Mission 2	GIMMEMY JETPACK	**Mission 15**	BIG BAD DRAGON
Mission 3	CONVEYORAMA	**Mission 16**	MONTROSSISBAD
Mission 4	BIGCITYNIGHTS	**Mission 17**	VOSAISBADDER
Mission 5	IEATNERFMEAT	**Mission 18**	JANGOISBADDEST
Mission 6	VOTE4TRELL	**TGC Cards**	GO FISH

Star Wars: Rogue Squadron 2: Rogue Leader

For the following unlockables, enter the 1st password at the Password screen. R2D2 will not beep for this password. Return to the Password screen and enter the 2nd password. R2D2 beeps to confirm a correct code entry.

Unlockable	1st Password	2nd Password
Ace Mode (See Note)	U!?!VWZC	GIVEITUP
All Tech Upgrades	AYZB!RCL	WRKFORIT
Asteroid Field Level	TVLYBBXL	NOWAR!!!
Car (See Note)	!ZUVIEL!!	BENZIN!.
Death Star Escape Level	PYST?OOO	DUCKSHOT
Endurance Level	?WCYBRTC	??MBC???
Imperial Shuttle (See Note)	AJHH!?JY	BUSTOUR
Level Select (See Note)	!??QWTTJ	CLASSIC
Millennium Falcon	MVPQIU?A	OH!BUDDY
Naboo Starfighter	CDYXF!?Q	ASEPONE!
Revenge on Yavin Level	OGGRWPDG	EEKEEK!
Slave I	PZ?APBSY	IRONSHIP
TIE Advanced X1 Prototype (Darth Vader's TIE)	NYM!UUOK	BLKHLMT!
TIE Fighter	ZT?!RGBA	DISPSBLE
Triumph of the Empire Level	AZTBOHII	OUTCAST!
Unlimited Lives	JPVI?IJC	RSBFNRL

Star Wars: Rogue Squadron 2: Rogue Leader (cont'd)

NOTE

In Ace mode, you just need to complete a level to get a gold rank.

NOTE

The Car code must be re-activated every time a new game session is started.

NOTE

The Imperial Shuttle can be piloted only in levels where an Imperial ship is normally used (for example, Revenge on Yavin). Press Ⓑ when flying the Imperial Shuttle and an automatic gun on the ship will fire.

NOTE

The Level Select code doesn't unlock the bonus missions.

Unlockable	Code
Art Gallery	Enter EXHIBIT! as a password. The "Art Gallery" option is unlocked at the Special Features menu.
Audio Commentary	Enter BLAHBLAH as a password. The "Audio Commentary" option is unlocked at the Special Features menu.
Credits	THATSME! as a password. The "Credits" option is unlocked at the Special Features menu.
Documentary	Enter ?INSIDER as a password. The "Documentary" option is unlocked at the Special Features menu.
In-Game Reset	Hold Ⓧ+Ⓨ+Ⓑ+START for about one and a half seconds.
Quick Mission Start	Hold Ⓛ+Ⓡ while selecting a mission to start the mission immediately with the default ship.
Sound Test	Enter COMPOSER as a password. The "Sound Test" option is unlocked at the Special Features menu.

Star Wars: Rogue Squadron 3: Rebel Strike

All codes are entered in the Passcodes menu in the Options.

NOTE

Some cheats will have two or more passwords. Enter the first one then enter the remaining codes.

Unlockable	Code
Ace Mode	YNMSFY?P, YOUDAMAN
All Ships for Versus	W!WSTPQB, FREEPLAY
All Single Player Missions	HYWSC!WS, NONGAMER
All Single Player Missions plus Bonus Missions	EEQQ?YPL
Art Gallery	!KOOLART
Asteroid Field Mission in Co-Op	RWALPIGC, NOWAYOUT
Black and White Mode	NOCOLOR?
Beggar's Canyon Race in Co-Op	FRLL!CSF, FARMBOY?

PSP Xbox PS2 GC GBA

Star Wars: Rogue Squadron 3: Rebel Strike (cont'd)

Credits	LOOKMOM!
Deathstar Escape Mission in Co-Op	YFCEDFRH, DSAGAIN?
Documentary	THEDUDES
Empire Strikes Back Arcade Game	!H!F?HXS, KOOLSTUF
Endurance Mission in Co-Op	WPX?FGC!, EXCERSIZ
Level Select for Co-Op Mode	SWGRCQPL, UCHEATED, CHE!ATER
Millennium Falcon	QZCRPTG!, HANSRIDE
Music Hall	HARKHARK
Naboo Starfighter	RTWCVBSH, BFNAGAIN
Rudy's Car	AXCBPRHK, WHATTHE?
Slave 1	TGBCWLPN, ZZBOUNTY
Star Wars Arcade Game	RTJPFC!G, TIMEWARP
Tie Advance in Co-Op	VDX?WK!H, ANOKSHIP
Tie Bomber	JASDJWFA, !DABOMB!
Tie Fighter in Co-Op	MCKEMAKD, ONESHOT!
Tie Hunter	FRRVBMJK, LOOKOUT!
Unlimited Lives	IIOUAOYE, WIMPIAM!

Star Wars: The Clone Wars

Unlockable	Code
All FMV Sequences	CINEMA
Campaign Level Select	GASMASK
Invincibility	1WITHFORCE
Multiplayer Level Select	FRAGFIESTA
Programming Team Photographs (See Note)	SAYCHEESE
Three Bonus Objectives for Prior Mission Marked Complete	YUB_YUB
Unlimited Secondary and Special Weapon	CHOSEN1
Battle Droid in Academy Geonosis Level	ROGERROGER
Clone Trooper in Academy Geonosis Level	FAKE FETT
Next Level	THRISNOTRY
Padme Amidala in Academy Geonosis Level	CORDE
Super Battle Droid in Academy Geonosis Level	WAT TAMBOR
Wookie in Academy Geonosis level	FUZZBALL
Ewok Song	Press ↑,↑,↓,↓,←,→,←,→,Ⓑ,Ⓐ,START at the Options screen or during gameplay.

Star Wars: The Clone Wars (cont'd)

NOTE

You must first unlock the "Sketchbook" option to view the Programming Team Photographs.

Starsky and Hutch

Unlockable	Code
Unlock Everything	Enter VADKRAM as a profile name.

Street Hoops

Unlockable	Objective
Alternate Clothing Colors	When buying clothes, press ↑ or ↓ to change the color of all your clothing.
Athens Minotaurs Team	Win the World Tournament three times. Note: This was accomplished under the Greatest of All Time difficulty setting.
Cypress Hill LowRider Music Video	Complete the game three or four times, depending on the difficulty setting.
Kinshasha Warriors Team	Win the World Tournament four times. Note: This was accomplished under the Greatest of All Time difficulty setting.
London Knights Team	Win the World Tournament two times. Note: This was accomplished under the Greatest of All Time difficulty setting.
Masta P Make Em Say Ugh and OOOHHWEE Music Video	Complete the game three or four times, depending on the difficulty setting.
Play as AO, Booger, Half Man-Half Amazing, Headache, Hot Sauce, Speedy, The Future, The Main Event	Before you start playing, you can choose which Professional Street Baller you want to use. After that, you use your team and go city to city. The team and player you choose may randomize the ballers. Continue playing and unlock a new baller in each city. You should have them all unlocked at the third-to-last court on your first run. Note: When unlocked, each baller costs $10,000.
Play as B Real, Muggs, BoBo, and the London Knights Team	Win the World Tournament twice. Note: This was accomplished under the Greatest of All Time difficulty setting.
Play as Cypress Hill, DJ Muggz, and BoBo	Win the World Tournament under the Greatest of All Time difficulty setting.
Play as Dennis Rodman	Play on Balla and get 10 or more rebounds. An easy way to do this is to play on 20 minutes.
Play as Half Man-Half Amazing	When playing in World Tournament mode, you play the Urban Hitmen. Defeat them to unlock Half Man-Half Amazing. Note: You need $10,000 to play as him.
Play as Lil' Romeo and Master P	Go to the Foot Action store and buy several thousand dollars of P. Miller clothes. Buy the most expensive pants, sweaters, hats, glasses, and sneakers for the five-man squad. Once you spend enough money, they appear outside the store.

Street Hoops (cont'd)

Play as Silk the Shocker	Win the Lord of the Court in Shakespeare Park.
Play as Xzibit	Finish the Lord of the Court challenge under any difficulty setting.
San Juan Coquis Team	Win the World Tournament once. Note: This was accomplished under the Balla difficulty setting.
Unlock Courts	To unlock the courts, you must play through World Tournament mode. When you unlock Coquis, you also unlock the San Juan, Puerto Rico, court. Play with them to unlock the London court and London team.
Unlock Street Hoops 3 and Street Hoops FMV sequences	Win the last two levels of the game (The African Village and Greese) to unlock two extra FMV sequences that contain parts from the making of the game and one of the mix tapes.
Volume 3 Mix Tape	Win the Lord of the Court at the Dome.
Volume 4 Mix Tape	Win the Lord of the Court at the Rucker.
Volume 5 Mix Tape	Win the Lord of the Court at West 4th Cage.
Xzibit Front 2 Back Music Video	Complete the game three or four times, depending on the difficulty setting.

Street Racing Syndicate

First enter ↑,↓,←,→ at the Title screen and then enter the following codes.

Unlockable	Code
96' Toyota Supra RZ in Arcade	SICKJZA
99' Mitsubishi Eclipse GS-T in Arcade	IGOTGST
04' Toyota Celica GT-S Action Package in Arcade	MYTCGTS
First Three Police Bust Are Given as Warnings	LETMEGO
Free Repair Once Per Game	FIXITUP
Pacman Vinyl	GORETRO
Subaru S202 STi in Arcade	SICKGDB

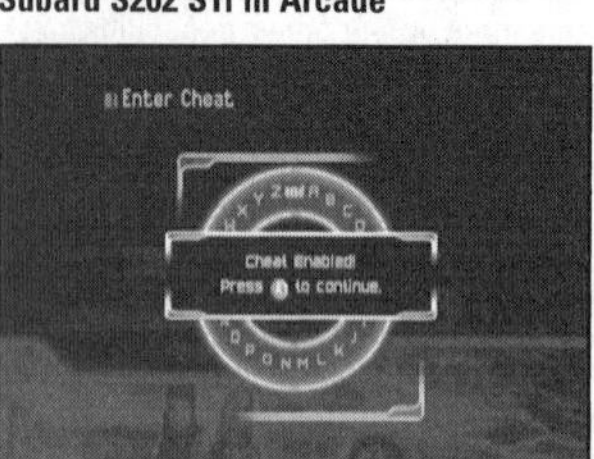

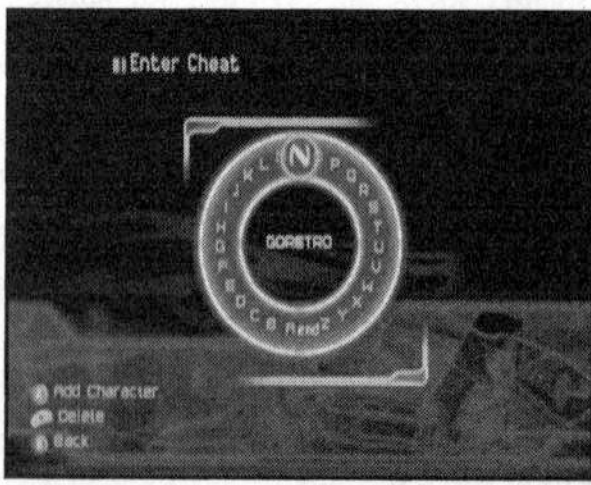

Super Mario Sunshine

Unlockable	Objective
Alternate Ending Screen	If you complete the game with 119 Shine Sprites or less, you get an ending screen in which el Piantissimo inspects the paintbrush. However, if you finish it with all 120 Shine Sprites, the ending screen shows all the characters in the game.
Another Alternate Ending	There are 240 Blue Coins and 120 Shine Sprites. You need 50 Shine Sprites to complete Level 7 on all seven stages to get to Level 8. You only need 117 Shine Sprites to complete the game to get one ending. Get the last three Shine Sprites to see a different ending. Get the shirt and glasses for a different appearing ending.

Super Mario Sunshine (cont'd)

Ending Bonus	Complete and save the game. Pay 10 coins to use a boat near the clock tower where Yoshi is found to return to the Airport level at the game's start. Additionally, you can get a shirt covered with Shine pictures from the man wearing sunglasses. He is the one who normally gives Mario sunglasses in the game.

Super Monkey Ball

Unlockable	Objective
Bonus Level	Select any difficulty setting and complete all normal levels. A bonus level will start during the credits. Get as many bananas as you can while avoiding the falling letters from the credits.
EX Levels	To unlock three EX levels, successfully complete Beginner mode without losing any lives.
Master Mode	Complete the game in Expert mode without using any continues.
Quick Finish in Monkey Race	During any Monkey Race on any setting, press L+R+A+X+Y to instantly finish the race.
Skip Credits	Hold L+R and repeatedly press A when you see the first words appear. Alternately, press A as soon as the credit scene appears.
Unlimited Continues	After you buy all three mini-games, for every 2,500 play points you get, you'll gain an extra continue. After you reach nine continues, the game gives you unlimited continues.

Super Monkey Ball 2

Unlockable	Objective
Bonus Levels	Select the Beginner difficulty setting, and complete all ten levels in World 1 without using any continues to unlock 10 Bonus Beginner levels. Select the Advanced difficulty setting, and complete all 30 levels in Worlds 2 through 4 without using any continues to unlock 10 Bonus Advanced levels. Select the Expert difficulty setting, and complete all 50 levels in Worlds 5 through 10 without using any continues to unlock 10 Bonus Expert levels.
Gift Option	Once you unlock all party games, the "Gift" option at the Options screen unlocks. by using play points, you can buy more lives in Challenge mode, in-game movies, and the staff credits.
Master Bonus Levels	Complete all 10 Master Mode levels without using any continues.
Master Difficulty Setting	Select the Expert difficulty setting, and complete all 50 levels in Worlds 5 through 10 and the 10 Bonus Expert levels without using any continues.
Party Games	It takes 2,500 play points to unlock a party game. The best way to rack up quick points is to play Challenge mode. Play the Beginner level a few times without continuing to earn extra stages that help your score skyrocket.

Superman: Shadow of Apokolips

Unlockable	Code
Everything Unlocked	I WANT IT ALL
Extra Difficulty	NAILS
Infinite Health	FIRST AID
Infinite Superpower	JUICED UP
Make Test of Strength Easy	SORE FINGER
No Superpower	JOR EL
Play as Clark Kent	SECRET IDENTITY

Superman: Shadow of Apokolips (cont'd)

Play as Parasite	FEELING DRAINED
Reverse Controls	SUPERMAN
Slow Motion Mode	SLOW MOTION
Turn off Time Limits	STOP THE CLOCK
All Character Biographies	INTERVIEW
All Intermission Sequences	POPCORN
All Level Attack Stages	SIGHTSEEING
Explore Metropolis Mode	WANDERER
Shooting Gallery and Item Hunt	CREEP
Silent Movie Mode	RETRO

Tak and the Power of Juju

To enter these codes, you must first unlock the cheat menu: press START to pause and enter B, X, Y, Y, B, X, Y, Y. To unlock the remaining codes, pause and enter the sequence listed.

Unlockable	Code
100 Feathers	B, Y, X, B, Y, X, B, Y
All Juju Power Ups	↑, →, ←, ↓, Y, X, B, ↓
All Moonstones	Y, Y, B, B, X, X, ←, →
All Plants	B, Y, X, ←, ↑, →, ↓, ↓
All Yorbels	↑, Y, ←, B, →, X, ↓, ↑

Tarzan: Untamed

Unlockable	Objective
Corkscrew Trick Move	Complete the Terk challenges in World 3 to unlock the Corkscrew trick move for the river surfing challenges.
Ground Tumble Trick Move	Complete the Terk challenges in World 1 to unlock the Ground Tumble trick move for jungle exploration.
Jane	Complete the Terk challenges in World 1 to unlock Jane in the waterskiing or river surfing challenges.
Porter	Complete the Terk challenges in World 2 to unlock Porter in the waterskiing or river surfing challenges.
Scarecrow Trick Move	Complete the Terk challenges in World 2 to unlock the Scarecrow trick move for the waterskiing challenges.
Terk the Monkey	Complete the three Terk challenges in the final levels of the game to unlock Terk.

Teenage Mutant Ninja Turtles

Enter these passwords in the Password menu.

Unlockable	Code
2x Defense for Donatello	MLMLS
2x Defense for Leonardo	LDSMS
2x Defense for Michelangelo	RLDDR
2x Defense for Raphael	SDRML
2x Power-Up for Donatello	MLSDS
2x Power-Up for Leonardo	RSDMM
2x Power-Up for Michelangelo	RLMSM

Teenage Mutant Ninja Turtles

Unlockable	Code
2x Power-Up for Raphael	RSSSR
Bonus Course 1	LSMMS
Bonus Course 2	SSLDM
Bonus Course 3	MSSLD
Bonus Course 4	SRLMD
Bonus Course 5	LSDRM
Casey Jones Mode	SRLMD
Donatello's Alternate Costume	RRSLR
Infinite Shurikens for Leonardo	SSLDM
Infinite Shurikens for Michelangelo	MSSLD
Leonardo's Alternate Costume	RSLMD
Leonardo's Improved Weapon	LMLSD
Michelangelo's Alternate Costume	RLSLS
Michelangelo's Improved Weapon	MSRMM
Playmates Toy Database	LSDRM
Raphael's Alternate Costume	SLSMM
Raphael's Improved Weapon	RDSRL
Sound Effects	DDDML
Splinter Mode	LSLML

Teenage Mutant Ninja Turtles 2: Battle Nexus

In the Options Menu, select "Passwords" to enter any of the codes listed in the following tables.

Unlockable Challenges	Code
Abyss	SDSDRLD
Endurance	MRMDRMD
Fatal Blow	LRSRDRD
Lose Shuriken	RLMRDSL

Unlockable Challenges	Code
Nightmare	SLSDRDL
Poison	DRSLLSR
Super Tough	RDSRMRL

Miscellaneous Unlockables	Code
New Nexus Outfit for Donatello	DSLRDRM
New Nexus Outfit for Leonardo	LMRMDRD
New Nexus Outfit for Michelangelo	MLMRDRM
New Nexus Outfit for Raphael	RMSRMDR
Playmates added to Bonus Materials	SRMLDDR

PSP Xbox PS2 GC GBA

Teenage Mutant Ninja Turtles 2: Battle Nexus (cont'd)

Unlockable Cheats	Code
All You Can Throw Shuriken	RSRLRSM
Health	DSRDMRM
Mighty Turtle	LSDRRDR
Pizza Paradise	MRLMRMR
Self Recovery	DRMSRLR
Squeaking	MLDSRDM
Super Defense Power	LDRMRLM
Super Offense Power	SDLSRLL
Toddling	SSSMRDD

NOTE

When selecting a turtle hold L to pick his New Nexus Outfit.

Tiger Woods PGA Tour 2004

Enter these passwords in the passwords menu.

Unlockable	Code
Ace Andrews	ACEINTHEHOLE
All Courses	ALLTHETRACKS
All Golfers	CANYOUPICKONE
Cedric the Entertainer	CEDDYBEAR
Dominic "The Don" Donatello	DISCOOKING
Downtown Brown	DTBROWN
Edwin "Pops" Masterson	EDDIE
Everything	THEKITCHENSINK
Hamish "Mulligan" McGregor	DWILBY
Moa "Big Mo" Ta'a Vatu	ICYONE
Solita Lopez	SHORTGAME
Sunday Tiger	4REDSHIRTS
Takeharu "Tsunami" Moto	EMERALDCHAMP
Tiger World Challenge	SHERWOOD TARGET
Val Summers	BEVERLYHILLS
"Yosh" Tanigawa	THENEWLEFTY

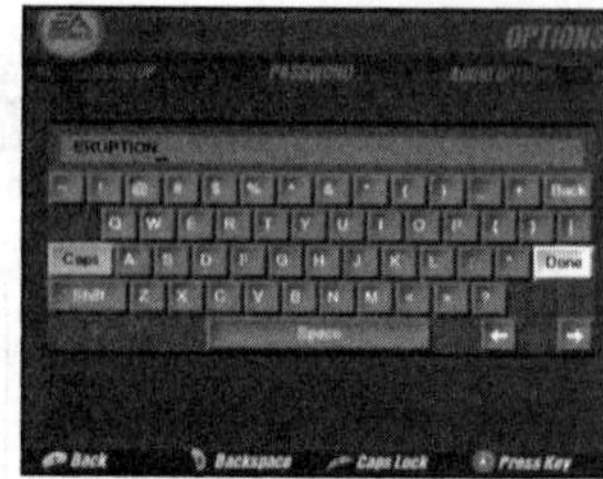

Timesplitters 2

Complete the following levels in Story mode under the Medium Difficulty setting to access the playable characters.

Level Reward	Playable Character
1853 Wild West Level Reward	Colonel
1895 Notre Dame Paris Level Reward	Notre Dame
1920 Aztec Ruins Level Reward	Golem
1932 Chicago Level Reward	Big Tony
1972 Atom Smasher Level Reward	Khallos

Timesplitters 2 (cont'd)

1990 Oblask Dam Siberia Level Reward	Mutant TimeSplitter
2019 NeoTokyo Level Reward	Sadako
2280 Return to Planet X Level Reward	Ozor Mox
2315 Robot Factory Level Reward	Machinist
2401 Space Station Level Reward	Reaper Splitter as a playable character in Arcade mode.

NOTE

Complete the level under the Easy difficulty setting to unlock the ending sequence.

Tom Clancy's Splinter Cell

Unlockable	Code
All Levels and Checkpoints	Enter LAMAUDITE for your name.

Tony Hawk's Pro Skater 3

Enter all codes in the Cheats Menu.

Unlockable	Code
All Characters	Freakshow
All Cheats	MARKEDCARDS
All Created Skaters	WEEATDIRT
All FMV Sequences	Popcorn
All Movies	POPCORN
Master Code	MarkedCards
Max Stats	MAXMEOUT
Super Stats	MaxMeOut
Unlimited Specials	Unlimited

NOTE

The characters unlocked by the "All Characters" cheat include Darth Maul, Wolverine, Officer Dick, Private Carrera, Ollie the Magic Bum, Kelly Slater, Demoness, and the Neversoft Eyeball Man.

TIP

An alternate way of getting all FMV sequences is to get gold medals in all three competitions in Career mode.

NOTE

The "Master Code" cheat unlocks all modes, such as "Snowboard," "Giant," and "First Person." It also unlocks the "Super Stats," "Always Perfect," "Perfect Manuals," and "Perfect Rails" cheats.

TIP

You can also unlock the same effect as the "Super Stats" cheat by completing all the goals in the game, and getting gold medals in all three competitions 14 times in Career mode (with a different skater each time).

TIP

Another way of achieving the effect of the "Unlimited Specials" code is to complete all the goals in the game, and get gold medals in all three competitions 12 times in Career mode (with a different skater each time).

Tony Hawk's Pro Skater 3 (cont'd)

Unlockable	Objective
A Day in the Life FMV Sequence	Complete all the goals in the game and get gold medals in all three competitions in Career mode with the Neversoft Eyeball.
All Highlight Tapes	Get gold medals in all three competitions in Career mode with a skater to unlock his or her tape.
Burnside Level from Tony Hawk's Pro Skater	Complete all the goals in the game and get gold medals in all three competitions six times in Career mode with a different skater each time.
Cruise Ship Level	Get any medal on all three competition levels.
Darth Maul	Complete all the goals in the game and get gold medals in all three competitions one time with any character in Career mode.
Demoness	Complete all the goals in the game and get gold medals in all three competitions 10 times in Career mode with a different skater each time.
Expert Mode	Complete all the goals in the game and get gold medals in all three competitions 20 times in Career mode with a different skater each time.
First-Person Mode	Complete all the goals in the game and get gold medals in all three competitions 22 times in Career mode with a different skater each time.
Huge Skater	Complete all the goals in the game and get gold medals in all three competitions 15 times in Career mode with a different skater each time.
Kelly Slater	Complete all the goals in the game and get gold medals in all three competitions eight times in Career mode with a different skater each time.
Kickflip Contest FMV Sequence	Complete all the goals in the game and get gold medals in all three competitions in Career mode with Private Carrera.
Moon Physics	Complete all the goals in the game and get gold medals in all three competitions 19 times in Career mode with a different skater each time.
Neversoft Bails FMV Sequence	Complete all the goals in the game and get gold medals in all three competitions in Career mode with Darth Maul.
Neversoft Friends FMV Sequence	Complete all the goals in the game and get gold medals in all three competitions in Career mode with Ollie the Magic Bum.
Neversoft Friends FMV Sequence	Complete all the goals in the game and get gold medals in all three competitions three times in Career mode using five bonus or created skaters.
Neversoft Makes FMV Sequence	Complete all the goals in the game and get gold medals in all three competitions in Career mode with Wolverine.
Neversoft Mascot	Complete all the goals in the game and get gold medals in all three competitions 21 times in Career mode with a different skater each time.
Neversoft Old School FMV Sequence	Complete all the goals in the game and get gold medals in all three competitions in Career mode with Demoness.
Officer Dick	Complete all the goals in the game and get gold medals in all three competitions three times in Career mode with a different skater each time.
Ollie the Magic Bum	Complete all the goals in the game and get gold medals in all three competitions seven times in Career mode with a different skater each time.

Tony Hawk's Pro Skater 3 (cont'd)

Perfect Balance for Manuals	Complete all the goals in the game and get gold medals in all three competitions 17 times in Career mode with a different skater each time.
Perfect Balance for Rails	Complete all the goals in the game and get gold medals in all three competitions 13 times in Career mode with a different skater each time.
Perfect Record	To get a perfect record for a skater, enable the following codes in order: "Level select," "All characters," "All FMV sequences," and "Master code."
Private Carrera	Complete all the goals in the game and get gold medals in all three competitions five times in Career mode with a different skater each time.
Pro Bails 2 FMV Sequence	Complete all the goals in the game and get gold medals in all three competitions in Career mode with a created skater.
Pro Bails FMV Sequence	Get medals (gold, silver, or bronze) in all three competitions in Career mode.
Pro Retro FMV Sequence	Complete all the goals in the game and get gold medals in all three competitions in Career mode with Officer Dick.
Roswell Level from Tony Hawk's Pro Skater	Complete all the goals in the game and get gold medals in all three competitions nine times in Career mode with a different skater each time.
Slater Surf FMV Sequence	Complete all the goals in the game and get gold medals in all three competitions in Career mode with Kelly Slater.
Slow Motion	Complete all the goals in the game and get gold medals in all three competitions 16 times in Career mode with a different skater each time.
Small Skater	Complete all the goals in the game and get gold medals in all three competitions 18 times in Career mode with a different skater each time.
Snowboard Mode	Complete all the goals in the game and get gold medals in all three competitions 11 times in Career mode with a different skater each time.
Warehouse Level from Tony Hawk's Pro Skater	Complete all the goals in the game and get gold medals in all three competitions three times in Career mode with a created skater.
Wolverine	Complete all the goals in the game and get gold medals in all three competitions two times in Career mode with a different skater each time.

Tony Hawk's Pro Skater 4

Enter all codes in the Cheats Menu.

Unlockable	Code
Always Special	GOLDEN
Daisy	(o)(o)
Matrix Mode	MRANDERSON
Moon Gravity	GIANTSTEPS
Perfect Manuals	2WHEELIN
Perfect Rails	BELIKEGEOFF
Unlock Everything	WATCH_ME_XPLODE

Tony Hawk's Pro Skater 3 (cont'd)

To unlock the following secret characters, create a new skater and enter one of the following passwords as the name.

Password	Password	Password	Password
#$%@!	Fritz	Maya's Daddy	Rick Thorne
Aaron Skillman	Gary Jesdanun	Meek West	Sik
Adam Lippmann	grjost	Mike Day	Stacey D
Andrew Skates	Henry Ji	Mike Lashever	Stacey Ytuarte
Andy Marchal	Jason Uyeda	Mike Ward	Team Chicken
Angus	Jim Jagger	Mr. Brad	Ted Barber
Atiba Jefferson	Joe Favazza	Nolan Nelson	Todd Wahoske
Ben Scott Pye	John Rosser	Parking Guy	Top Bloke
Big Tex	Jow	Peasus	Wardcore
Brian Jennings	Kenzo	Pete Day	Zac Zig Drake
Captain Liberty	Kevin Mulhall		
Chauwa Steel	Kraken		
Chris Peacock	Lindsey Hayes		
ConMan	Lisa G Davies		
Danaconda	Little Man		
Dave Stohl	Marilena Rixfor		
DDT	Mat Hoffman		
DeadEndRoad	Matt Mcpherson		

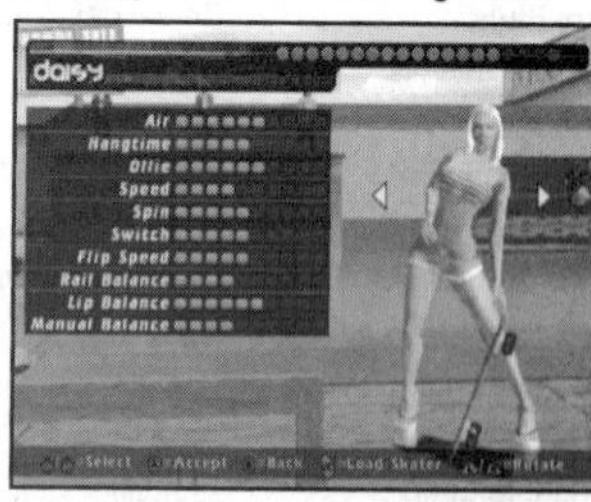

Tony Hawk's Underground

Unlockable	Code
Moon Gravity	getitup
Perfect Manuals	keepitsteady
Perfect Rails	letitslide
Perfect Skitches	rearrider
T.H.U.D.	NOOO!!

Tony Hawk's Underground 2

Enter all codes in the Cheats Menu.

Unlockable	Code
Natas Kaupas	oldskool
Nigel Beaverhausen	sellout
Perfect Rails	straightedge

Top Gun Combat Zones

Unlockable	Code
All Aircraft and Levels	Enter SHPONGLE as a name to unlock all aircraft and levels. The effects of the code are disabled if the game is saved.

True Crime: Streets of LA

While driving around in your car, go to the City Map menu to enter this first set of codes.

Unlockable	Code
All Bonuses	↑,→,↓,←,↑,Ⓐ
All Combat Moves	↑,↓,↑,↓,Ⓐ
All Driving Maneuvers	←,→,←,→,Ⓐ

True Crime: Streets of LA (cont'd)

All Fighting Skills	↑,↓,↑,↓,Ⓐ
All Gun Upgrades	→,←,→,←,Ⓐ
All Upgrades	↑,←,↓,←,↑,Ⓐ
Boost	Hold ↑ and press Ⓐ,Ⓐ,Ⓐ
Extra Car Mass	↓,↓,↓,Ⓐ
Impound Garage Cars	↑,→,↓,←,↑,Ⓐ
Lesser Car Mass	↑,↑,↑,Ⓐ
Snoop Dogg	R,L,↑,→,←,↓,Z,Z,Ⓐ,Y,X,Y

When you start a new game, enter the following passwords for your License Plate to use different skins for Nick.

Skin	Password
Asian Worker	HARA
Bartender	HAWG
Bum	B00Z
Commando	M1K3
Dirty Morales	BRUZ
Donkey	JASS
Gangsta Alt	TFAN
George	FATT
Jimmy Fu	MRFU
Lola Gees	B00B
Pimp	P1MP
Policeman Johnson	5WAT
Rosie	ROSA
Rosie in Lingerie	Hurt M3
Sewer Ghoul	J1MM
Street Punk	MNKY
Tattoo Concubines	TATS
The Chief	B1G1
Triad Butcher	PHAM

NOTE

After you enter the code for Snoop Dogg, get to a save point, then quit to the Main Menu. Continue your game; on the Chapter Select screen, you should see Snoop Dogg's face in the corner.

Tube Slider

Unlockable	Objective
Maximum Mode	Beat the game on Normal Mode.
New Track	Beat all of the Maximum Class races.
New Vehicle	Beat the extra race against the Spider.

Turok Evolution

Enter all codes in the Cheats menu.

Unlockable	Code
All Cheats	FMNFB
All Weapons	TEXAS
Big Heads	HEID
Demo Mode	HUNTER
Invincible	EMERPUS
Invisibility	SLLEWGH
Level Select	SELLOUT
Unlimited Ammo	MADMAN
Zoo Mode	ZOO

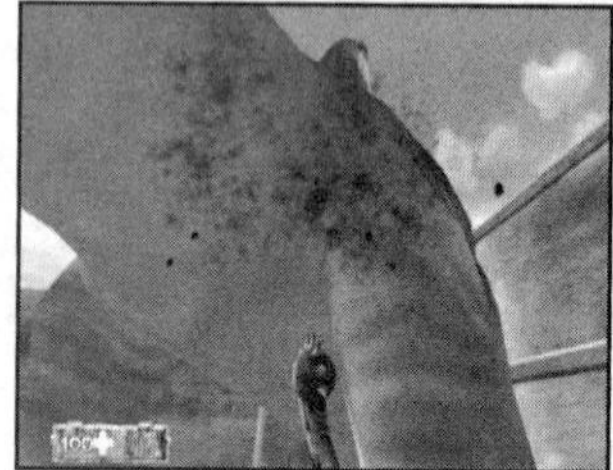

Ty the Tasmanian Tiger

All codes are entered during gameplay; do not pause the game.

Unlockable	Code
All Abilities	L, R, L, R, Y, Y, B, B, Y, B
Show Hidden Objects	L, R, L, R, Y, Y, X, B, B, X, Z, Z
Technorangs	L, R, L, R, Y, Y, Y, B, Y, B
Unlimited Life	L, R, L, R, Y, Y, Y, Y, X, X

Ultimate Muscle: Legends vs. New Generation

Unlockable Character	Objective
Blocken Jr.	Beat Story Mode as Jaeger.
Bone Cold	Collect 300 Toy Capsules.
Buffalo Man	Beat Story Mode as Dik Dik Van Dik.
Hanzo	Collect 200 Toy Capsules.
Kin Kotsu Man	Complete Story Mode with Bone Cold.
King Muscle	Beat Story Mode as Kid Muscle.
Panda Man	Complete Story Mode with Kin Kotsu Man.
Ramen Man	Beat Story Mode as Wally Tusket.
Robin Mask	Beat Story Mode as Kevin Mask.
Scar Face	Collect 100 Toy Capsules.
Sunshine	Beat Story Mode as Checkmate.
Terry Man	Beat Story Mode as Terry Kid.
The Ninja	Complete Story Mode with Hanzo.
Wars Man	Complete Story Mode with Scar Face.

Universal Studios Park Adventure

Unlockable	Objective
Attraction Mode	Get all eight stamps, then talk to Woody Woodpecker near the globe. Select the magic show when you talk to him. Allow the credits to finish, then return to the title screen. The option for Attraction mode will be unlocked.
Easy Money	Walk around the park, picking up trash and throwing it away.
Easy Points	Repeatedly watch the Waterworld Show to get 100 points each time.
Night Mode	Complete five attractions and the sun goes down.

Viewtiful Joe

Unlockable	Objective
Sylvia	Beat game on Adult Mode.

Wario World

To access the following unlockable, collect all eight treasures in the designated level.

Unlockable	Level
Dodge Balls	Greenhorn Ruins
UFO Assist	Wonky Circus
Jumpin' Rope	Beanstalk Way
Munch a Bunch	Pecan Sands
Trial Version 1—Wario Whirled	Greenhorn Forest
Trial Version 2—Heads Up	Horror Manor
Trial Version 3—Gold Digger	Shivering Mountains
Trial Version 4—Lickety-Split	Mirror Mansion

NOTE

Here's a special tip. Find all 40 Spritelings before beating the final boss to get the best castle and best ending.

Wave Race: Blue Storm

Unlockable	Code
Alternate Costumes	Highlight a racer, and press Z at the character selection screen.
Alternate Visualizations	Go to the Options screen, then select the audio settings. Press Z to change visualizations.
Arctic Bay Track	Complete the game in Championship mode under the Normal difficulty setting. This track is named Cool Ocean in the Japanese version of the game.
Control Loading Screen	Press the left analog stick while a track loads to control the water.
Control Replay	Use the right analog stick during a replay to control the view: ↑ to change camera angles. → to pan the camera around your character. ↓ to bring the view to water level. ← to switch to a first-person view.
Control Title Screen	Press the left analog stick when "Start" appears on the title screen to move it on the water. Press Z at the title screen to change the START button into a magnifying lens. Press Z again to change it back.

Wave Race: Blue Storm (cont'd)

Dolphin Park Stunt Track	Enter KTUPWNPD as a password to unlock this track in the Normal difficulty setting under Stunt mode. Enter 463YWNX3 as a password in the Japanese version of the game.
Expert Championship Tournament	Enter AJXY8P53 as a password to unlock an expert championship tournament on seven tracks.
Ghost Rider	To make the rider appear as a ghost, press ↑. Press ↓ to return to normal.
In-Game Reset	Hold Ⓧ+Ⓑ+START during gameplay.
La Razza Canal Time Attack Track	Enter MJV8LKL6 as a password to unlock this track under Time Attack mode.
La Razza Canal Track	Complete the game in Championship mode under the Advanced difficulty setting. This track is named Aqua Maze in the Japanese version of the game.
Lost Temple Lagoon Time Attack Track	Enter LQ3TRKTE as a password to unlock this track under Time Attack mode. Enter J784WMHF as a password in the Japanese version of the game.
Ride a Dolphin	Enter DLPHNMOD as a password to ride on the back of a dolphin in Free Run mode. You can still perform tricks on the dolphin, but you can only do back flips and barrel rolls.
Southern Island Stunt Track	Enter WCX5WP5A as a password to unlock this track in Stunt mode.
Strongwater Keep Track	Complete the game in Championship mode under the Expert difficulty setting. This track is named Victory Gate in the Japanese version of the game.
Time Attack Tournament Mode	Press Ⓧ+Ⓩ+START at the Options menu to unlock the "Password" selection. Passwords for various time attack tournaments may now be entered.
Trial Mode	Complete Tutorial mode under the Beginner and Master difficulty settings to unlock the "Trial" option on the tutorial menu.
Weather	Complete the Expert Championship in first, second, or third place, respectively, to unlock the weather conditions in Time Trial mode under the expert, advanced, or normal difficulties.

Wreckless

To enter this code, highlight Unlimited Time, then enter the code.

Unlockable	Code
Gold Rating for all Missions	Hold L+R+→, then press Z.

WWE Crush Hour

To access the following unlockable characters, beat Season Mode with the designated playable character.

Unlockable Character	Playable Character
Bradshaw	Brock Lesnar
Christian	Chris Jericho
D-Von Dudley	Bubba Ray Dudley
Hulk Hogan	The Rock

WWE Crush Hour (cont'd)

Lita	Matt Hardy
Ric Flair	The Big Show, Rob Van Dam, and Triple H
Stephanie McMahon	Kurt Angle
Vince McMahon	Face Vince (in the final battle).

Unlockable	Objective
Unlock All Vehicles/Level Select	Go to the player select screen and press Y, Z, X, L.
Unlock Demolition Derby Mode	Win a match without firing weapons.
Unlock Kevin Nash	Go to the player select screen and press L, X, Z, Y.

WWE WrestleMania X8

Unlockable	Objective
Chris Benoit	Win the WWE Undisputed Championship.
Original WWE SmackDown Arena	Win the WWE Undisputed Championship as The Rock.
Raven	Win the WWE Light Heavyweight Championship.
Rhyno	Win the WWE Hardcore Championship.
Ric Flair	Win the WWE European Championship.
Stacy Keibler	Win the WWE Tag Team Championship.
Vince McMahon	Win the WWE Intercontinental Championship.
WWE Royal Rumble 2001 Arena	Win the Royal Rumble with any Superstar.
WWE WrestleMania X7 Arena	Wrestle in all other arenas in Exhibition mode.

X-Men Legends

Enter this code at the main menu.

Unlockable	Code
Xtreme Costumes	↑,↑,→,←,↓,↓,START

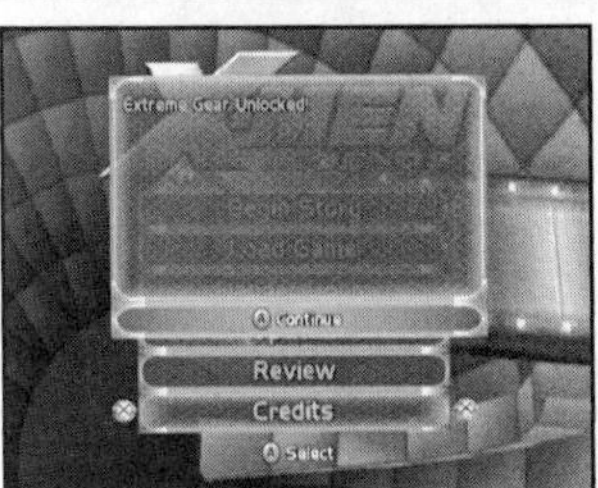

X2 Wolverine's Revenge

Unlockable	Code
All Cerebro Files	Ⓑ,X,Ⓑ,Y,Y,Y,R,R,Z
All Costumes	Ⓑ,X,Ⓑ,Y,Y,Y,L,L,Z
Invulnerability	Ⓑ,Ⓑ,X,X,Y,Y,X,X,X,L,L,R,R,Z
Level Select and Challenges	Ⓑ,X,Ⓑ,Y,Ⓑ,X,L,R,Z

Yu-Gi-Oh! Falsebound Kingdom

Enter the code during gameplay on a blank piece of land without pausing.

Unlockable	Code
Extra Money	↑,↑,↓,↓,←,→,←,→,Ⓑ,Ⓐ
Gold Coins	↑,↑,↓,↓,←,→,←,→,Ⓑ,Ⓐ

Zoocube

Description	Code
Ending Bonuses	Complete the Pacific Ocean level under the Classic difficulty setting to unlock the Gold difficulty setting and the Gulf of Mexico bonus level. Complete the Pacific Ocean level under the Gold difficulty setting to unlock the Platinum difficulty setting for the Gulf of Mexico level.
Warp Speed Setting	Complete the Pacific Ocean level under the Platinum difficulty setting.

Table of Contents - GBA

PSP Xbox PS2 GC GBA

Advance GTA

Unlockable	Objective
Formula 1 Mode	To access the extra Formula 1 mode, play through the Championship mode and beat all four of the classes with a first place in each race. You get a new car (Formula 1 racecar) after the last race. At the Menu screen, the Extra 2 option will be available.

Advance Rally

Unlockable	Objective
Co-Driver Mode	Win first place in all races in World Rally mode.
Hidden Track	Win first place in Co-Driver mode.

Advance Wars

Unlockable	Code
Advance Campaign Mode	Complete Campaign mode. Enter the Battle Maps screen and buy the "Advance Campaign" item for one coin. Hold SELECT and choose Campaign mode to begin an advanced campaign with a more difficult CPU opponent.
Deleted Saved Games	Hold L + R + SELECT when turning on the Game Boy Advance.
Field Training Bonuses	Complete Field Training mode to unlock the "War Room," "Campaign," "Design Maps," "Stats," and "Special Intel" options.
Ghost Mode	Hold Ⓑ during your turn.
In-Game Reset	Press START + SELECT + Ⓑ + Ⓐ during gameplay. See Caution
Quickly Finish Field Training	Select the final battle in Field Training mode. Win that battle to unlock all options that normally require Field Training to be completed.

CAUTION

In Game Reset Caution!

Do not use this while the Game Boy Advance is linked to a Gamecube or it may cause data loss.

Advance Wars 2: Black Hole Rising

Unlockable	Objective
Adder	Clear any Campaign Mode.
Colin	Recruit Grit or Olaf.
Drake	Clear the Green Earth Campaign.
Eagle	Clear the Green Earth Campaign.
Grit	Clear the Blue Moon Campaign.
Hachi	Clear any campaign on Hard Mode.
Hawke	Clear any Campaign Mode.
Jess	Recruit Drake or Eagle.
Kanbei	Clear the Yellow Comet Campaign.
Lash	Clear any Campaign Mode.
Nell	Earn an overall A rank in Campaign mode.
Olaf	Clear the Blue Moon Campaign.
Sensei	Recruit Kanbei or Sonja.

Advance Wars 2: Black Hole Rising (cont'd)

Unlockable	Objective
Sonja	Clear the Yellow Comet Campaign.
Sound Test	Beat Campaign mode with overall rank of A.
Sturm	Earn an overall A rank in Campaign mode.

Aggressive Inline

Unlockable	Code
All levels	At the Title Screen, press ↑,↓,↑,↓,←,→,Ⓑ,Ⓒ
All levels up to Deadman's Sewer	At the Title Screen, press Ⓛ,Ⓑ,Ⓡ,Ⓑ
All Skaters	Ⓛ,Ⓛ,Ⓑ,Ⓑ,Ⓡ,Ⓡ,Ⓛ,Ⓡ

Alienators: Evolution Continues

Unlockable	Code
Full Ammunition	RBJPXCKC
Level 2	MDKMZKCC
Level 3	BHSZSKTC
Level 4	ZKTSHKMC
Level 5	JLPFDKHB
Level 6	HMDBRKCB
Level 7	GLDKLKZB
Level 8	GLPKLKRB
Level 9	GLDJBKKF
Level 10	GLPJBKFF
Level 11	GLDKBKZF
Level 12	GLPKBKRF
Level 13	GLDJLKHD

American Idol

Enter the following codes as a password.

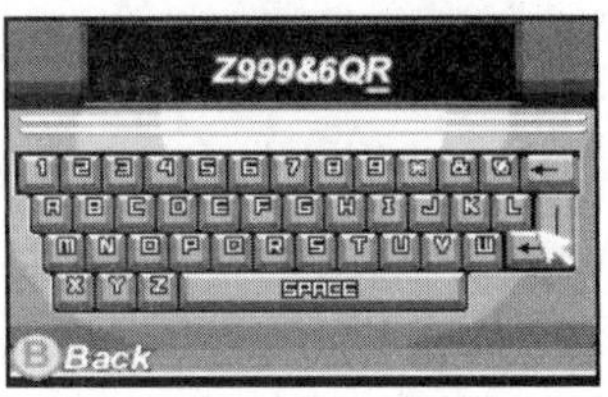

Unlockable	Code
Last three practice songs	Z999&6QR
More Costumes	HTH4&6CK

Army Men Advanced

Unlockable	Code
All Levels Unlocked	At the Password screen, enter NQRDGTPB.

Army Men: Operation Green

Unlockable	Code
Level 2: Workin' 9 til 5	5VKPR6*B
Level 3: With a Bucket, a Spade, and a Hand Grenade	5PK5LL*4
Level 4: Goin' Downtown	Y8DTF4HK
Level 5: Down on the Farm	62BVXHXY
Level 6: Baby, Light My Fire	MQ5310VP
Level 7: Here a Tan, There a Tan	SZQR6W1J
Level 8: The Rumble in the Jungle	44BQQCWH
Level 9: The Donkey Ride	F4J1ZRWG
Level 10: Top Brass in Trouble	FFOOWP36
Level 11: Jungle Fever	*HBNVVV4
Level 12: Spider's Web	85M3QCF*

Atlantis: The Lost Empire

Unlockable	Code
Level 2	BMQDNPJS
Level 3	BRZSGZDY
Level 4	BVMJFYLG
Level 5	B7JHPMHC
Level 6	C6XQLUNF
Final Level	COCNQQIY

Ballistic: Ecks vs. Sever 2

Enter the following words in the Password screen:

Unlockable	Code
All weapons	TOOLEDUP
Invincibility	DEATHWISH
Unlimited ammo	BIGPOCKET
Alternate sounds	HORNBLOW
Invisibility	DOYOUCME
Huge explosions	ACMEBANGS
Immobilized enemies	COLDFEET
Rapid fire	MYBIGUN

Level	Ecks Code	Sever Code
Two	SMOKEY	RAVEN
Three	BUTTERFLY	FIREFLY
Four	COVEY	BULLDOG
Five	TIGER	DRAGON
Six	HORNET	LOUDMOUTH
Seven	LITTERBUG	STINGER
Eight	MUSTANG	NAIL
Nine	SPECTRE	ZORRO
Ten	NIMROD	XRAY
Eleven	SPOOKY	REDDOG

Batman: Rise of Sin Tzu

Enter the following codes at the Main Menu while holding L+R.

Unlockable	Code
All Upgrades	↓,↑,↓,←,↓,→,↑,↓
All Rewards	←,↓,←,→,←,←,↓,→
God Mode	↑,→,↑,←,↓,←,↓,→
Unlimited Combo Meter	←,→,↓,↑,↑,↓,→,←

Batman Vengeance

Level	Normal Code	Advanced Code
Level 1	—	ARKHAM
Level 2	GOTHAM	WAYNE
Level 3	BATMAN	AMY
Level 4	BARBARA	NYGMA
Level 5	GRAYSON	CARRIE
Level 6	ROBIN	WESKER
Level 7	TIM	BULLOCK
Level 8	BATGIRL	GORDON
Level 9	FRIES	JONES
Level 10	VICTOR	OSWALD
Level 11	ALFRED	TALIA
Level 12	CATWOMAN	MONTOYA
Level 13	JAMES	SCARFACE
Level 14	DRAKE	CREEPER
Level 15	HARVEY	DENT
Level 16	SELINA	KYLE
Level 17	BATARANG	—
Level 18	BRUCE	—
Level 19	QUINZEL	—
Level 20	JACK	—
Level 21	EDWARD	—
View All Animations	NORA	—

Unlockable	Code
Unlimited Smoke Bombs	Enter LSMRTG as a password in a story or in Advance mode.

Britney's Dance Beat

Unlockable	Code
Activate Cheat Mode (All levels and bonuses)	Enter HMNFK as a password.

Castlevania: Aria of Sorrow

Description	Code/Objective
Don't Use Items	Enter "NOUSE" as your name.
Don't Use Souls	Enter "NOSOUL" as your name.
Get Best Ending	Collect all of the ancient books and beat Graham. You will then be taken to a fight against Chaos.
Boss Rush Mode	Beat the game to unlock Boss Rush mode.
Unlock Hard Mode	Beat the game and earn the good ending to unlock Hard Mode.
Julius Belmont	Beat the game once with Soma, then begin a new game and use the name "Julius."

Castlevania: Circle of the Moon

Description	Objective
Get the Shining Armor	Beat the Battle Arena in the chapel tower.
Unlock Fighter Mode	Beat the game twice (the second time in Magician mode). Your stats are higher then usual, but there are no DSS cards to collect.
Unlock Magician Mode	After you beat the game, enter the name "FIREBALL" at the Data screen. You will begin the game with all DSS Cards available right away.

Castlevania: Harmony of Dissonance

Unlockable	Code
Boss Rush Mode	Complete the game to unlock the Boss Rush option. There are three levels (easy, normal, and hard) that must be unlocked by playing each in succession, starting with easy.
Classic Simon	Unlock Boss Rush mode, then press ↑, ↑, ↓, ↓, ←, →, ←, →, Ⓑ, Ⓐ, SELECT at the Konami logo. Select Boss Rush mode to play as the NES version of Simon.
Hard Mode	Enter HARDGAME as a name after completing the game at least once. A voice at the start of the introduction confirms correct code entry.
No Magic	Enter NO MAGIC as a name after completing the game at least once.
Play as Maxim Kischine	Enter MAXIM as a name after completing the game at least once. He is faster and jumps higher than Belmont.
Sound Test Mode	Complete the game with the good ending (where you rescue Maxim and Lydie).

Castlevania: White Night Concerto

Unlockable	Code
Boss Rush Mode	Complete the game. There are three levels (easy, normal, and hard) that must be unlocked by playing each in succession, starting with easy.
Classic Simon	Unlock Boss Rush mode, then press ↑, ↑, ↓, ↓, ←, →, ←, →, Ⓑ, Ⓐ, SELECT at the Konami logo. Select Boss Rush mode to play as the NES version of Simon.
Hard Mode	Enter HARDGAME as a name after completing the game at least once. A voice at the start of the introduction confirms correct code entry.
No Magic	Enter NO MAGIC as a name after completing the game at least once.
Play as Maxim Kischine	Enter MAXIM as a name after completing the game at least once. He is faster and jumps higher than Belmont.
Sound Test Mode	Complete the game with the good ending (where you rescue Maxim and Lydie).

Chu Chu Rocket

Unlockable	Objective
Hard Mode	Complete Normal mode.
Special Mode	Complete Hard mode.
Mania Mode	Complete Special mode.

Classic NES Series: Bomberman

Level	Code
Level 1	NMIHPPBPCAFHABDPCPCH
Level 2	HIJDIJFJDLHFLOPDJDJN
Level 3	BAJDINANMJGGCPOOLOLG
Level 4	DJOLBGLGKGJAHIEMNMNN
Level 5	NMKGDDONMHLCGKKGKGKJ
Level 6	ABGKKBPHILHFLOPCPCPC
Level 7	FEBABGLEFLHFLOPCPCPA
Level 8	HIFEMIIABJGGCPOBABAN
Level 9	NMEFPHCMNJGGCPOBABAF
Level 10	JDGKKBPHILHFLOPGKGKL
Level 11	HIPCOHCMNLHFLOPEFEFG
Level 12	ABJDIFJKGGJAHIEPCPCN

Classic NES Series: Bomberman (cont'd)

Level	Code
Level 13	JDBABANOLJGGCPODJDJF
Level 14	ABNMKNAIHFAJNMMKGKGF
Level 15	ABIHPGLEFCNNJDBEFEFN
Level 16	ABABEMKJDAFHABDCPPCN
Level 17	JDDJOIIOLCNNJDBABOLH
Level 18	JDNMKLGHILHFLOPGKEFH
Level 19	DJABEKMPCFAJNMMOLFEL
Level 20	FEGKKJFNMAFHABDABOLN
Level 21	NMKGDDOIHJGGCPONMIHN
Level 22	NMCPIIIOLFAJNMMGKEFF
Level 23	NMPCOIIOLCNNJDBBAHIJ
Level 24	NMGKKEEHILHFLOPPCGKL
Level 25	HIKGDODCPGJAHIEPCGKJ
Level 26	ABHIMGLBANCLFEINMIHH
Level 27	MNGKKDOOLGJAHIEKGCPC
Level 28	OLDJOIIKGLHFLOPEFLOL
Level 29	IHJDIKMEFNCLFEINMIHF
Level 30	IHDJOIIKGLHFLOPMNJDA
Level 31	DJJDIDOOLFAJNMMEFLOC

Level	Code
Level 32	IHIHPBPCPNCBOLIHIJDH
Level 33	OLFEMANMNFADDJMABFEF
Level 34	MNDJOODJDHLPPCKBAMNA
Level 35	DJABEMKMNNCMIHIMNDJC
Level 36	BADJOIIIHAFDDJDIHOLA
Level 37	DJFEMPBPCGJKEFEEFBAC
Level 38	DJKGDIIIHJGBOLOABFEH
Level 39	DJCPIODFECNOBABABFEN
Level 40	IHEFPPBGKFAIMNMOLKGJ
Level 41	IHLOEHCMNNCMIHIIHOLJ
Level 42	DJEFPHCMNJGBOLOABFEH
Level 43	MNGKKIIOLGJKEFEKGPCJ
Level 44	BAPCOMKDJJGBOLODJIHJ
Level 45	OLNMKDOIHFAIMNMGKLOF
Level 46	OLIHPMKNMFAIMNMABFEH
Level 47	OLABEMKNMCNOBABPCEFL
Level 48	OLOLBFJGKGJKEFEFEPCL
Level 49	OLFEMFJGKLHPPCPLOMNL
Level 50	NMABEKMKGNCLFEIIHFEL

Classic NES Series: Metroid

Enter the following words in the Password screen:

Unlockable	Code
Samus with lots of weapons	JUSTIN BAILEY ------ ------
Invincibility and Unlimited Missiles	NARPAS SWORD0 000000 000000

Contra Advance The Alien Wars EX

Enter passwords in the passwords menu.

Unlockable	Password
Level 2 with 99 lives	Y4HC1B L5P212 34ZWF1
Level 3 with 99 lives	WXJD1Z JHSJ1Q KKNCY1
Level 5 with 99 lives	G3421N TDN51N C3BV2C
Level 6 with 99 lives	W3MJ1S J4VP1N YY24BD
Novice Level 2	11111N TYLH1Z FCS5H1
Novice Level 3	111113 TYLH1W BHZXZ1

PSP Xbox PS2 GC GBA

Contra Advance The Alien Wars EX (cont'd)

Novice Level 4	11111B TYLH1T XLGHSB
Normal Level 2	111111 TYLH1S 35MYH1
Normal Level 3	11111H TYLH1X QTTH1B
Normal Level 4	11111J TYLH1Z MY1RSB
Normal Level 5	11111V TYLH13 2D21LC
Normal Level 6	11111M TYLH1V CFDJDD

Crash Bandicoot: The Huge Adventure

Unlockable	Objective
Bonus level	Finish the game with a 100 percent completion. Play again and fight the final boss. Win the battle to play a level featuring mutated bosses.
Double Jump	Defeat N. Gin on the boss stage on the second floor to get the Double Jump.
Super Belly Flop	Get all the items.
Tornado Spin	Defeat Tiny on the boss stage on the third floor.
Turbo	Complete the game to unlock the ability to run faster in subsequent games. Hold L during gameplay to move faster.

Crash Bandicoot Purple: Ripto's Rampage

In the Mode Menu press L + R, and enter the following codes.

Unlockable	Code
100 Wumpa	CR4SH
200 Wumpa	G3CK0
500 Wumpa	C0FF33
All Intermission Sequences	CVTZ
Grenades	STR4WB3RRY or SVNB1R. Press the R to throw grenades
Green Pants	K1LL4Z
Kickin' It Old Skool! (Gray Game)	R3S3NTZ

Unlockable	Code
Mayan Jungle Card	WH1STL3
Orange Pants	BR3NT
Orangilicious Mode	L4MPP0ST
Purple Fever	WVMP4FR00T
Sewers Card	PH0N3T4G

TIP

Spyro Party USA Mini-Game

Hold L + R while powering up the Game Boy Advance

Crash Nitro Kart

Unlockable	Code
Crash Party USA	Hold both trigger buttons when turning on the game to access the mini game.

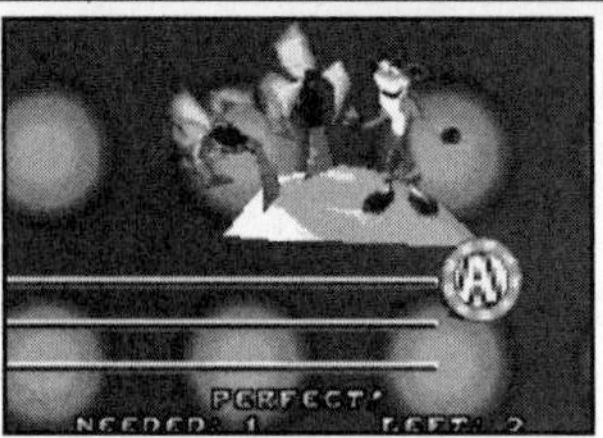

Crazy Taxi

Unlockable	Objective
City 2	Get a Crazy License ($10,000+) in City 1 on normal rules.

Cruis'n Velocity

Unlockable	Code
Level 1	HLDDRTSN
Level 2	HLDDSNST
Level 3	HLDDNRLN
Level 4	HLDDHVGD

CT Special Forces

Unlockable	Code
Level 2	1608
Level 3	2111
Final Level	1705
Unlock Special Characters	0202

Dark Arena

Enter the following codes as a password.

Unlockable	Code
All Keys	KNGHTSFR
All Maps	LMSPLLNG
All Weapons	THRBLDNS
Unlimited Ammunition	NDCRSDRT
Unlimited Health	HLGNDSBR
God Mode (This code activates unlimited health, all weapons, all keys, unlimited ammunition, all maps, and the level skip features.)	S_X_N—Note that the underscore ("_") indicates a space.
Level Skip	NFTRWLLH—Go to the Map screen, and press Select to advance to the next level.
Sound Effects Test	CRSDR—Enter the Game Options menu, then set "Sound FX" to Off, then back On to hear a random sound.

PSP
Xbox
PS2
GC
GBA

Dexter's Laboratory: Deesaster Strikes

For the following codes, pause gameplay, then enter code.

Unlockable	Code
Extra Life	Press L,L,R,R,L,R,L, L,L,R,L,L,R,R,L,L. Repeat to get more lives for a maximum of nine.
Extra Ray Gun Ammunition	Press L,R,R,R,L,L,R, R,L,L,L,L,R,L,L,R.
Faster Movement	Press L,R,R,R,R,L,R, L,R,R,L,L,R,L,R,R.
Faster Opponents	Press L,R,R,R,R,R,L, L,L,L,R,R,R,R,L,L.
Higher Jumps	Press L,L,R,R,R,R,R, R,L,L,R,R,L,L,L,R.
Invincibility	Press L,L,L,R,R,R,R, R,L,R,R,R,R,L,L,L.
Less Damage	Press L,R,R,R,R,L,L, L,R,L,L,L,L,L,L,R.
Reverse Controls	Press L,R,R,R,R,R,R, L,R,L,L,R,R,L,L,L.
Slower Opponents	Press L,L,R,R,R,L,R, R,R,L,L,R,R,L,L,R.
Stronger Dexter (Dexter can destroy robots more easily by punching or kicking for a limited amount of time.)	Press L,L,R,R,R,L,L, R,L,L,R,R,L,R,L,R.
Stronger Opponents	Press L,L,R,R,R,R,L, R,R,R,L,L,L,L,L,L,L.

Disney Princesses

Unlockable	Code
Unlock Extra Level	z8L5HGSCP4 x3tHlk0BtL

Donkey Kong Country

Unlockable	Code
Hero Mode	Complete the game with 100%, then start a new game and select two player mode.
Start with 50 Lives	Go to Start. On the Select a Game screen, highlight Erase. Then hold SELECT and press B,A,R,R,A,L.

Donkey Kong Country 2

Go to the Options menu and select Cheats. Enter the following words:

Donkey Kong Country 2 (cont'd)

Unlockable	Code
Level Select	FREEDOM
No DK Barrels	ROCKARD
No DK or Half-Way Barrels	WELLARD
Start with 15 Lives	HELPME
Start with 55 Lives	WEAKLING
Start with 10 Banana Coins	RICHMAN
Start with 50 Banana Coins	WELLRICH

Unlockable	Code
Credits	KREDITS

Doom

To access the following unlockables, press START to pause gameplay, hold L+R, then enter code.

Unlockable	Code
All Weapons, Items, and Keys	Ⓐ,Ⓑ,Ⓑ,Ⓐ,Ⓐ,Ⓐ,Ⓐ,Ⓐ.
Berserk	Ⓑ,Ⓐ,Ⓑ,Ⓐ,Ⓐ,Ⓐ,Ⓐ,Ⓐ.
Computer Map	Ⓑ,Ⓐ,Ⓐ,Ⓐ,Ⓐ,Ⓐ,Ⓐ,Ⓐ.
Disable God Mode	Ⓐ,Ⓐ,Ⓑ,Ⓐ,Ⓑ,Ⓑ,Ⓑ,Ⓑ.
God Mode	Ⓐ,Ⓐ,Ⓑ,Ⓐ,Ⓐ,Ⓐ,Ⓐ,Ⓐ.
Invincibility	Ⓑ,Ⓑ,Ⓑ,Ⓐ,Ⓐ,Ⓐ,Ⓐ,Ⓐ.
Level Skip (Use only in single-player games.)	Ⓐ,Ⓑ,Ⓐ,Ⓐ,Ⓑ,Ⓑ,Ⓑ,Ⓐ.
Radiation Suit	Ⓑ,Ⓑ,Ⓐ,Ⓐ,Ⓐ,Ⓐ,Ⓐ,Ⓐ.

Double Dragon Advance

In the Options screen, hold SELECT and enter the following codes.

Unlockable	Code
Ten Credits	L,R,↓,L,R,↓,L,R,→
Background Music Select	R,L,R,L
Expert Mode	↑,↑,↓,↓,←,→,←,→

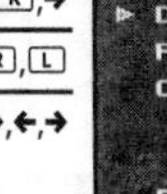

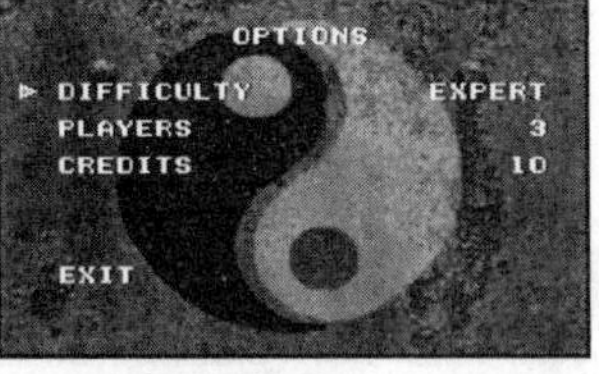

Dragon Ball Z: The Legacy of Goku

Unlockable	Code
Invincibility	↑, ↓, ←, →, Ⓑ, Ⓐ

Dragon Ball Z: Legend of Goku II

Unlockable	Objective
Alternative Ending	Unlock Mr. Satan and go to Level 50, then go to West City and break down the Level 50 door to ZZTV.
Gohan's Trophy	Go to Level 50 with Gohan, then go to the "50" gate outside Gingertown to collect the trophy.
Goku's Trophy	Finish the game.
Piccolo's Trophy	Go to Level 50 with Piccolo, then go to the "50" gate at Namek planet to collect the trophy.
Play as Hercule	Go to Level 50 with Gohan, Piccolo, Vegeta, and Trunks, then go to the character-specific "50" gates to collect trophies.
Trunks' Trophy	Go to Level 50 with Trunks, then go to the "50" gate at West City to collect the trophy.

Dragon Ball Z: Legend of Goku II (cont'd)

Unlock Mr. Satan (Hercule)	Get everyone but Goku to Level 50, then go through each character's Level 50 Area and collect their Character Trophies. Then beat the game and you'll get Goku's Trophy, with a message telling you that Mr. Satan is now playable.
Vegeta's Trophy	Go to Level 50 with Vegeta, then go to the "50" gate at Northern Mountains to collect the trophy.

Dragon Ball Z: Supersonic Warriors

Unlockable	Objective
Secret Final Battles	Complete story mode without losing once, then wait until after the credits. Note: Not all characters have a final battle.

Driven

Enter the following passwords as a code.

Unlockable	Code
All Cars and Tracks	29801
Game Stop Car	07913
Master Car	62972

Duke Nukem Advance

Cheat Mode	At anytime during the game, pause and enter ←, ↑, Ⓐ, ↑, ←, Ⓐ, START, SELECT

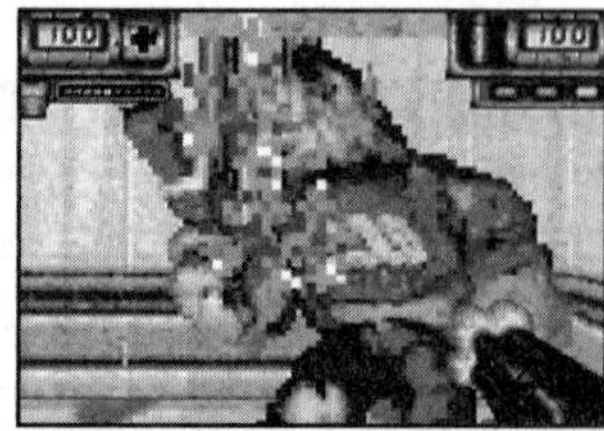

E.T.: The Extra-Terrestrial

Unlockable	Code
Level 2	↑,↑,Ⓐ,↓,↓,Ⓑ,[R],[L]
Level 3	←,↑,→,↓,[L],Ⓐ,[R],Ⓑ
Level 4	Ⓐ,←,Ⓑ,→,[L],↑,[R],↓
Level 5	[L],[R],[R],[L],Ⓐ,↑,Ⓑ,←
Level 6	[L],←,[R],→,Ⓐ,Ⓐ,Ⓑ,Ⓐ
Level 7	Ⓑ,[R],Ⓑ,[L],Ⓐ,↑,Ⓑ,↑
Level 8	↑,↑,Ⓐ,↓,↓,←,Ⓐ,Ⓑ
Level 9	→,Ⓑ,Ⓑ,←,↑,[R],[R],[L]
Level 10	←,←,Ⓐ,[L],→,→,Ⓑ,[R]

Earthworm Jim

To access the following unlockables, pause gameplay and enter code.

Unlockable	Code
Skip to Buttville	[L],Ⓐ,↑,[R],Ⓐ,[R],Ⓐ,SELECT
Skip to Down the Tubes	↑,[L],↓,Ⓐ,[R],Ⓐ
Skip to For Pete's Sake	[R],[L],[R],[L],Ⓐ,[R]
Skip to Level 5	[R],[L],Ⓐ,Ⓑ,Ⓑ,Ⓐ,[L],[R]
Skip to Snot a Problem	[R],↑,SELECT,[L],[R],←
Skip to What the Heck	SELECT,[R],Ⓑ,↓,[L]

Extreme Ghostbusters

Level	Password
Big Building Boss	8G20S86SC
Carnivorous and Hungry	WSFKP6WT3
Closer to the Underworld	MD*XN7KTJ
Ethereal Ball	MD2TK4XTK
In the Wings	MDZ9KK/T8
On Stage	WS0PJ6LTC
Racing 2	30J82JBMB
Racing 3	VD*PJKFTS
Racing 4	LDK9K6HTC
The Botanical Museum Final Boss	VSFPPMHT8
The Broadway Star Theater	VS31JL9TW
The Corridors	5PMDTF/K2
The Crypt	V8JNNVGLC
The Final Confrontation	MS29P7JTW
The Hall	HGBNL14VJ
The Offices	21QSR9JTS
The Main Aisle	BNKN34SMW

F-14 Tomcat

Level	Ace Code	Novice Code
Level 2	DHGJ	DHGJ KLFF
Level 3	KJTR DBPT	GSDF BFPT
Level 4	RVBP ZJVM	RRHC FDVM
Level 5	BMNQ YLNF	BPSX FDNF
Level 6	LFMS DNBQ	LDFS DTKQ
Level 7	PGHP CZNJ	PXSB SZNJ
Level 8	DKDG BPQK	DKXZ GZQK
Level 9	GSYP ZLCT	GKQB GHCT
Level 10	DCZX RPQR	DTRH RPFJ
Level 11	WRTN JYSX	WZPK JYZX
Level 12	JDPQ MLRT	JDZFLKFV
Level 13	SPBX BMRG	SPNG DRRG
Level 14	SPXP RGDH	SFGF JHDH
Level 15	LPFG NBGZ	LPFH PRFZ
Level 16	TQWJ GZHN	TDKZ XSHX
Level 17	BGJK SZPQ	DGBV KMNB

F-14 Tomcat (cont'd)

Level 18	PLMN HRTY	KJHG RJCB
Level 19	GLMR TRRC	VBMQ RWTP
Level 20	NHDJ PBCX	LKFD SPBV
Level 21	LCML FLTC	NHDC DKPM

F-Zero

Enter the following codes at the title screen.

Unlockable	Code
All Tracks	Ⓑ,[L],Ⓑ,Ⓐ,[R],Ⓑ,Ⓑ,Ⓐ,Ⓐ
Alternate Vehicles	Press Ⓐ,Ⓐ,Ⓑ,Ⓐ,[L],[R],Ⓐ,Ⓑ,[L]
Faster Vehicles	Ⓐ,Ⓑ,[L],Ⓐ,Ⓐ,[R],Ⓑ

Unlockable	Code
In-Game Reset	Press SELECT+START+Ⓐ+Ⓑ during gameplay.
Password Screen	Press [L],[R],START,[R],[L],SELECT at the machine selection screen in Grand Prix mode.
Slower Opponents	Press Ⓐ,[R],[L],Ⓑ,Ⓐ,Ⓐ,Ⓑ,[L] at the title screen.

Final Fight One

Unlockable	Code
Alpha Cody and Alpha Guy (Alpha Cody is bigger, and Alpha Guy is stronger.)	Press ← or → at the character selection screen to choose these fighters.
Change Control Settings	Pause gameplay and hold [L]+[R]+Ⓑ+Ⓐ.

Finding Nemo

Unlockable	Code
Level 2	Password: HZ51
Level 3	Password: ZZ51
Level 4	Password: 8061
Level 5	Password: QHP1
Level 6	Password: 8BP1
Level 7	Password: 73P1
Level 8	Password: 8MN2
Level 9	Password: 7452
Level Select and Access All Gallery Images	Password: M6HM

Fire Emblem

Unlockable	Objective
Canas	Visit the village in Chapter 16x (17x Hector).
Erk	Talk to Erk with Serra in Chapter 14.
Farina	Get Farina to talk to you in Chapter 25 (Hector Mode only). She will ask for 20,000 Gold in exchange for helping you in battle.
Fiora	Talk to Fiora with Florina in Chapter 18 (19 Hector).
Geitz	Talk to Geitz with Dart in Chapter 23 (24 Hector) if all lords' levels equal 50 or higher.
Guy	Talk to Guy with Matthew in Chapter 13.
Harken	Talk to Harken with Eliwood, Hector, or Isadora in Chapter 25 (27 Hector) if all magic users' level gain is larger than Fighters, Myrmidons,and Mercenaries.
Heath	Talk to Heath with any of your lords in Chapter 21 (22 Hector).
Fire Jaffar	Talk to him with Nino in Chapter 26 (28 Hector.) He won't join until the beginning of Chapter 26x (28x Hector.)

Fire Emblem (cont'd)

Unlockable	Objective
Karel	Talk to Karel with Lyn in Chapter 25 (27 Hector) if Fighters, Myrmidons, and Mercenaries' level gains are bigger than all your magic users.
Karla	In Chapter 31x, you must have a Warrior Bartre Level 5. Talk to Karla with Bartre. You must both survive in battle for one turn, then she will join you.
Legault	Talk to Legault with any of your lords in Chapter 19 (20 Hector).
Lucius	Talk to Lucius with Raven in Chapter 16 (17 Hector).
Nino	Talk to Nino with Lyn or your main lord in Chapter 26 (28 Hector).
Priscilla	Visit the lower-left village in Chapter 14.
Rath	Talk to Rath with Lyn in Chapter 21 (22 Hector).
Raven	Talk to Raven with Priscilla in Chapter 16 (17 Hector).
Renault	Visit the village in the northwest corner in Chapter 30 (32 Hector).
Vaida	Talk to Vaida with your main lord in Chapter 27 (29 Hector). Note: she won't appear if you killed her in Chapter 24 (26 Hector).
Wallace	Talk to Wallace with Lyn in Chapter 23 (24 Hector) if all lords' levels equal 49 or less.

Gekido Advance: Kintaro's Revenge

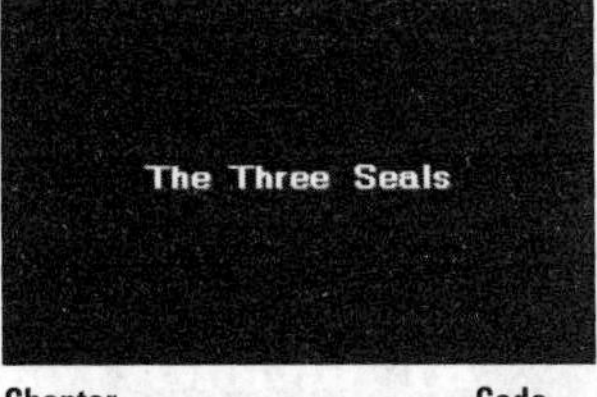

Chapter	Code
Chapter 2 The Three Seals	SACCO
Chapter 3 The Ancient Book	TAPPO
Chapter 4 Searching for Koji	TEMPO
Chapter 5 The Final Battle	BECCO

Golden Sun: The Lost Age

Unlockable	Code
Name all your party members	To give alternate names to Jenna, Sheba, and Pierrs, press SELECT, SELECT, SELECT while naming Felix. If you are playing a non-linked game, you may name Garet, Ivan, and Mia by pressing ↑,↓,↑,↓,←,→,←,→,↑,→,↓,←,↑, SELECT. A sound confirms correct code entry.
New Difficulties	Beat the game once to unlock the new difficulties. With your Clear Data save, select "New Game." Select "Yes" for Easy or "No" for Hard.

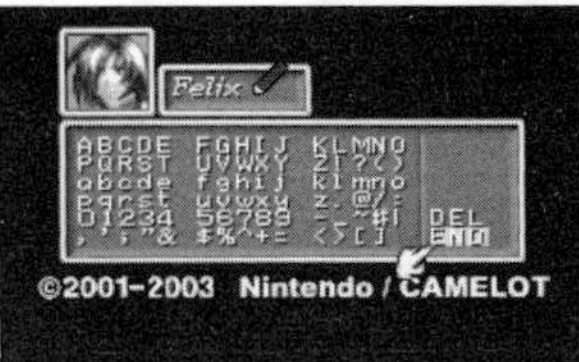

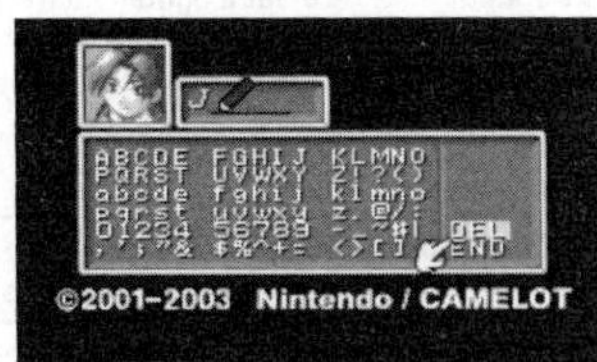

Gradius Galaxies

Unlockable	Code
All Power-Ups	Press START to pause gameplay, then press ↑,↑,↓,↓,L, R,L,R,B,A,START. See Caution Box.
Challenge A Mode	Complete the game to unlock the Challenge A option at the main menu.
Challenge B Mode	Complete the game in Challenge A mode.
Delete Saved Game	Enter the Options screen, highlight "Exit," then hold L+R+B and press START.
Self-Destruct	Press START to pause gameplay, then press ↑,↑,↓,↓,←,→,←,→,B,A,START.

CAUTION

The "All Power Ups" cheat can be used only a limited number of times until it causes your ship to self-destruct.

Grand Theft Auto Advance

Unlockable	Code
Location Coordinates	During gameplay, press and hold START + A + B.

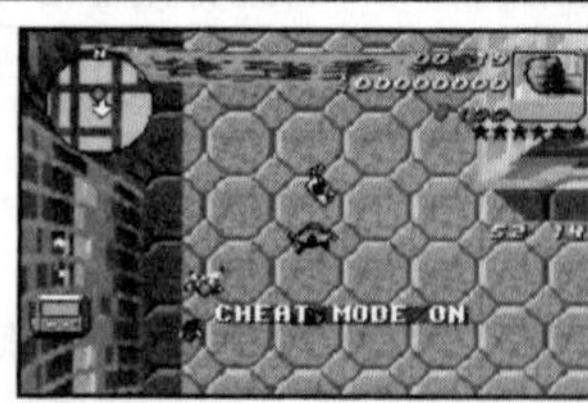

GT Advance 2

Input the following codes at the title screen.

Unlockable	Code
All Cars	Hold L+B and press ←.
All Tracks	Hold L+B and press →.
All Tune Ups	Hold L+B and press ↑.
Extra Modes	Hold L+B and press ↓.

GT Advance Championship Racing

Enter the following codes at the title screen.

Unlockable	Code
F1 Mode	Press and hold L+R, press ←,B. The Extra 2 option will be available.
Go-Kart Mode	Press and hold L+R, press →,B. The Extra 1 option will be available.
View Credits	Press and hold L+R, press ↑,B.

Guilty Gear X

Unlockables	Code
Alternate Costumes	Press START or SELECT when choosing a fighter at the character selection screen.
Dizzy	Defeat Dizzy's daredevil version in Survival mode. Alternately, defeat Dizzy on Stage 10 in Arcade mode.
Extra Mode	Defeat a fighter's daredevil version in Survival mode to unlock the extra mode for that fighter. The fighter's extra version can execute new moves and supers.
Fight as Dizzy or Testament	Press ↓,R,R,↑,START at the Press Start screen.
Original Mode	Complete the game in Survival mode to unlock the "Original Mode" selection at the Options screen.
Testament	Defeat Testament's daredevil version in Survival mode. Alternately, defeat Testament in Stage 9 and Dizzy on Stage 10 in Arcade mode.

Harry Potter and the Sorcerer's Stone

Unlockable	Code
Get 10 Extra Lives	Press SELECT,B,A,B,A,B,B,A,A during gameplay.

Hot Wheels Velocity X

Enter these passwords:

Unlock	Code
All cars	496-93-993
Everything	723-83-462

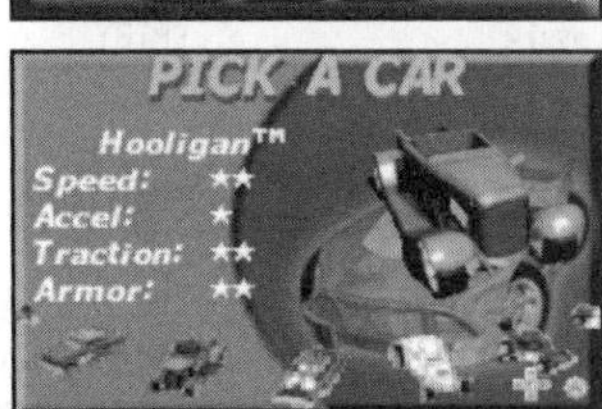

Ice Age

Enter the following codes as a password.

Unlockable	Code
Art Gallery	MFKRPH
Level Select	NTTTTT

Incredible Hulk

Unlockable	Code
Stage Skip	Pause the game, then press ↓,→,↓,→,←,←,←,↑.

Inspector Gadget: Advance Mission

Unlockable	Code
Big Ben: The Palace	*3RM33P
Big Ben: The Top	RHRM37P
Egypt: The Great Pyramid	*9R33XP
Egypt: The Valley of the Kings	RC7M27P
Statue of Liberty: In the Statue	*7*MM14
Statue of Liberty: The Flame of Liberty	*3HMLI4
The Great Wall: At the Foot of the Great Wall	*H*3M24
The Great Wall: On the Great Wall	R5*3MR4
The Tower: Higher than Anything	*CH3L24
The Tower: The Lift	R7H3L64
The Tower: The Tower Keeps Watch	R3*3M64

Iridion 3D

Unlockable	Code
All Levels	Go to the Password screen and enter S3L3CT0N,press OK, then return to the Password screen from the main menu and enter SH0WT1M3, then press OK.
View All Bosses	To view an end level boss, go to the Game Options screen and highlight "Start Level." Select your level, then highlight the option for "Start at Boss." Select "Yes," then "OK," and you will be at the boss fight!

Iridion II

Unlockable	Password
Finished Game	4RC8!
Jukebox	CH4LL
Level 2	9PTBY
Level 3	TYHLY
Level 4	9VDBW
Level 5	SLZGW
Level 6	TDZQ4
Level 7	5M!H6
Level 8	N59G6
Level 9	558GY
Level 10	54!H4
Level 11	PCGZW
Level 12	NPH74
Level 13	9GF46
Level 14	SOL46
Level 15	9!H84

Jackie Chan Adventures: Legend of the Dark Hand

Unlockable	Code
Activate Cheat Mode (Unlock all levels and scrolls)	Hold R and press Ⓑ,Ⓐ,←,↓,↑,→ at the Press Start screen. Alternately, hold R and press Ⓑ,Ⓐ,↑,↓,←,→.

James Bond 007: Nightfire

During gameplay, pause the game and input the following codes. A voice will confirm correct code entry.

Unlockable	Code
500 Bullets	Press R, ←, L, →, ↑, SELECT, →.
All Levels	Press R, ←, L, →, ↑, SELECT, R.
Invincibility	Press R, ←, L, →, ↑, SELECT, ←.

Jet Grind Radio

Unlockable	Objective
Hear the Sega Scream	Tap Ⓐ as the game boots.
Noise Tanks	Beat the Benten-Cho levels earning a Jet ranking.
Poison Jam	Beat the Kogane-Cho levels earning a Jet ranking.
Prof. K	Beat the game.
The Love Shockers	Beat the Shibuya-Cho levels earning a Jet ranking.

Jimmy Neutron: Boy Genius

Go to Enter Code in the Main Menu and enter the following passwords.

Jimmy Neutron: Boy Genius (cont'd)

Unlockable	Easy Mode Code	Hard Mode Code
Asteroid Field:	WM5DR5H3MCLB	2040YL61TT0T
Dungeon:	N?+94T1?DJXW	456N$DWBWM?F
Ending Scene:	3L!VPH26V7$8	+CLT3LD1TTSF
King Goobot:	BD5VVRDF3GXV	—
Poultra:	939BSYT41N0Z	XZ16F2F8NS$!
Yokian Moon:	KVZQG3Q50LZG	GGP6WCC273-3
Yokus:	—	2H?-!L81TT0K
Yokian Palace:	MMS-KXBVC4FS	+R6H!L91TT0F

Kao the Kangaroo

Enter one of the following icon passwords to skip to a specific level.

Level	Code
Ancient Ruins	Flag, Bomb, Kao's Face, Boxing Glove, Kao's Face.
Bear Peak	Frog, Frog, Kao's Face, Boxing Glove, Kao's Face.
Big Blizzard	Lamp, Palm Tree, Heart, Boxing Glove, Kao's Face.
Crocodile Island	Heart, Palm Tree, Lamp, Boxing Glove, Kao's Face.
Deadly Waterfall	Boxing Glove, Mushroom, Evergreen, Boxing Glove, Kao's Face.
Evil Descent	Owl, Butterfly, Bird, Boxing Glove, Kao's Face.
Frozen Lake	Bird, Key, Frog, Boxing Glove, Kao's Face.
Holy Temple	Bomb, Kao's Face, Boxing Glove, Boxing Glove, Kao's Face.
Hunter	Palm Tree, Lamp, Frog, Boxing Glove, Kao's Face.
Hypnodjin	Bomb, Flag, Coin, Boxing Glove, Kao's Face.
Ice Caves	Key, Key, Kao's Face, Boxing Glove, Kao's Face.
Island Shores	Coin, Heart, Palm Tree, Boxing Glove, Kao's Face.
Lightning Speed	Palm Tree, Heart, Coin, Boxing Glove, Kao's Face
Little Valley	Butterfly, Bird, Key, Boxing Glove, Kao's Face.
Lost Village	Evergreen, Fish, Owl, Boxing Glove, Kao's Face.
Megasaurus Ferocious	Fish, Owl, Butterfly, Boxing Glove, Kao's Face.
Mythical Caves	Mushroom, Evergreen, Fish, Boxing Glove, Kao's Face.
Neverending Slide	Flag, Coin, Heart, Boxing Glove, Kao's Face.
Peril Desert	Heart, Coin, Flag, Boxing Glove, Kao's Face.
Trade Village	Coin, Flag, Bomb, Boxing Glove, Kao's Face.

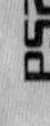

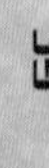
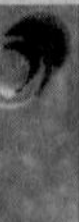

Konami Collector's Series: Arcade Advanced

Unlockable	Code
Frogger (Enhanced Graphics)	Press ↑,↑,↓,↓,←,→,←,→,Ⓑ,Ⓐ,START
Gyruss (Enhanced Graphics)	Press ↑,↑,↓,↓,←,→,←,→,Ⓑ,Ⓐ,START
Rush'n Attack (Two Extra Lives)	Press ↑,↑,↓,↓,←,→,←,→,Ⓑ,Ⓐ,START
Scramble (Enhanced Graphics)	Press ↑,↑,↓,↓,←,→,←,→,Ⓑ,Ⓐ,START
Time Pilot (Extra Stage)	Press ↑,↑,↓,↓,←,→,←,→,Ⓑ,Ⓐ,START
Yie Ar Kung Fu (Extra Fighters in Vs. Mode)	Press ↑,↑,↓,↓,←,→,←,→,Ⓑ,Ⓐ,START

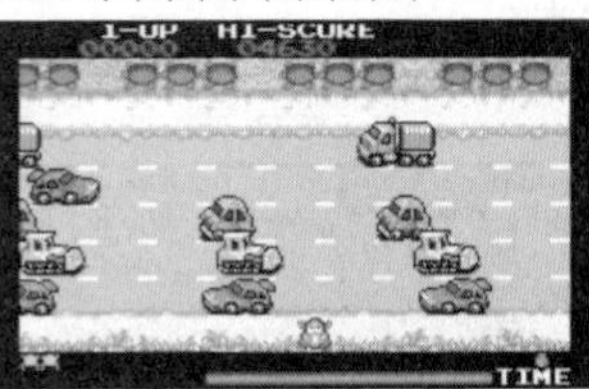

Lego: Bionicle

For the following codes, enter each as a name, then select "End," press Ⓐ,START,Ⓑ,START, then select "Quit Game," "Yes," then "No."

Unlockable	Code
Master Code	Enter B9RBRN.
Gali Mini-Game	Enter 9MA268. Alternately, complete the game as Gali.
Kopaka Snow Ball Sling Mini-Game	Enter V33673. Alternately, complete the game as Kopaka.
Lewa Mini-Game	Enter 3LT154. Alternately, complete the game as Lewa.
Onua Crab Dig Mini-Game	Enter 8MR472. Alternately, complete the game as Onua.
Pohatu Football Mini-Game	Enter 5MG834. Alternately, complete the game as Pohatu.
Tahu Lava Surf Mini-Game	Enter 4CR487. Alternately, complete the game as Tahu.

Lilo and Stitch

Use the following icon combinations as passwords to skip to specific levels.

Unlockable	Code
Beach	Stitch, Stitch, Stitch, Stitch, Stitch, Stitch, Stitch.
End	Pineapple, Pineapple, Pineapple, Pineapple, Stitch, Stitch, Stitch.
Escape!	Stitch, Scrump, UFO, Gun, Rocket, Scrump, UFO.
Final Challenge	Lilo, Pineapple, Flower, Pineapple, Gun, Gun, Stitch.
Junkyard Planet	UFO, Rocket, Stitch, Rocket, Rocket, Scrump, Stitch.

Lilo and Stitch (cont'd)

Unlockable	Code
Mothership	UFO, Scrump, Stitch, Rocket, UFO, Stitch, UFO.
Rescue	Flower, Scrump, UFO, Gun, Gun, Gun, UFO.
Space Cruiser	Lilo, Rocket, Stitch, Rocket, Rocket, Scrump, Stitch.

WELCOME TO SCUM. AN ASTEROID JUNKYARD. YOUR SHIP WAS TOTALLY DESTROYED IN THE CRASH.

Lion King

Unlockable	Code
Level 2	63NSBY
Level 3	80FSBX8
Level 4	GV9NSN2
Level 5	8WNF2NB
Level 6	2V10FWO
Level 7	Q9B2WHV
Level 8	D3J8P3V
Level 9	VPD+XKJ
Level 10	456P67L

Lord of the Rings: Return of the King

Unlockable	Code
Smeagol	Complete the game with 2000 or more kills.

Mario Kart Super Circuit

Unlockable	Objective
Alternate Title Screen	Complete all circuits in all classes to change the background color of the title screen.
Control Player Selection Screen	Press L to shoot a green shell or press R to jump at the character selection screen.
Delete Game	Hold L+R+B+START and turn on the system to delete the current saved data.
Special Cup Circuit	Win a gold cup in all races to unlock the Special Cup circuit.
Super Mario Kart tracks	Get 100 coins or more by the end of the cup to unlock extra tracks. Press L or R to view and play them. Once you get an "A" rank on every cup in every class, you unlock all of the original courses from Super Mario Kart.
Waluigi	Win every cup (50, 100, 150) and get gold medals in everything, including the secret levels.

Medal of Honor: Underground

God Mode Go to Options and enter "MODEDEDIEU" as a password.

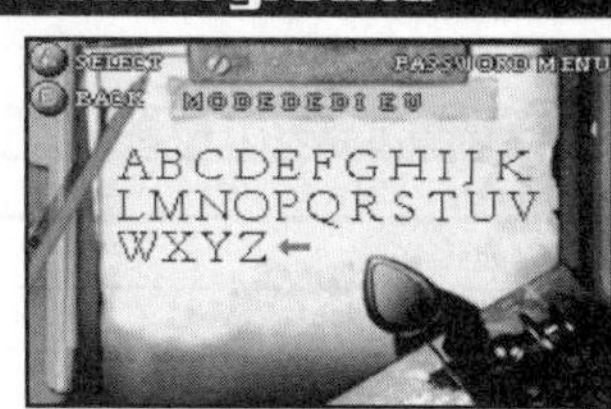

Unlockable	Easy Mode Level Passwords	Medium Mode Level Passwords	Hard Mode Level Passwords
Level 1	TRILINGUE	IRRADIER	DOSSARD
Level 2	SQUAME	FRIMAS	CUBIQUE
Level 3	REVOLER	ESCARGOT	CHEMIN

Medal of Honor: Underground (cont'd)

Unlockable	Easy Mode Level Passwords	Medium Mode Level Passwords	Hard Mode Level Passwords
Level 4	FAUCON	DEVOIR	BLONDEUR
Level 5	UNANIME	COALISER	BLESSER
Level 6	ROULIS	BASQUE	AVOCAT
Level 7	RELAVER	ROBUSTE	AFFINER
Level 8	POUSSIN	SOYEUX	LAINE
Level 9	PANOPLIE	TERRER	MESCLUN
Level 10	NIMBER	VOULOIR	NORME
Level 11	NIAIS	COUVERT	ORNER
Level 12	KARMA	VOYANCE	PENNE
Level 13	INCISER	PIGISTE	QUELQUE
Level 14	GADOUE	NOMMER	REPOSE
Level 15	FUSETTE	JETER	SALIFIER
Level 16	EXCUSER	ENJAMBER	TROPIQUE
Level 17	ENRICHIR	MORPHE	VOTATION

Mega Man and Bass

Unlockable	Code
Delete Database	(SELECT)+(START)+(A)+(B)+(L)+(R)

Men in Black: The Series

Enter the following codes as passwords.

Unlockable	Code
All Weapons	LLWPNSDD
Ending	NFNTMMDD
Episode 2: Forest Landing Site	FCHTRMNS
Episode 3: Alien Technology Lab	HSDSHSBS
Episode 4: Rocket Silo	MXNMSNNG
Episode 5: MIB Safehouse	THXBXSCK
Episode 6: Halloween in Manhattan	NNTNDWNY
Invincibility	LVFRVRDD
Unlimited Ammunition and Game's Ending	NFNTMMDD

MLB Slugfest 2004

Unlockable	Code
1920 Mode	(B),(B),(A),(A),(A),(A),(R),(R),↑
All Fielders Run	(B),(A),(A),(A),(R),(R),↑
Backwards Fielders	(B),(B),(B),(B),(A),(A),(A),(A),(R),(R),(R),(R),→
Fireworks	(B),(A),(A),(A),(A),(R),→
Ghost Fielders	(B),(B),(B),(A),(R),(R),(R),↓
Nuke Ball	(B),(B),(B),(A),(A),(A),(A),(R),(R),(R),↑
Skull Ball	(B),(B),(B),(A),(A),(R),(R),(R),←

Monsters, Inc.

Unlockable	Code	Unlockable	Code
Level 2	SJBOGS	Level 13	LTD!SK
Level 3	MKB2Z7	Level 14	ZTFZD8
Level 4	VPB971	Level 15	BYY2NL
Level 5	LLCOBK	Level 16	M2F9S7
Level 6	8PW2DY	Level 17	LYGOBO
Level 7	NQWOJF	Level 18	1FZ2CJ
Level 8	WRC9SQ	Level 19	F2Z2FM
Level 9	3RC!94	Level 20	F2Z2KR
Level 10	XRDZB1	Level 21	PNG!TL
Level 11	YRX2DQ	Level 22	WRG!!C
Level 12	3NX2JX		

Mortal Kombat: Tournament Edition

Description	Objective
Bo' Rai Cho Fatality	Beat Tag Team Mode with every character (except Noob Saibot & Sektor).
Cyrax Fatality	Defeat ten opponents in Survival Mode with Cyrax.
Drahmin	Beat 1P Tag Team mode on Normal+ difficulty with any team.
Drahmin Fatality	Purchase in the Krypt.
Hsu Hao	Beat 1P Arcade Mode on Normal+ difficulty.
Hsu Hao Fatality	Purchase in the Krypt.
Johnny Cage Fatality	Purchase in the Krypt.
Mavado Fatality	Purchase in the Krypt.
Nitara Fatality	Purchase in the Krypt.
Noob Saibot	Beat both 1P Arcade and Tag Team modes with every other character (except Sektor). Then beat 1P Arcade mode on Hard difficulty with Scorpion with his "Reaper Scorpion".
Noob Saibot Fatality	Beat Tag Team mode with a team of Noob Saibot and Scorpion.
Quan Chi Fatality	Beat Tag Team mode with a team of Quan Chi and Sareena.
Raiden Fatality	Defeat ten opponents in Survival Mode with Raiden.
Reptile	Beat 1P Arcade Mode with every character (except for Sektor and Noob Saibot) on Normal+ difficulty.
Reptile Fatality	Purchase in the Krypt.
Sareena Fatality	Purchase in the Krypt.
Scorpion Fatality	Defeat ten opponents in Survival Mode with Scorpion.
Sektor	Link to MK:DA.
Sektor Fatality	Beat Tag Team mode with a team of Sektor and Cyrax.
Shang Tsung Fatality	Beat Tag Team mode with a team of Shang Tsung and Quan Chi.

The Muppets: On With the Show

Enter the following codes as a password.

Description	Code
All Games	J09J4
Hard mode & Pigs In Space w/ 30 stars	H08L2
Medium difficulty w/ 30 stars	G07n0

Nancy Drew: Haunted Mansion

Level	Password
Briefcase	Sheep, Tiger, Horse, Ox
Chinese Room	Ox, Horse, Tiger, Sheep
Chinese Room 2	Rooster, Boar, Rabbit, Dragon
Entry Door	Dragon, Rabbit, Boar, Rooster
Hallway Door	Snake, Monkey, Dog, Rat
Peep Hole	Rat, Dog, Monkey, Snake

NBA Jam 2002

Description	Code
Extra Points	When you're shooting the ball, go to center court and throw. Sometimes you'll get lucky and get up to nine points if you sink it. However, you could get as little as one point.
Beach and Street Courts	Enter LHNGGDBLBJGT as a password.
Playoffs	Enter MKJLBFQBLDGH as a password to be in the playoffs as the Toronto Raptors.

NFL Blitz 2002

To activate Cheat Mode, press L,B,A, to enter the following codes on the match-up screen in Exhibition mode.

Description	Code
No Random Fumbles	L,L,L,B,B,A,R
Ogre Field	L,B,B,B,A,A,R
Shadow Players	L,L,L,B,A,A,A,R
Snow Field	L,L,B,B,A,A,A,A,A,R
Unlimited Turbo	L,L,L,L,B,B,B,A,A,R

NHL 2002

Description	Code
Bonus Teams and Extra Creation Points	Wait for Demo mode to begin, then hold SELECT and rapidly tap L,R repeatedly. When the demonstration is about to end, press START, but keep SELECT held while tapping L,R. Keep tapping until you hear a voice say "It's in the game." If you do it correctly, you should get the Budcat and Tiburon teams in Exhibition mode and 1,000 points for creating a player.
Zamboni in Introduction Sequence	Hold R+L and power on the Game Boy Advance.

No Rules Get Phat

Enter one of the following passwords to skip to a specific level.

Description	Code
Boss 1	13TYNLP18J34
Boss 2	PPTDDLS18J26
Boss 3	K7RFNLKH8J39
Boss 4	TFQFNL9H8J2R
Level 2	DPTYNLP17ZM!
Level 3	NKTDDLS18J24
Level 4	JTRFNLKH8J3v

Pac-Man Collection

Here are the passwords for the last five levels of Pac Attack

Description	Code
Level 96	YLW
Level 97	PNN
Level 98	SPR
Level 99	CHB
Level 100	LST

Peter Pan: Return To Neverland

Enter one of the following passwords to skip to a specific level.

Level	Code
Beach	PGCMMD
Forest	CNCGKG
Jungle	RGCKYD
Ship	ZGWYCR

Pirates of the Caribbean: The Curse of the Black Pearl

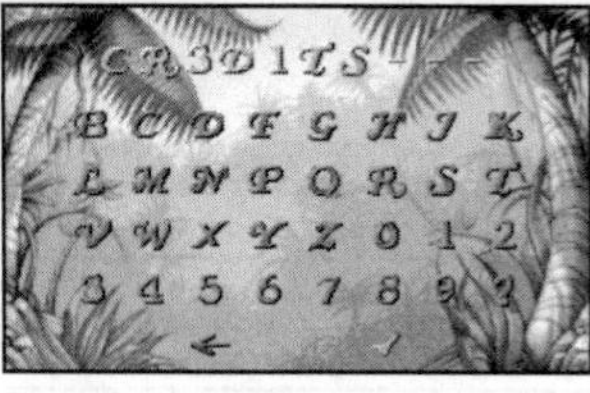

From the Main Menu, choose Continue Game and enter any of the following passwords.

Pirates of the Caribbean: The Curse of the Black Pearl (cont'd)

From the Main Menu, choose Continue Game and enter any of the following passwords.

Unlockable	Code
Enemies are more aggressive/harder	G3N1VS
Game credits	CR3D1TS
Infinite Lives	1MMORT4L
Picture of a baby	L1TTLVN
Start with Triple Cannons, Sabre and Pistol	GOOD13S
Soldiers and pirates become sheep	SH33P
Unlimited cannonballs and bullets	BVLL1TZ

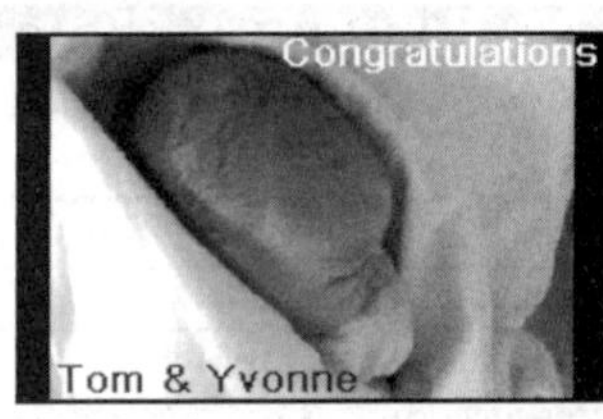

Pitfall: The Mayan Adventure

Description	Code
Infinite Continues	Use all your lives in the first level, then tap Ⓑ,Ⓑ,Ⓑ when the Continue screen comes up. The counter stops counting down and you're able to continue forever.
View All Levels	Enter L,SELECT,Ⓐ,SELECT,R,Ⓐ,L,SELECT. Press SELECT+L or SELECT+R to scroll through the levels. Press ← to make the boomerang appear around the word "Start."

Planet of the Apes

Enter the following passwords to skip to a specific level.

Level	Code	Level	Code
Level 2	64N4HY	Level 8	QK6293
Level 3	F5BMGF	Level 9	JDDUTJ
Level 4	B1SKZR	Level 10	046PJ#
Level 5	76FNHB	Level 11	3#9QLS
Level 6	P7GRXK	Level 12	C12KYY
Level 7	6B7VM#	Level 13	CBCYPH

Pokemon Ruby

Description	Code
1-5 victories	Calcium
6 or more victories	Bright Powder
50 Victories in a row	Award Ribbon
100 Victories in a row	Gold Shield

Pokemon Pinball Ruby and Sapphire

Unlockable	Objective
Groudon Bonus Stage	Get the hole after evolving a Pokemon, catching or hatching three Pokemon. This is only on the Ruby Field.
Kyogre Bonus Stage	Get the hole after evolving a Pokemon, catching or hatching three Pokemon. This is only on the Sapphire Field.
Rayquaza Bonus Stage	Get the hole after evolving a Pokemon, catching or hatching three Pokemon. This is on both fields.

Pokemon Sapphire

Description	Code
1-5 victories	Calcium
6 or more victories	Bright Powder
50 Victories in a row	Award Ribbon
100 Victories in a row	Gold Shield

Power Rangers Time Force

Enter one of the following passwords to skip to a specific level.

Description	Code
Level 2	DBBR
Level 3	GCB5
Level 4	HCB9
Final Battle	8QSD

Rayman 3: Hoodlum Havoc

Description	Objective
Unlock Bonus Levels with Link to Nintendo GameCube	Once you have collected at least 100 orbs, link your GBA to your GCN to purchase bonus levels.

Rayman Advance

Description	Code
Unlimited Continues	Go to the Continue screen and press ↑,↓,→,←, then START.

Razor Freestyle Scooter

Enter one of the following passwords to skip to a specific level.

Description	Code
Aircraft Carrier Completed	VDY3ZJ6LJVCQBF
Circus Completed	ZBF4GJ5VJVCQBF
Construction Site Completed	QHY4LJ2LHZCQBF
Scooter Park Completed	SBY5VJ4BJVCQBF
Shopping Mall Completed	QLY67J3BJVCQBF
Sports Stadium Completed	7JY4GJZBJVCQBF

Ready 2 Rumble Boxing: Round 2

Enter the following codes at the Main Menu.

Description	Code
Unlock Michael Jackson	Highlight the Arcade option, then press ←,←,→,→,←,→,L+R. You'll hear a cheering noise if you entered the code correctly.
Unlock Rumble Man	Highlight CHAMPIONSHIP, then press ←,←,→,←,→,→,←,→,L+R. You'll hear some cheering, then you can play as Rumble Man.
Unlock Shaquille O'Neal	Highlight the Survival option, then press ←,←,←,←,→,→,←,←,→,L+R.

Revenge of Shinobi

Description	Password
Level Select	Enter 67MB FNNG VL&Y FWZ5.

Ripping Friends

Enter this code in the Password screen.

Unlockable	Code
Level Select	→, L, ↑, ↓, B, ←, ←, →, ←

River City Ransom EX

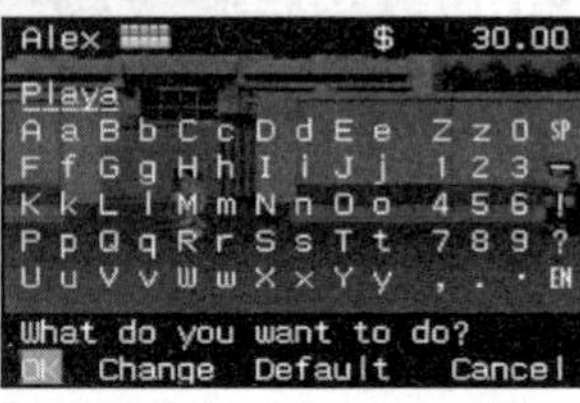

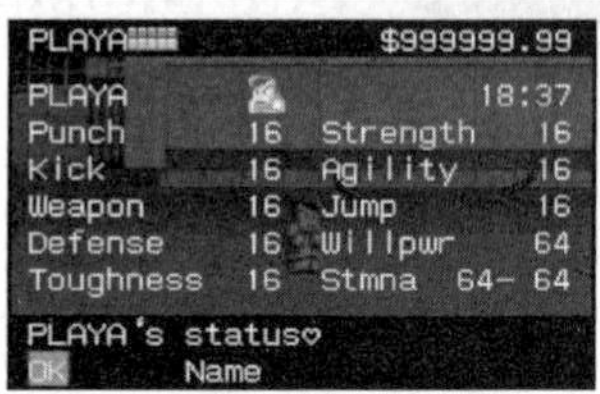

Enter the following case sensitive codes in the Name Change screen under the Status menu.

Unlockable	Name
$999,999	PLAYA
Custom Char	XTRA0
Custom Move	XTRA2
Custom Self	XTRA1
Delete Saved Games	ERAZE
Maximum Stats	DAMAX

Robotech: The Macross Saga

Enter these codes in the Title Screen. There will be a chicken clucking if the code is entered correctly.

Unlockable	Code
All Characters	↓, ↓, ↓, ↓, ↓, R, R
Level Select	↑, ↓, ↑, ↓, L, R, L, R
Max Upgrades	↑, →, ↓, ←, R, L, L, L
Unlimited Lives	→, →, →, ↑, ↑, L, L

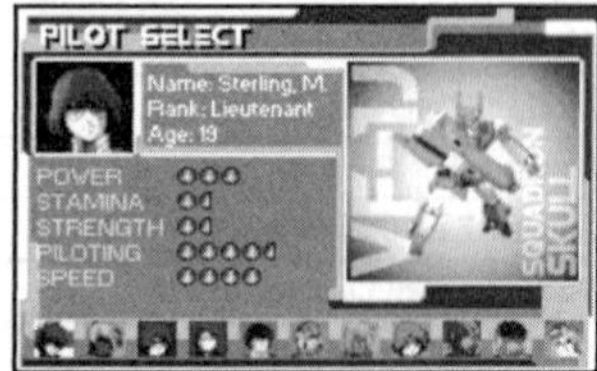

Rocket Power: Dream Scheme

Enter one of the following passwords to skip to a specific level.

Description	Password
After Elementary School	2V74BFDG
After Mad Town	MFKGTB!R
After Neighborhood	?FXX6BLJ
After Ocean Shores Beach	4GWD!KL1
After Spooky Woods	2L!DZHS8
After Town Square	6!LN99V5
Dr. Stepatone's Hideout	TW1ST3R!
End	B!P356BT

Rugrats Castle Capers

Enter one of the following passwords to skip to a specific level.

Level	Code
Level 2	QGPCJNWXGWCB
Level 3	QQTKJYWLGKGF
Level 4	CTKLJKGLSCQR
Level 5	RLPTKKGLWKWP
Level 6	FZLDVHMMDQRB
End	JSJRJKSLXCFJ

Scooby Doo!

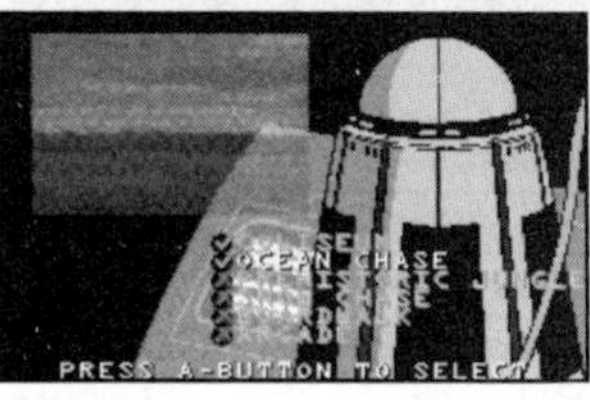

Enter the following codes as passwords.

Unlockable	Code
Coliseum Level	MXP#2VBL
Ocean Chase Level	CHBB5VBX
Prehistoric Jungle Level	5S@C7VB8

Scooby-Doo 2: Monsters Unleashed

Unlockable	Code
Alternate ending	SD2
Final Level: Scooby vs. Masked Guy	5DBY3MT8

PSP Xbox PS2 GC GBA

Scorpion King: Rise of the Akkadian

Description	Code
Level Select	Enter the following character colors at the Password screen: Blue, Green, Green, Blue.
Play as Cassandra	Enter Mathayus, Menmon, Isis, Mathayus as a password to play as Cassandra with all runes.

The Scorpion King Sword of Osiris

To enter these codes, select continue from the main menu.

Unlockable	Code
Level Select	Blue, Green, Green, Blue

Unlockable	1st Quest level codes	2nd Quest level codes
Level 1	—	Red, Purple, Green, Red
Level 2	Green, Purple, Green, Blue	Red, Blue, Purple, Yellow
Level 3	Red, Blue, Purple, Yellow	Yellow, Blue, Yellow, Purple
Level 4	Purple, Yellow, Green, Yellow	Purple, Red, Blue, Yellow
Level 5	Red, Yellow, Green, Purple	Red, Blue, Red, Green
Level 6	Red, Green, Yellow, Red	Red, Yellow, Green, Yellow

Serious Sam Advance

Level	Easy Mode Password	Normal Mode Password	Hard Mode Password
Amon Thule	HEXMODE	OPEE	WOLF
Baths of Diocletian	NEED	OWL	LIMO
Caesar's Palace	WAFTY	MOOPAY	MOCKNEY
Gladiator School	COINAGE	FRYUP	MADEUP
Praetorian Fort	NORTHERN	FILLY	MIRROR
Pyramid Entrance	BADDUN	BETTERER	CHIPPER
Slave Compound	BOBBINS	PILCH	FORREST
Slave Quarters	TOAST	BEVIL	BEAK
The Forum of Mars	GAMES	DUCKAROO	FOZZER
Temple of Herkat Lower	MNIP	KIPPAGE	TITHES
Tomb of Ramses	MEGAMUNT	HORSE	EYE

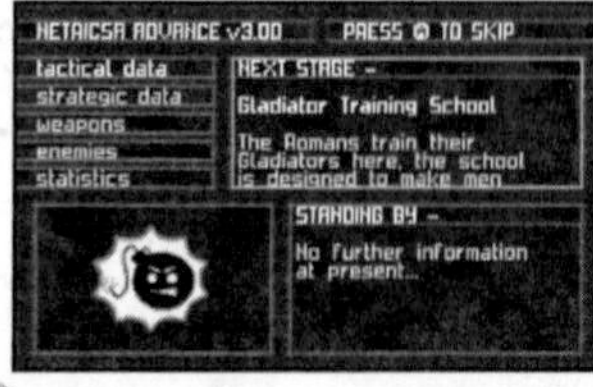

The Simpsons: Road Rage

Unlockable	Code
All cars, levels and bonuses	Maggie, Willy, Bart, Chief Wiggum, Apu, Moe, Krusty, Barney
All characters	Bart, Bart, Lisa, Lisa, Marge, Marge, Barney, Barney

Sonic Advance

Description	Objective
Hidden Sound Test Mode Songs	To get more than the 39 default songs in Sound Test mode, complete The Moon Zone, Extra mode, or unlock the Super Sonic Ending. Three additional songs will be available.
Moon Zone	Collect all seven Emeralds for all characters. Complete the game as Sonic to unlock the Moon Zone.
Tails as Partner (Tails will follow you during the game, but can't be controlled.)	Highlight Sonic at the character selection screen and press ↑. Next, highlight Tails and press ↓. Then, highlight Knuckles and press L. Finally, highlight Amy and press R. Now you can highlight Sonic and press Ⓐ to select him.

Sonic Adventure 2

Unlockable	Objective
Amy	Beat the game and get all seven Chaos Emeralds with Cream, Knuckles, Sonic, and Tails.
Bonus Level	Beat the game and collect all of the Chaos Emeralds with Amy, Cream, Sonic, Tails and Knuckles.
Boss Option in Time Attack	Beat the game and collect all Chaos Emeralds with three characters.
Cream	Finish the Leaf Forest level as Sonic.
Knuckles	Finish the Sky Canyon level as Sonic.
Sound Test	Beat the game and collect all Chaos Emeralds with two characters.
Tails	Finish the Music Plant level as Sonic.
Tiny Chao Garden	Beat the game and collect all Chaos Emeralds.

Space Channel 5

Description	Code
Self Play	Hold L+R during the game, then press ↑,←,Ⓐ,←,Ⓐ,↓,→,Ⓑ,→,Ⓑ.

Spider-Man

Description	Objective
Ending Bonus	Complete the game to unlock the level select option at the Main Menu. Press START during gameplay to choose a new level.
Movie Clips	Take pictures on every level to unlock all movie clips.
Unlock Cheat Mode	Complete the game, collecting all of the small red spiders and taking the pictures on each stage to unlock the cheats (armor upgrade, strength enhancement, and level cheat) in the Secrets menu.

Sponge Bob Squarepants: SuperSponge

Enter the following passwords to skip to a specific level.

Description	Code	Description	Code
Level 1	BGNR	Level 11	WFXM
Level 2	CLMB	Level 12	MNTL
Level 3	KVNF	Level 13	QGAV
Level 4	WKGA	Level 14	LXHK
Level 5	DFVJ	Level 15	HGCD
Level 6	NGPS	Level 16	CNXK
Level 7	WMCV	Level 17	LKKV
Level 8	XNAD	Level 18	PVHS
Level 9	HPJQ	Level 19	JAST
Level 10	QHDG	Final Level	WMBT

Sports Illustrated for Kids Baseball

Select Season Mode, pick a team and in Team Management choose Cheat Code. Enter the following codes to unlock the specified players.

Player	Code
Eddie Penn (2B)	SIKSTAR
George Stocks (P)	TARGETPLYR
Keith Fisher (3B)	GAMESTOP
Mark Modesto (RF)	GOCIRCUIT
Michael Quince (1B)	BESTBUYSTR
Nateo Geooni (CF)	EBRULES
Riley Waters (SS)	BAMSTAR
Tecumseh Brown (LF)	SIKPOWER

Sports Illustrated for Kids Football

Select Season Mode, pick a team and choose Cheat Code. Enter the following codes to unlock the specified player.

Player	Code
Eddie Brown (LRB/ROLB)	EBPLAYER
Hal Church (LG/LOLB)	RZONESTAR
Mac Marshall (RRB/FS)	BAMPLYR
Mark Haruf (QB/SS)	CIRCUITFUN
Rob Lewis (LRB/ROLB)	SIKPOWER

Sports Illustrated for Kids Football

Ryan Hunter (RRB/SS)	TARGETSTAR
Sammy Rivera (LE/RILB)	TOUCHDOWN
Sandy Sanders (RE/LOLB)	SIKSTAR
Wayne Selby (C/RT)	BESTBUYPWR

Spy Hunter

Description	Code
Arcade Mode	Enter EDACRA as a name.
Delete High Scores	Press ↑,↑,↓,Ⓛ,Ⓡ,Ⓛ at the Copyright screen.
Delete Saved Games	Press ←,←,→,←,→,→ at the Copyright screen.
Super Agent Mode	Complete the game with all Primary Objectives and Secondary Objectives.

Spy Kids 3D: Game Over

Description	Code
3-D Picture 13 of Juni's cycle	Enter ZR19 as a password.

Spyro: Season Of Ice

Enter the following codes at the title screen when "Press Start" appears.

Description	Code
99 Lives	Press ←,→,→,→,↓,↑,→,↑,Ⓐ.
All Keys	Press Ⓛ+SELECT.
Level Portals Opened (All level portals can be opened without collecting the required fairies.)	Press ↑,↑,↓,↓,←,→,↑,↓,Ⓐ.
Unlimited Health in Sparx Worlds	Press ↓,↑,↑,↓,←,→,→,←,Ⓐ.
Unlimited Weapons in Sparx Worlds	Press ↓,→,↑,←,←,↑,→,↓,Ⓐ.
Unlock All Levels	Press ↓,↓,↑,↑,←,→,↑,↓,Ⓐ.
Warp	Press ←,→,→,←,↑,←,←,→,Ⓐ.
Warp Unlock All Levels	Press ↓,↑,↓,←,→,↑,←,↑,Ⓐ.

For extra Sparkx weapons, press →,↑,→,←,↓,↑,←,↓,Ⓐ at the title screen. Then, use one of the following commands during gameplay in Sparx worlds.

Unlockable Weapons	Code
Homing Bombs	↓+SELECT
Invincibility Shield	↑+SELECT
Rapid Fire	←+SELECT
Smart Bomb	→+SELECT

Spyro Orange: The Cortex Conspiracy

At the Game Mode Menu, press the L + R buttons together to activate the code entry screen, then enter the following codes.

Unlockable	Code
100 Gems	V1S10NS
200 Gems	T4P10C4
Enemies are sheep	SH33P
Gray Game	G3MZ
Hidden Card	V4N1LL4
Hidden Card	S0YB34N
Orange Game	SP4RX
Orange Spyro	SPYR0
Purple Game	P0RT4L
Spyro's flame is replaced with sheep	B41S0KV

TIP

Crash Party USA Mini-Game

Hold L + R while powering up the Game Boy Advance

Star Wars: Episode II Attack of the Clones

Enter the following passwords to skip to a specific level.

Description	as Jedi Knight	as Padawan
Level 2	BJDGGM	BHDBGJ
Level 3	BJFGHM	BHFBHJ
Level 4	BJGGDM	BHGBDJ
Level 5	BJHGFM	BHHBFJ
Level 6	BJKGCM	BGKBCK
Level 7	BJLGSM	BGLBSK
Level 8	BJMGTM	BGMBTK
Level 9	BJNGQM	BGNBQK
Level 10	BJPGRM	BGPBRK
Level 11	BGQGNP	BGQBNK
Final Level	—	BGRBPK

Star Wars: Flight of the Falcon

Unlockable	Code
Episode IV	TGHK
Episode V	8TV2
Episode VI	TSB2
Bonus Level	RRV2
All Levels and Bonus Game	4?6C

Star Wars: Jedi Power Battles

Enter the following passwords to skip to a specific level.

Level	as Darth Maul	as Mace Windu	as Obi Wan	as Qui Gon
Level 2	VCJ0D2J	VC1LCGF	WFJ3BPG	VHS3BFG
Level 3	VCJ0G*J	VCJCC6F	XFJ3BYG	VMN3BFG
Level 4	VCJ0JKK	VC1CCFG	YFJ3B6G	VRL3BFG
Level 5	VCJ0LTK	VCJDCPG	ZFJ3BFH	VWL3BFG
Level 6	VCJ0N2K	VC1DCYG	0FJ3BPH	V0L3BYG
Level 7	VCJ0Q1K	VCJPCFH	1FJ3BYH	V4N3BFH
Level 8	VCJ0SFK	VC1FCFH	2FJ3B6H	V8N3BPH
Level 9	VCJ0VPK	VCJGCPH	3FJ3BFJ	VCP3BYH
Level 10	VCJ0XYK	VC1GCYH	4FJ3BPJ	VHR3BFJ

Unlockable	Code
Final Battle	NBJ3L6H
Level Select (Upper levels for all three characters)	G1V34LL

Stuart Little 2

Level	Code
Level 1	1377
Level 2	1487
Level 3	2278
Level 4	6366
Level 5	6787
Level 6	5778
Level 7	5688
Level 8	6678
Level 9	6588
Level 10	6216
Level 11	7614
Level 12	7421

Super Dodgeball Advance

Description	Objective
Dream Team A: the Shooters	Win Special Championship for the second time.
Dream Team B: the Rockets	Win Championship mode once.
Dream Team C: Iron Men	Win Special Championship mode once.
Special Championship	Beat the Rocket team in the finals of Championship mode.

TIP

Rank Climbing Tip

To climb the ranks quickly during Championship mode, always challenge the top team. If you win, you'll move halfway up the list each time. In four matches, you could be playing for Number One!

PSP Xbox PS2 GC GBA

Super Puzzle Fighter II Turbo

Secret Character	Code
Play as Akuma	Highlight Morrigan, hold SELECT, and press ↓,↓,↓,←,←,←,Ⓐ.
Play as Anita	Highlight Morrigan, press SELECT, and move the pointer to highlight Donovan and press Ⓐ.
Play as Dan	Highlight Morrigan, hold SELECT, and press ←,←,←,↓,↓,↓,Ⓐ.
Play as Hsien-Ko paper Talisman	Highlight Morrigan, press SELECT, move the pointer to highlight Hsien-Ko, and press Ⓐ.
Select Devilot	Highlight Morrigan, hold SELECT, and press ←,←,←,↓,↓,↓,Ⓐ as the timer hits 10.

Superman: Countdown to Apokolips

Description	Code
All Levels	APLsXp
Level 2	Q#aaTa
Level 3	g#ab2o
Level 4	A#asAp

Teenage Mutant Ninja Turtles

Unlockable	Code
Level 1	LSMMS
Level 2	SSLDM
Level 3	MSSLD
Level 4	SRLMD
Level 5	LSDRM

Teenage Mutant Ninja Turtles 2: Battle Nexus

Unlockable	Battle Mode Passwords	Race Mode Passwords
Course 16	DDRSMSR	RDLDSMD
Course 17	SMRDLML	MDSMSDM
Course 18	LMSLSRS	SRMLDDR

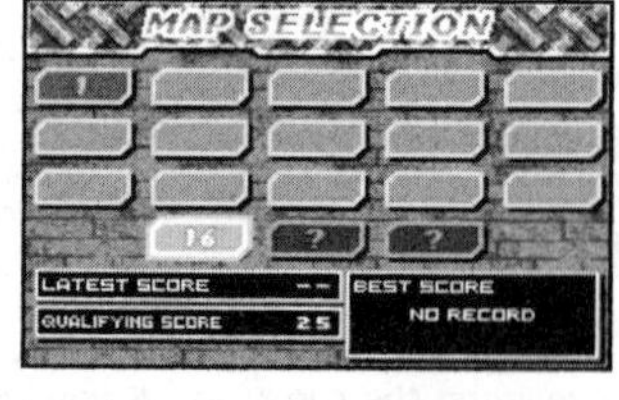

TIP

At the Title Screen, press ↑, ↑, ↓, ↓, ←, →, ←, →, Ⓑ, Ⓐ. This displays "COWABUNGA" when players clear the Story Mode

Tekken

Description	Code
All Modes and Characters	Hold Ⓐ+Ⓑ and press L,R,R,L,L,↑,↑,R at the Main Menu. Note: You may need to repeat this two or three times before it activates.
Alternate Costumes	Press L, R, or START at the character selection screen.
Fight as Heihachi	Complete the game with all nine characters. Heihachi will appear next to Hworang and Paul at the character selection screen.
Team Battle Modes	Complete Arcade mode as Heihachi to unlock the Versus Team Battle options.

Tom Clancy's Splinter Cell

Description	Objective
Extra Missions	Link to the Nintendo GameCube version of Splinter Cell to download extra missions.
Unlock Another Bonus Mission	Find all the safes in missions one through nine.
Unlock Bonus Mission	Beat levels one to five with a completion rate of 60% or higher.

Tony Hawk's Pro Skater 2

Enter the following button presses at the Main Menu or while paused during gameplay.

Description	Code
All Levels Unlocked and Maximum Money	Hold R, then press Ⓑ,Ⓐ,←,↓,Ⓑ,←,↑,Ⓑ,↑,←,←.
Happy Face Blood	Hold R, then press START,Ⓐ,↓,Ⓑ,Ⓐ,←,←,Ⓐ,↓.
Set Time to Zero	Hold R, then press ←,↑,START,↑,→.
Turn Off the Blood!	Hold R, then press Ⓑ,←,↑,↓,←,START,START.
All Levels	Hold R, then press Ⓐ,START,Ⓐ,→,↑,↑,↑,↓,↓,↑,↑,↓.
Cheats	Hold R, then press Ⓑ,Ⓐ,↓,Ⓐ,START,START,Ⓑ,Ⓐ,→,Ⓑ,→, Ⓐ,↑,←. The following cheats are now available: Perfect Balance, Always Special, Stud Mode, Sim Mode, Moon Physics, and Always Zoom.
Disco Zoom	Hold R, then press ←,Ⓐ,START,Ⓐ,→,START,→,↑,START.
Mindy	Hold R, then press Ⓐ,←,←,↑,→,Ⓑ,Ⓐ,START at the main menu.
Spider-Man	Hold R, then press ↑,↑,↓,↓,←,→,←,→,Ⓑ,Ⓐ,START.
Unlimited Air	Hold R, then press ←,Ⓐ,START,Ⓐ,→,↑,START. Now every time you ollie, hold Ⓑ to fly. It's hard to control at first, but you can use L and R to go left and right, ↑ and ↓ to go forward and back, Ⓑ to rise, and Ⓐ to hover.

Top Gear Rally

Enter the following codes as a new file name.

Unlockable	Code
Hovercraft	HOVERCAR
RC-Car	RCRACERS
All Roadside Obstacles Become Cows	ROGUEOPS

Ultimate MUSCLE

Description	Objective
Sgt. Kinnikuman	Beat survival mode on hard difficulty.
Young Buffaloman	Beat survival mode on normal difficulty.
Young King Muscle	Beat story mode once on easy difficulty without losing.
Young Ramenman	Beat 3 on 3 mode on normal difficulty.

Wario Land 4

Unlockable	Objective
Super Hard Difficulty Setting	Complete the game under the Hard difficulty setting. Then start a new game, and you can now select the Super Hard difficulty setting.
Wario Karaoke	Enter the sound room and highlight the "Exit" option. Press SELECT+START+R+L+↑ to unlock Wario Karaoke. Alternately, get gold crowns by collecting over 10,000 coins in all levels to unlock the Wario Karaoke (music test) option.
Wario Karaoke Control	Press ↑ or ↓ to change the pitch of the song. Press ← or → to change the tempo of the song. Press L or R to toggle between a green CD, yellow CD, or just the lyrics.

Wario Ware Inc

Unlockable	Code
Boss Game	Beat the standard game.
Easy Game	Beat Wario in the standard game.
Hard Game	Score 15 or more in the Thrilling game.
Mini-Games	Win 25 games in Jimmy's stages to unlock full versions of Dr. Wario, Fly Swatter, and Wario's Sheriff.
Music Test	Go to the Options screen,then go to the Name Entry screen. Select Yes, then press [[6]] to go to the Music Test screen.
Pyoro	Play every single game for every character to unlock Pyoro.
Pyoro II	Earn a medal on every game in Grid Mode.
Staff Page	Beat the standard game to unlock the Staff Page.
Thrilling Game	Earn a high score while beating the Easy game.

Wild Thornberrys: Chimp Chase

Enter one of the following passwords to skip to a specific level.

Description	Code
Arctic 1	6GRHJ74W
Arctic 2	KF3W?6Jr
Arctic 3	MR8594NJ
End	M661M8LB
Jungle 2	4S7JXTJ3
Jungle 3	473H1SZD
Outback 1	8!YJCDH4
Outback 2	!!2VKJFS
Outback 3	NDC4SJ3S
Plains 1	B147T3B2
Plains 2	4DZZFB7F
Plains 3	Y5TSGWK2

Wild Thornberrys: The Movie

Enter the following as a password.

Unlockable	Code
Level Select	HB5F

Wing Commander: Prophecy

Enter the following codes at the start screen.

Description	Code
Invincibility	↑,↓,Ⓐ,Ⓑ,←,→,L,L,R,R,Ⓑ,Ⓐ
Mission Select	↑,↑,L,R,↓,↓,Ⓐ,Ⓐ,Ⓑ,Ⓐ
View Alien Ships in Tactical Database	R,L,Ⓐ,Ⓐ,Ⓐ,Ⓑ,↑,←,↓,→,↑,Ⓐ

Wolfenstein 3D

For the following unlockables, press START to pause gameplay, hold L+R, then enter code.

Description	Code
Advance to Boss Level	Press Ⓐ,Ⓑ,Ⓐ,Ⓐ,Ⓑ,Ⓑ,Ⓐ,Ⓐ. The sound of a siren confirms correct code entry. When the game is resumed, you start at the current boss.
All Weapons, Keys, Ammo, and Health	Press Ⓐ,Ⓑ,Ⓑ,Ⓐ,Ⓐ,Ⓐ,Ⓐ,Ⓐ. A shout confirms correct code entry. All weapons and keys are unlocked and your health and ammunition are restored.
God Mode	Press Ⓐ,Ⓐ,Ⓑ,Ⓐ,Ⓐ,Ⓐ,Ⓐ,Ⓐ. A sound confirms correct code entry.
Skip Level	Press Ⓐ,Ⓑ,Ⓐ,Ⓐ,Ⓑ,Ⓑ,Ⓑ,Ⓐ. The sound of a door opening confirms correct code entry. When the game is resumed, you start on the next level.

NOTE

If you use the Skip Level code on Level 1, you go to the secret floor!

X2 Wolverine's Revenge

Description	Code
Double jumps	Hold L at the slot Select screen and press SELECT,←,↑,↓,↓,↑,↓.
Invincibility	Hold L at the slot Select screen and press ↓,↑,↓,↓,↑,↓,SELECT.
Regenerate with Claws Extended	Hold L at the slot Select screen and press →,↑,↓,→,←,SELECT,SELECT.
Unlock New Costumes	At the main menu, quickly press ↑,↓,↑,↓,←,→,←,→,Ⓑ,Ⓐ.

XXX

Description	Code
Completion Bonuses (Options for infinite health and ammunition are unlocked.)	After defeating Yorgi in Level 12, the credits appear. At the end of the credits, go to "Extras."

PSP Xbox PS2 GC GBA

Yoshi's Island

Unlockable	Code
Bonus Games	On the Stage Select Screen press and hold SELECT and press L, L, B, A, R

Yu-Gi-Oh! The Duelist of the Roses

Unlockable	Code
Ancient Tree of Enlightenment	EKJHQ109
Aqua Dragon	JXCB6FU7
Barrel Dragon	GTJXSBJ7
Beast King of the Swamp	QXNTQPAX
Birdface	N54T4TY5
Blast Sphere	CZN5GD2X
Change of Heart	SBYDQM8B
Crush Card	SRA7L5YR
Dark Hole	UMJ10MQB
Dragonseeker	81EZCH8B
EarthShaker	Y34PN1SV
Elf's Light	E5G3NRAD
Exodia: The Forbidden One	37689434
Fairy King Truesdale	YF07QVEZ
Fairy's Gift	NVE7A3EZ
Goblin Fan	92886423
Gravity Bind	0HNFG9WX
Greenkappa	YBJMCD6Z
Harpy's Feather Duster	8HJHQPNP
Horn of the Unicorn	S14FGKQ1
Left Arm of the Forbidden One	A5CF6HSH
Magician of Faith	GME1S3UM
Meteor Dragon	86985631
Mimicat	69YDQM85
Mirror Wall	53297534
Mystical Capture Chains	N1NDJMQ3
Robotic Knight	S5S7NKNH
Royal Decree	8TETQHE1
Seiyaryu	2H4D85J7
Serpentine Princess	UMQ3WZUZ
Slate Warrior	73153736
Swordsman From A Foreign Land	CZ81UVGR
SwordStalker	AH0PSHEB
Tactical Warrior	054TC727

Yu-Gi-Oh! Eternal Duelist Soul

Enter these passwords in the Password menu.

Enter the following passwords for Exodia Pieces

33396948	07902349	70903634
44519536	08124921	08058240

Yu-Gi-Oh! Eternal Duelist Soul (cont'd)

The following passwords are for cards.

Card	Password
Ancient Elf	93221206
Ansatsu	48365709
Beaver Warrior	32452818
Blue Eyes White Dragon	89631139
Book of Secret Arts	91595718
Celtic Guardian	91152256
Change of Heart	04031928
Claw Reacher	41218256
Curse of Dragon	28279543
Dark Magician	46986414
Doma the Angel of Silence	16972957
Dragon Zombie	66672569
Feral Imp	41392891
Fissure	66788016
Gaia	06368038
Giant Soldier of Stone	13039848
Great White	13429800
Magical Ghost	46474915
Mammoth Graveyard	40374923
Man-Eating Bug	54652250
Man-Eating Treasure Chest	13723605
Monster Reborn	83764718
Mystical Elf	15025844
Neo the Magic Swordsman	50930991
Reinforcements	17814387
Silver Fang	90357090
Summoned Skull	70781052
The Stern Mystic	87557188
Trap Hole	04206964
Waboku	12607053
Winged Dragon	87796900
Witty Phantom	36304921

Yu-Gi-Oh! The Falsebound Kingdom

Unlockable	Objective
Armored Zombie	Use Call of the Grave on Zanki.
B. Skull Dragon	Red-Eyes B. Dragon+Summoned Skull
Black Luster Soldier	Use Black Luster ritual on Gaia the Fierce Knight.
Blue-Eyes Ultimate Dragon	Three Blue Eyes
Chimera the Flying Mythical Beast	Berformat+Gazelle
Cosmo Queen	Dark Elf+Mystical Elf
Crimson Sunbird	Mavelus+Winged Eagle
Dragon Zombie	Use Call of the Grave on Crawling Dragon.
Gaia the Dragon Champion	Gaia the Fierce+Curse of Dragon
Gate Guardian	Kazejin+Suijin+Sanga
Magician of Black Chaos	Use Black Luster ritual on Dark Magician.
Metalzoa	Use Metal Morph on Zoa.
Meteor B. Dragon	Meteor Dragon+ Red Eyes Black Dragon

Yu-Gi-Oh! The Falsebound Kingdom (cont'd)

Unlockable	Objective
Rabid Horseman	Battleox+Mystic Horseman
Red Eyes Black Metal Dragon	Use Metal Morph on Red Eyes Black Dragon.
Thousand Dragon	Baby Dragon+Time Wizard
Twin Headed Thunder Dragon	Two Headed King Rex+Thunder Dragon
Valkyrion	Alpha+Beta+Gamma

TIP

To get some free money, enter this code while playing on a Black Piece of land: ↑,↑,↓,↓,←,→,←,→,Ⓑ,Ⓐ. The game will laugh and say "Yu, Yu". You will then be rewarded with 537 gold.

Yu-Gi-Oh! Reshef of Destruction

Enter the following codes as passwords.

Unlockable	Code
7 Colored Fish	23771716
Abyss Flower	40387124
Acid Crawler	77568553
Acid Trap Hole	41356845
Air Marmot Of Nefa	75889523
Akakieisu	38035986
Akihiron	36904469
Alinsection	70924884
All-Seeing Goddess	53493204
Alligator's Sword	64428736
Alpha The Magnet Warrior	99785935
Amazon Of The Seasons	17968114
Amazon Sword Women	94004268
Ameba	95174353
Amphibious Bugroth	40173854
Ancient Brain	42431843
Ancient Elf	93221206
Ancient Jar	81492226
Ancient One of the Forest	14015067
Ancient Sorcerer	36821538
Ancient Tool	49587396
Blue Eyes White Dragon	89631139
Dark Magician	46986414
Dragon Zombie	66672569
Harpie Lady	76812113
Life Eater	52367652
Lisark	55210709
Mushroom Man	14181608
Mystical Elf	15025844

Yu-Gi-Oh! Reshef of Destruction (cont'd)

Unlockable	Code
Penguin Knight	36039163
Summoned Skull	70781052
Sword Arm of Dragon	13069066
Witty Phantom	36304921
Puts Beta The Magnet Warrior in the Shop	39256679
Puts Dark Magician Knight in Grandpa's Shop	50725996
Puts Harpie's Feather Duster in the Shop	18144506
Puts Knight's Title in Grandpa's Shop	87210505

Yu-Gi-Oh! Worldwide Edition: Stairway to the Destined Duel

To access these cheats, go to the main map, press R, then go to the Misc Menu. Select Password and enter these codes to unlock the corresponding card for your deck.

Description	Code
30,000-Year White Turtle	11714098
4-Starred Ladybug of Doom	83994646
7 Colored Fish	23771716
7 Completed	86198326
Abyss Flower	40387124
Acid Crawler	77568553
Acid Trap Hole	41356845
Air Eater	08353769
Air Marmot of Nefariousness	75889523
Akakieisu	38035986
Akihiron	36904469
Alinsection	70924884
Alligator's Sword	64428736
Alligator's Sword Dragon	03366982
Alpha the Magnet Warrior	99785935
Amazon Archer	91869203
Amazon of the Seas	17968114
Ameba	95174353
Amphibian Beast	67371383
Amphibious Bugroth	40173854
Ancient Brain	42431843
Ancient Elf	93221206
Ancient Jar	81492226
Ancient Lizard Warrior	43230671
Ancient One of the Deep Forest	14015067
Ancient Sorcerer	36821538
Ancient Telescope	17092736
Ancient Tool	49587396
Ancient Tree of Enlightenment	86421986
Ansatsu	48365709
Anthrosaurus	89904598
Anti Raigeki	42364257
Anti-Magic Fragrance	58921041
Appropriate	48539234
Aqua Chorus	95132338
Aqua Dragon	86164529
Aqua Madoor	85639257
Aqua Snake	12436646
Aqua Spirit	40916023
Arlownay	14708569
Arma Knight	36151751
Armaill	53153481
Armed Ninja	09076207
Armored Glass	36868108
Armored Lizard	15480588
Armored Rat	16246527
Armored Starfish	17535588
Armored Zombie	20277860
Attack and Receive	63689843
Axe of Despair	40619825
Axe Raider	48305365
Baby Dragon	88819587

Yu-Gi-Oh! Worldwide Edition: Stairway to the Destined Duel (cont'd)

Backup Soldier	36280194
Banisher of the Light	61528025
Baron of the Fiend Sword	86325596
Barox	06840573
Barrel Dragon	81480460
Barrel Lily	67841515
Barrel Rock	10476868
Basic Insect	89091579
Bat	72076281
Battle Ox	05053103
Battle Steer	18246479
Battle Warrior	55550921
Bazoo the Soul-Eater	40133511
Beaked Snake	06103114
Bean Soldier	84990171
Beast Fangs	46009906
Beast of Gilfer	50287060
Beastking of the Swamps	99426834
Beautiful Beast Trainer	29616941
Beautiful Headhuntress	16899564
Beaver Warrior	32452818
Behegon	94022093
Bell of Destruction	83555666
Berfomet	77207191
Beta the Magnet Warrior	39256679
Bickuribox	25655502
Big Eye	16768387
Big Insect	53606874
Big Shield Gardna	65240384
Binding Chain	08058240
Bio-Mage	58696829
Bio Plant	07670542
Bite Shoes	50122883
Black Dragon Jungle King	89832901
Black Illusion Ritual	41426869
Black Pendant	65169794
Blackland Fire Dragon	87564352
Bladefly	28470714
Blast Juggler	70138455
Blast Sphere	26302522
Blind Destruction	32015166
Block Attack	25880422
Blocker	34743446
Blue-Eyed Silver Zombie	35282433
Blue-Eyes Toon Dragon	53183600
Blue-Eyes Ultimate Dragon	23995346
Blue-Eyes White Dragon	80906030
Blue Medicine	20871001
Blue-Winged Crown	41396436
Boar Soldier	21340051
Bolt Escargot	12146024
Bolt Penguin	48531733
Bombardment Beetle	57409948
Bone Mouse	21239280
Boneheimer	98456117
Boo Koo	68963107
Book of Secret Arts	91595718
Bottom Dweller	81386177
Boulder Tortoise	09540040
Bracchio-Raidus	16507828
Brave Scizzar	74277583
Breath of Light	20101223
Bright Castle	82878489
Bubonic Vermin	06104968
Burglar	06297941
Burning Land	24294108
Burning Spear	18937875
Buster Blader	78193831
Call of the Dark	78637313
Call of the Grave	16970158
Call of the Haunted	97077563
Candle of Fate	47695416
Cannon Soldier	11384280
Card Destruction	72892473
Card of Safe Return	57953380
Castle of Dark Illusions	00062121
Castle Walls	44209392
Catapult Turtle	95727991
Ceasefire	36468556
Celtic Guardian	91152256

Yu-Gi-Oh! Worldwide Edition: Stairway to the Destined Duel (cont'd)

Ceremonial Bell	20228463
Chain Destruction	01248895
Chain Energy	79323590
Change of Heart	04031928
Change Slime	18914778
Charubin the Fire Knight	37421579
Chimera the Flying Mythical Beast	04796100
Chorus of Sanctuary	81380218
Chosen One	21888494
Claw Reacher	41218256
Clown Zombie	92667214
Cockroach Knight	33413638
Cold Wave	60682203
Collected Power	07565547
Confiscation	17375316
Copy Cat	26376390
Corroding Shark	34290067
Crass Clown	93889755
Crawling Dragon	67494157
Crawling Dragon #2	38289717
Crazy Fish	53713014
Crimson Sentry	28358902
Crimson Sunbird	46696593
Crow Goblin	77998771
Crush Card	57728570
Cure Mermaid	85802526
Curse of Dragon	28279543
Curse of Fiend	12470447
Curse of the Masked Beast	94377247
Curtain of the Dark Ones	22026707
Cyber Commander	06400512
Cyber Falcon	30655537
Cyber Harpie	80316585
Cyber Jar	34124316
Cyber Saurus	89112729
Cyber Shield	63224564
Cyber Soldier	44865098
Cyber Soldier of Darkworld	75559356
Cyber-Stein	69015963
Cyber-Tech Alligator	48766543
Cyclon Laser	05494820
Dancing Elf	59983499
Dancing Fairy	90925163
Dark Artist	72520073
Dark Assailant	41949033
Dark Bat	67049542
Dark Chimera	32344688
Dark Elf	21417692
Dark Energy	04614116
Dark-Eyes Illusionist	38247752
Darkfire Dragon	17881964
Darkfire Soldier #1	05388481
Darkfire Soldier #2	78861134
Dark Gray	09159938
Dark Hole	53129443
Dark Human	81057959
Dark King of the Abyss	53375573
Dark Magic Curtain	99789342
Dark Magician	46986414
Dark Necrofear	31829185
Darkness Approaches	80168720
Dark Plant	13193642
Dark Prisoner	89558090
Dark Rabbit	99261403
Dark Sage	92377303
Dark Shade	40196604
Dark Spirit of the Silent	93599951
Dark Titan of Terror	89494469
Dark Witch	35565537
Darkworld Thorns	43500484
Dark Zebra	59784896
Deal of Phantom	69122763
Deepsea Shark	28593363
Deepsea Warrior	24128274
De-Fusion	95286165
Delinquent Duo	44763025
De-Spell	19159413
Destiny Board	94212438
Destroyer Golem	73481154
Destruction Punch	05616412

PSP Xbox PS2 GC GBA

Yu-Gi-Oh! Worldwide Edition: Stairway to the Destined Duel (cont'd)

Dharma Cannon	96967123
Dice Armadillo	69893315
Dig Beak	29948642
Dimensional Warrior	37043180
Dimensionhole	22959079
Disk Magician	76446915
Dissolverock	40826495
Djinn the Watcher of the Wind	97843505
DNA Surgery	74701381
Dokuroizo the Grim Reaper	25882881
Dokuroyaiba	30325729
Doma the Angel of Silence	16972957
Doron	00756652
Dorover	24194033
Dragon Capture Jar	50045299
Dragoness the Wicked Knight	70681994
Dragonic Attack	32437102
Dragon Piper	55763552
Dragon Seeker	28563545
Dragon Statue	28563545
Dragon Treasure	01435851
Dragon Zombie	66672569
Dream Clown	13215230
Drill Bug	88733579
Driving Snow	00473469
Droll Bird	97973387
Drooling Lizard	16353197
Dryad	84916669
Dunames Dark Witch	12493482
Dungeon Worm	51228280
Dust Tornado	60082869
Earthbound Spirit	67105242
Earthshaker	60866277
Eatgaboon	42578427
Ekibyo Drakmord	69954399
Eldeen	06367785
Electric Lizard	55875323
Electric Snake	11324436
Electro-Whip	37820550
Elegant Egotist	90219263
Elf's Light	39897277
Embryonic Beast	64154377
Emperor of the Land and Sea	11250655
Empress Judge	15237615
Empress Mantis	58818411
Enchanted Javelin	96355986
Enchanting Mermaid	75376965
Eradicating Aerosol	94716515
Eternal Draught	56606928
Eternal Rest	95051344
Exchange	05556668
Exile of the Wicked	26725158
Exodia the Forbidden One	33396948
Eyearmor	64511793
Fairy Box	21598948
Fairy Dragon	20315854
Fairy Guardian	22419772
Fairy Meteor Crush	97687912
Fairy of the Fountain	81563416
Fairy's Gift	68401546
Fairywitch	37160778
Faith Bird	75582395
Feral Imp	41392891
Fiend Kraken	77456781
Fiend Reflection #1	68870276
Fiend Reflection #2	02863439
Fiend's Hand	52800428
Fiend Sword	22855882
Final Destiny	18591904
Final Flame	73134081
Fire Eye	88435542
Firegrass	53293545
Fire Kraken	46534755
Fire Princess	64752646
Fire Reaper	53581214
Fire Sorcerer	27132350
Fireyarou	71407486
Fissure	66788016
Flame Cerebrus	60862676

Yu-Gi-Oh! Worldwide Edition: Stairway to the Destined Duel (cont'd)

Flame Champion	42599677
Flame Dancer	12883044
Flame Ghost	58528964
Flame Manipulator	34460851
Flame Swordsman	40502030
Flame Viper	02830619
Flash Assailant	96890582
Flower Wolf	95952802
Flying Fish	31987274
Flying Kamakiri #1	84834865
Flying Kamakiri #2	03134241
Flying Penguin	05628232
Follow Wind	98252586
Forced Requisition	74923978
Forest	87430998
Frenzied Panda	98818516
Frog the Jam	68638985
Fungi the Musk	53830602
Fusion Gate	33550694
Fusionist	01641882
Fusion Sage	26902560
Gadget Soldier	86281779
Gaia	06368038
Gaia Power	56594520
Gaia the Dragon Champion	66889139
Gaia the Fierce Knight	00603060
Gale Dogra	16229315
Gamble	37313786
Gamma the Magnet Warrior	11549357
Ganigumo	34536276
Garma Sword	90844184
Garma Sword Oath	78577570
Garnecia Elefantis	49888191
Garoozis	14977074
Garuda the Wind Spirit	12800777
Garvas	69780745
Gate Deeg	49258578
Gate Guardian	25833572
Gatekeeper	19737320
Gazelle the King of Mythical Beasts	05818798
Gearfried the Iron Knight	00423705
Gemini Elf	69140098
Genin	49370026
Germ Infection	24668830
Ghoul with an Appetite	95265975
Giant Flea	41762634
Giant Germ	95178994
Giant Mech-Soldier	72299832
Giant Rat	97017120
Giant Red Seasnake	58831685
Giant Scorpion of the Tundra	41403766
Giant Soldier of Stone	13039848
Giant Trunade	42703248
Giant Turtle Who Feeds on Flames	96981563
Gift of the Mystical Elf	98299011
Giganto	33621868
Giga-tech Wolf	08471389
Giltia the D. Knight	51828629
Girochin Kuwagata	84620194
Goblin Attack Force	78658564
Goblin Fan	04149689
Goblin's Secret Remedy	11868825
Goddess of Whim	67959180
Goddess with the Third Eye	53493204
Gokibore	15367030
Golgoil	07526150
Gorgon Egg	11793047
Graceful Charity	79571449
Graceful Dice	74137509
Gradius	10992251
Grand Tiki Elder	13676474
Grappler	02906250
Gravedigger Ghoul	82542267
Gravekeeper's Servant	16762927
Graverobber	61705417
Graverobber's Retribution	33737664

PSP Xbox PS2 GC GBA

Yu-Gi-Oh! Worldwide Edition: Stairway to the Destined Duel (cont'd)

Graveyard and the Hand of Invitation	27094595
Gravity Bind	85742772
Great Bill	55691901
Great Mammoth of Goldfine	54622031
Great White	13429800
Greenkappa	61831093
Green Phantom King	22910685
Griffore	53829412
Griggle	95744531
Ground Attacker Bugroth	58314394
Ground Collapse	90502999
Gruesome Goo	65623423
Gryphon Wing	55608151
Guardian of the Labyrinth	89272878
Guardian of the Sea	85448931
Guardian of the Throne Room	47879985
Gust	73079365
Gust Fan	55321970
Gyakutenno Megami	31122090
Hane-Hane	07089711
Haniwa	84285623
Happy Lover	99030164
Hard Armor	20060230
Harpie Lady	76812113
Harpie Lady Sisters	12206212
Harpie's Brother	30532390
Harpie's Feather Duster	18144506
Harpie's Pet Dragon	52040216
Hayabusa Knight	21015833
Headless Knight	05434080
Heavy Storm	19613556
Hercules Beetle	52584282
Hero of the East	89987208
Hibikime	64501875
High Tide Gyojin	54579801
Hinotama	46130346
Hinotama Soul	96851799
Hiro's Shadow Scout	81863068
Hitodenchak	46718686
Hitotsu-Me Giant	76184692
Holograh	10859908
Horn Imp	69669405
Horn of Heaven	98069388
Horn of Light	38552107
Horn of the Unicorn	64047146
Hoshiningen	67629977
Hourglass of Courage	43530283
Hourglass of Life	08783685
House of Adhesive Tape	15083728
Humanoid Slime	46821314
Humanoid Worm Drake	05600127
Hunter Spider	80141480
Hurricail	15042735
Hyo	38982356
Hyosube	02118022
Hyozanryu	62397231
Hysteric Fairy	21297224
Ice Water	20848593
Illusionist Faceless Mage	28546905
Ill Witch	81686058
Imperial Order	61740673
Infinite Cards	94163677
Infinite Dismissal	54109233
Insect Armor with Laser Cannon	03492538
Insect Barrier	23615409
Insect Imitation	96965364
Insect Queen	91512835
Insect Soldiers of the Sky	07019529
Inspection	16227556
Invader from Another Dimension	28450915
Invader of the Throne	03056267
Invigoration	98374133
Invitation to a Dark Sleep	52675689
Island Turtle	04042268
Jam Breeding Machine	21770260
Jam Defender	21558682
Jar Of Greed	83968380

Yu-Gi-Oh! Worldwide Edition: Stairway to the Destined Duel (cont'd)

Jellyfish	14851496
Jigen Bakudan	90020065
Jinzo	77585513
Jinzo #7	32809211
Jirai Gumo	94773007
Job-Change Mirror	55337339
Jowgen the Spiritualist	41855169
Judge Man	30113682
Just Desserts	24068492
Kagemusha of the Blue Flame	15401633
Kageningen	80600490
Kairyu-Shin	76634149
Kaiser Dragon	94566432
Kamakiriman	68928540
Kaminari Attack	09653271
Kaminarikozou	15510988
Kamionwizard	41544074
Kanan the Swordmistress	12829151
Kanikabuto	84103702
Kappa Avenger	48109103
Karate Man	23289281
Karbonala Warrior	54541900
Key Mace	01929294
Key Mace #2	20541432
Killer Needle	88979991
King Fog	84686841
King of Yamimakai	69455834
Kiseitai	04266839
Kojikocy	01184620
Korogashi	32569498
Kotodama	19406822
Koumori Dragon	67724379
Krokodilus	76512652
Kumootoko	56283725
Kunai with Chain	37390589
Kurama	85705804
Kuriboh	40640057
Kuwagata A	60802233
Kwagar Hercules	95144193
Kycoo the Ghost Destroyer	88240808
La Jinn the Mystical Genie of the Lamp	97590747
Labyrinth Tank	99551425
Lady Assailant of the Flames	90147755
Lady of Faith	17358176
Lady Panther	38480590
LaLa Li-oon	09430387
LaMoon	75850803
Larvas	94675535
Laser Cannon Armor	77007920
Last Day of Witch	90330453
Last Warrior from Another Planet	86099788
Last Will	85602018
Laughing Flower	42591472
Launcher Spider	80703020
Lava Battleguard	20394040
Left Arm of the Forbidden One	07902349
Left Leg of the Forbidden One	44519536
Legendary Sword	61854111
Leghul	12472242
Leogun	10538007
Leo Wizard	04392470
Lesser Dragon	55444629
Lightforce Sword	49587034
Lightning Blade	55226821
Lightning Conger	27671321
Limiter Removal	23171610
Liquid Beast	93108297
Lisark	55210709
Little Chimera	68658728
Little D	42625254
Living Vase	34320307
Lord of the Lamp	99510761
Lord of Zemia	81618817
Lucky Trinket	03985011
Luminous Spark	81777047
Lunar Queen Elzaim	62210247
Mabarrel	98795934

PSP Xbox PS2 GC GBA

Yu-Gi-Oh! Worldwide Edition: Stairway to the Destined Duel (cont'd)

Card	Code
Machine Attacker	38116136
Machine Conversion Factory	25769732
Machine King	46700124
Mad Sword Beast	79870141
Madjinn Gunn	43905751
Mage Power	83746708
Magic Cylinder	62279055
Magic Jammer	77414722
Magic Thorn	53119267
Magical Ghost	46474915
Magical Hats	81210420
Magical Labyrinth	64389297
Magic-Arm Shield	96008713
Magician of Faith	31560081
Maha Vailo	93013676
Maiden of the Moonlight	79629370
Major Riot	09074847
Makiu	27827272
Malevolent Nuzzler	99597615
Mammoth Graveyard	40374923
Man Eater	93553943
Man-Eater Bug	54652250
Man-Eating Black Shark	80727036
Man-Eating Plant	49127943
Man-Eating Treasure Chest	13723605
Manga Ryu-Ran	38369349
Marie the Fallen One	57579381
Marine Beast	29929832
Maryokutai	71466592
Masaki the Legendary Swordsman	44287299
Mask of Brutality	82432018
Mask of Darkness	28933734
Mask of Dispel	30765952
Mask of Restrict	29549364
Mask of the Accursed	56948373
Mask of Weakness	57882509
Masked Clown	77581312
Masked Sorcerer	10189126
Master & Expert	75499502
Mavelus	59036972
Mech Bass	50176820
Mech Mole Zombie	63545455
Mechaleon	94412545
Mechanical Snail	34442949
Mechanical Spider	45688586
Mechanicalchaser	07359741
Meda Bat	76211194
Mega Thunderball	21817254
Megamorph	22046459
Megasonic Eye	07562372
Megazowler	75390004
Megirus Light	23032273
Melchid the Four-Face Beast	86569121
Meotoko	53832650
Mesmeric Control	48642904
Messenger of Peace	44656491
Metal Detector	75646520
Metal Dragon	09293977
Metal Fish	55998462
Metal Guardian	68339286
Metalmorph	68540058
Metalzoa	50705071
Michizure	37580756
Midnight Fiend	83678433
Millennium Golem	47986555
Millennium Shield	32012841
Milus Radiant	07489323
Minar	32539892
Minomushi Warrior	46864967
Minor Goblin Official	01918087
Miracle Dig	06343408
Mirror Force	44095762
Mirror Wall	22359980
Misairuzame	33178416
Molten Destruction	19384334
Mon Larvas	07225792
Monster Egg	36121917
Monster Eye	84133008
Monster Reborn	83764718

Yu-Gi-Oh! Worldwide Edition: Stairway to the Destined Duel (cont'd)

Monster Recovery	93108433
Monster Tamer	97612389
Monstrous Bird	35712107
Monsturtle	15820147
Moon Envoy	45909477
Mooyan Curry	58074572
Morinphen	55784832
Morphing Jar	33508719
Morphing Jar #2	79106360
Mother Grizzly	57839750
Mountain	50913601
Mountain Warrior	04931562
Mr. Volcano	31477025
Muka Muka	46657337
Multiply	40703222
Muse-A	69992868
Mushroom Man	14181608
Mushroom Man #2	93900406
Musician King	56907389
M-Warrior #1	56342351
M-Warrior #2	92731455
Mysterious Puppeteer	54098121
Mystery Hand	62793020
Mystic Box	25774450
Mystic Clown	47060154
Mystic Horseman	68516705
Mystic Lamp	98049915
Mystic Plasma Zone	18161786
Mystic Probe	49251811
Mystic Tomato	83011277
Mystical Capture Chain	63515678
Mystical Elf	15025844
Mystical Moon	36607978
Mystical Refpanel	35563539
Mystical Sand	32751480
Mystical Sheep #1	30451366
Mystical Sheep #2	83464209
Mystical Space Typhoon	05318639
Neck Hunter	70084224
Necrolancer the Timelord	61454890
Needle Ball	94230224
Needle Worm	81843628
Negate Attack	14315573
Nekogal #1	01761063
Nekogal #2	43352213
Nemuriko	90963488
Neo the Magic Swordsman	50930991
Night Lizard	78402798
Nightmare Scorpion	88643171
Nightmare's Steelcage	58775978
Nimble Momonga	22567609
Niwatori	07805359
Nobleman of Crossout	71044499
Nobleman of Extermination	17449108
Numinous Healer	02130625
Nuvia the Wicked	12953226
Obese Marmot of Nefariousness	56713552
Octoberser	74637266
Ocubeam	86088138
Offerings to the Doomed	19230407
Ogre of the Black Shadow	45121025
One-Eyed Shield Dragon	33064647
One Who Hunts Souls	03606209
Oni Tank T-34	66927994
Ooguchi	58861941
Ookazi	19523799
Orion the Battle King	02971090
Oscillo Hero	82065276
Oscillo Hero #2	27324313
Overdrive	02311603
Painful Choice	74191942
Pale Beast	21263083
Panther Warrior	42035044
Paralyzing Potion	50152549
Parasite Paracide	27911549
Parrot Dragon	62762898
Patrol Robo	76775123
Peacock	20624263

Yu-Gi-Oh! Worldwide Edition: Stairway to the Destined Duel (cont'd)

Pendulum Machine	20404030
Penguin Knight	36039163
Penguin Soldier	93920745
Petit Angel	38142739
Petit Dragon	75356564
Petit Moth	58192742
Phantom Dewan	77603950
Phantom Ghost	61201220
Polymerization	24094653
Pot of Greed	55144522
Pot the Trick	55567161
Power of Kaishin	77027445
Pragtical	33691040
Premature Burial	70828912
Prevent Rat	00549481
Princess of Tsurugi	51371017
Prisman	80234301
Prohibition	43711255
Protector of the Throne	10071456
Psychic Kappa	07892180
Pumpking the King of Ghosts	29155212
Punished Eagle	74703140
Queen Bird	73081602
Queen of Autumn Leaves	04179849
Queen's Double	05901497
Raigeki	12580477
Raimei	56260110
Rain of Mercy	66719324
Rainbow Flower	21347810
Rainbow Marine Mermaid	29402771
Raise Body Heat	51267887
Rare Fish	80516007
Ray & Temperature	85309439
Reaper of the Cards	33066139
Red Archery Girl	65570596
Red Medicine	38199696
Red-Eyes B. Dragon	74677422
Red-Eyes Black Metal Dragon	64335804
Red-Moon Baby	56387350
Reinforcements	17814387
Relinquished	64631466
Remove Trap	51482758
Respect Play	08951260
Restructer Revolution	99518961
Return of the Doomed	19827717
Reverse Trap	77622396
Revival Jam	31709826
Rhaimundos of the Red Sword	62403074
Right Arm of the Forbidden One	70903634
Right Leg of the Forbidden One	08124921
Riryoku	34016756
Riryoku Field	70344351
Rising Air Current	45778932
Roaring Ocean Snake	19066538
Robbin' Goblin	88279736
Rock Ogre Grotto #1	68846917
Rock Ogre Grotto #2	62193699
Rock Spirit	82818645
Rocket Warrior	30860696
Rogue Doll	91939608
Root Water	39004808
Rose Spectre of Dunn	32485271
Royal Command	33950246
Royal Decree	51452091
Royal Guard	39239728
Rude Kaiser	26378150
Rush Recklessly	70046172
Ryu-Kishin	15303296
Ryu-Kishin Powered	24611934
Ryu-Ran	02964201
Saber Slasher	73911410
Saggi the Dark Clown	66602787
Salamandra	32268901
Sand Stone	73051941
Sangan	26202165
Science Soldier	67532912
Scroll of Bewitchment	10352095

Yu-Gi-Oh! Worldwide Edition: Stairway to the Destined Duel (cont'd)

Sea Kamen	71746462
Sea King Dragon	23659124
Seal of the Ancients	97809599
Sebek's Blessing	22537443
Sectarian of Secrets	15507080
Senju of the Thousand Hands	23401839
Serpent Marauder	82742611
Seven Tools of the Bandit	03819470
Shadow Ghoul	30778711
Shadow of Eyes	58621589
Shadow Specter	40575313
Shadow Spell	29267084
Share the Pain	56830749
Shield & Sword	52097679
Shining Abyss	87303357
Shining Fairy	95956346
Shining Friendship	82085619
Shovel Crusher	71950093
Silver Bow and Arrow	01557499
Silver Fang	90357090
Sinister Serpent	08131171
Skelengel	60694662
Skelgon	32355828
Skull Dice	00126218
Skull Invitation	98139712
Skull Lair	06733059
Skull Mariner	05265750
Skull Red Bird	10202894
Skull Servant	32274490
Skull Stalker	54844990
Skullbird	08327462
Sky Dragon	95288024
Slate Warrior	78636495
Sleeping Lion	40200834
Slot Machine	03797883
Snake Fang	00596051
Snakeyashi	29802344
Snatch Steal	45986603
Sogen	86318356
Solemn Judgment	41420027
Solemn Wishes	35346968
Solitude	84794011
Solomon's Lawbook	23471572
Sonic Bird	57617178
Sonic Maid	38942059
Sorcerer of the Doomed	49218300
Soul Hunter	72869010
Soul of Purity and Light	77527210
Soul of the Pure	47852924
Soul Release	05758500
Souls of the Forgotten	04920010
Sparks	76103675
Spear Cretin	58551308
Spellbinding Circle	18807108
Spherous Lady	52121290
Spike Seadra	85326399
Spikebot	87511987
Spiked Snail	98075147
Spirit Elimination	69832741
Spirit Message "A"	94772232
Spirit Message "I"	31893528
Spirit Message "L"	30170981
Spirit Message "N"	67287533
Spirit of Flames	13522325
Spirit of the Books	14037717
Spirit of the Breeze	53530069
Spirit of the Harp	80770678
Spirit of the Mountain	34690519
Spirit of the Winds	54615781
Spiritualism	15855454
St. Joan	21175632
Stain Storm	21323861
Star Boy	08201910
Steel Ogre Grotto #1	29172562
Steel Ogre Grotto #2	90908427
Steel Scorpion	13599884
Steel Shell	02370081
Stim-Pack	83225447
Stone Armadiller	63432835
Stone D.	68171737

Yu-Gi-Oh! Worldwide Edition: Stairway to the Destined Duel (cont'd)

Stone Ghost	72269672
Stone Ogre Grotto	15023985
Stop Defense	63102017
Stuffed Animal	71068263
Succubus Knight	55291359
Summoned Skull	70781052
Summoner of Illusions	14644902
Supply	44072894
Supporter in the Shadows	41422426
Swamp Battleguard	40453765
Sword Arm of Dragon	13069066
Sword Hunter	51345461
Sword of Dark Destruction	37120512
Sword of Deep-Seated	98495314
Sword of Dragon's Soul	61405855
Swords of Revealing Light	72302403
Swordsman from a Foreign Land	85255550
Swordsman of Landstar	03573512
Swordstalker	50005633
Synchar	75646173
Tailor of the Fickle	43641473
Tainted Wisdom	28725004
Takriminos	44073668
Takuhee	03170832
Tao the Chanter	46247516
Tatsunootoshigo	47922711
Temple of Skulls	00732302
Tenderness	57935140
Tentacle Plant	60715406
Terra the Terrible	63308047
That Which Feeds on Life	52367652
The 13th Grave	00032864
The All-Seeing White Tiger	32269855
The Bewitching Phantom Thief	24348204
The Bistro Butcher	71107816
The Cheerful Coffin	41142615
The Dark Door	30606547
The Drdek	08944575
The Earl of Demise	66989694
The Emperor's Holiday	68400115
The Eye of Truth	34694160
The Fiend Megacyber	66362965
The Forceful Sentry	42829885
The Forgiving Maiden	84080938
The Furious Sea King	18710707
The Gross Ghost of Fled Dreams	68049471
The Immortal of Thunder	84926738
The Inexperienced Spy	81820689
The Judgment Hand	28003512
The Last Warrior from Another Planet	86099788
The Legendary Fisherman	03643300
The Little Swordsman of Aile	25109950
The Masked Beast	49064413
The Melting Red Shadow	98898173
The Portrait's Secret	32541773
The Regulation of Tribe	00296499
The Reliable Guardian	16430187
The Rock Spirit	76305638
The Shadow Who Controls the Dark	63125616
The Shallow Grave	43434803
The Snake Hair	29491031
The Statue of Easter Island	10262698
The Stern Mystic	87557188
The Thing That Hides in the Mud	18180762
The Unfriendly Amazon	65475294
The Unhappy Maiden	51275027
The Wandering Doomed	93788854
The Wicked Worm Beast	06285791
Thousand Knives	63391643
Thousand-Eyes Idol	27125110
Thousand-Eyes Restrict	63519819
Three-Headed Geedo	78423643
Three-Legged Zombies	33734439
Thunder Dragon	31786629
Tiger Axe	49791927

Yu-Gi-Oh! Worldwide Edition: Stairway to the Destined Duel (cont'd)

Time Seal	35316708
Time Wizard	71625222
Toad Master	62671448
Togex	33878931
Toll	82003859
Tomozaurus	46457856
Tongyo	69572024
Toon Alligator	59383041
Toon Mermaid	65458948
Toon Summoned Skull	91842653
Toon World	15259703
Torike	80813021
Tornado Bird	71283180
Tornado Wall	18605135
Torrential Tribute	53582587
Total Defense Shogun	75372290
Trakadon	42348802
Trap Hole	04206964
Trap Master	46461247
Tremendous Fire	46918794
Trent	78780140
Trial of Nightmare	77827521
Tribute to the Doomed	79759861
Tripwire Beast	45042329
Turtle Bird	72929454
Turtle Raccoon	17441953
Turtle Tiger	37313348
Turu-Purun	59053232
Twin Long Rods #1	29692206
Twin Long Rods #2	78984772
Twin-Headed Fire Dragon	78984772
Twin-Headed Thunder Dragon	54752875
Two-Headed King Rex	94119974
Two-Mouth Darkruler	57305373
Two-Pronged Attack	83887306
Tyhone	72842870
Tyhone #2	56789759
Type Zero Magic Crusher	21237481
UFO Turtle	60806437
Ultimate Offering	80604091
Umi	22702055
Umiiruka	82999629
Unfriendly Amazon	65475294
United We Stand	56747793
Unknown Warrior of Fiend	97360116
Upstart Goblin	70368879
Uraby	01784619
Ushi Oni	48649353
Valkyrion the Magna Warrior	75347539
Vengeful Bog Spirit	95220856
Vermillion Sparrow	35752363
Versago the Destroyer	50259460
Vile Germs	39774685
Violent Rain	94042337
Violet Crystal	15052462
Vishwar Randi	78556320
Vorse Raider	14898066
Waboku	12607053
Wall of Illusion	13945283
Warrior Elimination	90873992
Warrior of Tradition	56413937
Wasteland	23424603
Water Element	03732747
Water Girl	55014050
Water Magician	93343894
Water Omotics	02483611
Waterdragon Fairy	66836598
Weather Control	37243151
Weather Report	72053645
Wetha	96643568
Whiptail Crow	91996584
White Dolphin	92409659
White Hole	43487744
White Magical Hat	15150365
Wicked Dragon with the Ersatz Head	02957055
Wicked Mirror	15150371
Widespread Ruin	77754944
Wilmee	92391084
Windstorm of Etaqua	59744639

Yu-Gi-Oh! Worldwide Edition: Stairway to the Destined Duel (cont'd)

Card	Password
Wing Eagle	47319141
Wing Egg Elf	98582704
Winged Cleaver	39175982
Winged Dragon, Guardian of the Fortress #1	87796900
Winged Dragon, Guardian of the Fortress #2	57405307
Winged Egg of New Life	42418084
Wings of Wicked Flame	92944626
Wingweaver	31447217
Witch of the Black Forest	78010363
Witch's Apprentice	80741828
Witty Phantom	36304921
Wodan the Resident of the Forest	42883273
Wolf	49417509
Wood Clown	17511156
Wood Remains	17733394
World Suppression	12253117
Worm Drake	73216412
Wow Warrior	69750536
Wretched Ghost of the Attic	17238333
Yado Karu	29380133
Yaiba Robo	10315429
Yamadron	70345785
Yamatano Dragon Scroll	76704943
Yami	59197169
Yaranzo	71280811
Yashinoki	41061625
Yormungarde	17115745
Zanki	30090452
Zarigun	10598400
Zoa	24311372
Zombie Warrior	31339260
Zombyra the Dark	88472456
Zone Eater	86100785

Unlockable Character	Objective
Duke Devlin	Defeat the following characters at least one time: Yugi Moto, Tea, Joey, Bakura, Seto Kaiba, Ishizu, Rex, Weevil, Solomon, Mai, Espa Roba, Mako, Mokuba, Bandit Keith, Maximillion Pegasus, Seeker/Rare Hunter, Strings, Odion, Umbra & Lumis, Arkana, Marik, and Shadi.
Mokuba	You have to lose 5 duels. It doesn't matter which duelist you lose to.
Pegasus	Obtain a Toon World card. Search around Battle City and he shows up as a duelist you haven't fought yet.
Shadi and the Rare Hunters	Complete Marik's little Phantom Pyramid.

Unlockable	Code
100 Lives	Hold L at the slot Select screen and press →,→,→,→,→,→,→.
All Power-Ups	Hold L at the slot Select screen and press →,←,→,←,→,←,→.
Free Mode (No Restrictions)	Beat all the limitation duels once.
Ghost Hideout	Beat all of the Ghosts (i.e. Rare Hunter, Strings, Arkana) at least once. After you beat the last Ghost, there is a cutscene with Grandpa Yugi and Tea. Tea leads you, possessed, to the Ghosts Hideout where you duel. After that, you duel with other Ghosts/Rare Hunters until you get to the final stage where you face Marik. After you complete the Ghosts Hideout, you unlock all of the Ghosts/Rare Hunters to challenge and play freely.